Lecture Notes in Computer Science

Lecture Notes in Artificial Intelligence 15941

Founding Editor

Jörg Siekmann

Series Editors

The series Lecture Notes in Artificial Intelligence (LNAI) was established in 1988 as a topical subseries of LNCS devoted to artificial intelligence.

The series publishes state-of-the-art research results at a high level. As with the LNCS mother series, the mission of the series is to serve the international R & D community by providing an invaluable service, mainly focused on the publication of conference and workshop proceedings and postproceedings.

Peggy Cellier · Bernhard Ganter · Rokia Missaoui
Editors

Conceptual Knowledge Structures

Second International Joint Conference, CONCEPTS 2025
Cluj-Napoca, Romania, September 8–12, 2025
Proceedings

Springer

Editors
Peggy Cellier
INSA Rennes
Rennes, France

Bernhard Ganter
Dresden University of Technology
Dresden, Sachsen, Germany

Rokia Missaoui
Universite du Quebec en Outaouais
Gatineau, QC, Canada

ISSN 0302-9743 ISSN 1611-3349 (electronic)
Lecture Notes in Artificial Intelligence
ISBN 978-3-032-03363-5 ISBN 978-3-032-03364-2 (eBook)
https://doi.org/10.1007/978-3-032-03364-2

LNCS Sublibrary: SL7 – Artificial Intelligence

This Springer imprint is published by the registered company Springer Nature Switzerland AG
The registered company address is: Gewerbestrasse 11, 6330 Cham, Switzerland

Preface

In September 2024, the three established conference series ICCS, CLA, and ICFCA were held together for the first time. The joint conference, called CONCEPTS 2024, took place in Cádiz, Spain. This marked the beginning of a new series of conferences, which is now being continued with the *2nd International Joint Conference on Conceptual Knowledge Structures* (CONCEPTS 2025), held in Cluj Napoca, Romania, from September 8 to September 12, 2025. It brings together the 29th International Conference on Conceptual Structures (ICCS), the 19th International Conference on Formal Concept Analysis (ICFCA), and the 18th International Conference on Concept Lattices and Their Applications (CLA).

Submissions of significant and original research were invited on topics relevant to the conference. They were subject to single-blind peer review by following three different modalities: journal-track papers, regular papers, and short papers. A total of 46 contributions were submitted from authors all over the world (13 for the journal track and 33 regular or short papers) and presented to three independent reviewers each. Twenty-five regular and two short papers were accepted, most of these after revision. Accepted journal-track papers are published in a special issue of the *International Journal of Approximate Reasoning*, while this volume contains the accepted 25 regular and 2 short papers distributed into four topical sections: Methodology (8 papers); Patterns, Clusters, Visualization and Software (6 papers); Data Analysis (5 papers); and Theory (8 papers).

We are reviving a tradition that originated in the ICFCA conference series. On occasion, "historical papers" were included in the conference proceedings, i.e., previously published papers that had a groundbreaking influence on the field of research. We thank the authors for their permission.

We would like to thank Christian Săcărea, who is responsible for organizing and running the conference as General Chair, and his team for the smooth cooperation. We are also deeply grateful to the members of the Program Committee for their outstanding efforts in reviewing nearly 50 papers, and often more, when we consider revised versions.

We would like to conclude this preface by acknowledging the support and confidence of Springer in publishing this volume, supporting the efforts to establish a new series of conferences which promotes advances in formal concept analysis, conceptual structures, and related areas.

Our thanks also go to the organizations that sponsored this event: The Babeş-Bolyai University of Cluj-Napoca, the Romanian Ministry of Education and Research, SAS Analytical Solutions S.R.L., and the Raiffeisen Bank Romania.

July 2025

Peggy Cellier
Bernhard Ganter
Rokia Missaoui

Organization

General Chair

Christian Săcărea	Babeş-Bolyai University, Cluj-Napoca, Romania

Local Organization Committee

Christian Săcărea	Babeş-Bolyai University, Cluj-Napoca, Romania
Diana Cristea	Babeş-Bolyai University, Cluj-Napoca, Romania
Diana Şotropa	Babeş-Bolyai University, Cluj-Napoca, Romania

Program Chairs

Peggy Cellier	IRISA/INSA Rennes, France
Bernhard Ganter	TU Dresden, Germany
Rokia Missaoui	Université du Québec en Outaouais, Canada

Executive Board

Jaume Baixeries	Polytechnic University of Catalonia, Spain
Radim Belohlavek	Palacký University Olomouc, Czech Republic
Tanya Braun	University of Münster, Germany
Madalina Croitoru	University of Montpellier, France
Sébastien Ferré	University of Rennes, France
Sergei Kuznetsov	HSE University, Moscow, Russia
Rokia Missaoui	Université du Québec en Outaouais, Canada
Amedeo Napoli	LORIA, Nancy, France
Sergei Obiedkov	TU Dresden, Germany
Manuel Ojeda-Aciego	University of Malaga, Spain
Uta Priss	Ostfalia University of Applied Sciences, Wolfenbüttel, Germany
Gerd Stumme	University of Kassel, Germany

Program Committee

Jaume Baixeries	Polytechnic University of Catalonia, Spain
Alexandre Bazin	LIRMM, Montpellier, France
Mike Behrisch	Technische Universität Wien, Austria
Sadok Ben Yahia	Technology University of Tallinn, Estonia
Radim Belohlavek	Palacký University Olomouc, Czech Republic
Karell Bertet	La Rochelle University, France
Inma P. Cabrera	Universidad de Málaga, Spain
Peggy Cellier	IRISA/INSA Rennes, France
Maria E. Cornejo Piñero	University of Cádiz, Spain
Christophe Demko	La Rochelle University, France
Xavier Dolques	Université de Strasbourg, France
Dominik Dürrschnabel	Universität Kassel, Germany
Sébastien Ferré	IRISA université de Rennes, France
Bernhard Ganter	TU Dresden, Germany
Alain Gely	Université de Lorraine, France
Tom Hanika	University of Hildesheim, Germany
Tobias Hille	University of Kassel, Germany
Marianne Huchard	LIRMM, Univ. Montpellier, France
Mohamed Hamza Ibrahim	American University of Sharjah, UAE
Dmitry Ignatov	HSE University, Moscow, Russia
Mehdi Kaytoue	Infologic R&D, France
Blaise Blériot Koguep Njionou	Université de Dschang, Cameroon
Francesco Kriegel	TU Dresden, Germany
Sergei Kuznetsov	HSE University, Moscow, Russia
Leonard Kwuida	Bern University of Appl. Sciences, Switzerland
Florence Le Ber	Université de Strasbourg, France
Pierre Martin	University of Montpellier, France
Jesús Medina	University of Cádiz, Spain
Rokia Missaoui	University of Quebec in Outaouais, Canada
Amedeo Napoli	LORIA, Université de Lorraine, France
Sergei Obiedkov	TU Dresden, Germany
Manuel Ojeda-Aciego	Universidad de Málaga, Spain
Jan Outrata	Palacký University Olomouc, Czech Republic
Tim Pattison	Defence Science and Techn. Group, Australia
Carmen Peláez-Moreno	Univ. Carlos III de Madrid, Spain
Uta Priss	Ostfalia U. Appl. Sci., Wolfenbüttel, Germany
Sandor Radeleczki	University of Miskolc, Hungary
Eloísa Ramírez Poussa	Universidad de Cádiz, Spain
Sebastian Rudolph	TU Dresden, Germany
Baris Sertkaya	Frankfurt Univ. of Applied Sciences, Germany

Henry Soldano	Université Paris 13, France
Petko Valtchev	Université du Québec à Montréal, Canada
Gerd Stumme	University of Kassel, Germany
Martin Trnecka	Palacký University Olomouc, Czech Republic
Francisco J. Valverde-Albacete	Univ. Rey Juan Carlos, Madrid, Spain

External Reviewer

Chao Zhang	Shanxi University, China

A Historical Paper

The following pages are a reprint of a seminal publication contributed by Radim Bělohlávek and Vilém Vychodil to the CLA 2005 conference. Their research group at Palacký University in Olomouc, Czech Republic, subsequently developed the theory of fuzzy concept analysis substantially through numerous publications.

The original version of this paper is available from the CEUR Workshop Proceedings at https://ceur-ws.org/Vol-162/. A follow-up by Bělohlávek "written for people familiar with ordinary concept lattices who would like to learn about fuzzy concept lattices" was published under the title *"What is a fuzzy concept lattice? II"* in volume 6743 of the Springer LNAI series.

What is a fuzzy concept lattice?*

Radim Bělohlávek and Vilém Vychodil

Department of Computer Science, Palacky University, Olomouc Tomkova 40, CZ-779 00 Olomouc, Czech Republic
{radim.belohlavek,vilem.vychodil}@upol.cz

Abstract. The paper is an overview of several approaches to the notion of a concept lattice from the point of view of fuzzy logic. The main aim is to clarify relationships between the various approaches.

Keywords: formal concept analysis · fuzzy logic · fuzzy attribute

1 Introduction

Formal concept analysis (FCA) deals with a particular kind of analysis of data which, in the basic setting, has the form of a table with rows corresponding to objects, columns corresponding to attributes, and table entries containing 1's and 0's depending on whether an object has or does not have an attribute (we assume basic familiarity with FCA and refer to [24] for information). The basic setting is well-suited for attributes which are crisp, i.e. each object of the domain of applicability of the attribute either has (1) or does not have (0) the attribute. Many attributes are fuzzy rather than crisp. That is to say, it is a matter of degree to which an object has a (fuzzy) attribute. For instance, when asking whether a man with a height of 182 cm is tall, one probably gets an answer like "not completely tall but almost tall" or "to a high degree tall", etc. A natural idea, developed in fuzzy logic [12, 28, 31], is to assign to an object a truth degree to which the object has a (fuzzy) attribute. Degrees are taken from an appropriate scale L of truth degrees. A favorite choice of L is the real unit interval [0, 1] or some subset of [0, 1]. Then, we can say that a man with a height of 182 cm is tall to a degree, say, 0.8. Doing so, the entries of a table describing objects and attributes become degrees from L instead of values from $\{0, 1\}$ as is the case of the basic setting of FCA.

FCA provides means to process tables with degrees from a scale L. Namely, one can consider a table with degrees from L a many-valued context and use a so-called conceptual scaling [24]. There is, however, another way to process such data tables. The way is based on considering the table entries as truth degrees in fuzzy logic and proceed analogously as we do in the basic setting of FCA, just "replacing classical (bivalent) logic

Supported by grant No. 1ET101370417 of GA AV CR and by institutional support, research plan MSM 6198959214.

with fuzzy logic". Recently, the second way gained a considerable interest. The structures which result this way are called fuzzy concept lattices, fuzzy Galois connections, etc. However, the particular approaches, and hence the resulting structures, differ.

The basic aim of this paper is to compare them and to show some of the basic relationships between them. Due to a limited scope, we omit some technical details (mostly proofs). These are left for a full version of this paper.

Note that we do not study mathematical or any other (like epistemic) relationships of the discussed "fuzzy logic approaches" to the above-mentioned possibility of using conceptual scaling. This, again, is left for a forthcoming paper.

2 Why fuzzy logic in formal concept analysis and a basic standpoint

2.1 Why fuzzy logic in formal concept analysis?

The main reason is the following. FCA is based on working with formulas like "an object belongs to (a set) A iff it has all attributes from (a set) B". In the basic setting (i.e., table entries contain 0's and 1's), this is done in classical logic. When the truth degrees in a data table are taken from scale L, do the same as in the basic setting of FCA, only "replace classical logic by fuzzy logic". Doing so, the results of FCA in a fuzzy setting will have the same verbal interpretation as those in the classical setting. Namely, the underlying formulas are the same in both the fuzzy setting and the classical setting and the difference is only in the interpretation of the formulas (many-valued interpretation in fuzzy setting vs. bivalent interpretation in classical setting).

2.2 A basic standpoint: first-order fuzzy logic

However, "replace classical logic by fuzzy logic" is ambiguous. Namely, there are several ways to perform the "replacement". Nevertheless, there is a way which might be considered direct and simple. Namely, one can use a framework of first-order fuzzy logic (and fuzzy relations) the same way as one uses first-order classical logic (and classical relations) in the basic setting of FCA. Since the standpoint of a first-order logic (and relations) is simple and easy to understand, we take it for a basic standpoint in our paper. It is the one to which we compare the other approaches. In the rest of this section, we recall some basic concepts we need. We refer to [12, 28, 30] for further information.

As a set of truth degrees equipped with suitable operations (truth functions of logical connectives) we use a complete residuated lattice i.e. an algebra $\mathbf{L} = \langle L, \wedge, \vee, \otimes, \rightarrow, 0, 1\rangle$ such that $\langle L, \wedge, \vee 0, 1\rangle$ is a complete lattice with 0 and 1 being the least and greatest element of L, respectively; $\langle L, \otimes, 1\rangle$ is a commutative monoid (i.e. $\otimes$ is commutative, associative, and $a \otimes 1 = 1 \otimes a = a$ for each $a \in L$); $\otimes$ and $\rightarrow$ satisfy so-called adjointness property: $a \otimes b \leq c$ iff $a \leq b \rightarrow c$; for each $a, b, c \in L$. Elements a of L are called truth degrees (usually, $L \subseteq [0, 1]$). $\otimes$ and $\rightarrow$ are (truth functions of) "fuzzy conjunction" and "fuzzy implication". By $\mathbf{L}^U$ (or L^U) we denote the collection of all fuzzy sets in a universe U, i.e. mappings A of U to L. For $A \in L^U$ and $a \in L$, a set ${}^aA = \{u \in U \mid A(u) \geq a\}$ is called an a-cut of A.

2.3 What else than a first-order fuzzy logic?

Other approaches can be based on working with the truth degrees from L in the data table in any way which, if taking $L = \{0, 1\}$, yields the same what we have in the basic setting of FCA (we will see some of them later). Of course, this requirement follows from a requirement saying that we want to have a generalization of the basic setting of FCA. If the requirement is satisfied, we can consider the results (over a general scale L of truth degrees) as "having the same meaning as in the basic setting of FCA".

3 Overview and comparison of existing approaches to fuzzy concept lattices

A common point of all of the presented approaches is the notion of a fuzzy context, i.e. the input data. Let L be a scale of truth degrees. L might be a support set of some structure $\mathbf{L} = \langle L, \dots \rangle$ of truth degrees like a complete residuated lattice described above. Then, a fuzzy context (L-context, or $\mathbf{L}$-context) is a triplet $\langle X, Y, I \rangle$ where X and Y are sets of objects and attributes, respectively, and $I : X \times Y \to L$ is a fuzzy relation (L-relation, $\mathbf{L}$-relation) between X and Y. A degree $I(x, y) \in L$ is interpreted as a degree to which object x has attribute y. Note that if one takes $L = \{0, 1\}$ then the notion of a fuzzy context coincides in an obvious way with the notion of an (ordinary) context.

3.1 Basic setting of FCA

To fix notation for further reference, we recall the following [24]. A formal context (formal counterpart to a data table) is a triplet $\langle X, Y, I \rangle$ where X and Y are sets of objects and attributes, respectively, and $I \subseteq X \times Y$ is a binary relation "to have" ($\langle x, y \rangle \in I$ means that object x has attribute y). A formal concept in $\langle X, Y, I \rangle$ is a pair $\langle A, B \rangle$ of a set $A \subseteq X$ of objects and a set $B \subseteq Y$ of attributes such that

$$B \text{ is the collection of all attributes shared by all objects from } A \tag{1}$$

$$A \text{ is the collection of all objects sharing all the attributes from } B. \tag{2}$$

For $A \subseteq X$ and $B \subseteq Y$, put

$$A^{\uparrow} = \{y \mid \text{ for each } x \in A : \langle x, y \rangle \in I\}, \tag{3}$$

$$B^{\downarrow} = \{x \mid \text{ for each } y \in B : \langle x, y \rangle \in I\}. \tag{4}$$

This says that, $A^{\uparrow}$ is the set of all attributes from Y shared by all objects from A, and $B^{\downarrow}$ is the set of all objects from X sharing all attributes from B. Therefore, a formal concept is a pair $\langle A, B\rangle$ for which $A^{\uparrow} = B$ and $B^{\downarrow} = A$. For a formal concept $\langle A, B\rangle$, A is called an extent (collection of objects covered by $\langle A, B\rangle$), B is called an intent (collection of attributes covered by $\langle A, B\rangle$). Denote by $\mathcal{B}(X, Y, I)$ the set of all formal concepts in $\langle X, Y, I\rangle$, i.e. $\mathcal{B}(X, Y, I) = \{\langle A, B\rangle \mid A^{\uparrow} = B, B^{\downarrow} = A\}$. Introduce a relation $\leq$ on $\mathcal{B}(X, Y, I)$ by $\langle A_1, B_1\rangle \leq \langle A_2, B_2\rangle$ iff $A_1 \subseteq A_2$ (or, equivalently $B_2 \subseteq B_1$). The structure $\langle \mathcal{B}(X, Y, I), \leq\rangle$, i.e. set $\mathcal{B}(X, Y, I)$ equipped with $\leq$, is called a concept lattice of $\langle X, Y, I\rangle$. Basic structure of concept lattices is described by the so-called main theorem of concept lattices [24, 39].

3.2 The approach by Burusco and Fuentes-Gonzáles

Burusco and Fuentes-Gonzáles are the authors of the first paper on FCA in a fuzzy setting. Namely, in [21], they proceed as follows. Let $\mathbf{L} = \langle L, \leq, ', \oplus, 0, 1\rangle$ be a structure such that $\langle L, \leq, 0, 1\rangle$ is a complete lattice bounded by 0 and 1, $'$ be a unary operation of complementation, and $\oplus$ be a t-conorm on L (i.e. a binary operation which is associative, commutative, and has 0 as its neutral element). For an L-context $\langle X, Y, I\rangle$, define mappings $^{\uparrow} : L^X \to L^Y$ and $^{\downarrow} : L^Y \to L^X$ by

$$A^{\uparrow}(y) = \textstyle\bigwedge_{x\in X} (A(x)' \oplus I(x, y)), \tag{5}$$

$$B^{\downarrow}(x) = \textstyle\bigwedge_{y\in Y} (B(y)' \oplus I(x, y)), \tag{6}$$

for $A \in L^X$ and $B \in L^Y$. Furthermore, put $\mathcal{B}(X, Y, I) = \{\langle A, B\rangle \in L^X \times L^Y \mid A^{\uparrow} = B, B^{\downarrow} = A\}$ and define a partial order $\leq$ on $\mathcal{B}(X, Y, I)$ by $\langle A_1, B_1\rangle \leq \langle A_2, B_2\rangle$ iff $A_1 \subseteq A_2$ (iff $B_2 \subseteq B_1$).

Note first that for $L = \{0, 1\}$, $'$ being a classical negation (i.e. $0' = 1$ and $1' = 0$), and $\oplus$ being a classical disjunction (i.e. $a \oplus b = \max(a, b)$), $\mathcal{B}(X, Y, I)$ equipped with $\leq$ coincides in an obvious way with the ordinary concept lattice.

In [21], the authors show that $\mathcal{B}(X, Y, I)$ equipped with $\leq$ is a complete lattice and show some of the basic properties of $^{\uparrow}$ and $^{\downarrow}$. However, $^{\uparrow}$ and $^{\downarrow}$ do not satisfy some useful properties which hold true in the classical case, like $A \subseteq A^{\uparrow\downarrow}$ a $B \subseteq B^{\downarrow\uparrow}$. The authors extended (generalized) their approach later to include so-called implication operators [22]. Note also that the authors discussed other extensions of FCA in their setting, see e.g. [23]. But since some useful properties are missing in their approach, we stop our visit to this approach here and leave a more detailed discussion to a full paper.

3.3 The approach by Pollandt and Bělohlávek

Pollandt [36] and, independently, Bělohlávek ([3] is the first publication, an overview can be found in [12]), elaborated the following approach which turned out to be a feasible way to develop FCA and related structures in a fuzzy setting. Let $\mathbf{L}$ be a complete residuated lattice (see above). The choice of a residuated lattice structure, and particularly the adjointness property of conjunction and implication turns out to be a crucial property. Let $\langle X, Y, I\rangle$ be an $\mathbf{L}$-context, i.e. $I : X \times Y \to L$. For fuzzy sets $A \in L^X$ and $B \in L^Y$, consider fuzzy sets $A^{\uparrow} \in L^Y$ and $B^{\downarrow} \in L^X$ (denoted also $A^{\uparrow_I}$ and $B^{\downarrow_I}$) defined by

$$A^{\uparrow}(y) = \bigwedge_{x \in X}(A(x) \to I(x, y)), \tag{7}$$

$$B^{\downarrow}(x) = \bigwedge_{y \in Y}(B(y) \to I(x, y)). \tag{8}$$

Using basic rules of predicate fuzzy logic [12, 28], one can easily see that $A^{\uparrow}(y)$ is the truth degree of "y is shared by all objects from A" and $B^{\downarrow}(x)$ is the truth degree of "x has all attributes from B". That is, (7) and (8) properly generalize (3) and (4). Putting

$$\mathcal{B}(X, Y, I) = \{\langle A, B\rangle \mid A^{\uparrow} = B,\ B^{\downarrow} = A\},$$

$\mathcal{B}(X, Y, I)$ is the set of all pairs $\langle A, B\rangle$ such that (a) A is the collection of all objects that have all the attributes of (the intent) B and (b) B is the collection of all attributes that are shared by all the objects of (the extent) A. Elements of $\mathcal{B}(X, Y, I)$ are called formal concepts of $\langle X, Y, I\rangle$; $\mathcal{B}(X, Y, I)$ is called a (fuzzy) concept lattice (**L**-concept lattice) of $\langle X, Y, I\rangle$. Note that as in the case of Burusco and Fuentes-Gonzáles, both the extent A and the intent B of a formal concept $\langle A, B\rangle$ are in general fuzzy sets. This corresponds to the fact that in general, concepts apply to objects and attributes to various intermediate degrees, not only 0 and 1. Putting

$$\langle A_1, B_1\rangle \leq \langle A_2, B_2\rangle \quad \text{iff} \quad A_1 \subseteq A_2 \quad (\text{iff } B_1 \supseteq B_2) \tag{9}$$

for $\langle A_1, B_1\rangle, \langle A_2, B_2\rangle \in \mathcal{B}(X, Y, I)$, $\leq$ models the subconcept-superconcept hierarchy in $\mathcal{B}(X, Y, I)$.

Note that if **L** is a two-element Boolean algebra, i.e. $L = \{0, 1\}$, the notions of an **L**-context, a formal concept, and an **L**-concept lattice coincide with the ordinary notions [24].

For this approach, several issues of FCA have been generalized:

- Main theorem of **L**-concept lattices has two versions. The first one deals with the above defined ordinary partial order on formal concepts (a proof via reduction to the ordinary case can be found in [36] and in [9], a direct proof can be found in [8]). The second one deals with a fuzzy order on formal concepts, see [14]. In particular, $\mathcal{B}(X, Y, I)$ is a complete lattice w.r.t. $\leq$.
- Related structures like Galois connections and closure operators are studied in [5, 10, 11].
- A direct algorithm for generating all formal concepts based on Ganter's algorithm [24] is presented in [13].
- Issues which are degenerate in the ordinary case have been studied, see e.g. [6, 7].
- Several further issues like many-valued contexts, relationship to approximate reasoning, attribute implications are studied in [36]. Attribute implications are studied also in [16, 17, 19, 20].

3.4 The aproach by Yahia *et al.* and Krajči

Yahia [40] and, independently, Krajči [32] proposed the following approach, called "one-sided fuzzy approach" by Krajči. Note first that the approaches are not the same but the only difference is that for an L-context $\langle X, Y, I\rangle$, Yahia's definitions yield what Krajči's definitions yield for $\langle Y, X, I^{-1}\rangle$ with $I^{-1} \in L^{Y\times X}$ defined by $I^{-1}(y, x) = I(x, y)$, i.e. the approaches are the same up to the roles of objects and attributes. Note also that both Yahia and Krajči consider $L = [0, 1]$.

For an L-context $\langle X, Y, I\rangle$, define mappings $f : 2^X \to L^Y$ (assigning a *fuzzy set* $f(A) \in L^Y$ of attributes to a *set* $A \subseteq X$ of objects) and $h : L^Y \to 2^X$ (assigning a *set* $h(B) \subseteq$ of objects to a *fuzzy set* $B \in L^Y$ of attributes) by

$$f(A)(y) = \textstyle\bigwedge_{x\in A} I(x, y) \tag{10}$$

and

$$h(B) = \{x \in X \mid \text{ for each } y \in Y : B(y) \leq I(x, y)\}. \tag{11}$$

Then, put

$$\mathcal{B}_{f,h}(X, Y, I) = \{\langle A, B\rangle \in 2^X \times L^Y \mid f(A) = B, h(B) = A\}.$$

The set $\mathcal{B}_{f,h}(X, Y, I)$, equipped with a partial order $\leq$ defined by (9) is what Yahia and Krajči call a (one-sided) fuzzy concept lattice (it is, indeed, a complete lattice [32, 40]). Note that extents of concepts from $\mathcal{B}_{f,h}(X, Y, I)$ are crisp sets while the intents are fuzzy sets. Needless to say, one can modify this approach and have fuzzy extents and crisp intents.

The following theorem (partly contained in [32, Observation 2]) shows a basic hint to the relationship of f and h, and $^{\uparrow}$ and $^{\downarrow}$ defined by (7) and (8).

Theorem 1 For $A \subseteq X$ and $B \in L^Y$ and $^{\uparrow}$ and $^{\downarrow}$ defined by (7) and (8), we have

$$f(A) = A^{\uparrow}, \qquad \text{and} \qquad h(B) =^{1} (B^{\downarrow}).$$

Proof Easy, omitted due to lack of space.

Here, $A^{\uparrow}$ for A means $A'^{\uparrow}$ where A' is a fuzzy set in X corresponding to A, i.e. $A'(x) = 1$ for $x \in A$ and $A'(x) = 0$ for $x \notin A$. Therefore, f and h can be expressed by $^{\uparrow}$ and $^{\downarrow}$. In fact, $\mathcal{B}_{f,h}(X, Y, I)$ is isomorphic to (and, in fact, almost the same as) a substructure of Pollandt's and Bělohlávek's **L**-concept lattice $\mathcal{B}(X, Y, I)$. The details will be shown in the next section.

3.5 Crisply generated fuzzy concepts

In [15], when dealing with the problem of a possibly large number of formal concepts in Pollandt's and Bělohlávek's **L**-concept lattice $\mathcal{B}(X, Y, I)$, the authors proposed the following approach. Instead of considering the whole $\mathcal{B}(X, Y, I)$, they consider only its part $\mathcal{B}_c(X, Y, I) \subseteq \mathcal{B}(X, Y, I)$ consisting of what they call crisply generated fuzzy concepts: $\langle A, B\rangle \in \mathcal{B}(X, Y, I)$ is called crisply if there is a crisp (i.e., ordinary) set $B_c \subseteq Y$ of attributes such that $A = B_c^{\downarrow}$ (and thus $B = B_c^{\downarrow\uparrow}$). Then, $\mathcal{B}_c(X, Y, I) = \{\langle A, B\rangle \in \mathcal{B}(X, Y, I) \mid \text{ there is } B_c \subseteq Y : A = B_c^{\downarrow}\}$. Restricting oneself to crisply generated fuzzy concepts, one eliminates "strange" concepts like concepts $\langle A, B\rangle$ such that for any $x \in X$ and $y \in Y$ we have $A(x) = 1/2$ and $B(y) = 1/2$ which might be difficult to interpret.

Note that in the modified approach of Yahia and Krajči, extents are fuzzy sets and intents are crisp sets while in case of crisply generated concepts, both extents and intents are in general fuzzy sets. As the next theorem shows, this is only a negligible difference since there is a natural isomorphism between the lattice of "one-sided fuzzy concepts" and the lattice of crisply generated fuzzy concepts:

Theorem 2 For an **L**-context $\langle X, Y, I\rangle$, the "one-sided fuzzy concept lattice" $\mathcal{B}_{f,h}(X, Y, I)$ with fuzzy extents and crisp intents (equipped with the above-defined partial order) is a complete lattice which is isomorphic to $\mathcal{B}_c(X, Y, I)$ (equipped with a partial order inherited from $\mathcal{B}(X, Y, I)$). Moreover, there exists an isomorphism such that for the corresponding concepts $\langle A, B\rangle \in \mathcal{B}_{f,h}(X, Y, I)$ and $\langle C, D\rangle \in \mathcal{B}_c(X, Y, I)$ we have $A = C$ and $B =^1 D$.

Proof Omitted due to lack of space (use definitions and Theorem 1).

For further properties of crisply generated fuzzy concepts we refer to [15].

3.6 The approach of Snášel, Vojtáš *et al.*

Another approach appeared in [38] and in a series of related papers. The basic idea is to consider, for a given L-context $\langle X, Y, I\rangle$, formal contexts $\langle X, Y, {}^aI\rangle$ for $a \in K$ for a suitable subset $K \subseteq L$. That is, one takes a-cuts ${}^aI = \{\langle x, y\rangle \mid I(x, y) \geq a\}$ of the original fuzzy relation I for each $a \in K$. K contains truth degrees which are considered important, relevant, sufficiently covering L, etc. Since ${}^aI$ is an ordinary relation, $\langle X, Y, {}^aI\rangle$ is an ordinary formal context. Therefore, one can apply (ordinary) formal concept analysis to each $\langle X, Y, {}^aI\rangle$. Particularly, one can form concept lattices $\mathcal{B}(X, Y, {}^aI)$. All $\mathcal{B}(X, Y, {}^aI)$'s are then "merged" into a structure $\bigsqcup_{a\in K} \mathcal{B}(X, Y, {}^aI)$ defined by

$$\bigsqcup_{a\in K} \mathcal{B}(X, Y, {}^aI) = \{\langle A, B\rangle \mid A \in \mathrm{Ext}({}^aI) \text{ for some } a \in K;$$
$$B \text{ is a multiset in } Y \text{ with } B(y) = |\{a \in K;\ A \in \mathrm{Ext}({}^aI),\ y \in A^{\uparrow_{aI}}\}|\}.$$

$\bigsqcup_{a\in K} \mathcal{B}(X, Y, {}^aI)$ then represents the resulting structure derived from the fuzzy context $\langle X, Y, I\rangle$. Here, $\mathrm{Ext}({}^aI) = \{A \subseteq X \mid \langle A, A^{\uparrow_{aI}}\rangle \in \mathcal{B}(X, Y, {}^aI)\}$ denotes the set of all extents of formal concepts from $\mathcal{B}(X, Y, {}^aI)$. Recall that a multiset may contain multiple occurrences of elements. Therefore, a multiset B in a universe set Y may be understood as a function assigning to each $y \in Y$ a nonnegative integer $B(y)$ (the number of occurrences of y in B). That is, $\bigsqcup_{a\in K} \mathcal{B}(X, Y, {}^aI)$ contains pairs $\langle A, B\rangle$ where A is the extent of some formal concept of ${}^aI$, and B is a multiset of attributes with $B(y)$ being the number of cut-levels $a \in K$ for which A is an extent of $\langle X, Y, {}^aI\rangle$ and y belongs to $A^{\uparrow_{aI}}$.

Although this approach is very different from the other ones, there is still the following relationship:

Theorem 3 For a linearly ordered complete residuated lattice **L** of truth values with $a \otimes b = \min(a, b)$ and any truth degree $a \in L$ we have

$$\mathrm{Ext}({}^aI) = \{{}^aA \mid \langle A, B\rangle \in \mathcal{B}_c(X, Y, I)\}.$$

Proof Omitted due to lack of space.

Therefore, extents of concepts from $\bigsqcup_{a\in K}\mathcal{B}(X, Y, {}^{a}I)$ are just a-cuts of (crisply generated) concepts from $\mathcal{B}_c(X, Y, I)$. A more detailed discussion is left to a full paper.

3.7 Concept lattices and Galois connections with hedges

As a generalization of both fuzzy concept lattcies of Pollandt and Bělohlávek and lattices of crisply generated fuzzy concepts, the authors proposed the following approach in [18]. The approach consists in emplyoing, as parameters, two unary functions on L, called hedges. For a complete residuated lattice $\mathbf{L}$, a (truth-stressing) hedge is a unary function * satisfying (i) $1^* = 1$, (ii) $a^* \leq a$, (iii) $(a \to b)^* \leq a^* \to b^*$, (iv) $a^{**} = a^*$, for all $a, b \in L$. A hedge * is a (truth function of) logical connective "very true" [29]. The largest hedge (by pointwise ordering) is identity, the least hedge is globalization which is defined by $a^* = 1$ for $a = 1$ and $a^* = 0$ for $a < 1$.

Given an $\mathbf{L}$-context $\langle X, Y, I\rangle$, one can proceed as follows. Let $*_X$ and $*_Y$ be hedges (their meaning will become apparent later). For $\mathbf{L}$-sets $A \in \mathbf{L}^X$ ($\mathbf{L}$-set of objects), $B \in \mathbf{L}^Y$ ($\mathbf{L}$-set of attributes) we define $\mathbf{L}$-sets $A^{\uparrow} \in \mathbf{L}^Y$ ($\mathbf{L}$-set of attributes), $B^{\downarrow} \in \mathbf{L}^X$ ($\mathbf{L}$-set of objects) by

$$A^{\uparrow}(y) = \bigwedge_{x\in X}\big(A(x)^{*_X} \to I(x, y)\big),$$
$$B^{\downarrow}(x) = \bigwedge_{y\in Y}\big(B(y)^{*_Y} \to I(x, y)\big).$$

We put $\mathcal{B}(X^{*_X}, Y^{*_Y}, I) = \{\langle A, B\rangle \in \mathbf{L}^X \times \mathbf{L}^Y \mid A^{\uparrow} = B, B^{\downarrow} = A\}$. For $\langle A_1, B_1\rangle, \langle A_2, B_2\rangle \in \mathcal{B}(X^{*_X}, Y^{*_Y}, I)$, put $\langle A_1, B_1\rangle \leq \langle A_2, B_2\rangle$ iff $A_1 \subseteq A_2$ (or, iff $B_2 \subseteq B_1$; both ways are equivalent). Operators $^{\downarrow}, ^{\uparrow}$ form a so-called Galois connection with hedges [18]. $\langle \mathcal{B}(X^{*_X}, Y^{*_Y}, I), \leq\rangle$ is called a *concept lattice with hedges* induced by $\langle X, Y, I\rangle$ (it is, indeed, a complete lattice [18]). The following is the basic relationship to the above described approaches.

Theorem 4 For ^{*_X} and ^{*_Y} being identities, $\mathcal{B}(X^{*_X}, Y^{*_Y}, I)$ coincides with $\mathcal{B}(X, Y, I)$ (fuzzy concept lattice of Pollandt and Bělohlávek). For ^{*_X} being identity and ^{*_Y} being globalization, $\mathcal{B}(X^{*_X}, Y^{*_Y}, I)$ coincides with $\mathcal{B}_c(X, Y, I)$ (set of all crisply generated fuzzy concepts).

Note, however, that there are other choices of ^{*_X} and ^{*_Y} possible. As demonstrated in [18], ^{*_X} and ^{*_Y} can be seen as parameters controlling the size of the resulting $\mathcal{B}(X^{*_X}, Y^{*_Y}, I)$.

3.8 Krajči's generalized concept lattice

In [33, 34, 35], Krajči studies a so-called generalized concept lattice. In the previous approaches to concept lattices, formal concepts are defined as certain pairs $\langle A, B\rangle$ where for A and B we can have the following possibilities: both A and B are crisp sets, both A and B are fuzzy sets, A is crisp and B is fuzzy, A is fuzzy and B is crisp. Krajči suggests to consider three sets of truth degrees in general, namely, a set L_X (for objects), L_Y (for attributes), and L (for degrees to which objects have attributes, i.e. table entries).

Given sets X and Y of objects and attributes, one can consider a fuzzy context as a triplet $\langle X, Y, I\rangle$ where I is an L-relation between X and Y, i.e. $I \in L^{X\times Y}$. Furthermore, one can consider L_X-sets A of objects and L_Y-sets B of attributes, i.e. $A \in L_X^X$ and $B \in L_Y^Y$. Furthermore, Krajči assumes that L_X and L_Y are complete lattices and L is a partially ordered set. For convenience, we denote all the partial orders (on L_X, L_Y, and L) by $\leq$. Likewise, infima and suprema in both $\langle L_X, \leq\rangle$ and $\langle L_Y, \leq\rangle$ will be denoted by $\bigwedge$ and $\bigvee$.

In order to define arrow-operators, Krajči assumes that there is an operation $\otimes$: $L_X \times L_Y \to L$ satisfying

$$a_1 \leq a_2 \text{ implies } a_1 \otimes b \leq a_2 \otimes b, \tag{12}$$

$$b_1 \leq b_2 \text{ implies } a \otimes b_1 \leq a \otimes b_2, \tag{13}$$

$$\text{if } a_j \otimes b \leq c \text{ for each } j \in J \text{ then } (\textstyle\bigvee_{j\in J} a_j) \otimes b \leq c, \tag{14}$$

$$\text{if } a \otimes b_j \leq c \text{ for each } j \in J \text{ then } a \otimes (\textstyle\bigvee_{j\in J} b_j) \leq c, \tag{15}$$

for each index set J and all $a, a_j \in L_X$, $b, b_j \in L_Y$, and $c \in L$. That is, we have a three-sorted structure $\langle L_1, L_2, L, \otimes, \leq, \dots\rangle$ of truth degrees. Call such a structure $\langle L_1, L_2, L, \otimes, \leq, \dots\rangle$ satisfying (12)–(15) Krajči's structure.

Then, Krajči introduces mappings $^{\nearrow} : L_X^X \to L_Y^Y$ and $^{\swarrow} : L_Y^Y \to L_X^X$ by

$$A^{\nearrow}(y) = \bigvee\{b \in L_Y \mid \text{ for each } x \in X : A(x) \otimes b \leq I(x, y)\}, \tag{16}$$

$$B^{\swarrow}(x) = \bigvee\{a \in L_X \mid \text{ for each } y \in Y : a \otimes B(y) \leq I(x, y)\}, \tag{17}$$

and defines a formal concept in $\langle X, Y, I\rangle$ as a pair $\langle A, B\rangle \in L_X^X \times L_Y^Y$ satisfying $A^{\nearrow} = B$ and $B^{\swarrow} = A$.

At first sight, it looks like there is no adjointness involved. Also, compared to (7) and (8), (16) and (17) seem a bit complicated. However, the following theorem shows that Krajči's structure $\langle L_1, L_2, L, \otimes, \leq, \dots\rangle$ can be looked at as a three-sorted structure with two implication connectives satisfying adjointness-like conditions.

Theorem 5 (residuated structure for generalized concept lattices) Let L_1, L_2 be complete lattices and L be a partially ordered set (all partial orders are denoted by $\leq$).

(1) For a Krajči's structure $\langle L_1, L_2, L, \otimes, \leq, \dots\rangle$ define for $c \in L_1$, $d \in L_2$, and $p \in L$,

$$c \to_1 p = \bigvee\{d \in L_2 \mid c \otimes d \leq p\}, \tag{18}$$

$$d \to_2 p = \bigvee\{c \in L_1 \mid c \otimes d \leq p\}. \tag{19}$$

Then we have the following form of adjointness:

$$c \otimes d \leq p \quad \text{iff} \quad c \leq d \to_2 p \quad \text{iff} \quad d \leq c \to_1 p. \tag{20}$$

(2) If $\langle L_1, L_2, L, \otimes, \to_1, \to_2, \dots\rangle$ satisfies (20), then $\langle L_1, L_2, L, \otimes, \leq, \dots\rangle$ is a Krajči's structure.

Proof Omitted due to lack of space.

Then, arrow operators have the form similar to (7) and (8).

Theorem 6 (arrows via residuum for generalized concept lattices) We have

$$A^{\nearrow}(y) = \bigwedge_{x \in X} (A(x) \rightarrow_1 I(x, y)), \tag{21}$$

$$B^{\swarrow}(x) = \bigwedge_{y \in Y} (B(y) \rightarrow_2 I(x, y)). \tag{22}$$

Proof Omitted due to lack of space.

Due to Theorem 5, a structure $\langle L_1, L_2, L, \otimes, \rightarrow_1, \rightarrow_2, \ldots \rangle$ satisfying (20) can be called a three-sorted complete residuated lattice. Theorems 5 and 6 show that Krajči's approach can be seen as another approach (a very general one) in the framework of residuated structures of truth degrees.

A main theorem for a generalized concept lattice is presented in [33]. In particular, each generalized concept lattice is a complete lattice. Note furthermore that in a recent paper [35], Krajči shows that each concept lattice with hedges is isomorphic to some generalized concept lattice. The question of whether each generalized concept lattice is isomorphic to some concept lattice with hedges seems to be an open problem.

4 Concluding remarks

- As mentioned above, we did not discuss the relationship of the approaches presented here with so-called conceptual scaling of fuzzy contexts considered as many-valued contexts. This issue will be discussed in a forthcoming paper.
- Proofs of the results presented here, more detailed comments, further results, and examples will be presented in a full version of this paper. In particular, we did not discuss concept lattices and related structures over structures of truth degrees equipped with non-commutative conjunction. This has been developed in [25, 26]. A discussion of relationships to this approach will also be included in the full paper.

References

1. Arnauld A., Nicole P.: *La logique ou l'art de penser*. 1662. Also in German: *Die Logik oder die Kunst des Denkens*. Darmstadt, 1972.
2. Barbut, M., Monjardet, B.: *L'ordre et la classification, algèbre et combinatoire, tome II*. Hachette, Paris (1970).
3. Bělohlávek, R.: Lattices generated by binary fuzzy relations (extended abstract). In: Abstracts of the Fourth International Conference on Fuzzy Sets Theory and Its Applications, p. 11. Slovakia, Liptovsky Jan (1998).
4. Bělohlávek R.: Fuzzy concepts and conceptual structures: induced similarities. Joint Conf. Inf. Sci'.98 Proceedings, Vol. I, pp. 179–182, Durham, USA,: [Assoc. Intel, Machinery (1998)0-9643456-7-6]

5. Bělohlávek, R.: Fuzzy Galois connections. *Math. Log. Quart.* **45**(4), 497–504 (1999).
6. Bělohlávek, R.: Logical precision in concept lattices. *J. Logic and Computation* Vol. **12** No. 6(2002), 137–148.
7. Bělohlávek, R.: Similarity relations in concept lattices. *J. Logic Comput.* **10**(6), 823–845 (2000).
8. Bělohlávek, R.: Lattices of fixed points of fuzzy Galois connections. *Math. Logic Quarterly* **47**(1), 111–116 (2001).
9. Bělohlávek, R.: Reduction and a simple proof of characterization of fuzzy concept lattices. *Fundamenta Informaticae* **46**(4), 277–285 (2001).
10. Bělohlávek, R.: Fuzzy closure operators. *J. Math. Anal. Appl.* **262**, 473–489 (2001).
11. Bělohlávek R.: Fuzzy closure operators II. *Soft Computing* **7**(2002) 1, 53–64.
12. Bělohlávek, R.: *Fuzzy Relational Systems: Foundations and Principles.* Kluwer Academic/Plenum Publishers, New York (2002).
13. Bělohlávek R.: Algorithms for fuzzy concept lattices. Proc. Fourth Int. Conf. on Recent Advances in Soft Computing. Nottingham, United Kingdom, 12–13 December, 2002, pp.67–68 (extended abstract); pp. 200–205 (full paper on the included CD). [ISBN 1-84233-0764]
14. Bělohlávek, R.: Concept lattices and order in fuzzy logic. *Ann. Pure Appl. Logic* **128**, 277–298 (2004).
15. Bělohlávek, R., Sklenář, V., Zacpal, J.: Crisply Generated Fuzzy Concepts. In: B. Ganter and R. Godin (Eds.): ICFCA 2005, *Lecture Notes in Computer Science* **3403**, pp. 268–283, Springer-Verlag, Berlin/Heidelberg, 2005.
16. Bělohlávek R., Chlupová M., Vychodil V.: Implications from data with fuzzy attributes. AISTA 2004 in Cooperation with the IEEE Computer Society Proceedings, 2004, 5 pages, ISBN 2–9599776–8–8.
17. Bělohlávek R., Vychodil V.: Implications from data with fuzzy attributes vs. scaled binary attributes. In: FUZZ-IEEE 2005, The IEEE International Conference on Fuzzy Systems, May 22–25, 2005, Reno (Nevada, USA), pp. 1050–1055 (proceedings on CD), abstract in printed proceedings, p. 53, ISBN 0–7803–9158–6.
18. Bělohlávek R., Vychodil V.: Reducing the size of fuzzy concept lattices by hedges. In: FUZZ-IEEE 2005, The IEEE International Conference on Fuzzy Systems, May 22–25, 2005, Reno (Nevada, USA), pp. 663–668 (proceedings on CD), abstract in printed proceedings, p. 44, ISBN 0–7803–9158–6.
19. Bělohlávek R., Vychodil V.: Fuzzy attribute logic: attribute implications, their validity, entailment, and non-redundant basis. In: Yingming Liu, Guoqing Chen, Mingsheng Ying (Eds.): *Fuzzy Logic, Soft Computing & Computational Intelligence: Eleventh International Fuzzy Systems Association World Congress* (Vol. I), 2005, pp. 622–627. Tsinghua University Press and Springer, ISBN 7–302–11377–7.
20. Bělohlávek R., Vychodil V.: Fuzzy attribute logic: syntactic entailment and completeness. *Proceedings of the 8th Joint Conference on Information Sciences*, 2005, pp. 78–81, ISBN 0–9707890–3–3.
21. Burusco, A., Fuentes-Gonzáles, R.: The study of the L-fuzzy concept lattice. *Mathware & Soft Computing* **3**, 209–218 (1994).
22. Burusco A., Fuentes-Gonzáles R.: Concept lattice defined from implication operators. *Fuzzy Sets and Systems* (2000).

23. Burusco, A., Fuentes-Gonzáles, R.: Contexts with multiple weighted values. *Int. J. Uncertainty, Fuzziness and Knowledge-Based Systems* (2001).
24. Ganter, B., Wille, R.: *Formal Concept Analysis. Mathematical Foundations.* Springer-Verlag, Berlin (1999).
25. Georgescu, G., Popescu, A.: Concept lattices and similarity in non-commutative fuzzy logic. *Fundamenta Informaticae* **53**(1), 23–54 (2002).
26. Georgescu, G., Popescu, A.: Non-commutative Galois connections. *Soft Computing* **7**, 458–467 (2003).
27 Goguen J. A.: The logic of inexact concepts. *Synthese* **18**(1968-9), 325–373.
28. Hájek, P.: *Metamathematics of Fuzzy Logic.* Kluwer, Dordrecht (1998).
29. Hájek, P.: On very true. *Fuzzy sets and systems* **124**, 329–333 (2001).
30. Höhle, U.: On the fundamentals of fuzzy set theory. *J. Math. Anal. Appl.* **201**, 786–826 (1996).
31. Klir, G.J., Yuan, B.: *Fuzzy Sets and Fuzzy Logic. Theory and Applications.* Prentice Hall, Upper Saddle River, NJ (1995)
32. Krajči, S.: Cluster based efficient generation of fuzzy concepts. *Neural Network World* **5**, 521–530 (2003).
33. Krajči S.: The basic theorem on generalized concept lattice. In Bělohlávek R., Snášel V.: *CLA,: Proc. of 2nd Int. Workshop,* Ostrava **2004**, 25–33 (2004).
34. Krajči S.: A generalized concept lattice. *Logic J. of IGPL* (to appear).
35. Krajči S.: Every concept lattice with hedges is isomorphic to some generalized concept lattice. Submitted to *CLA 2005, Proc. of 3nd Int. Workshop.*
36. Pollandt, S.: *Fuzzy Begriffe.* Springer-Verlag, Berlin/Heidelberg (1997).
37. Takeuti, G., Titani, S.: Globalization of intuitionistic set theory. *Annal of Pure and Applied Logic* **33**, 195–211 (1987).
38. Ďuráková D., Krajči S., Snášel V., Vojtáš P.: Conceptual structures. Arbeitstagung Allgemeine Algebra, 2002.
39. Wille R.: Restructuring lattice theory: an approach based on hierarchies of concepts. In: Rival I.: *Ordered Sets.* Reidel, Dordrecht, Boston, 1982, 445–470.
40. Yahia S., Jaoua A.: Discovering knowledge from fuzzy concept lattice. In: Kandel A., Last M., Bunke H.: *Data Mining and Computational Intelligence*, pp. 167–190, Physica-Verlag, 2001.

Contents

Patterns, Clusters, Visualization and Software

Data Analysis

Theory

Methodology

Conceptual Topic Aggregation

Klara M. Gutekunst[1,2], Dominik Dürrschnabel[1,2,3(✉)], Johannes Hirth[1,2], and Gerd Stumme[1,2]

[1] Knowledge and Data Engineering Group, University of Kassel, Kassel, Germany
klara.gutekunst@uni-kassel.de,
{duerrschnabel,hirth,stumme}@cs.uni-kassel.de
[2] Interdisciplinary Research Center for Information System Design, University of Kassel, Kassel, Germany
[3] Baden Wuerttemberg Cooperative State University Mosbach, Mosbach, Germany

Abstract. The vast growth of data has rendered traditional manual inspection infeasible, necessitating the adoption of computational methods for efficient data exploration. Topic modeling has emerged as a powerful tool for analyzing large-scale textual datasets, enabling the extraction of latent semantic structures. However, existing methods for topic modeling often struggle to provide interpretable representations that facilitate deeper insights into data structure and content.

In this paper, we propose FAT-CAT, an approach based on Formal Concept Analysis (FCA) to enhance meaningful topic aggregation and visualization of discovered topics. Our approach can handle diverse topics and file types – grouped by directories – to construct a concept lattice that offers a structured, hierarchical representation of their topic distribution.

In a case study on the ETYNTKE dataset, we evaluate the effectiveness of our approach against other representation methods to demonstrate that FCA-based aggregation provides more meaningful and interpretable insights into dataset composition than existing topic modeling techniques.

Keywords: Topic Modeling · FCA · NLP · Text Mining · Hierarchical Topic Representation · Semantic Analysis

1 Introduction

Investigating large, unstructured datasets with diverse file types is a common challenge, especially in domains such as tax investigation. When leaks potentially involving tax fraud emerge, human analysts must sift through unknown data to find relevant evidence. To support this task, we propose using concept lattices to structure the data hierarchically, enabling efficient identification of meaningful topics and patterns.

Current methods such as LDA, BERTopic, and Top2Vec can be used for the identification of topics in documents. However, these techniques do not leverage

P. Cellier et al. (Eds.): CONCEPTS 2025, LNAI 15941, pp. 3–18, 2025.
https://doi.org/10.1007/978-3-032-03364-2_1

the intrinsic hierarchical structure of the topics encapsulated in the documents. One attempt in the realm of FCA [7] is to overcome this shortcoming by creating document-topic relations and use the concept lattice as a hierarchical representation. However, as they work on independent and homogeneous documents, which are exclusively of textual nature, this method lacks the ability to aggregate information.

In this work, we introduce FCA-based Aggregation for Topics using Conceptual Analysis and Taxonomies (FAT-CAT), which integrates Natural Language Processing (NLP) with FCA, leveraging their complementary strengths to structure and visualize relationships within data. Thereby, we can incorporate heterogenous data, consisting of different data types and content. The main contributions of this work are:

(a) Our approach integrates non-textual image data.
(b) We employ FCA to aggregate topic information effectively, facilitating insight combination across multiple directories.
(c) FAT-CAT is designed to operate with minimal training requirements, utilizing pre-trained, off-the-shelf models and thereby removing the necessity for extensive training.
(d) We demonstrate through a case study on a real-world dataset, how the approach can support a human analyst.
(e) We provide an open-source implementation, accessible on GitHub[1].

The structure of this paper is as follows: In Sect. 2, we review relevant literature. Section 3 presents foundations, followed by Sect. 4, which details our proposed methodology FAT-CAT. In Sect. 5, we present three baseline strategies. Section 6 outlines implementation details of our approach. In Sect. 7, we present a case study on a real-world dataset, including results and an empirical assessment of our approach alongside the baselines. Finally, we conclude with Sect. 8 and outline potential directions for future research.

2 Related Work

The authors of [4] apply FCA to a Twitter dataset to extract insights into the topics present. In their methodology, tweets serve as objects, while words occurring within the tweets act as attributes. They assume that tweets forming a formal concept, i.e., those sharing the same terminology, correspond to the same topic. Upper concepts in the resulting concept lattice represent general topics, whereas lower-level concepts reflect more specific themes. However, a key limitation of their approach is the excessive number of concepts generated, making interpretation challenging. To mitigate this, they introduce upper and lower frequency thresholds, discarding terms whose occurrence falls outside these predefined bounds, arguing that the former are too general and the latter too specific

[1] https://github.com/KlaraGtknst/text_topic (29.01.2025) & https://github.com/KlaraGtknst/clj_exploration_leaks (29.01.2025).

for meaningful analysis. While their approach provides valuable means as how to derive topic structures from text data, it relies purely on term frequency as attributes rather than leveraging the semantic relationships inherent in topic models, as we do in this work.

The authors of [12] employ FCA to structure topic representations derived from a topic model. They construct two matrices: One capturing document-topic probabilities obtained through their ILDA model and another representing topic-word probabilities, restricted to the top ten words per topic. Unlike our approach, which automatically derives hierarchical relationships, their method relies on manual categorization of topics into broader thematic groups. These manually curated categories are subsequently visualized using a FCA-inspired order diagrams to reflect topic generalization. In contrast, our approach seeks to infer hierarchical topic structures automatically, without requiring manual intervention.

According to [14], Hierarchical Latent Dirichlet Allocation (hLDA) organizes extracted topics into a tree, and requires documents with clear structure and rigorous style. Since our approach aims to analyze the structure of diverse data rather than demanding a specific structure, we do not employ hLDA. Moreover, we chose to employ FCA since trees give less structural information than lattices.

The authors of [10] also leverage FCA to structure topic hierarchies. They utilize LDA for topic modeling, encoding documents based on the distribution of topics. Similar to our approach, they introduce a thresholding mechanism to retain only relevant topics per document. However, a major divergence lies in their reliance on HowNet, a linguistic knowledge base. Their primary objective is to facilitate precise querying, using a concept lattice to provide a more nuanced representation of documents beyond mere word-level indexing. To manage the complexity of the lattice, they eliminate concepts whose attribute sets exhibit excessively high or low support. While effective for information retrieval, their approach differs from ours in fundamental ways. The focus of our approach is uncovering hierarchical relationships within topic structures across the dataset, rather than enhancing document retrieval. We do not discard high-support concepts, as they provide crucial insights into overarching themes.

Our approach builds on the work of the authors of [7] who propose extracting two relational structures from topic models. The first structure is a weighted document-topic relation, i.e., which topics t_i are present in which documents d_j. The second structure is a weighted topic-word relation, i.e., which words w_k are present in which topics t_i. These relations are subsequently used to derive incidence matrices, as visualized in Tables 1 and 2.

To compute a binary relation from the document-topic relation, they apply a thresholding approach, while for the term-topic relation, they retain only the top n words per topic. Subsequently, the authors compute the formal concepts of high support. Their approach enables a structured representation of topic hierarchies, which they demonstrate on academic papers from machine learning conferences. The approach lacks the possibility to compare subsets of the whole dataset, which might stem from an organization of files into directories.

Table 1. Document-topic relation

Documents	Topics			
	t_1	t_2	$\cdots$	t_n
d_1	$w_{1,1}$	$w_{1,2}$	$\cdots$	$w_{1,n}$
d_2	$w_{2,1}$	$w_{2,2}$	$\cdots$	$w_{2,n}$
$\vdots$	$\vdots$	$\vdots$	$\ddots$	$\vdots$
d_l	$w_{l,1}$	$w_{l,2}$	$\cdots$	$w_{l,n}$

Table 2. Term-topic relation

Terms	Topics			
	t_1	t_2	$\cdots$	t_n
s_1	$\hat{w}_{1,1}$	$\hat{w}_{1,2}$	$\cdots$	$\hat{w}_{1,n}$
s_2	$\hat{w}_{2,1}$	$\hat{w}_{2,2}$	$\cdots$	$\hat{w}_{2,n}$
$\vdots$	$\vdots$	$\vdots$	$\ddots$	$\vdots$
s_l	$\hat{w}_{l,1}$	$\hat{w}_{l,2}$	$\cdots$	$\hat{w}_{l,n}$

By contrast, our approach addresses this limitation by explicitly incorporating cross-directory topic structures, allowing for a more comprehensive analysis of thematic relationships spanning multiple data sources. Furthermore, our method is not restricted to only textual data.

3 Foundations

Formal Concept Analysis (FCA). The mathematical theory of FCA [5] is a method to analyze relational data in a hierarchical structure. The triple $\mathbb{K} :- (G, M, I)$ defines the *formal context*. G is the set of *objects*, M is the set of *attributes*, and $I \subseteq G \times M$ is the *incidence relation*, which describes when an object g has an attribute m. The object derivation $(\cdot)' : \mathcal{P}(G) \to \mathcal{P}(M)$ defines for any subset $A \subseteq G$ as $A' :- \{m \in M \mid \forall g \in A : (g, m) \in I\}$. The attribute derivation $(\cdot)' : \mathcal{P}(M) \to \mathcal{P}(G)$ is defined for any subset $B \subseteq M$ as $B' :- \{g \in G \mid \forall m \in B : (g, m) \in I\}$. The same notation $(\cdot)'$ is used for both derivation operators. A formal concept of $\mathbb{K}$ is a pair (A, B) where $A \subseteq G$ and $B \subseteq M$ satisfy the conditions $A' = B$ and $B' = A$. The set $\mathfrak{B}(\mathbb{K})$ denotes all formal concepts of $\mathbb{K}$. The concept lattice $\underline{\mathfrak{B}}(\mathbb{K}) :- (\mathfrak{B}(\mathbb{K}), \leq)$ is defined by the set of all formal concepts with the order relation $(A, B) \leq (C, D)$ if and only if $A \subseteq C$.

Image Captioner. An image captioner is a tool to generate textual descriptions from images. In this paper, we specifically employ the Generative Image-to-text Transformer (GIT)[2] model [11]. It is a straightforward generative model comprising an image encoder and a text decoder. The image encoder is a Contrastive Learning-pretrained, Swim-like vision transformer, which outputs a flattened 2D representation of the image. This vector is then projected into D dimensions before being passed to the text decoder, a transformer module, which generates coherent textual descriptions. This pre-trained model has the ability to generate meaningful captions without the need for custom training, enabling us to seamlessly integrate visual information into our topic modeling process.

[2] https://huggingface.co/microsoft/git-base (29.01.2025).

Top2Vec. The pre-trained topic model Top2Vec [2], which is employed in this study, embeds texts into the same vector space as words and topics. This is particularly advantageous, as it allows for semantic similarity calculations between texts, words, and topics. The model encodes texts using a multilingual Universal Sentence Encoder (USE) model [13], supporting 16 languages, which is crucial for working with diverse datasets containing multiple languages. The documents are first embedded into a 300-dimensional space, then reduced to 5 dimensions and finally clustered into topics. Due to the modular design of our approach, it is straightforward to substitute Top2Vec with alternative topic modeling algorithms, such as BERTopic, that offer comparable functionality.

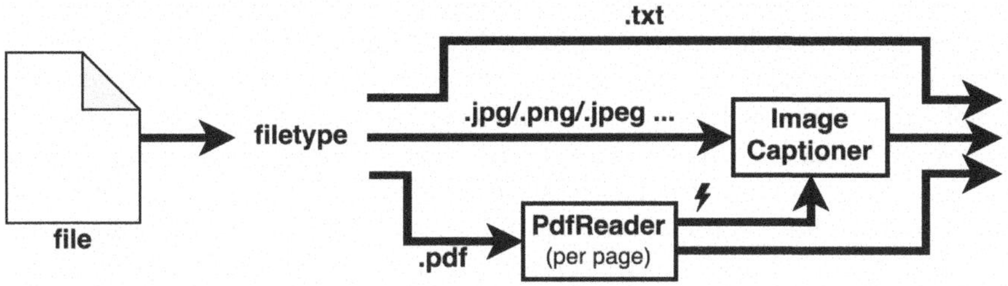

Fig. 1. Visual representation of the workflow for extracting text from the data files. If a page of a PDF document contains no text or raises an error during extraction, the image captioner is used to generate a textual description of the image of that page.

TITANIC. Computing concept lattices for large datasets presents a significant challenge, as the size of a concept lattice can grow exponentially with respect to the size of the context. Consequently, complete visualizations of large concept lattices may obscure important hierarchical relationships within the data, hindering human interpretation. To address this issue, [9] introduced the TITANIC algorithm, which computes iceberg concept lattices. An iceberg concept lattice includes only the top-level concepts, specifically those corresponding to frequent attribute sets.

The authors define a minimum support threshold, $minsupp \in [0, 1]$, below which attribute sets are not considered frequent. An attribute set $B \subseteq M$ is deemed frequent in $\mathbb{K}$ if its support

$$supp(B) = \frac{|B'|}{|G|}$$

meets or exceeds the *minsupp* threshold. A concept (A, B) is considered frequent if its intent B constitutes a frequent attribute set. The iceberg concept lattice of a context $\mathbb{K}$ comprises all such frequent concepts.

4 Method

The *FCA-based Aggregation for Topics using Conceptual Analysis and Taxonomies (FAT-CAT)* methodology introduced in this paper outlines a systematic workflow for deriving the directory-topic concept lattice of a dataset. First, we extract the text from the data files. The processing of text-related fields follows a distinct workflow, as shown in Fig. 1.

By employing a topic model, specifically the Top2Vec model, we extract the topics of the documents. While the model typically returns only one topic per document, we retrieve the top ten topics for each document to capture a broader range of thematic content. Additionally, the model provides topic scores, topic words, and word scores, which we leverage to derive document-topic relationships, as proposed by [7] (cf. Table 1). These topics are assigned real values $w_{i,j} \in \mathbb{R}$, which indicate the relevance of a respective topic t_i to document d_j. Next, these weights are row-normalized. The binary document-topic incidence matrix is then created by applying a threshold δ, which helps in determining the most relevant topics to each document. If $w_{i,j} \geq \delta$, topic t_i is present in document d_j. The threshold is the first value such that the density of thresholded weights is below a certain density threshold. With accordance to [7], we set the density threshold to 0.1 to obtain a reasonably sparse binary incidence leading to a comprehensibly sized concept lattice including the most important topics. The computation resulting in $\delta = 0.09$ is visualized in Fig. 2. After δ is determined, we obtain the binary document-topic incidence matrix

$$\mathcal{D}_\delta(i,j) = \begin{cases} 1 & \text{if } w_{i,j} \geq \delta, \\ 0 & \text{else.} \end{cases}$$

This matrix serves as the foundation for understanding how topics are distributed across different directories.

Compared to the approach of Hirth and Hanika [7], we aggregate the binary document-topic incidence matrices from all directories to gain a broader understanding of the dataset's topic structure as a whole. The workflow is visualized in Fig. 3.

We adopt the TITANIC algorithm as it generates interpretable concept lattices from large datasets, making it well-suited for our study. For each directory, we compute an iceberg concept lattice. We focus on high-support concepts because their attribute sets represent topics that are consistently present across

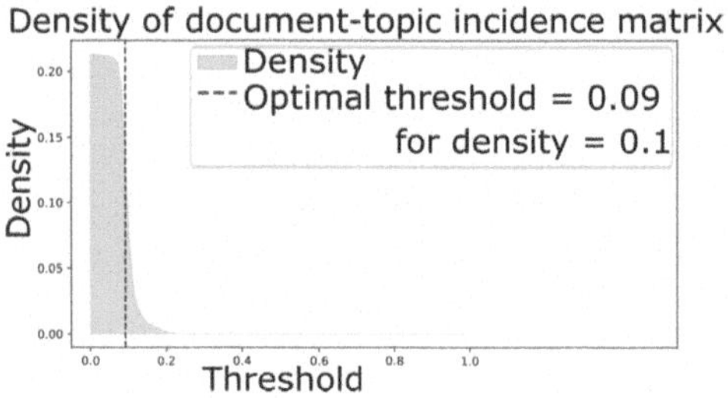

Fig. 2. Computation of threshold δ such that the resulting thresholded binary document-topic incidence $\mathcal{D}_\delta$ has a density of $\frac{|\mathcal{D}_\delta|}{|D \times T|} = 0.1$.

Table 3. Weighted directory-topic relation. The weights $\tilde{w}_{i,j} \in \{0,1\}$ represent whether a topic t_j is present in a directory $\hat{d}_i$.

Directories	Topics			
	t_1	t_2		t_n
$\hat{d}_1$	$\tilde{w}_{1,1}$	$\tilde{w}_{1,2}$	$\cdots$	$\tilde{w}_{1;n}$
$\hat{d}_2$	$\tilde{w}_{2,1}$	$\tilde{w}_{2,2}$	$\cdots$	$\tilde{w}_{2,n}$
$\vdots$	$\vdots$	$\vdots$	$\ddots$	$\vdots$
$\hat{d}_k$	$\tilde{w}_{k,1}$	$\tilde{w}_{k,2}$	$\cdots$	$\tilde{w}_{k,n}$

many documents in a directory. These frequent topics capture broader themes that are widely distributed throughout the respective directory, making them ideal for constructing a representative set of attributes. The minimum support is a parameter that should be chosen according to the degree of detail in which the data ought to be explored. According to the experience of the authors, a starting parameter of 0.1 is recommendable. The sequence of frequent concepts over multiple directories is then used to build the incidence matrix presented in Table 3. This aggregation allows for a hierarchical investigation of the dataset, where more general topics appear at the top of the hierarchy and more specific topics are found towards the bottom.

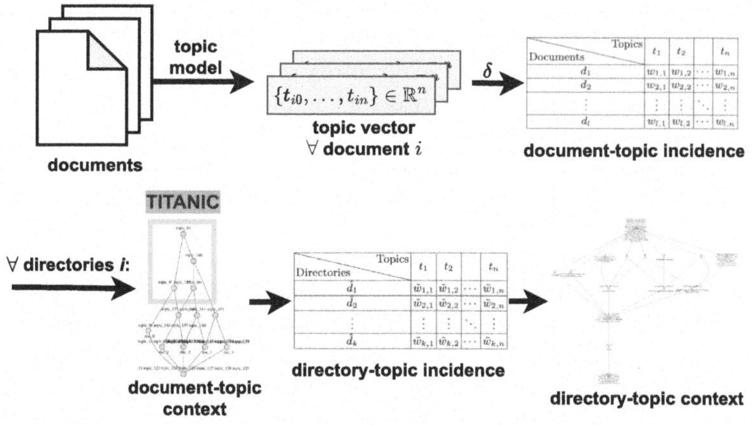

Fig. 3. Workflow for deriving the directory-topic concept lattice.

5 Baselines

The following sections outline common topic visualization strategies serving as baselines for our approach. We begin with word clouds, a simple, frequency-based visualization baseline of the most common words in a document. Next, we describe the Embedding - Dimension Reduction (EDR) approach that clusters low-dimensional embeddings of the documents by directories. We then explore Clustering Named Entities (CNE).

Word Clouds. An initial approach for visualizing topics involves using word clouds, a simple and intuitive method for displaying the most frequent words in a document. A word cloud is a visual representation of text data where words are displayed in varying sizes based on their frequency or importance. It helps identify key themes and trends in textual content at a glance. Since we are interested in the content of the directories, we generate word clouds for each directory in the dataset. The Figs. 9a and 9b show examples of word clouds.

Embedding - Dimension Reduction (EDR). The second baseline approach EDR, whose workflow is illustrated in Fig. 4, aims to cluster documents by directories to investigate whether the files within a directory exhibit semantic similarity in terms of content. To achieve this, the text from the files is embedded with the Sentence-BERT (SBERT) model in a vector space such that distance correlates with semantic dissimilarity. Subsequently, dimensionality reduction is employed to enable visualization via a scatter plot. For this baseline we tried the three different dimensionality reducing algorithms Principal Component Analysis (PCA), Uniform Manifold Approximation and Projection for Dimension Reduction (UMAP), and t-Distributed Stochastic Neighbor Embedding (t-SNE) (cf. Fig. 10) and settled on t-SNE, as the other two empirically lacked the ability to clearly separate of the data points. The directory names serve as class labels for the files, i.e., they give the color of the presented points. To make the method applicable to large-scale datasets, the directory names are preprocessed to reduce the number of classes. Specifically, directory names that contain more than 50% numerical characters are replaced with the label "numbers", while any remaining directory names containing numbers have the numbers stripped. Directory names with fewer than five alphabetic characters are replaced with the label "chars".

Clustering Named Entities (CNE). The baseline CNE builds on Named Entity Recognition (NER), which identifies and classifies entities into predefined categories, such as organizations, locations, dates, and other relevant terms [1]. Thereby, NER provides a method for categorizing text. The NER workflow, as shown in Fig. 5, begins with truncating the text to meet the input length constraints of the `nlp` object. The NER model is then applied to the text, restructuring the identified Named Entitys (NEs) so that each entity category functions as a key mapping to a list of corresponding NEs. This structure allows for the efficient retrieval of named entities by category, facilitating their use in subsequent analyses.

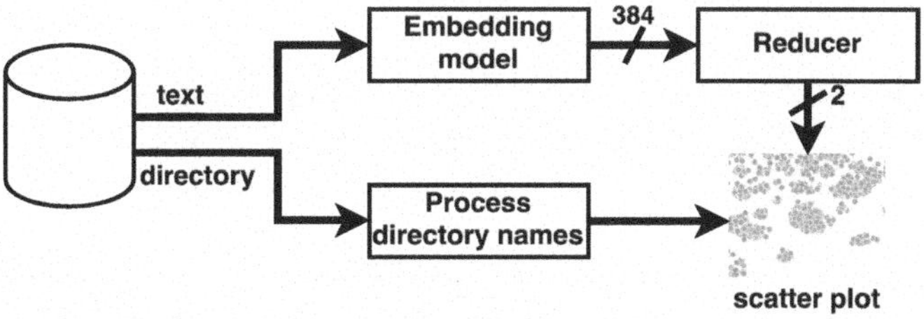

Fig. 4. Illustration of the dimensionality reduction process for document embeddings colored by directory labels. The embedding model SBERT omits 384 dimensional embeddings for each text. They are reduced to two dimensions using PCA, UMAP or t-SNE. The directory names are preprocessed to group similar ones and reduce the number of classes since they are used to color the points in the scatter plot.

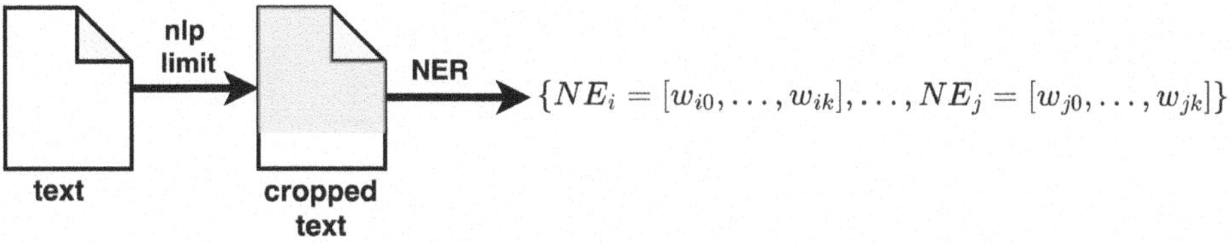

Fig. 5. Visual representation of the workflow from text processing to the structure storing NEs for a given document.

In this baseline, we disregard the hierarchical directory structure and focus on the clustering of NEs for distinct categories. The approach of clustering of NEs has been proposed by [1]. The workflow of this baseline is illustrated in Fig. 6. First, NER is applied to all texts. While [1] replaces similar NEs with a single version, referred to as soft entity linking, we omit this step, though it may improve clustering results.

Subsequently, NEs are embedded using a language model that produces embeddings comparable via cosine similarity. This study employs the pre-trained Word2Vec model. For each NE category i, the $N = 50$ most frequent NEs are extracted. A symmetric $N \times N$ similarity matrix is computed for the most frequent NEs within each category, using cosine similarity as a similarity measure. Each row of the similarity matrix is treated as the feature vector of a given NE. These NEs are then clustered using the k-Means algorithm, with $k = 5$. We chose $k = 5$ as a reasonable number of clusters for the NE categories, after consulting the elbow method across multiple NE categories as displayed in Fig. 7. Choosing more than five clusters does not substantially increase the compactness of the clusters. Both N and k are hyperparameters which can be optimized.

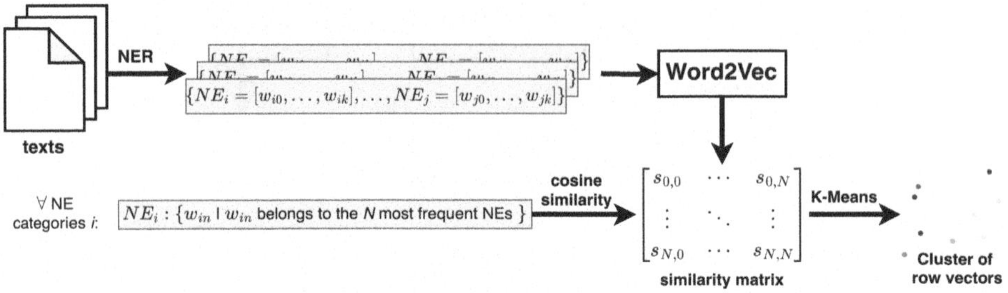

Fig. 6. Illustrates the workflow for deriving a clustering of the NE categories i.

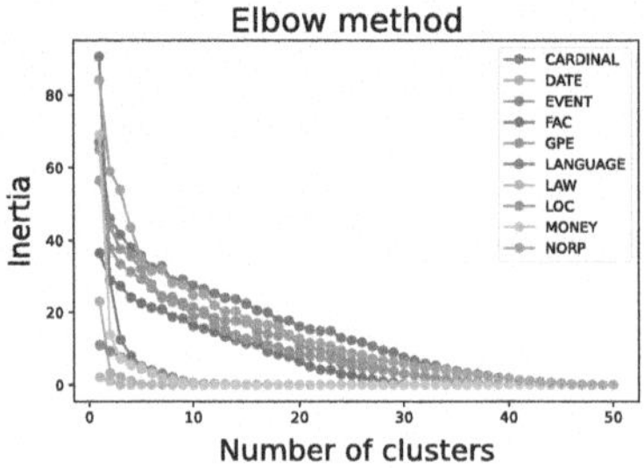

Fig. 7. Elbow method for selecting k in k-means across selected NE categories.

6 Implementation

This section details the implementation of the key components of our approach. Several FCA tools used in this work are implemented by the `conexp-clj` library [6]. We derive iceberg concept lattices via the TITANIC algorithm. We choose a minimum support threshold of 0.1 as we usually observed around 15 concepts which is a reasonable amount to be readable by a human analyst. For text visualization via word clouds, we utilize the Python library `wordcloud`[3] which is employed with its default parameters. To extract NEs, we employ the pre-trained `en_core_web_sm` pipeline from the spaCy library, serving as the `nlp` object. This lightweight model, trained on English text, provides a general-purpose pipeline for tagging, parsing, lemmatization, and NER[4]. However, this implementation is constrained to a maximum of 10^6 tokens[5].

7 Case Study

To assess the applicability of our approach FAT-CAT, we apply our method alongside three baselines to the ETYNTKE dataset. The next section describes

[3] https://github.com/amueller/word_cloud (01.02.2025).
[4] https://spacy.io/models (13.02.2025).
[5] https://spacy.io/api/language (30.01.2025).

the dataset, followed by an evaluation of our approach against baseline techniques.

7.1 Dataset

The dataset utilized in this study, referred to as Everything You Need To Know Ever (ETYNTKE)[6], comprises approximately 101 GB of images, text documents, and other file types uploaded in 2015. It covers a diverse range of topics, including politics, weaponry, and computer science, providing a rich and varied foundation for extracting semantic insights. This diversity is particularly suited for the application of our FCA approach, as it enables the exploration of patterns across multiple domains, showcasing the versatility of the methodology.

Structurally, the dataset follows a hierarchical organization, with files arranged in folders and subfolders. The presence of malformed files, which cannot be opened or read, adds an additional layer of complexity, making the dataset an ideal challenge for testing the robustness and adaptability of our approach.

The large size, heterogeneity, and hierarchical structure of ETYNTKE make it an ideal candidate for applying our FAT-CAT methodology, as we can leverage the organizational structure in our approach. Its variety of content, along with the potential inconsistencies in its organization, provides a comprehensive testbed for exploring how NLP and FCA can work together to extract meaningful insights and structure complex datasets.

7.2 FAT-CAT

The lattice resulting from the ETYNTKE dataset is illustrated in Fig. 8. Topics, represented by numbers above the nodes, propagate downward to transitive adjacent nodes. Consequently, every node connected to and below node 94 also contains topic 94. Topics associated with higher nodes are more common among directories, whereas lower nodes contain more specific topics found in fewer directories. The uppermost node represents topics shared across all directories. In this case, no such topic exists. Ranges of consecutive topic numbers are denoted by their lowest and highest IDs, separated by a hyphen. A subset of topic words for a selection of topic IDs is given in Table 4. The topic model successfully merged content from different languages into single, unified topics, indicating it captures cross-lingual semantic similarity. The concept lattice then organizes these topics by structural relationships, enabling a hierarchical investigation of the dataset through the ordering of concepts. While the topic model extracts and clusters semantic content, the concept lattice structures and contextualizes these clusters to support exploratory analysis. As directories propagate upwards, lower nodes correspond to fewer directories.

[6] https://archive.org/details/ETYNTKE (29.01.2025).

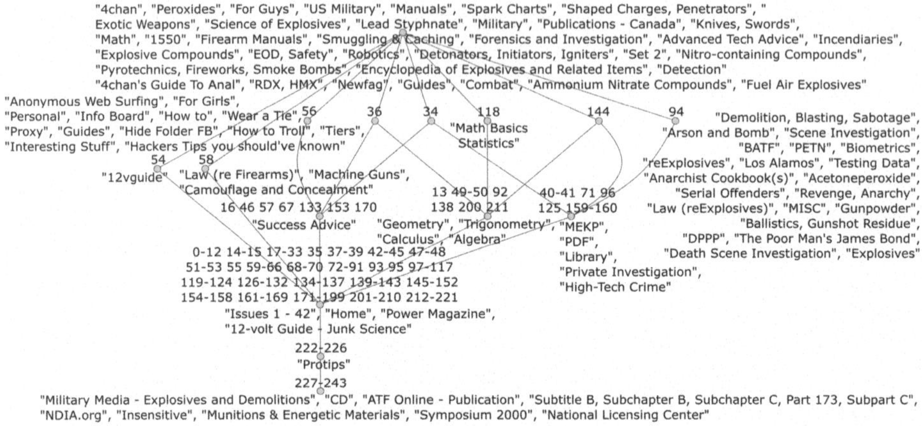

Fig. 8. Concept lattice representing the directory-topic incidence of the dataset ETYNTKE. The numbers correspond to topic IDs, with each topic characterized by 50 words, as determined by the Top2Vec model. A subset of the topic IDs is mapped to corresponding terms in Table 4. The text entries below the nodes represent directory names.

A motif is a statistically significant subgraph or pattern [8]. The presence of such structural patterns, which can be identified in Fig. 8, including both contranominal and ordinal motifs, suggests promising opportunities for analysis. In accordance with expectations, the directories at the bottom of the graph, which are considered the most specific in terms of topic categorization, predominantly contain subdirectories. It is noteworthy that the only directory present at both the highest level of the directory hierarchy and the bottom node is the `Military` directory. With respect to content, some directories exhibit intriguing thematic associations. The `High-Tech Crime` directory, for instance, comprises topics related to explosives, while the `Success Advice` directory additionally features content concerning chemicals. The top node of the ordinal motif, which aggregates the incoming edges, introduces philosophical content. Consequently, the content of directories positioned at the lowermost levels of the graph, which predominantly comprise subdirectories, encompasses a greater proportion of philosophical subjects in comparison to directories positioned at more elevated levels within the graph and, in some cases, the directory hierarchy of the dataset.

Our approach FAT-CAT enables us to explore large datasets without the need for manual inspection of each document. The hierarchical structure of the concept lattice offers insights into the relationships between topics, facilitating a deeper understanding of how different themes interconnect across directories. However, it is important to note that while this approach offers valuable insights, the visual representation may not be intuitive to all users, particularly those unfamiliar with concept lattices or FCA. The topics are represented by their IDs, because the space is too limited to display 50 words per topic.

Table 4. Subset of translated topic IDs and their top 5 descriptive words for the directory-topic concept lattice.

Topic ID	Topic Words				
34	gun	weapons	rifles	pistol	firearm
36	terminological	nonverbal	linguist	codeword	longtext
54	microelectron	microkernels	microparticle	microphysics	microcosmic
56	pythonpath	pythonmac	python_version	python_object	pythonpowered
58	nuclear	hazardous	explosive	nanotoxicity	chernobyl
94	project	fundraiser	donation	volunteering	charity

7.3 Baselines

Word Clouds. These word clouds not only provide an overview of the directory's content based on the most frequent terms in the directory but also allow identifying directories noteworthy of further inspection. Intuitively, if the words of a word cloud do not align with the expected content of the directory name, or if a word cloud includes terms of particular relevance, one can consider the directory in further data mining. While word clouds are intuitive and simple to interpret, they have limitations. They only display the most frequent words, which may not fully represent the semantic relationships between terms. Moreover, the quality of the word clouds is dependent on the quality of the text extraction process (cf. Fig. 1). Furthermore, by inspection of the word clouds for the directories `Military` and `Spytech`, respectively displayed in Fig. 9a and 9b, it becomes evident that it is complicated to compare the content of different directories.

Embedding - Dimension Reduction (EDR). Ideally, the dimensionality reduction algorithm should separate the clusters of documents associated with different directories. Although t-SNE provides the best separation among the reducer algorithms, the large number of directories results in too many classes to distinguish, as shown in Fig. 10. Consequently, this approach is not well-suited for

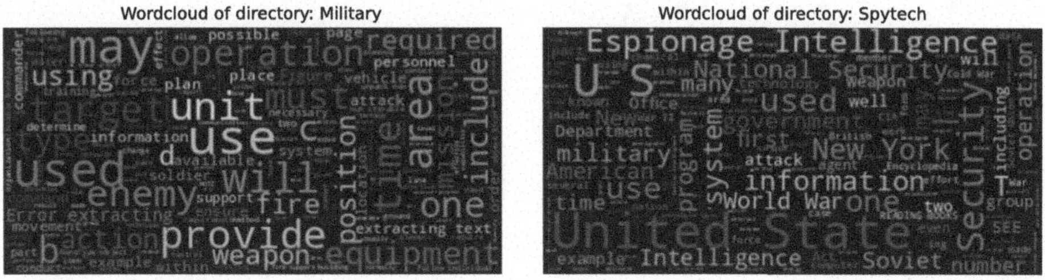

(a) **`Military`** (b) **`Spytech`**

Fig. 9. Wordcloud visualisations for selected directories.

datasets of this size, since it is difficult to extract meaningful clusters from the reduced embeddings, as the colors become too similar.

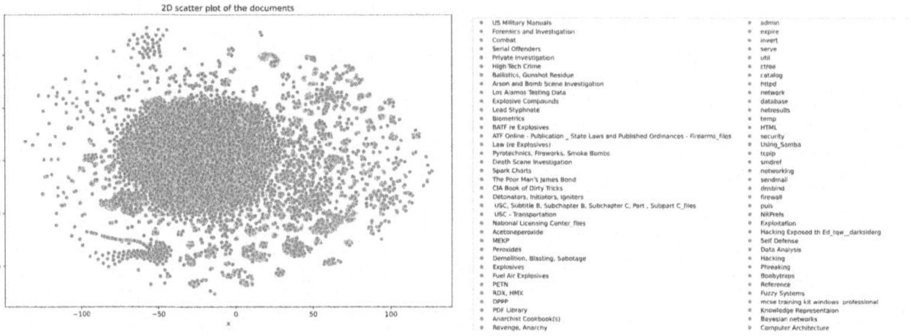

Fig. 10. Scatter plot of document embeddings reduced to two dimensions using t-SNE, colored by directory labels.

Clustering Named Entities (CNE). This baseline is based on entity categories, in contrast to our FAT-CAT, which relies on the hierarchical directory structure of the dataset. A visualization of the clustering of the NE category `LANGUAGE` is shown in Fig. 11. It reveals that the approach effectively separates programming languages, such as *C++*, from spoken languages. Most language families[7] are grouped together. However, as with the NER process, entities are often incorrectly categorized, e.g., *False*. Although some patterns in the class members can be observed, neither the topological clusters nor the clustering results provide clear or accurate information. Overall, this approach does not yield meaningful insights into the data's structure.

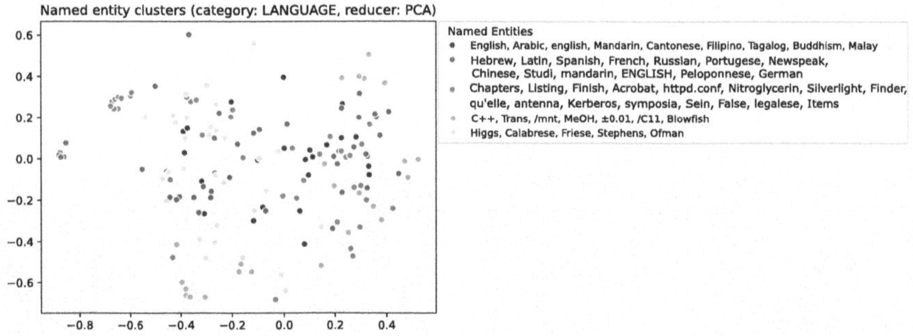

Fig. 11. Clustering of NEs of the category `LANGUAGE`.

[7] https://www.omniglot.com/writing/langfam.htm? (01.02.2025).

7.4 Empirical Comparison

In this section, we compare different approaches for analyzing directory content, assessing their strengths and limitations. Our evaluation demonstrates that the proposed FCA-based method FAT-CAT offers superior insights into the dataset's structure.

Word clouds provide an intuitive overview by highlighting frequently occurring terms, enabling the identification of noteworthy directories. However, they fail to capture semantic relationships and depend heavily on the text extraction quality. Additionally, comparing multiple directories using word clouds is challenging due to their unstructured nature. In contrast, embedding-based visualization techniques allows directly comparing directories based on their content. Not only does the quality of the reducers affect the results, but the large number of directories also complicates the interpretation of the visualization. This approach is therefore ineffective for large-scale datasets. NER-based clustering of category entities suffers from frequent misclassification. Moreover, the resulting clusters neither exhibit clear patterns nor provide meaningful structural insights into the content of directories, making this method unreliable for data analysis. Our proposed FCA-based approach enables a hierarchical exploration of directory topics without requiring manual document inspection. Although the visualization is less intuitive for non-experts, this method remains the most effective for uncovering the relationships between directory topics. Among the evaluated methods, FAT-CAT proves to be the most effective for structured data exploration.

8 Conclusion and Future Work

In this paper, we proposed a method for analyzing structures in an unknown dataset of diverse content, and compared it to three baseline methods. In the case study, we found that our approach FAT-CAT is better suited for exploring and visualizing topics across multiple directories than the baseline techniques. While word clouds offer a quick overview, and embedding-based methods attempt clustering, neither approach provides sufficient clarity for the large dataset of the case study. NER clustering is unreliable due to misclassification. In contrast, FCA enables hierarchical and systematic topic analysis, making it the preferred method despite requiring expertise for interpretation.

However, our approach has some limitations. Visualizing topic names directly in the concept lattice leads to visual clutter, while using only topic IDs makes the lattice hard to interpret for a human. To solve this, one may experiment with interactive versions where mouseover effects reveal topic details. Additionally, the quality of image captioning and topic modeling might limit the expressiveness of the computed concept lattices.

Currently, FAT-CAT's results do not provide any insight into the dataset's directory hierarchy. However, this structural information could be highly valuable when considered alongside the topic hierarchy of the directories. Therefore, future work could explore integrating both sources of information to enhance the analysis.

In this work, we employed Top2Vec [2] as the topic modeling technique. While newer models, such as C-Top2Vec [3], have been introduced, we opted for Top2Vec due to its ability to represent documents using a single-vector format. This approach allows for topic aggregation by counting the occurrences of topics across the documents in a directory. In contrast, C-Top2Vec supports multi-vector document representation, which would provide a more granular description of individual documents and the dataset as a whole. Future work could explore and evaluate the performance of C-Top2Vec in comparison to Top2Vec for this purpose.

References

1. Alsudais, A., Tchalian, H.: Clustering prominent named entities in topic-specific text corpora (2019)
2. Angelov, D.: Top2vec: distributed representations of topics. arXiv preprint arXiv:2008.09470 (2020)
3. Angelov, D., Inkpen, D.: Topic modeling: contextual token embeddings are all you need. In: Findings of the Association for Computational Linguistics: EMNLP 2024, pp. 13528–13539 (2024)
4. Cigarrán, J., Castellanos, Á., García-Serrano, A.: A step forward for topic detection in twitter: an FCA-based approach. Expert Syst. Appl. **57**, 21–36 (2016)
5. Ganter, B., Wille, R.: Formal Concept Analysis: Mathematical Foundations. Springer (2024)
6. Hanika, T., Hirth, J.: Conexp-Clj-a research tool for FCA. ICFCA (Supplements) **2378**(70–75), 346 (2019)
7. Hirth, J., Hanika, T.: The geometric structure of topic models. CoRR abs/2403.03607 (2024). https://doi.org/10.48550/ARXIV.2403.03607
8. Hirth, J., Horn, V., Stumme, G., Hanika, T.: Ordinal motifs in lattices. Inf. Sci. **659**, 120009 (2024)
9. Stumme, G., Taouil, R., Bastide, Y., Pasquier, N., Lakhal, L.: Computing iceberg concept lattices with titanic. Data Knowl. Eng. **42**(2), 189–222 (2002)
10. Wang, F., Wang, N., Cai, S., Zhang, W.: Dynamically constructing semantic topic hierarchy through formal concept analysis. Multimedia Tools Appl. **82**(5), 7267–7292 (2023)
11. Wang, J., et al.: GIT: a generative image-to-text transformer for vision and language. arXiv preprint arXiv:2205.14100 (2022)
12. Wang, K., Wang, F.: Topic-feature lattices construction and visualization for dynamic topic number. J. Syst. Sci. Inf. **9**(5), 558–574 (2021)
13. Yang, Y., et al.: Multilingual universal sentence encoder for semantic retrieval. arXiv preprint arXiv:1907.04307 (2019)
14. Yu, D., Xu, D., Wang, D., Ni, Z.: Hierarchical topic modeling of twitter data for online analytical processing. IEEE Access **7**, 12373–12385 (2019)

The Geometric Structure of Topic Models

Johannes Hirth[1] and Tom Hanika[2](✉)

[1] Knowledge and Data Engineering Group, University of Kassel, Kassel, Germany
hirth@cs.uni-kassel.de

[2] Intelligent Information Systems, University of Hildesheim, Hildesheim, Germany
tom.hanika@uni-hildesheim.de

Abstract. Topic models are a popular tool for clustering and analyzing textual data. Despite their widespread use in research and application, in-depth analysis methods for topic models are still an important subject of research. Modern methods for interpreting topic models are based on simple visualizations, such as similarity matrices, top-term lists or low-dimensional embeddings, which can only be explained to a limited extent.

In this paper we develop a fundamentally different incidence geometric method for analysing and interpreting topic models. For this, we derive ordinal structures from flat topic models, such as non-negative matrix factorization. These enable the analysis of the topic model in a higher (order) dimension and the possibility of extracting conceptual relationships between several topics at once. Due to the use of conceptual scaling, our approach does not introduce any artificial topical relationships, such as artifacts of feature or dimension compression.

We introduce and demonstrate the applicability of our approach based on a topic model derived from a corpus of scientific papers taken from 32 top machine learning venues.

Keywords: Explainable AI · Topic Models · Geometric Visualization

1 Introduction

Topic models are a popular tool for analyzing text through clustering and have a vast application domain such as recommendation systems [7,12,24], sentiment analysis [42,44], and text summarization [33,38]. They discover groups or hierarchies of topics in text corpora using various techniques. Using the computed topics one may classify new text samples within the topic space. Furthermore, the (frequently) underlying vector space may help to understand the original text corpus and the inter-topic relations of the documents. Thus, topic models are an excellent tool for a structural analysis of large text corpora. This is particularly true when background information about corpus entities, such as authors, venues, places, publishers, research groups, is used. This allows, e.g., deriving (temporal) trajectories for such entities [34,36,41] as well as identifying social network relations between them [27,35].

The vast majority of topic models encode relationships between topics and terms, e.g., LDA or NMF [25]. Common methods that aim at explaining and

P. Cellier et al. (Eds.): CONCEPTS 2025, LNAI 15941, pp. 19–34, 2025.
https://doi.org/10.1007/978-3-032-03364-2_2

interpreting this relation rely on interpreting the elements of the underlying vector space $\mathbb{R}^t$, where t denotes the number of topics. Yet, conventional (plot based) methods must perform a dimension reduction since $t > 3$ in all practical cases. This (often) non-linear reduction can result in (heavily) distorted representations.

Fundamentally different to this are methods that are rooted in ordinal data analysis [6,15,40]. We contribute to this line of research by conceiving the topic-term relationship as a geometric incidence structure. This approach was identified as fruitful not only for topic models, but for explaining term based methods all together, such as large language models [5]. We show how these corresponding conceptualizations allow for rich interpretations of topic models and how to extract explainable patterns from them. The latter are based on ordinal motifs [23]. Our main contribution is the formalization of a novel diagrammatic language for comprehensively visualizing topic models.

We demonstrate our approach based on a well researched topic model that was derived from a large corpus of scientific works within the realm of machine learning [34]. The results show that our method is capable of capturing insights about authors and research venues from the corpus data.

2 Related Work

Several methods to interpret topic models have been proposed. Some of them represent the document-topic relation through vector space models [34,36]. This allows the reader to visually interpret this relation through proximity in two or three dimensional diagrams. Common methods for this are multidimensional scaling [30] or t-distributed stochastic neighborhood embedding [29].

Other explanation approaches follow a more relational notion. A very simple method is to compute a relation based on topic-topic correlation. This is, for example, computed using cosine similarities between topics in a vector space model [34]. Some topic models, like the *Correlation Topic Model* (CTM) [4], allow for directly inferring this relation from the model and present it in a graph structure. Extensions have been proposed that would facilitate a hierarchical interpretation of this relationship. These extensions are based on clustering techniques [3].

With our work, we contribute to the explainability of topic models based on relations that are defined on the data, i.e., documents-topics and term-topics relations. These are often weighted [32] and are *scaled* to binary relations [13]. A basic investigation of the derived (binary) relations are visualizations using bipartite graphs [9]. Based on these graphs, simple (tree shaped) hierarchies can be inferred by applying hierarchical clustering methods [1]. A benefit of hierarchical interpretations is that one can infer topic-topic relations of higher arity from them. On top of that, they allow for assessing the overall *global* structure of a data set. However, tree structures are very limited [21] in their expressiveness. For instance, there is only a single path connecting two nodes.

A hierarchical structure that is not limited by this property can be computed using *Formal Concept Analysis* [14] (FCA). With FCA, we compute from the bipartite graph the set of all maximal bi-cliques. These exhibit a natural order relation which results in a lattice structure, called the *concept lattice*. An application of concept lattices on documents-topics and term-topics relations has been shown to be useful for organizing discussion forums in educational software [10]. We further elaborate on this later. We expand on FCA based methods by transferring new SOTA [22,23] explanation approaches for concept lattices towards topic modeling. These allow for a novel global interpretation of the topic model structure. A different, yet related line of research is the computation of hierarchical topic models [8,16,26] and FCA based scientometric studies [11,31]. Multiple visualization techniques have been proposed for their explanation [37].

3 Incidence Relations in Topic Models

To eventually employ Formal Concept Analysis (FCA) [14], we are required to properly identify incidences that naturally occur in topic models.

Almost every topic model TM exhibits at least two fundamental relations, i.e., the topics for any document $d \in D$ and the terms for a given topic $t \in T$. These relations are often weighted, e.g., a document d_i might have topic t_j with a weight of $w_{i,k} \in [0,1]$, as depicted in Fig. 1. The document-topic matrix can be extracted by embedding each document $d \in D$ by the topic model TM into the topic space, i.e., computing $\mathrm{TM}(d_i) = (w_{i,1}, \ldots, w_{i,n})$. For the computation of the term-topic matrix there are multiple options depending on the used TM method. Based on both matrices we can infer incidence relations $\mathcal{D} \subseteq D \times T$ and $\mathcal{S} \subseteq S \times T$ in the following way. A natural approach is to apply threshold values to the weights. For the document-topic matrix we select a value $\delta \in [0,1]$, which results in the *document-topic-incidence* $\mathcal{D}_\delta$. Hence, $(d,t) \in \mathcal{D}_\delta$ iff the weight for (d,t) in the document-topic matrix is greater than or equal to δ. For the *term-topic-incidence* $\mathcal{S}$ we act differently. We extract for each topic the top-n terms, i.e., the n entries in the respective column from the term-topic matrix with the greatest values. For a term $s \in S$ and a topic $t \in T$ is $(s,t) \in \mathcal{S}_n$ iff the weight of (s,t) is among the top-n weights in column t in the term-topic matrix.

FCA. Due to the limited space, we have refrained from a formal introduction and refer to Ganter and Wille [14], from which we use the standard notation. The SOTA on analyzing TM with FCA is to derive a formal context from the document-topic $\mathcal{D}$ and the term-topic relation $\mathcal{S}$ [10]. This is done by applying thresholds to both relations. Our approach for the term-topic relation is different to that.

$D \backslash T$	t_1	t_2	...	t_n
d_1	$w_{1,1}$	$w_{1,2}$		$w_{1,n}$
d_2	$w_{2,1}$	$w_{2,2}$		$w_{2,n}$
...				
d_l	$w_{l,1}$	$w_{l,2}$		$w_{l,n}$

$S \backslash T$	t_1	t_2	...	t_n
s_1	$\hat{w}_{1,1}$	$\hat{w}_{1,2}$		$\hat{w}_{1,n}$
s_2	$\hat{w}_{2,1}$	$\hat{w}_{2,2}$		$\hat{w}_{2,n}$
...				
s_k	$\hat{w}_{k,1}$	$\hat{w}_{k,2}$		$\hat{w}_{k,n}$

Fig. 1. The weighted term-topic (right) and document-topic relations (left).

4 Conceptual Views

We extend the basic modeling from the last section by means of *ordinal motifs* [22,23]. These motifs are ordinal substructures that allow for a rich interpretation of the underlying data. We demonstrate our approach based on an already published and extensively discussed topic model [34], hereinafter referred to as SSH21. This model was built using 35,200 scientific publications from machine learning, retrieved via the *Semantic Scholar Open Research Corpus* [2]. The employed topic modeling technique is *non-negative matrix factorization* [25], a widely used procedure that has several advantages with respect to explainability. We may stress at this point that our notion is agnostic with respect to the topic modeling technique. The topic model consists of twenty-two [34, Table 4.1] topics which were manually assigned based on the top ten terms per topic. The training corpus and therefore the resulting topic model has 14828 terms.

Computing Incidence Relations. To set the threshold for computing $\mathcal{D}$ we normalize the document-topic matrix by row using $\delta \in [0, 1]$. The goal [28] is to derive a sparse $\mathcal{D}$. Documents are then mainly represented by their most important topics and this leads to a comprehensibly sized concept lattice. At the same time, however, one may lose substantial parts of the concept lattice structure. We therefore decided for a density based approach. That is $|\mathcal{D}|/|D \times T|$, which is depicted on the left in Fig. 2. A feature of our approach is to provide tailored result for investigating corpus entities of interest, such as particular authors or venues. To address this, one may choose δ depending on the distribution of documents in the corpus with respect to a selected entity. For example, we computed different values of δ for four different authors and machine learning venues, see Fig. 2. For this we considered only those documents that were co-authored by author a or published at venue v. The result is an induced sub-context of the $\mathcal{D}_\delta$ formal context. The entities were selected because they have been discussed in detail in previous literature [34,36]. For our further analyses, we have opted for the value $\delta = 0.25$ based on Fig. 2. The threshold for $\mathcal{S}$ will be discussed in Sect. 4.2.

Conceptual Data Reduction. Formal Concept Analysis has a rich tool-set of data reduction methods. A particular feature of these tools is that they

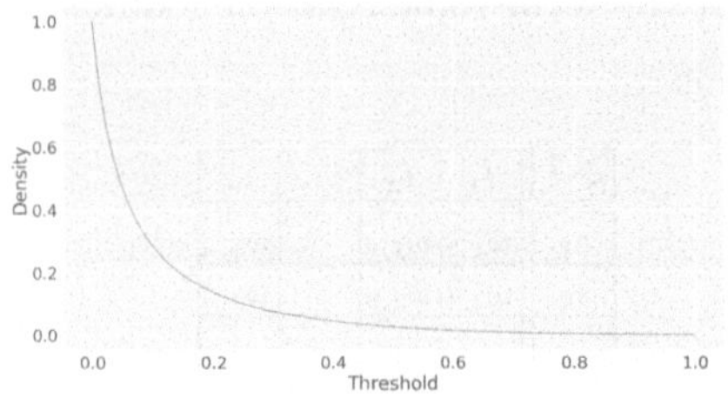

Author	0.1	0.2	0.25	0.3	0.4	0.5
Sebastian Thrun	398	89	51	31	18	13
Bernhard Schölkopf	640	144	80	51	20	17
Dieter Fox	342	66	42	28	15	10
Wolfgang Nejdl	387	94	58	39	19	14
ECML	568	173	108	74	37	20
RecSys	389	83	60	47	21	11
NeurIPS	2366	405	212	142	66	22
Neural Networks	1368	261	155	107	43	21

Fig. 2. The density of the document-topic relation for given thresholds (left) and the concept lattice sizes of induced sub-contexts for given entities and thresholds (right).

Table 1. The table displays the number of objects, attributes, the density and the number of concepts of the context derived from $\mathcal{D}$ for four authors and four venues. The sixth column depicts the number of concepts in the 2, 8-core and the last column the number of concepts after applying TITANIC with a minimum support value of 3%.

	documents (objects)	topics (attributes)	density	concepts	core concepts	view concepts
Sebastian Thrun	266	22	0.055	51	11	11
Bernhard Schölkopf	522	22	0.059	80	50	22
Dieter Fox	244	22	0.057	42	16	15
Wolfgang Nejdl	387	22	0.059	58	28	21
ECML	639	22	0.061	108	52	25
RecSys	856	22	0.058	60	29	23
NeurIPS	6233	22	0.060	212	202	25
Neural Networks	3521	22	0.061	155	144	21

allow for controlling the (conceptual) error [17,18,20]. For our work, we rely on TITANIC [39] and *pq*-cores [19]. The overall goal is to compute comprehensible representations of comprehensible size, i.e., fifty concepts.

The ***pq*-core** of $\mathcal{D}$ is the largest subset of documents $H \subseteq D$ and topics $S \subseteq T$ such that each document $d \in H$ has at least p topics and every topic $t \in S$ has at least q documents in $\mathcal{D}$. This method can easily be restricted to a proper subset of the documents, e.g., all documents belonging to some entity, and we call the result *core topics* of said entity. Finding well suited parameters p, q is supported by a measure for importance [19], which leads here to the pair $(p, q) = (2, 8)$.

The `TITANIC` algorithm computes the hierarchy of formal concepts in a top down fashion, with respect to a pre-defined (monotone) importance parameter. Commonly the support function $\text{supp}_{\mathbb{K}} : \text{Int}(\mathbb{K}) \to [0, 1]$ is used, where $\text{supp}_{\mathbb{K}}(B) := {}^{|B'|}/_{|G|}$. The `TITANIC` algorithm computes the hierarchy of all formal concepts that satisfy a minimum threshold value $c \in [0, 1]$. The result is called iceberg concept lattice, i.e., a *join-semilattice*. In our case study on the `SSH21` topic model we found the value $c = 0.03$ to be sufficient. The result of both methods is shown in the last two columns of Table 1.

4.1 The Resulting Conceptual View and Interpretation

In Fig. 3 we depict the iceberg concept lattice for the researcher Bernhard Schölkopf[1] $\mathfrak{B}_{\text{BS}}$ (top) and Wolfgang Nejdl[2] $\mathfrak{B}_{\text{WN}}$ (bottom). We employ order diagrams with a particular *short-hand* notation as follows: each concept is represented by a node in the diagram. For example the node annotated with *Support Vector Machines* is the concept (A, B) that collects all documents that share the

[1] https://dblp.org/pid/97/119.html.
[2] https://dblp.org/pid/n/WolfgangNejdl.html.

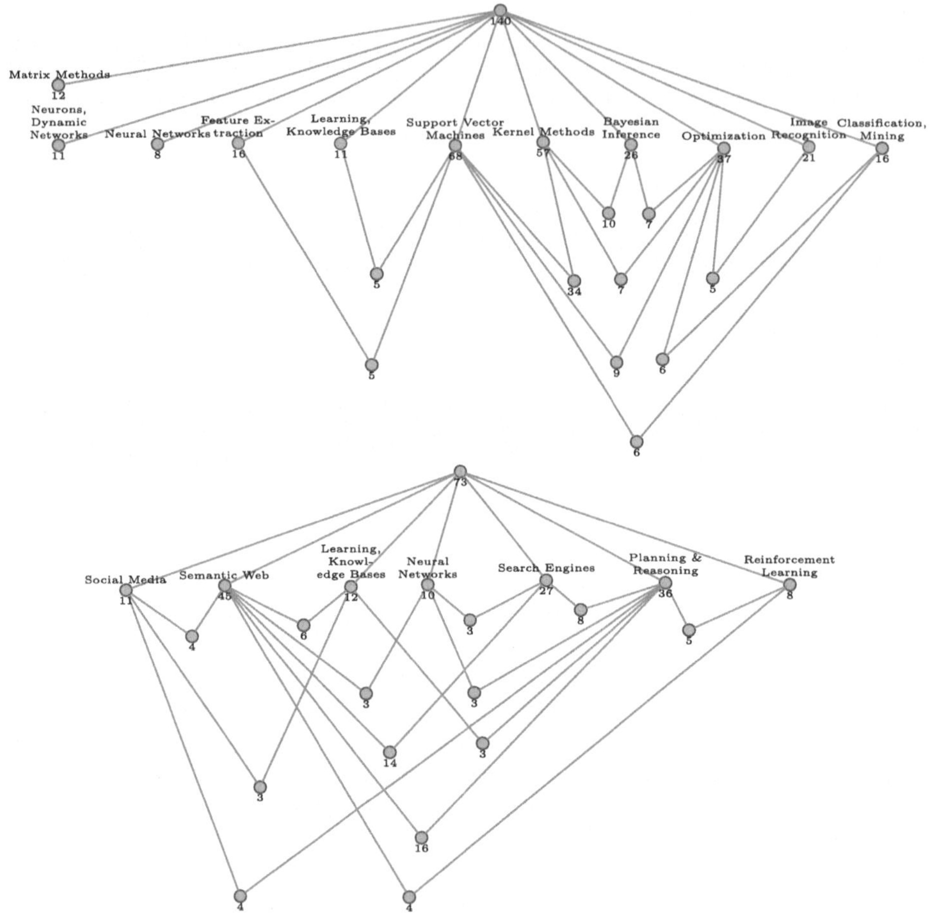

Fig. 3. The iceberg-CL for the entities B. Schölkopf (top) and W. Nejdl (bottom).

topic $B = \{\textit{Support Vector Machines}\}$. In classical FCA one annotates all these documents below the node. Due to their large quantity, we annotated only their number, i.e., $|A| = 68$. The connection between two nodes indicates that the corresponding concepts are in subconcept relation. For example, the node in the bottom right annotated by 6 is a subconcept of the concept with the intent *Support Vector Machines*. It is also a subconcept of the concept with the intent *Classification, Mining*. The extent size 6 indicates that there are six documents in $\mathcal{D}$ of Bernhard Schölkopf that have the topics *Support Vector Machines* and *Classification, Mining*. In general, the larger concept in the subconcept relation is placed higher in the diagram and the topic names (attributes) are annotated atop the largest concept that they are contained in. The top most concept bears no annotation. Hence, there is no topic that is shared by all documents.

In $\mathfrak{B}_{\text{WN}}$ we observe that only seven topics out of twenty-two were identified as core topics of Wolfgang Nejdl. The most frequent topic is *Semantic Web* which occurs in forty-five documents. Out of these, sixteen also have the *Planning & Reasoning* topic and fourteen are also associated to *Search Engines*. The second most frequent topic is *Planning & Reasoning*, which occurs in thirty-six documents. Overall, the $\mathfrak{B}_{\text{WN}}$ iceberg concept lattice has twenty-one concepts. Such a comprehensive representation of the thematic distribution of an author is not possible with other methods as far as we know. With this structural approach, we overcome the limitations of commonly used methods that are based on filtering topics by frequency. For example, selecting the strongest topic signals would result in a total ordered ranking without structural insights.

We present the same analysis for Bernhard Schölkopf ($\underline{\mathfrak{B}}_{\text{BS}}$) and can identify twenty-two concepts comprised of eleven core topics. The most supported and structurally important topics are *Support Vector Machines* with sixty-eight documents and *Kernel Methods* with fifty-seven documents. The topics coincide in thirty-four documents. The large overlap of these topics is not surprising due to the close connection between SVMs and kernel methods.

Apart from the individual analysis of an entity's topic structure, our approach does also allow for an in-depth cross entity comparisons. Comparing $\underline{\mathfrak{B}}_{\text{BS}}$ and $\underline{\mathfrak{B}}_{\text{WN}}$ we observe that both authors have two topics in common, namely *Learning Knowledge Bases* and *Neural Networks*. Despite that, these topics are completely differently interconnected within their respective research. While Wolfgang Nejdl studies *Learning Knowledge Bases* in the context of *Semantic Web, Social Media* and *Planning & Reasoning*, Bernhard Schölkopf studies *Learning Knowledge Bases* in the context of *Support Vector Machines*. An analog differentiation can be found for *Neural Networks*.

Ordinal Motifs in Lattices: The geometric aspects of our analysis method allow the application of *ordinal motifs*. This method for interpreting concept hierarchies was proposed by Hirth et al. [23] and is capable of explaining concept lattices [22] based on common scales, i.e., ordinal patterns. In detail, this method extracts sub-structures within the concept hierarchy and provides visual *geometric* interpretations. We shortly discuss the three types of ordinal motifs that occurred in our data. It is quite possible that for other data sets other ordinal motifs might occur. Nonetheless, our method can be applied analogously.

The *nominal ordinal motif* is a simple structure that reflects the incomparability (Fig. 4) of the related elements (topics). A slightly more expressive structure results by adding an additional (artificial) + object as the meet of all elements of the motif. This motif can be observed in real world data, for example, it occurs in Fig. 5 (see concept with the term *learning*). Equipped with the + version of the ordinal motif, we will demonstrate a novel geometric drawing technique Sect. 5. The *crown motif* can be identified by its *zig-zag* pattern that reflects that there is a *round-trip* or a cycle along topics and documents (see Fig. 4, second row). We were able to identify many crown ordinal motifs in $\underline{\mathfrak{B}}_{\text{BS}}$ and $\underline{\mathfrak{B}}_{\text{WN}}$. The largest crown ordinal motif in $\underline{\mathfrak{B}}_{\text{BS}}$ is a cycle over the topics (*SVM*, *KM*, *BI*, *O*, *Class*, *SVM*). In $\underline{\mathfrak{B}}_{\text{WN}}$ we find many cycles on four elements,

$\mathbb{N}_3$	r	g	b
1	×		
2		×	
3			×
+	×	×	×

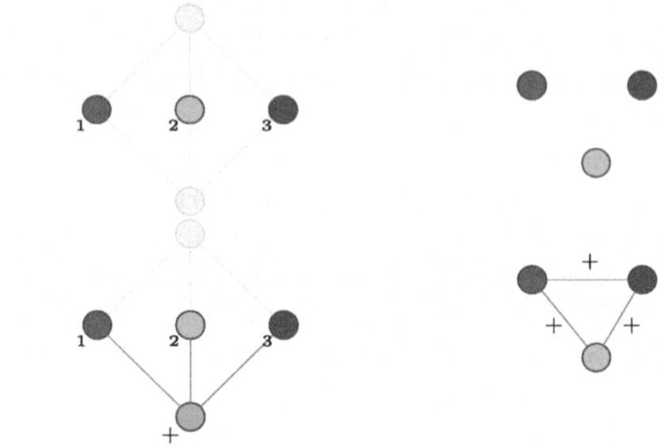

$\mathbb{C}_{10}$	a	b	c	...	i	j
1	×	×				
2		×	×			
3			×			
...						
9					×	×
10	×					×

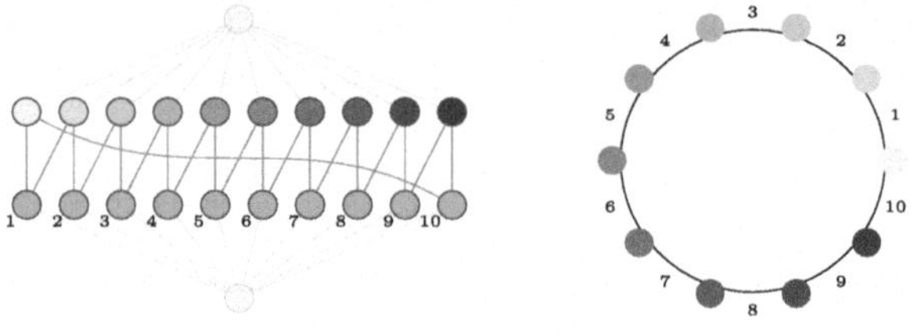

$\mathbb{B}_3$	r	g	b
c		×	×
p	×		×
y	×	×	

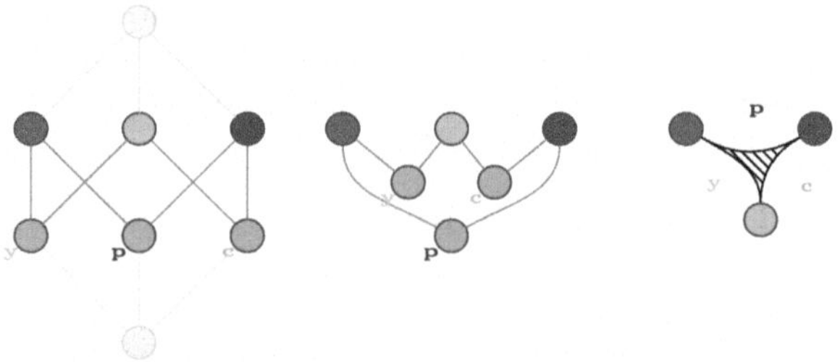

Fig. 4. The nominal (top) crown (middle) and contranominal (bottom) ordinal motif in context (left), concept lattice (middle) and geometric drawing style (right) representation. The nominal context $[N]_3$ has an optional + object and two different display styles based on the existence of this element. The contranominal ordinal motif has an additional layout, namely the tulip layout, for its inner concepts.

e.g., (*SemW*, *LKB*, *PR*, *SM*, *SemW*). The occurrence of such a motif may reflect a topic based cycle within the research history of an author. Hence, these cycles constitute interesting candidates for a temporal topical analysis.

Finally, the *contranominal ordinal motif* can be visually identified by the tulip layout in the lattice diagrams. This motif reflects that there is a unique set of documents for any combination of topics. Moreover, this type of motif represents a densely explored area within the topic space. By explored, we refer to the research activities of the respective entity, e.g., an author. For example, within

$\mathfrak{B}_{\text{WN}}$ we find that *Social Media*, *Semantic Web* and *Learning Knowledge Base*, or *Semantic Web*, *Neural Networks* and *Search Engines* constitute a contranominal structure. Furthermore, we find within $\mathfrak{B}_{\text{BS}}$ the contranominal motifs *Support Vector Machines*, *Kernel Methods* and *Optimization*, or *Support Vector Machines*, *Optimization*, *Classification*. The involved topics are structurally important within $\mathfrak{B}_{\text{BS}}$, i.e., within the research of *Bernhard Schölkopf*.

Concluding this section we want to stress that the presented analysis can be conducted for any type of entity within a topic model or the whole topic model all-together. Moreover, we will elaborate on this basic usage of ordinal motifs in Sect. 5 by a novel geometric drawing method.

4.2 The Conceptual Term-Topic Structure

The topic-term relation $\mathcal{S}$ also entails important information on the SSH21 topic model. It allows us to explain the topics of SSH21 via terms $s \in S$. We inferred $n = 10$ is reasonable for the top-n parameter, as it results in about fifty formal concepts. This parameter choice is common in the literature [10, 34], independently of our requirement on a low number of concepts.

We depict the concept lattice of $\mathcal{S}_{10}$ in Fig. 5 and omitted the (unsupported) bottom concept. From this we can infer dependencies in terms of their shared terms. For example, the topics *Kernel Methods* and *Support Vector Machines* are connected via the term *kernels*. Analogously, the topics *Neural Networks* and *Graphs* are connected via the term *nodes*. We highlighted several contranominal and crown ordinal motifs. For example, the topics *Search Engines*, *Semantic Web* and *Social Media* are of contranominal structure with the terms *web*, *user* and *content* being responsible. Another example is the set of topics *Planning & Reasoning*, *Matrix Methods* and *Leaning Knowledge Bases*, which are also of contranominal structure with the terms *domain*, *learning* and *knowledge*. Hence, in both cases these terms are pair-wise differently used in the SSH21 topic model and therefore in the research corpus D. An example crown motif is given by the sub-structure highlighted in red spanned by *Classification*, *Neural Networks*, *Neurons and Dynamic Networks* to *Reinforcement Learning* and back to the *Classification*.

The proposed method allows for a novel and meaningful structural analysis of topic models. In particular, our method is capable of identifying dependencies in the topic space, such as the cycles between topics that emerges from the crown motif. In summary, the conceptual structure of $\mathcal{S}_{10}$ allows for a global and deep investigation of topic models such as SSH21.

5 The Geometric Structure

The study of ordinal motifs allows for further geometric interpretation of the sub-structures within the topic space. In the last section, we analyzed the topic model with singular ordinal motifs at a time. Now the goal is to access the comprehensive geometric structure. The *geometric structure* of a (contextual)

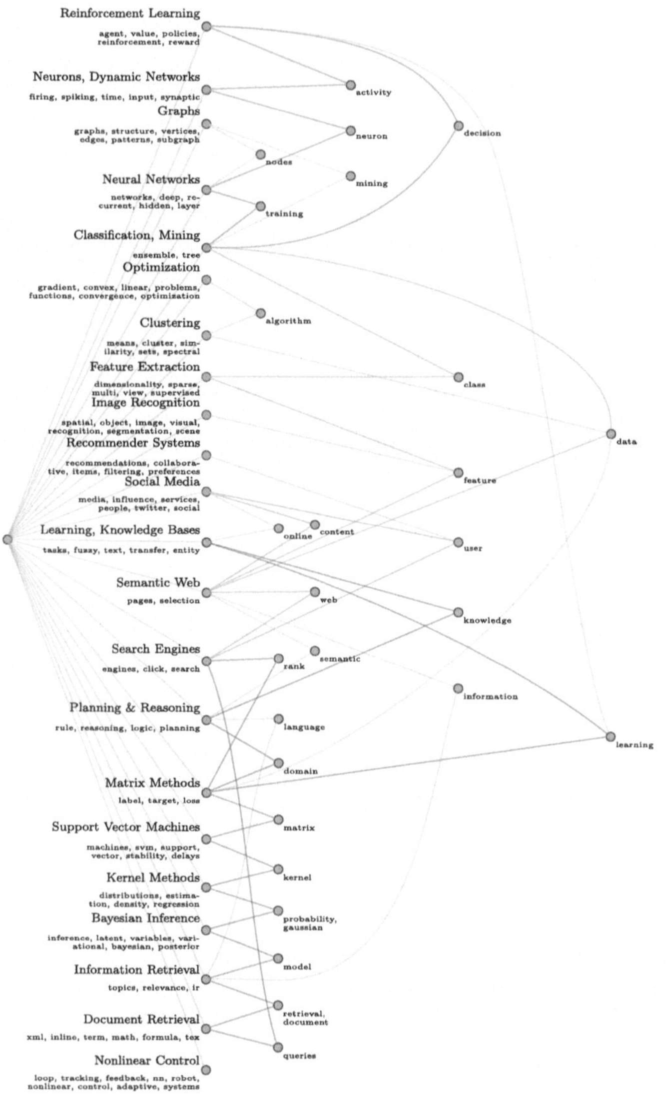

Fig. 5. The iceberg-CL of the term-topic relation of the `SSH21` topic model. Edges of the same color comprise an ordinal motive.

data set is a multi-relational hypergraph structure. In this hypergraph every hyperedge relation encodes one type of ordinal motif $\mathcal{S}_1, \ldots, \mathcal{S}_n$.

Definition 1 (Geometric Structure). *For a context* $\mathbb{K} := (G, M, I)$ *and families of ordinal motifs* $\mathcal{S}_1, \ldots, \mathcal{S}_n$ *the* geometric structure *of* $\mathbb{K}$ *with respect to* $\mathcal{S}_1, \ldots, \mathcal{S}_n$ *is a multi-hypergraph* $(M, E_1, \ldots, E_n)$ *where* $E_i := \{N \subseteq M \mid N \text{ is of ordinal motif type } \mathcal{S}_i \text{ in } \mathbb{K}\}$.

An attribute set $N \subseteq M$ is of ordinal motif type $\mathcal{S}$, if the concept lattice of $\mathbb{K}[G, N]$ (i.e., $\mathbb{K}$ restricted to the attributes N) resembles a concept lattice of $\mathcal{S}$. For example, $\mathbb{K}[G, N]$ is of crown type iff the concept lattice $\mathfrak{B}(\mathbb{K}[G, N])$ has a fence pattern (cf. Fig. 4). We may note that we do not impose any particular choice of $\mathcal{S}_i$. The selection of suitable ordinal motifs [23] is up to the analyst. The question *"Is* $\mathbb{G}, \mathbb{N}$ *of ordinal motif type?"* is a formal decision problem called the *ordinal motif problem*. Its computational complexity was investigated in Hirth et al. [23]. Within this work all problem instances are in P [22].

5.1 Geometric Structure Diagram

We make the geometric structure human accessible through a diagrammatic presentation. For this we define a set of drawing rules for each ordinal motif type, which we then apply to `SSH21`. The resulting figure is called *geometric drawing* of $\mathbb{K}$. This method is inspired by the geometric representations introduced by R. Wille [43]. In this geometric drawing, every attribute $m \in M$ (i.e., topic for `SSH21`) is represented by a node. The hyperedges of an ordinal motif type are drawn as connections between nodes. Each ordinal motif type has its own drawing style to ensure that they can be distinguished. The connection lines are annotated by the objects $g \in G$ (i.e., terms for `SSH21`) that induce the respective ordinal motif. This allows for deriving explanations of ordinal motifs both in terms of the attributes they connect and the objects they entail.

We present the drawing rules for each type of ordinal motifs in greater detail: **Nominal:** There are two cases of nominal ordinal motifs that we distinguish with respect to the objects they entail. In case there is an object $g \in G$ that supports all attributes N, i.e., $g \in N'$, we draw an edge between all pairs of attributes $n_1, n_2 \in N$ and annotate the connecting lines by g. Otherwise, no edge is drawn. A prototypical example for both cases is shown in Fig. 4 (top right). **Crown:** This ordinal motif does not require their own drawing rule. Instead, they can be read from (closed) cycles of nominal ordinal motifs. Yet, two conditions need to be satisfied: (1) Objects must not occur more than once along a cycle. (2) No other edges, apart from the cycle edges connect cycle attributes. A prototypical example for the crown ordinal motif on ten elements is depicted in Fig. 4 (middle right). **Contranominal:** This motif encodes that any subset $D \subseteq N$ is supported by a unique set of objects $H \subseteq G$. Therefore, they reflect a densely connected part within the conceptual structure. Our drawing shall reflect this by applying the drawing rule: contranominal hyperedges of size n are drawn by a filled n-polygon that connects the attributes N. The edge between two attributes $n_1, n_2 \in N$ then annotated by all objects that they have in common, i.e., by the objects $\{n_1, n_2\}'$. Prototypical examples for contranominal ordinal motifs of size three can be found in Fig. 4 (bot right). **Ordinal:** This motif type encodes rankings among the attributes. In such a motif, the greatest element subsumes all the incidences of a smaller attribute. We reflect this in the diagram by the drawing rule: an attribute (node) is drawn such that it overlaps the next lower ranked attribute (node). For this kind of motif, objects are annotated next to nodes. At each attribute (node) we annotate all objects

$\mathbb{I}_4$	a	b	c	d
$\leq a$	×			
$\leq b$	×	×		
$\leq c$	×	×	×	
$\leq d$	×	×	×	×
$\geq a$	×	×	×	×
$\geq b$		×	×	×
$\geq c$			×	×
$\geq d$				×

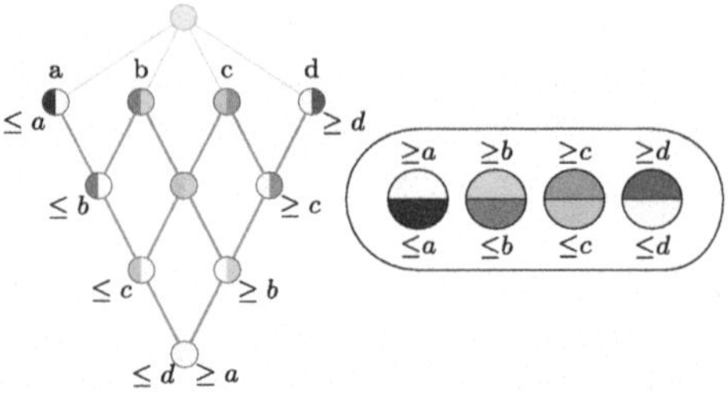

Fig. 6. Interordinal motif: formal context, concept lattice and geometric drawing style

such that there is no lower ranked attribute that is in incidence with this object. This procedure is in accordance to the short-hand notation of FCA line diagrams. **Interordinal:** This motif encodes two ordinal motifs of ordinal type, whose rankings on the attributes are complementary to each other. We have depicted an example on four elements in Fig. 6. To display this motif one draws an hyperedge that encloses the motif's attributes. The objects are annotated next to the attribute nodes based on the two rankings and the ordinal drawing rule. Objects from the same ranking are to be drawn on the same side of the hyperedge.

5.2 The Geometric Structure of SSH21

Figure 7 depicts the geometric drawing of SSH21. The drawing includes nominal, contranominal and crown ordinal motifs. There are no non-trivial ordinal or interordinal types in the topic model structure. This fact is, however, not surprising, since the topics within a topic model are optimized to be independent of each other. For readability reasons, we abbreviated the terms and topics.

We have highlighted ordinal motifs in the same color as in the last section. The representation of the relations in the geometric drawing is fundamentally different to line diagrams. By design, in the drawing it is easier to identify ordinal motifs. For example, we can easily read from the diagram that there are eight contranominal ordinal motifs. Out of the twenty-two topics, *Semantic Web* (SW) occurs in five contranominal ordinal motifs and is therefore structurally very important within the topic model. This is followed by the *Matrix Methods* (MM) topic which occurs in four contranominal ordinal motifs. In contrast to line diagrams, this information is easy to infer from the geometric drawing. The *Non-Linear Control* (NLC) topic is very isolated and does not exhibit any (non-trivial) connection to other topics. Crown ordinal motifs can easily be read from the structure as (closed) cycles. For example, we find *NN – Class – RL – NDN –NN* (red) and *SW – IR – DR – SE – SW*.

We invite the reader to compare the geometric drawing to classical approaches such as topic-topic heatmaps and t-SNE embeddings. Based on this comparison, we argue that geometric drawings of topic models allow for a non-flat analysis of the inter-topic relation and their respective terms.

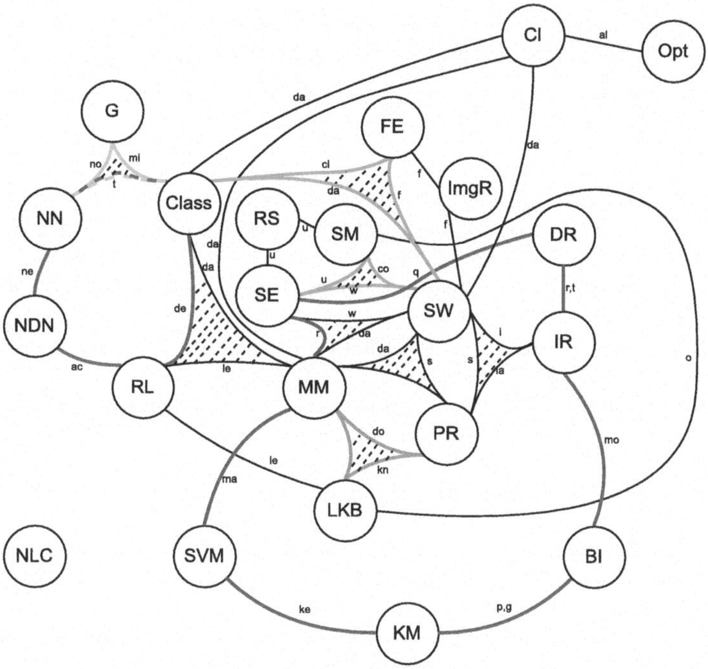

Fig. 7. The geometric drawing of the SSH21 topic model for top-ten terms. Topic and term names are abbreviated for better readability.

6 Limitations and Conclusion

With our work, we proposed a comprehensive approach for analyzing and visualizing high dimensional topic models. In principle, this method is applicable to arbitrary matrix shaped data sets. We have shown that our method is capable of capturing insights about researchers and venues from the realm of machine learning research. Moreover, we teased how conceptual structures can be used to track the change in their topics.

As the present work has established a robust link between topic models and their conceptual analysis, we envision several directions for future work. First, the absence of (non-trivial) ordinal and interordinal motifs within the analyzed topic model is not surprising. This due to the fact that topic models optimize to compute independent (non-nesting) topics. Yet, this is not true in the case of hierarchical topic modeling. The logical next step is to apply our methods to these models, e.g., HLDA or PAM [8,16,26,45].

Second, within the research field of human-computer interaction, we propose to conduct a user study in order to gather statistical evidence. Moreover, this may reveal new insights into the developed geometric drawings and potentially their visual optimization. Third, in order to conduct a study, as proposed above, a difficult algorithmic task has to be solved. Although, the geometric drawings are well-defined, their algorithmic computation is an open problem.

References

1. Akhtar, N., Javed, H., Ahmad, T.: Hierarchical summarization of text documents using topic modeling and formal concept analysis. In: Balas, V.E., Sharma, N., Chakrabarti, A. (eds.) Data Management, Analytics and Innovation. AISC, vol. 839, pp. 21–33. Springer, Singapore (2019). https://doi.org/10.1007/978-981-13-1274-8_2
2. Ammar, W., et al.: Construction of the literature graph in semantic scholar. arXiv preprint arXiv:1805.02262 (2018)
3. Aznag, M., Quafafou, M., Jarir, Z.: Leveraging formal concept analysis with topic correlation for service clustering and discovery. In: 2014 IEEE ICWS, pp. 153–160 (2014)
4. Blei, D., Lafferty, J.: A correlated topic model of Science. Ann. Appl. Stat. **1**, 17–35 (2007)
5. Bradley, T.-D., Gastaldi, J.L., Terilla, J.: The structure of meaning in language: parallel narratives in linear algebra and category theory. Not. Am. Math. Soc. **71**, 174–185 (2024)
6. Castellanos, A., Cigarrán, J., García-Serrano, A.: Formal concept analysis for topic detection: a clustering quality experimental analysis. Inf. Syst. **66**, 24–42 (2017)
7. Chen, J., et al.: Exploiting word embedding for heterogeneous topic model towards patent recommendation. Scientometrics **125**(3), 2091 (2020)
8. Cigarrán, J.M., Castellanos, Á., García-Serrano, A.M.: A step forward for topic detection in Twitter: an FCA-based approach. Expert Syst. Appl. **57**, 21–36 (2016)
9. Crossno, P.J., et al.: TopicView: visually comparing topic models of text collections. In: 2011 IEEE 23rd International Conference on Tools with Artificial Intelligence, pp. 936–943 (2011)
10. Distante, D., Fernandez, A., Cerulo, L., Visaggio, A.: Enhancing online discussion forums with topic-driven content search and assisted posting. In: Fred, A., Dietz, J.L.G., Aveiro, D., Liu, K., Filipe, J. (eds.) IC3K 2014. CCIS, vol. 553, pp. 161–180. Springer, Cham (2015). https://doi.org/10.1007/978-3-319-25840-9_11
11. Doerfel, S., Jäschke, R., Stumme, G.: Publication analysis of the formal concept analysis community. In: Domenach, F., Ignatov, D.I., Poelmans, J. (eds.) ICFCA 2012. LNCS (LNAI), vol. 7278, pp. 77–95. Springer, Heidelberg (2012). https://doi.org/10.1007/978-3-642-29892-9_12
12. Du, Y., Meng, X., Zhang, Y.: CVTM: a content-venueaware topic model for group event recommendation. IEEE Trans. Knowl. Data Eng. **32**(7), 1290–1303 (2019)
13. Ganter, B., Wille, R.: Conceptual scaling. In: Roberts, F. (ed.) Applications of Combinatorics and Graph Theory to the Biological and Social Sciences, pp. 139–167. Springer, New York (1989). https://doi.org/10.1007/978-1-4684-6381-1_6
14. Ganter, B., Wille, R.: Formal Concept Analysis: Mathematical Foundations. Springer (2024)
15. Hanika, T., Stumme, G., Dürrschnabel, D.: Towards ordinal data science. Trans. Graph Data Knowl. **1** (2023)
16. Griffiths, T., et al.: Hierarchical topic models and the nested Chinese restaurant process. In: Advances in Neural Information Processing Systems, vol. 16 (2003)

17. Hanika, T., Hirth, J.: Exploring scale-measures of data sets. In: Braud, A., Buzmakov, A., Hanika, T., Le Ber, F. (eds.) ICFCA 2021. LNCS (LNAI), vol. 12733, pp. 261–269. Springer, Cham (2021). https://doi.org/10.1007/978-3-030-77867-5_17
18. Hanika, T., Hirth, J.: Quantifying the conceptual error in dimensionality reduction. In: Braun, T., Gehrke, M., Hanika, T., Hernandez, N. (eds.) ICCS 2021. LNCS (LNAI), vol. 12879, pp. 105–118. Springer, Cham (2021). https://doi.org/10.1007/978-3-030-86982-3_8
19. Hanika, T., Hirth, J.: Knowledge cores in large formal contexts. Ann. Math. Artif. Intell. **90**(6), 537–567 (2022)
20. Hanika, T., Hirth, J.: On the lattice of conceptual measurements. Inf. Sci. **613**, 453–468 (2022)
21. Hanika, T., Hirth, J.: Conceptual views on tree ensemble classifiers. Int. J. Approx. Reason. **159**, 108930 (2023)
22. Hirth, J., et al.: Automatic textual explanations of concept lattices. In: Ojeda-Aciego, M., Sauerwald, K., Jäschke, R. (eds.) ICCS 2023. LNCS, pp. 138–152. Springer, Cham (2023). https://doi.org/10.1007/978-3-031-40960-8_12
23. Hirth, J., et al.: Ordinal motifs in lattices. Inf. Sci. **659**, 120009 (2024)
24. Kawai, M., Sato, H., Shiohama, T.: Topic model-based recommender systems and their applications to cold-start problems. Expert Syst. Appl. **202**, 117129 (2022)
25. Lee, D.D., Seung, H.S.: Learning the parts of objects by non-negative matrix factorization. Nature **401**(6755), 788–791 (1999)
26. Li, W., McCallum, A.: Pachinko allocation: DAG-structured mixture models of topic correlations. In: Proceedings of the 23rd International Conference on Machine Learning, pp. 577–584 (2006)
27. Liao, Z., et al.: Core-reviewer recommendation based on pull request topic model and collaborator social network. Soft. Comput. **24**, 5683–5693 (2020)
28. Lin, T., et al.: The dual-sparse topic model: mining focused topics and focused terms in short text. In: Chung, C.-W., et al. (eds.) WWW, pp. 539–550. ACM (2014)
29. Van der Maaten, L., Hinton, G.: Visualizing data using t-SNE. J. Mach. Learn. Res. **9**(11), 2579–2605 (2008)
30. Mead, A.: Review of the development of multidimensional scaling methods. J. Roy. Stat. Soc. Ser. D (Stat.) **41**(1), 27–39 (1992)
31. Poelmans, J., Ignatov, D.I., Viaene, S., Dedene, G., Kuznetsov, S.O.: Text mining scientific papers: a survey on FCA-based information retrieval research. In: Perner, P. (ed.) ICDM 2012. LNCS (LNAI), vol. 7377, pp. 273–287. Springer, Heidelberg (2012). https://doi.org/10.1007/978-3-642-31488-9_22
32. Ramos, J., et al.: Using TF-IDF to determine word relevance in document queries. In: Proceedings of the First Instructional Conference on Machine Learning, vol. 242, no. 1, pp. 29–48. Citeseer (2003)
33. Roul, R.K.: Topic modeling combined with classification technique for extractive multi-document text summarization. Soft. Comput. **25**, 1113–1127 (2021)
34. Schaefermeier, B., Stumme, G., Hanika, T.: Topic space trajectories. Scientometrics **126**(7), 5759–5795 (2021)
35. Schäfermeier, B., Hirth, J., Hanika, T.: Research topic flows in co-authorship networks. Scientometrics **128**(9), 5051–5078 (2022)
36. Schäfermeier, B., Stumme, G., Hanika, T.: Mapping Research Trajectories. arXiv preprint arXiv:2204.11859 (2022)

37. Smith, A., Hawes, T., Myers, M.: Hiearchie: visualization for hierarchical topic models. In: Proceedings of the WS on Interactive Language Learning, Visualization, and Interfaces, pp. 71–78 (2014)
38. Srivastava, R., et al.: A topic modeled unsupervised approach to single document extractive text summarization. Knowl.-Based Syst. **246**, 108636 (2022)
39. Stumme, G., et al.: Computing iceberg concept lattices with TITANIC. Data Knowl. Eng. **42**(2), 189–222 (2002)
40. Sun, F., Li, Y., Zhang, Z.: A tool for visualizing topic evolution in large text collections. In: 2013 IEEE 13th International Conference on Advanced Learning Technologies, pp. 53–54 (2013)
41. Takizawa, P.A.: Using a topic model to map and analyze a large curriculum. PLoS ONE **18**(4), e0284513 (2023)
42. Venugopalan, M., Gupta, D.: An enhanced guided LDA model augmented with BERT based semantic strength for aspect term extraction in sentiment analysis. Knowl.-Based Syst. **246**, 108668 (2022)
43. Wille, R.: Geometric representation of concept lattices. In: Optiz, O., et al. (eds.) Conceptual and Numerical Analysis of Data, pp. 239–255. Springer, Heidelberg (1989). https://doi.org/10.1007/978-3-642-75040-3_17
44. Yin, H., et al.: Sentiment analysis and topic modeling for COVID-19 vaccine discussions. World Wide Web **25**(3), 1067–1083 (2022)
45. Zhao, H., et al.: Inter and intra topic structure learning with word embeddings. In: International Conference on Machine Learning, pp. 5892–5901. PMLR (2018)

Relational Concept Analysis and Graph-FCA in Practice: Analyzing Multi-relational Data

Vanessa Fokou[1], Peggy Cellier[2], Xavier Dolques[1], Sébastien Ferré[2], and Florence Le Ber[1](✉)

[1] Université de Strasbourg, ENGEES, CNRS, ICube UMR 7357, 67000 Strasbourg, France
{vfokou,dolques}@unistra.fr, florence.leber@engees.unistra.fr
[2] Univ Rennes, CNRS, Inria, INSA Rennes, IRISA - UMR 6074, Rennes, France
{peggy.cellier,Sebastien.Ferre}@irisa.fr

Abstract. Relational Concept Analysis (RCA) and Graph-FCA (GCA) are two extensions of Formal Concept Analysis (FCA) to multi-relational data. Whereas similar when restricted to some specific inputs and parameters, RCA and GCA processes are different and can be applied to a variety of multi-relational data. Analysts should thus be guided to choose between the two methods, their parameters, and the data model, according to the queries to solve. In this paper, we focus on the processing of n-ary relationships, how they can be modeled, and the impact of the chosen model and the chosen method on query answering.

Keywords: Relational Concept Analysis · Graph-FCA · Multi-relational Data · Query · N-ary Relationship

1 Introduction

In many areas of real life, data are multi-relational, which makes it possible to capture several types of interaction between entities. Representing and analyzing such data is necessary to understand complex phenomena involving several entities. For instance, in the research community, a researcher may be affiliated with several institutions, collaborate with different researchers, and organize events with other researchers. Querying and analyzing this type of data requires appropriate methods. Formal Concept Analysis (FCA) [11] is a mathematical framework based on lattice theory that aims to discover conceptual structures on tables that describe objects by their attributes (called formal contexts). FCA has been successfully used for analyzing, mining, and exploring tabular data. This has led to several extensions of FCA to complex data, notably Relational Concept Analysis (RCA) [20] for binary multi-relational data and Graph-FCA (GCA) [8] for labeled hyper-graphs (with edges of any arity). Other approaches

This research is supported by ANR project SmartFCA (ANR-21-CE23-0023).

P. Cellier et al. (Eds.): CONCEPTS 2025, LNAI 15941, pp. 35–50, 2025.
https://doi.org/10.1007/978-3-032-03364-2_3

have been proposed, such as Power Context Family [23] and Triadic Concept Analysis [16]. These approaches aim to extract conceptual structures from multi-relational data in the same way that FCA extracts conceptual structures from binary tables. We focus here on GCA and RCA: the two methods have some similarities [10], but their processes are different, leading to different results, and it is interesting to study their behaviors with regard to data characteristics and to analysts' questions. In particular, GCA directly handles n-ary relations, while RCA is limited to binary relations and requires transformations to handle n-ary relations. Other differences can be noticed: cycle processing, the ability to derive n-ary concepts, the automatic integration of inverse relations, and the use of quantifiers. It is therefore important and interesting to analyze these differences to see to what extent they can be complementary according to the objectives of the analysis.

In this paper, we compare RCA and GCA from a practical point of view on their ability to fulfill user queries according to their difference in the processing of n-ary relations, and we also discuss the readability of the results. This work is a preliminary step towards the aim of bringing closer and combining both approaches in a practical way. The remainder of the paper is organized as follows. Section 2 presents the related work while Sect. 3 introduces the fundamental notions of RCA and GCA and provides an overview of their differences. Section 4 explores the ability of RCA and GCA to answer analysis questions involving ternary relationships with an emphasis on their complementarities. Section 5 concludes and gives a few perspectives.

2 Related Work

Representing relational data is a recurrent question in many domains, from databases [13,21] to data mining [7]. Description Logics [2] (DL) language offers a collection of constructors for expressing relational information using role restrictions. Some works combine FCA and DL for a richer representation. For example, [3] uses FCA methods to support the hierarchical representation in the bottom-up construction of knowledge bases and [12] combines FCA and DL to compute clusters in a knowledge graph, similarly to RCA. Indeed RCA can manage relational structures, but only binary relations. Relations with high arities must be transformed to be processed by RCA: in [15], two encoding models are used to transform a ternary relation, reification and decomposition. The authors evaluate these two encodings on their number of concepts and their ability to answer a replacement scenario regarding pesticide plants. A practical comparison of RCA, GCA, and Triadic Concept Analysis (TCA) [16], has been carried out on real data for modeling indeterminate values in ternary data (consisting of one ternary relation) [14]. In this work, the focus is on the processing of ternary relations for RCA since TCA and GCA can directly handle any ternary relation. On the RCA side, different encodings including reification and decomposition have been used to transform the ternary relation. In addition, an encoding of the ternary relation into binary relations for GCA illustrates the ease of interpreting the results compared to its results on the ternary relation. The authors compare the three approaches on their concepts, flexibility, readability, and ease of use. The more general question of encoding complex relational data has been considered in [5]: the authors propose to use design patterns formalizing recurring encodings in RCA with regards to data characteristics and analysis questions.

Besides, relational data analysis requires the manipulation and the navigation of complex representations. Efforts have been made to help the analyst in this work, especially for RCA. In [1], the authors present a query-based navigation approach that helps an expert to explore a concept lattice family. In [18] overlays on the RCAExplore tool [6] are suggested to guide the user in the choice of scaling quantifiers and to help interpret the results. Another way of making the analysis easier is to summarize the lattice family into an ordered set of graphs – close to GCA patterns – as proposed by [17] to explore qualitative temporal data. In this approach, graphs are constructed for all concepts of a chosen main lattice. This hierarchy of graphs therefore provides an overview for answering queries on entities in this main lattice. Regarding GCA, different graphical representation of the concepts have been proposed: graph patterns to emphasize the relational structures in the data, and concept hierarchies to emphasize the generalization ordering between concepts. In [9], the authors explore different modellings of natural language syntactic structures.

Finally, no systematic comparison of RCA and GCA has been conducted, except in the work of [10], which have compared the outputs of the two methods when used on a common ground, highlighting how cycles are processed differently. Nevertheless, the respective ability of RCA and GCA to answer user queries and how their differences can be complementary is still to be addressed.

3 Preliminaries

In this section, we recall the main notions of RCA and GCA and provide an overview of their differences.

3.1 Relational Concept Analysis (RCA)

RCA aims at extending FCA to take multiple formal contexts with relations between their objects [20]. The idea is to represent the information contained in the relations through special relational attributes, to enhance the description of objects in the formal contexts. RCA takes as input data a Relational Context Family (RCF). An RCF is a pair (**K**,**R**) where: $\mathbf{K} = \{\mathcal{K}_i\}_{i=1..n}$ is a set of object-attribute contexts (formal contexts) $\mathcal{K}_i = (O_i, A_i, I_i)$, and $\mathbf{R} = \{r_k\}_{k=1..m}$ is a set of object-object contexts (relational contexts) r_k where $r_k \subseteq dom(r_k) \times ran(r_k)$, and $dom(r_k), ran(r_k) \in \{O_i\}_{i=1..n}$ are respectively the domain and range of r_k. Figure 1 shows an example of an RCF made of two formal contexts introducing `Researcher` and institution (`Inst`) respectively and one relational context (`is_affiliated_to`) indicating which institution a researcher is affiliated to. This means that $dom($`is_affiliated_to`$) =$

Researcher	n_pub_sup_10	n_pub_inf_10	n_cit_inf_20	n_cit_sup_20	researcher
R1	×		×		×
R2	×			×	×
R3		×		×	×
R4	×		×		×
R5		×		×	×
R6	×			×	×

Inst	company	university	France	Romania	inst
I1		×	×		×
I2		×		×	×
I3	×			×	×
I4	×		×		×

is_affiliated_to	I1	I2	I3	I4
R1			×	
R2		×		
R3				×
R4				×
R5			×	
R6	×			

Fig. 1. An RCF about researchers and their affiliations.

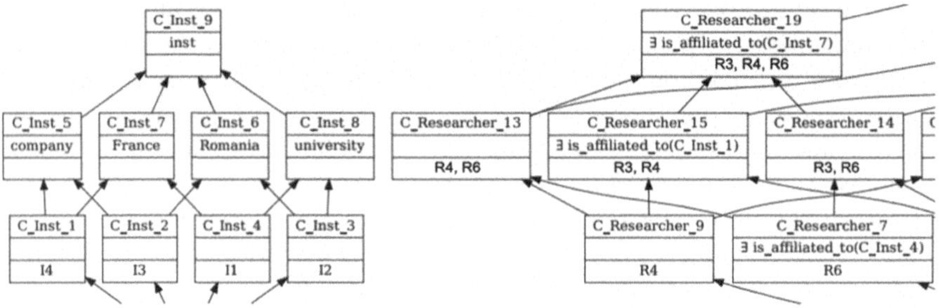

Fig. 2. Lattices (excerpt) obtained from the RCF in Fig. 1.

$O_{Researcher}$ and $ran(\texttt{is\_affiliated\_to}) = O_{Inst}$. The researcher entities $\{\texttt{R1},\ldots,\texttt{R6}\}$ are described by the number of publications, which can be lower than 10 (n_pub_inf_10) or greater than 10 (n_pub_sup_10), and the number of citations, which can be lower than 20 (n_cit_inf_20) or greater than 20 (n_cit_sup_20). The institution entities $\{\texttt{I1},\ldots,\texttt{I4}\}$ are described by their type (university, company) and by their country (France, Romania).

RCA builds concepts in an iterative way. Initially, concepts are built for each formal context, e.g. lattice of $\mathcal{K}_{\texttt{Inst}}$ (left of Fig. 2): in this representation, arrows represent the subsumption relation between concepts and each concept is represented with three sections containing, from top to bottom, the identifier (e.g. C_Inst_7), the (reduced) intent and the (reduced) extent of the concept respectively. At the next step, the relational contexts r_k are used to form relational attributes that express the relation between objects of $dom(r_k)$ and concepts built on $ran(r_k)$. For instance, the relational attribute $\exists$ is_affiliated_to (C_Inst_7) is assigned to $\{\texttt{R3, R4, R6}\}$ in concept C_Researcher_19 (right lattice of Fig. 2, extents are complete for the sake of clarity), because *they are affiliated to an institution* in C_Inst_7. Various quantifiers (e.g. $\exists\forall$, $\supseteq$) can be used to form the relational attributes [4]. The number of iterations in the RCA process depends on the data model, and the RCA process ends when the families of lattices of two consecutive steps are isomorphic.

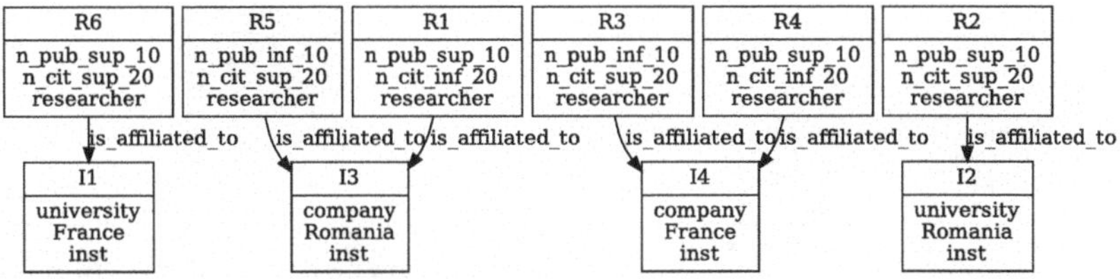

Fig. 3. Graph context corresponding to the RCF in Fig. 1.

3.2 Graph-FCA (GCA)

GCA [8] is an extension of FCA for hyper-graphs. GCA takes as input data a *graph context* which is defined as an incidence relation between *tuples* of objects and attributes. Formally, a graph context is a triple $K = (O, A, I)$, where O is a set of objects, A is a set of attributes, and $I \subseteq O^* \times A$ is an incidence relation between object tuples $\overline{o} = (o_1, \ldots, o_k) \in O^*$, for any arity k, and attributes $a \in A$. In a graph context, objects represent nodes, and attributes represent hyper-edge labels. An incidence $((o), a)$ describes object o by attribute a like in FCA. An incidence $((o_1, o_2), a)$ relates object o_1 to object o_2 through a binary relation a like in RCA. An incidence $((o_1, \ldots, o_n), a)$ represents an n-ary relationship and an alternative notation of $((o_1, \ldots, o_n), a)$ for readability is $a(o_1, \ldots, o_n)$. Finally, unary attributes are used to label nodes and n-ary attributes are used to label edges connecting n nodes. For instance, in the graph context shown in Fig. 3, the unary incidence `company(I3)` describes institution `I3` as a `company` and the binary incidence `is_affiliated_to(R5, I3)` expresses the fact that researcher `R5` *is affiliated to* institution `I3`.

Given a graph context $K = (O, A, I)$, we introduce the extensional representation (called *object relation*) and the intensional representation (called *Projected graph Pattern - PGP*) in GCA. An object relation is a set $R \subseteq O^k$ of tuples of objects, for some arity k. For $k = 1$, the object relation is a set of objects, which corresponds in GCA to the extensional representation of so-called unary concepts. In the scope of this work, the following definitions are limited to unary concepts[1]. Let $\mathcal{V}$ be an infinite set of variables. A graph pattern $P \subseteq \mathcal{V}^* \times A$ is a set of n-ary edges with variables as nodes, and attributes as labels. A PGP is then defined as a couple $Q = (\overline{x}, P)$ where P is a graph pattern and $\overline{x} \in \mathcal{V}^*$ is called the projection tuple. The *description* of any object o is then defined by the PGP $Q(o) = ((o), I)$. The intent of a finite non-empty set of objects R, denoted by $int(R)$, is the intersection of the description of all of objects in R: $int(R) = \bigcap_{o \in R} Q(o)$. Conversely, the extension of a unary PGP Q is defined as the set of objects whose description contains Q: $ext(Q) = \{o \in O \mid Q \subseteq Q(o)\}$. A graph concept is then a pair (R, Q) such that $R = ext(Q)$ and $Q = int(R)$ where R is the *extent* and Q is the *intent*.

[1] GCA also processes n-ary concepts, which are concepts whose extensions are object relations of arity n, i.e. sets of n-tuples of objects.

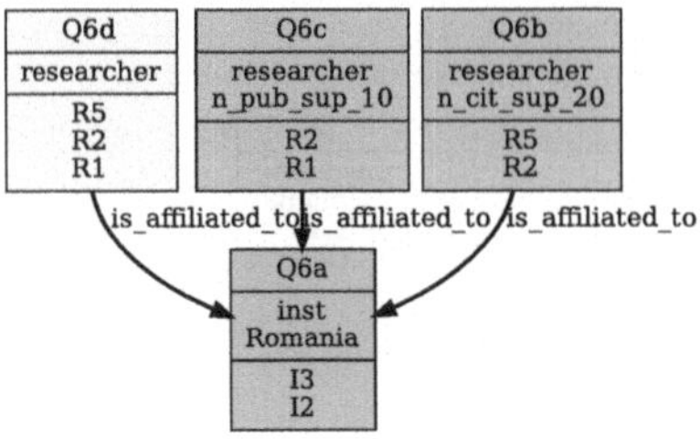

Fig. 4. Pattern P6 (excerpt) of the graph context of Fig. 3.

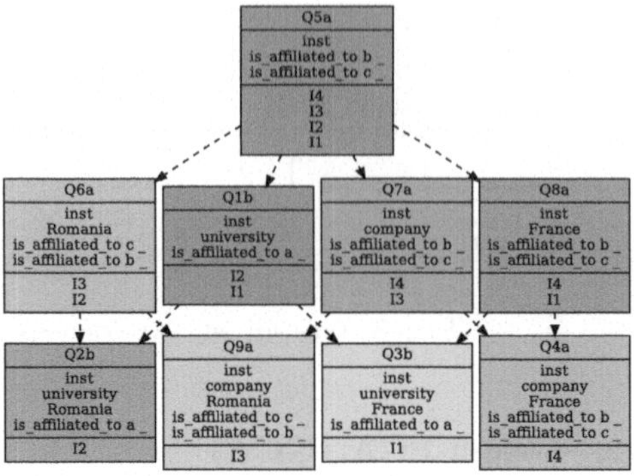

Fig. 5. Concept hierarchy of the `institution` category.

For instance, {(R5), (R2)} is an object relation of arity 1 in the current example. It corresponds in FCA to the set of objects {R5, R2}. Figure 4 shows a graph pattern (P6) extracted from the patterns of the graph context presented in Fig. 3. Each node x identifies a unary concept (e.g., Q6d) along with its extent (here, {R1, R2, R5}). The concept intent is the PGP $((x), P)$, where P is the subgraph containing node x and all the nodes useful for describing x i.e., the pattern core (bright color nodes). For instance, let us name P_{abc} the pattern core of pattern P6 (Fig. 4). P_{abc} consists of concepts Q6a, Q6b and Q6c, so $int(Q6c) = ((c), P_{abc})$ (because Q6c belong to P_{abc}) and $int(Q6d) = ((d), P6)$.

The GCA tool also provides a lattice view as an alternative to the pattern view. For a sake of place, we only present the concept hierarchy of the `institution` category as shown in Fig. 5. In this hierarchy view, relations between nodes are represented by textual labels in the description of the nodes along with unary relations. For instance, the relation `is_affiliated_to` between nodes Q6b and Q6a in pattern P6 (Fig. 4) is represented by the edge [`is_affiliated_to b _`] in the description part of Q6a in Fig. 5. In general, the GCA tool does not display a bottom concept with empty extent and a top concept with empty intent. This hierarchy view of GCA concepts appears as a family of concept hierarchies, one for each category of objects, similarly to RCA.

3.3 Differences Between RCA and GCA

RCA and GCA are two extensions of FCA for multi-relational data with the objective of capturing the relationships between objects in the computation of concepts. Besides some common features studied in [10], RCA and GCA have many differences, as briefly discussed below:

Quantifiers: GCA uses (implicitly) only the existential quantifier, while RCA has a number of other quantifiers ($\exists\forall$, $\supseteq$, or with percentages), which can be used to satisfy more precise queries, such as: the group of institutions where 50% of researchers have a number of publications lower than 10 (`n_pub_inf_10`). The answer in the running example is {`I3, I4`}. A second query could be: institutions whose *all* researchers have a number of citations > 20, the answer is {`I1, I2`}.

Results Presentation: RCA results is a family of concept lattices - one lattice for each category of objects - interconnected by relational attributes. The difficulty lies in navigating between lattices when the dataset grows, and thus tools have been proposed to summarize or simplify the representation. GCA has three output modes: only showing hierarchies such as RCA, only showing relational patterns (graph patterns), or showing the two combined. The latter is the richest representation but it is more difficult to grasp and the pattern view highlights the different structures and connections between elements.

Process: from an algorithmic point of view, RCA concepts are computed through a fixed-point iteration of FCA, while GCA relies on graph intersection. This intersection of graphs which corresponds to the categorical product of graphs, enables GCA to automatically consider inverse relations. On the RCA side, the integration of inverse relations is not automatic and depends on the needs of the analysis. RCA and GCA each have a set of options for controlling the results. RCA offers different quantifiers for relations and can use different algorithms for calculating concepts, such as iceberg [22] and AOC-poset [19]. By default, all concepts are calculated. Regarding GCA, there are several options such as: `-only-cores` to restrict the generation to pattern cores, `-minsupp N` to restrict the output to unary concepts that have an extent size higher or equal to N.

N-ary Concepts: RCA is limited to computing unary concepts, unlike GCA, which also computes $n(> 1)$-ary concepts (called n-ary relational concepts). The extents of n-ary concepts are sets of n-tuples of objects and the intents are graph patterns with a focus on n nodes. In the same way that unary concepts represent groups of elements with common characteristics, n-ary concepts represent groups of relationships with common characteristics. For instance, on pattern `P6` shown in Fig. 4, the concept of *Romania's institutions and their researchers* can be defined as the binary concept $Q6(a, d)^2$ of extension {`(I2,R2)`, `(I3,R1)`, `(I3,R5)`}.

N-ary Relations Processing: RCA is limited to binary relationships, whereas GCA is designed to directly handle n-ary relationships. Therefore, n-ary relationships need to be transformed into binary relationships for RCA [15]. This is discussed further in the following.

4 Exploring Multi-relational Data with RCA and GCA

As said before, the analysis of multi-relational data may require modeling choices such as n-ary relationship representation and this choice can affect user query answering. This section presents a dataset and two user questions that are used to illustrate the effect of data modeling on RCA and GCA answers. We also discuss the readability of their results as well as their complementarity.

[2] Notation representing the projection onto nodes a and d of pattern P6.

4.1 Data and User Queries

For this study, we use the graph context depicted in Fig. 6, which extends the graph context about researchers and their affiliations shown in Fig. 3. It models a network of researchers, their affiliations and activities such as conference organization and the publication of papers[3].

This graph context is made up of 5 categories of objects. The `researcher` entities {`R1,...,R6`} and institutions (`inst`) {`I1,...,I4`} as described in Sect. 3.1. The `paper` entities {`P1,...,P4`} are described by their type (`journal`, conference (`cf`)) and by the fact that they have been cited (`cited`). The `role` entities {`g_chair, p_chair, l_organizer`} (for general chair, program chair and local organizer respectively) and the conference (`conf`) entities {`ICCS, ICFCA, CLA`} have no attributes. It contains the binary relation `is_affiliated_to`, the ternary relations `publish(researcher, paper, inst)` which means that a researcher publishes a paper with an affiliation and `organize(researcher, conf, role)` which means that a researcher organizes a conference with a given role. GCA uses ellipse nodes to represent $n(> 2)$-ary relations and uses numbers to indicate the position of entities in the relationship. For ternary relationships, these numbers range from 1 to 3, for instance, `organize(R4, ICFA, p_chair)` in Fig. 6. The user can address several queries on such a dataset; here are two of them:

- *query1*: the group of institutions whose researchers have organized a conference;
- *query2*: the group of researchers who have published papers and are affiliated to a French institution.

To solve some queries, inverse relationships need to be integrated into RCA data. For instance, to answer *query1*, the inverse of the relation `is_affiliated_to` must be added in the RCF to link `institution` entities to `researcher` entities. After that, the second stage consists in filtering groups of researchers according to the organization of conferences by verification of the intents of the researchers' concepts. On the contrary, thanks to the categorical product of graphs, GCA automatically integrates inverse relationships. Thus the links between groups of institutions and groups of researchers are directly expressed in the GCA results, as shown by the concept hierarchy of `institution` category (Fig. 5) computed on the graph context in Fig. 3.

4.2 Modeling Ternary Relationships

RCA requires initial modeling for n-ary relations, and such modeling is not without consequences, as it can lead to the loss of structural information. The question that arises is how to model n-ary relations efficiently in the RCA way. Regarding GCA, the question relates to the difficulty of interpreting patterns computed directly on n-ary relations. We explore how each of the RCA (according to data modeling) and GCA approaches satisfies *query1* and *query2*.

[3] It should be noted that this graph context only represents an excerpt of what such a graph could be for a community of researchers in a given field (e.g., FCA).

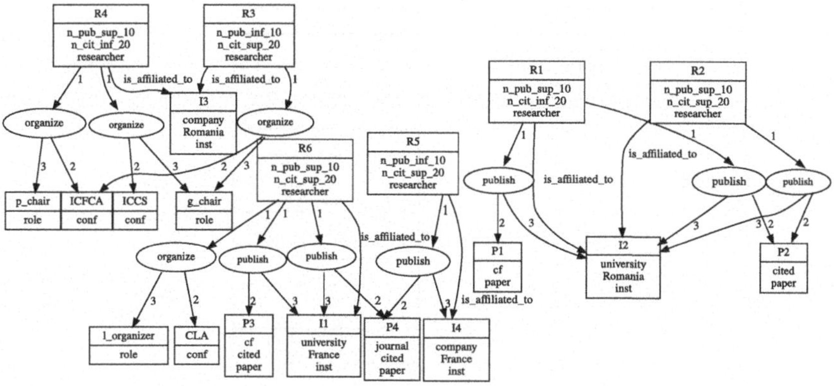

Fig. 6. A graph context about the researchers and their activities.

RCA and Ternary Relationships. To answer *query1* and *query2* with RCA, we use the encodings in [14,15] to model the ternary relations:

1. *reification*: consists of reifying the ternary relation as a new formal context whose objects are 3-tuples of the relation. Formally, a relation $r(A, B, C)$ is transformed into 3 binary relations: $r1(ABC, A)$, $r2(ABC, B)$, and $r3(ABC, C)$;
2. *decomposition*: consists of decomposing a relation $r(A, B, C)$ respectively into a chain of 2 binary relations $r1(A, B)$ and $r2(B, C)$ [14], or into 3 binary relations: $r1(A, B)$, $r2(B, C)$, and $r3(A, C)$ [15];
3. *partitioning*: consists of partitioning a ternary relation $r(A, B, C)$ on the entities of B into a set of binary relations $\{b_i(A, C)\}_{b_i \in B}$ [14].

Of these encodings, reification does not lead to a loss of information, decomposition can lead to a loss of structural information, and partitioning leads to a loss of connectivity.

Reification. The relations `publish` and `organize` are reified by creating new formal and relational contexts. For illustration, `organize(researcher, conf, role)` is reified by adding a formal context `organization (Org)` – without attributes – whose entities are 3-tuples representing the instances of `organize` and 3 relational contexts linking `Org` entities to the initial entities: `is_about (Org, conf) with_role(Org, role)` and, `is_done_by(Org, researcher)`.

With reification, RCA without inverse relations produces 61 concepts (without bottom concepts[4]) and contains the answer to *query2* but not *query1*. After adding the inverse relations[5], RCA produces 99 concepts; among them, concept `C_Inst_12` gives the answer to *query1*. Figure 7 shows the extract of RCA

[4] In the following, we do not consider bottom concepts in the RCA and GCA results.
[5] In the following, inverse relationships are added to the RCA data.

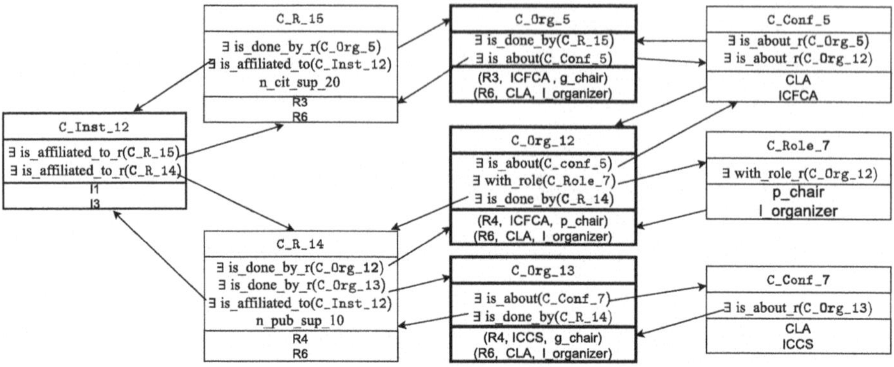

Fig. 7. RCA description of the specific intent of concept `C_Inst_12` (reification).

concepts linked to `C_Inst_12`. Arrows represent relational attributes between concepts, and relations ending with "_r" represent inverse relations. The extent of `C_Inst_12` is {`I1, I3`}. Its intent expresses that they are institutions whose researchers (`C_R_14, 15`) are in link with `Org` concepts (`C_Org_5, 12, 13`) – concepts of reified entities into 3-tuples. By analyzing the intent of these `Org` concepts, we find all the information concerning each group of organization i.e., the researchers, the institutions and the roles of researchers in organizing conferences.

For *query2*, its result is {`R5, R6`}, the extent of concept `C_R_13` whose intent expresses the fact that they are researchers affiliated to French institutions {`I1, I4`} and involved in publication in concept `C_Publish_8` of extension {`(R5, P4, I4), (R6, P4, I1)`}. Like `organization` concepts, `publication` concept intents indicate all the information about a publication: researchers, the paper and the affiliations associated to the publication. We can satisfy more specific queries such as: all researchers affiliated to *university institutions* and who have published conference and journal papers.

Chain Decomposition. The ternary relations are encoded as a chain of two binary relations. The relation `organize(researcher, conf, role)` is encoded by `is_organize_by(conf, researcher)` and `has_role(researcher, role)`, expressing the fact that a conference is organized by a researcher and a researcher has a role. The relationship `publish(researcher, paper, inst)` is encoded by `is_publish_by(paper, researcher)` and `belong_to(researcher, inst)`, expressing that a paper is published by a researcher and a researcher belongs to an institution (like the relation `is_affiliated_to`).

With chain decomposition, RCA produces a total of 59 concepts containing the answers to *query1* and *query2*. Figure 8 depicts `C_R_13` that answers to *query2*: its intent expresses the fact that researchers {`R5, R6`} are affiliated to French institutions {`I1, I4`} and have published paper `P4` (`C_Paper_1`). There is no specific indication that a paper is published by a researcher with a *given affiliation* unlike reification. Regarding *query1*, its answer is {`I1, I3`},

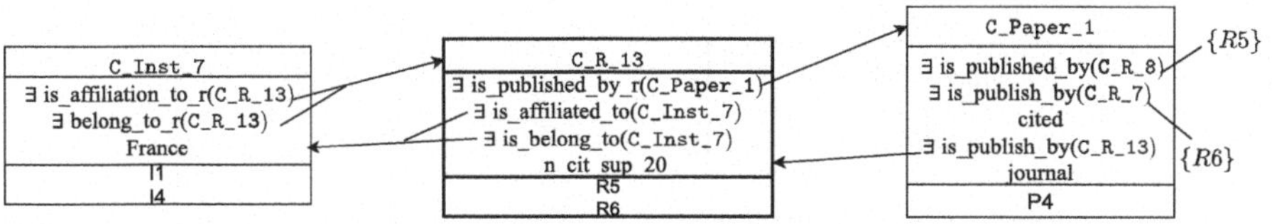

Fig. 8. RCA description of the specific intent of C_R_13 (chain decomposition).

the extent of concept C_Inst_11 whose intent expresses that they are institutions with researchers who have roles and have organized conferences. As in the case of the relation publish, its does not specifically indicate that a conference is organized by a researcher with a *given role*. We also note that the relation has_role(researcher, role) is not very significant because a researcher has a role in respect of its participation in the organization of a conference. Indeed, chain decomposition leads to a loss of structural information because it does not capture the global dependency between entities.

Partitioning. The relation organize(researcher, conf, role) is partitioned on role entities into a set of relations $\texttt{role}_i$(researcher, conf) for each $\texttt{role}_i$ in role. For instance, p_chair(R4, ICFCA) means that researcher R4 is the program chair of ICFCA. Regarding publish(researcher, paper, inst), a partitioning on institution entities leads to instances of the form I4(R5, P4) meaning that researcher R5 publishes paper P4 with affiliation I4. However, this partitioning leads to a loss of connectivity, as institution entities are also involved in the relation is_affiliated_to, and the same entity is split between an object and a relation. For the same reasons, a partitioning of publish on researcher entities is not desirable, as they are involved in other relationships (is_affiliated_to and organize)[6]. Consequently, the only possibility is partitioning on paper entities, which gives relations $\texttt{paper}_i$(researcher, inst) for each $\texttt{paper}_i$ in paper.

With this partitioning, RCA produces 37 concepts containing the answer to *query2* but not *query1*. Indeed, institution entities are described by their researchers (through is_affiliated_to_r) who are described by their *affiliations* and *roles*. Since researchers have occupied *different roles* in the organization of conferences, the set of researchers who have organized conferences does not form a concept. Consequently, the set of institutions characterized by such researchers does not itself form a concept, which explains the absence of answers to *query1*. Regarding *query2*, its result is {R5, R6} the extent of C_R_13 depicted in Fig. 9. Its intent expresses that {R5, R6} are affiliated to French institutions {I1, I4} and have published P4 with affiliations {I1, I4}. However, we have no information on the features of P4 unlike reification and chain decomposition (see Fig. 8). Partitioning captures the *global dependency between entities*, but also leads to a

[6] In [14], partitioning was applied to a dataset composed of a single ternary relationship, so no conflicts were possible.

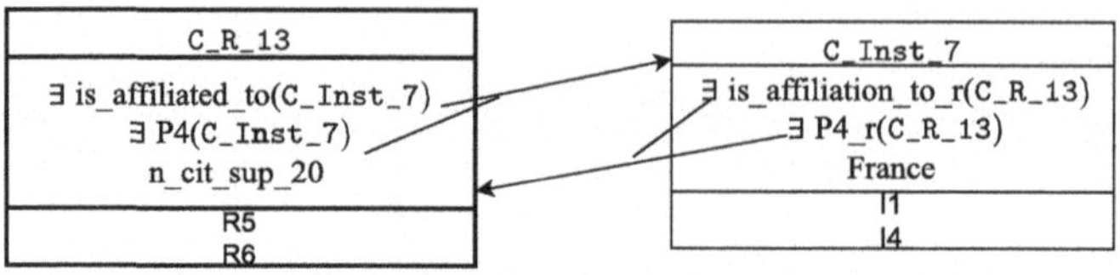

Fig. 9. RCA description of the specific intent of concept `C_R_13` (partitioning).

loss of *features* of partitioned objects, and thus to the loss of the corresponding category concepts. In our case, we lose the concepts of `role` and `paper`.

GCA and Ternary Relationships. GCA on the initial data (called GCA-ternary) produces 9 patterns and 63 concepts. The answers to *query1* and *query2* are respectively contained in patterns `P7` (Fig. 10) and `P9` (Fig. 11). As in the graph context, ternary relations are indicated by ellipse nodes in graph patterns.

The solution to *query1* regarding institutions whose researchers have *organized* a conference is {`I1`, `I3`}, the extent of concept `Q7a` of `P7` (Fig. 10). Pattern `P7` captures the organization of conferences by researchers, indicating the associated roles and affiliations. It shows all the researchers who have organized a conference (`Q7m`), their affiliations (`Q7a`), all the conferences that have been organized (`Q7i`), and the roles assumed by the researchers (`Q7h`) in the organization of the conferences. The answer to *query2* about researchers who have *published* papers and are affiliated to a French institution is {`R5`, `R6`}, the extent of concept `Q9k` of pattern `P9` shown in Fig. 11. As we can see in this pattern, `Q9k` generalizes concepts `Q9f` and `Q9e`. Concept `Q9f` represents researchers who have published a paper and are affiliated to a French institution which is a `university` and `Q9e` represents researchers who have published a paper and are affiliated to a French institution which is a `company`. Concepts `Q9f` and `Q9e` answer more specific queries about the publication of papers by researchers. Through a pattern, many queries can be solved because each concept of a pattern represents a query and its answer: the query is defined by the concept intent and the answer by its extent. For instance, the answer of the query "researchers who have *organized* conferences and have *published* papers" is {`R6`} the extent of `Q9f` (Fig. 11). GCA graph patterns highlight the different connections between concepts.

As mentioned earlier (Sect. 3.2), in the hierarchical view of GCA patterns, $n(>1)$-ary relations are replaced by textual labels in concept descriptions. For illustration, the ternary relation `publish(Q9k, Q9c, Q9i)` (linking concepts `Q9k, Q9c, Q9i`) of pattern `P9` will be represented by the label `[publish_c i]` in the intensional part of `Q9k` meaning that: for each researcher `k` ∈ `Ext(Q9k)`, there exists a paper `c` ∈ `Ext(Q9c)` and an institution `i` ∈ `Ext(Q9i)` such that `publish(k, c, i)` is verified. Naturally, the greater the arity of a relation, the more difficult it is to read and interpret the concept intents in natural language. This may raise questions about potential encodings of n-ary relations in order to facilitate the interpretation of GCA concept intents. Should n-ary relations be

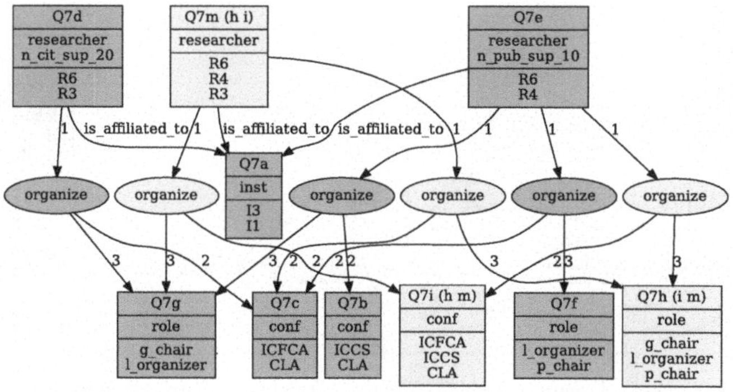

Fig. 10. Pattern P7 extracted from patterns of the graph context in Fig. 6.

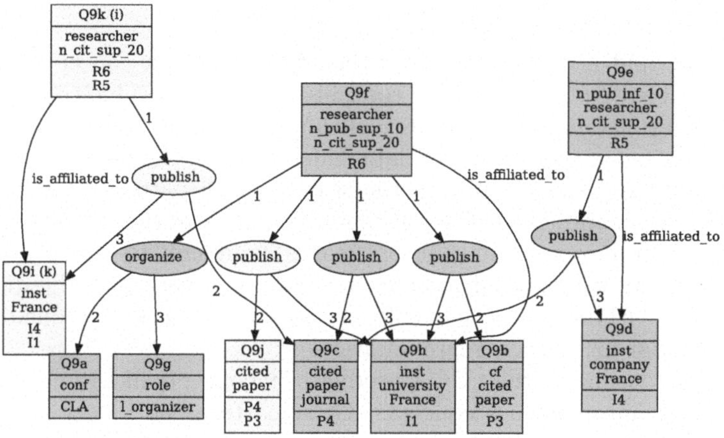

Fig. 11. Pattern P9 extracted from patterns of the graph context in Fig. 6.

encoded into binary relations to make the interpretation of GCA patterns more accessible? In the following comparison, we also performed GCA on the three encodings applied to RCA data.

4.3 Comparison and Discussion

GCA-ternary (i.e., on the initial data) produces a total of 63 concepts, 9 graph patterns containing 7 automorphic concepts (different occurrences of the same concept[7]). Like RCA, GCA produces 99 concepts on reified data. The 36 supplementary concepts are induced by the reified entities and does not impact the concepts for the initial categories which remains unchanged. Furthermore, the number of graph patterns remains unchanged (9), whereas their size (number

[7] The duplication of concepts in GCA is sometimes required to properly represent the graph patterns that exhibit symmetries.

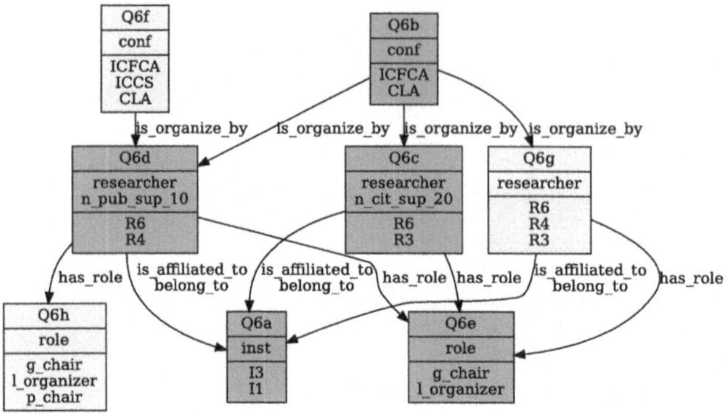

Fig. 12. Equivalent of pattern P7 in Fig. 10.

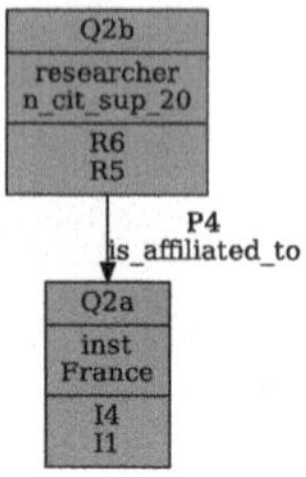

Fig. 13. Pattern P2.

of concepts per pattern) increases with the addition of new concepts and consequently the increase of automorphic concepts: 110 automorphic concepts versus 7 with GCA-ternary. These results reveal the disadvantages that reification can bring: the increase in the size of the data which leads to the increase in the number of concepts and the increase in the size of graph patterns. GCA does not favor reification: in addition to introducing new concepts, the significant increase in the number of automorphic concepts makes it difficult to read and interpret graph patterns. In terms of advantages, reification preserves all the dimensions of the relation without any loss of information, it manages relations of various arities by standardizing their representation.

With chain decomposition, GCA produces 59 concepts like RCA, 9 patterns, and contains 4 automorphics concepts. GCA patterns no longer have ternary relationships (ellipse nodes) and look simpler to read. Figure 12 shows the equivalent of pattern P7 (Fig. 10) with chain decomposition. Like with RCA, there is a loss of structural information and the possible introduction of ambiguities. For illustration, if an entity is shared between two binary relations, it becomes difficult, even impossible, to reconstruct the original relation. Regarding partitioning, GCA produces 37 concepts, 11 patterns (with no automorphic concepts). Partitioning produced fewer concepts, which can be explained by the fact that it leads to the loss of concepts from partitioned categories. This results in smaller, less rich patterns (in terms of links between entities). Figure 13 depicts pattern `P2` that contains the answer to *query2*: the extent of concept `Q2b`. As we can see, the features of paper `P4` have been lost. This pattern `P2` corresponds to the RCA excerpt depicted in Fig. 9.

It is important to note that these different encodings can be applied to relations with arities greater than 3 and that the choice should depend on the analysis questions, because according to the queries to be solved, one encoding may be more appropriate than another. For instance, *partitioning* on the relation `organize` does not answer to *query1*. The analyst can even consider combined encodings. For illustration, the modeling of a relation $r(A, B, C, D, E)$ of arity 5 can first consist of its decomposition into a chain of 2 ternary relations

$r1(A, B, C)$ and $r2(C, D, E)$, followed by the reification of $r1$ and partitioning of $r2$. Finally, the difference in the number of concepts between the GCA-ternary results (63 concepts) and those of GCA on *chain decomposition* (59) and *partitioning* (37) illustrates the loss of information of these encodings and therefore the reduced possibility of satisfying some queries depending on data modeling. However, these encodings can be used in GCA (with the same consequences as in RCA) to *simplify* GCA patterns that become more complex for relations of *high arity*: it is a trade-off between simplicity of analysis and loss of information (e.g., pattern presented in Fig. 12 versus pattern P7 in Fig. 10).

5 Conclusion and Future Work

This work compares RCA and GCA on their ability to answer user queries, focusing on the processing of ternary relations. GCA directly handles ternary relations (and n-ary relations in general) while RCA is limited to binary relations. We use three encodings (reification, chain decomposition, and partitioning) to model RCA data. We have shown the impact of these encodings in terms of information loss, data increase and, consequently, query solving. We have also modeled the GCA data using these encodings and it appears that chain decomposition and partitioning lead to graph patterns that are easier to read and interpret. This exploration and comparison of ternary relationship modeling for RCA/GCA analysis has to be extended and deepened on real datasets, to study both the complexity induced by the various encodings and the actual readability of the results.

In a future work, we will further compare the ability of RCA and GCA in terms of query solving by exploring other differences such as: n-ary concepts, cycles processing, and quantifiers. We plan to propose a framework for choosing data encoding models (reification, decomposition, partitioning, etc.) and methods (RCA, GCA, etc.) according to the analysis questions.

References

1. Azmeh, Z., Huchard, M., Napoli, A., Hacene, M.R., Valtchev, P.: Querying relational concept lattices. In: CLA, vol. 11, p. 377. Citeseer (2011)
2. Baader, F., Calvanese, D., Mcguinness, D., Nardi, D., Patel-Schneider, P.: The Description Logic Handbook: Theory, Implementation, and Applications. Cambridge University Press (2003)
3. Baader, F., Sertkaya, B.: Applying formal concept analysis to description logics. In: Eklund, P. (ed.) ICFCA 2004. LNCS (LNAI), vol. 2961, pp. 261–286. Springer, Heidelberg (2004). https://doi.org/10.1007/978-3-540-24651-0_24
4. Braud, A., Dolques, X., Huchard, M., Le Ber, F.: Generalization effect of quantifiers in a classification based on relational concept analysis. Knowl.-Based Syst. **160**, 119–135 (2018)
5. Braud, A., Dolques, X., Huchard, M., Le Ber, F., Martin, P.: Relational concept analysis in practice: capitalizing on data modeling using design patterns. In: Dürrschnabel, D., López Rodríguez, D. (eds.) ICFCA 2023. LNCS, vol. 13934, pp. 166–182. Springer, Cham (2023). https://doi.org/10.1007/978-3-031-35949-1_12

6. Dolques, X., Braud, A., Huchard, M., Le Ber, F.: RCAExplore, a FCA based tool to explore relational data. In: Workshop "Applications and Tools of Formal Concept Analysis" (ICFCA 2019), pp. 1–5 (2019)
7. Džeroski, S.: Multi-relational data mining: an introduction. SIGKDD Explor. **5**, 1–16 (2003)
8. Ferré, S., Cellier, P.: Graph-FCA: an extension of formal concept analysis to knowledge graphs. Discret. Appl. Math. **273**, 81–102 (2020)
9. Ferré, S., Cellier, P.: Modeling complex structures in graph-FCA: illustration on natural language syntax. In: Workshop ETAFCA (ICFCA 2022), pp. 1–6 (2022)
10. Fokou, V., Cellier, P., Dolques, X., Ferré, S., Le Ber, F.: Comparing relational concept analysis and graph-FCA on their common ground. In: Cabrera, I.P., Ferré, S., Obiedkov, S. (eds.) CONCEPTS 2024. LNCS, vol. 14914, pp. 63–79. Springer, Cham (2024). https://doi.org/10.1007/978-3-031-67868-4_5
11. Ganter, B., Wille, R.: Formal Concept Analysis: Mathematical Foundations. Springer (1999)
12. Hodo, F., Pranav, S., Sertkaya, B.: Clustering knowledge graphs using concept lattices. In: Description Logics. CEUR Workshop Proceedings (2023)
13. Jones, T.H., Song, I.Y.: Binary equivalents of ternary relationships in entity-relationship modeling: a logical decomposition approach. J. Database Manag. (JDM) **11**(2), 12–19 (2000)
14. Keip, P., Ferré, S., Gutierrez, A., Huchard, M., Silvie, P., Martin, P.: Practical comparison of FCA extensions to model indeterminate value of ternary data. In: CLA 2020. CEUR-WS Proceedings, vol. 2668, pp. 197–208 (2020)
15. Keip, P., et al.: Effects of input data formalisation in relational concept analysis for a data model with a ternary relation. In: ICFCA 2019, pp. 191–207 (2019)
16. Lehmann, F., Wille, R.: A triadic approach to formal concept analysis. In: Ellis, G., Levinson, R., Rich, W., Sowa, J.F. (eds.) ICCS-ConceptStruct 1995. LNCS, vol. 954, pp. 32–43. Springer, Heidelberg (1995). https://doi.org/10.1007/3-540-60161-9_27
17. Nica, C., Braud, A., Dolques, X., Huchard, M., Le Ber, F.: Extracting hierarchies of closed partially-ordered patterns using relational concept analysis. In: Haemmerlé, O., Stapleton, G., Faron Zucker, C. (eds.) ICCS 2016. LNCS (LNAI), vol. 9717, pp. 17–30. Springer, Cham (2016). https://doi.org/10.1007/978-3-319-40985-6_2
18. Ouzerdine, A., Braud, A., Dolques, X., Huchard, M., Le Ber, F.: Adjusting the exploration flow in relational concept analysis: an experience on a watercourse quality dataset. In: AKDM, vol. 9, pp. 175–198. Springer, Cham (2022)
19. Petersen, W.: A set-theoretical approach for the induction of inheritance hierarchies. Electron. Notes Theor. Comput. Sci. **53**, 296–308 (2004)
20. Rouane-Hacene, M., Huchard, M., Napoli, A., Valtchev, P.: Relational concept analysis: mining concept lattices from multi-relational data. Ann. Math. Artif. Intell. **67**, 81–108 (2013)
21. Song, I.Y., Jones, T.H.: Ternary relationship decomposition strategies based on binary imposition rules. In: 11th ICDE, pp. 485–492. IEEE (1995)
22. Stumme, G., Taouil, R., Bastide, Y., Pasquier, N., Lakhal, L.: Computing iceberg concept lattices with Titanic. Data Knowl. Eng. **42**(2), 189–222 (2002)
23. Wille, R.: Conceptual graphs and formal concept analysis. In: Lukose, D., Delugach, H., Keeler, M., Searle, L., Sowa, J. (eds.) ICCS-ConceptStruct 1997. LNCS, vol. 1257, pp. 290–303. Springer, Heidelberg (1997). https://doi.org/10.1007/BFb0027878

Reduced Subcontext Completion in Lattices and Concept Lattices

Christophe Demko[1(✉)], Jérémy Richard[1,2], Martin Waffo Kemgne[1], Cyril Faucher[1], and Karell Bertet[1]

[1] L3I - Laboratoire Informatique, Image et Interaction - EA 2118, La Rochelle, France
christophe.demko@univ-lr.fr

[2] LAERO, CNRS, IRD - Observatoire Midi-Pyrenees, Toulouse, France

Abstract. Lattices and concept lattices are fundamental structures in mathematics and computer science, providing a robust framework for understanding order and hierarchy in various domains. The completion of a lattice, particularly through the Dedekind-MacNeille completion, is a well-established process that embeds a partially ordered set into a complete and minimal lattice. However, this process often results in the generation of a large and complex lattice, which may not be necessary or efficient for all applications.

In this article, we introduce the concept of reduced subcontext completion, a novel approach that focuses on modifying an existing reduced subcontext rather than generating the entire sublattice. This method is analogous to the Dedekind-MacNeille completion but aims to maintain a simplified reduced subcontext while maintaining the join and meet operations, making it more practical for certain applications. We will first apply this approach to general lattice elements and then extend it to concept lattice elements, demonstrating its versatility and potential.

Unlike traditional methods that seek to represent the complete sublattice corresponding to a known (possibly enlarged) context, our approach calculates a reduced subcontext representing the smallest sublattice encompassing the given elements or concepts. This distinction highlights the radical difference between the two methods and underscores the efficiency and practicality of the ReducedSubcontextCompletion algorithm, particularly in concept lattices.

Keywords: Completion · Subcontexts · Sublattices · Reduced Contexts · Irreducible · AOC-posets

1 Introduction and Motivations

Building on the teachings and theoretical concepts of Formal Concept Analysis and lattice theory, the NextPriorityConcept algorithm was introduced by Christophe Demko and Karell Bertet in 2020 [2]. It proposes a way to use user-guided Formal Concept Analysis for complex and heterogeneous data. Within

P. Cellier et al. (Eds.): CONCEPTS 2025, LNAI 15941, pp. 51–66, 2025.
https://doi.org/10.1007/978-3-032-03364-2_4

a constantly evolving ecosystem, the algorithm is directly integrated into the **GALACTIC** platform[1] (for **GA**lois **LA**ttices, **C**oncept **T**heory, **I**mplicational systems, and **C**losures). With this platform, the user chooses characteristics to represent the type of data to be processed, descriptions that describe a dataset, and strategies that describe how the data will be analyzed.

The particularity of the NextPriorityConcept algorithm is that it integrates the notion of monadic predicates in a generic way, used by descriptions and strategies. A user can thus mix different descriptions and strategies to analyze heterogeneous data from the same dataset. The result is concepts that integrate multiple types of data, enabling the analysis of complex and heterogeneous data.

The deluge of patterns generated by description spaces adapted to each data type makes it impractical to compute the full concept lattice. In practice, only a domain-expert data analyst can guide the exploration of relevant concepts in such rich datasets, which justifies the need for an interactive system. The user can change strategies during the analysis, from a naive "fine-grained" strategy that generates all possible concepts, to more "coarse-grained" strategies that are better suited at the beginning of the analysis. Since the strategies are only used to discover new concepts, it is possible to consider an interactive analysis mechanism where the analyst can discover and select the concepts of interest, as only they know the semantics of their data.

This requires maintaining a lattice structure that respects the operations of supremum and infimum. As a result, we focus on exploring only a sublattice, ensuring that the extracted knowledge remains valid in the complete structure. To optimize this task, our approach consists of working with reduced subcontexts rather than with the sublattices themselves, because the existing bijection between these two types of representations allows for the reconstruction of one from the other.

We therefore need an algorithm capable of maintaining a reduced (sub)context of the concepts explored by the user. More precisely, the problem we address considers a lattice structure $\mathbb{L}$ and a subset A of L, and consists of computing the minimum sublattice $\phi(A)$ of $\mathbb{L}$ containing A and maintaining the supremum and infimum in $\mathbb{L}$.

To support this, we store lattices and sublattices via their reduced (sub)contexts, which underscores the importance of the algorithm presented in this paper for incrementally updating or directly computing them. While artificial data allow us to illustrate the capabilities and time complexity of our algorithms (using the number of generated concepts as a proxy for time), a full validation of our approach will ultimately rely on real-world experiments guided by expert analysts.

We exhibit the structure of all the sublattices of $\mathbb{L}$, and the isomorphic structure of all its reduced subcontexts, in order to highlight and characterize the operators inside these structures which allow composing sublattices and subcontexts of $\mathbb{L}$. We characterize these operators through a processing chain composed of an extension process of a reduced context to include new elements, iterated

[1] https://galactic.univ-lr.fr/.

until saturation, following by a reduction process to its irreducible elements. We develop two algorithms capable of performing this task for lattices in general, and for concept lattices in particular using the properties of the AOC-poset.

Section 2 explore the theoretical foundations of reduced subcontext completion and illustrate its application through examples. By doing so, we hope to provide a comprehensive understanding of this innovative approach and its potential benefits in various fields. Subsection 3.1 presents the algorithm for lattices in general and Subsect. 3.2 presents the algorithm for concept lattices. The last section gives some experimentations.

2 Reduced Subcontext Completion: Main Issue and Description

2.1 Definitions

Definition 1 (Finite Lattice). *A finite lattice is an algebraic structure in mathematics* $\mathbb{L} = \langle X, \leq, \vee, \wedge \rangle$ *where* $\langle X, \leq \rangle$ *is a finite partially ordered set in which every pair of elements* (x, y) *of* $X \times X$ *has an upper bound (supremum or join), denoted* $x \vee y$*, and a lower bound (infimum or meet), denoted* $x \wedge y$*.* ◊

In the rest of the document, only finite lattices are considered. A lattice can be represented graphically by its Hasse diagram (cf. Fig. 1a), which consists of retaining only the relations of $\langle X, \leq \rangle$ limited to the transitive and reflexive reduction of called the covering relation $\langle X, \prec \rangle$
where: $\prec := \{(x, y) \in X \times X | x \leq y \text{ and } x \leq z \leq y \implies z = x \text{ or } z = y\}$

In a lattice $\mathbb{L} = \langle X, \leq, \vee, \wedge \rangle$, there are certain particular or notable elements such as the maximum, the minimum, the co-atoms, the atoms, and the join and meet irreducibles:

maximum It is the greatest element of the lattice and can be defined by $1_{\mathbb{L}} = \bigvee X$. There is no maximum element in a lattice when $X = \emptyset$.
minimum It is the smallest element of the lattice and can be defined by $0_{\mathbb{L}} = \bigwedge X$. There is no minimum element in a lattice where $X = \emptyset$.
co-atoms These are the immediate predecessors of the maximum element and can be defined by $\{x \in X | x \prec 1_{\mathbb{L}}\}$. This set is empty when $|X| \leq 1$.
atoms These are the immediate successors of the minimum element and can be defined by $\{x \in X | 0_{\mathbb{L}} \prec x\}$. This set is empty when $|X| \leq 1$.
join-irreducible These are the elements $j \in X$ that are not the join of other elements. They have the particularity of having only one predecessor j^- such that $j^- \prec j$, and $j^- = \vee_{x<j} x$. The set of join-irreducible elements is denoted $J_{\mathbb{L}}$ and can be defined by $J_{\mathbb{L}} = \{j \in X \mid j > \vee_{x<j} x\}$. This set is empty when $|X| \leq 1$.
meet-irreducible These are the elements $m \in X$ that are not the meet of other elements. They have the particularity of having only one successor m^+ such that $m \prec m^+$, and $m^+ = \wedge_{x>m} x$. The set of meet-irreducible elements is denoted $M_{\mathbb{L}}$ and can be defined by $M_{\mathbb{L}} = \{m \in X \mid m < \wedge_{x>m} x\}$. This set is empty when $|X| \leq 1$.

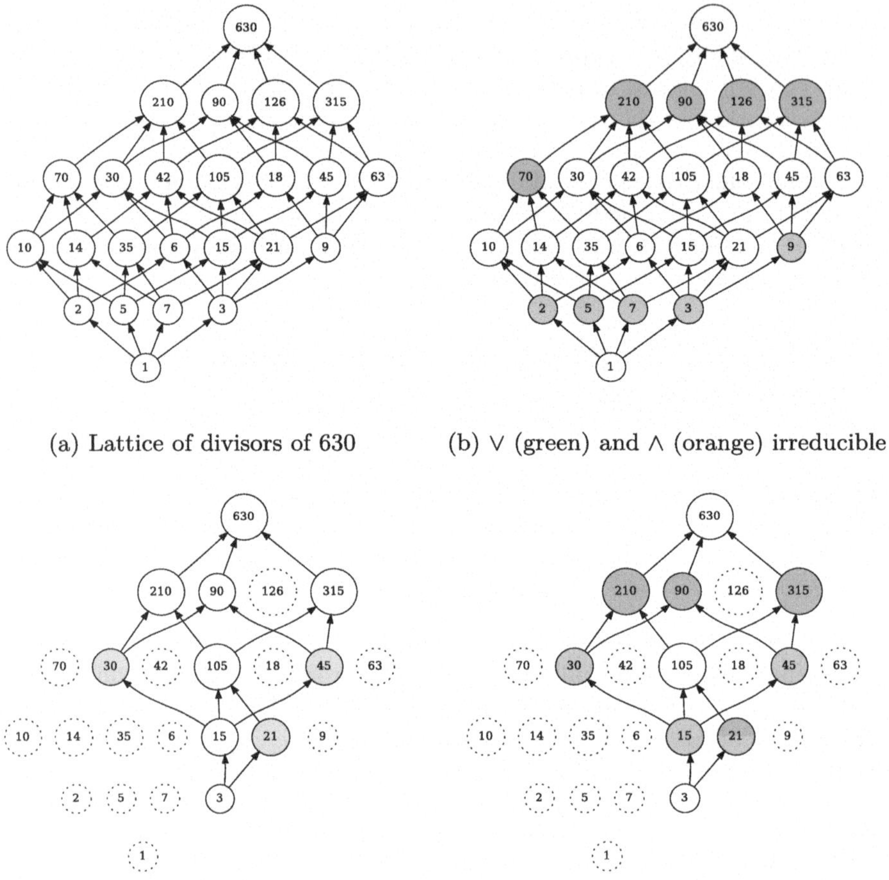

(a) Lattice of divisors of 630 (b) ∨ (green) and ∧ (orange) irreducible

(c) Sublattice completion for $\{21, 30, 45\}$ (d) ∨ and ∧ irreducible of the completion

Fig. 1. Hasse diagrams of the divisors of 630 and its completion for $\{21, 30, 45\}$.

The irreducible table $\langle J_{\mathbb{L}}, M_{\mathbb{L}}, \leq\rangle$ encodes the lattice $\mathbb{L}$ since any element $x \in X$ can be obtained as a join or a meet: $x = \bigvee_{j \in J_{\mathbb{L}} | j \leq x} j$ or equivalently $x = \bigwedge_{m \in M_{\mathbb{L}} | m \geq x} m$. The existing bijection between $\mathbb{L}$ and $\langle J_{\mathbb{L}}, M_{\mathbb{L}}, \leq\rangle$ allows for the reconstruction of one from the other [1]. This table is also named the reduced context of $\mathbb{L}$ in Formal Concept Analysis.

2.2 Main Issue

Given a lattice structure $\mathbb{L} = \langle X, \leq, \vee, \wedge\rangle$ and a subset $A \subseteq X$, we address the issue of computing the reduced context of the minimum sublattice $\phi(A)$ of $\mathbb{L}$ containing A.

Definition 2 (Sublattice completion). *Given a lattice structure* $\mathbb{L} = \langle X, \leq, \vee, \wedge\rangle$ *and a subset* $A \subseteq X$ *such that* $\langle A, \leq\rangle$ *forms a poset, the calculation of the sublattice completion* $\phi(A) = X' \supseteq A$ *maintaining the join and meet operations consists of finding a sublattice* $\mathbb{L}' = \langle X' \supseteq A, \leq, \vee, \wedge\rangle$ *of* $\mathbb{L}$ *such that* X' *is minimum.* $\Diamond$

For example, the Fig. 1a shows the lattice $\langle X_d, \leq_d, \vee_d, \wedge_d\rangle$ of divisors of 630 where $x \leq_d y$ if x is a divisor of y, $x \vee_d y = \text{GCD}(x, y)$ and $x \wedge_d y = \text{LCM}(x, y)$. The Fig. 1c shows the sublattice completion of $A = \langle\{21, 30, 45\}, \leq_d\rangle$ respecting $\vee_d$ and $\wedge_d$.

Our approach is similar to that developed by Dedekind-MacNeille that compute the completion of a poset A into a minimal lattice. We compute the completion $\phi(A)$ maintaining the join and meet operations in $\mathbb{L}$. However, this completion generates larger sublattices (the DM completion of $\langle\{21, 30, 45\}\rangle$ consists only of adding a top and a bottom).

In our issue, clearly, $\phi(A)$ is uniquely defined. It corresponds to the Dedekind-MacNeille completion of the poset A respecting the $\vee$ and $\wedge$ operators. This operation ϕ can be likened to a closure operator since it is extensive (if A is not a lattice, then $\phi(A)$ forms the smallest sublattice encompassing A, and if A is a lattice, then $\phi(A)$ is equal to A), increasing (the smallest sublattice of A encompasses the smallest sublattice of A' if $A' \subseteq A$) and idempotent (the smallest sublattice encompassing $\phi(A)$, i.e. $\phi(\phi(A))$ is equal to the sublattice $\phi(A)$). Therefore, we can define the lattice of all sublattices of $\mathbb{L}$:

Definition 3 (Lattice of sublattices). *The set of sublattices of* $\mathbb{L}$*, denoted by* $\mathcal{S}(\mathbb{L})$ *is equipped with a lattice structure* $\langle \mathcal{S}(\mathbb{L}), \sqsubseteq_{\mathcal{S}}, \sqcup_{\mathcal{S}}, \sqcap_{\mathcal{S}}\rangle$ *where for each couple of lattices* $\mathcal{S}(\mathbb{L}) \ni \mathbb{L}_1 = \langle X_1 \subseteq X, \leq, \vee, \wedge\rangle$ *and* $\mathcal{S}(\mathbb{L}) \ni \mathbb{L}_2 = \langle X_2 \subseteq X, \leq, \vee, \wedge\rangle$*:*

- $\mathbb{L}_1 \sqsubseteq_{\mathcal{S}} \mathbb{L}_2$ *if* $X_1 \subseteq X_2$
- $\mathbb{L}_1 \sqcup_{\mathcal{S}} \mathbb{L}_2 = \langle \phi(X_1 \cup X_2), \leq, \vee, \wedge\rangle$
- $\mathbb{L}_1 \sqcap_{\mathcal{S}} \mathbb{L}_2 = \langle X_1 \cap X_2, \leq, \vee, \wedge\rangle$ $\Diamond$

Since any lattice can be reconstructed from its reduced context, it is more computationally efficient to generate the reduced context instead of a sublattice. From the bijection between lattices and reduced contexts, we derive the set $\mathcal{R}(\mathbb{L})$ of reduced subcontexts of $\mathbb{L}$ from the set $\mathcal{S}(\mathbb{L})$ of its sublattices:

Definition 4 (Lattice of reduced subcontexts). *The set of reduced subcontexts of* $\mathbb{L}$*, denoted by* $\mathcal{R}(\mathbb{L})$*, is the set of reduced contexts of the sublattices of* $\mathbb{L}$*, and is equipped with a lattice structure* $\langle \mathcal{R}(\mathbb{L}), \sqsubseteq_{\mathcal{R}}, \sqcup_{\mathcal{R}}, \sqcap_{\mathcal{R}}\rangle$*. Given two sublattices* $\mathbb{L}_1$ *and* $\mathbb{L}_2$ *of* $\mathbb{L} = \langle X, \leq, \vee, \wedge\rangle$*, and their reduced contexts* $K_{\mathbb{L}_1}$ *and* $K_{\mathbb{L}_2}$*, we define:*

- $K_{\mathbb{L}_1} \sqsubseteq_{\mathcal{R}} K_{\mathbb{L}_2}$ *iff* $\mathbb{L}_1 \sqsubseteq_{\mathcal{S}} \mathbb{L}_2$
- $K_{\mathbb{L}_1} \sqcup_{\mathcal{R}} K_{\mathbb{L}_2}$ *iff* $\mathbb{L}_1 \sqcup_{\mathcal{S}} \mathbb{L}_2$
- $K_{\mathbb{L}_1} \sqcap_{\mathcal{R}} K_{\mathbb{L}_2}$ *iff* $\mathbb{L}_1 \sqcap_{\mathcal{S}} \mathbb{L}_2$ $\Diamond$

The computation of the completion by ϕ that we propose in this paper relies on the characterization of $\sqcup_{\mathcal{R}}$ that allows to generate the reduced subcontext of any sublattice of $\mathbb{L}$ in an incremental way. Therefore, the problem we address consider the more general case of the completion by A from a given reduced subcontext of $\mathbb{L}$, and is formulated as the reduced subcontext completion as follows:

Definition 5 (Reduced subcontext completion). *Given a lattice structure* $\mathbb{L}\langle X, \leq, \vee, \wedge\rangle$, *a sublattice* $\mathbb{L}' = \langle X', \leq, \vee, \wedge\rangle$ *of* $\mathbb{L}$ *represented by its reduced subcontext* $K_{\mathbb{L}'} = \langle E_{\mathbb{L}'}, F_{\mathbb{L}'}, \leq\rangle$ *and a subset* $A \subseteq X$, *the calculation of the reduced subcontext completion consists of finding the reduced subcontext* $K_{\mathbb{L}''} = \langle E_{\mathbb{L}''}, F_{\mathbb{L}''}, \leq\rangle$ *of the sublattice* $\mathbb{L}'' = \langle X'', \leq, \vee, \wedge\rangle$ *of* $\mathbb{L}$ *such that* $\mathbb{L}''$ *is the sublattice completion maintaining the join and meet operations of the poset* $\langle E_{\mathbb{L}'} \cup F_{\mathbb{L}'} \cup A, \leq\rangle$. ◊

The reduced subcontext completion of A given $\mathbb{L}$ is a special case where $\mathbb{L}'$ is a singleton. In the next sections, we will characterize the operators $\sqsubseteq_{\mathcal{R}}$, $\sqcup_{\mathcal{R}}$ and $\sqcap_{\mathcal{R}}$ before providing our algorithm for the reduced subcontext completion issue.

2.3 Reduced Subcontext Completion

First of all, we precise the definition of a reduced context $K_{\mathbb{L}}$ of a lattice $\mathbb{L} = \langle X, \leq, \vee, \wedge\rangle$ including the special case where $\mathbb{L}$ is a singleton.
$K_{\mathbb{L}} = \langle E_{\mathbb{L}} \subseteq X, F_{\mathbb{L}} \subseteq X, \leq\rangle$ is a binary relation between two minimum sets of elements $E_{\mathbb{L}}$ and $F_{\mathbb{L}}$, allowing the reconstruction of any element of the lattice. Two cases may arise:

- The case where $|X| > 1$: in this case, $E_{\mathbb{L}}$ is equal to the join-irreducible elements $J_{\mathbb{L}}$, and $F_{\mathbb{L}}$ is equal to the meet-irreducible elements $M_{\mathbb{L}}$.
- The case where $|X| \leq 1$: in this case, the domain $E_{\mathbb{L}}$ and codomain $F_{\mathbb{L}}$ are equal to X.

Definition 6 (Reduced context). *The reduced context* $K_{\mathbb{L}}$ *defined from a lattice* $\mathbb{L} = \langle X, \leq, \vee, \wedge\rangle$ *is completely defined by a couple of minimal subsets* $(E_{\mathbb{L}} \subseteq X, F_{\mathbb{L}} \subseteq X)$ *equipped with the binary relation* $\leq$ *(* $(E_{\mathbb{L}}, F_{\mathbb{L}}) = (J_{\mathbb{L}}, M_{\mathbb{L}})$ *if* $|X| > 1$ *else* (X, X)*).* ◊

Therefore, all the elements from the lattice $\mathbb{L}$ can be generated from the reduced context $K_{\mathbb{L}}$ using the three (four) equations below:

- the maximum element of $\mathbb{L}$ (if it exists) can be computed by $1_{\mathbb{L}} = \bigvee E_{\mathbb{L}}$
- the minimum element of $\mathbb{L}$ (if it exists) can be computed by $0_{\mathbb{L}} = \bigwedge F_{\mathbb{L}}$
- each element x of X can be computed by $x = 1_{\mathbb{L}} \wedge \bigwedge_{f \in F_{\mathbb{L}} | f \geq x} f$ or equivalently by $x = 0_{\mathbb{L}} \vee \bigvee_{e \in E_{\mathbb{L}} | e \leq x} e$

Definition 7 (Subcontext). *Given a lattice* $\mathbb{L} = \langle X, \leq, \vee, \wedge \rangle$, *a subcontext* K *is a restriction of the relation* $\leq$ *between two subsets* $E, F \subseteq X$: $K = \langle E, F, \leq \rangle$ ◊

We can note that the reduced context $K_{\mathbb{L}}$ of the lattice $\mathbb{L}$ is a particular subcontext of $\mathbb{L}$.

Table 1. Reduced context and subcontexts of the divisors of 630

	70	90	126	210	315
2	✓	✓	✓	✓	
3		✓	✓	✓	✓
5	✓	✓		✓	✓
7	✓		✓	✓	✓
9		✓	✓		✓

(a) Reduced context of lattice in Fig. 1b

	210	315
21	✓	✓

(b) Subcontext for $\{21\}$ and $\{210, 315\}$

	21	210	315
21	✓	✓	✓

(c) Extension by $\epsilon_\vee$ of Table 1b

	21	210	315
21	✓	✓	✓
105		✓	✓
210		✓	
315			✓

(d) Extension by $\epsilon_\wedge$ of Table 1c

	21	105	210	315	630
21	✓	✓	✓	✓	✓
105		✓	✓	✓	✓
210			✓		✓
315				✓	✓
630					✓

(e) Saturation of the subcontext of Table 1d

	21	210	315
105		✓	✓
210		✓	
315			✓

(f) Subcontext reduction of Table 1e

Definition 8 (Extensions of subcontexts). *The extension of a subcontext* $K = \langle E, F, \leq \rangle$ *either on the domain or either on the codomain is defined using the couple of functions* $\epsilon_\vee$ *and* $\epsilon_\wedge$ *(extension of* F *and* E*):*

$$\epsilon_\vee : 2^X \to 2^X \qquad E \mapsto \{ \bigvee E' \mid \emptyset \subset E' \subseteq E \} \qquad\qquad \epsilon_\wedge : 2^X \to 2^X \qquad F \mapsto \{ \bigwedge F' \mid \emptyset \subset F' \subseteq F \}$$

The subcontext extension of K *by* $\epsilon_\vee$ *and by* $\epsilon_\wedge$ *is given by* $\epsilon_\vee^\square(K)$ *and* $\epsilon_\wedge^\square(K)$*:*

$$\epsilon_\vee^\square : \quad \mathcal{K}(\mathbb{L}) \to \mathcal{K}(\mathbb{L}) \quad \langle E, F, \leq \rangle \mapsto \langle E, \epsilon_\vee(E) \cup F, \leq \rangle \qquad\qquad \epsilon_\wedge^\square : \quad \mathcal{K}(\mathbb{L}) \to \mathcal{K}(\mathbb{L}) \quad \langle E, F, \leq \rangle \mapsto \langle \epsilon_\wedge(F) \cup E, F, \leq \rangle$$

◊

Example 1 (Subcontext extension). The Table 1b gives an example of a subcontext of the lattice of the divisors of 630 whose domain equals $E = \{21\}$ and whose codomain equals $F = \{210, 315\}$. The Table 1c gives the extension by $\epsilon_\vee$ of the subcontext of Table 1b and the Table 1d gives the extension by $\epsilon_\wedge$ of the subcontext of Table 1c.

These two functions $\epsilon_\vee$ and $\epsilon_\wedge$ can be composed and repeated to obtain a saturation of the subcontext where the final domain equals the final codomain and can be equipped with a sublattice structure of $\mathbb{L}$.

Lemma 1 (Subcontext saturation). *Given a lattice $\mathbb{L} = \langle X, \leq, \vee, \wedge \rangle$, and $A \subseteq X$, there exists $n \in \mathbb{N}$ such that $\langle (\epsilon_\vee \circ \epsilon_\wedge)^n(A), \leq, \vee, \wedge \rangle$ is a sublattice of $\langle X, \leq, \vee, \wedge \rangle$ which is the sublattice completion $\phi(A)$ of $\langle A, \leq \rangle$ preserving join and meet, i.e. $\phi = (\epsilon_\vee \circ \epsilon_\wedge)^n$ is a closure operator on X* ◊

Example 2 (Subcontext saturation). The Table 1e gives the saturation of the subcontext of Table 1b. $\langle \{21, 105, 210, 315, 630\}, \leq, \vee, \wedge \rangle$ forms a sublattice of the divisors of 630 and is the sublattice completion of $\langle \{21, 210, 315\}, \leq \rangle$.

It is not necessarily useful to keep all the elements generated by the operations $\epsilon_\vee$ and $\epsilon_\wedge$, since some elements of the domain can be generated by other elements of the domain using the join operation (similarly for the codomain, where some elements of the codomain can be generated by other elements of the codomain using the meet operation). If the domain and the codomain are not reduced to the same singleton, we can also remove the minimum element from the domain if it is the meet of the elements of the codomain (and reciprocally we can remove the maximum element from the codomain if it is the join of the elements of the domain).

Definition 9 (Subcontext reduction). *We can define the reduction operation, $\theta^\square$*

$$\begin{aligned} \theta^\square : \quad & \mathcal{K}(\mathbb{L}) \to \mathcal{K}(\mathbb{L}) \\ & \langle E, F, \leq \rangle \mapsto \langle E' \subseteq E, F' \subseteq F, \leq \rangle \end{aligned}$$

where:

$$\left. \begin{aligned} E' &= \left\{ j \in E | j > j^- = \bigvee\nolimits_{x \in E | x < j} x \right\} \setminus \{\bigwedge F\} \\ F' &= \left\{ m \in F | m < m^+ = \bigwedge\nolimits_{y \in F | y > m} y \right\} \setminus \{\bigvee E\} \end{aligned} \right| \begin{array}{l} \text{if } E \neq F \\ \text{or } \max(|E|, |F|) > 1 \end{array}$$

($E' = E$ and $F' = F$ if E and F are the empty set or the same singleton) ◊

Lemma 2. *The reduction of a satured subcontext computes the join-irreducible as the domain and the meet-irreducible as the codomain, i.e. the reduced subcontext. The extension of a reduced subcontext by $\epsilon_\vee^\square \circ \epsilon_\wedge^\square$ gives a satured subcontext.* ◊

Example 3 (Subcontext reduction). The Table 1f gives the reduction of the subcontext of Table 1e. $\langle \{21, 105, 315\}, \{21, 210, 315\}, \leq \rangle$ forms the reduced subcontext of the sublattice $\langle \{21, 105, 210, 315, 630\}, \leq, \vee, \wedge \rangle$ of the divisors of 630.

The extension of a reduced context to include new elements, iterated until saturation, following by a reduction process to its irreducible elements allows to characterize the operators of the lattice of reduced subcontext $\mathcal{R}(\mathbb{L})$:

Lemma 3. *Given two reduced subcontexts of* $\mathcal{R}(\mathbb{L})$, $K_{\mathbb{L}_1} = \langle E_{\mathbb{L}_1}, F_{\mathbb{L}_1}, \leq \rangle$ *and* $K_{\mathbb{L}_2} = \langle E_{\mathbb{L}_2}, F_{\mathbb{L}_2}, \leq \rangle$ *where* $\mathbb{L}_1 = \langle X_1, \leq, \vee, \wedge \rangle$ *and* $\mathbb{L}_2 = \langle X_2, \leq, \vee, \wedge \rangle$ *are two sublattices of* $\mathbb{L} = \langle X, \leq, \vee, \wedge \rangle$

- $K_{\mathbb{L}_1} \sqsubseteq_{\mathcal{R}} K_{\mathbb{L}_2}$ *if* $\forall x \in \{0_{\mathbb{L}_1}\} \cup E_{\mathbb{L}_1}$ *or* $\forall x \in \{1_{\mathbb{L}_1}\} \cup F_{\mathbb{L}_1}$, $x = 1_{\mathbb{L}_2} \wedge \bigwedge_{f \in F_{\mathbb{L}_2} | f \geq x} f$ *(or equivalently* $x = 0_{\mathbb{L}_2} \vee \bigvee_{e \in E_{\mathbb{L}_2} | e \leq x} e$*); i.e. it is sufficient that the minimum (resp. maximum) and the join-irreducible (resp. meet-irreducible) elements of* $\mathbb{L}_1$ *can be generated by the elements of* $\mathbb{L}_2$.
- $K_{\mathbb{L}_1} \sqcup_{\mathcal{R}} K_{\mathbb{L}_2} = \theta^{\square}(\langle X', X', \leq \rangle)$ *where* $X' = \phi(E_{\mathbb{L}_2} \cup F_{\mathbb{L}_1} \cup E_{\mathbb{L}_1} \cup F_{\mathbb{L}_1})$ *(in practice, the calculation does not need all of this union); i.e. the join between* $K_{\mathbb{L}_1}$ *and* $K_{\mathbb{L}_2}$ *is equal to the reduced context generated by the union of all the irreducible elements of* $\mathbb{L}_1$ *and* $\mathbb{L}_2$*, since they allow the generation of all the elements of their respective lattices.*
- $K_{\mathbb{L}_1} \sqcap_{\mathcal{R}} K_{\mathbb{L}_2} = \theta^{\square}(\langle X', X', \leq \rangle)$ *where* $X' = \{x \in \{0_{\mathbb{L}_1}\} \cup E_{\mathbb{L}_1} | x \in X_2\}$ *(or* $\{x \in \{1_{\mathbb{L}_1}\} \cup F_{\mathbb{L}_1} | x \in X_2\}$, $\{x \in 0_{\mathbb{L}_2} \cup E_{\mathbb{L}_2} | x \in X_1\}$, $\{x \in \{1_{\mathbb{L}_2}\} \cup F_{\mathbb{L}_2} | x \in X_1\}$*); i.e. the meet between* $K_{\mathbb{L}_1}$ *and* $K_{\mathbb{L}_2}$ *is the reduced context of the elements common to* $\mathbb{L}_1$ *and* $\mathbb{L}_2$ *that can be generated from the irreducible elements common to both* $\mathbb{L}_1$ *and* $\mathbb{L}_2$. ♢

3 Algorithms

In this section, we propose three algorithms for the *Reduced Subcontext Completion* problem described in Definition 5: two algorithms for the general case of lattices with a completion for a subset A of elements (Sect. 3.1), and one algorithm for the case of concept lattices with a completion for a set C of concepts (Sect. 3.2).

3.1 Algorithm for the General Case

Consider a reduced subcontext $K_{\mathbb{L}'} = \langle J_{\mathbb{L}'}, M_{\mathbb{L}'}, \leq \rangle$ of a sublattice $\mathbb{L}' = \langle X', \leq, \vee, \wedge \rangle$ of a lattice structure $\mathbb{L} = \langle X, \leq, \vee, \wedge \rangle$. We want to compute the subcontext reduced completion of $K_{\mathbb{L}'}$ by addition of $A \subseteq X$.

The Algorithm 1 is the literal transcription of the presented method by extension of saturation (**while** loop lines 9–17) then reduction to irreducibles (lines 18–29) described in the previous section. The special case of the empty subcontext is trivial and not described in the algorithms.

Algorithm 1: Naive ReducedSubcontextCompletion for general lattices

```
Input: K = ⟨J, M, ≤⟩ a non-empty reduced subcontext of ⟨X, ≤, ∨, ∧⟩ and
       A ⊆ X;
Output: The new reduced subcontext induced by K and A
1 ← ⋁J // Old top
0 ← ⋀M // Old bottom
A ← A ∪ {0, 1} // Add old top and bottom to A
1 ← 1 ∨ ⋁A // New top
0 ← 0 ∧ ⋀A // New bottom
E′ ← J ∪ A // Initial ∨-irreducible candidates
F′ ← M ∪ A // Initial ∧-irreducible candidates
E ← F ← ∅
while E ≠ E′ or F ≠ F′ do
    E ← E′; F ← F′; E′ ← F′ ← ∅
    // Extend to new ∧-irreducible: F′ ← ε∨(E)
    foreach X ⊆ E such that X ≠ ∅ do
        F′ ← F′ ∪ {∨X}
    end
    // Extend to new ∨-irreducible: E′ ← ε∧(F)
    foreach X ⊆ F such that X ≠ ∅ do
        E′ ← E′ ∪ {∧X}
    end
end
// Keep ∨-irreducible: J′ ← {j ∈ E | j > ∨_{x∈E|x<j} x} \ {0}
J′ ← ∅
foreach j ≠ 0 ∈ E do
    j⁻ ← 0
    foreach x ∈ E < j do j⁻ ← j⁻ ∨ x
    if j > j⁻ then J′ ← J′ ∪ {j}
end
// Keep ∧-irreducible: M′ ← {m ∈ F | m < ∧_{y∈F|y>m} y} \ {1}
M′ ← ∅
foreach m ≠ 1 ∈ F do
    m⁺ ← 1
    foreach y ∈ F > m do m⁺ ← m⁺ ∧ y
    if m < m⁺ then M′ ← M′ ∪ {m}
end
return ⟨J′, M′, ≤⟩
```

The Algorithm 2 is an optimized version of Algorithm 1. This algorithm has been proposed by Jérémy Richard in its phD thesis [6] and works incrementally for each $a \in A$. More specifically, if we denote $A = \{a_1, a_2, \ldots, a_n\}$, the algorithm successively calculates the reduced subcontext of the smallest sublattice containing $J_{\mathbb{L}'} \cup M_{\mathbb{L}'} \cup \{a_1\}$, then the smallest sublattice containing $J_{\mathbb{L}'} \cup M_{\mathbb{L}'} \cup \{a_1, a_2\}$ by adding a_2, and so on, until the reduced subcontext of the smallest sublattice containing $J_{\mathbb{L}'} \cup M_{\mathbb{L}'} \cup A$. Thus, for each a_i, the reduced subcontext calculated in the previous step is updated, and the reduction to irreducible at each iteration.

By comparaison, several algorithms exist in the literature to compute the Dedekind-MacNeille completion, but to our knowledge, there are no algorithms that compute the completion maintening the join and meet operation which is a different problem. We can cite that of Ganter and Kuznetsov [4] whose complexity is given as a function of the size of the outputs $\mathcal{O}(cn^2w) = \mathcal{O}(cn^3)$ where n is the number of elements of the input partial order, c is the number of elements of the completion and w is the width of the partial order (the size of its largest antichain).

Algorithm 1 computes and stores all the elements of the sublattice before reduction, with a complexity that depends on the size c of the sublattice that is exponential in the worst case. Algorithm 2 is an optimized version which avoid being exponential in memory by keeping all the lattice elements before reduction at each iteration, therefore an exponential complexity in time, but not in memory.

3.2 Algorithm for Concept Lattices

Definition 10 (Concept lattice). *A concept lattice is defined from a context $\mathcal{K} = \langle G, M, I \rangle$, which defines a Galois connection (α, β) that allows the generation of the concepts $(A, B) \in \mathcal{B}(\mathcal{K})$ of the concept lattice $\mathcal{CL}(\mathcal{K}) = \langle \mathcal{B}(\mathcal{K}), \leq, \vee, \wedge \rangle$:*

$$\begin{aligned} \alpha : 2^G &\rightarrow 2^M \\ A &\mapsto \{m \in M \mid \forall g \in A, (g, m) \in I\} \end{aligned} \qquad \begin{aligned} \beta : 2^M &\rightarrow 2^G \\ B &\mapsto \{g \in G \mid \forall m \in B, (g, m) \in I\} \end{aligned}$$

A concept (A, B) is in $\mathcal{B}(\mathcal{K})$ if and only if $B = \alpha(A)$ and $A = \beta(B)$. Concepts of $\mathcal{B}(\mathcal{K})$ are ordered by:

$$(A, B) \leq (A', B') \iff A \subseteq A' \equiv B \supseteq B'$$

And the join and meet operations are defined by:

$$\begin{aligned} \vee : \quad \mathcal{B}(\mathcal{K}) \times \mathcal{B}(\mathcal{K}) &\rightarrow \mathcal{B}(\mathcal{K}) \\ (A_1, B_1) \ , \ (A_2, B_2) &\mapsto (\beta \circ \alpha(A_1 \cup A_2), B_1 \cap B_2) \end{aligned}$$

$$\begin{aligned} \wedge : \quad \mathcal{B}(\mathcal{K}) \times \mathcal{B}(\mathcal{K}) &\rightarrow \mathcal{B}(\mathcal{K}) \\ (A_1, B_1) \ , \ (A_2, B_2) &\mapsto (A_1 \cap A_2, \alpha \circ \beta(B_1 \cup B_2)) \end{aligned}$$

◊

Algorithm 2: ReducedSubcontextCompletion for general lattices

```
Input: K = ⟨J, M, ≤⟩ a non-empty reduced subcontext of ⟨X, ≤, ∨, ∧⟩ and
       A ⊆ X;
Output: The new reduced subcontext induced by K and A
// See lines 1-8 of Algorithm 1
J' ← J
M' ← M
while E ≠ E' or F ≠ F' do
    E ← E'; F ← F'; E' ← F' ← ∅
    foreach x ∈ E ∪ F do
        // Extend to new irreducible
        foreach e ∈ J' ∪ M' do
            r⁻ ← e ∧ x
            r⁺ ← e ∨ x
            if r⁻ ≠ 0 then E' ← E' ∪ {r⁻}
            if r⁺ ≠ 1 then F' ← F' ∪ {r⁺}
        end
        // Keep ∨ and ∧ irreducible. See lines 18-29 of Algorithm 1
    end
end
return ⟨J', M', ≤⟩
```

In a concept lattice, in addition to particular elements of general lattices, there are certain particular or notable elements such as the set of object concepts and the set of attribute concepts [5].

object concepts These are the concepts that introduce a new object g. A concept (A, B) is an object concept if there exists $g \in G$ such that $g \in A$ but $g \notin A'$ for all $(A', B') < (A, B)$. The join-irreducible elements are included in the set of object concepts.

attribute concepts These are the concepts that introduce a new attribute m. A concept (A, B) is an attribute concept if there exists $m \in M$ such that $m \in B$ but $m \notin B'$ for all $(A', B') > (A, B)$. The meet-irreducible elements are included in the set of attribute concepts.

The poset formed by the object and attribute concepts is called the AOC-poset.

Reduced Subcontext Completion. In the case of concept lattices, the issue is to compute the reduced context completion for a subset of concepts $C \subseteq \mathcal{B}(\mathcal{K})$ given a reduced subcontext $K = \langle J_{\mathbb{L}}, M_{\mathbb{L}}, \leq \rangle$ of a sublattice of the concept lattice $\langle \mathcal{B}(\mathcal{K}), \leq, \vee, \wedge \rangle$ of the context $\mathcal{K} = \langle G, M, I \rangle$.

First of all, we introduce the two functions ϵ_G $(2^{\mathcal{B}(\mathcal{K})} \rightarrow 2^{\mathcal{B}(\mathcal{K})})$ and ϵ_M $(2^{\mathcal{B}(\mathcal{K})} \rightarrow 2^{\mathcal{B}(\mathcal{K})})$ which limit $\epsilon_\wedge$ and $\epsilon_\vee$ to the extension of a subcontext to the sets of object concepts and attribute concepts using C and a given top and bottom elements 1 and 0: $\epsilon_G(C) = \left\{1 \wedge \bigwedge_{(A,B) \in C | g \in A} (A, B) | g \in G\right\}$ and $\epsilon_M(C) = \left\{0 \vee \bigvee_{(A,B) \in C | m \in B} (A, B) | m \in M\right\}$.

It is easy to prove that all elements of (A, B) of C can be generated by all elements of $\epsilon_G(C)$ or by all elements of $\epsilon_M(C)$: $(A, B) = \bigvee_{(A',B') \in \epsilon_G(C) | A' \subseteq A}(A', B')$ and $(A, B) = \bigwedge_{(A',B') \in \epsilon_M(C) | B' \subseteq B}(A', B')$.

Lemma 4. *The function* ϵ_G *and* ϵ_M *composed iteratively with a maximum of* $\min(|G|, |M|$ *steps (since they traverse the concept lattice top-down and bottom up)) allow to produce the set of object concepts* $\mathcal{B}_G$) *and the set of attribute concepts* $\mathcal{B}_M$ *of* C*:* $\mathcal{B}_G^C = (\epsilon_G \circ \epsilon_M)^{n \leq \min(|G|,|M|)}(C)$ *and* $\mathcal{B}_M^C = (\epsilon_M \circ \epsilon_G)^{n \leq \min(|G|,|M|)}(C)$ ◊

Algorithm 3 limit the extension of a subcontext to the sets of object concepts and attribute concepts using Lemma 4 (lines 9–25) and then filters them to obtain only the irreducible elements (lines 26–37). Let $g = |G|$, $m = |M|$, $c = |C|$, $m_K = |M_K|$, $j_K = |J_K|$; since the saturation is limited by $\min(g, m)$, the complexity in time becomes polynomial, and more precisely Algorithm 3 has a cubic time complexity of $O(g^2(c + m_K) + m^2(c + j_K)) + \min(g, m)gm(g + m))$. The complexity in memory, $O((g + m)^2)$, is quadratic in function of $g + m$ since the size of $\mathcal{B}_G^C$ is equal to g concepts and the size of $\mathcal{B}_M^C$ is equal to m concepts.

4 Experiments

The first experimentation[2] illustrates our algorithm's ability to reduce the flood of patterns with the formal context of the lenses[3] dataset. Computing the full lattice of all Boolean attributes results in a lattice with 130 concepts. If the data analyst is only interested in the concepts related to the 'tear production' attributes, our algorithm will compute the reduced subcontext completion for the concepts/closures of both boolean attributes 'tear production: reduced' and 'tear production: normal', which correspond to a four concepts lattice. This lattice is a sublattice of the whole lenses lattice, with the same information within the concepts, both in extent and in intent, and the knowledge extracted from the concept where 'tear production: reduced' appears (e.g., the implication 'tear production: reduced' → 'class: no contact lenses') also holds true in the full context.

The second experiment focuses on the execution times of the three algorithms. We generated random contexts consisting of $|M| = 10$ attributes and a number of objects proportional to $0.05 \cdot 2^{|M|}$ and $0.10 \cdot 2^{|M|}$. The probability that an object is related to an attribute also varied, with values of 0.3, 0.5, and 0.7. We computed the reduced subcontext completion for random generated concepts using Algorithm 1 for general lattices, and Algorithm 2 and Algorithm 3 for concept lattices. We used a degraded version of the Algorithm 2 (One pass Concept lattices) and Algorithm 3 (Incremental Concept lattices) by adding elements one by one instead of all at once, in order to truly compare it to the algorithm

[2] All experiments are visible at https://galactic.univ-lr.fr/docs/algebras/concept/latest/ in the *Learning* section.

[3] https://archive.ics.uci.edu/dataset/58/lenses.

Algorithm 3: ReducedSubcontextCompletion for concept lattices

Input: $K = \langle J_K, M_K, \leq \rangle$ a non-empty reduced subcontext of $\mathcal{K}$, $\langle G, M, I \rangle$ the initial context and $C \subseteq \mathcal{B}(\mathcal{K})$;

Output: The new reduced subcontext induced by K and C

$1 \leftarrow \bigvee J_K$ `// Old top`
$0 \leftarrow \bigwedge M_K$ `// Old bottom`
$C \leftarrow C \cup \{0, 1\}$ `// Add old top and bottom to` C
$1 \leftarrow 1 \vee \bigvee C$ `// New top`
$0 \leftarrow 0 \wedge \bigwedge C$ `// New bottom`
$\mathcal{B}'_G \leftarrow C \cup J_K$ `// Initial object concepts candidates`
$\mathcal{B}'_M \leftarrow C \cup M_K$ `// Initial attribute concepts candidates`
$\mathcal{B}_G \leftarrow \mathcal{B}_M \leftarrow \emptyset$
while $\mathcal{B}'_G \neq \mathcal{B}_G$ *or* $\mathcal{B}'_M \neq \mathcal{B}_M$ **do**
    $\mathcal{B}_G \leftarrow \mathcal{B}'_G$; $\mathcal{B}_M \leftarrow \mathcal{B}'_M$; $\mathcal{B}'_G \leftarrow \mathcal{B}'_M \leftarrow \emptyset$
    `// Extend to new object concepts:` $\mathcal{B}'_G \leftarrow \epsilon_G(\mathcal{B}_M)$
    foreach $g \in G$ **do**
        $g' \leftarrow 1$
        foreach $(A, B) \in \mathcal{B}_M$ *such that* $g \in A$ **do**
            $g' \leftarrow g' \wedge (A, B)$
        end
        $\mathcal{B}'_G \leftarrow \mathcal{B}'_G \cup \{g'\}$
    end
    `// Extend to new attribute concepts:` $\mathcal{B}'_M \leftarrow \epsilon_M(\mathcal{B}_G)$
    foreach $m \in M$ **do**
        $m' \leftarrow 0$
        foreach $(A, B) \in \mathcal{B}_G$ *such that* $m \in B$ **do**
            $m' \leftarrow m' \vee (A, B)$
        end
        $\mathcal{B}'_M \leftarrow \mathcal{B}'_M \cup \{m'\}$
    end
end
`// Keep ∨-irreducible:` $J'_K \leftarrow \left\{ j \in \mathcal{B}_G | j > 0 \vee \bigvee_{c \in \mathcal{B}_G | c < j} c \right\}$
$J'_K \leftarrow \emptyset$
foreach $j \in \mathcal{B}_G$ **do**
    $j^- \leftarrow 0$
    foreach $c \in \mathcal{B}_G < j$ **do** $j^- \leftarrow j^- \vee c$
    if $j > j^-$ **then** $J'_K \leftarrow J'_K \cup \{j\}$
end
`// Keep ∧-irreducible:` $M'_K \leftarrow \left\{ m \in \mathcal{B}_M | m < 1 \wedge \bigwedge_{c \in \mathcal{B}_M | c > m} c \right\}$
$M'_K \leftarrow \emptyset$
foreach $m \in \mathcal{B}_M$ **do**
    $m^+ \leftarrow 1$
    foreach $c \in \mathcal{B}_M > m$ **do** $m^+ \leftarrow m^+ \wedge c$
    if $m < m^+$ **then** $M'_K \leftarrow M'_K \cup \{m\}$
end
return $\langle J'_K, M'_K, \leq \rangle$

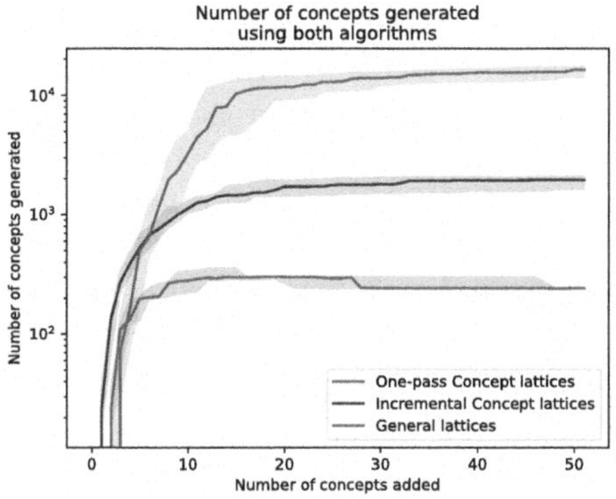

(a) $|G| = 0.05 \cdot 2^{|M|}$, $p((g, m) \in I) = 0.30$

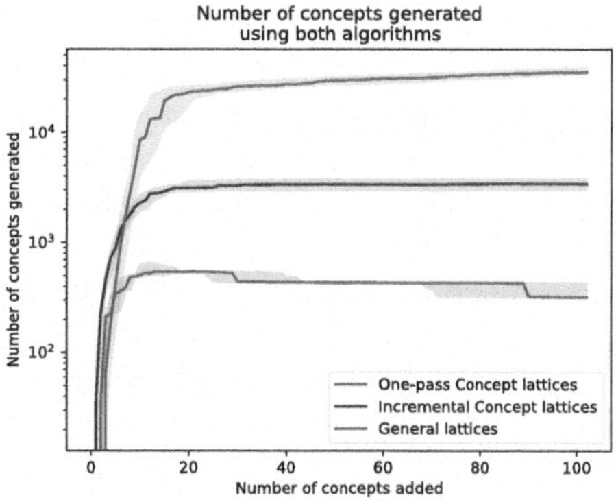

(b) $|G| = 0.10 \cdot 2^{|M|}$, $p((g, m) \in I) = 0.30$

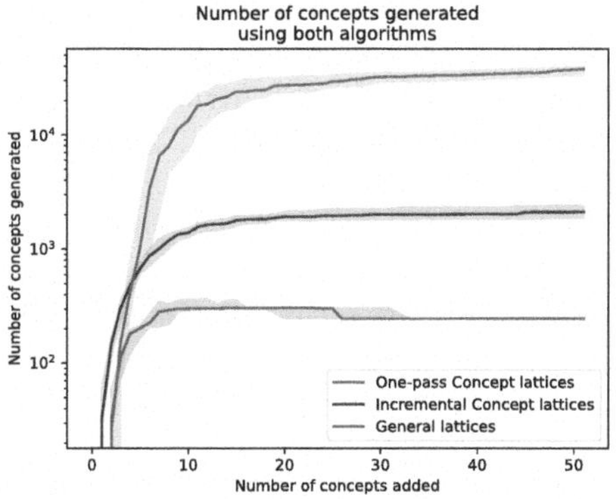

(c) $|G| = 0.05 \cdot 2^{|M|}$, $p((g, m) \in I) = 0.50$

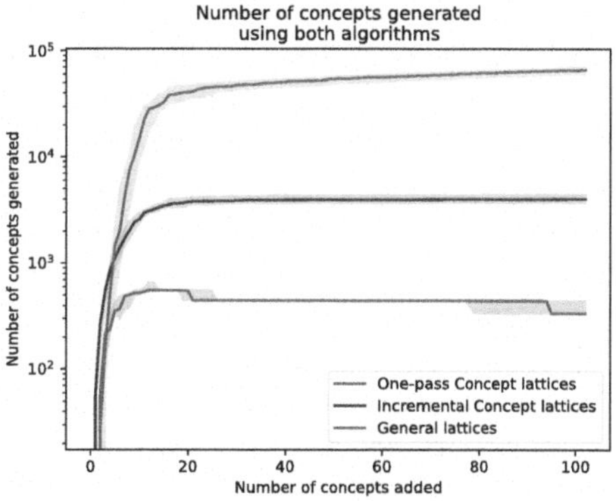

(d) $|G| = 0.10 \cdot 2^{|M|}$, $p((g, m) \in I) = 0.50$

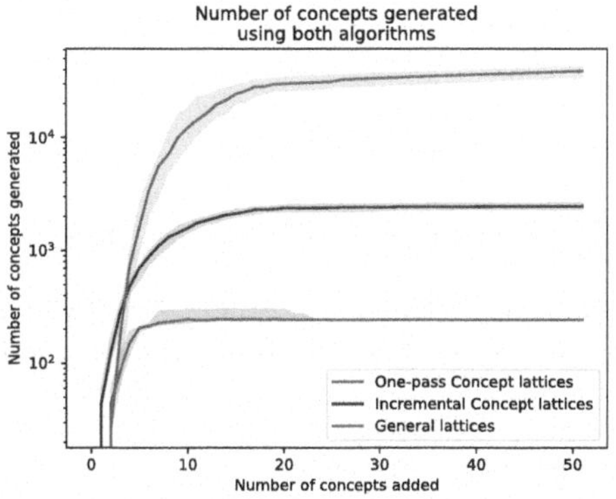

(e) $|G| = 0.05 \cdot 2^{|M|}$, $p((g, m) \in I) = 0.70$

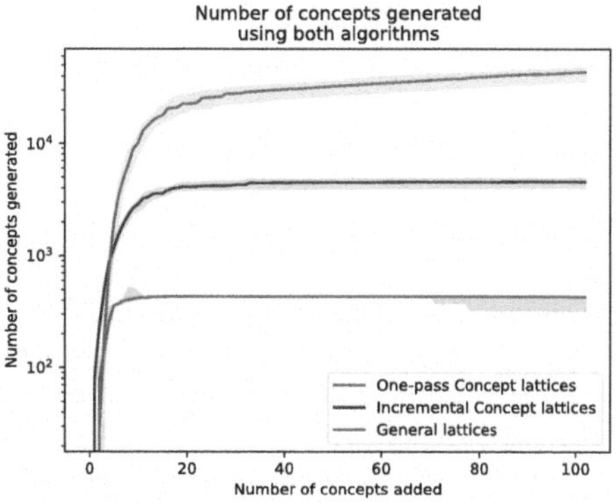

(f) $|G| = 0.10 \cdot 2^{|M|}$, $p((g, m) \in I) = 0.70$

Fig. 2. $|M| = 10$, 30 runs per experience, median curve framed by the first and third quartiles.

dedicated to general lattices. Instead of generating random concepts by closing randomly selected subsets of objects or attributes—a strategy that often results in the top concept—we adopted a progressive construction approach. Each random concept is generated by simultaneously expanding from both the top and bottom of the lattice, incrementally adding objects or attributes at random (with a slight bias based on the number of objects and attributes) until they converge into a single valid concept. The results are shown in Fig. 2, with a clear advantage for Algorithm 2 dedicated to concept lattices. It is also noted that it stabilizes on a plateau when it can no longer evolve the reduced subcontext, i.e., when it has reached the reduced context of the global lattice.

5 Conclusion and Perspectives

In this article, we have defined the problem of calculating the reduced subcontext from an existing reduced subcontext and a set of elements to be added to it. We proposed two algorithms to solve this problem for general lattices and concept lattices. This ensures a (sub-)lattice structure that provides a theoretical foundation for the extracted implication and association rules.

We are currently working on establishing a similar type of algorithm where the data is no longer represented by a set of binary attributes but is embedded in convex geometries [3], each with the property of being meet-distributive. This will allow us to refine our interactive analysis method for data scientists by offering them the reduced subcontext at any moment during their exploration, i.e., during their concept creation.

Acknowledgments. This study was funded by the ANR-21-CE23-0023 project.

Disclosure of Interests. The authors have no competing interests to declare that are relevant to the content of this article.

References

1. Barbut, M., Monjardet, B.: Ordre et classification: algèbre et combinatoire. Hachette (1970)
2. Demko, Ch., Bertet, K., Faucher, C., Viaud, J.F., Kuznetsov, S.O.: NextPriorityConcept: a new and generic algorithm computing concepts from complex and heterogeneous data. Theoret. Comput. Sci. **845**, 1–20 (2020)
3. Demko, Ch., Bertet, K., Viaud, J.F., Faucher, C., Mondou, D.: Description lattices of generalised convex hulls. Int. J. Approx. Reason. 109269 (2024)
4. Ganter, B., Kuznetsov, S.O.: Stepwise construction of the Dedekind-MacNeille completion. In: Mugnier, M.-L., Chein, M. (eds.) ICCS-ConceptStruct 1998. LNCS, vol. 1453, pp. 295–302. Springer, Heidelberg (1998). https://doi.org/10.1007/BFb0054922
5. Ganter, B., Wille, R.: Formal Concept Analysis, 2nd edn. Springer, Heidelberg (2024)
6. Richard, J.: De la capture de trajectoires de visiteurs vers l'analyse interactive de comportement après enrichissement sémantique. Ph.D. thesis, La Rochelle University (2023). https://theses.fr/2023LAROS012

Limitations of Attribute Derivations for Approximating User-Based Attribute Weighting

Stefan Schneider[1(✉)], Armin Schulz[3], Steven Verheyen[2], and Andreas Nürnberger[1]

[1] Data and Knowledge Engineering Group, Faculty of Computer Science, Otto von Guericke University Magdeburg, Universitätsplatz 2, 39106 Magdeburg, Germany
stefan.schneider@sschneider.de

[2] Brain and Cognition, Department of Psychology, Education and Child Studies, Erasmus University Rotterdam, Post Box 1738, 3000 DR Rotterdam, The Netherlands

[3] Department of Computer Science and Media, Brandenburg University of Applied Science, Magdeburger Straße 50, 14770 Brandenburg an der Havel, Germany
http://www.dke.ovgu.de

Abstract. In large object-attribute matrices, irrelevant attributes often bias derived conceptual orderings. Attribute weights can be helpful to directly reduce the number of attributes. User-based attribute weighting methods allow the user to express attribute weights themselves in a structured form. A major drawback of user-based attribute weighting is that additional user judgments are required. Therefore, approximating attribute weights from existing object-attribute matrix data (or incidence-based attribute weighting) is an interesting alternative. This study investigates the usefulness of attribute derivations, which are popular measures of incidence-based attribute weighting, for approximating user-based attribute weights. For the analysis, we use an established general domain concept dataset. We observe a correlation between the first-order attribute derivation and user-based attribute weights. However, this correlation only applies to exemplar data with more than 100 concrete attributes and not to category data with significantly fewer abstract attributes. Our analysis includes two well-known methods for user-based attribute weighting: feature importance ratings and feature generation frequencies. Our results show that first-order attribute derivation is the preferred incidence-based attribute weight based on a restricted set of attributes. The application of different sampling methods indicates that these methods differ in terms of their suitability for categories. This limitations of attribute derivations needs to be considered by theories and algorithms for attribute weighting.

Keywords: formal context · attribute weighting · user-based attribute weighting · attribute derivation

P. Cellier et al. (Eds.): CONCEPTS 2025, LNAI 15941, pp. 67–90, 2025.
https://doi.org/10.1007/978-3-032-03364-2_5

1 Introduction

What is required to describe a concept sufficiently? According to Zadeh's Fuzzy Sets approach [36], a concept can be described by grouping a set of entities together on the basis of some assertion, or some criterion or a rule—the so-called concept's extension. While the extension represents the concept as a black box, it is also possible to describe it as a white box, as Hampton's Attribute Inheritance Model [13] illustrates. It assumes that there is an idea associated with the concept, which includes the set of associated attributes and possibly complex structured knowledge descriptions - the so called concept's intension. Since the extension and intension of a concept are intertwined [26], it has been proposed to determine a concept based on a collection of attributes, objects, and their relationships represented through binary data. Following such a hybrid approach, an object-attribute matrix is used to derive a hierarchical conceptual order using models such as Formal Concept Analysis (FCA) [35] or HICLAS [6,26].

Although the hybrid approach allows for a linked structural representation of objects and their associated attributes, it is still necessary that only characteristic attributes are present in the existing attribute set. It is a well-known problem that FCA quickly generates a large number of concepts, as the number of concepts increases exponentially with the size of an object-attribute matrix [18]. It can also be assumed that the correctness of the conceptual order is negatively influenced by attributes that do not contain relevant information. The challenges involved in using high-dimensional Euclidean data representations make this consideration obvious. These challenges are usually discussed in connection with the phenomenon of the "curse of dimensionality" [21]. One of these phenomena concerns the impact of the ratio of relevant and irrelevant attributes on the separability of data [37]. The inclusion of irrelevant attributes leads to an additive noise effect. It has been shown that distance concentration (= The ratio of the variance of the length of any point vector with the length of the mean point vector converges to zero with increasing data dimensionality.), another phenomenon of the curse of dimensionality, can be avoided if there are not too many irrelevant attributes [10]. The observation that a high-dimensional relevant attribute space can lead to more plausible results than a low-dimensional space supports this view [31]. The challenges posed by the high dimensionality of binary data representations have also been discussed using methods for determining optimal intrinsic dimensionality [15,28]. Nevertheless, it has already been shown that in Euclidean space, intrinsic dimensionality alone is not sufficient to avoid the distance concentration effect, which is why attribute relevance must also be taken into account [10].

The described problem of using irrelevant attributes results from the fact that all attributes present in the attribute set need to be processed. According to binary data analysis of object-attribute relationships, conceptual knowledge is completely represented by the use of an object-attribute matrix and no further implicit knowledge can be expressed. It has also been pointed out that usually only a subset of that concept is relevant to the user and that further background knowledge can be used to focus on the user's relevant concept [4]. The relative importance of attributes, expressed by attribute weights, is an interesting approach to enable the user to take any kind of background knowledge into account directly with just a single metric. Attribute weights have already been used to eliminate concepts that are unsuitable or unnatural for a particular purpose [2]. In this respect, the concept of attribute weighting seems to be very powerful. On the one hand, it allows the user to express each type of influencing factor that is modeled with just one value, while on the other hand, these values can be used very flexibly to filter out relevant from irrelevant attributes. Attribute weights thus enable a direct reduction in the number of attributes.

When using attribute weights, it is an open question how these weights can be captured in a valid way. User-based attribute weighting tries to avoid leaving the ranking of attributes to the intuition of the researchers involved. Instead, structured methods such as feature importance ratings are used to support each individual user in weighting the given attributes [7]. A major drawback of user-based attribute weighting is that additional user judgements are required to infer attribute weights. While attribute weights are typically expressed by the user, it has recently been suggested that incidence data alone can be used to approximate these weights [16]. Such an incidence-based approach to attribute weighting does not allow for flexible contextualization of users' background knowledge, as originally intended. However, in contrast to user-based attribute weighting, no additional user data is required, which makes such an approach more cost-effective. Therefore, approximating attribute weights from existing object-attribute matrix data is an interesting alternative.

In this study, we aim to provide some practical guidance for evaluating the usefulness of methods for incidence-based attribute weighting by identifying the extent to which they approximate user-based attribute weighting. To this end, we use a well-established general domain data set and analyze the extent to which incidence-based attribute weighting approximates user-based attribute weighting.

2 Attribute Weights in Formal Contexts

We use philosophical considerations of context-dependent meaning by FCA [34]. The starting point for using FCA is an object-attribute matrix called a formal context. This represents the context of a collection of concepts and allows for rigorous analysis and derivation of those concepts, making them "formal" in a mathematical sense. Following the terminology of FCA, a formal context $\mathbb{K} := (G, M, I)$ consists of two sets, G and M, with I in relation to G and M. The elements of G are defined as objects and the elements of M are defined as attributes of the formal context $\mathbb{K}$. To express that an object $g \in G$ is related to an attribute $m \in M$, we write it as gIm or $(g, m) \in I$ and read that the object g has the attribute m. I is also defined as the context incidence relation [12].

Attribute weights are an additional component based on a given formal context. They are one way of channeling a user's background knowledge. We follow the basic terminology by Belohlavek and Macko [2] and assume that the weights to be assigned to attributes form a partial ordering $\langle W, \leq \rangle$. (Weights are elements $w \in W$.) A popular case used in various methods of data analysis as well as in our paper is $\langle W, \leq \rangle = \langle \mathbb{R}_0^+, \leq \rangle$ (weights are reals). Given a formal context $\mathbb{K}$ and a partially ordered set $\langle W, \leq \rangle$ of weights, we assume that there is an assignment of weights w from W to attributes m element of M, i.e. that a function

$$w : M \rightarrow W$$

is specified. The rule of thumb is that the more important the attribute, the larger the weight assigned to it. In this paper, attribute weights are only comparable within a formal context $\mathbb{K}$. An attribute weight value of w becomes true only for a given object set O and attribute set A. In Sect. 3 we present candidate functions to estimate w.

3 Principles of Attribute Weighting

Currently, user-based and incidence-based attribute weights play a crucial role in the binary data analysis of object attribute relationships in both category representation and FCA. In category representation, attribute weights are used to derive similarity structures between objects [8,9,14,22] while in the field of FCA they are used to simplify the process of deriving hierarchical conceptual structures by pruning the formal context [16]. In the following section, we will compare how attribute weights are embedded in FCA and consider which principles of attribute weights from category representation could be interesting for the area of FCA.

In the field of FCA, various other approaches such as methods for dimensionality reduction (e.g. Singular Value Decomposition [24], Correlation Dimensions [28]), formal concepts (e.g. Geometric sets [15,17]), constraints (e.g. attribute dependency formulas [4]) or grouping (e.g. attribute clarifying and reducibility [16]) have been proposed as an alternative to user-based attribute weights. All these methods serve the purpose of simplifying a formal context $\mathbb{K}$ in order to reduce the size of the hierarchical conceptual structure to be created. The special thing about user-based attribute weights is that they allow the user to determine how the original formal context is simplified without requiring access to incidence data and calculations based on it. User-based attribute weights allow different aspects of a user's background knowledge to be channeled into just one metric. In contrast to attribute dependency formulas as constraints [3,4], attribute weights [2] can be used not only to reduce the size of the concept lattice after computation, but also to reduce the size of a formal context before a concept lattice has been calculated [16]. In addition, only a threshold parameter is required, which selects the relevant attributes from the complete attribute set M for pruning a formal context and simplifying a concept lattice. More formally, the goal of attribute selection is to identify a set $N \subseteq M$ of the most relevant attributes for a cardinality $n \in \mathbb{N}$, i.e., an element from $\{N \subseteq M \| N| = n \wedge n(N)$ maximal $\}$. N is called the maximal relevant set [16].

Recent contributions on the use of attribute weights for FCA have focused on incidence-based weighting measures. Existing approaches are either entropy-based (i.e., the Entropic Relevance Approximation (ERA) and its simplification Iterative Maximal Relevant Set (IRMS), both proposed by Hanika et al. [16]), or network-based (i.e., δ-adjustment by Dürrschnabel et al. [11]). With ERA the impact of the reduction of $\mathbb{K}$ by N is expressed by

$$ERA(N) = \frac{|\mathfrak{B}(\mathbb{K}_{\overline{N}})|}{|\mathfrak{B}(\mathbb{K})|} \cdot \frac{E(\mathbb{K}_{\overline{N}})}{E(\mathbb{K})}.$$

The smaller $ERA(N)$, the more relevant N is considered to be for $\mathbb{K}$. So the relevance is measured by the loss of concepts and entropy when comparing $\mathfrak{B}(\mathbb{K})$ with $\mathfrak{B}(\mathbb{K}_{\overline{N}})$. There are two proposals for computing the *object information entropy* $E(\mathbb{K})$. The *Shannon entropy*

$$ERA_{SE}(\mathbb{K}) = \sum_{g \in G} -\frac{|g''|}{|G|} log_2 \left(\frac{|g''|}{|G|}\right)$$

and the *object entropy*

$$ERA_{OE}(\mathbb{K}) = \frac{1}{|G|} \sum_{g \in G} \left(1 - \frac{|g''|}{|G|}\right).$$

To determine the maximal relevant attribute set N, the $\binom{n}{|M|}$ ERA-values for all subsets in $\binom{M}{n}$ need to be calculated. This includes the construction of all the reduced concept lattices. With ERA, the existing set of attributes is always used to determine which attribute product has the highest relevance. ERA approaches are therefore significantly more complex and their effort increases exponentially with the number of attributes. As a more efficient alternative, IRMS takes only the attribute with the highest relevance and sets it as the default. IRMS is specified as an iterative approach. Instead of testing every subset of size n (as usually done with ERA) we construct $N \subseteq M$ by first considering all singleton sets $\{m\} \subseteq M$. Consequently, in every step i where X is the so far constructed set, we find $x \in M$ such that $r(X \cup \{x\}) \geq r(X \cup \{m\})$ for all $m \in M$. This approach requires the computation of only $n \cdot |M| - (n-1) \cdot n/2$ different relative relevances and their comparison.

In contrast to that entropy-based measures, δ-adjustment has been proposed. The δ-adjustment determines the influence of an attribute on the concept lattice. Essential to the determination is the acquisition of contranominal scales in so-called k-cubic sub-contexts of a certain formal context. While entropy-based measures emphasize the approximation of attribute weights by incidence data, δ-adjustment focuses exclusively on their significance for conceptual structuring. The attempt to provide a pruned formal context as input was explicitly formalized by the maximum relevant set. Nevertheless, the proposed incidence-based attribute weighting methods for FCA have in common that they all require the calculation of a complete concept lattice to determine the attribute weights.

In category representation, it is assumed that a graded category structure is present. The typicality of elements in the category, expressed by typicality ratings [22] captures the general intuition that some exemplars are more representative than others. A typicality gradient is assumed, whereby some exemplars (exemplar: objects) are more typical or representative of the category (category: set of exemplars) than others (e.g. [7,31]). According to prototype theory, the typicality of category exemplars is based on the extent to which they possess attributes that are characteristic of the concept (i.e. based on the similarity of the exemplars to the category prototype or to other exemplars). The notion of graded category structures implies that a concept cannot be fully determined by the use of attributes, but they do provide useful insights into the concept representation [29]. Instead, concepts are viewed as consisting of a prototype representation with an allowable degree of distortion [14,22].

Along these lines, user-based attribute weights were used to calculate similarities between exemplars. To this end, several feature-based similarity measures were presented. The most influential among those measures is perhaps the contrast model by Tversky [29]. The basic premise of the contrast model is that the similarity between two objects depends on a linear combination of their common and dinstinctive attributes. Tversky's observations confirmed that using a combination of common and distinctive attributes is the best way to predict pairwise similarity judgments between objects. The contrast model has also been used to predict typicality gradients [8]. Various other insights were gained regarding the role of user-based attribute weighting in feature-based similarity measures. Using user-based attribute weights to derive similarity measures achieves a higher degree of homogeneity in the participants' responses and shows a better match between similarity and its representation than judgements of similarity [9]. The prediction of empircal variables such as typicality ratings also benifits from weighting of the features [9,31].

4 Outline

While it is recognized that attributes offer a window into the concept's representation [19], the selection of attributes, possibly based on an attribute ranking, is still an open issue. Instead of defining an attribute ranking purely based on a researcher's intuition, feature generation tasks have been proposed to support each individual user in the structured acquisition of attributes. Feature generation tasks assume that the mention of an attribute by a user is an indicator of its importance. With feature generation tasks, exemplar typicality can be predicted from attributes generated for the exemplars of a superordinate-level category [22] as well as on the basis of attributes generated for the category labels [14] themselves - or both [1].

With classical feature generation tasks, no reproducible ranking of attributes can usually be derived. One problem is that important attributes are not always mentioned by the user because they are considered too general (for example, the attributes such as <*larger than a pencil*>, <*slower than a jet*> and

<*rarely found in office buildings*> can be applied to many more concepts than <*dog*>) [19]. Another problem is that attributes are only mentioned for certain objects, although they may be applicable to other objects [30]. Since feature generation tasks are suspectible to these problems, it has been suggested to count the frequency with which an attribute is generated across all users, also known as *feature generation frequencies* [7]. This approach is based on the observation that the frequency with which a feature is generated in response to a particular concept is a significant predictor of the time required to verify whether the feature is true of the concept [1]. While feature generation frequencies aim to achieve reproducible results, they do not cover differences between user groups.

This is particularly problematic because it has been observed that one group of participants in a study generated some attributes more frequently than others in response to a semantic cue [23]. There might be systematic differences between users in the importance or relevance of certain attributes for concepts [32] (e.g. "Three people may disagree as to whether chess and hiking are Sports, because one believes Sports should have competitive and gamelike attributes, while the other two only label activities that require physical effort Sports" [33]). Therefore, it seems plausible that users can directly indicate the importance of an attribute. This approach has already been proposed by using *feature importance ratings* [7,26]. Participants rate the subjective importance of individual attributes for a particular concept, for instance by providing a rating on a Likert scale. An advantage is that all participants consider all existing attributes, whereas in generation, each participant only considers a subset.

Feature generation frequencies and feature importance ratings have in common that the attribute ranking is derived from user judgements or user-based attribute weighting methods. A major drawback of user-based attribute weighting methods is that additional user judgements are required to infer attribute weights. Instead of using these user-based attribute weighting methods, incidence-based attribute weighting seems to be an interesting alternative. These methods allow to determine the weighting of attributes based solely on a specific formal context. Taking the incidence distribution into account, statements about the general applicability of objects [9] and attributes are derived, which are interpreted as an indicator for the weighting of attributes.

Using a derivation operator, these properties are referred to as first- and second-order attribute derivation, which are already used in existing methods for attribute weighting [16]. The derivation operator $(\cdot)'$ for $A \subseteq G$ and $B \subseteq M$ is defined as follows: For a set $A \subseteq G$ of objects we define $A' = \{m \in M \mid \forall g \in A : gIm\}$ (the set of attributes common to the objects in A). Correspondingly, for a set $B \subseteq M$ of attributes we define $B' = \{g \in G \mid \forall m \in B : gIm\}$ (the set of objects which have all attributes in B). The double application of $(\cdot)'$ refers to applying the derivation operator twice. This is a closure operator, i.e. $(\cdot)''$ is extensive, idempotent, and monotone. The closure operator is extensive since the closure of a set contains the original set or for every set $X, X \subseteq X''$. The closure operator is idempotent since applying the closure operator to an already closed set doesn't change it or $(X'')'' = X''$. And the closure operator is monotone (or increasing) since it preserves the subset relationship which means if $X \subseteq Y$, then $X'' \subseteq Y''$. Together these properties ensure that the double application of the derivation operator behaves as a closure operator. Sets $A \subseteq G$, $B \subseteq M$, such that $A = A''$ and $B = B''$ are said to be closed.

In this study, we want to investigate whether attribute derivations can be used to approximate user-based attribute weighting methods. Whether user judgments can be predicted from incidence data was already part of the introduction of HICLAS [26], which was intended to demonstrate the plausibility of this model. The HICLAS model is a clustering technique based on Boolean decomposition that is applied directly to a formal context $\mathbb{K} := (G, M, I)$. Unlike FCA, HICLAS first generates a simplified model with a series of bundles that simplifies the incidence structure of the given formal context before calculating a conceptual order. By creating a model based on the incidence data, a Jaccard goodness-of-fit index can be calculated for the individual objects and attributes. This measure can be interpreted as a measure of prototypicality (for the objects) and of attribute importance (for the attributes).

In an initial study [26], a HICLAS solution including only one bundle tested whether a differentiation between members and non-members of a category corresponds to characterising and non-characterising attributes of judged membership of the general (undifferentiated) categories. From seven domains (*kitchen utensils*, *furniture*, *vehicles*, *fruits*, *vegetables*, *fish* and *birds*), 30 objects were selected per domain. In a separate experiment with 32 participants, as many attributes as possible had to be named for each domain, with between 8 and 16 attributes selected for each domain based on the frequency with which the attributes were generated. The binary incidence data were provided by 4 participants in a fuzzy manner using a 5-point Likert scale, indicating whether an object had an attribute or not, where $+2$ = 'definitely yes,' 0 = 'unsure,' and -2 = 'definitely no.' The incidence data of all participants were summed and dichotomized to obtain a binary input context. To assess plausibility, the goodness-of-fit values for the individual objects from the HICLAS model were correlated with the user rated category membership (i.e., the typicality ratings). Significant correlations were observed in six of the domains analyzed, with the exception of furniture. The correlations ranged between .55 and .90, with a median of .76.

Another study [5] also evaluated the predictability of typicality ratings using Jaccard goodness-of-fit values for the objects derived from the calculated HICLAS model. In addition, it was tested whether a HICLAS solution can reproduce a plausible conceptual order. The data came from the Leuven Concept Data [7] with two aggregated domains, namely animals (a matrix with 129 exemplars and 225 category level attributes, including 30 mammals with 52 attributes, 30 birds with 58 attributes, 23 fish with 70 attributes, 26 insects with 60 attributes, 20 reptiles and amphibians with 70 attributes) and artifacts (a matrix with 166 exemplars and 300 category level attributes, including 27 musical instruments with 71 attributes, 27 tools with 73 attributes, 30 vehicles with 74 attributes, 29 items of clothing with 79 attributes, 33 kitchen utensils with 62 attributes, and 20 weapons with 54 attributes). The incidence data were provided by 4 participants, with the results being summed and dichotomized using the majority rule. The HICLAS solution included five bundles for animals and six bundles for the artifacts domain. By comparing the goodness-of-fit incidences for objects with typicality ratings for animals that represent a non-overlapping concept hierarchy, significant correlations (except for mammals) between .43 and .66 were observed (median of .54). The goodness-of-fit incidences for artifacts representing an overlapping concept hierarchy were compared with their typicality ratings. Only the correlations for clothing .60 and tools .64 were significant (median of .62).

Together, the contributions presented so far show that incidence data, i.e., Jaccard similarity scores for objects, can be used to predict user typicality ratings, whereby the number of concepts to be determined (referred to as bundles in HICLAS) in the model and the size of the attribute set limit the quality of the approximation. The present results suggest that the more complex the modeling, the more uncertain the predictability becomes. While [26] uses no more than 16 attributes as input and the model consists of only one bundle, a strong correlation of .76 is achieved. In contrast, the second study [5] processes up to 300 attributes that form five/six bundles, which only leads to moderate to weak correlations of 62 (non-overlapping category) and .54 (overlapping category). Prediction problems arise in particular when the objects in the concept hierarchy are overlapping and one object can be assigned to multiple bundles. In this case, fewer domains yield significant correlations with the typicality ratings.

Both studies focus on predicting typicality ratings based on goodness-of-fit values derived from incidence data on the object side. The prediction of user-based attribute weights, which indicate the attribute importance, based on incidence data, has not yet been studied. In this study, we focus specifically on attribute-related connections and attempt to reproduce existing findings to a certain extent. We assume that the prediction of user-based attribute weights is uncertain when a large number of attributes are given and the model to be formed contains a large number of concepts. To achieve a situation of complex conceptual order, we choose a simple FCA setting without additional modeling components. Such a setting is, in the sense of HICLAS, an extreme case in which modeling is identical to reality. We choose first- and second-order attribute derivations as two basic measures for incidence-based attribute weighting that can be derived from a simple FCA setup.

In the following, we evaluate the correlation between the feature generation frequency and feature importance ratings and the first and second attribution derivation of a formal context. The analysis is based on the Leuven Concept Data, which has already been introduced. In contrast to other established large binary datasets (e.g. found in [28]), the Leuven Concept Data include user-based attribute weights together with incidence data, which enables a direct comparison with incidence-based attribute weights.

5 Method

Unless otherwise specified, all of the data in this study were taken from the normed semantic category data set called the Leuven Concept Data reported in [7]. Detailed descriptions of the methods employed to collect these data can be found in [7,23], and so we will restrict the following to merely describing the data. While the Leuven Concept Data comprises three data classes, we focus in this study on two of them, the results of a feature generation task (class 2) and a large-scale formal context originally referred to as an 'exemplar by attribute applicability matrix' (class 3). The present study focuses on 15 semantic categories. Five of the categories were taken from the categories of animals (mammals, birds, fish, insects, and reptiles), 6 from the categories of artifacts (kitchen utensils, musical instruments, clothing, weapons, vehicles, and tools), 2 from the category of foods (fruits and vegetables), and 2 from the category of activities (sports and professions). Each of the categories contained between 20 and 33 exemplars. The selected exemplars cover a wide range of typicality, and the reliability of the typicality ratings that were also included in the Leuven Concept Data was very high (reliability for all categories above .90, except for insects with .87).

Feature-by-Exemplar Matrices
The feature-by-exemplar matrix used was created in two steps with separate tasks. Step 1 comprised a feature generation task and Step 2 a feature applicability judgement task. While the objects of this matrix were in any case the exemplars of each category, their attributes were determined by a feature generation task performed by 1003 participants. For each semantic category, attributes with two levels of abstraction were generated, namely exemplar level and category level attributes. To generate exemplar-level attributes, the participants in the study were presented with an exemplar term (e.g., "Pelikan") as a stimulus and asked to name attributes based on it. At the category level, the stimulus consisted of just a category label (e.g., "birds"). After preprocessing the named attributes, an ordered overall list was created that contained 156 to 382 attributes at the exemplar level and 21 to 39 at the category level. Feature importance ratings for all preprocessed exemplar level and category level attributes over 15 domains were provided by 84 participants. The feature importance ratings of an attribute for every domain include ratings by 12 participants.

On the basis of the list of attributes and objects, a feature applicability task was constructed. At the exemplar level, binary incidence data were collected between object-attribute relations in a study with 51 participants. Each participant described the incidence data for one to three matrices, resulting in a total of four matrices for each semantic category. At the category level, four participants filled in the incidence for all semantic categories, which also resulted in four matrices per semantic category. Each cell in a given matrix has the structure of a usual formal context $\mathbb{K} := (G, M, I)$ with unique incidence values I, which contain either a 1 or a 0 and indicate the applicability of each attribute-object relation.

User-Based Attribute Weighting

Feature Generation Frequencies: Feature generation frequencies can be determined when a feature generation task has been conducted with multiple, usually many, participants. In general, feature generation frequencies are a distribution measure that indicates how often an attribute is generated accross participants [7]. The more participants associate an attribute with a stimulus, the more important the attribute is. Note also the associated description of how to perform the feature generation task. Participants are usually encouraged to name as many different attributes as possible that they consider typical.

Feature Importance Ratings: Ordinal feature ratings are an alternative to feature generation frequencies to measure the importance of attributes through direct user ratings based on a set of already generated attributes [7,27]. Feature importance ratings are based on the assumption that different attributes listed for a particular object may differ in their relevance to the object. To apply the feature importance rating, the user is asked to rate how important or relevant they consider the attributes to be for the category on a 7-point Likert scale, ranging from -3 (for a very unimportant feature) to +3 (for a very important feature).

Incidence-Based Attribute Weighting

Attribute Derivation 1: Navarro and Perfors (2010) [20] have proposed using attribute derivation 1 to determine attribute weights. If many objects have a true incidence for a particular attribute, this results in high values for attribute derivation 1, which can be interpreted to mean that the attribute can be assigned to many objects in the formal context.

Attribute Derivation 2: Attribute derivation 2 takes the objects from attribute derivation 1 and calculates how many attributes the respective object set has in common for each added object subset.

6 Analyses

The following correlation analysis is performed independently of a specific domain and user by calculating the *median* Pearson correlation coefficient or $\tilde{\rho}$ across all 15 conceptual categories of the Leuven Concept Data. This aggregation is based on the measurement of Pearson's correlation coefficient ρ and significance level p for each individual category and the incidence data for each individual user.

We compute the correlations between feature generation frequencies *frequency*, the feature importance ratings *importance*, attribute derivation 1 *AD1*, and attribute derivation 2 AD2. The *frequency* of an attribute f_i was normalized across the entire attribute set n using $\hat{f}_i = \frac{f_i}{\sum_{i=1}^{n} f_i}$. We recoded the *importance* scale of an attribute i_j from $[-3, +3]$ to $[1, 7]$, which provides identical results. We take the average of the feature importance ratings provided by all 12 participants to obtain *importance*. To calculate *AD1* and *AD2*, we use the incidence data of the individual participants and normalize *AD1* $ad1_k$ at the object level

$\hat{ad1}_k = \frac{a'_k}{|O|}$ and *AD2* at the attribute level $\hat{ad2}_k = \frac{b'_k}{|A|}$. The data for this analysis can be downloaded from the GitHub repository of one of the authors: https://github.com/itchy2385/robust/.

The correlation analysis is performed separately at the exemplar level *exe* and the category level *cat*, since the attributes may vary depending on their level of abstraction in the feature generation task [25]. The Leuven Concept data at the category and exemplar levels differ not only in their degree of abstraction but also in the number of attributes listed. At the category level, there is a $1:1$ ratio between objects and attributes, while at the exemplar level, there is a $1:10$ ratio between objects and attributes. To check whether a ratio of $1:1$ at the exemplar level can influence the approximation quality, we select 10% of the given attributes randomly $exe10r$, based feature generation frequencies (highest values first) $exe10f$ and feature importance ratings (highest values first) $exe10i$, the associated attribute weights, and the associated incidence data for each domain and measure the correlation again.

An overview of the results of the correlation analysis can be found in the following Table 1. This overview relates *frequency*, *importance*, *AD1*, and *AD2* using *median* and compares the results for the different levels (exe, $exe10r$, $exe10f$, $exe10i$, and cat) separately.

Correlation Analysis (Overview)

Table 1. Correlation analysis based on the median correlation values across all 15 Leuven concept domains. Values highlighted in bold indicate the highest correlation strength in the comparison group. The comparison group include variants exemplar level exe, 10 percent of all randomly selected exemplar attributes $exe10r$, 10 percent selected based on the feature generation frequencies $exe10f$ and feature importance ratings $exe10i$ as well as the category level cat.

variables	frequency	importance
importance exe	.27	-
importance exe10r	**.56**	-
importance exe10f	.55	-
importance exe10i	**.56**	-
importance cat	.46	-
AD1 exe	.29	.46
AD1 exe10r	.51	.54
AD1 exe10f	.56	.56
AD1 exe10i	**.68**	**.72**
AD1 cat	.38	.45
AD2 exe	−.17	−.30
AD2 exe10r	−.40	−.47
AD2 exe10f	.00	−.52
AD2 exe10i	**−.55**	**−.63**
AD2 cat	−.36	−.44

A table with all observed correlation values for the individual categories p with the observed significance levels $* : p < .05, ** : p < .01, *** : p < .001$ is also added to the Appendix in the following correlation tables: Correlation analysis at the exemplar level (Table 2), the exemplar level with 10% randomly selected (Table 3), 10% by feature generation frequencies (Table 4), 10% by feature importance ratings (Table 5) and the category level (Table 6). In addition to the overview of the correlation analysis, a detailed correlation analysis table is added to Table 7 in the Appendix. This table also contains minimum min and maximum max correlation values and summarizes the correlation analysis for all 15 categories any, the non-overlapping categories $1 : n$ (i.e., animals) and the overlapping categories $n : m$ (i.e., artifacts). The division into non-overlapping and overlapping categories had already led to differences in the quality of the approximation of typicality ratings based on incidence data [5,26]. Therefore, we want to investigate whether these differences can also be observed at the attribute level.

First, we compare the correlation between the two user-based attribute weighting methods, *frequency* and *importance*. Both variables attempt to indicate attribute importance, which is why we assume that *importance* and *frequency* should be positively correlated. At the exemplar level, the correlation strength is not good $\tilde{\rho} : .27$ ($\rho : [.17, .43]$ with significant observations in all 15 domains except professions. In a sample of 10% of the attributes, the correlation strength generally reached a moderate correlation level $exe10r$ reached $\tilde{\rho} : .56$ ($\rho : [.38, .65]$ with significant correlations for birds, kitchen utensils, vegetables, and vehicles; $exe10f$ reached $\tilde{\rho} : .55$ ($\rho : [.42, .68]$ with significant correlations for birds, kitchen utensils, mammals, and tools; and $exe10i$ reached $\tilde{\rho} : .56$ ($\rho : [.54, .59]$ with significant correlations for birds and weapons. Compared to the sample-level correlations, the moderate median correlation at the category level is lower, with a similar range of correlation values $\tilde{\rho} : .46$ ($\rho : [.39, .62]$, which can be explained by significant observations in more domains (i.e., birds, fruit, kitchen utensils, mammals, musical instruments, reptiles, sports, vegetables, vehicles, weapons). While it seems reasonable to consider *importance* and *frequency* against the same background at the category level, it is essential to analyze them separately at the exemplar level. The same background can also be assumed between both variables in the sample versions of the exemplar level, but only for certain domains, depending on the sampling method.

Second, we examined the observed correlations between *frequency*, *importance*, and *AD1* and expect a positive correlation in both cases. Note: In the following, we only mention categories with significant correlations according to the majority rule (i.e., significance for at least 3 out of 4 users). The results only hold at the exemplar level: Both *frequency* and *importance* correlate positively with *AD1*. *AD1* correlates moderately with *importance* $\tilde{\rho} : .46$ ($\rho : [-.31, .65]$ not significant for professions created by user 3 and user 4), but only weakly $\tilde{\rho} : .29$ ($\rho : [.16, .50]$) with *frequency* (significant across all domains and users). Furthermore, the correlation at the category level between *AD1* and *frequency* is $\tilde{\rho} : .38$ ($\rho : [-.37, .52]$ for birds and insects), *importance* $\tilde{\rho} : .45$ ($\rho : [-.42, .66]$

for birds, fish, fruit, insects, kitchen utensils, musical instruments, occupations, sports, and tools) in a similar range of values between weak and moderate correlation strength. At the exemplar level, *AD1* cannot even approximately express *frequency*, but it can reflect *importance* to a certain extent. At the category level, the use of *AD1* to approximate *frequency* and *importance* should also be critically questioned, whereby its applicability is additionally limited to certain domains. The results at the category level show that the approximation of *frequency* by *AD1* is much more limited than the approximation of *importance*.

Third, due to the double application of the deriviation operator, *AD2* should correlate negatively with *frequency* and *importance*. The observations show that *AD2* correlates weak negatively with *frequency* ($\tilde{\rho}: -.17$ ($\rho: [-.30, -.10]$ with significant results for all domains expect clothing and kitchenutensils) *importance* ($\tilde{\rho}: -.30$ ($\rho: [-.46, .26]$ over all domains and all users) at the exemplar level. On the category level a negative correlation can be also observed. For *frequency* ($\tilde{\rho}: -.36$ ($\rho: [-.44, -.33]$ only for tools) and *importance* ($\tilde{\rho}: -.44$ ($\rho: [-.66, .40]$ for fish, insects, kitchenutensils and tools) a similar level of the correlation strength on the border between weak to moderate exists. Based on these observations, *AD2* is generally not suitable for approximating *frequency* or *importance* on exemplar level and needs to be might be an option on category level but only for certain domains.

Fourth, using the exemplar attributes 10% of the samples, we examine the influence of the size of the attribute set between *AD1* and *frequency*, *importance*. If an exemplar-based attribute sampling $exe10r$, $exe10f$, $exe10i$ achieves a higher correlation strength than the observed correlation at the category level *cat*, this would indicate that the degree of abstraction in feature generation is relevant, which has already been pointed out by others [25]. In contrast to *exe*, *AD1* achieves a moderate correlation strength that is similar in value for both *frequency* and *importance*, by sampling exemplar attributes randomly or based on feature generation frequencies *exe10r*: *Frequency* $\tilde{\rho}: .51$ ($\rho: [.33, .68]$ for birds, professions, reptiles, and vehicles) compared to *importance* $\tilde{\rho}: .54$ ($\rho: [.40, .75]$ for birds, kitchen utensils, musical instruments, sports, tools, vegetables, vehicles, and weapons); *exe10f*: *frequency* $\tilde{\rho}: .56$ ($\rho: [.44, .85]$ for birds, fish, insects, kitchen utensils, mammals, and sports) vs. *importance* $\tilde{\rho}: .56$ ($\rho: [-.56, .75]$ for birds, clothing, fruit, insects, kitchen utensils, mammals, and tools); By using feature importance ratings sampled exemplar attribute a strong correlation between AD1 and frequency, importance can been observed - *exe10i*: *frequency* $\tilde{\rho}: .68$ ($\rho: [.57, .89]$ for birds, clothing, and fruit) vs. *importance* $\tilde{\rho}: .72$ ($\rho: [-.91, .90]$ for birds, insects, reptiles, tools, and vehicles). Compared to the correlation results at category level *cat* with a maximum correlation strength of .52, $exe10i$ is notably larger, which also applies to a lesser extent to $exe10r$ and $exe10f$. From this consideration, it can be concluded that the degree of abstraction in feature generation plays a decisive role in the quality of the approximation to user-based attribute weights using *AD1*. These results also indicate that, depending on the method used for attribute sampling at the exemplar level, significant correlations between *AD1* and *frequency* or *importance* can only be observed for certain domains. It is noteworthy that even with random attribute sampling at the exemplar level, better correlations were observed than when considering correlations with all attributes at the exemplar level.

Fifth, in addition to the correlation analysis of all 15 Leuven concept data domains, we compare the correlation values of the categories animals and artifacts, which are examples of non-overlapping and overlapping concept hierarchies that have been investigated previously [5]. The concepts in a non-overlapping concept hierarchy are defined in such a way that each object can be assigned to only one concept. In contrast, overlapping concept hierarchies are ill-defined in that objects can be assigned to one or more concepts. Following existing investigations by Ceuleman et al., we assume that the correlation for non-overlapping domains or $1:n$ is stronger than for overlapping domains or $n:m$ domains. For this analysis, we focus on correlations based on *AD1* in comparison to *frequency* and *importance*. While on exemplar level *frequency* to *AD1* by $1:n$ domains achieve weak to moderate correlations $\tilde{\rho}:.39$ ($\rho:[.16,.50]$), $n:m$ domains show weaker correlations $\tilde{\rho}:.29$ ($\rho:[.19,.42]$). Considering the results on exemplar level of the correlations between *importance* and *AD1*, we observe that $1:n$ and $n:m$ domains achieve similar moderate correlation results ($1:n$: $\tilde{\rho}:.48$ ($\rho:[.27,.65]$) and $n:m$: $\tilde{\rho}:.48$ ($\rho:[.36,.61]$)). At the category level, we observe similar correlation strengths between $1:n$: $\tilde{\rho}:.39$ ($\rho:[.34,.49]$) and $n:m$: $\tilde{\rho}:.39$ ($\rho:[.33,.52]$) through the approximation of *AD1* to *frequency* and through the approximation of *AD1* and *importance* ($1:n$: $\tilde{\rho}:.50$ ($\rho:[.36,.61]$); $n:m$: $\tilde{\rho}:.43$ ($\rho:[.32,.66]$). If we look at the results of the sampling methods $exe10f$ and $exe10i$ for approximating the *frequency* at the sample level, we can see stronger correlation results for $1:n$ compared to $n:m$ for $exe10f$ ($1:n$: $\tilde{\rho}:.68$ ($\rho:[.51,.85]$) ; $n:m$: $\tilde{\rho}:.49$ ($\rho:[.44,.55]$)) and $exe10i$ ($1:n$: $\tilde{\rho}:.79$ ($\rho:[.65,.89]$) ; $n:m$: $\tilde{\rho}:.60$ ($\rho:[.57,.79]$)) as well. In contrast, by approximating *importance*, we obtain similar results for $exe10f$ ($1:n$: $\tilde{\rho}:.65$ ($\rho:[.50,.75]$) ; $n:m$: $\tilde{\rho}:.54$ ($\rho:[.41,.73]$)) and $exe10i$ ($1:n$: $\tilde{\rho}:.64$ ($\rho:[.53,.88]$) ; $n:m$: $\tilde{\rho}:.78$ ($\rho:[.73,.90]$)) as well. According to these results, $1:n$ domains can be approximated more easily than $n:m$ domains if *frequency* is to be approximated. However, this does not apply to the approximation of *importance*.

Sixth, the research design follows a complex conceptual approach. Without any modeling component, which is present when using HICLAS, we assumed that in a traditional FCA environment, a large number of concepts are formed when the attribute set is large. In such an FCA environment, *AD1* and *AD2* are two incidence-based attribute weighting measures that can only rank attributes using a given formal context. By focusing only on the correlation results of *AD1* and *AD2* at the exemplar level, we can conclude that none of the correlations are large in absolute terms for approximating user-based attribute weights. There are still many variances that need to be explained, which points to a general limitation of the incidence-based attribute weighting measures $AD1$ and $AD2$ used. Based on this consideration, it is assumed that *importance* or *frequency* should be used as the gold standard. However, these variables also do not correlate very well, so it is unclear which of them should actually serve as the gold standard. In addition, there are individual differences in both the incidences and the feature ratings, so it is questionable how well these can be reconciled. To this end, future work should investigate the extent of individual differences.

7 Discussion

We conducted a first study to determine whether incidence-based attribute weighting techniques can be used to approximate user-based attribute weighting techniques. To do this, we evaluated the correlations between feature generation frequencies and feature importance ratings on the one hand, and first- and second-order attribute derivation on the other. We applied a correlation analysis to the Leuven Concept data [7] that had already been used to predict typicality ratings from incidence data [5,26]. In this study, we measure the correlation between user-based and incidence-based attribute weights using Pearson correlation. These measure indicate whether an approximation is predictable and certain. Correlation analysis by calculating cross-domain ranges of correlation values, including the median, provides the best measure for general guidance on the principles of attribute weighting.

In line with previous research [20], the analysis in this paper shows that it is possible in principle to approximate user-based attribute weights from incidence data, but that this approach is subject to limitations. The limitations observed can be summarized as follows: It must be taken into account that the feature importance ratings and the feature generation frequencies measure different aspects of attribute importance. Choosing second-order attribute derivation is questionable and first-order attribute derivation needs to be preferred. On exemplar level including a large attribute set, feature generation frequencies cannot be predicted using the first-order attribute derivation, but feature importance ratings. In general, caution should be exercised when predicting attribute weights using first-order attribute derivation, as the predictions deviate considerably from user-based attribute weights.

This analysis not only provides new insights into the limitations of approximating user-based attribute weights using incidence-based attribute weights, but also highlights the role of the complexity of a formal context.

A first complexity problem concerns the type of conceptual order that is intended in the data. In this context, previous research [5,26] already distinguished between formal contexts that allow a $1 : n$ order between objects and concepts (concepts can contain multiple objects, but each object must be assigned to exactly one concept) and those that allow an $n : m$ order (an object can be assigned to multiple concepts at the same time). The results of Ceulemans [5] already suggest that formal contexts that allow a $1 : n$ conceptual order can be better approximated at the object level than those that allow an $n : m$ conceptual order. In this study, we investigated whether these observations also apply at the attribute level. We compared the correlation results between attribute derivation 1 and the user-based attribute weights for domains $1 : n$ and $n : m$ separately. On exemplar level including its sampled versions, the correlation results between attribute derivation 1 and the feature generation frequencies show that $1 : n$ conceptual orders achieve a greater correlation strength than $n : m$, which indicated that $1 : n$ are more easily to approximate. At the exemplar level, including their sample versions, the correlation results between first-order attribute derivation and the feature generation frequencies show that $1 : n$ conceptual orders achieve a greater correlation strength than $n : m$. This suggests that $1 : n$ orders are easier to approximate in this scenario. In contrast, the correlation results between first-order attribute derivation and feature importance ratings show that both types achieve more or less the same degree of approximation.

A second complexity problem concerns the attribute set. The Leuven Concept Data [7] divided attributes that were derived from the category and exemplar levels using a feature generation task. The reason for this separation was that the two types differ in their degree of abstraction due to the way the feature generation task was applied [25]. At the category level, features had to be generated, only the category name (e.g., "birds") was specified, whereas at the exemplar level, features were generated by representing the individual exemplar of a category (e.g., "owl"). Furthermore, both types refer to the same set of objects, but differ in the relative object-attribute ratio. At the category level the ratio is $1 : 1$ (which more or less means that in a formal context with 30 objects, 30 attributes were determined) whereas at exemplar level the ratio is $1 : 10$ (which more or less means that with 30 objects, 300 attributes were determined). In this study, a subset of 10% was selected by different methods (randomly, by feature generation frequencies and by feature importance ratings) from the attribute set to obtain a ratio of $1 : 1$ as at the category level. The results showed that the first-order attribute derivation correlates more strongly with user-based attribute weights when attributes are selected at the exemplar level at random or based on the feature generation frequencies compared to the category level. This demonstrated that the degree of abstraction of the attributes also plays a decisive role in the approximation of user-based attribute weights. Furthermore, it should be noted that sampling exemplar attributes based on feature importance ratings yielded a stronger correlation than all other methods. Such a strong correlation in the approximation of user-based attribute weights by first-order attribute derivation when sampling based on feature importance ratings clearly shows that the selection of the most important attributes can offer an additional advantage.

In general, this study questions the way we apply conceptual orders using formal contexts. Many algorithms have been proposed in the past to improve the basic notion of FCA. These algorithms are often explained and evaluated using very simple examples, whereby the formal contexts only comprised small sets of objects and attributes with incidence data. More recent developments attempt to develop FCA algorithms that can be used in real-world application scenarios, where the number of objects and attributes is often very large [16]. While some applications have been evaluated while maintaining a small attribute set [11,16], other contributions also address the challenge of having many attributes [15,28]. One strategy for dealing with large formal contexts is to leave the input data unchanged and calculate a concept lattice on this basis. Such an approach becomes formally problematic because the FCA calculation and visualization of the concept lattice become too complex. In this direction, the use of constraints and attribute weights to simplify the calculation and visualization was an improvement [2,3]. Nevertheless, the results of this study show that large formal contexts mean that incidence-based attribute weights can only approximate user-based attribute weights to a limited extent.

Approximation of user-based attribute weights at the exemplar level was generally not possible, with the exception of first-order attribute derivation and feature importance ratings, although the quality of the approximation must be questioned here as well. When the size of the attribute set was restricted (as specified at the category level and in the sample versions of the exemplar level), the approximation improved, but only within a certain range of categories. Surprisingly, user-based attribute weights can be approximated better even with random attribute selection at the exemplar level than when using large attribute sets at the exemplar level. Ultimately, however, there was no incidence-based attribute weighting method for small attribute sets that generally provided a good approximation. It follows that it is advisable to limit the size of the attribute set by searching for a suitable feature selection method that is permissible within the given domain.

It should also be noted that the number of concepts that need to be created based on a specific formal context is another important criterion that influences the complexity of the formal context. The correlation results for the approximation of user-based attribute weights at the exemplar level also stem from the chosen basic FCA setting, which typically leads to a very large number of concepts to be generated. The results of Ceulemans and Storms [5,26], who observed a strong correlation between typicality ratings and Jaccard distances, suggest that even with a simple model, better correlations with user-based attribute weights can be achieved. In general, this work could be a starting point for considering the use of HICLAS-like modeling in the sense of FCA. A second question that also arises is whether (without using a modeling approach) it is sufficient to reduce the number of attributes, e.g., through attribute weighting or correlation dimensions [15,28], in order to obtain a valid conceptual order.

This contribution is based on the idea that incidence-based attribute weighting could be an interesting alternative to user-based attribute weighting. While user-based approaches require attribute weights to be determined separately for each user, incidence-based approaches allow this data to be obtained entirely from existing incidences. The question remains open whether it is fundamentally possible to approximate user-based attribute weights from incidence data, or whether other measures are required. This would be an argument for considering other methods of user-based attribute weighting in the future, rather than approximating the existing ones.

8 Conclusion

In summary, it can be said that the approximation of feature importance ratings and feature generation frequencies through first- or second-order attribute derivation is questionable on exemplar level. An improved approximation can been achieved by attribute selection. In the current study, two common methods of user-based attribute weighting were used as the gold standard in comparison to incidence-based attribute weighting. Both methods correlate not very well, for that it is not clear which of them should be chosen as gold standard. It should be noted that feature importance ratings and feature generation frequencies also have their own disadvantages when determining attribute weights. The methods require either a large number of users or a high level of effort on the part of users to evaluate the attributes. Further these methods are also proned to individual differences in perceived importance. Researchers should thus carefully way the pros and cons of both user-based and incidence-based attribute weights when considering them to restrict the attribute set.

Appendix

1. **A1**: $corr(frq, imp)$
2. **A2**: $corr(frq, ad1_{USER1})$
3. **A3**: $corr(frq, ad1_{USER2})$
4. **A4**: $corr(frq, ad1_{USER3})$
5. **A5**: $corr(frq, ad1_{USER4})$
6. **A6**: $corr(frq, ad2_{USER1})$
7. **A7**: $corr(frq, ad2_{USER2})$
8. **A8**: $corr(frq, ad2_{USER3})$
9. **A9**: $corr(frq, ad2_{USER4})$
10. **B1**: $corr(imp, ad1_{USER1})$
11. **B2**: $corr(imp, ad1_{USER2})$
12. **B3**: $corr(imp, ad1_{USER3})$
13. **B4**: $corr(imp, ad1_{USER4})$
14. **B5**: $corr(imp, ad2_{USER1})$
15. **B6**: $corr(imp, ad2_{USER2})$
16. **B7**: $corr(imp, ad2_{USER3})$
17. **B8**: $corr(imp, ad2_{USER4})$

Table 2. Leuven Concept Data Correlation Table by Domain - Exemplar

domain	A1	A2	A3	A4	A5	A6	A7	A8	A9	B1	B2	B3	B4	B5	B6	B7	B8
Birds	.43***	.49***	.41***	.38***	.50***	−.15*	−.20**	−.21**	−.22***	.50***	.54***	.51***	.53***	−.30***	−.24***	−.25***	−.30***
Clothing	.25***	.36***	.32***	.27***	.33***	−.12	−.15*	−.12	−.15*	.53***	.46***	.60***	.49***	−.34***	−.37***	−.41***	−.34***
Fish	.39***	.41***	.44***	.47***	.49***	−.25**	−.25**	−.19*	−.30***	.54***	.54***	.65***	.50***	−.35***	−.28***	−.35***	−.33***
Fruit	.28***	.28***	.26***	.28***	.20**	−.21**	−.16*	−.21**	−.18**	.44***	.39***	.37***	.38***	−.21**	−.19**	−.27***	−.22***
Insects	.26***	.22**	.21**	.25***	.25***	−.15*	−.12	−.18*	−.15*	.27***	.41***	.45***	.39***	−.20**	−.36***	−.46***	−.37***
Kitchenutensils	.25***	.29***	.22***	.23***	.29***	−.09	−.10	−.08	−.14*	.45***	.36***	.37***	.42***	−.30***	−.24***	−.25***	−.24***
Mammals	.32***	.43***	.38***	.39***	.40***	−.17**	−.16**	−.21***	−.27***	.46***	.47***	.42***	.45***	−.1	−.3***	−.26***	−.23***
Musicalinstruments	.21**	.19**	.23***	.23***	.23***	−.13	−.14*	−.14*	−.16*	.50***	.57***	.60***	.61***	−.16*	−.37***	−.34***	−.40***
Professions	.02	.49***	.25***	.41***	.44***	−.11*	−.10	−.14**	−.10*	−.13*	−.31***	−.08	−.04	−.22***	.26***	.06	−.28***
Reptiles	.31***	.24**	.22**	.25***	.16*	−.15*	−.17*	−.20**	−.17*	.44***	.49***	.44***	.52***	−.28***	−.43***	−.34***	−.39***
Sports	.17**	.22***	.25***	.31***	.22***	−.14**	−.16**	−.12*	−.13*	.36***	.39***	.40***	.37***	−.12*	−.12*	−.05	−.14**
Tools	.20***	.29***	.27***	.34***	.31***	−.19**	−.16**	−.16**	−.19***	.46***	.46***	.49***	.49***	−.35***	−.35***	−.28***	−.31***
Vegetables	.18**	.21***	.21***	.22***	.23***	−.13*	−.12*	−.11	−.12*	.61***	.63***	.63***	.59***	−.31***	−.34***	−.30***	−.31***
Vehicles	.42***	.29***	.33***	.31***	.42***	−.18**	−.18**	−.22***	−.25***	.49***	.51***	.39***	.57***	−.35***	−.29***	−.25***	−.38***
Weapons	.37***	.29***	.25***	.26***	.32***	−.15*	−.12	−.21**	−.21**	.47***	.4***	.41***	.37***	−.33***	−.25***	−.29***	−.26***

Table 3. Leuven Concept Data Correlation Table by Domain - Exemplar Random Sample 10 percent

domain	A1	A2	A3	A4	A5	A6	A7	A8	A9	B1	B2	B3	B4	B5	B6	B7	B8
Birds	.64**	.62**	.48*	.56**	.51*	−.16	−.20	−.25	−.29	.60**	.58**	.54**	.57**	−.35	−.29	−.17	−.52*
Clothing	−.07	.07	.16	−.05	.06	−.14	−.18	−.18	.01	.39	.29	.65***	.42*	−.5*	−.32	−.59**	−.52**
Fish	−.17	.25	−.01	.13	.09	−.33	−.15	−.14	−.21	.20	.27	.39	.33	−.29	.04	−.19	−.40
Fruit	.32	.07	.07	.40	.21	−.39	−.18	−.25	−.32	−.02	.02	.04	−.06	−.09	−.09	−.11	−.03
Insects	.31	−.16	−.02	.01	−.10	−.10	−.05	−.16	.08	.12	.43	.53*	.44*	−.24	−.27	−.36	−.43*
Kitchenutensils	.38*	.54**	.35	.36*	.35	−.10	−.15	−.07	−.15	.47**	.33	.44*	.41*	−.34	−.29	−.22	−.37*
Mammals	.23	.20	.27	.41*	.39*	−.41*	−.36	−.39*	−.47*	.28	.41*	.31	.34	−.35	−.52**	−.40*	−.49**
Musicalinstruments	.31	.28	.24	.19	.29	−.30	−.5*	−.40	−.42	.58**	.68***	.62**	.63**	−.08	−.50*	−.63**	−.45*
Professions	−.03	.56***	.38*	.66***	.64***	−.34*	−.18	−.34*	−.06	−.16	−.40*	−.15	−.11	.35*	.56***	.34*	−.27
Reptiles	.40	.68**	.58*	−.04	.63**	−.31	−.17	−.01	−.19	.57*	.26	−.21	.47	−.51*	−.28	−.03	−.15
Sports	.31	.17	.33*	.43**	.10	−.19	−.25	−.27	−.19	.33*	.50**	.46**	.31	−.15	−.20	−.10	−.15
Tools	.21	.05	.09	.12	.17	−.34	−.22	−.21	−.37	.48**	.63***	.48*	.54**	−.36	−.43*	−.31	−.36
Vegetables	.49**	.40*	.35	.33	.39*	−.15	−.21	−.18	−.17	.67***	.75***	.64***	.68***	−.34	−.49**	−.47**	−.39*
Vehicles	.65***	.30	.50**	.48**	.63***	−.27	−.22	−.29	−.40*	.42*	.54**	.33	.67***	−.32	−.23	−.16	−.38*
Weapons	.30	.02	−.07	.05	.09	.01	.08	−.11	−.21	.52*	.68**	.47*	.51*	−.41	−.36	−.45	−.12

Table 4. Leuven Concept Data Correlation Table by Domain - Exemplar Feature Generation Frequencies ranked sample 10 percent

domain	A1	A2	A3	A4	A5	A6	A7	A8	A9	B1	B2	B3	B4	B5	B6	B7	B8
Birds	.68***	.85***	.68***	.63**	.84***	−.26	−.41	−.33	−.44	.67**	.66**	.60**	.65**	−.45*	−.25	−.22	−.45*
Clothing	.13	.55**	.49*	.33	.41	−.27	−.32	−.16	−.28	.47*	.41*	.27	.53**	−.33	−.37	−.23	−.50*
Fish	.50	.68**	.60*	.48	.74**	−.45	−.36	−.39	−.39	.60*	.33	.49	.68**	−.63*	.18	−.12	−.29
Fruit	.31	.40	.32	.46*	.35	−.32	−.18	−.28	−.23	.60**	.32	.47*	.47*	−.51*	−.03	−.22	−.12
Insects	.43	.29	.56*	.51*	.53*	−.27	−.36	−.28	−.35	.50*	.55*	.66**	.55*	−.56**	−.50*	−.52*	−.58**
Kitchenutensils	.42*	.51*	.40	.47*	.45*	−.23	−.17	−.21	−.22	.48*	.50*	.56**	.54**	−.40	−.26	−.61**	−.35
Mammals	.66***	.76***	.52*	.68***	.77***	−.18	−.18	−.22	−.33	.75***	.62**	.65**	.71***	−.31	−.33	−.15	−.29
Musicalinstruments	−.12	.01	.05	−.00	.03	−.14	−.20	−.18	−.19	.62**	.62**	.61**	.56*	−.00	−.20	−.17	−.15
Professions	−.24	.44	.14	−.03	−.04	−.21	−.10	−.13	−.36	−.29	−.56**	−.15	−.16	.39	.72***	.49*	.41
Reptiles	.36	.16	.12	.61*	.28	.13	−.16	−.38	−.19	.52	.33	.72**	.55	−.55*	−.74**	−.65*	−.70**
Sports	.30	.80***	.51*	.69***	.51*	−.29	−.35	−.32	−.26	.28	.39	.40	.37	−.05	−.13	−.03	−.07
Tools	.43*	.33	.37	.44*	.52**	−.30	−.15	−.25	−.33	.49*	.60**	.73***	.56**	−.48*	−.52**	−.57**	−.48*
Vegetables	.01	.11	.35	.12	.14	−.29	−.3	−.25	−.09	.30	.51*	.53*	.23	−.38	−.17	−.32	−.11
Vehicles	.11	−.00	.08	.02	.12	−.13	−.24	−.14	−.19	.32	.48*	.33	.50*	−.41*	−.31	−.11	−.25
Weapons	.33	−.06	.03	.16	.10	−.19	−.13	−.36	−.24	.48	.48	.60*	.52*	−.39	−.22	−.63*	−.28

Table 5. Leuven Concept Data Correlation Table by Domain - Exemplar Feature Importance Ratings ranked sample 10 percent

domain	A1	A2	A3	A4	A5	A6	A7	A8	A9	B1	B2	B3	B4	B5	B6	B7	B8
Birds	.54*	.86***	.72**	.65**	.77***	−.68**	−.55*	−.36	−.54*	.53*	.59*	.58*	.56*	−.32	−.33	−.25	−.20
Clothing	.05	.7**	.57*	.48	.79***	−.38	−.40	−.32	−.44	.32	.05	.50	.31	−.42	−.31	−.56*	−.48
Fish	.33	.66	.75*	.14	.82*	−.54	−.61	−.39	−.44	.69	.57	.88**	.68	−.64	−.34	−.76*	−.66
Fruit	.50	.64*	.65*	.61*	.43	−.53	−.45	−.35	−.35	.77**	.83***	.69*	.71**	−.61*	−.77**	−.54	−.63*
Insects	.24	.71	.89**	.82*	.64	−.24	−.63	−.50	−.58	.32	.19	.30	−.11	−.55	.04	−.25	.35
Kitchenutensils	.29	−.03	−.03	−.04	−.08	−.21	−.24	.14	.13	−.02	.32	.21	.16	−.08	−.38	.01	.15
Mammals	.43	−.16	−.13	.23	.07	−.27	−.13	−.27	−.32	−.01	.09	.2	.17	−.10	−.10	−.06	−.04
Musicalinstruments	.03	−.09	.01	.40	−.14	.16	.33	.08	.07	.26	.62	.61	.7	.26	.01	−.60	−.08
Professions	.50	−.44	−.54	−.45	−.37	.54	.80	.88*	.73	−.70	−.73	−.91*	−.19	.93**	.78	.81	.29
Reptiles	.27	−.07	.18	.25	.19	.12	−.11	−.14	−.15	.61	.70*	.76*	.69*	−.41	−.16	−.33	−.40
Sports	−.35	.08	.11	.01	.04	−.28	−.34	−.37	−.32	.58	.49	.72*	.61*	−.26	−.37	−.39	−.26
Tools	.39	.60*	.43	.45	.60*	−.62*	−.17	−.10	−.53	.78**	.78**	.78**	.78**	−.59*	−.44	−.63*	−.57
Vegetables	.52	.12	.59*	.50	.59*	−.37	−.37	−.38	−.27	.05	.68*	.27	.23	−.08	−.53	−.36	−.32
Vehicles	.48	.36	.40	.59	.47	−.47	−.40	−.47	−.47	.80**	.90***	.86***	.73*	−.51	−.79**	−.67*	−.54
Weapons	.59*	.07	.15	.41	.33	−.09	−.03	−.31	−.28	.28	−.02	.28	.43	−.36	−.01	−.46	−.45

Table 6. Leuven Concept Data Correlation Table by Domain - Category

domain	A1	A2	A3	A4	A5	A6	A7	A8	A9	B1	B2	B3	B4	B5	B6	B7	B8
Birds	.62***	.36	.39*	.45*	.38*	−.26	−.25	−.32	−.21	.47*	.53**	.58**	.56**	−.32	−.24	−.28	−.39*
Clothing	.28	.38*	.24	.13	.31	−.33*	−.25	−.18	−.30	.30	.19	.28	.14	−.44**	−.29	−.35*	−.22
Fish	.34	.15	.30	.21	.24	−.04	−.12	−.07	−.11	.54**	.45*	.61***	.53**	−.55**	−.26	−.47**	−.55**
Fruit	.54**	−.10	−.25	−.03	−.27	.02	.11	.12	.26	−.37*	−.41*	−.17	−.42*	.01	.08	.14	.16
Insects	.25	.34*	.34*	.35*	.18	−.27	−.19	−.23	−.19	.21	.37*	.55***	.37*	−.25	−.63***	−.66***	−.43**
Kitchenutensils	.53***	.33*	.17	.30	.30	−.20	−.10	−.23	−.17	.46**	.38*	.32*	.43**	−.43**	−.37*	−.35*	−.12
Mammals	.46**	−.07	−.06	−.07	.01	.15	.16	.18	.12	.36*	.29	.37*	.34	−.42*	−.29	−.25	−.41*
Musicalinstruments	.41*	.06	.16	.30	.29	−.06	−.13	−.26	−.12	.42**	.43**	.33*	.53***	−.27	−.44**	−.11	−.47**
Professions	.35	.18	.21	.34	.25	−.10	−.16	−.25	−.16	.54*	.53*	.54*	.61**	−.35	−.22	−.42	−.25
Reptiles	.54***	.22	.49**	.43**	.24	−.07	−.30	−.13	−.12	.19	.38*	.33	.23	−.07	−.33	−.31	−.17
Sports	.39*	−.32	−.37*	−.31	−.35*	.10	.31	.24	.27	−.30	−.42*	−.38*	−.40*	.18	.33	.37*	.23
Tools	.18	.32	.40*	.28	.52**	−.35*	−.37*	−.15	−.44**	.65***	.66***	.59***	.56***	−.46**	−.50**	−.44**	−.51**
Vegetables	.39*	−.29	−.09	−.09	−.29	−.12	−.05	−.06	−.18	−.20	.07	−.02	.02	.03	−.15	−.28	−.19
Vehicles	.46**	.22	.18	.25	.27	.04	−.02	−.05	−.17	.29	.34*	.32	.21	.08	−.15	−.09	−.09
Weapons	.46**	−.02	−.08	−.13	.02	−.19	.15	.26	−.21	−.11	−.13	−.18	−.13	.08	.09	.40*	−.08

Table 7. Correlation analysis (detailed)

variables correlation	frequency			importance		
	med	min	max	med	min	max
importance (1:n) exe	.32	.26	.43	-	-	-
importance (1:n) exe10r	.64	.64	.64	-	-	-
importance (1:n) exe10f	.67	.66	.68	-	-	-
importance (1:n) exe10i	.54	.54	.54	-	-	-
importance (1:n) cat	.50	.46	.62	-	-	-
importance (n:m) exe	.25	.20	.42	-	-	-
importance (n:m) exe10r	.52	.38	.65	-	-	-
importance (n:m) exe10f	.42	.42	.43	-	-	-
importance (n:m) exe10i	.59	.59	.59	-	-	-
importance (n:m) cat	.46	.41	.53	-	-	-
importance (any) exe	.27	.17	.43	-	-	-
importance (any) exe10r	.56	.38	.65	-	-	-
importance (any) exe10f	.55	.42	.68	-	-	-
importance (any) exe10i	.56	.54	.59	-	-	-
importance (any) cat	.46	.39	.62	-	-	-
AD1 (1:n) exe	.39	.16	.50	.48	.27	.65
AD1 (1:n) exe10r	.56	.39	.68	.55	.41	.60
AD1 (1:n) exe10f	.68	.51	.85	.65	.50	.75
AD1 (1:n) exe10i	.79	.65	.89	.64	.53	.88
AD1 (1:n) cat	.39	.34	.49	.50	.36	.61
AD1 (n:m) exe	.29	.19	.42	.48	.36	.61
AD1 (n:m) exe10r	.50	.36	.63	.53	.41	.68
AD1 (n:m) exe10f	.49	.44	.55	.54	.41	.73
AD1 (n:m) exe10i	.60	.57	.79	.78	.73	.90
AD1 (n:m) cat	.39	.33	.52	.43	.32	.66
AD1 (any) exe	.29	.16	.5	.46	−.31	.65
AD1 (any) exe10r	.51	.33	.68	.54	−.4	.75
AD1 (any) exe10f	.56	.44	.85	.56	−.56	.75
AD1 (any) exe10i	.68	.57	.89	.72	−.91	.9
AD1 (any) cat	.38	−.37	.52	.45	−.42	.66
AD2 (1:n) exe	−.19	−.30	−.15	−.30	−.46	−.20
AD2 (1:n) exe10r	−.44	−.47	−.39	−.50	−.52	−.40
AD2 (1:n) exe10f	.00	.00	.00	−.56	−.74	−.45
AD2 (1:n) exe10i	−.61	−.68	−.54	−.76	−.76	−.76
AD2 (1:n) cat	.00	.00	.00	−.47	−.66	−.39
AD2 (n:m) exe	−.16	−.25	−.14	−.32	−.41	−.16
AD2 (n:m) exe10r	−.45	−.50	−.40	−.50	−.63	−.37
AD2 (n:m) exe10f	.00	.00	.00	−.51	−.63	−.41
AD2 (n:m) exe10i	−.62	−.62	−.62	−.63	−.79	−.56
AD2 (n:m) cat	−.36	−.44	−.33	−.44	−.51	.4
AD2 (any) exe	−.17	−.30	−.10	−.30	−.46	.26
AD2 (any) exe10r	−.40	−.50	−.34	−.47	−.63	.56
AD2 (any) exe10f	.00	.00	.00	−.52	−.74	.72
AD2 (any) exe10i	−.55	−.68	.88	−.63	−.79	.93
AD2 (any) cat	−.36	−.44	−.33	−.44	−.66	.40

References

1. Ashcraft, M.H.: Property dominance and typicality effects in property statement verification. J. Verb. Learn. Verb. Behav. **17**, 155–164 (1978)
2. Belohlavek, R., Macko, J.: Selecting important concepts using weights. In: Valtchev, P., Jäschke, R. (eds.) ICFCA 2011. LNCS (LNAI), vol. 6628, pp. 65–80. Springer, Heidelberg (2011). https://doi.org/10.1007/978-3-642-20514-9_7
3. Bělohlávek, R., Sklenář, V.: Formal concept analysis constrained by attribute-dependency formulas. In: Ganter, B., Godin, R. (eds.) ICFCA 2005. LNCS (LNAI), vol. 3403, pp. 176–191. Springer, Heidelberg (2005). https://doi.org/10.1007/978-3-540-32262-7_12
4. Belohlavek, R., Vychodil, V.: Formal concept analysis with background knowledge: attribute priorities. IEEE Trans. Syst. Man Cybern. Part C **39**(4), 399–409 (2009). https://doi.org/10.1109/TSMCC.2008.2012168
5. Ceulemans, E., Storms, G.: Detecting intra-and inter-categorical structure in semantic concepts using HICLAS. Acta Psychologica **133**(3), 296–304 (2010)
6. De Boeck, P., Rosenberg, S.: Hierarchical classes: model and data analysis. Psychometrika **53**(3), 361–381 (1988)
7. De Deyne, S., et al.: Exemplar by feature applicability matrices and other Dutch normative data for semantic concepts. Behav. Res. Methods **40**, 1030–1048 (2008)
8. Dry, M.J., Storms, G.: Features of graded category structure: generalizing the family resemblance and polymorphous concept models. Acta Psychologica **133**(3), 244–255 (2010)
9. Dry, M.J., Storms, G.: Similar but not the same: a comparison of the utility of directly rated and feature-based similarity measures for generating spatial models of conceptual data. Behav. Res. Methods **41**(3), 889–900 (2009)
10. Durrant, R.J., Kabán, A.: When is 'nearest neighbour' meaningful: a converse theorem and implications. J. Complex. **25**(4), 385–397 (2009)
11. Dürrschnabel, D., Koyda, M., Stumme, G.: Attribute selection using contranominal scales. In: Braun, T., Gehrke, M., Hanika, T., Hernandez, N. (eds.) ICCS 2021. LNCS (LNAI), vol. 12879, pp. 127–141. Springer, Cham (2021). https://doi.org/10.1007/978-3-030-86982-3_10
12. Ganter, B., Wille, R.: Formal Concept Analysis: Mathematical Foundations. Springer (2012)
13. Hampton, J.A.: Inheritance of attributes in natural concept conjunctions. Mem. Cogn. **15**(1), 55–71 (1987)
14. Hampton, J.A.: Polymorphous concepts in semantic memory. J. Verb. Learn. Verb. Behav. **18**(4), 441–461 (1979)
15. Hanika, T., Hille, T.: What is the intrinsic dimension of your binary data?–and how to compute it quickly. In: Cabrera, I.P., Ferré, S., Obiedkov, S. (eds.) CONCEPTS 2024. LNCS, vol. 14914, pp. 97–112. Springer, Cham (2024). https://doi.org/10.1007/978-3-031-67868-4_7
16. Hanika, T., Koyda, M., Stumme, G.: Relevant attributes in formal contexts. In: Endres, D., Alam, M., Şotropa, D. (eds.) ICCS 2019. LNCS (LNAI), vol. 11530, pp. 102–116. Springer, Cham (2019). https://doi.org/10.1007/978-3-030-23182-8_8
17. Hanika, T., Schneider, F.M., Stumme, G.: Intrinsic dimension of geometric data sets (2022)
18. Kuznetsov, S.O.: On computing the size of a lattice and related decision problems. Order **18**(4), 313–321 (2001)

19. McRae, K., et al.: Semantic feature production norms for a large set of living and nonliving things. Behav. Res. Methods **37**(4), 547–559 (2005)
20. Navarro, D.J., Perfors, A.F.: Similarity, feature discovery, and the size principle. Acta Psychologica **133**(3), 256–268 (2010)
21. Pestov, V.: Intrinsic dimension of a dataset: what properties does one expect? In: IJCNN 2007, pp. 2959–2964. IEEE (2007)
22. Rosch, E., Mervis, C.B.: Family resemblances: studies in the internal structure of categories. Cogn. Psychol. **7**, 573–605 (1975)
23. Ruts, W., et al.: Dutch norm data for 13 semantic categories and 338 exemplars. Behav. Res. Methods Instrum. Comput. **36**(3), 506–515 (2004)
24. Snášel, V., et al.: On concept lattices and implication bases from reduced contexts. ICCS Suppl. **8**, 83–90 (2008)
25. Storms, G., De Boeck, P.: Formal models for intracategorical structure that can be used for data-analysis. In: Lamberts, K., Shanks, D. (eds.) Knowledge, Concepts, and Categories, pp. 439–459. UCL Press, London (1997)
26. Storms, G., Mechelen, I.V., Boeck, P.D.: Structural analysis of the intension and extension of semantic concepts. Eur. J. Cogn. Psychol. **6**(1), 43–75 (1994)
27. Storms, G., et al.: Dominance and noncommutativity effects in concept conjunctions: extensional or intensional basis? Mem. Cogn. **21**(6), 752–762 (1993)
28. Tatti, N., et al.: What is the dimension of your binary data? In: Sixth International Conference on Data Mining (ICDM 2006), pp. 603–612. IEEE (2006)
29. Tversky, A.: Features of similarity. Psychol. Rev. **84**(4), 327 (1977)
30. Tversky, B., Hemenway, K.: Objects, parts, and categories. J. Exp. Psychol. Gen. **113**(2), 169 (1984)
31. Verheyen, S., Ameel, E., Storms, G.: Determining the dimensionality in spatial representations of semantic concepts. Behav. Res. Methods **39**, 427–438 (2007)
32. Verheyen, S., Storms, G.: A mixture approach to vagueness and ambiguity. PLoS ONE **8**(5), e63507 (2013)
33. Verheyen, S., White, A., Égré, P.: Revealing criterial vagueness in inconsistencies. Open Mind **3**, 41–51 (2019)
34. Wille, R.: Formal concept analysis as mathematical theory of concepts and concept hierarchies. In: Ganter, B., Stumme, G., Wille, R. (eds.) Formal Concept Analysis. LNCS (LNAI), vol. 3626, pp. 1–33. Springer, Heidelberg (2005). https://doi.org/10.1007/11528784_1
35. Wille, R.: Restructuring lattice theory: an approach based on hierarchies of concepts. In: Ferré, S., Rudolph, S. (eds.) ICFCA 2009. LNCS (LNAI), vol. 5548, pp. 314–339. Springer, Heidelberg (2009). https://doi.org/10.1007/978-3-642-01815-2_23
36. Zadeh, L.A.: Fuzzy sets. Inf. Control **8**(3), 338–353 (1965)
37. Zimek, A., Schubert, E., Kriegel, H.-P.: A survey on unsupervised outlier detection in high-dimensional numerical data. Stat. Anal. Data Mining ASA Data Sci. J. **5**(5), 363–387 (2012)

Moregraph: Metadata-Driven Enterprise Architecture Using Conceptual Structures

Simon Polovina[1,2](✉), Richard Fallon[3], and Mahpara Saleem[4]

[1] Department of Computing and Digital Technologies, Sheffield Hallam University, Sheffield, UK
S.Polovina@shu.ac.uk
[2] Simile Logics Limited, Sheffield, UK
simon@similelogics.ltd
[3] Red Rooster IT, Vienna, Austria
richard@fallon.at
[4] Mahaz Tech Enterprise Limited (MTE), Manchester, UK
mahpara@mahaztechenterprise.com

Abstract. Enterprise Architecture (EA) enables organisations to articulate their business purpose, from strategy to execution, without incurring technical debt. Data infrastructures underpin their EA, enabling organisations to derive their purpose from their data landscape. Metadata, a crucial aspect of this infrastructure, is a human construct that gives meaning to the data and shapes the organisation's EA. The data objects referenced by metadata, however, are usually encapsulated inside applications. The Moregraph application visualises the data objects and their relations, unrestricted by application boundaries, thus allowing the data objects to express their semantics directly at a more precise level of granularity. Conceptual Graphs are used to maintain the requirements for Moregraph's conceptual structure, which is then implemented using SAP Graph to access the data objects in SAP Business Accelerator Hub. As these data objects are clean core, they can be extended or compared by organisations to address their technical debt at the same level of granularity, with further opportunities for application and Application Programming Interface (API) rationalisation. From these experiences alongside SAP as the representative case study, Moregraph advances metadata-driven enterprise architecture and informs the direction of future work.

Keywords: Enterprise Architecture · Technical Debt · Metadata · Data Object · Clean Core · Conceptual Graphs · Business Data Graphs · SAP Graph

1 Introduction

Enterprise Architecture (EA) recognises that enterprises arise from and are sustained by human endeavours that recognise market or societal gaps. To meet the challenges of these gaps, enterprises become organisations with defined business roles and processes. EA functions enable organisations to articulate their

P. Cellier et al. (Eds.): CONCEPTS 2025, LNAI 15941, pp. 91–106, 2025.
https://doi.org/10.1007/978-3-032-03364-2_6

humanly defined business purpose and align their strategy, structure, and systems to fulfil that purpose, ensuring that all these assets optimally contribute [9]. These assets include the IT (Information Technology) landscape, notorious for its technical debt. This debt is the present-day, light-speed, digital-era organisational debt classically known as bureaucracy [2,6]. Computers bring productivity to human creativity that characterises the enterprise, hence IT's success, but at the potential cost of technical debt. Solution Architecture aligns IT with human creativity, as articulated in the organisation's Business Architecture, under EA's overall control, to address this issue[1]. In this overall landscape, data is pivotal.

Furthermore, metadata sets the data context. For example, the data in Electronic Medical Records (EMR) in healthcare is complex. Therefore, EMR uses metadata to make healthcare data intelligible [20]. Indeed, the metamodel that underpins EA itself is based on metadata, as it is itself an entity-relationship diagram that illuminates the pathways between strategy and technology and is elegantly depicted by LeanIX's metamodel diagram [11]. Metadata describes a business's understanding of enterprise data through data objects [7,14]. Metadata is ultimately a human construct, capturing the mindset of business stakeholders and employees in their roles, which collectively define the purpose of an enterprise as a human endeavour; hence, metadata's value to EA.

The paper is thus organised as follows. The research question is identified and justified, supported by a single-case study research method, which is exemplified by the selection of SAP as the case study. Moregraph and its ability to address technical debt through clean core metadata integration in Solution Architecture are introduced. Moregraph's conceptual structure leverages Conceptual Graphs, which capture Moregraph's requirements, specifications, and updates. This conceptual structure motivated the development of the Moregraph application, which included the selection of SAP Graph, SAP's Business Hub Accelerator, and consideration of alternatives outside SAP, to demonstrate metadata-driven Enterprise Architecture (EA). Related research, current limitations and future work are discussed, culminating in the paper's research contributions in its concluding remarks, followed by the references.

2 Research Method

2.1 Research Question

Our research question is "How can Moregraph better drive Clean Core Strategy through Metadata-driven Enterprise Architecture?". This question focuses on the role of Moregraph in achieving clean core, which is a modern approach to maintaining system reliability while enabling agility and digital transformation. Clean core strategies are therefore increasingly important for organisations

[1] For more background information about EA, there is a helpful resource at https://www.leanix.net/en/blog/enterprise-architecture-terms-to-know-glossary. Although this content is from a vendor, it provides a lucid glossary of EA and its terminology across all its dimensions without being overly product-biased. For example, we refer to the Data Object derived from that glossary alongside many others.

looking to minimise customisations within their core systems while leveraging cloud-based solutions. The likely or intended impacts include Moregraph driving clean core, through metadata-driven enterprise architecture, providing valuable insights into improving system efficiency, reducing technical debt, and enhancing scalability.

2.2 Case Study

In support of our research question, we selected a single-case study research method, as it enabled us to advance the theory and its practical application within a single case, rather than managing across multiple cases. Related research, such as the value co-creation of AI in industrial markets through a single case study in healthcare, underscores these benefits [12]. SAP's Business Technology Platform (BTP) was the single case study in research that examined the role of knowledge boundary resources in platform ecosystems [8].

We also chose SAP as the case study for our topic due to its market-leading significance and leadership in the enterprise software industry. SAP's comprehensive suite of applications and services provides a robust platform for business and technological innovations, as well as best practices that extend beyond SAP to the broader business computing ecosystem, such as via its Business Technology Platform (BTP). SAP's 2024 Annual Report[2] showed a total revenue of €32.5 billion, marking a 9% increase from the previous year. The cloud segment achieved €14.2 billion in revenue, up by 18% year-over-year. SAP serves over 440,000 customers in more than 180 countries. The company invests €4.5 billion in research and development. Additionally, SAP's sustainability initiatives, including a 30% reduction in greenhouse gas emissions compared to 2020, highlight its dedication to responsible business practices.

Our evaluation covered all the data objects that are publicly available in the SAP Business Accelerator Hub's Graph Navigator[3]. The number of data objects in that resource comprises SAP SuccessFactors (sap.hcm, 999), SAP S/4HANA ERP (sap.s4, 1479), and SAP Cloud for Customer (sap.c4c, 2027)[4]. The sum of these data objects is $999 + 1479 + 2027 = 4505$. These objects encompass most of SAP's central systems, thereby providing a representative, enterprise-scale metadataset of data objects on which to base our study. As they are documented in SAP Business Accelerator Hub, they are all clean core. SAP Graph (sap.graph) adds a further 55 data objects that interconnect the 4505 clean core data objects, bringing the total to 4560. We intentionally added another small number of custom data objects (6) as a simple test of how the 4560 data objects can be accessed with custom-coded data objects outside of the clean core without incurring technical debt.

[2] https://www.sap.com/investors/.

[3] https://api.sap.com/graph.

[4] An overview of these systems can be found at https://www.sap.com/products/hcm.html, https://www.sap.com/uk/products/erp.html, and https://support.sap.com/en/alm/solution-manager/expert-portal/public-cloud-operations/sap-hybris-cloud-for-customer.html, respectively.

Given all the above, SAP is an exemplary subject for a detailed and informative case study.

3 Moregraph

The Moregraph application identifies data objects across and within applications, thereby revealing technical debt at a more precise level of granularity, as it is unrestricted by application boundaries. To convey Moregraph's essence and how it fulfils this purpose, Fig. 1 depicts Moregraph's conceptual structure as a Conceptual Graph.

3.1 Moregraph's Conceptual Structure

Arising from Sowa's original work and as part of the wider endeavour in Conceptual Structures [18], Conceptual Graphs enable humans to draw concepts intuitively while developing the underlying complex relationships at both logical and mathematical levels. Their graphical nature makes them accessible to both humans and machines, combining human creativity with computer productivity for knowledge representation, reasoning, and artificial intelligence. They have multiple modern-day interpretations [3, 13,15]. The Conceptual Graph shown by Fig. 1 was produced to capture the requirements for Moregraph. This graph enables the key concepts that comprise Moregraph to be captured expressively, with each concept in Fig. 1 documented as follows. Taken together, Moregraph's formal purpose is revealed.

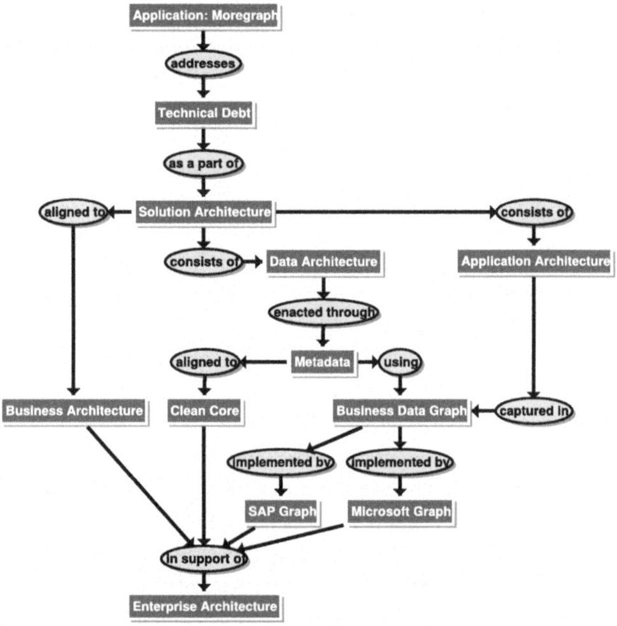

Fig. 1. Moregraph as a Conceptual Graph.

Technical Debt. As stated earlier, Moregraph's modus operandi investigates technical debt by interconnecting data objects from multiple applications that do not hinder the investigation, adopting **Clean Core** as described shortly.

Solution Architecture, Business Architecture, and Enterprise Architecture (EA). Moregraph aligns Solution to Business Architecture concepts in support of EA, the culminating concept in Fig. 1. **Solution Architecture** consists of **Data Architecture** and **Application Architecture**, with a pathway from **Data Architecture** to **Metadata**, described earlier and **Clean Core**, which is described next.

Clean Core. In software engineering, "clean core" leverages clean code [10]. Clean core refers to a design philosophy where the central, essential part of a software system is kept simple, well-organised, and free from unnecessary complexity. Clean core refines clean code into reusable code that any enterprise can leverage, as all enterprises share a common structure and do not need to customise more than 5% of the code in their IT systems. The other 95% is not unique, as 80% is code that is generic to all enterprises, such as accounting or human resources and in the purchasing-to-sales cycle. Industry-specific software accounts for the other 15%, which covers functionalities tailored to the specific needs of an industry sector. For example, a healthcare organisation might need software for patient management, whereas a retail business might need inventory management systems. While these percentages are not hard and fast, they reflect a common understanding in contemporary enterprise software development [1]. Clean core, therefore, significantly reduces development time and costs. Customising only the necessary parts allows enterprises to focus their resources on areas that truly differentiate them. This technical debt risk is simultaneously reduced to at most 5% of the organisation's IT landscape. Clean core furthermore extends the core, rather than modifying it, thus not breaking the core itself. Equally, updates to the core do not break the customisation extensions, forming an implementable contract that further avoids technical debt, which becomes even less than 5%, especially if 'no' or 'low' code alternatives to full custom coding are adopted [19]. A clean core enables future updates and migrations (e.g., from on-premise solutions to the Cloud) to be completed with fewer technical issues. The success of clean core is exemplified in an industrial context by SAP [17]. Moregraph takes clean core to the finer-grained data object level of granularity, demonstrated in Sect. 4.

Business Data Graph, and SAP Graph. SAP Graph is a Business Data Graph because it provides a unified API for accessing data objects across SAP and non-SAP systems and applications, reflecting a connected graph of business data objects [4]. SAP Graph identifies opportunities for simplifying API management, as the other APIs can be encapsulated and replaced by SAP Graph's navigation with fewer APIs, thus making API rationalisation possible. SAP Graph's focus is on the **Data Architecture**-oriented data objects in place of the applications where those objects happen to be processed. **Application Architecture** is also captured as shown in Fig. 1 because SAP Graph adds the application name as a metadata attribute to a data object. These features are demonstrated in

Sect. 4. **Microsoft Graph** is another example of Business Data Graphs, which are not SAP-specific.

3.2 Moregraph's Application Architecture

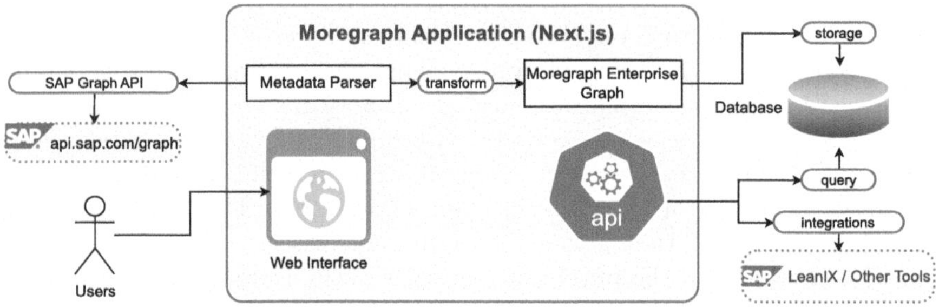

Fig. 2. Moregraph's Application Architecture.

The implementation of the Moregraph application is scoped by the Conceptual Graph in Fig. 1 and the definitions provided in Subsect. 3.1. Fig 2 depicts Moregraph's application architecture. The Moregraph application is built using *Next.js*, a React framework for creating high-performance, feature-rich web applications, and *TypeScript*, a language designed for developing large-scale applications. These choices enable Moregraph to focus on integrating and visualising enterprise data objects by connecting to SAP Graph APIs. Additionally, to demonstrate connectivity with other applications, it integrates with SAP LeanIX, but is not limited to SAP applications. The system ingests metadata, transforms it into an enterprise graph, and stores it in a PostgreSQL database for querying and interaction through a web interface and API layer. It features the following components:

1. **SAP Graph API Integration**. The application connects to the SAP Graph API in the SAP Business Accelerator Hub's Graph Navigator, referred to earlier, and fetches enterprise metadata from the 4505 data objects across three core SAP applications interconnected by SAP Graph's 55 data objects. This metadata is ingested in raw form and passed to the internal parsing system. Future planned work includes other APIs, such as Microsoft Graph[5].
2. **Metadata Parser**. This component parses the incoming metadata from the SAP Graph API. It leverages SAP Graph's interconnectivity and normalises the data objects and relationships into a canonical format suitable for graph construction. The metadata parser also handles mapping and cleansing logic to prepare for graph generation.

[5] https://learn.microsoft.com/en-us/graph/overview.

3. **Moregraph Enterprise Graph.** This component converts the parsed metadata into an internal graph structure that represents the data objects, applications, and interdependencies. It performs transformation logic to structure data as a directed, typed graph, and encapsulates core graph logic and domain relationships.
4. **Database.** The enterprise graphs are stored in a relational schema within a PostgreSQL database layer that supports the efficient querying of nodes, edges, and metadata properties.
5. **API.** The Application Programming Interface (API) layer exposes the enterprise graphs and related data via RESTful APIs. It handles authentication, business logic, and orchestrates database queries. It also mediates between the frontend and external integrations, such as LeanIX.
6. **LeanIX Integration.** The API interface with SAP LeanIX enables the creation of Data Objects and their associated applications in the LeanIX EA software tool[6]. Alternatively, Moregraph can export content as Excel spreadsheets in a format that can be imported into LeanIX or tailored for import to other tools. We have also explored and piloted an earlier integration with the Essential Project, an open-source non-SAP EA tool, with initial success that we plan to take forward [16].
7. **Web Interface.** Using Next.js frontend capabilities, enhanced with UI5 Web Components through a React wrapper[7], Moregraph produces dynamic web pages for end-users to query the enterprise graph that the application automatically visualises, explore metadata, and discover further insights, including clean core.

4 Demonstration

As shown by Fig. 2 and the narrative supplied in Sect. 3.2, the Moregraph application ingested the publicly available, clean core reference architecture documented in SAP's Business Hub Accelerator (*api.sap.com*). Together with SAP Graph, Moregraph interconnects the three pivotal SAP systems and all their data objects described in Sect. 2.2. These applications were: 1) sap.s4: SAP S/4HANA ERP (Enterprise Resource Planning), 2) sap.c4c: SAP Sales & Service Cloud CRM (Customer Relationship Management), and 3) sap.hcm: SAP SuccessFactors HCM (Human Capital Management).

4.1 Navigating the Clean Core

Figure 3 shows an extract of the resulting visualisation instantiated with the interconnected 4560 data objects (sap.graph, sap.s4, sap.c4c, and sap.hcm) and the flow directions between each data object.

[6] https://docs-eam.leanix.net/reference/available-apis.
[7] https://github.com/SAP/ui5-webcomponents-react.

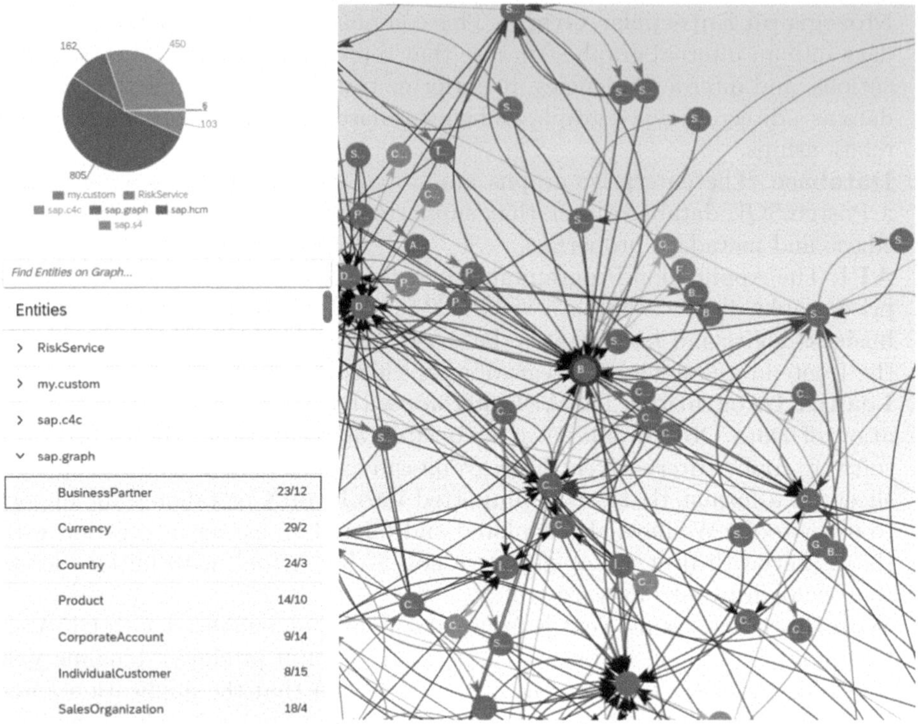

Fig. 3. Moregraph's visualisation from api.sap.com

Figure 4 shows a *drill-down* into one of these data objects: BusinessPartner. The figure reveals that Moregraph, through SAP Graph, has interlinked the corresponding data object A_BusinessPartner in sap.s4: S/4HANA and BusinessPartnerCollection in sap.c4c: SAP Sales & Service Cloud.

When we select A_BusinessPartner in sap.s4 or BusinessPartnerCollection in sap:c4c, the navigation takes us into the heart of these systems, as shown by Fig. 5 and Fig. 6, respectively. While both figures primarily consist of the colour coding of those systems, the interconnections with sap.graph with its colour coding remain evident in both figures, including the pie chart on the left-hand side. A similar exercise from BusinessUser would point to the sap.hcm data objects, shown in Fig. 7.

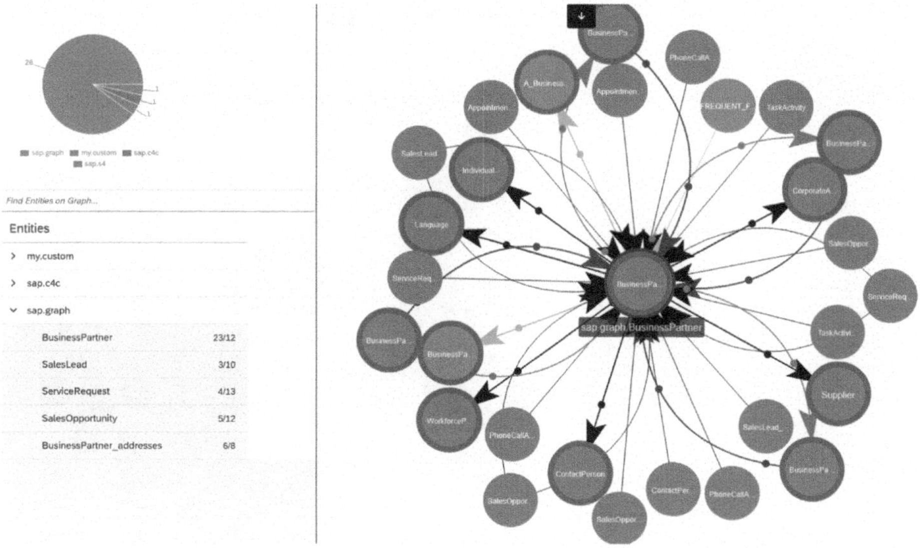

Fig. 4. Drill-down to the sap.graph BusinessPartner Data Object

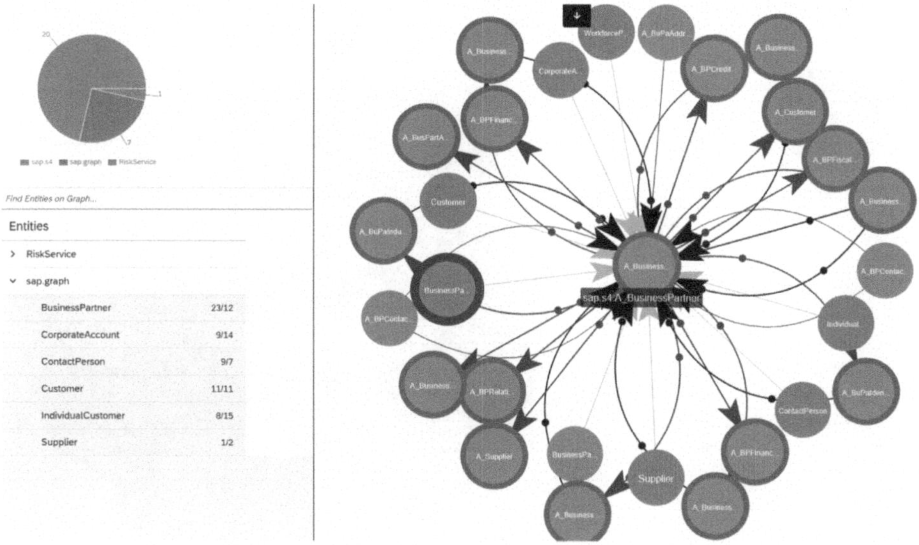

Fig. 5. Drill-down to the sap.s4 A_BusinessPartner Data Object

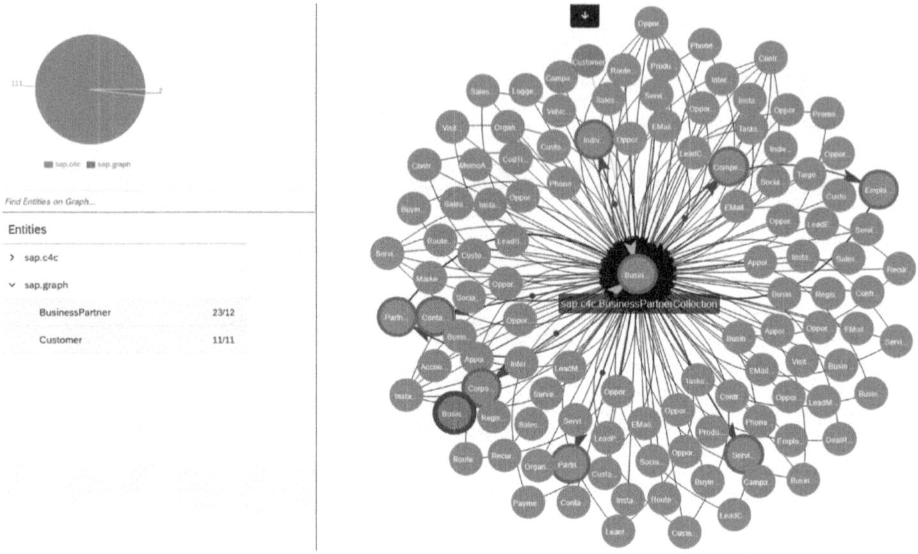

Fig. 6. Drill-down to the sap.c4c BusinessPartnerCollection Data Object

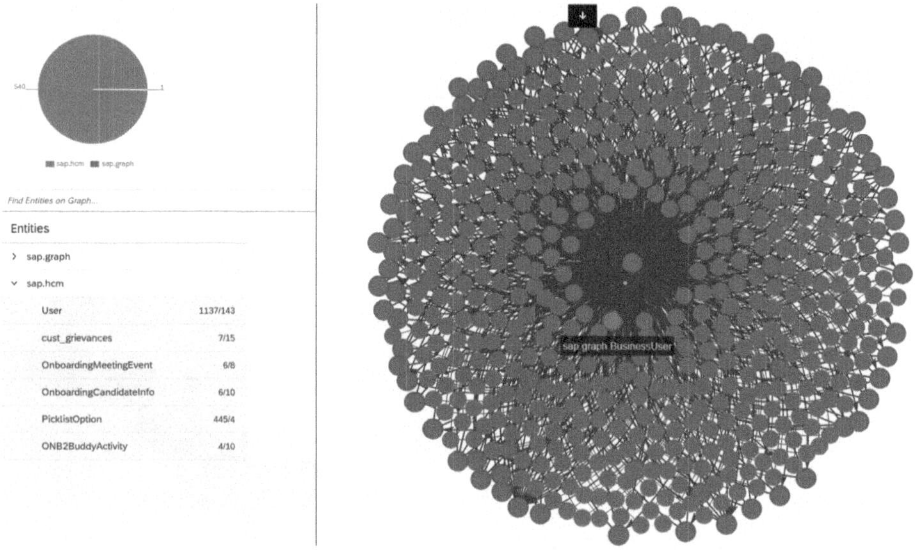

Fig. 7. Drill-down from the sap.graph BusinessUser Data Object to sap.hcm

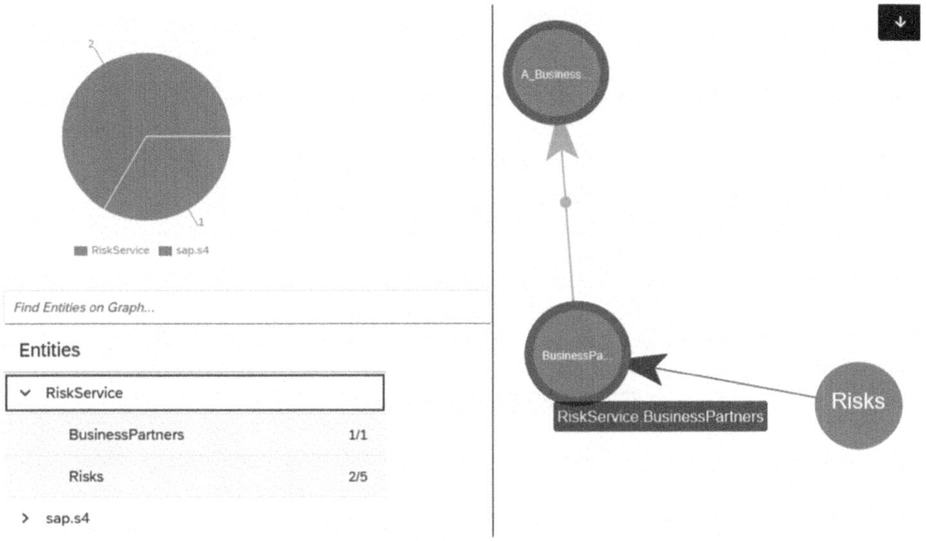

Fig. 8. sap.s4 RiskService extension

4.2 Extending the Clean Core

The link to a custom non-SAP FREQUENT_FLYER application shown towards the top-right and in the pie chart of Fig. 4 demonstrates a use case where SAP Graph, hence Moregraph, is not restricted to SAP systems. Notably, the link is clean core as this custom application has *not* modified the BusinessPartner data object. We similarly linked a custom extension to RiskService from A_BusinessPartner in S/4HANA[8]. Figure 8 illustrates this extension, which is linked from Fig. 5 and is visible towards the bottom right of that diagram and the associated pie chart. Unlike FREQUENT_FLYER, which is an application in its own right, RiskService modifies A_BusinessPartner by extending it, thus following the clean core strategy articulated by SAP [17]. This extension has likewise not modified the core.

4.3 A Pathway to Clean Core

With the above Sects. 4.1 and 4.2 in mind, we considered data objects in typical organisational landscapes that were not clean core to identify a pathway to how they could become clean core. One such exemplar is shown in Listing 1.1

Listing 1.1. Product example that's not Clean Core

```
<edmx:DataServices ...>
  <Schema Namespace="SEPMRA_PROD_MAN"... />
```

[8] This example is taken from https://learning.sap.com/learning-journeys/build-side-by-side-extensions-on-sap-btp.

```
    <EntityType Name="Product">
      <Key>
        <PropertyRef Name="ProductID"/>
      </Key>
      <Property Name="ProductID" ... />
      <Property Name="Name" ... />
      <Property Name="Price" ... />
      <!-- Custom Field added directly into standard object -->
      <Property Name="LegacySystemFlag" ... />
    </EntityType>
    <EntityContainer Name="SEPMRA_PROD_MAN_Entities">
      <!-- Overwriting standard EntitySet -->
      <EntitySet Name="Products"
          EntityType="SEPMRA_PROD_MAN.Product" ... />
    </EntityContainer>
  </Schema>
</edmx:DataServices>
```

The XML extract depicted in Listing 1.1 highlights a typical situation where a) a custom field has been directly added (`LegacySystemFlag` in this case), and b) an entity type has been overwritten (`SEPMRA_PROD_MAN.Product` in this case), causing mutable access to the standard data create/update/delete operations on SAP-delivered data objects. It is evident from these two commonplace issues in a data object where a clean core-compliant metadata extension could replace that data object if it is to be retained, leading to its reconnection with the standard Product data object, thus reunited with the clean core 4560 data objects and visualised in Moregraph in the same way as shown by Fig. 8 for the RiskService extension.

4.4 Evaluation

Moregraph navigated to the individual data objects and applied clean core extensions at the metadata level, integrated custom applications, and included a pathway for hitherto non-clean core custom data objects. Notably, Moregraph can navigate through all the data objects, rather than being constrained by the broader application interfaces. This navigation level is akin to the Solution Data Flow Diagram familiar to EA[9].

Moregraph also provides an alternative means of reusing reference architecture content using the Business Hub Accelerator (api.sap.com/graph) alongside the capability or process-oriented methods in which that reference content is presently structured[10].

Furthermore, the existing capability or process-oriented reference architecture content also points to the same reference solution architecture at

[9] More specifically, in the SAP Enterprise Architecture Methodology Guide (https://help.sap.com/docs/SAP_ENTERPRISE_ARCHITECTURE_FRAMEWORK and search for 'Solution Data Flow Diagram').

[10] Refer to the previous footnote's link, but this time search for 'Reference Architecture Content'.

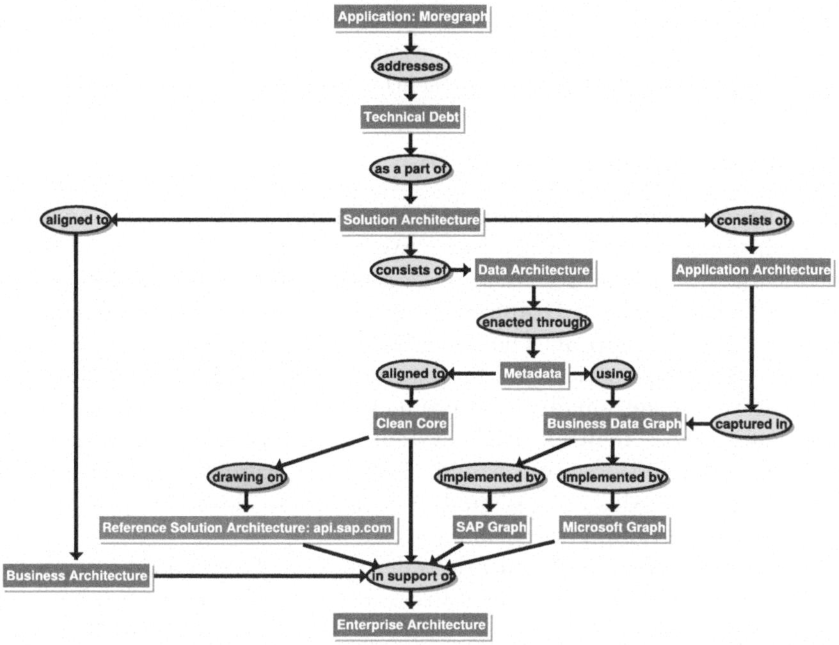

Fig. 9. Moregraph Conceptual Graph with the Reference Solution Architecture join.

api.sap.com, thereby demonstrating alignment with it when accessed through the novel metadata route. This new knowledge can be joined to the original Conceptual Graph in Fig. 1, resulting in Fig. 9, which highlights the new join. In the pursuit of addressing **Technical Debt**, Moregraph has consequently advanced **Clean Core** to **Data Architecture**, hence **Enterprise Architecture**, and added **Reference Solution Architecture: api.sap.com**.

5 Discussion

5.1 Related Research

Knowledge and property graphs were also considered powerful alternatives to SAP Graph. Knowledge graphs emphasise semantic relationships and use triples (such as subject-predicate-object) to manage and infer knowledge, often employing ontologies for precise data description. Property graphs represent entities and their relationships using nodes and edges, with properties attached to both, making them suitable for dynamic schema changes and complex queries. Moregraph, however, focused on SAP Graph as it is based on business data graphs. Business data graphs provide a unified API for accessing data objects across heterogeneous systems, simplifying data integration and enabling Moregraph to interconnect applications through their data objects, rather than managing complex data connections. Therefore, the convenience of SAP Graphs' generally available, wide-ranging implementation by SAP, together with the relative simplicity of business data graphs, presently meets Moregraph's needs.

5.2 Limitations and Future Work

While we have demonstrated Moregraph's research contribution, it has yet to be tested with other substantial use cases. We are in the early stages of two such industrial use cases. The first is an organisation that seeks the integration of SAP Graph with Microsoft Graph in its clean core journey, thus demonstrating Moregraph's broader appeal. The second allows another organisation to seamlessly interrogate their current data infrastructure at the data object level across the entire development, quality, and production (D/Q/P) software development life cycle and across multiple ERP systems resulting from the acquisition of other organisations. Moregraph would visually identify the data object differences (D/Q/P) from this use case and indicate where clean core principles have been adhered to, including the techniques shown in Sect. 4.

Like many others, both organisations desire to 'fit-to-standard', which means not revisiting what is already known. Instead, those risks are pushed back to the software vendor, e.g., SAP, who in turn has the opportunity to demonstrate that their standardised software does meet 95% of all their customers' needs through a rich, tested, and well-maintained common core. Customisations are then the exception rather than the norm, as organisations are freed to focus their IT budgets on their 5% core differentiating activities that distinguish their enterprise from the others in their industry sector.

Conceptual Graphs could potentially play a far bigger role in future work, as they emphasise logical structure in a human-digestible form, as lucidly depicted in Fig. 1. Similarly, Formal Concept Analysis with its mathematical underpinning can be used in conjunction with Conceptual Graphs [3], or from related work [5]. We will also explore how Artificial Intelligence (AI) agents can analyse the data objects of an organisation's landscape across all their SAP and non-SAP applications, thus aligning its non-clean core data objects with clean core opportunities as an automated service in Moregraph.

6 Concluding Remarks

The Moregraph application automatically visualises the data objects and their relations within and between applications. It offers the eradication of technical debt by enabling clean core to be applied to the detailed granularity of data objects within and across applications. While SAP Graph already identifies opportunities for rationalising APIs, Moregraph extends SAP Graph, and thus Business Data Graphs as a whole, to efficiently discover and display *all* the interconnected APIs and locate their data objects, as demonstrated in Sect. 4. Moregraph's navigations help to identify the deviances from standard data objects caused by an organisation's over-customised data objects outside of its distinctive

'5%'. As SAP Graph captures application information, and Moregraph can visualise all the interconnected data objects, it becomes possible to identify opportunities for both API and application rationalisation, where applications add too little or even negative value from their data objects, exposed by Moregraph.

These experiences facilitate the organisation's return to a fit-to-standard approach by establishing a clean core at the detailed Data Architecture level, as opposed to the Application Architecture level, where the application's boundaries encapsulate that detail, thus causing valuable insights to remain undiscovered. Moregraph's conceptual structure, implementation, and demonstration have begun the journey to advance Metadata-driven Enterprise Architecture (EA). It has set the direction for an organisation's journey toward eradicating technical debt and to advance it further through our future work.

Acknowledgments. The authors are grateful for the invaluable contributions towards this work made by Lorenzo Ramirez—additionally, Stephanie Lewellen and her colleagues who were on the SAP Graph beta program team at SAP. We also thank Truc Huynh and Zairul Jilani from the Department of Computing and Digital Technologies at Sheffield Hallam University through the local Digital Innovation for Growth (DIfG) programme.

Disclosure of Interests. The authors have no competing interests to declare relevant to this article's content.

References

1. Abendroth, A., Bender, B., Gronau, N.: The evolution of original ERP customization: a systematic literature review of technical possibilities. In: Proceedings of the 26th International Conference on Enterprise Information Systems, pp. 17–27. SCITEPRESS - Science and Technology Publications, Angers (2024). https://doi.org/10.5220/0012305500003690. https://www.scitepress.org/DigitalLibrary/Link.aspx?doi=10.5220/0012305500003690
2. Ahmad, M.O., Al-Baik, O.: Beyond technical debt unravelling organisational debt concept. In: Proceedings of the 39th ACM/SIGAPP Symposium on Applied Computing, SAC '24, pp. 802–809. Association for Computing Machinery, New York (2024). https://doi.org/10.1145/3605098.3635913
3. Andrews, S., Polovina, S.: Exploring, reasoning with and validating directed graphs by applying formal concept analysis to conceptual graphs. In: Croitoru, M., Marquis, P., Rudolph, S., Stapleton, G. (eds.) GKR 2017. LNCS (LNAI), vol. 10775, pp. 3–28. Springer, Cham (2018). https://doi.org/10.1007/978-3-319-78102-0_1. http://www.springer.com/gb/book/9783319781013
4. Bendelac, C.: Introduction to SAP Graph (2021). https://community.sap.com/t5/technology-blogs-by-sap/part-1-introduction-to-sap-graph/ba-p/13503946
5. Bendimerad, A., Mathonat, R., Remil, Y., Kaytoue, M.: Exploiting formal concept analysis for data modeling in data lakes. In: Cabrera, I.P., Ferré, S., Obiedkov, S. (eds.) Conceptual Knowledge Structures, pp. 270–285. Springer, Cham (2024). https://doi.org/10.1007/978-3-031-67868-4_18
6. Grinyer, P.H., Yasai-Ardekani, M.: Strategy, structure, size and bureaucracy. Acad. Manag. J. **24**(3), 471–486 (1981). https://doi.org/10.5465/255569. https://journals.aom.org/doi/abs/10.5465/255569

7. Inmon, W.H., O'Neil, B., Fryman, L.: Business Metadata: Capturing Enterprise Knowledge. Morgan Kaufmann, Burlington (2010)
8. Kauschinger, M., Schreieck, M., Krcmar, H.: The role of knowledge boundary resources for platform ecosystems insights and design implications from SAP's Business Technology Platform. R&D Manag. **54**(3), 470–495 (2024). https://doi.org/10.1111/radm.12644. https://onlinelibrary.wiley.com/doi/abs/10.1111/radm.12644
9. Kotusev, S., Kurnia, S., Dilnutt, R., van de Wetering, R.: The structuring of enterprise architecture functions in organizations. Bus. Inf. Syst. Eng. **66**(4), 465–488 (2024). https://doi.org/10.1007/s12599-023-00845-4
10. Latte, B., Henning, S., Wojcieszak, M.: Clean code: on the use of practices and tools to produce maintainable code for long-living, vol. 2308, pp. 96–99. Stuttgart (2019). http://CEUR-WS.org
11. LeanIX: LeanIX Meta Model (2025). https://docs-eam.leanix.net/docs/meta-model
12. Leone, D., Schiavone, F., Appio, F.P., Chiao, B.: How does artificial intelligence enable and enhance value co-creation in industrial markets? An exploratory case study in the healthcare ecosystem. J. Bus. Res. **129**, 849–859 (2021). https://doi.org/10.1016/j.jbusres.2020.11.008. https://www.sciencedirect.com/science/article/pii/S0148296320307517
13. Luger, G.F.: Association-based representations: frames, conceptual graphs, WordNet, and FrameNet. In: Artificial Intelligence: Principles and Practice, pp. 321–339. Springer, Heidelberg (2025). https://doi.org/10.1007/978-3-031-57437-5_14
14. Olesen-Bagneux, O.: The Enterprise Data Catalog. O'Reilly, Newton (2023)
15. Quintero, R., Torres-Ruiz, M., Saldaña-Pérez, M., Guzmán Sánchez-Mejorada, C., Mata-Rivera, F.: A conceptual graph-based method to compute information content. Mathematics **11**(18), 3972 (2023). https://doi.org/10.3390/math11183972. https://www.mdpi.com/2227-7390/11/18/3972
16. Saleem, M., Polovina, S.: Towards metadata-driven enterprise architecture by integrating SAP graph and essential project. In: Proceedings of MOVE2024: The Second International Measuring Ontologies for Value Enhancement Workshop. pp. In press – to be updated. CEUR-WS (2025). https://ceur-ws.org/
17. SAP: RISE with SAP | ERP Clean Core Strategy (2025). https://www.sap.com/products/erp/rise/methodology/clean-core.html
18. Sowa, J.F.: Conceptual graphs for representing conceptual structures. In: Conceptual Structures in Practice. Chapman and Hall/CRC, Boca Raton (2009)
19. Sufi, F.: Algorithms in low-code-no-code for research applications: a practical review. Algorithms **16**(2), 108 (2023). https://doi.org/10.3390/a16020108. https://www.mdpi.com/1999-4893/16/2/108
20. Xu, B.: Healthcare data analytics: using a metadata annotation approach. J. Manag. Anal. **3**(2), 136–151 (2016)

LLM-Assisted Relational Concept Analysis for Class Model Restructuring

Hani Guenoune[1], Alain Gutierrez[1], Marianne Huchard[1], Mathieu Lafourcade[1], Pierre Martin[2,3(✉)], André Miralles[1,4], and Huaxi Zhang[5]

[1] LIRMM, Univ. Montpellier, CNRS, Montpellier, France
[2] CIRAD, UPR AIDA, 34398 Montpellier, France
pierre.martin@cirad.fr
[3] AIDA, Univ. Montpellier, CIRAD, Montpellier, France
[4] INRAE - UMR TETIS - Territoires, Environnement, Télédétection et Information Spatiale, Montpellier, France
[5] EPROAD, UR 4669, Université de Picardie Jules Verne, Amiens, France

Abstract. Formal Concept Analysis (FCA) and Relational Concept Analysis (RCA) have been used to assist software engineers restructure class models, with the aim of factoring common elements (e.g., attributes, methods) and revealing new abstractions, e.g., superclasses. Their foundations, based on lattice theory, lack "common-sense" knowledge to assess whether derived concepts correspond to relevant abstractions and, if so, to name them appropriately. This paper presents a methodology that combines FCA/RCA with Large Language Models (LLMs) to provide such assistance. Our approach builds on the existing literature by taking advantage of LLMs to address the naming problem of an entity (e.g. a class) and assess its relevancy. The results of several LLMs are compared and are encouraging.

Keywords: Formal Concept Analysis · Relational Concept Analysis · Grounding Problem · LLM · UML · Class model refactoring

1 Introduction

The design of class models and more specifically their specialization/generalization hierarchy has been a central issue since the beginning of object-orientation in the domains of programming, modeling, database, and knowledge representation (e.g. in ontology development). It remains an essential step in the specification and modernization of a software system, with specific challenges when the integration or interoperability of several systems are at stake.

As reported in [13], many ad-hoc methods were initially proposed, all with the main objective of restructuring a hierarchy of classes to obtain a well-organized set of domain concepts, with the appropriate hierarchical levels and structure. In 1990s, the paper by Godin and Mili [9] was the trigger of a long series of works based on Formal Concept Analysis (FCA). The structural benefits of using FCA for this task are numerous, as detailed in Sect. 2. To go beyond the logical

P. Cellier et al. (Eds.): CONCEPTS 2025, LNAI 15941, pp. 107–123, 2025.
https://doi.org/10.1007/978-3-032-03364-2_7

structuring and integrate semantics into the process, it is however useful to leverage other techniques, such as a lexico-semantic resource or an ontology.

With the advent of LLM, another door opens to complement the structural benefits of FCA. LLM may be a relevant source of "common sense" knowledge due to the amount of modeling and descriptive documents ingested. We hypothesize that combining FCA, to maintain a structuring process on solid tracks, and LLM, to complement it with domain knowledge, is an approach that deserves to be explored.

In this paper, we build upon work initiated in [1], where anonymous FCA concepts are given a name thanks to LLM prompting. With regard to the complexity of UML models, we use FCA in its Relational Concept Analysis (RCA) extension, the outputs of which are particularly complex to understand. The question addressed in the paper is therefore to assess the ability of LLMs to exploit RCA model restructuring, by assessing the relevance of the concepts identified and by naming them. This assessment aims to enrich the software designers' analytical process and support evidence-based design decisions.

In Sect. 2, we present how FCA and RCA are leveraged to improve the factorization in a class model. It is illustrated with a reduced class metamodel and one simple class model instance of this metamodel. Section 3 presents the LLM-based methodology to address the limitations of using only FCA and RCA, then applies it to a simple and representative UML class model and to a real class model. Related work is presented in Sect. 4, while Sect. 5 synthesizes the proposal and describes future work.

2 FCA/RCA-Based Class Model Refactorization

Extract Superclass Refactoring (ESR), including its variants, plays a central role in conceptual model (e.g., UML class models) design, as it consists in identifying new abstractions among the classes that can take the form of concrete or abstract classes or interfaces [7,16]. It is triggered by the identification of similarities between two classes C_1 and C_2 (e.g. similar attributes, roles in associations or operations). The identified common part is moved into a new class, which is added as a superclass of C_1 and C_2. ESR can be applied locally by modern Integrated Development Environments (e.g. Eclipse or IntelliJ IDEA). The limit of such approach is that there is no guarantee that a maximal factorization will be achieved. E.g. if we consider the simple UML class model of Fig. 1, a superclass of `Rainfall`, `Wind`, and `RainReport` classes can be obtained by factorizing the operation `print()`. Another independent superclass of `Rainfall` and `Wind` classes may be obtained by factorizing the operation `print()` and the attributes `measuringDate` and `measureQuality`, which conducts to a lack of a complete factorization of the operation `print()`. As mentioned in [7], a complete refactoring, conducted at the level of the whole model, is needed to get a consistent structure.

2.1 FCA-Assisted ESR at the Class Model Level

FCA [8] has been leveraged since the 1990s, with the seminal work of Godin and Mili [9], to improve factorization and abstraction at the level of the whole class

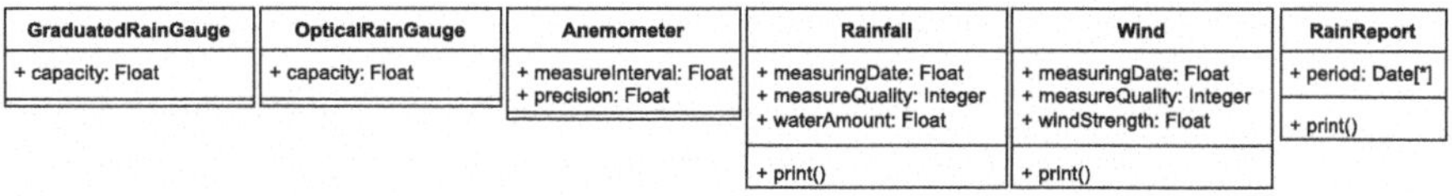

Fig. 1. A UML class model for weather measurement.

model. We explain how it works using the very simple example of weather measurement. The first step consists to encode, in a formal context, parts of the UML class model that the designer considers to be important for the refactoring. The UML model comes usually with an inheritance hierarchy which, in this case, is flattened. The formal context for weather measurement is shown in Table 1. The classes are represented as the context-objects ; the UML attributes and operations are represented as the context-attributes. Applying FCA to this context produces the concept lattice shown in Fig. 2. Concepts are *anonymous*. In the representation[1], a grey concept introduces a single UML class, e.g. C_Class_12 which introduces `Anemometer`. Assuming that the designer does not wish to reconsider the initial UML classes, these concepts are kept as classes and their connection to other concepts indicates their position in the inheritance hierarchy, ensuring part of the compactness by limiting the number of inheritance links. An orange concept introduces more than one UML class, e.g. C_Class_10 which introduces `GraduatedRainGauge` and `OpticalRainGauge`, as both share the `capacity` attribute and do not have any distinguishing attribute or operation. A blue concept does not introduce an UML class and is a pure factorization concept, that may correspond to an interesting abstraction (to clarify organization or extension points in the UML model). E.g. C_Class_17 factorizes `print`. In the two last cases, a new name has to be assigned.

FCA ensures that the refactored model is the most compact structure in the sense of a graph, i.e. with the smallest number of nodes and edges, and with a maximal factorization (no left redundancies). Some obstacles to the current FCA application remain, such as the need for a preliminary standardization of the vocabulary as the model may contain synonyms or hyperonyms, or other issues connected to terms similarity, and the need for naming the new super-classes and the need for evaluating their pertinence. In particular, FCA may generate accidental clustering, by grouping in a single new superclass, attributes and operations that correspond to different class responsibilities. The orange color concept (in Fig. 2) is a special clustering case, where the pertinence of merging the two classes may be questioned. FCA may also suggest classes with low interest (e.g. containing a single attribute with no real significance for founding a concept, like 'uid') that would complicate the design. This is where LLM can help, e.g., by suggesting additional attributes or operations to classes with few attributes, or by confirming that two classes correspond to the same conceptual entity and should be merged providing a name to this new abstraction.

[1] All conceptual structures are computed with FCA4J. https://www.lirmm.fr/fca4j.

Table 1. Class Context encoding the UML class model of Fig. 1.

Class	capacity	measureInterval	precision	measuringDate	measureQuality	waterAmount	windStrength	period	print
GraduatedRainGauge	x								
OpticalRainGauge	x								
Anemometer		x	x						
Rainfall				x	x	x			x
Wind				x	x		x		x
RainReport								x	x

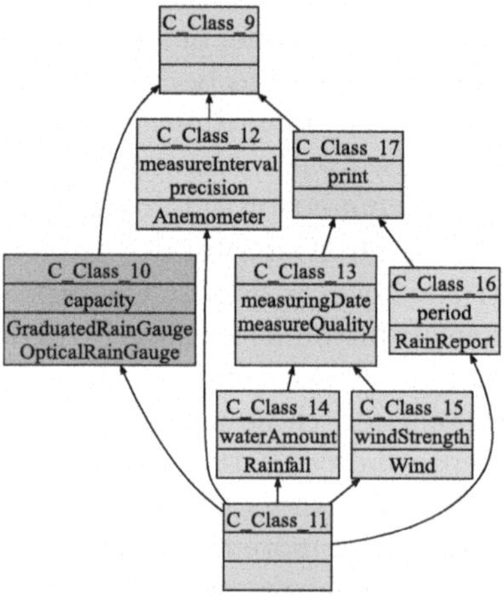

Fig. 2. The concept lattice resulting from the application of FCA to the formal context of Table 1 presented in a simplified representation: only introduced attributes and objects appear in the concept. A grey concept introduces a single UML class. An orange concept introduces more than one UML class. A blue concept does not introduce any UML class. It corresponds to a pure factorization concept. (Color figure online)

2.2 RCA-Assisted ESR at the Class Model Level

FCA is a relevant tool to deal with class models that can easily be encoded in a binary table, but it hardly deals with complex class models with associations, and more generally when all elements of the class model deserve to be considered for abstraction as shown in previous work [6]. Relational Concept Analysis (RCA) has been introduced to address this issue, with UML refactoring as a first motivating application in [17]. RCA considers a data model that takes the form of a simplified entity-relationship model, encoded in a *Relational Context Family (RCF)* composed of formal and relational contexts. In the case of UML refactoring, the data model is a more or less simplified UML metamodel. In our example (see Table 2), entities are classes and roles, respectively described by attributes and operations, and their name. Two unidirectional relations connect a class to its roles (`hasRole`) and a role to its type (`hasType`). In the RCF, each kind of entity is represented by a formal context: Entity `Class` and `Role` are respectively represented by the formal contexts `FC Class` and `FC Role`. Each unidirectional association is represented in a relational context: Association **hasRole** and **hasType** are respectively represented by the relational contexts **RC hasRole** and **RC hasType**. A simple UML model, such as the one presented in Fig. 3 that extends the weather model, is then encoded by filling in the contexts. Here are a few examples from Table 2: FC Class is similar to Table 1; FC Role describes 4 roles (each UML association end is a different object): two **measuredRainfall** roles, one issued from **GraduatedRainGauge (GRG)** and the other one from **OpticalRainGauge (ORG)**; In RC hasRole, Class GRG is connected to **GRG::measuredRainfall**; In RC hasType, Role **GRG::measuredRainfall** is connected to **Rainfall**.

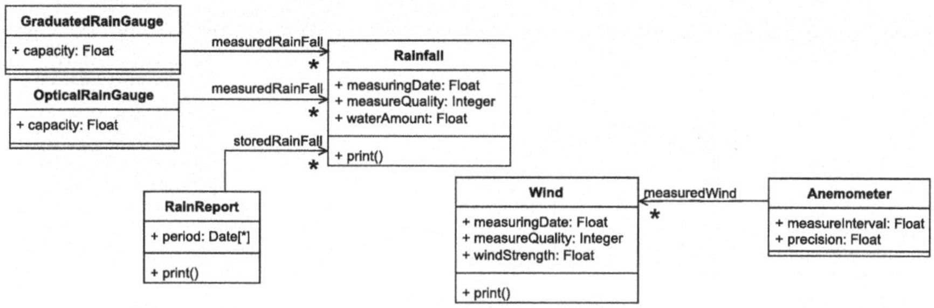

Fig. 3. The UML class model for weather measurement extended with unidirectional associations.

Table 2. Class Context encoding the UML class model of Fig. 3.

FC Class	capacity	measureInterval	precision	measuringDate	measureQuality	waterAmount	windStrength	period	print
GraduatedRainGauge	x								
OpticalRainGauge	x								
Anemometer		x	x						
Rainfall				x	x	x			x
Wind				x	x		x		x
RainReport								x	x

FC Role	measuredRainfall	measuredWind	storedRainfall
GRG::measuredRainfall	x		
ORG::measuredRainfall	x		
A::measuredWind		x	
RR::storedRainfall			x

RC hasRole	GRG::measuredRainfall	ORG::measuredRainfall	A::measuredWind	RR::storedRainfall
GraduatedRainGauge	x			
OpticalRainGauge		x		
Anemometer			x	
Rainfall				
Wind				
RainReport				x

RC hasType	GraduatedRainGauge	OpticalRainGauge	Anemometer	Rainfall	Wind	RainReport
GRG::measuredRainfall				x		
ORG::measuredRainfall				x		
A::measuredWind					x	
RR::storedRainfall				x		

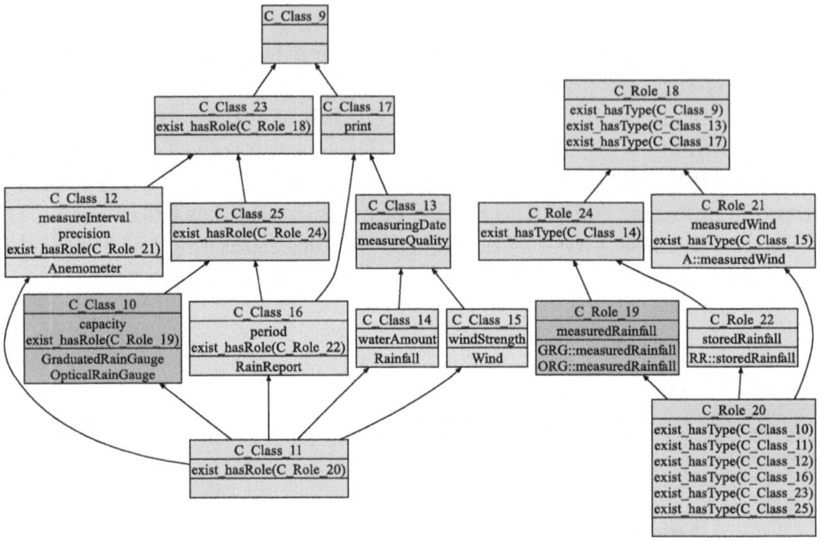

Fig. 4. The lattices of Classes and Roles at the end of the RCA process.

RCA applies FCA iteratively. At step 0, only formal contexts are used to build concept lattices, one per formal context of the RCF. Then, each formal context FC is extended with relational attributes derived from each relational context RC, s.t. FC is the source. Each relational attribute indicates how objects of FC are connected to concepts of the target formal context of RC. For example, at Step 0, C_Role_19 groups `GRG::measuredRainfall` and `ORG::measuredRainfall` as both are named `measuredRainfall`. At step 1, `FC Class` is extended with relational attributes coming from `RC hasRole`. A relational attribute has the form $qRel(Conc)$, where q is a logical quantifier (e.g. $\exists$), Rel is a relational context from a source FC to a target FC, and $Conc$ is a concept of the target FC. For instance, $\exists hasRole(C\_Role\_19)$ is a new attribute in the extended `FC Class`. Relational attributes are assigned to objects depending their logical semantics. For instance $\exists hasRole(C\_Role\_19)$ is assigned to `GraduatedRainGauge` and `OpticalRainGauge` because both classes have one role with type is in C_Role_19 extent. At a step $n \geq 1$, new concept lattices are built using each FC extended with the relational attributes formed with the concepts of step $n-1$, the RC whose FC is a source and a selected logical operator. For more details, see [17]. The concept lattices obtained at the end of the process are shown in Fig. 4. Relational attributes correspond to references to concepts in the same lattice or from another lattice. E.g., C_Role_24 contains a reference to C_Class_14 through relational attribute $\exists\_hasType(C\_Class\_14)$ meaning that it groups roles having `Rainfall` as type. The relational attribute introduced in C_Class_25 points to C_Role_24, meaning that the grouped classes have a role that has `Rainfall` as type. In order to ease the reading for end users, we leverage rewriting techniques detailed in [11] as follows: the target concept

C of a relational attribute is replaced by the attributes of C intent restricted to the introduced attributes. When the intent contains more than one introduced attribute, they are connected with symbol &. When the intent contains no introduced attribute, it is replaced by the attributes of the (full) intent of C, that are thus all inherited and appear after symbol /_INH_/. This is made recursively when an introduced attribute is itself a relational one. For example, $\exists hasRole(C\_Role\_24)$ is rewritten $\exists hasRole(\exists hasType(C\_Class\_14))$, then $\exists hasRole(\exists hasType(waterAmount))$. Figure 5 shows a suggested UML model. In a real process driven by a software engineer, each proposal of class is evaluated. Here, we keep them all for the sake of explanation. Each class concept of Fig. 4 is suggested as a class. E.g. Concept C_Class_17 is suggested and gives rise to the anonymous UML class C_Class_17 of Fig. 5 which factorizes *print*; Concept C_Class_10 is suggested as the merging class *RainGauge*. Concept C_Class_25 is suggested as the anonymous UML class C_Class_25, which holds anonymous role pointing to class *RainFall*. As in the case of FCA, RCA operates at the logical level, but does not operates at the meaning. This is where LLM can help the software engineer analyze the suggestions and produce the final restructured model. E.g. LLM could consider Concept C_Class_17 of little interest, except as the interface for displayable items; C_Class_10 could be kept as a superclass of the two classes of rain gauges, with LLM suggesting new distinguishing attributes.

In the following section of the paper, we have used a variant of RCA, i.e. RCA-AOC, which computes AOC-posets instead of lattices [3]. AOC-poset is a suborder of the concept lattice that only contains concepts introducing at least one object or one characteristic. Using such variant, a class which does not introduce a characteristic or does not represent an initial class cannot be present in the model. This restriction is guided by two concerns. First (for attribute-introducer concepts), by mainstream practice in model design, where a new abstract class introduction is guided by the existence of non-inherited shared characteristics, i.e. characteristics that need to be explicitly grouped ("declared") in a code structure (existing, or to be created). Second, object-introducer concepts represent initial classes, and must be preserved as code structure.

3 Leveraging LLM to Assist Class Model Refactorization

In the previous section, we have shown with a simple UML metamodel and model how concepts can be used to suggest new classes on the basis of common characteristics. There is, however, a gap between the RCA world and the software engineering (SE) world, where the use of RCA results by software engineers requires either a training or a specific tool that transforms concepts and concept lattices into suggestions for the domain model. The question explored in this section is an instantiation of the general question "Can LLM help in translating artifacts from RCA world to another domain world, and exploit the translation for conducting a task in this domain?". The addressed domain here is SE, and the required task consists in proposing relevance scores and names for concepts that correspond here to classes. The crucial issue in this translation is to enable LLM

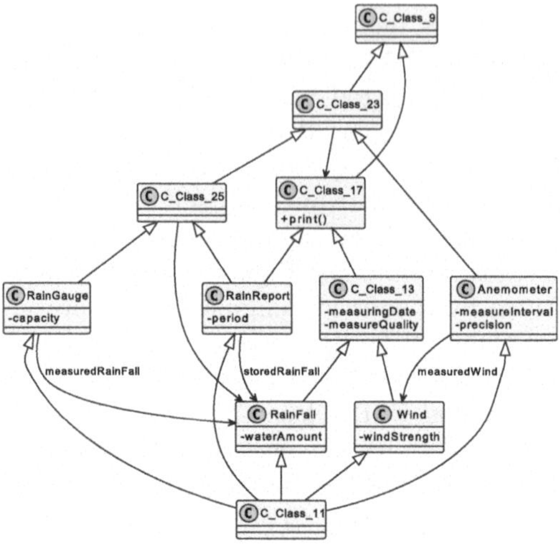

Fig. 5. The suggested UML model, using the content of the lattices from Fig. 4.

to understand the concept content, especially the relational attributes, either before or after rewriting them. In this section, we first introduce an example using a realistic UML metamodel and a simple Books-EBooks model. We present a prompt designed to achieve the task. Finally, we analyze the results of its use for the Books-EBooks model, compared to an analysis made by human participants. Then we apply the approach to a real model. Data of the analysis are available online[2], as well as the used RCA tool[3] and the modeling tool[4].

3.1 The Books-Ebooks Example

Figure 6 shows a UML model presenting several features to be reviewed. Operation *display*() appears in three different classes. *Book* and *EBook* classes share a significant number of common attributes (e.g. *title*, *author*, *editor*). *BookShelf* and *EReader* share similarly named roles (*storedItem*). *LoanRecord* and *EReader* (resp. *BookShelf*) both are in relation to *EBook* (resp. to *Book*). The model is encoded with a UML metamodel composed of four FC, i.e. for classes, attributes, roles, and operations. Four RC associate the classes to their attributes, to their operations, and to their roles, and the roles to their ending class. Applying RCA-AOC to this model provides four connected AOC-posets, provided by RCA tool in the form of a file in Graphviz (dot) textual syntax, that can be used to produce an image (e.g., Fig. 4). At the end of the RCA-AOC process, 36 relational attributes were built, including 23 in the class concept AOC-poset. These 23 relational attributes may include the other 13 during the rewriting operation. There are 5 RCA-AOC

[2] https://gite.lirmm.fr/fca4j/companion-data-for-rca-uml-llm.
[3] FCA4J v 0.4.5 https://www.lirmm.fr/fca4j/.
[4] https://plantuml.com/fr/, https://www.planttext.com/.

steps, and the number of imbrication of relational attributes ranges from 1 to 5. A class concept (not considering the bottom) contains between 1 and 8 relational attributes. As the metamodel presents a cycle, relational attributes may have complex shape, whether before or after rewriting, such as (after rewriting): *exist_hasRole (exist_hasTypeEnd(/_OBJ_/BookShelf &EReader &Book & EBook &LoanRecord) &exist_hasTypeEnd (exist_hasAttribute(loanDate) & exist_hasAttribute(itemStatus) &exist_hasAttribute(title) &exist_has Attribute (authors) &exist_hasAttribute(editor)) &exist_hasTypeEnd(exist_hasOperation (display)))*[5].

Without rewriting, the complexity comes from the need to navigate from one AOC-poset to another, and understand the meaning of operators. This is why it is necessary to transform the output for end users. For LLM, which are capable of interpreting complex textual syntax when it is adequately explained, the challenge lies in crafting such explanations within a prompt. Once the LLM demonstrates proficiency in understanding the syntax, it can be expected to provide meaningful insights and recommendations regarding the concepts.

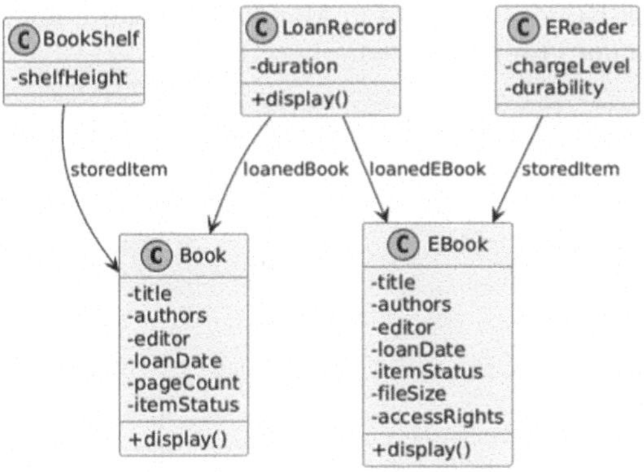

Fig. 6. The Books-Ebooks model before refactoring.

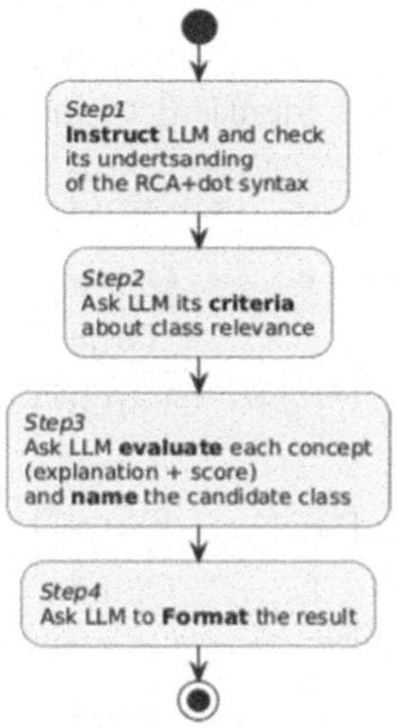

Fig. 7. The 4-step Prompt.

3.2 Prompt Design

The prompt, whose text is available online, is drafted in Fig. 7. It is composed of four steps. Step 1 instructs LLM and checks it can correctly report what it captures from RCA and the dot file. Step 2 asks LLM to elaborate on SE criteria related to the task, to focus its analysis. Step 3 asks LLM to proceed to the analysis, producing explanations, relevance score and name for candidate classes. Step 4 asks LLM to format the result. The prompt is designed to be applied on a specific dot file resulting from FCA4J, which contains the serialization of the AOC-posets (or concept lattices), with rewritten relational attributes as

[5] The special term '/_OBJ_/' introduces the extent (objects) of the target concept of the relational attribute. This has to be given to LLM in the prompt.

described in Sect. 2. In addition, to ensure that LLM has sufficient information, and given that the concepts will be analyzed separately by LLM, the concept description includes the top-to-bottom inherited characteristics and the bottom-to-top inherited objects, increasing the difficulty of reading. Although the prompt may look quite complex, it is actually produced from a single reusable template that integrates well-known prompting techniques including role conditioning, few-shot examples, and chain-of-thought reasoning. Based on those, we built an agent that can automatically execute a series of prompts and commands to fully automate the process.

3.3 Application to the Books-EBooks Example

In this section, we analyze the results obtained with the prompt applied to the Books-EBooks example. Eleven conversations have been conducted using various LLMs (see Table 3). We experimented with several state-of-the-art LLMs[6]. We focused on so-called "thinking models" and chose those that demonstrated strong reasoning ability and performed well on our specific needs.

Table 3. LLMs evaluated on the Book-EBooks example in March 2025, and numbers of terms identical to most used class names they provided.

ConversationId	LLM	LLM version	# Terms identical to most used class names
Gemini_1	Gemini	pro2.5 2	12
Grok_1	Grok	3 thinking	12
ChatGPT_1	ChatGPT	o1	10
Grok_2	Grok	3 thinking	9
ChatGPT_2	ChatGPT	o1	8
Claude_1	Claude	3.7 thinking 2	7
ChatGPT_3	ChatGPT	o1	7
Gemini_2	Gemini	pro2,5	7
DeepSeek	DeepSeek	V3	6
Claude_2	Claude	3,7 sonnet no think	6
Phind	Phind	2.0, 70B model	5

Answers to Step 1 were reviewed by the co-authors in order to assess whether each LLM has analyzed correctly the syntax of RCA and dot format. The human review revealed no error. However, because the review was carried out by humans—even experts—it inevitably retains a degree of subjectivity. Similarly, Step 2 answers were reviewed by one co-author to check whether each LLM has sufficient knowledge about the principles of object-oriented design. All LLMs report these principles without difficulty, as they are widely found in SE literature. There is no particular point to note about the formatting in Step 4, which was made quite correctly.

[6] LMArena leaderboard https://lmarena.ai/leaderboard. Visited 2025/04/19 [5].

With regards to Step 3 results, several aspects were assessed. Six co-authors analyzed the RCA results, made more readable by manual transformation (see Fig. 8), and answered the same questions as LLM in Step 3. Then we looked at variability in answers of human participants and of the LLM about name and score provided for each potential class, by calculating the minimum, maximum, mean, and standard deviation on the score and occurrences of the most commonly used class names. The results are presented in Table 4, and in Fig. 9 for more details on the distribution of names. Regarding the names given by LLM, when the average score is high and the standard deviation very low, the chosen names are quite similar. But for C_Kclass_34, for instance, there is a high variation in the proposed names, the average score is high, and the standard deviation is higher than for the other class names. Regarding the names given by participants, it is interesting to note that there is more dispersion, even for high scores. Regarding the scores, standard deviation varies from 0 to 0.328 for participants and from 0.106 to 0.223 for LLM. Variation in LLM answers and in participant answers are quite similar, and a little higher in one case for participants on a particularly questionable concept.

We also evaluated if LLM answers on the suggested names are relevant and similar to those of participants (see columns 6 and 11 of Table 4). An empty cell in Table 4 corresponds to answers indicating that the participant could not find a meaningful name in the book domain, e.g. "bottom", "absurd", "?", "<none>". In this simple yet representative example, we obtained encouraging results showing that with the provided background and context LLM was able to produce relevant and informed results, based on RCA outputs.

Table 4. Evaluation of classification by Humans and LLMs.

Concept	Human					**LLM**				
	Min score	Max score	Average score	Standard Deviation	Most used names (# out of 6)	Min score	Max score	Average score	Standard Deviation	Most used class names (# out of 11)
C_Kclass_28	0	0	0	0		0	0.3	0.0625	0.106	N/A (5)
C_Kclass_29	0.7	1	0.95	0.122	Book (2)	0.9	1	0.9875	0.035	Book (9) PhysicalBook (2)
C_Kclass_30	0.7	1	0.95	0.122	EBook (5)	0.9	1	0.9875	0.035	EBook (9)
C_Kclass_31	0.7	1	0.917	0.133	BookShelf (3)	0.8	1	0.9625	0.074	BookShelf (10)
C_Kclass_32	0.7	1	0.917	0.133	EReader (3)	0.8	1	0.9625	0.074	Ereader (10)
C_Kclass_33	1	1	1	0	LoanRecord (5)	0.9	1	0.9875	0.035	LoanRecord (10)
C_Kclass_34	0.8	1	0.933	0.082	Document (2)	0.4	0.9	0.8375	0.177	LibraryItem (3) Publication (3) MediaItem (2)
C_Kclass_35	0.2	1	0.6	0.328	Displayable (2)	0.5	0.8	0.6375	0.151	Displayable (9 + 2)
C_Kclass_36	0.5	1	0.65	0.187	*scattered*	0.2	0.8	0.4875	0.223	ItemContainer (2) StorageContainer (2) StorageUnit (2)
C_Kclass_38	0	0.1	0.0167	0.041		0.1	0.4	0.2125	0.125	N/A (5)
C_Kclass_45	0	0.1	0.0167	0.041		0.1	0.5	0.25	0.131	N/A (4)
C_Kclass_46	0	0.2	0.05	0.084		0.1	0.5	0.25	0.131	N/A (4)

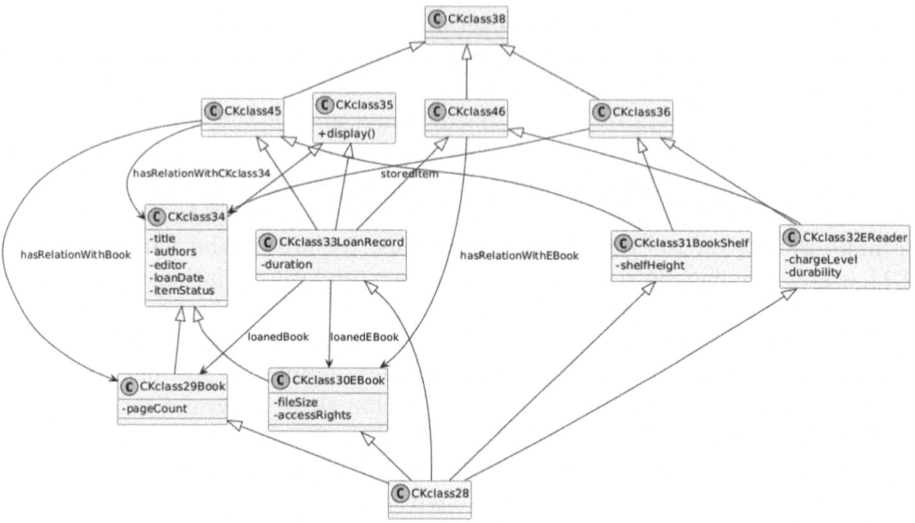

Fig. 8. The Books-Ebooks model after refactoring.

3.4 Application to a Real-Life IS: EIS Pesticides

We tested our approach on the UML model created in the EIS Pesticides project [19]. This project aimed to build an information system to contribute to the reduction of the environmental impact of pesticides. This system was designed and modeled in UML, and implemented with PostGreSQL and PostGIS in order to share knowledge and data on several watersheds monitored by Irstea research units[7]. It has been used to carry out both pesticide and IT research during several projects over a decade[8]. The model and the system have been continuously enriched in response to project requirements, to reach a total of ~170 classes.

We selected an advanced version of the UML model, which contains 170 classes, 185 attributes, 5 operations, 94 roles, and 94 associations. We considered the class concepts built at step 1 of the RCA-AOC process. 49 of these concepts do not introduce any UML class, meaning that they are candidates to be added in the UML model as new factorization superclasses. We reduced the prompt, because LLMs still have constraints in context length. While models like Gemini 2.5 Pro claim to support 1 million tokens, we observed a slight performance drop when feeding them long contexts. In future versions with stronger context processing, this limitation could naturally be lifted. In particular, we do not feed the prompt with the initial UML model, and only reason, score and names are requested. We ran the prompt six times with chatGPT o3 and Gemini 2.5 Pro in the same morning, and then analyzed the results.

[7] ADBX (Bordeaux, France) et MALY (Lyon, France).

[8] EIS Pesticides and IEPAP (ANR Carnot), Miriphyque (ANR), Maeveau, EQUIPE (Ecophyto), Modchar2 and IMAS (Agence de l'Eau Adour Garonne), SIGOUAGRO (OFB).

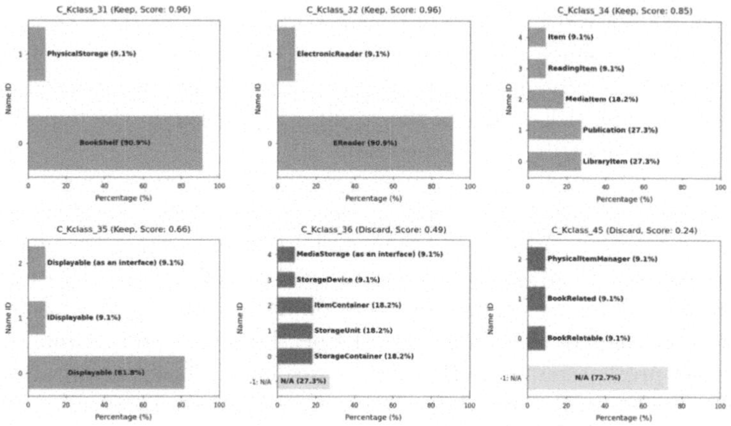

Fig. 9. Distribution of class names with a score between 0.24 and 0.96. A green (resp. orange) boxe corresponds to a concept for which the answer of most of LLMs to question (1) is Yes keep or Maybe (resp. No keep). (Color figure online)

Gemini was very optimistic about the scores and the usefulness, with an overall average score of 0.9. It gives a good score (e.g. 0.7) even when it notes a concept 'highly abstract', such as the concept that factorizes attribute 'comment'. ChatGPT was more moderate (the overall average score is 0.65) and sometimes assigned low scores to highly abstract concepts. When looking at the most frequently suggested names, Gemini's proposals are stable, whereas ChatGPT's are more scattered. For our expert, this variability was not a problem, as long as the suggested names stay within the same semantic field, and was rather a useful source of insight for refining judgment and choosing the best solution.

The main lesson is that the expert was able to assess the relevance and accuracy of answers, which have a meaning with professional terms. Therefore, they can be considered to improve the model. E.g. reading a LLM analysis for a concept which introduces the attribute 'slope', factorized from linear (1D) and polygonal (2D) elements in a proposed class named 'SlopedNetworkElement', the expert considered it to be questionable as grouping linear and polygonal elements below a common superclass is not relevant: but he was interested to add a factorization superclass above the three linear-element classes. These results provide encouraging evidence for adopting FCA and RCA in this task: an LLM can translate their solid, yet complex, outputs into clear, actionable insights while also handling the post-processing steps.

4 Related Work

FCA/RCA Based Class Model Refactorization. The need to normalize class model hierarchies arose very early in object-oriented paradigm development. The first attempt to solve this problem appeared in [9], imitating approaches to database schema normalization. A large range of research work, described in [13], has been carried out since the seminal paper of Godin and Mili at OOPLSA'93, benefiting from FCA advances. The experiments were mainly focused on reducing construction time [10] or size of the results [15], based on the hypothesis that users with FCA skills will handle the results.

FCA and LLM Combined Approaches. Recent approaches combine FCA and LLM. Triadic Concept Analysis (TCA) and LLM prompting are combined in [2] to assist the specification of a software system. TCA is used to extract the logic of a family of systems in the targeted domain, while LLM is used to guide the designers in their option choices to define the new system. Our inspiration source for the present paper is [1] and its associated oral presentation, where authors introduce prompt templates to leverage LLM to name anonymous concepts produced by FCA. RCA results, used here, are however more complex.

LLM and Class Model Building Assistance. LLMs are widely explored for dealing with software engineering tasks as developed in the systematic literature survey of [12], which shows that a major work was dedicated to software development and generation at that time. Cámara et al. [4] report that there is few work on the use of LLM for modeling tasks. They investigate the use of ChatGPT to assist software modeling. They identified that the task of UML class model building from text, unlike code generation, was not yet satisfactorily addressed, with a lack of consistency and repeatability. They also found that better results are obtained in OCL constraints generation. In [14], authors explore the generation, from natural language requirements, of a UML class diagram and the corresponding code ensuring bi-directional traceability between the two. In [20], authors evaluate how LLM can help students to design UML models (use case diagram, class diagram, sequence diagram) from the description of a case study. They conclude that LLM can make relevant suggestions, but its instability and occasional errors in the results require vigilance. In our work, we do not address UML class model generation from text. The addressed task consists to refactor an existing class model and bring out new abstractions. We investigate how, based on a systematic and sound refactoring performed using RCA, LLM is able to help the software designer select the relevant abstractions from the RCA results. The challenge is to teach LLM how to read complex RCA outputs.

5 Conclusion

In this paper, we revisited the use of RCA to assist software engineers in the task of improving the structure of a class model, factoring out common characteristics, and highlighting new abstractions. We proposed and applied a method based on prompting LLM to provide this assistance and assessing the results, with encouraging results. It is important to note that, in restructuring activities, designers usually analyze excerpts of models focused on a topic, rather than a whole model where many topics are mixed, with a likely inadequate factorization.

As future work, we would like to explore the impact of several variants. E.g., rewriting relational attributes using objects (classes) could help. Prompting LLM without giving concept extents should also be explored to evaluate the impact of the initial class names on the results. By stopping at each step of the RCA process, it will be possible to examine the proposed improvements and retain the relevant ones. Regarding the use of results, UML supports multiple inheritance, and it is preferable to retain it at the analysis level. The model can then serve as an ontology, as a conceptual database model, or as a basis for generating code in an object-oriented programming language. C++ and Python support multiple inheritance natively, whereas Java provides it through interfaces implemented by classes. Depending on the target, a design-level UML model will be produced that may—or may not—transform multiple inheritance into single inheritance, as described in [18]. During this transformation, the LLM could suggest whether each concept should be treated as a class or as an interface. As explained, we currently favour the AOC-poset over the complete lattice because, in practice, designers rarely define a class that has no attributes or operations. This choice was a pragmatic compromise in the era before LLM assistance. Today, however, a step-wise exploration of the full lattice becomes feasible, as an LLM can propose plausible characteristics for any class that initially lacks them.

In this paper, we focused on the question of analyzing whether LLM can exploit RCA results, regarding the initial SE task. We thus plan to develop a two-branch process to propose a factorization, one branch corresponding to the present work and the other one using only LLM, which will be combined in the following step. We also deem it useful to conduct an analysis of using LLMs in this context, comparing the approach with both an in-house assistance tool (without LLM) and considering the human expertise invested in each scenario. The study would examine environmental footprint, performance, output quality, computation time, and, crucially, the models' capacity to learn and to capitalize on both company-specific and general knowledge.

Acknowledgments. The authors would like to thank Gonzalo A. Aranda-Corral and Miguel A. Rodriguez-Roman for sharing thoughts about the approach. They also thank the anonymous reviewers for their relevant feedback that helped improving this paper. This work was supported by the ANR SmartFCA project, Grant ANR-21-CE23-0023 of the French National Research Agency.

References

1. Aranda-Corral, G., Bundy, A., Borrego-Díaz, J., Chan, P.: Grounding problem in formal concept analysis by means of large language models. In: Ws. Late Breaking Advances on Conceptual Structures @ Concepts 2024 (2024). https://concepts2024.uca.es/lbacs/
2. Bazin, A., Gutierrez, A., Huchard, M., Martin, P., Zhang, Y.H.: Variability-driven user-story generation using llm and triadic concept analysis. In: 20th International Conference on Evaluation of Novel Approaches to Software Engineering (ENASE) (2025). https://doi.org/10.5220/0013360500003928

3. Berry, A., Gutierrez, A., Huchard, M., Napoli, A., Sigayret, A.: Hermes: a simple and efficient algorithm for building the AOC-poset of a binary relation. Ann. Math. Artif. Intell. 45–71 (2014). https://doi.org/10.1007/s10472-014-9418-6
4. Cámara, J., Troya, J., Burgueño, L., Vallecillo, A.: On the assessment of generative AI in modeling tasks: an experience report with ChatGPT and UML. Softw. Syst. Model. **22**(3), 781–793 (2023). https://doi.org/10.1007/s10270-023-01105-5
5. Chiang, W.L., et al.: Chatbot arena: an open platform for evaluating LLMs by human preference (2024). https://doi.org/10.48550/arXiv.2403.04132
6. Dao, M., Huchard, M., Hacène, M.R., Roume, C., Valtchev, P.: Improving generalization level in UML models *iterative cross generalization in practice*. In: Wolff, K.E., Pfeiffer, H.D., Delugach, H.S. (eds.) ICCS-ConceptStruct 2004. LNCS (LNAI), vol. 3127, pp. 346–360. Springer, Heidelberg (2004). https://doi.org/10.1007/978-3-540-27769-9_23
7. Fowler, M.: Refactoring - Improving the Design of Existing Code -. Addison Wesley object technology series, 2nd edn. Addison-Wesley, Boston (2018)
8. Ganter, B., Wille, R.: Formal Concept Analysis: Mathematical Foundations. Springer, Heidelberg (1999)
9. Godin, R., Mili, H.: Building and maintaining analysis-level class hierarchies using galois lattices. In: OOPSLA '93, vol. 28, pp. 394–410 (1993)
10. Godin, R., Mili, H., Mineau, G.W., Missaoui, R., Arfi, A., Chau, T.T.: Design of class hierarchies based on concept (galois) lattices. Theory Appl. Obj. Syst. **4**(2), 117–134 (1998)
11. Gutierrez, A., Huchard, M., Martin, P., Zhang, Y.H.: Empowering Relational Concept Analysis using Large Language Model knowledge delivery (2025)
12. Hou, X., et al.: Large language models for software engineering: a systematic literature review. ACM Trans. Softw. Eng. Methodol. **33**(8) (2024). https://doi.org/10.48550/arXiv.2308.10620
13. Huchard, M.: Analyzing inheritance hierarchies through formal concept analysis: a 22-years walk in a landscape of conceptual structures. In: Sakkinen, M. (ed.) Proceedings of WS. MASPEGHI@ECOOP 2015, pp. 8–13. ACM (2015)
14. Kanuka, H., Koreki, G., Soga, R., Nishikawa, K.: Exploring the ChatGPT approach for bidirectional traceability problem between design models and code (2023). https://arxiv.org/abs/2309.14992
15. Miralles, A., Molla, G., Huchard, M., Nebut, C., Deruelle, L., Derras, M.: Class model normalization - outperforming formal concept analysis app. with AOC-posets. In: Proceedings of the 12th CLA, vol. 1466, pp. 111–122. CEUR-WS.org (2015). https://ceur-ws.org/Vol-1466/paper09.pdf
16. Opdyke, W.F., Johnson, R.E.: Creating abstract superclasses by refactoring. In: Kwasny, S.C., Buck, J.F. (eds.) Proceedings of the ACM 21th CSC, pp. 66–73 (1993)
17. Rouane-Hacène, M.R., Huchard, M., Napoli, A., Valtchev, P.: Relational concept analysis: mining concept lattices from multi-relational data. Ann. Math. Artif. Intell. **67**(1), 81–108 (2013). https://doi.org/10.1007/s10472-012-9329-3
18. Rumbaugh, J., Blaha, M., Premerlani, W., Eddy, F., Lorensen, W.: Object-Oriented Modeling and Design. Prentice-Hall Inc., Upper Saddle River (1991)
19. Vernier, F., et al.: EIS pesticides: an environmental information system to characterize agricultural activities and calculate agro-environmental indicators at embedded watershed scales. Agric. Syst. **122**, 11–21 (2013). https://doi.org/10.1016/j.agsy.2013.07.005

20. Wang, B., Wang, C., Liang, P., Li, B., Zeng, C.: How LLMs aid in UML modeling: an exploratory study with novice analysts. In: IEEE International Conference on Software Services Engineering, SSE, pp. 249–257 (2024). https://doi.org/10.48550/arXiv.2404.17739

Empowering Relational Concept Analysis Using Large Language Model Knowledge Delivery

Alain Gutierrez[1], Marianne Huchard[1], Pierre Martin[2,3](✉), and Huaxi Zhang[4]

[1] LIRMM, Univ. Montpellier, CNRS, Montpellier, France
[2] CIRAD, UPR AIDA, 34398 Montpellier, France
pierre.martin@cirad.fr
[3] AIDA, Univ. Montpellier, CIRAD, Montpellier, France
[4] EPROAD, UR 4669, Université de Picardie Jules Verne, Amiens, France

Abstract. Relational concept analysis (RCA) computes and represents relational datasets as lattices of concepts and implications. This approach relies on the computation of relational attributes which capture quantified relationships between objects and concepts. However, interpreting this representation is challenging for end-users. FCA experts must combine relational attributes from different concept lattices to obtain a complete formulation, while domain experts (e.g., software engineers, agronomists) face the additional difficulty of extracting meaning from these mathematical structures. This paper proposes an approach to address this issue by leveraging Large Language Models (LLMs). It comprises two main components: (1) the generation of a textual description of relational attributes; (2) the design of a generic prompt that enables LLM to produce a natural-language description of RCA artifacts using the generated textual description. The approach is illustrated using representative implications from a real-world agroecological dataset.

Keywords: Formal Concept Analysis · Relational Concept Analysis · LLM · RCA attribute rewriting

1 Introduction

Formal Concept Analysis (FCA, [11]) is an established approach in the field of symbolic AI, among other logic-based approaches, that guarantees accurate results. However, the interpretation of FCA results is mainly accessible to FCA experts and needs post-processing to be accessible to domain experts. The recent advent of LLMs may provide a solution to this issue, through the reformulation of implications into natural language.

FCA analyzes a tabular set of binary data provided as input and returns either data classified in a concept lattice or implications. In this paper, we address the implications. An implication is a logical formulation consisting of two parts joined by the connector →, where the left and right parts of this connector

P. Cellier et al. (Eds.): CONCEPTS 2025, LNAI 15941, pp. 124–139, 2025.
https://doi.org/10.1007/978-3-032-03364-2_8

indicate the premise and its conclusion respectively. Software for navigating in sets of implications remains dedicated to FCA experts [20].

Several FCA extensions have been developed to address more complex structures, such as Polyadic Concept Analysis [2], GraphFCA [10], and Relational Concept Analysis (RCA) [19] for n-ary, graphical, and multi-relational datasets respectively. In the case of a multi-relational dataset, the structure of the data model can vary from a simple UML class model to a complex one containing cycles. Understanding concept lattices and implications built using RCA is even more complex than with FCA. For the implications, their understanding requires to navigate the concepts computed by RCA, easier to visualize in the lattices. Thus computing lattices is also a need. To make implications accessible to domain experts, the solution proposed in this paper consists of rewriting them by unfolding the concept content, and then converting them into natural-language text using an LLM.

Figure 1 gives an overview of our contributions. The original RCA process, presented in the left-hand part of Fig. 1, consists of preprocessing a raw dataset (step 1 of the process) according to a simplified UML class model, used to filter the elements of interest for a planned analysis, to produce a formal dataset. The latter is analyzed through RCA software to obtain a set of implications. To deliver an intelligible formulation of implications, i.e. expressed in plain text, the process, presented in this paper, consists, once step 1 has been completed, of producing self-contained **rewritten implications** by enhancing RCA computation (step 2) and then taking advantage of LLM. The latter consists of (i) defining a prompt template, describing RCA implication syntax that includes generic parts to consider specific domain aspects, which are instantiated (step 3) using knowledge on the UML model and additional domain information to build the final prompt, and (ii) computing **intelligible implications** using LLM (step 4).

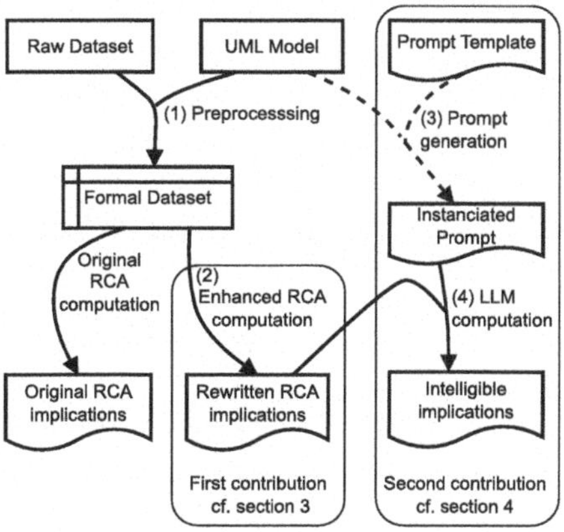

Fig. 1. Outline of the process, presented in this paper, converting relational dataset into implications expressed in plain text. A solid and a dotted line represent respectively a sofware computation and a manual operation.

The paper is organized as follows. Section 2 introduces FCA and RCA. This section shows that one difficulty in reading RCA results lies in the understanding of relational attributes, i.e. the elements built by RCA to encompass quantified relationships between data. Section 3 presents the approach to rewrite relational attributes and implications. Section 4 introduces the principles of the proposed prompts and shows results of the approach applied to a dataset in agroecology. Related work is presented in Sect. 5. We conclude and give perspectives of this work in Sect. 6.

2 Relational Concept Analysis and the Challenge of Interpretation

Basics on FCA and RCA. We sketch here the main notions of FCA and RCA; for a complete formal treatment the reader is referred to [11] and [19], which we cannot reproduce here owing to space constraints. One noticeable feature of FCA is its capacity to structure and analyze data given under the form of a formal context (FC) $\mathcal{K} = (G, M, I)$ where G is a set of objects, M is a set of attributes, and $I \subseteq G \times M$ is the incidence relation indicating which object owns which property [11]. The first main output of FCA is a concept lattice computed using two functions $\alpha : \mathcal{P}(G) \rightarrow \mathcal{P}(M)$ and $\beta : \mathcal{P}(M) \rightarrow \mathcal{P}(G)$, such that $\forall X \subseteq G\ \alpha(X) = \{y \in M | \forall x \in X, (x, y) \in I\}$ and $\forall Y \subseteq M$, $\beta(Y) = \{x \in G | \forall y \in Y, (x, y) \in I\}$. The concept lattice $\mathcal{L}$ computed from $\mathcal{K}$, also denoted $\mathcal{L}(\mathcal{K})$, is the set of concepts $\{(X, Y) | X \subseteq G, Y \subseteq M, \alpha(X) = Y \text{and } \beta(Y) = X\}$, provided with a partial order relation based on inclusion of concept extents. For a concept $C = (X, Y)$, X is the concept extent, denoted as $Extent(C)$, and Y is the concept intent, denoted as $Intent(C)$. A concept (X_{sub}, Y_{sub}) is a sub-concept of a concept (X_{sup}, Y_{sup}) when $X_{sub} \subseteq X_{sup}$. Figure 2 (right-hand side) shows an excerpt of the concept lattice computed for FC `Ingredient` presented in Table 1 (the bottom concept has been hidden). In figures, concepts are presented in a simplified form, where only introduced[1] objects and attributes are shown. For instance `CIng11` is a subconcept of `CIng10`. Its extent is composed of bottom-up inherited objects: $\{shallot, mushroom, tomato, eggplant\}$. Its intent is $\{vege, vegan\}$, with *vegan* introduced `CIng11` and *vege* top-down inherited.

The second main output of FCA is implication sets [11]. An implication has the form $Pr \rightarrow Co$, where $Pr \subseteq M$ and $Co \subseteq M$. The implication indicates that all objects owning the attributes in the premise Pr also own those in the conclusion Co. An implication has a *support*, which is the number of objects that own the Pr attributes. An example of implication for FC `Ingredient` is $\{summer\} \rightarrow \{vege\}$ with support 3 (i.e., *goatcheese*, *tomato*, and *eggplant*).

RCA [19] is an FCA extension introduced to structure and analyze multi-relational data. Input data take the form of a *relational context family* (RCF), which roughly follows a simplified UML class model. An RCF is a pair $(\mathcal{C}, \mathcal{R})$ such that: $\mathcal{C} = \{\mathcal{C}_i = (\mathcal{G}_i, \mathcal{M}_i, \mathcal{I}_i)\}$ is a set of FC (object-attribute relations). The attributes of any $\mathcal{M}_i$ are called primitive attributes. $\mathcal{R} = \{r \mid r \subseteq \mathcal{G}_i \times \mathcal{G}_j\}$ is a set of relations r (object-object relations, or relational contexts RC) from objects of a *source context* $src(r) = \mathcal{C}_i$ to objects of a *destination context* $dest(r) = \mathcal{C}_j$. $r(o)$ denotes the *image* of $o \in \mathcal{G}_i$ by relation r. For instance, the RCF presented in Table 1 is composed of three FC and two RC, corresponding respectively to entities (pizzerias, pizzas, ingredients) and relationships (serves, contains). The associated UML class model depicts pizzerias as serving pizzas composed of various ingredients. In RCA, a concept groups together objects sharing primitive attributes, such as FCA, but also sharing relations to other objects, and

[1] We use the term "introduced" instead of "generating" to emphasize the position of the object or attribute in the concept lattice visualization.

Table 1. Example of relational context family.

Pizzeria	IdHappizzy	IdEataly	IdLafelicita	IdSmallitaly
happizzy	×			
eataly		×		
lafelicita			×	
smallitaly				×

Pizza	Idchevrette	IdForest	IdViolet	IdStjacques
chevrette	×			
forest		×		
violet			×	
stjacques				×

Ingredient	vege	vegan	spring	summer	autumn
goatcheese	×			×	
burrata	×		×		
scallop			×		
tomato	×	×		×	
shallot	×	×			×
mushroom	×	×			×
eggplant	×	×		×	

serves	chevrette	forest	violet	stjacques
happizzy	x	x		
eataly		x	x	
lafelicita			x	
smallitaly	x			x

contains	goatcheese	burrata	scallop	tomato	shallot	mushroom	eggplant
chevrette	x			x			
forest					x	x	
violet				x			x
stjacques		x	x				

by extension, relations with concepts grouping these objects together. This is made through *relational scaling*, that adds *relational attributes* in the formal contexts [19]. The form of a relational attribute is $qr(C)$, where q is a quantifier, r a relation and C a concept. An example of relational attribute is ∀∃ `contains(CIng10)`, which means "contains at least one and only ingredients of `CIng10` extent", i.e. vegetarian ingredients.

In general, for an RCF $(\mathcal{C}, \mathcal{R})$, FC $\mathcal{C}_i = (\mathcal{G}_i, \mathcal{M}_i, \mathcal{I}_i)$ of $\mathcal{C}$ is extended using the set R of relations in $\mathcal{R}$, for which $\mathcal{C}_i$ is the source, and a set of scaling operators $\mathcal{Q}$ (i.e. quantifiers, e.g. $\exists$ or $\forall\exists$) associated with the relations of R, via a mapping $\rho : \mathcal{R} \rightarrow \mathcal{Q}$. The extension FC $\mathcal{C}_i^+ = (\mathcal{G}_i, \mathcal{M}_i^+, \mathcal{I}_i^+)$, which extends $\mathcal{C}_i$ with relational attributes, is defined as follows: $\mathcal{M}_i^+ = \mathcal{M}_i \cup \{qr(C) \mid q \in \mathcal{Q}, r \in R, \rho(r) = q,\ C \in \mathcal{L}(dest(r))\}$, and $\mathcal{I}_i^+ = \mathcal{I}_i \cup \{(o, qr(C)) \mid C = (E, I)\ and\ conforms(q, E, r(o))\}$. $conforms(\exists, E, r(o))$ is true when $E \cap r(o) \neq \emptyset$, meaning that o is connected by r to at least one element in E. $conforms(\forall\exists, E, r(o))$ is true when $r(o) \neq \emptyset$, and $r(o) \subseteq E$, meaning that o is connected by r to at least one element in E and only to elements in E. The set of all extended FC is $\mathcal{C}^+ = \{\mathcal{C}_i^+ \mid \mathcal{C}_i \in \mathcal{C}\}$.

To be computed, RCA follows an iterative process: step $s, s \in \{0, ..n\}$, builds (1) the concept lattices of FCs in the RCF (these FCs are extended when $s \geq 1$) and (2) a new RCF $(\mathcal{C}^+, \mathcal{R})$ using the built concepts to generate or update relational attributes. Table 2 shows the extended FCs for pizzas and pizzerias at step $s = 1$. In the pizzas extended FC, the new relational attributes point to ingredient concepts. For instance, ∀∃ `contains(CIng10)` is shared by *chevrette*, *forest*, and *violet*, since all their ingredients are in `CIng10` extent. The process stops when a fix-point is reached (i.e. there is no more modification of the concept lattices or the extended FCs) or once the number of steps defined by the user has been reached. Figure 2 shows an excerpt of the concept lattices at the end of the process. Interestingly, in this figure, even if *chevrette* and *forest* do not share any

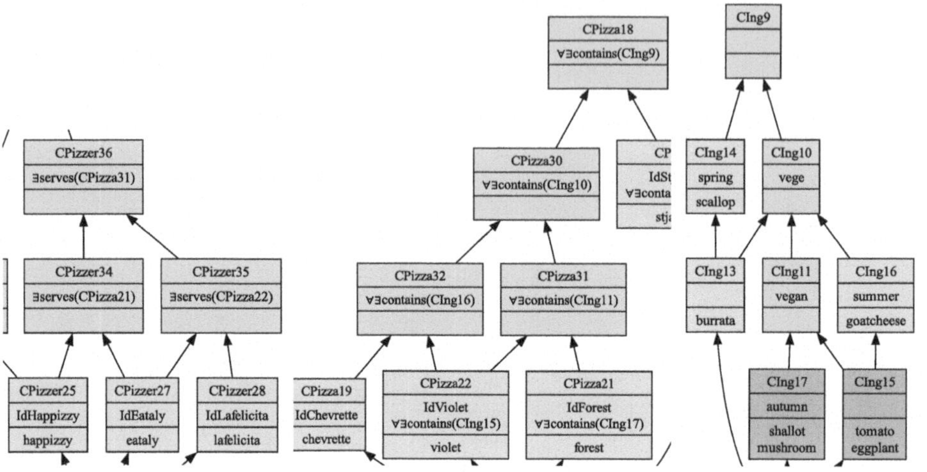

Fig. 2. Excerpt of concept lattices of pizzerias (left), pizzas (middle), and ingredients (right) with relational attributes, at the end of the RCA computation process. The lattices were built using FCA4J [12] and wording was then simplified for an easier reading, i.e. reduced name length and use of mathematical symbols.

primitive attribute, and do not contain common ingredients, as they have only ingredients in the extent of `CIng10` (*vege* ingredients), they share, with *forest*, the relational attribute ∀∃ `contains(CIng10)` and thus are grouped in `CPizza30`. Similarly *violet* and *forest* share ∀∃ `contains(CIng11)` (only *vegan* ingredients) and are grouped in `CPizza31`. Therefore pizzerias *happizy*, *eataly*, and *lafelicita* share ∃ `contains(CPizza31)` and are grouped in `CPizzer36` which introduces this attribute. Using RCA, each extended formal context $\mathcal{C}_i^+$ contains relational attributes, and can be used to compute implications. An example of implication for the extended pizzerias when the fixpoint is reached is:
{∃ `serves(CPizza21)`} → {∃ `serves(CPizza31)`} (support 2).

Interpretation of RCA by Non-specialists. RCA artifacts (i.e. concepts, lattices, and implications) are difficult for domain experts to interpret, as reading the results needs grasping the content of relational attributes by navigating from one lattice to another. E.g. to interpret the implication {∃ `serves(CPizza21)`} → {∃ `serves(CPizza31)`}, one has to consult the pizza lattice and observe that `CPizza21` introduces ∀∃ `contains(CIng17)`, the latter referring to the ingredient lattice, where `CIng17` is the group of ingredients that are better in autumn. After a similar navigation to interpret the conclusion, the implication meaning can be established, revealing that "If a pizzeria serves at least one pizza having all its ingredients in those that are better in autumn, then it also serves at least one pizza whose all ingredients are vegan". To establish this interpretation, the three components of the relational attributes were considered: the quantifier, the relation, and the concept from the targeted lattice. For each relational attribute of each lattice concept, this rewriting is carried out until the primitive attributes are obtained, to be fully understood.

Table 2. The extended formal contexts Pizza and Pizzeria at step $s = 1$.

Pizza	IdChevrette	IdForest	IdViolet	IdStjacques	∃∀contains(CIng9)	∃∀contains(CIng10)	∃∀contains(CIng11)	∃∀contains(CIng12)	∃∀contains(CIng13)	∃∀contains(CIng14)	∃∀contains(CIng15)	∃∀contains(CIng16)	∃∀contains(CIng17)
chevrette	x				x	x						x	
forest		x			x	x	x						x
violet			x		x	x	x				x	x	
stjacques				x	x					x			

Pizzeria	IdHappizzy	IdEataly	IdLafelicita	IdSmallitaly	∃serves(CPizza18)	∃serves(CPizza19)	∃serves(CPizza20)	∃serves(CPizza21)	∃serves(CPizza22)	∃serves(CPizza23)
happizzy	x				x	x		x		
eataly		x			x			x	x	
lafelicita			x		x				x	
smallitaly				x	x	x				x

The aim of rewriting a relational attribute is to make it fully explicit. Thus, firstly, an introduced attribute must be differentiated from an inherited one, as an introduced attribute is specific to a concept and identifies the objects of its extent, while an inherited attribute is shared with objects located outside the concept extent. Secondly, a rewritten relational attribute must indicate whether the handled concept is located at the top or at the bottom of the lattice, as it contains respectively all its objects or all its attributes, otherwise lists them. Thirdly, when the data model contains a cycle, a circular reference from a relational attribute of the concept on itself can be expected. Informing that the iterative process was stopped to prevent endless rewriting is mandatory. Finally, RCA-AOC, i.e. a variant of RCA, computes AOC-posets [4] instead of lattices. The AOC-poset is the suborder of the concept lattice restricted to concepts introducing at least one object or one attribute. In this variant, concepts existing at one step s can disappear at a later step t. By construction, this situation results at step t in relational attributes that refer to concepts which no longer exist.

3 Relational Attribute and Implication Rewriting

This section introduces our first contribution, i.e. the rewriting of relational attributes. We first consider the four cases previously introduced, i.e., inheritance, disappearing concept, circular reference, and a concept at the bottom or at the top of the lattice. We present a solution for handling the different cases, discuss possible alternatives, and describe the rewriting algorithm. All of these variants are implemented in the FCA4J software library[2].

[2] https://www.lirmm.fr/fca4j/.

Inheritance in the Rewriting of Relational Attributes. In the basic case, the rewriting consists to recursively 'unfold' a relational attribute by replacing the target concept by the attributes introduced in its intent when any. The symbol & (meaning "and") is inserted between attributes located in the same concept to separate them. The recursion stops when there are no more relational attribute to unfold. For example (Fig. 2), in `CPizzer34`, ∃ `serves(CPizza21)` is rewritten replacing `CPizza21` by the attributes introduced in its intent, giving ∃ `serves(IdForest&` ∀∃ `contains(CIng17))`. ∀∃ `contains(CIng17))` is then rewritten with the attribute *autumn* introduced in `CIng17` intent, giving ∀∃ `contains(autumn)`. Finally ∃ `serves(CPizza21)` is rewritten as ∃ `serves(IdForest &` ∀∃ `contains(autumn))`, an expression which no longer contains target concept. If the target concept does not introduce attributes, the entire intent is used instead. Therefore, all the attributes are inherited and are preceded by the tag `/_INH_/` in the attribute rewriting. For example (Fig. 2), in `CPizzer35`, ∃ `serves(CPizza22)` is rewritten ∃ `serves(IdViolet &` ∀∃ `contains(CIng15))`, then since `CIng15` does not introduce attribute, and $Intent(CIng15) = \{vege, vegan, summer\}$, the final rewriting is ∃ `serves(IdViolet &` ∀∃ `contains(/_INH_/ vege & vegan & summer))`.

Disappearing Concepts. In an AOC-poset, any concept introduces at least one attribute or at least one object. During its computation using RCA-AOC, a concept can disappear from one step to another, because it introduces neither object nor attribute. Let us consider a concept C which, at some step i, has an empty introduced intent and necessarily a non empty introduced extent $\{o_1, o_2, ...o_n\}$. If at one or several computation steps j, such that $j > i$ during the building of the new RCF, the objects $o_1, o_2, ...o_n$ acquire new attributes (necessarily relational), such that each o_x acquires an attribute that o_y, $x \neq y$ does not acquire, then the introduced extent of C will be emptied. Thus at some step k, $k > i$, C disappears. We illustrate this phenomenon using a simple example. Table 3 shows a RCF where pizzas contain ingredients imported from various countries. In Fig. 3 that shows Step 0, `CIng7` has an empty introduced intent, with *basil* and *olive* objects in its introduced extent. Figure 4 shows Step 1. `CIng7` disappeared at this step because *olive* acquired ∃ `importedFrom(CCountry15)` and *basil* acquired ∃ `importedFrom(CCountry14)`. The adopted rewriting solution, to inform of this disappearance, consists of giving the introduced objects of the extent (that potentially provides less information than a full initial intent, but is shorter) preceded by the tag `/_OBJ_/`. E.g. ∃ `contains(CIng7)` in `CPizza24` is rewritten ∃ `contains(/_OBJ_/ basil & olive)`.

Circular References. Cyclic models may cause circular references in the relational attributes. In the RCF of Table 4, a food is produced in a country, and (people of) a country consume a lot of some food. Excerpts of the concept lattices before rewriting are shown in Fig. 5. Two cases may occur.

In the case where a relational attribute refers to the concept that introduces it, the tag `_SELF_` is inserted in the attribute rewriting to mention this self-reference. E.g. ∃ `r(_SELF_)` then means "has at least one r link to an object of

Table 3. Relational context family with countries, pizzas, and ingredients to illustrate disappeared concepts.

Pizza	large	small	thick	thin
chevrette	x			
forest		x		
omozza			x	
otomme				x

Ingredient	italian	french	meet	fish
mozzarella		x		
tomme	x			
basil	x	x		
olive	x	x		
chicken	x	x	x	
salmon	x	x		x

Country	coastline	peninsula	alps	archipelago
france	x			
italy		x		
greece			x	
switzerland				x

contains	mozzarella	tomme	basil	olive	chicken	salmon
chevrette		x			x	
forest	x					x
omozza	x					
otomme		x				

importedFrom	france	italy	greece	switzerland
mozzarella		x	x	
tomme	x			x
basil	x			
olive		x		
chicken	x			
salmon		x		

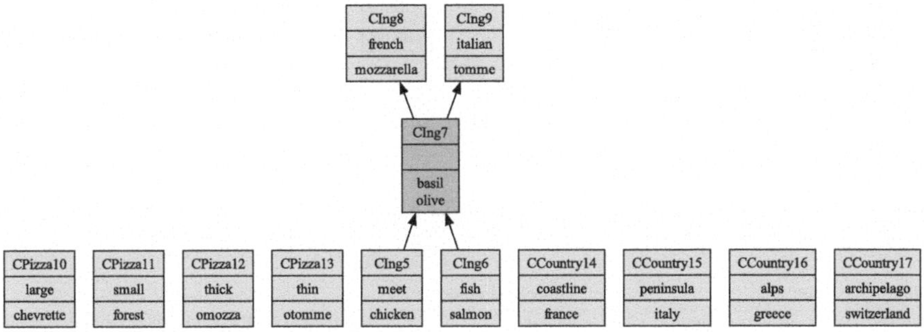

Fig. 3. AOC-posets of pizzas, ingredients, and countries of RCF Table 3 with relational attributes rewritten using the **rai** variant, at Step 0.

this same concept". E.g. Attribute ∃ `consumesALotOf(CFood11)` in `CCountry6` is rewritten as ∃ `consumesALotOf(`∃ `isProducedIn(CCountry6))`, then as ∃ `consumesALotOf(`∃ `isProducedIn(_SELF_))`.

Otherwise, when a relational attribute does not refer to its introducing concept but refers to a concept already included in its rewriting, then the rewriting provides the concept extent preceded by the tag `/_OBJ_/`. E.g. (with parts hidden to focus on this rewriting) Attribute ∃ `isProducedIn(CCountry6))` is rewritten first in `CFood11` as ∃ `isProducedIn(...&` ∃ `consumesALotOf(CFood8) & ...))`, and second as ∃ `isProducedIn(...&` ∃ `consumesALotOf (/_INH_/ ...` ∃ `isProducedIn(CCountry6) .... & ...))`. As `CCountry6` has already been visited, to avoid endless rewriting, it is replaced by `/_OBJ_/ France` which is the introduced extent of `CCountry6`, giving ∃ `isProducedIn(...&` ∃ `consumesALotOf(/_INH_/ ... &` ∃ `isProducedIn(/_OBJ_/ France) ... & ...))`.

The Top and Bottom Concept Cases. When the top concept ⊤ does not introduce attributes, which would be attributes common to all objects, the tag `_ALL_OBJECTS_` is substituted to ⊤, to make the expression more readable. E.g. ∃ `r(_ALL_OBJECTS_)` can be read "has at least a r link to one object". Similarly,

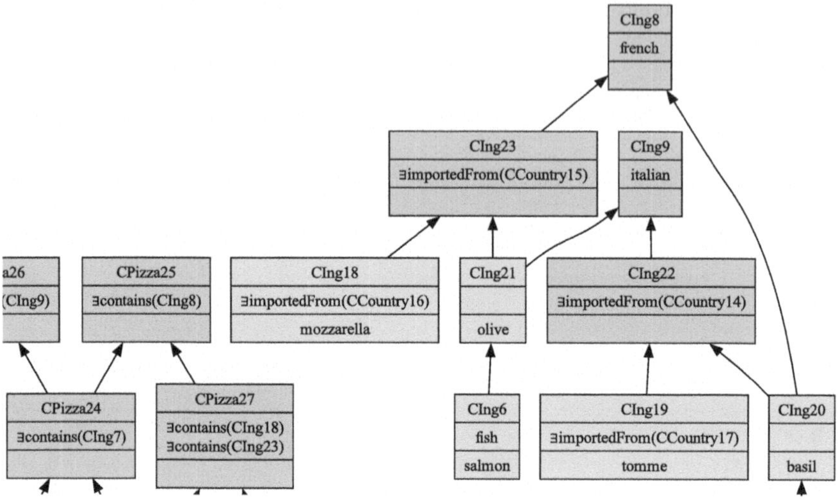

Fig. 4. Excerpts of the AOC-posets of pizzas, ingredients and countries of RCF Table 3 at Step 1.

Table 4. Relational context family with food and countries to illustrate circular references.

Food	seed	root
Manioc		x
Colza	x	
Parsnip	x	x
Ginseng	x	x

Country	Europe	Asia
France	x	
China		x

isProducedIn	France	China
Manioc		
Colza	x	x
Parsnip	x	
Ginseng		x

consumesALotOf	Manioc	Colza	Parsnip	Ginseng
France		x		
China	x			

when the bottom concept $\bot$ is referred, the tag `_ALL_ATTRIBUTES_` is substituted to $\bot$. E.g. $\exists$ `r(_ALL_ATTRIBUTES_)` can be read "has at least a r link to one object which owns all attributes". Such objects are rarely found in real datasets. For example in `CPizza18` (Fig. 2), $\forall\exists$ `contains(CIng9)` is rewritten $\forall\exists$ `contains(_ALL_OBJECTS_)`, as $Intent(CIng9) = \emptyset$ (top concept).

Variants Included in FCA4J. The adopted solution to handle critical rewriting cases presented above, precised using tags, is implemented in FCA4J. This solution corresponds to the variant **rai** (**r**ewriting/**a**ttributes/**i**ntroduced.) Two other variants were implemented in FCA4J. In variant **ra** (**r**ewriting/**a**ttributes), the target concept C of a relational attribute is also recursively rewritten using its introduced attributes. When C intent does not contain introduced attributes, C is not replaced. In variant **ri** (**r**ewriting/**i**nherited), the target concept C of a relational attribute is always replaced by the attributes of the entire intent of C (introduced attributes and inherited attributes). Inherited attributes are preceded by the tag `/_INH_/`.

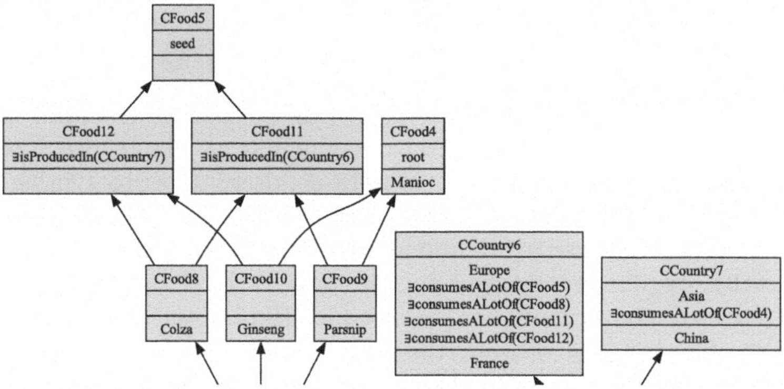

Fig. 5. Excerpts of the AOC-posets of food and countries of RCF Table 4 before rewriting.

The Rewriting Algorithm. Algorithm 1 presents the rewriting procedure, restricted to variant **rai** which is used for implications in this paper. In the algorithm, for a concept $C = (X, Y)$, we use the set of introduced attributes, i.e. $IntroducedAtt(C) = \{a \in Y | \forall C_{sup} = (X_{sup}, Y_{sup}) \in \mathcal{L}(dest(r)), C \leq C_{sup}, a \notin Y_{sup}\}$, and the set of introduced objects, i.e. $IntroducedObj(C) = \{o \in X | \forall C_{sub} = (C_{sub}, Y_{sub}) \in \mathcal{L}(dest(r)), C \geq C_{sub}, o \notin X_{sub}\}$. The algorithm applies to an attribute at Step i, and stores the visited concepts for dealing with circular references. The primitive attributes are kept unchanged by the rewriting (Lines 1–2). Lines 3–4 deal with the self-reference case, where a relational attribute refers to the concept where it is introduced. In Lines 5–15, the concept in the relational attribute is present and not yet visited. It is replaced by its introduced attributes if any (Lines 6–7), or alternatively by its inherited attributes if any, or by tags (Lines 10–15). If the top does not introduce attribute, it is replaced by a tag (Line 15). In Lines 16–26, the cases of disappeared concepts or already visited concepts are managed with rewriting by introduced objects (Lines 17–18), by whole extent (Lines 20–22), or by tags (Lines 23–26).

Implication Rewriting. Rewriting the implications means only rewriting the relational attributes. The rewriting variant to use depends on the kind of analysis expected by the domain expert. For instance, variant **ra** can be used for initial implication mining, where the appearance of a concept name indicates that a more complex analysis is skipped. This reduces the interpretation work. Moreover, as implications are computed from the extended formal contexts, one can expect that variant **ri** should be avoided to limit redundancies. In the experiment presented in the next section, we use variant **rai** which is more complete than **ra**, without the redundancies introduced by **ri**.

4 Delivering RCA Artifacts with LLM

This section introduces our second contribution, i.e., the delivery of intelligible implications by LLM to a domain expert. This work is applied to a concrete dataset. The designed prompts and all data mentioned in this section are available online[3]. The software implementing the proposal is FCA4J version 0.4.5.

Agroecological Dataset. The dataset [15] is an excerpt of scientific literature data collected by the Knomana[4] initiative. Knomana seeks to provide farmers with botanical products based on local flora as alternatives to synthetic pesticides and antimicrobials. The dataset comprises 5 FC (i.e., `ProtSystem`, `Plant`, `Crop`, `Pest`, and `OrganismInfo`) and 6 RC (i.e., `uses`, `protects`, `controls`, `pl_CharactBy`, `cr_CharactBy`, and `pe_CharactBy`). FC `Plant`, `Crop`, and `Pest` represent respectively a plant (used to produce the botanical product), a crop, and a pest. These 3 FC contain the species, the genus, and the family of each organism according to the taxonomy. Each of these FC is related to FC `OrganismInfo`, using respectively RC `pl_CharactBy`, `cr_CharactBy`, and `pe_CharactBy`, to know whether the organism is consumed and used as a medicine. FC `ProtSystem` represents the agricultural crop protection systems (ACPS). The latter reifies the ternary relation of an ACPS that uses (RC `uses`) a plant (FC `Plant`) to protect (RC `protects`) a crop (FC `Crop`) to `control` (RC `controls`) a pest (FC `Pest`). The dataset contains 600 organisms and 721 ACPS.

Prompt Template. We designed a prompt template complying with the recommendations of OpenAI[5] and literature [16,21]. It aims to be instantiated for a variety of relational datasets. It is divided into five sections. The first one describes the context of the rewriting, i.e., the thematic domain. It also introduces RCA and the objective of the prompt. The second and third sections describe the syntax of the relational attributes and the syntax of RCA implications respectively. These two sections are the tricky parts of the prompt as presenting this syntax clearly is a need to avoid LLM misunderstanding the expected work. The two last sections consist of asking LLM to reformulate an implication in natural language while applying particularities of the implications in the domain if any.

Instantiated Prompt. In the prompt instantiated for Knomana, we indicate that the context concerns ACPS and provide a description of the dataset. In the syntax implication section, we introduce two specific codifications: i) for Boolean attributes (regarding consumed/not consumed and used/not used as medicine characteristics) and ii) for species name provided with the abbreviation sp. (i.e. an unknown species from the genus such as Mentha sp. corresponding to an unknown species of mint) and spp. (i.e. several unknown species from a genus). In addition, we add a rule to limit redundancies in the implication due to the taxonomy encoding. It consists of removing the most general taxonomic levels for each organism, i.e. the family name when the genus is precised, and the genus name and the family name when the species name is precised.

[3] https://gite.lirmm.fr/fca4j/companion-data-for-rca-knomana-implications-llm/.
[4] https://www.knomana.org/en.
[5] https://platform.openai.com/docs/guides/prompt-engineering.

Results Provided by LLM. The implications used for this evaluation are part of the Duquenne-Guigues basis of implications computed for the Knomana dataset, as it is a non redundant implication set of minimal cardinality. 1391 implications, with support > 0, were computed for FC `ProtSystem`. We selected ten representative implications, with a varying number of relational attributes. A total of 4 LLM sessions for the 10 implications were conducted: three using Gemini-2.5-pro-exp-03-25 and one using chatGPTo3. We chose Gemini as it ranks first on the LMArena leaderboard[6] [5] on assessing human preferences. chatGPTo3 was used to be another source of reformulation. LLM reformulation examples are shown in Table 5 for one representative implication.

Table 5. An implication and two reformulations by LLM.

`exist_controls(PeSpecies_ SpodopteraLitura & exist_pe_CharactBy(Species_SpodopteraLitura)), exist_controls(PeFamily_Noctuidae & exist_pe_CharactBy(Family_ Noctuidae)& exist_pe_CharactBy(Food_)& exist_pe_CharactBy(Medical_)) => exist_controls(PeGenus_Spodoptera & exist_pe_CharactBy(Genus_ Spodoptera)), exist_protects (exist_cr_CharactBy(Medical_X))`	"Whenever a system controls the moth *Spodoptera litura*—a pest that is neither eaten nor used medicinally—the crop it protects is used as a medicinal plant." *by LLM chatGPTo3, Computed 18 April 2025* "if the ACPS controls the pest species Spodoptera litura (which implies Genus Spodoptera and Family Noctuidae), that cannot be consumed and cannot be used as a medication, then the ACPS protects a crop that can be used as a medication." *by LLM Gemini 2.5, Computed 18 April 2025*

The 40 reformulations are intelligible and easy to compare with the initial implications for expert familiar with FCA. We checked the correctness and completeness of the 40 reformulations provided by LLMs (cf. Table 6). Among these 40, 38 are correct, i.e., 31 contain complete and non redundant information, 1 includes redundant information, and 6 exhibit omissions. In the 2 incorrect reformulations, which concern the same implication having the highest number of relational attributes (i.e., 26), an error occurred in the interpretation of the encoding of Boolean-valued attributes. As lesson learned, developing the prompts to make LLM rewrite an implication built by RCA required a strong expertise leveraging different techniques (e.g., Chain of Thought, Few Shot). The results allow any domain expert understanding implications despite RCA formalism. The very few misinterpretations can be resolved by improving the prompts.

5 Related Work

LLMs are now part of increasingly diverse processing chains, e.g., [14]. To our knowledge, the only work which combines FCA and LLM to deliver a kind of interpretation is [1] (and slides of the talk), where authors propose prompt

[6] https://lmarena.ai/leaderboard. Visited 2025/04/19.

Table 6. Overall metrics for the reformulation of the 10 implications by LLMs.

	support	#rel. attrib.	taxo	sp./spp.	#complete/correct	#misinterpretation	#redundancy	#omission
i1	10	10			4			
i2	1	26	x	x	1	2		1
i3	20	8			4			
i4	222	10			3			1
i5	32	10	x		3			1
i6	380	12	x		3			1
i7	43	8			4			
i8	50	10			4			
i9	594	10	x		3			1
i10	80	10	x		2		1	1

templates for LLM to give names to anonymous FCA concepts. Another work [3] combines Triadic Concept Analysis (TCA) and LLM prompting for software system specification assistance in the context of software product lines.

Several solutions for delivering RCA results to domain experts have been proposed in the literature. Some are based on graphs, such as [8] that produces model transformation patterns in the software domain, [9] that exploits hierarchies of concepts graphs, and [18] which leverages hierarchies of closed partially-ordered patterns (CPO-patterns) to build more specifically sequential patterns. Visualization tools are proposed, such as RCAviz [13] which allows to navigate between the different lattices, and needs the domain expert to have been trained to understand them. FCAvizIR [17] is another visualization tool, dedicated to navigate RCA implications, which is based on a form of relational attribute rewriting provided by a previous version of the library FCA4J [12]. Several works have introduced a form of relational attribute rewriting by intents, which is the only direction that has been used in practical cases [6,7,17,23] to our knowledge. This rewriting was done in the context of the interpretation of RCA implications. In [6,7], an ad-hoc algorithm has been applied to a dataset whose data model has no cycle. The rewriting uses attributes. In [23], circular data models are considered, but circular dependencies are avoided. When a target concept is rewritten, it is replaced by the intent of the concept as it was at the creation time (and not at the current step) of the concept. Since at the creation time, the relational attributes refer to concepts created at previous steps, they are recursively rewritten until only primitive attributes are found. In [22], it is suggested to use Concept generators.

In this paper, given that domain experts are rarely familiar with graph representations and with FCA/RCA, and that our aim is to leverage LLM to exploit the result, we explore the rewriting of relational attributes into plain text. Compared to existing rewriting techniques, we address the problem of disappearing concepts and circular dependencies, and we allow different rewriting variants concerning the inherited attributes/objects.

Algorithm 1: Rewriting attributes

Input: x: an attribute (primitive or relational) introduced in concept C_{int}
$\mathcal{L}^i(\text{dest}(r))$: concept lattice of target formal context of r at step i
$L_{Visited}$: the list of concepts already visited in the rewriting chain
Output: the rewriting of x

if *x is a primitive attribute* **then**
  return x
// Self-reference
if $x = qr(C)$ *and* $C_{int} = C$ **then**
  return $qr(\_SELF\_)$
// Referenced concept is present in $\mathcal{L}^i(\text{dest}(r))$ and not yet visited
if $x = qr(C)$ *and* $C_{int} \neq C$ ***and*** $C \in \mathcal{L}^i(dest(r))$ ***and*** $C \notin L_{Visited}$ **then**
  if $IntroducedAtt(C) = \{a_1, \ldots, a_n\} \neq \emptyset$ **then**
    return $qr\big(R[a_1] \wedge \ldots \wedge R[a_n]\big)$
  else
    if $Intent(C) \neq \emptyset$ **then**
      if $|Intent(C) = \{a_1, \ldots, a_n\}| \neq |\mathcal{A}_i^+|$ **then**
        // All attributes are inherited - but not Bottom
        return $qr\big(/\_INH\_/\ R[a_1] \wedge \cdots \wedge R[a_n]\big)$
      else
        // Bottom
        return $qr(\_ALL\_ATTRIBUTES\_)$
    else
      // Top with no introduced attribute
      return $qr(\_ALL\_OBJECTS\_)$
// Referenced concept has disappeared or is already visited
if $x = qr(C)$ *and* $C_{int} \neq C$ ***and*** $\big(C \notin \mathcal{L}^i(dest(r))$ ***or*** $C \in L\_Visited\big)$ **then**
  if $IntroducedObj(C) = \{o_1, \ldots, o_n\} \neq \emptyset$ **then**
    return $qr\big(/\_OBJ\_/\ o_1 \wedge \cdots \wedge o_n\big)$
  else
    if $Extent(C) = \{o_1, \ldots, o_n\} \neq \emptyset$ **then**
      if $|Extent(C)| \neq |O_i|$ **then**
        // Objects introduced or inherited
        return $qr\big(/\_OBJ\_/\_INH\_/\ o_1 \wedge \cdots \wedge o_n\big)$
      else
        // Top inheriting all objects
        return $qr(\_ALL\_OBJECTS\_)$
    else
      // Bottom without objects
      return $qr(\_ALL\_ATTRIBUTES\_)$

6 Conclusion

To enable domain experts to understand the results computed by RCA, this paper presents a set of variants for rewriting relational attributes. Unfolding the concepts and using tags makes relational attributes intelligible without reading the lattice. We developed a generic prompt to make LLM reformulate implications and we apply it to a concrete dataset. We aim to insert the process in visualization tools such as FCAvizIR to enable domain expert interaction.

In a next step, we will conduct a larger evaluation on other parts of the Knomana dataset, and use metrics from Information Retrieval (i.e., precision, recall, and F-measure) to evaluate the reformulation at the implication level and the relational attribute level. We will also leverage this approach in another application domains, in particular the software engineering domain for enhancing existing tasks where FCA and RCA have proven their effectiveness.

Finally, we plan to develop concept rewriting and use LLM to summarize concept lattices. This will require to use LLM configurations with large working memory, as large concept lattices may be considered.

Acknowledgments. The authors thank the anonymous reviewers for their valuable comments that helped improving the paper. This work was supported by the French National Research Agency under the Investments for the Future Program, referred as ANR-16-CONV-0004 (#Digitag) and ANR SmartFCA, Grant ANR-21-CE23-0023 of the French National Research Agency.

References

1. Aranda-Corral, G., Bundy, A., Borrego-Díaz, J., Chan, P.: Grounding problem in formal concept analysis by means of large language models. In: Ws. Late Breaking Advances on Conceptual Structures @ Concepts 2024 (2024). https://concepts2024.uca.es/lbacs/
2. Bazin, A., Galasso, J., Kahn, G.: Polyadic relational concept analysis. Int. J. Approx. Reason. **164**, 109067 (2024)
3. Bazin, A., Gutierrez, A., Huchard, M., Martin, P., Zhang, Y.H.: Variability-driven user-story generation using LLM and triadic concept analysis. In: 20th International Conference on Evaluation of Novel Approaches to Software Engineering (ENASE) (2025)
4. Berry, A., Gutierrez, A., Huchard, M., Napoli, A., Sigayret, A.: Hermes: a simple and efficient algorithm for building the aoc-poset of a binary relation. Ann. Math. Artif. Intell. **72**(1–2), 45–71 (2014)
5. Chiang, W.L., et al.: Chatbot arena: an open platform for evaluating LLMs by human preference (2024)
6. Dolques, X., Le Ber, F., Huchard, M., Grac, C.: Performance-friendly rule extraction in large water data-sets with AOC posets and relational concept analysis. Int. J. Gen. Syst. **45**(2), 187–210 (2016)
7. Dolques, X., Braud, A., Huchard, M., Le Ber, F.: RCAexplore, a FCA based tool to explore relational data. In: ICFCA, vol. 2378, pp. 55–59. CEUR (2019)

8. Dolques, X., Huchard, M., Nebut, C., Reitz, P.: Learning transformation rules from transformation examples: an approach based on relational concept analysis. In: 2010 14th IEEE International Enterprise Distributed Object Computing Conference Workshops, pp. 27–32 (2010)
9. Ferré, S., Cellier, P.: How hierarchies of concept graphs can facilitate the interpretation of RCA lattices? In: Proceedings of CLA, vol. 2123, pp. 69–80. CEUR (2018)
10. Ferré, S., Cellier, P.: Graph-fca: an extension of formal concept analysis to knowledge graphs. Disc. Appl. Math. **273**, 81–102 (2020)
11. Ganter, B., Wille, R.: Formal Concept Analysis: Mathematical Foundations. Springer, Heidelberg (1999)
12. Gutierrez, A., Huchard, M., Martin, P.: FCA4J: a java library for relational concept analysis and formal concept analysis. In: ETAFCA 2022@CLA2022. CEUR Workshop Proceedings, vol. 3308, pp. 207–212 (2022)
13. Huchard, M., Martin, P., Muller, E., Poncelet, P., Raveneau, V., Sallaberry, A.: RCAviz: exploratory search in multi-relational datasets represented using relational concept analysis. Int. J. Approx. Reason. **166**, 109123 (2024)
14. Liu, Z., et al.: Make LLM a testing expert: bringing human-like interaction to mobile GUI testing via functionality-aware decisions. In: Proceedings of 46th ICSE. ACM (2024)
15. Martin, P., et al.: Dataset on Noctuidae species used to evaluate the separate concerns in conceptual analysis: application to a life sciences knowledge base (2021). https://doi.org/10.18167/DVN1/HTFE8T
16. Mondal, S., Bappon, S.D., Roy, C.K.: Enhancing user interaction in chatgpt: characterizing and consolidating multiple prompts for issue resolution. In: 21st IEEE/ACM International Conference on Mining Software Repositories, pp. 222–226. ACM (2024)
17. Musslin, L., et al.: FCAvizIR: exploring relational data set's implications using metrics and topics. In: CONCEPTS 2024. LNCS, vol. 14914, pp. 132–148. Springer, Heidelberg (2024). https://doi.org/10.1007/978-3-031-67868-4_10
18. Nica, C., Braud, A., Le Ber, F.: Rca-seq: an original approach for enhancing the analysis of sequential data based on hierarchies of multilevel closed partially-ordered patterns. Disc. Appl. Math. **273**, 232–251 (2020)
19. Rouane-Hacène, M.R., Huchard, M., Napoli, A., Valtchev, P.: Relational concept analysis: mining concept lattices from multi-relational data. Ann. Math. Artif. Intell. **67**(1), 81–108 (2013)
20. Saab, N., Huchard, M., Martin, P.: Evaluating formal concept analysis software for anomaly detection and correction. In: Proceedings of (CLA 2022). CEUR Workshop Proceedings, vol. 3308, pp. 213–218. CEUR-WS.org (2022)
21. Schulhoff, S., Ilie, M., Balepur, N., Kahadze, K., et al.: The prompt report: a systematic survey of prompting techniques (2024). https://arxiv.org/abs/2406.06608
22. Wajnberg, M.: Analyse relationnelle de concepts: une méthode polyvalente pour l'extraction de connaissance. Thèse de doctorat, Univ. du Québec à Montréal & Univ. de Lorraine (2020)
23. Wajnberg, M., Valtchev, P., Lezoche, M., Panetto, H., Massé, A.B.: Mining process factor causality links with multi-relational associations. In: Proceedings of K-CAP 2019, pp. 263–266. ACM (2019)

Patterns, Clusters, Visualization and Software

Towards Explainable Clustering in Process Mining and Sequential Pattern Mining: A Formal Framework

Marwa Trabelsi[1], Salah Eddine Boukhetta[2(✉)], Damien Mondou[1], Karell Bertet[1], Sébastien Amoury[1], Noura Joudieh[1], Rouaa Wannous[1], Cyril Faucher[1], Christophe Demko[1], Ronan Champagnat[1], and Alain Bouju[1]

[1] La Rochelle University, 23 Av. Albert Einstein, 17000 La Rochelle, France
{marwa.trabelsi,damien.mondou,karell.bertet,sebastien.amoury, noura.joudieh,rouaa.wannous,cyril.faucher,christophe.demko, ronan.champagnat,alain.bouju}@univ-lr.fr

[2] Aneo, 122 Av. du Général Leclerc, 92100 Boulogne-Billancourt, France
sboukhetta@aneo.fr

Abstract. In this paper, we propose a unified framework to enhance the explainability of clustering results by bridging methodologies from Trace Clustering in Process Mining and Sequence Pattern Mining. Our approach formalizes a common representation that transforms event logs and trajectories into structured sequences, ensuring consistency across sequential data types. We first introduce a systematic process for converting raw data into structured sequences, allowing for a coherent analysis of logs and trajectories. We then explore various clustering techniques, including Trace Clustering in Process Mining, Sequential Pattern Mining, and the `GALACTIC` approach, emphasizing their role in uncovering interpretable behavioral patterns. Through real-world dataset examples, on which we conducted behavioral pattern extraction studies, we demonstrate how integrating these methodologies enables a more comprehensive understanding of sequential data. Furthermore, we construct an event log and derive a process model from clusters obtained via Sequence Pattern Mining, illustrating how specific patterns contribute to cluster emergence. This structured approach enhances interpretability and provides a foundation for future research on explainable clustering.

Keywords: Explainable clustering · Trace clustering in Process mining · Sequential pattern mining

1 Introduction

The growing digitalization of our interactions generates large amounts of sequential data, from event logs in digital platforms [10,11] to trajectories in the physical world [12,15]. Despite their differences, both represent time-evolving sequences valuable for understanding behaviors, optimizing processes, and supporting decisions. However, analyzing such data is challenging due to its high

P. Cellier et al. (Eds.): CONCEPTS 2025, LNAI 15941, pp. 143–160, 2025.
https://doi.org/10.1007/978-3-032-03364-2_9

dimensionality and variability. Traditional clustering methods, while effective for grouping similar data points, these techniques often lack native mechanisms for interpreting the behavioral meaning behind the clusters. Furthermore, two approaches are widely used to analyze and cluster sequential data. Trace Clustering in Process Mining, which groups similar traces of users and builds process models that provide a clear view of how the process is executed [1], and Sequence Pattern Mining, which discovers frequent subsequences revealing structural patterns. While often used separately, combining them can enhance the explainability of clustering outcomes [8].

This paper introduces then a **unified framework** to analyze event logs and trajectories by representing them as activity sequences. By integrating Trace Clustering with Sequence Pattern Mining and the `GALACTIC` approach, we extract meaningful patterns within clusters and visualize them through process models. Built upon Formal Concept Analysis, `GALACTIC` offers a flexible and interpretable way to explore patterns in heterogeneous and sequential data. Real-world examples demonstrate how this synergy yields richer insights and a deeper understanding of sequential data.

The remainder of this paper is organized as follows. Section 2 presents the transformation of raw event logs and trajectories into a unified sequence representation, enabling cross-domain analysis. Section 3 introduces our unified framework for sequence clustering, which combines techniques from Process Mining, Sequential Pattern Mining, and the `GALACTIC` approach to enhance interpretability. Section 4 describes the datasets used to illustrate the approach, covering both digital and physical-world sequential data. Section 5 reports preliminary results that demonstrate the framework's potential for behavioral analysis through interpretable, cluster-based process models. Finally, Sect. 6 summarizes the main contributions and outlines directions for future work.

2 From Logs/Trajectories to Sequences

2.1 Logs Formalization : From Logs to Sequences

An event log captures a specific activity that takes place at a particular point in time and is associated with a unique case. It typically includes three core elements: a case ID (an identifier), the activity that occurred, and a timestamp indicating the exact time of the activity. In most cases, when extracted from information systems, event logs contain raw data representing user actions. To analyze user behavior, it is essential to extract ordered sequences of actions from raw logs. However, raw logs often lack structured activity information, requiring a **preprocessing enrichment step** [10, 14]. This step leverages domain knowledge and semantic interpretation to map raw data r to meaningful activities. This process can be formalized as:

$$E = \{(u, a, t) \mid u \in U, a \in A, t \in T \text{ and } r \models (u, a, t)\} \subseteq U \times A \times T \qquad (1)$$

where U represents the set of users, A the set of possible actions, and T the set of timestamps. Each triplet (u, a, t) corresponds to a log entry r describing the execution of an action $a \in A$ by user $u \in U$ at time t.

User-Centric Projection. First, we extract from E the trace E_u for each user $u \in U$, which contains all actions performed by the user. This transformation shifts the focus from global logs to a collection of user-specific traces, formally defined as:

$$(E_u = \{(a,t) \mid (u,a,t) \in E\})_{u \in U} \tag{2}$$

At this stage, the dataset is a collection of individual user traces E_u, enabling personalized analysis

Temporal Ordering. Next, for each user u, we sort the actions in E_u based on their timestamps to obtain the chronological sequence S_u. This transformation ensures that actions are analyzed in their natural order of occurrence, and the dataset is a family of individual user sequences S_u of length s_u:

$$(S_u = \langle (a_i, t_i)_{i \leq s_u} \in E_u \mid t_i < t_{i+1} \rangle)_{u \in U} \tag{3}$$

After this step, the dataset consists of structured user action sequences, facilitating the clustering for behavior modeling using process mining. In this paper, to simplify notations, we denote a temporal sequence by $S_u = \langle (a_i, t_i) \rangle$ instead of $\langle (a_i, t_i) \rangle_{i \leq s_u}$.

2.2 Trajectories Formalization: From Trajectories to Sequences

The raw trajectory of a mobile object is a list of GPS track sorted by timestamps. The analysis of trajectories consists in analysing the following dataset of trajectories where U is the set of mobile objects, and t_u is the length of the trajectory T_u of the mobile object $u \in U$:

$$(T_u = \langle (gps_j, t_j) \mid t_j < t_{j+1} \rangle_{j \leq t_u})_{u \in U} \tag{4}$$

A raw trajectory encoded as a sequence of coordinates gps_j provides no information about the context in which the object evolves. The raw trajectories are enriched into temporal sequence of activities in the following way:

Semantic Enrichment of Trajectories into Activities. Let us introduce the user's domain of activities by A, where each activity $a \in A$ is deduced from the geographical information gps_j by an enrichment $gps_j \models a$. Other parameters can be considered for this enrichment, such as the speed of the object for example. Each raw trajectory T_u for the object u is then replaced by the enriched trajectory E_u, and the dataset is a collection of enriched trajectory E_u:

$$(E_u = \langle (a_j, t_j) \mid (gps_j, t_j) \in T_u \text{ and } gps_j \models a_j \in A \rangle_{j \leq t_u})_{u \in U} \tag{5}$$

Time-Segmentation. When activities are similar activities at consecutive timestamps, they are grouped together and we obtain a collection of individual interval sequence S_u of activities of length $s_u \leq t_u$:

$$(S_u = \langle (a_i, [t_i, t_k]) \mid a_i = a_j \text{ for } i \leq j \leq k \rangle_{i \leq s_u})_{u \in U} \tag{6}$$

2.3 Summary : Unified Framework

The transformation from raw data to structured sequences follows different treatments depending on whether we are dealing with event logs or trajectories. A key distinction lies in the transition from sets to ordered sequences, ensuring a coherent representation of sequential data. Table 1 summarizes the different steps involved in structuring logs and trajectories: For event logs, the process begins with an initial dataset representing user interactions as sets of events. These are then projected in a user-centric manner to retain only relevant action-time pairs. Finally, an explicit temporal ordering is applied, producing a structured sequence where each action is associated with a specific timestamp. In contrast, trajectories start as sequential GPS traces annotated with timestamps. These are then mapped to semantic informations (e.g. locations or speed), converting raw GPS data into relevant activity representations. Rather than a single timestamp per action, trajectories typically involve time intervals that define the duration of activities. A key contribution of the unified framework is that it highlights the data processing steps where domain expertise is required, symbolized by $\models$. For event logs, expert knowledge is essential to extract relevant (u, a, t) triples. For trajectories, expertise is involved during the enrichment phase that maps raw GPS data to semantically meaningful activities. Depending on the analysis objective, two simplified representations can be adopted : (1) **Temporal sequences** $S_u = \langle a_i, t_i \rangle$ instead of interval sequences $S_u = \langle a_i, [t_i, t_k] \rangle$ for trajectories when focusing on discrete event occurrences rather than durations. (2) **Simplified sequences** $S_u = \langle a_i \rangle$ where only the ordered list of actions is retained, while timestamps are implicitly preserved through their sequence order.

Table 1. Transformation of event logs and trajectories into structured sequences

Logs	(1) Initial data:	$E = \{(u, a, t) \mid r \models (u, a, t)\}$
	(2) User-centric projection:	$(E_u = \{(a, t)\})_{u \in U}$
	(3) Temporal ordering:	$(S_u = \langle (a_i, t_i) \rangle)_{u \in U}$
Trajectories	(1) Initial data:	$(T_u = \langle (gps_j, t_j) \rangle)_{u \in U}$
	(2) Semantic trajectories:	$(E_u = \langle (a_j, t_j) \mid gps_j \models a_j \rangle)_{u \in U}$
	(3) Time-segmentation:	$(S_u = \langle (a_i, [t_i, t_k]) \rangle)_{u \in U}$

3 Sequence Clustering

This study focuses on sequence clustering, which can be applied to various types of data, such as event logs or trajectories. Different clustering methods can be used depending on the nature of the data and the specific objectives of the analysis. A distinction is generally made between partitioning and hierarchical approaches. ***Partitioning or density-based algorithms*** distribute the data into k groups, with two types of membership: exclusive, where each data point belongs to a single cluster, and non-exclusive, where a data point can belong to multiple clusters. Well-known partitioning-based algorithms include K-Means and K-Medoids, which, given an integer k, find a partition that minimizes the variance within each group. Density-based approaches such as DBSCAN [7] and OPTICS [13] offer an alternative by identifying clusters based on data density. ***Hierarchical algorithms*** compute a hierarchy where each cluster is a subcluster of its parent(s). These methods are classified into two types: divisive (top-down) methods, which iteratively split groups starting from the entire dataset, and agglomerative (bottom-up) methods, which progressively merge items into larger clusters. A partition can be extracted from a hierarchy by selecting clusters based on an appropriate criterion. Hierarchical Agglomerative Clustering (HAC) [13] is a widely used approach that constructs a cluster hierarchy using a distance matrix between data points. These methods are well-suited for numerical data or data for which a distance or similarity measure is available.

When dealing with sequential data, clustering methods are typically applied by defining suitable distance or similarity measures between sequences. However, these approaches often lack mechanisms to naturally reveal the underlying behavioral patterns shared within each cluster. Process mining techniques (Sect. 3.1) address this limitation by deriving descriptive models directly from clustered event logs. Likewise, Sequential Pattern Mining (Sect. 3.2) enables a structural analysis of raw sequences, offering both clustering and pattern-based characterization without relying on intermediate vector representations.

3.1 Trace Clustering in Process Mining

Process mining is an interdisciplinary field that bridges data science and process science, leveraging event logs generated by information systems to analyze, monitor, and improve business processes [1]. Process discovery is a fundamental component of process mining, aimed at constructing a process model from an event log. Process models provide a structured representation of processes, enabling their formalization. Various formalisms exist, such as BPMN models, Petri nets, and Directly Follows Graphs (DFGs). These formalisms primarily focus on modeling the control flow of activities. Several metrics are employed to assess the quality of a process model.

Trace clustering is a specific type of clustering applied to event logs in process mining. It focuses on grouping execution traces (i.e., sequences of events or activities) that exhibit similar behavior. The goal is to improve process discovery, conformance checking, and performance analysis by distinguishing different process variants that may be hidden within a complex, heterogeneous event log. Several approaches exist for trace clustering, each differing in how traces are represented and compared. In this study, we focus on two main approaches: **trace-based** clustering, where traces are preserved as ordered event sequences, and **feature-based** clustering, where traces are transformed into structured feature vectors encoding statistical properties such as event frequency, time intervals, or frequent subsequence patterns [14]. The process begins with the preprocessing and extraction of traces, representing process instances or users as **sequences** of activities. Noise filtering and log cleaning can be applied at this stage to remove incomplete or inconsistent traces. Once extracted, traces are represented either as sequences or as feature vectors, depending on the chosen approach [1]. To group similar traces, an appropriate distance measure is applied. trace-based clustering commonly relies on similarity measures such as Levenshtein distance, while feature-based clustering favors vector similarity measures like Euclidean distance or cosine similarity. In some cases, clustering algorithms such as DBSCAN or Mean Shift can be directly applied to feature vectors without explicitly computing pairwise distances. Once clustering is performed using classical clustering methods, the resulting clusters are analyzed to ensure they provide meaningful insights into process variations. Evaluation occurs at two levels: first, during the clustering phase, where metrics such as the silhouette score assess coherence and separation; second, during the process modeling phase, where the relevance and clarity of the discovered process models are examined. Each cluster leads to the discovery of a corresponding process model, providing a clair and structured representation of the underlying sequences [1].

3.2 Sequential Pattern Mining

Sequential Pattern Mining (SPM) is similar to hierarchical clustering in its goal of extracting a hierarchy of frequent sequential patterns, each describing a cluster of data, subject to a minimum support threshold as input. The process follows an agglomerative approach: beginning with a pattern encompassing the entire dataset, it iteratively divides clusters until the resulting patterns meet the frequency threshold. Unlike traditional clustering, which relies on similarity or distance metrics, SPM identifies maximal common subsequences shared by multiple sequences. These patterns represent the longest recurring ordered subsequences that appear frequently across different data instances. This property enhances interpretability, making SPM particularly suitable for decision-support systems, as it uncovers meaningful structures within event sequences. Alternatively, SPM can serve as a preprocessing step, where extracted patterns acting as features enhance sequence clustering by capturing meaningful similarities before applying conventional clustering techniques. A comprehensive survey by Fournier [8] details these developments. Sequential pattern mining traces its origins to the 1990s with Agrawal and Srikant's pioneering work. They extended the Apriori algorithm for frequent itemset mining to sequences, proposing the Generalized Sequential Patterns (GSP) algorithm. Subsequent advancements, such as PrefixSpan and SPADE, improved efficiency. However, early methods faced challenges: excessive computational time, overwhelming pattern volumes, and redundancy. Closed patterns (e.g., CloSpan) addressed redundancy by focusing on maximal subsequences. Further refinements incorporated constraints like maximum subsequence length, regular expressions, and inter-item gaps. When sequences include timestamps $\langle (a_i, t_i) \rangle$, temporal pattern mining enriches analysis by incorporating time constraints. For example, in movement data, a pattern $\langle L1, L2 \rangle$ lacks temporal context visits to $L1$ and $L2$ could occur hours or months apart. By enforcing temporal proximity, such constraints eliminate irrelevant patterns with large time gaps, improve expressiveness, and reduce redundancy.

3.3 Conceptual Analysis and GALACTIC Approach

An alternative and effective approach leverages Formal Concept Analysis (FCA), a mathematical framework where a concept is defined as a pair: a maximal subgroup of data (extent) and the attributes they share (intent). Each concept can be seen as either a closed pattern or a data cluster, depending on whether its intent or extent is considered. The complete set of concepts naturally forms a hierarchical structure known as the concept lattice, where the root concept contains all data. The concept lattice is uniquely defined by the relationship between data and their attributes, governed by the Galois connection. FCA-based methods exploit the algebraic and structural properties of lattices and closure operators to analyze data efficiently. To extend FCA beyond binary data, the pattern structures formalism generalizes the Galois connection to handle complex data types, such as sequences [5].

Inspired by pattern structures, GALACTIC provides a flexible framework for describing and exploring heterogeneous data using generic predicates. A concept in GALACTIC consists of a data cluster and a set of predicates that depend on the data type, whether numerical, binary, categorical, or more complex. For instance, numerical data can be described by predicates such as "is lesser/-greater than x," while sequence data can be described by predicates like "match x as a subsequence" or "match x as a prefix". The concept lattice is computed using the NextPriorityConcept algorithm [6] through a divisive approach, which starts from the cluster/concept that encompasses all data along with their shared description in terms of predicates. Each concept is then successively divided into predecessor concepts, for which new descriptions are computed. These concepts are computed on demand and do not need any kind of preprocessing. Beyond data description, GALACTIC integrates various exploration strategies to navigate through the numerous patterns generated. These strategies range from exhaustive approaches, considering all possible subgroups, to more targeted methods optimizing pattern selection and reducing the deluge of patterns. Several descriptions and strategies have been implemented for classical data types, among them, the *Numerical* description $\delta_N(V)$ of a set of numerical values $V = v_1..v_n$ that considers the max and min values of V as descriptive predicates. Sequence data analysis was incorporated into the GALACTIC platform [3], introducing descriptions and strategies for simple sequences, temporal sequences, and interval sequences. For simple sequences, the *Maximal Common Subsequences*, noted as $\delta_{MCS}(\{S_u\}_{u\in U})$, represents the maximal common subsequences shared by a set of sequences $\{S_u\}_{u\in U}$, and the Prefixed Common Subsequences $\delta_{PCS}(\{S_u\}_{u\in U})$, capture their longest common prefix. In addition to a *Naive* strategy σ_{SN} which is exhaustiv, the *Augmented* strategy σ_{SA} for simple sequences is proposed to reduce the number of generated concepts. Descriptions have also been implemented for temporal and interval sequences, among which we can mention the *Maximal Common Interval* description δ_{MCI}.

3.4 Behavior Extraction Through Clustering of Temporal and Sequential Patterns: Unified Framework

User log traces and object trajectories exhibit inherent structural similarities, as they both represent sequences of user activities over time. Extracting representative user behaviors from such sequences requires robust clustering techniques capable of handling both temporal and structural variations. More formally, given a set of users U, the clustering problem can be defined as follows:

Input: Collection of sequences $(S_u)_{u \in U}$
Output: Collection of n clusters of users $(C_k \mid C_k \subseteq U)_{k=1..n}$

Different clustering paradigms have been explored in the literature to identify patterns within sequential data. The choice of method affects the structure and interpretability of the extracted clusters:
Partitioning vs. Hierarchical Clustering: The set of clusters $(C_k)_{k=1..n}$ may form a strict partition where each user belongs to only one cluster, or a hierarchical structure where clusters may be nested, allowing for multi-level behavioral representation.
Process Mining Integration: In process mining, trace clustering is enhanced by associating each discovered cluster with a process model M_k, yielding a structured representation $(C_k, M_k)_{k=1..n}$, where M_k provides a graphical (process model) and executable abstraction of the clustered behaviors.
Sequential Pattern Mining: In contrast, sequential pattern mining leverages maximal subsequences P_k extracted from sequences to generate clusters based on recurring behavior patterns, leading to $(C_k, P_k)_{k=1..n}$.
Conceptual Clustering with `GALACTIC`: The `GALACTIC` framework extends clustering by integrating logic-based conceptual structures that encapsulate both the cluster C_k and its descriptive pattern P_k. These patterns may represent frequent subsequences, maximal prefixes, or structural predicates, resulting in $(C_k, P_k)_{k=1..n}$.

Table 2. Comparison of clustering approaches

	Structure	Computational Complexity
Trace clustering	Partition-based	Polynomial (traditional methods) Requires tuning to extract partitions
Sequential Pattern Mining	Hierarchical	Exponential (pattern explosion) Requires tuning to extract partitions
`GALACTIC`	Conceptual	Polynomial vs Exponential (prefix/subsequence) Strategies to limit pattern explosion

As shown in Table 2, different clustering approaches exhibit varying computational complexities based on their structure and the methods used. In Process Mining, trace clustering benefits from vector-based representations, enabling algorithms like k-means and HAC to operate with polynomial complexity, ensuring a manageable number of clusters through partitioning. However, these methods require careful tuning of parameters such as the number of clusters or distance metrics, which can impact computational efficiency. In contrast, Sequential Pattern Mining-based clustering inherently forms hierarchical structures, potentially leading to an exponential number of clusters and requiring costly computations of maximal common subsequences. Even when extracting a final partition from such a hierarchy, the intermediate hierarchical clustering step remains computationally expensive. To address these challenges, the `GALACTIC` framework optimizes clustering by limiting hierarchical growth and ensuring that maximal prefix computations remain polynomial, significantly reducing computational overhead while maintaining meaningful structural representations. These different approaches, while distinct, share complementary objectives and can be leveraged together to enhance the clustering process.

4 Datasets

In Sect. 2, we introduced a unified approach for analyzing event logs and trajectory data, applying trace clustering and sequential pattern mining to handle temporal or simple sequences. To illustrate this approach, we used five diverse datasets[1], on which we conducted behavioral pattern extraction studies, grouped into two distinct categories of interactions. The **first category** includes three event logs datasets that capture human-robot interactions and user navigation on Moodle and within the Digital Library. The **second category** includes two datasets dedicated to trajectory analysis: one tracking the movements of tourists in La Rochelle, France, and the other monitoring seal trajectories. Each dataset is transformed into a collection of user sequences of actions/activities, after which various clustering methods can be applied. Below, we describe how each dataset is structured, preprocessed, and clustered, illustrating the interplay of process mining and sequential pattern mining. To provide a comprehensive understanding, we employ a unified formalism to describe these different approaches (Tables 3, 4, 5, 6, and 7). This formalism highlights the divergences and convergences between methods, while also proposing potential synergies for future researches.

4.1 Human-Robot Interactions Logs

Data Representation: This dataset was collected during experiments conducted as part of the Fête de la Science [11], a national event in France aimed at promoting science to the general public. The goal of the experiment was to present three artworks to participants through an interactive quiz, delivered orally by the Nao robot. Each question in the serious game encouraged players to explore the museum in search of the answer before returning to the robot to continue the game. Players could interact with Nao at any time, simply by

[1] All the described datasets are documented in the published references; more details can be found therein.

having their badge visually recognized by the robot. A total of 46 participants took part in the experiment, generating 2,720 logs. These logs were extracted from the robot to analyze and identify player behaviors. The objective was to adapt the game scenario to different player profiles by adjusting specific parameters that control the game's progression. More formally, there is a set of logs $E = \{(u, a, t)\}$ where u is a player and a is a human-robot interaction. The simple sequences were extracted from the logs (see Sect. 2.1) to obtain a sequence $S_u = \langle a_i \rangle$ for each player u.

Partitioning Clustering: `GALACTIC` was first used to perform hierarchical clustering. Each concept (C_k, P_k) defines a cluster of players $C_k \subseteq U$, characterized by a predicate P_k. The *Prefix Common Subsequence* δ_{PCS} (see part 3.3) was chosen as the description method, as it is better suited than the *Maximal Common Subsequences* approach due to the game having a unique entry point for all players. The *Augmented* strategy was then applied to refine concepts into sub-concepts. At the boundary of the hierarchy, only the most specific clusters that is, clusters not included in any larger qualifying cluster and meeting a minimum frequency threshold were selected. These clusters, along with an outliers cluster C_0, form a partition of the users. The resulting partition categorizes players with varying levels of granularity depending on the chosen threshold. A semantic interpretation can be assigned to each cluster C_k based on its predicate.

Table 3. Human-robot interactions logs

Input Data	Logs $E = \{(u, a, t) \mid u \in U, a \in A\}$ U set of players, A set of interactions
Preprocessing	Extraction of simple sequences $(S_u = \langle a_i \rangle)_{u \in U}$
Hierarchical clustering	With `GALACTIC` $((C_k, P_k) \mid C_k \subseteq U)_{k=1..n}$ where $P_k = \delta_{PCS}((S_u)_{u \in C_k})$
Partitioning	Selection of maximal clusters of $\{(C_k, P_k) \mid k \leq n \text{ and } \frac{\lvert C_k \rvert}{\lvert U \rvert} \geq sup.\} \cup (C_0, \delta_{PCS}((S_u)_{u \in C_0}))$

4.2 Moodle Platform

Data Representation: Moodle, a widely used learning management system in universities and educational institutions, maintains a logging system that captures users' activities (e.g. taking courses, submitting assignments or attempting quizzes) at any point in time. This dataset was collected from Frederick University (Cyprus). It includes event logs from 471 students across 65 Computer Science courses (2018-2022). A typical Moodle log records user activity with a timestamp, user name (action initiator), and affected user (if applicable). It specifies the Moodle component (e.g., assignment, file module) and event context (course/resource). Each entry includes a description with user/resource details, the event's origin (web or other), and the IP address. The goal of this study is to extract learner profiles based on their behavior in Moodle. The raw logs first undergo cleaning, preprocessing, and enrichment using the `Moodle2EventLog` tool proposed by [9]. More formally, raw logs r are structured into activity information (u, a, t) by this preprocessing step, and they obtain a set of logs $E = \{(u, a, t)\}$ where u is a learner and a is an activity. The simple sequences were extracted from the logs using the user-centric projection from Sect. 2.1 to obtain a simple sequence $S_u = \langle a_i \rangle$ for each learner $u \in U$.

FSS-Based Hierarchical Clustering: The second step involves clustering students based on their learning behavior rather than mere interactions. To achieve this, the enriched event logs are first vectorized using the improved Frequent Sub-Sequence (FSS) encoding method adapted for Moodle logs, as described in [10]. The objective of FSS encoding is to represent each trace by its underlying learning patterns. This method begins by mining frequent patterns of semantic activities using the PrefixSpan algorithm where patterns corresponds to frequency maximal substrings, i.e. maximal subsequences without gap, each extracted pattern FSS is encoding using the following formula:

$$Encoding(FSS) = f_{FSS} \sum_{i=1}^{n-1} f_{a_i} f_{a_{i+1}} f_{r_{i,i+1}} \tag{7}$$

where f_{FSS} represents the frequency of the extracted FSS, $n = |FSS|$ is the length of the sequence (number of events), f_{a_i} is the frequency of event a_i in the event logs E, and $f_{r_{i,i+1}}$ denotes the frequency of the direct succession of two consecutive events a_i and a_{i+1} in the FSS. This transformation ensures that sequences or traces are primarily represented by meaningful learning patterns FSS rather than isolated interactions. Traces that do not contain any identified FSS patterns are discarded as unrepresentative. The resulting encoded values are then scaled to a range of [0,1], and clustering is performed on these numerical vectors using HAC with Ward linkage and Euclidean distance. Finally, a process discovery algorithm was applied to each cluster to uncover a process model that characterizes the behavior and learning profiles of students within that cluster. The evaluation was conducted in two steps: first, by assessing the clustering results using the Silhouette score and Davies-Bouldin index; and second, by evaluating the quality of the generated process models.

Table 4. Moodle interactions logs

Input Data	Logs $E = \{(u, a, t) \mid u \in U, a \in A\}$ U set of students, A set of actions performed on Moodle
Preprocessing	Extraction of simple sequences $(S_u = \langle a_i \rangle)_{u \in U}$
Hierarchical clustering	With ward linkage $(C_k \mid C_k \subseteq U)_{k=1..n}$ using the distance between the vectorized (S_u)
Clustering visualization	Clusters $((C_k, M_k) \mid C_k \subseteq U)_{k=1..n}$ C_k is enriched with its descriptive models M_k.

4.3 Digital Library Logs

Data Representation: The dataset consists of simulated digital library logs modeling user search behaviors within **Digital Libraries (DLs)**. Simulation provides a controlled environment with access to ground truth, facilitating approach validation. User traces are categorized into three types: *Lookup traces*, where users retrieve specific documents with minimal interactions via direct search or structured browsing; *Borderline traces*, where users explore a well-defined subject using multiple search methods and filtering; *Exploratory traces*, where users conduct open-ended searches across diverse topics with advanced search functionalities [4]. Formally, each user u has a sequence of actions $S_u = \langle a_i \rangle$ belonging to one of these categories, with an associated length $|S_u|$. The dataset includes 100 traces: 40 lookup, 30 borderline, and 30 exploratory. Exploratory traces, being the most complex, span over 10 activity types with a total of 310 events. Borderline traces involve 6 activity types and 170 events, while lookup traces are limited to 5 activity types with 140 events.

Hierarchical Clustering: Building on this DL data, a novel methodology for grouping user traces was introduced prior to the modeling phase using the `GALACTIC` framework, which generates hierarchical concepts $\{(C_k, P_k)\}$ that serve as the foundation for trace grouping using the *Maximal Common Subsequence* description δ_{MCS} and the Augmented strategy (see part 3.3) for the sequences S_u, and the numerical description δ_N for the lengths of the sequences. Patterns P_k are composed of predicates issued from $\delta_{MCS}((S_u)_{u \in C_k})$, and $\delta_N((|S_u|)_{u \in C_k})$ that describe the common behavior of users in each cluster.

Partitioning Clustering: A partitioning clustering is deduced from the hierarchy using a score between each trace S_u and the pattern P_k of each cluster C_k containing u. More precisely, this scoring integrate the edit distance (i.e. the minimum number of insertions, deletions, and substitutions required to transform one sequence to another) between S_u and the predicates obtained by δ_{MCS}, and a numerical distance between the length $|S_u|$ and the predicates obtained by δ_N. Each user trace S_u is assigned to the cluster that maximizes its score, ensuring that it is retained in only one cluster C_k of the hierarchy. This results in a partition of U into clusters $C_{k'} \subseteq C_k$, where empty clusters are discarded. GALACTIC generates between 18 and 22 meaningful concepts for cardinality values ranging from 15 to 30. With the proposed scoring method, the partitioning perfectly recovered the three predefined event log classes with 100% accuracy. Notably, cardinalities below 15 yielded four clusters, while values above 30 led to a coarser grouping into two clusters.

Table 5. Digital Library Interactions Logs

Input Data	Simple sequences with length of the sequence $(S_u = \langle a_i \rangle, \lvert S_u \rvert)_{u \in U}$, $u \in \{$Borderline, Lookup, Exploratory$\}$
Hierarchical clustering	With Galactic $((C_k, P_k) \mid C_k \subseteq U)_{k=1..n}$ where $P_k = \delta_{MCS}((S_u)_{u \in C_k}) \cup \delta_N((\lvert S_u \rvert)_{u \in C_k})$
Partitioning clustering	Selection of the non-empty clusters $\{(C_{k'}, P_k) \mid k \leq n \text{ and } C_{k'} = \{u \mid k = \arg\max_j(sc(u, P_j))\}$
Clustering visualization	Selected clusters $\{(C_{k'}, P_k, M_{k'})\}$ $C_{k'}$ is enriched with its descriptive models $M_{k'}$

4.4 Tourism Data

Data Preparation: The Geoluciole dataset [12] consists of GPS trajectories recorded in La Rochelle, France, during the summer of 2019. It was collected from tourists visiting the city on vacation. This dataset includes 108 individual trajectories, recorded using a developed application that captured participants' positions every 30 s throughout their stay. By associating GPS coordinates with the different districts of La Rochelle, for each tourist u, each trajectory $T_u = \langle (gps_j, t_j) \rangle$ was transformed into a temporal sequence D_u as described in Sect. 2.2: a semantic enrichment by $(gps_j, t_j) \models_D a^D$, where a^D is a district of the city, and a time-segmentation. Through a similar enrichment and time segmentation process, two other interval sequences were constructed from the trajectory T_u: W_u is derived from the enrichment $(gps_j, t_j) \models_W a^W$ where a^W is a weather description such as *cloudy* or *sunny* ; B_u is derived from $(gps_j, t_j) \models_B a^B$ where a^B is a beach of la Rochelle, or *no beach* when the visitor is not at the beach. With the aim of a multi-sequences and heterogeneous analysis, the average daily temperature tp_u for the tourist u is added to the dataset.

Hierarchical Clustering: In order to focus on visitors going to the beach, the analysis is conducted on beach-related visits in relation to the weather. Using the GALACTIC framework, tourist trajectories $(T_u)_{u \in U}$ were clustered based on the *Maximal Common Interval* description δ_{MCI} applied to the two temporal sequences: B_u, and W_u. Additionally, the *numerical description* δ_N was applied to the average daily temperature tp_u. This process resulted in a hierarchy of concepts $((C_k, P_k))_{k=1..n}$, where each cluster C_k is characterized by **rich patterns** P_k composed of predicates derived from $\delta_{MCI}((W_u)_{u \in C_k})$, $\delta_{MCI}((B_u)_{u \in C_k})$, and

$\delta_N((tp_u)_{u \in C_k})$, effectively capturing common tourist behaviors within each cluster. The GALACTIC framework generated 93 concepts, among which some revealed valuable insights. For instance, one concept highlighted a strong correlation between *rainy* and *no beach*, indicating that tourists tend to forgo beach visits when it rains. While this may seem intuitive, it demonstrates how the predicates computed by GALACTIC can effectively extract behavioral patterns from data.

Table 6. Tourists' trajectories

Input data	Trajectories $(T_u = \langle (gps_j, t_j) \rangle)_{u \in U}$ U set of tourists
Preprocessing	Three interval sequences and a value $(D_u = \langle (a_i^D, t_i) \rangle, W_u = \langle (a_i^W, t_i) \rangle, B_u = \langle (a_i^B, t_i) \rangle, tp_u)_{u \in U}$ D_u (District), W_u (Weather), B_u (Beach)
Hierachical clustering	With GALACTIC $((C_k, P_k) \mid C_k \subseteq U)_{k=1..n}$ $P_k = \delta_{MCI}((W_u)_{u \in C_k}) \cup \delta_{MCI}((B_u)_{u \in C_k}) \cup \delta_N((tp_u)_{u \in C_k})$

4.5 Seal Trajectories

Data Representation: Captured data of seals moving between their haulout sites along the coasts of the English Channel or in the Celtic and Irish Seas are collected using Global Navigation Satellite System (GNSS) systems provided by SMRU. The dataset consists of 14 seals, represented as U, with trajectories composed of sequences of spatio-temporal points [15]. One real seal trajectory dataset from 2020 and 2021 includes 388 014 raw GPS measurements, denoted as T_u. These datasets serve to analyze seal behavior within groups and identify simultaneous activities occurring in the same location. Four meta-data were included into the trajectory and related to the moving objects that are sd_j (surface dur), dd_j (dive dur), md_j (max dive depth) and tad_j (time allocation at depth). Based on expert interests, the analysis focuses on three primary activities: A =*Foraging, Resting, Traveling* deduced through semantic rules established by domain experts, i.e. $(sd_j, dd_j, md_j, tad_j) \models a_j \in A$. As described in [15], trajectories are converted into interval sequences S_u by time segmentation of similar activities a_i occurring at consecutive timestamps. These sequences are enriched with $zone_i$, representing an approximation of the spatial information gps_i as a decimal point, corresponding to a discretization into 10km × 10km spatial zones

Hierarchical Clustering: To extract insights from trajectories, the GALACTIC platform is utilized. The primary objective is to automatically classify seals into groups based on simultaneous activities occurring in the same time and zone location. The interval sequences $(S_u)u \in U$ are described using the *Maximal Common Interval* description δ_{MCI}. The obtained patterns $P_k = \delta_{MCI}((S_u)_{u \in C_k})$ describes both the common activities and the zone of each group C_k since the sequences integrate these two information. 24 concepts were obtained showing that some seals performed the same activities in the same zones, some of these concepts revealed seals performing either the same activity or simply being present in the same zone. For example, one concept includes two seals performing *Resting* at the one decimal point zone (49.3, −1.1) during the periods 03/06/2021 to 11/06/2021 and 13/06/2021 to 24/06/2021.

Table 7. Seals' trajectories

Input data	Trajectories $(T_u = \langle (gps_j, t_j, sd_j, dd_j, md_j, tad_j) \rangle)_{u \in U}$ U set of seals
Preprocessing	Interval-based sequences. A ={Foraging, Resting, Traveling} $(S_u = \langle (\{a_i, zone_i\}, [t_i, t_k]) \rangle)_{u \in U}$
Hierarchical clustering	With GALACTIC $((C_k, P_k) \mid C_k \subseteq U)_{k=1..n}$ $P_k = \delta_{MCI}((S_u)_{u \in C_k})$

5 Preliminary Results

To demonstrate the explainability of the proposed framework, we discovered process models corresponding to identified clusters within the robot event logs dataset [2], as illustrated in Fig. 1. The figure depict the extracted DFG from one computed cluster, obtained through partitioning clustering. The model visually represents the sequences of activities performed by players within the cluster. In the DFG[2], each box corresponds to an activity, while the directed arcs represent transitions between activities. The frequency of transitions is also displayed on each arc, indicating the number of times a particular transition occurs in the event log. Red elements denote predicates P_k, indicating the initial activities of the 34 players in the cluster, while blue elements represent all activities observed within the cluster. It is important to note that not all activities are necessarily performed by every player. For instance, cluster C_2 comprises 34 players who agreed to participate and listened to the first question. All players in this cluster answered the various questions correctly, which explains the absence of the "incorrect answer" activity in the corresponding process model.

[2] In DFGs, the • represents the start node, and a ■ represents the end node.

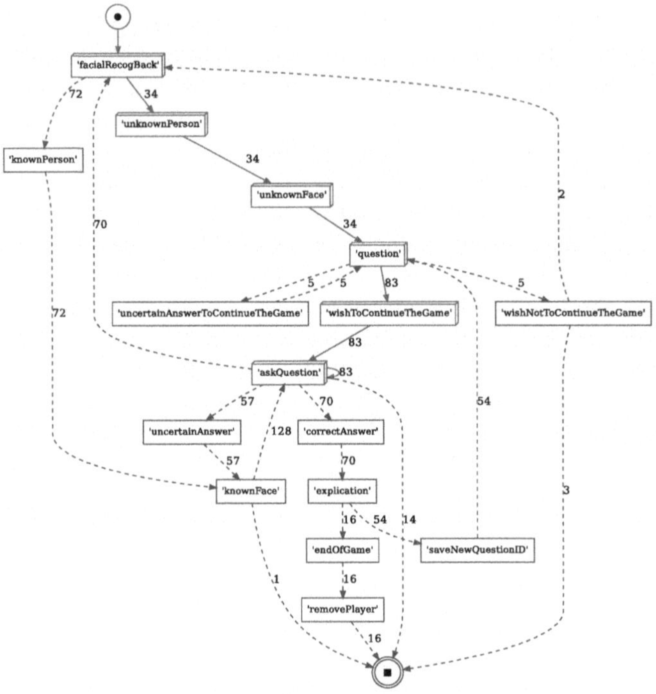

Fig. 1. Model M_2 of cluster C_2 in blue with P_2 in red (Color figure online)

6 Conclusion and Perspectives

This article presents a unified framework for analyzing both event logs and user trajectories by transforming them into sequences of activities. The process begins with the formalization of a common representation, enabling the conversion of heterogeneous data sources into temporal or simple sequences, with input from domain experts. We then identify suitable unsupervised learning techniques to cluster these sequences and extract meaningful insights. In the context of Process Mining (PM), Trace Clustering (TC) involves transforming event logs into sequences, optionally vectorizing them, applying clustering techniques, and discovering process models based on the resulting clusters. Complementary to this, Sequential Pattern Mining (SPM) offers a hierarchical clustering approach, while GALACTIC enriches these results with descriptive patterns, enhancing the interpretability of the clustering outcomes. This preliminary study highlights the added value of PM in interpreting clusters obtained through Sequential Pattern Mining SPM and GALACTIC, demonstrating how these techniques together provide a structured and comprehensible representation of user behaviors through process models. By integrating techniques from TC, SPM, and GALACTIC, our framework improves both the clarity and relevance of sequence clustering. A key contribution is the introduction of enriched triplets (C_k, P_k, M_k), where C_k represents clusters, P_k the associated predicates, and M_k the corresponding process models. This representation facilitates semantic interpretation, supports model evaluation, and enables scenario simulation, thus strengthening both explainability and adaptability.

As future work, we plan to deepen the integration of predicates P_k to further enhance cluster interpretability. In particular, we propose applying `GALACTIC`'s pattern extraction strategies within each cluster to identify distinctive behavioral patterns. We also aim to develop a comprehensive evaluation framework that combines PM-based quality metrics (e.g., fitness, precision, generalization) with SPM-based clustering metrics. A central goal of this integration is to assess the behavioral consistency within clusters and the fidelity of the corresponding process models.

References

1. Van der Aalst, W.: Process Mining: Data Science in Action. Springer (2016)
2. Amoury, S., Bertet, K., Mondou, D.: Clustering of serious game traces using formal concept analysis. In: International Conference on Intelligent Data Engineering and Automated Learning. pp. 287–299. Springer (2024)
3. Boukhetta, S.E., Demko, C., Richard, J., Bertet, K.: Sequence mining using fca and the nextpriorityconcept algorithm. In: Concept Lattices and Their Applications 2020. vol. 2668, pp. 209–222 (2020)
4. Boukhetta, S.E., Trabelsi, M.: Formal concept analysis for trace clustering in process mining. In: International Conference on Conceptual Structures. pp. 73–88. Springer (2023)
5. Buzmakov, A., Egho, E., Jay, N., Kuznetsov, S.O., Napoli, A., Raïssi, C.: On mining complex sequential data by means of fca and pattern structures. Int. J. Gen Syst **45**(2), 135–159 (2016)
6. Demko, C., Bertet, K., Faucher, C., Viaud, J.F., Kuznetsov, S.O.: Nextpriorityconcept: a new and generic algorithm computing concepts from complex and heterogeneous data. Theoret. Comput. Sci. **845**, 1–20 (2020)
7. Ester, M., Kriegel, H.P., Sander, J., Xu, X.: A density-based algorithm for discovering clusters in large spatial databases with noise. In: Proceedings of the Second International Conference on Knowledge Discovery and Data Mining (KDD). vol. 96, pp. 226–231 (1996)
8. Fournier-Viger, P., Lin, J.C.W., Kiran, R.U., Koh, Y.S., Thomas, R.: A survey of sequential pattern mining. Data Sci. Patt. Recogn. **1**(1), 54–77 (2017)
9. Joudieh, N., van der Aalst, W., Champagnat, R., Rabah, M., Nowakowski, S.: Moodle2eventlog: A tool for pedagogically-driven log enrichment and analysis. In: Proceedings of the 17th International Conference on Computer Supported Education - vol. 1. pp. 452–463 (2025)
10. Joudieh, N., Trabelsi, M., Champagnat, R., Rabah, M., Eteokleous, N.: Using trace clustering to group learning scenarios: an adaptation of fss-encoding to moodle logs use case. In: Proceedings of CSEDU (2). pp. 247–254 (2024)
11. Mondou, D.: Temporal automata for robotic scenario modeling with cit framework. Multimedia Tools and Applications **83**(22), 61261–61286 (2024)
12. Richard, J., Savarit, G., Boukhetta, S.E., Faucher, C., Bertet, K., Demko, C.: Discover spatio-temporal clusters from trajectory data enhanced by heterogeneous

contextual knowledge using fca and the nextpriorityconcept algorithm. In: Cordero, P., Kridlo, O. (eds.) CEUR Workshop Proceedings
13. Song, M., Günther, C.W., Van der Aalst, W.M.P.: Trace clustering in process mining. In: Proceedings of the International Conference on Business Process Management (BPM). pp. 109–120. Springer (2008)
14. Trabelsi, M., Suire, C., Morcos, J., Champagnat, R.: A new methodology to bring out typical users' interactions in digital libraries. In: Proceedings of the 2021 ACM/IEEE Joint Conference on Digital Libraries (JCDL). pp. 11–20. IEEE (2021)
15. Wannous, R., Boukhetta, S.E., Vincent, C.: Handling knowledge over moving object trajectories using formal concept analysis. In: Proceedings of the International Joint Conference on Conceptual Knowledge Structures. pp. 233–253. Springer (2024)

A Proposal for Building a Compact and Tunable Representation of a Concept Lattice Based on Clustering

Jaume Baixeries[1], Alexandre Bazin[2], Jérôme David[3], and Amedeo Napoli[4(✉)]

[1] Universitat Politécnica de Catalunya, Computer Science Department, 08034 Barcelona, Catalonia, Spain
jbaixer@cs.upc.edu

[2] Université de Montpellier, CNRS, LIRMM, F-34095 Montpellier, France
alexandre.bazin@lirmm.fr

[3] Université Grenoble Alpes, Inria, CNRS, Grenoble INP, LIG, 38000 Grenoble, France
jerome.david@inria.fr

[4] Université de Lorraine, CNRS, Loria, 54000 Nancy, France
amedeo.napoli@loria.fr

Abstract. A concept lattice provides a model of a dataset that can be navigated and explored by an analyst in an interactive way, except when the concept lattice is too large. Such a problem can be overcome by building a representation of the whole concept lattice that keeps a reasonable size and that can be interpreted by the analyst. Relying on previous work about link key discovery, we revisit in this paper an approach based on Formal Concept Analysis (FCA) and Agglomerative Hierarchical Clustering (AHC) applied to a set of concepts for building a representative set of clusters. Accordingly, we propose an AHC algorithm that (a) efficiently computes this representative set, and (b) respects the ordinal structure of the original concept lattice. A set of experiments performed over real datasets shows the effectiveness of our approach.

Keywords: Formal Concept Analysis · Agglomerative Hierarchical Clustering · Concept Lattice Representation · Representative Set · Order Preservation

1 Introduction

This study is a follow-up of a preceding work about the discovery of link keys for data interlinking in RDF datasets [1,2]. A link key can be seen as a rule identifying pairs of individuals in two different RDF datasets that represent the same real-world entity. Link keys can be discovered thanks to Formal Concept Analysis (FCA) [14], where they correspond to concepts in a specific concept lattice. The conditions related to a link key are materialized by the intent of the corresponding concept while the pairs of identified individuals constitute the extent of the concept. In general, the number of link keys can be very large

P. Cellier et al. (Eds.): CONCEPTS 2025, LNAI 15941, pp. 161–177, 2025.
https://doi.org/10.1007/978-3-032-03364-2_10

making their interpretation quite hard and raising the following representation problem: is it possible to design a *compact* and *representative set* of link keys preserving a maximal number of identity links and providing navigation and interpretation capabilities to a domain analyst?

Following this track, the objective of this paper is to propose a general method for concept lattice reduction based on Agglomerative Hierarchical Clustering (AHC [15,21]). In the long term, we aim at building a tool for the graphical exploration and interpretation of a concept lattice thanks to a mapping between the concept lattice and a hierarchical partition of clusters –aka dendrogram. The granularity of the partition may be tuned by allowing an analyst to navigate the representation of a concept lattice going from a coarser clustering to a finer clustering thanks to the variation of a cut-level related to a dendrogram. Among the approaches relating clustering and FCA, the present approach is original and proposes a reliable, readable, and interpretable summary of a concept lattice. There are many possible applications such as data cleaning (duplicate detection), data exploration with a variable precision, concept interpretation, and knowledge representation in a particular domain.

More precisely we aim at constructing a compact and representative set of clusters offering interactive data analysis capabilities. Finding such a representative set is not an easy task and relies on various constraints and a compromise. Firstly, a cluster consists of a subset of concepts, where one specific concept should be selected as the "medoid", i.e., the barycenter which minimizes the distances to all other concepts in the cluster, or the supremum or infimum of the cluster if any. The representative set, abbreviated as RepSet, is composed of such medoids, one per cluster. Secondly, the RepSet set should be kept small while the largest number of objects in the concept lattice should be preserved. The size of the RepSet is related to the number of clusters it includes and is measured by a "compression rate". Thirdly, the number of preserved objects is another suitable property to be considered when computing the RepSet, which is related to the "proportion of preserved objects" (PPO) attached to the medoids composing the RepSet. Optimizing at the same time the compression rate and the proportion of preserved objects entails a controversy, but an acceptable compromise can be achieved.

For building the RepSet, we propose the CLClust algorithm that is based on AHC [15,21]. As input, CLClust takes a concept lattice denoted as CTL, a dissimilarity measure defined with respect to (w.r.t.) the concept extents, a linkage criterion, and a cutting level. As output CLClust returns a set of clusters from which a RepSet can be issued, composed of the medoids selected in the clusters. Moreover, CLClust applies AHC to FCA for reducing a possibly large concept lattice in satisfying a third constraint, i.e., the set of concepts in a cluster should respect as well as possible the ordering of concepts in CTL, as this is the case for example when a cluster corresponds to a sublattice in CTL.

In particular, this AHC process can be regarded as a general method for concept lattice reduction based on a similarity between concepts. Indeed this contrasts the reduction of a concept lattice about link keys presented in [1], which is based on crisp equality between sets in FCA and in partition pattern structures. Here the constraint of crisp equality is relaxed and replaced by a dissimilarity used to build a partition of concepts.

The summary of the paper is as follows. In Sect. 2 we propose a review of papers related either to clustering and FCA or to reduction of concept lattices. Then, in Sect. 3 we introduce the properties of a RepSet, while in Sect. 4 we present the CLClust algorithm for building such a RepSet. Section 5 reports experiments performed on different datasets that demonstrate the effectiveness of the present approach and the efficiency of the algorithm in terms of lattice reduction, before conclusion.

2 Related Work

Many different methods introduced to reduce the complexity of a concept lattice are based on the clustering of the set of concepts. For example, there is a summary of classical clustering algorithms used in FCA in [22] (Sect. 2.9), mostly based on constructing clusters of concepts and then lattice of clusters, while alternative techniques are limiting the number of detected concepts by selecting some relevant subset or in building a new concept hierarchy.

Clustering relies on the definition of different measures to compute the similarity or proximity of concepts in order to apply a clustering algorithm. For example, three similarity measures are presented in [3], while a method combines the k-means algorithm with a quality measure in [16]. A method based on fuzzy k-means is described in [6] while [23] proposes a distance functions and a related clustering algorithm. Finally, [11] relies on pattern structures [13] and on SOFIA algorithm [8] to discover cluster candidates, and then introduces an algorithm to select non-overlapping clusters from the candidate set. In all cases the goal is the reduction of the size of the concept lattice.

Although remaining one of the main methods to reduce the dimension of a concept lattices, some alternative techniques to clustering have appeared. An extensive survey in [4] presents a classification of concept lattice reduction methods into three main categories: context pre-processing (reducing the number of attributes and yet preserving the structure of the lattice), elimination of non-essential distinctions (methods that highlight the most significant features) and concept filtration (a relevance criterion to choose formal concepts, objects, or attributes).

Another approach is presented in [10], where the reduction of a context is performed according to the properties of the implications holding in the context, while in [18] axial concepts are used to cluster data that are difficult to separate in plain FCA.

Finally, we mention some papers more related to the present paper based on the use of a congruence relation for reducing the concept lattice. In [5] a weaker notion of congruence to reduce a concept lattice is proposed, while in [9], revisited in [17], authors construct a quotient lattice based on an equivalence relation. In [25] the authors investigate how a congruence relation can be used to decompose a lattice into meaningful parts. A close approach was presented before in [24], where authors were studying the decomposition of a lattice into smaller parts using the so-called subdirect decompositions into factors.

3 Properties of a Representative Set of Concepts

It is well-known that the number of concepts in a concept lattice can be very large. Thus it can be convenient, e.g., for an interactive analysis, to build a compact *representative set* of concepts, denoted hereafter as a RepSet. Such a RepSet can be viewed as a summary capturing as much as possible the content of the original set of concepts. In the present case, the construction of a RepSet is based on the application of AHC to an original CTL. The output of AHC is a hierarchy of clusters where a "medoid", acting as a representative of the cluster, can be selected in each cluster. The medoid in a cluster can be defined in different ways, e.g., as the barycenter minimizing the distances to all other concepts in the cluster, or the supremum/infimum of the set of concepts in a cluster when they exist.

Then, given a set of clusters generated by the AHC process, the RepSet is composed of a set of selected medoids and should satisfy three properties. The first property, "ensure a *maximal preservation of the ordinal structure of the CTL*", is related to the clustering process itself. The two other properties, namely "observe a *high compression rate*" and "observe a *high proportion of preserved objects*" should be satisfied by the RepSet as better as possible. Moreover, it should be noticed that, given a CTL, the RepSet is not unique and depends on the selection of the medoids. Below we formally present and discuss these properties.

The Preservation of CTL Ordering
One requirement in applying AHC and then building the RepSet is to preserve the CTL ordering in the clustering. In particular, a cluster corresponds to a sublattice whenever the lower bound $x \wedge y$ and the upper bound $x \vee y$ of any pair of concepts x and y are also included in the cluster. In the present case, based on the fact that the dissimilarity measure used in the AHC process and introduced in the next section is not a congruence, only a "local preservation" of the lattice ordering can be achieved. However, in the CLClust algorithm, there exists an option constraining all clusters to be convex, i.e., a cluster corresponds to a chain or a sublattice in CTL.

In particular, congruences and ordering preservation are detailed in [5] while a general and extensive discussion about the preservation of a poset ordering is proposed in [7].

The Compression Rate of aRepSet w.r.t. CTL.
A RepSet should be minimal in size, i.e., the smaller the number of medoids in a RepSet the better the compression rate. The compression rate CR of a RepSet w.r.t. CTL is calculated as follows:

$$\text{CR}(\text{RepSet}, CTL) = 1 - \frac{|\text{RepSet}|}{|CTL|}$$

where $\top$ and $\bot$ are included in CTL, and |RepSet| denotes the number of medoids in CTL. The compression rate is ranging from 0 to 1, and the best values are close to 1, i.e., |RepSet| is small compared to |CTL|. It is equal to 0 when |RepSet| = |CTL|, i.e., there is no compression at all. The compression rate cannot be equal to 1 as the RepSet cannot be empty, i.e., it is assumed that there exists at least one concept whose extent is not empty.

The Proportion of Preserved Objects (PPO)
In general a clustering process focuses on objects and this explains why we are more interested in maximizing the proportion of preserved objects than in maximizing the proportion of preserved attributes (the latter is an option that should be studied in future work).

Then a RepSet. should preserve a maximal number of objects, i.e., the higher the number of objects lying in an extent and preserved in the RepSet the better the representativeness of the RepSet. The proportion of preserved objects PPO is calculated as follows:

$$PPO(\text{RepSet}, CTL) = \frac{|\bigcup_{md_i \in \text{RepSet}} Ext(md_i)|}{|G|}$$

where md_i denotes a medoid in the RepSet, and $|G|$ denotes the cardinality of the set of objects G which is assumed to be not empty. The proportion of preserved objects PPO ranges in $]0, 1]$, cannot be equal to zero, and is equal to 1 when all objects are preserved, i.e., RepSet = CTL.

The two former properties are in opposition as, for achieving a reliable and maximal representativeness, the number of medoids composing a RepSet should be low while the proportion of preserved objects should be high. Thus the compression rate and the proportion of preserved objects cannot be simultaneously optimized, but a good compromise can be achieved, i.e., discovering a relatively small set of medoids forming the RepSet and maximizing the compression rate, while retaining a relatively high number of preserved objects, in respecting at the best CTL local ordering.

In the next section, we make precise the construction of a RepSet, starting from a CTL and using agglomerative hierarchical clustering.

4 The CLClust Algorithm for Building a RepSet

4.1 Characteristics of the AHC Process in CLClust

The CLClust algorithm (see Function 1) constructs a hierarchy of clusters thanks to AHC [15,21]. The AHC process takes as input the set of concepts in CTL and builds a hierarchical partition of clusters. As usual, AHC is based on a bottom-up strategy, starting with each concept as a singleton cluster and then successively merging pairs of clusters w.r.t. their dissimilarity. AHC stops when all clusters are merged into a top cluster.

AHC relies on two main parameters, i.e., (i) a *dissimilarity* measure between concepts, and (ii) a *linkage criterion* for inserting a new element into a cluster. The dissimilarity between two concepts c_1 and c_2 is defined as follows:

$$\delta(c_1, c_2) = 1 - \frac{|Ext(c_1 \wedge c_2)|}{|Ext(c_1 \vee c_2)|}$$

where $c_1 \vee c_2 \neq \bot$ and $Ext(c)$ is the function returning the extent of concept c. The dissimilarity δ ranges from 0 to 1 and exhibits the following properties:

(i) $\delta(c_1, c_2) = 0$ iff $c_1 = c_2$ (no dissimilarity),
(ii) $\delta(c_1, c_2) = \delta(c_2, c_1)$ (symmetry),
(iii) $\delta(c_1, c_2) = 1$ iff $ext(c_1 \wedge c_2) = 0$.

In (iii), the lower bound of c_1 and c_2 is $\bot$ and then c_1 and c_2 are not comparable in CTL. However, when c_1 and c_2 are comparable, we may observe that the closer c_1 is to c_2 the smaller $\delta(c_1, c_2)$. For example, if $c_1 \leq c_2$, then $\delta(c_1, c_2) = 1 - |Ext(c_1)|/|Ext(c_2)|$ as $c_1 \wedge c_2 = c_1$ and $c_1 \vee c_2 = c_2$. In this way, given a concept say c_1, the least dissimilar concept c_2 from c_1 is in either the *lower cover* or the *upper cover* of c_1. In particular, intervals of concepts in CTL can be preserved and the following proposition can be stated:

Proposition 1. (see *[2]). If $c_1 \leq c_2 \leq c_3$ in CTL then $\delta(c_1, c_2) \leq \delta(c_1, c_3)$.*

This proposition, that is also discussed and proven in [2], introduces the "cover property in AHC", i.e., given three concepts, c_1, c_2, and c_3 such that $c_1 \leq c_2 \leq c_3$, c_2 will be agglomerated before c_3, and the ordering between c_1 and c_2 in CTL is locally preserved in the cluster (about metrics and order see also [20]). More precisely, the proposition ensures that, given a concept c_i lying in a cluster K_ℓ, the next concept c_j to be agglomerated in K_ℓ w.r.t. c_i is the concept the least dissimilar to c_i, and c_j is necessarily lying in the lower cover or the upper cover of c_i. In particular, this is in agreement with the properties of a RepSet, to preserve as well as possible the CTL ordering. It should be noticed that the full preservation of sublattices in the clustering requires the use of a *congruence* as explained in [5].

The second parameter required in AHC is related to the distance $dclust(X, Y)$ between two clusters X and Y, actually between a cluster and a singleton cluster. There are several alternatives detailed in [15,21]. The classical candidates are *single linkage* based on "min", *complete linkage* based on "max", and average linkage based on "mean distance". The CLClust algorithm relies on *complete linkage*, i.e., $dclust(X, Y) = \max_{x \in X, y \in Y} \delta(x, y)$.

It should be noticed that when complete linkage connects two clusters, say $X = \{x_1, x_2\}$ and $Y = \{y\}$, then the pair exhibiting the max of the dissimilarities, say x_1 and y, is selected. As x_1 and x_2 are already verifying the cover property, say $x_1 \leq x_2$, where $\leq$ denotes the lattice ordering, then x_1 and y will also be comparable. These two configurations may happen, either $y \leq x_1 \leq x_2$ or $x_1 \leq x_2$ and $x_1 \leq y$. This shows that the concept lattice ordering is again locally respected within the new cluster $X \cup Y = \{x_1, x_2, y\}$.

obj./att.	a	b	c	d	e	f	g	h	i	j	k
0	x					x			x		
1	x	x									
2			x								
3	x		x	x			x			x	x
4	x		x		x		x			x	x
5	x		x	x			x			x	x
6	x		x				x			x	x
7	x		x					x			
8										x	x
9	x		x	x	x		x			x	x

Fig. 1. The context for the running example.

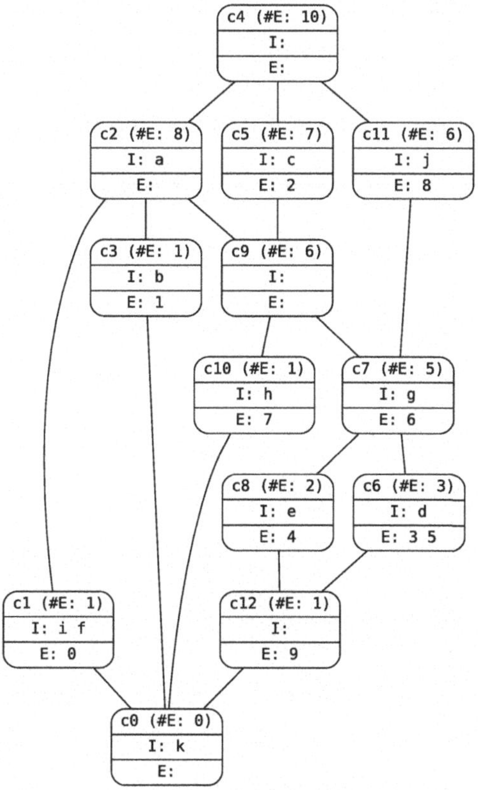

Fig. 2. The CTL lattice for the running example.

Table 1. Dissimilarity table between concepts lying in CTL. Only values in bold are needed by the CLClust algorithm.

	c_0	c_1	c_2	c_3	c_4	c_5	c_6	c_7	c_8	c_9	c_{10}	c_{11}	c_{12}
c_0													
c_1	**1.**												
c_2	1	**0.88**											
c_3	**1.**	1	**0.88**										
c_4	1	0.9	**0.2**	0.9									
c_5	1	1	0.4	1	**0.3**								
c_6	1	1	0.62	1	0.7	0.57							
c_7	1	1	0.38	1	0.5	0.29	**0.4**						
c_8	1	1	0.75	1	0.8	0.71	0.8	**0.6**					
c_9	1	1	**0.25**	1	0.4	**0.14**	0.5	**0.17**	0.67				
c_{10}	**1.**	1	0.88	1	0.9	0.86	1	1	1	**0.83**			
c_{11}	1	1	0.5	1	**0.4**	0.5	0.5	**0.17**	0.67	0.5	1		
c_{12}	**1.**	1	0.88	1	0.9	0.86	**0.67**	0.8	**0.5**	0.83	1	0.83	

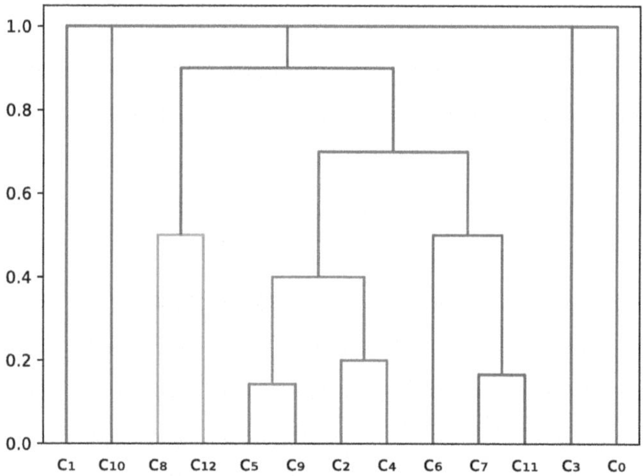

Fig. 3. Dendrogram built by AHC set up based on δ and complete linkage.

4.2 The CLClust Algorithm at Work

Let us now explain how the CLClust algorithm works in practice and propose a concrete example. AHC is initialized by computing all $\delta(x, y)$ between singleton clusters x and y and recording in a dissimilarity table, as shown in Table 1. However, in CLClust, thanks to the cover property in Proposition 1, only dissimilarities between neighboring candidates are computed, marked in bold in Table 1. Instead of computing $n.(n-1)/2$ dissimilarity values where n is the number of clusters as in AHC, a much smaller number should be computed in CLClust, depending on the number of neighbors of the concept under study.

Moreover, at each step of AHC, the dissimilarity table should be updated, requiring the computation of $n-2$ dissimilarity values, i.e., the number of clusters minus the two clusters that are merged. Again, in CLClust, due to the cover property, this number is much smaller as it only involves neighbor concepts. This particular aspect is illustrated in the next section where the running times of standard AHC and CLClust are compared.

As a concrete example, the CTL in Fig. 2 whose context is shown in Fig. 1 contains 13 concepts. Thus there are 78 dissimilarity values to compute at initialization. However, as shown in the dissimilarity table in Table 1, the computation is restricted to pairs of neighbor concepts, and only 18 values are calculated in practice. At first iteration, concepts c_5 and c_9 are merged as their dissimilarity value is 0.14, the merging involving the minimal dissimilarity. Then only 5 values need to be updated among the 11 possibilities at the next step (i.e., $n-2=11$ where $n=13$). When two dissimilarities are equal, the pair of comparable concepts, if any, is preferred in the merging.

It should be noticed that, with complete linkage, it may be necessary at some steps to calculate values that were not previously computed. For example, calculating the similarity between (c_5, c_9) (after merging) and c_2 requires computing the similarity value between c_2 and c_5 which was not already computed.

The CLClust algorithm stops when all clusters are merged into one final cluster corresponding to the whole set of concepts. The output can be visualized as a *dendrogram*, i.e., a tree-based representation as shown in Fig. 3. In such a dendrogram, clusters are determined thanks to a *cutting level*. Setting a cutting level mainly depends on the objectives of the analyst. More importantly, setting a cutting level will determine the RepSet. For example, a cutting level of 0.8 will give 6 clusters and a compression rate of $1 - 6/13 \simeq 0.54$, i.e., $\{c_1\}$, $\{c_{10}\}$, $\{c_8, c_{12}\}$, $\{c_2, c_4, c_5, c_9, c_6, c_7, c_{11}\}$, $\{c_3\}$, and $\{c_0\}$, with the related RepSet $\{\{c_1\}, \{c_{10}\}, \{c_8\}, \{c_7\}, \{c_3\}, \{c_0\}\}$. By contrast, a cutting level of 0.55 will give 7 clusters and a compression rate of $1 - 7/13 \simeq 0.46$, i.e., $\{c_1\}$, $\{c_{10}\}$, $\{c_8, c_{12}\}$, $\{c_2, c_4, c_5, c_9\}$, $\{c_6, c_7, c_{11}\}$, $\{c_3\}$, and $\{c_0\}$, with the related RepSet $\{\{c_1\}, \{c_{10}\}, \{c_8\}, \{c_4\}, \{c_7\}, \{c_3\}, \{c_0\}\}$. In the next section, we show how the compression rate and the proportion of preserved objects vary with the setting of the cutting level.

Even though the combination of dissimilarity $\delta(x, y)$ and complete linkage is compatible with lattice ordering, this is not sufficient to guarantee the whole partitioning into convex sublattices. The algorithm may produce non-convex groupings when the supremum is already associated with a cluster or in the event of a tie in dissimilarity values (this tie being arbitrarily resolved). Therefore the CLClust algorithm is extended with an option forcing the partitioning into convex sublattices.

CLClust algorithm makes use of a priority queue to store pairs of clusters and their associated distance values in ascending order. It first computes and adds distance values between every pair of neighboring concepts (lines 4–7). Then the algorithm adopts the following greedy approach (lines 8–21). It iteratively extracts and merges the pair of clusters having the smallest distance values (lines 10–11). If the convexity is forced (line 13), the new cluster is added to the queue only if it is effectively convex. The convexity of a cluster is satisfied if the cluster has an infimum, a supremum, and if each concept in the cluster is lying in the interval between the infimum and the supremum. The addition of a cluster consists in iterating over the queue and recalculating every distance value where one of the elements belongs to the new cluster (lines 15–21).

Algorithm 1. The function CLClust iteratively builds the hierarchy of clusters, minimizing the number of dissimilarity values to be computed.

```
 1: function CLCLUST(L : a lattice, forceConvexity : Boolean)
 2:     values ← createMinPriorityQueue()
 3:     ▷ Computing dissimilarity between a concept and concepts in its cover ◁
 4:     for x ∈ L do
 5:         for y ∈ cover(x, L) do
 6:             d ← δ(x, y)
 7:             add(values, ⟨x, y⟩, d)
 8:     while size(values) > 1 do
 9:         ▷ Select and merge the clusters with the smallest dissimilarity ◁
10:         ⟨x, y⟩, d ← extractMin(values)
11:         clust ← createClust(x, y, d)
12:         ▷ Check cluster convexity if needed ◁
13:         if (¬forceConvexity or isConvex(clust)) then
14:             ▷ Update the dissimilarity values based on complete linkage ◁
15:             for all (⟨x′, y′⟩, d′) ∈ values do
16:                 if ( x = x′ or y = x′ ) then
17:                     add(values, ⟨clust, y′⟩, dclust(clust, y′))
18:                     remove(values, ⟨x′, y′⟩)
19:                 else if ( x = y′ or y = y′ ) then
20:                     add(values, ⟨clust, x′⟩, dclust(clust, x′))
21:                     remove(values, ⟨x′, y′⟩)
        return extractMin(values)
```

5 Experiments

The CLClust algorithm is evaluated by using two series of experiments. Firstly, we demonstrate that CLClust builds a RepSet more efficiently w.r.t. running time than a classical AHC algorithm. We also discuss the variations related to the setting of a cutting level in the dendrogram. Secondly, the experiments evaluate both the qualities of the clusters, and the behavior of CLClust w.r.t. precision and recall in a supervised setting. These results confirm the effective capabilities of the CLClust algorithm in building a compact RepSet from a concept lattice.

Table 2. Statistics about the datasets considered in the experiments.

dataset	#concepts	#attributes	#objects
abalone	254	9	64
atom-sites	1,034	12	41
bridges	1,266	12	63
fd-reduced-250k-30	351	26	313
flight-1k-30c	3,058	19	288
flights-20–500k	490	12	23
glass	134	10	36
iris	27	5	10
page-blocks	254	11	27
wine	117	14	76

5.1 Datasets and Protocol

The experiments are performed on 10 different datasets from the UC Irvine Machine Learning Repository[1] displayed in Table 2. Every dataset is transformed as a reduced and clarified context, possibly leading to a reduction of the initial numbers of objects and attributes. The AddIntent algorithm [19] is used to compute the concept lattices whose concept count is shown in column #concepts in Table 2 . Moreover, all experiments have been conducted on a laptop equipped with an Intel(R) Core(TM) i7-10875H CPU @ 2.30GHz and 8GB of memory dedicated to the JVM.

5.2 Evaluation of the CLClust Algorithm

The two main aspects evaluated hereafter are the performance of the CLClust algorithm compared with a classical AHC algorithm and the quality of the partitioning. The experiments were carried out with four configurations based on different variations of the two following parameters: (i) the clustering method, i.e., CLClust or AHC algorithms, (ii) the convexity of a cluster is imposed or not.

For every dataset and every configuration, the running time for clustering and the number of required dissimilarities are recorded. The results are presented in Figs. 4 and 5. Figure 4 only shows the three datasets in which the clustering procedure takes at least 1 s.

As expected, configurations based on CLClust algorithm are more efficient than those based on a classical AHC algorithm, as shown in Fig. 4. In addition, the variation CLClust-convex works faster in general. In the case of AHC, convexity checking generates additional computational costs. In CLClust-convex,

[1] https://archive.ics.uci.edu/.

the convexity requirement reduces the number of possible groupings and therefore the number of dissimilarities to be computed as shown in Fig. 5. In line with these observed runtimes, Fig. 5 shows that the CLClust algorithm significantly reduces the number of calculated dissimilarities. This reduction is even more radical when the convexity constraint is enforced. The number of calculated dissimilarities is divided on average by 3.6, with significant differences between datasets. The gain in terms of execution time is even greater than the gain in terms of calculated values: reducing the number of dissimilarities also reduces the size of the priority queue and the number of updates during grouping (lines 15–21 of Algorithm 1).

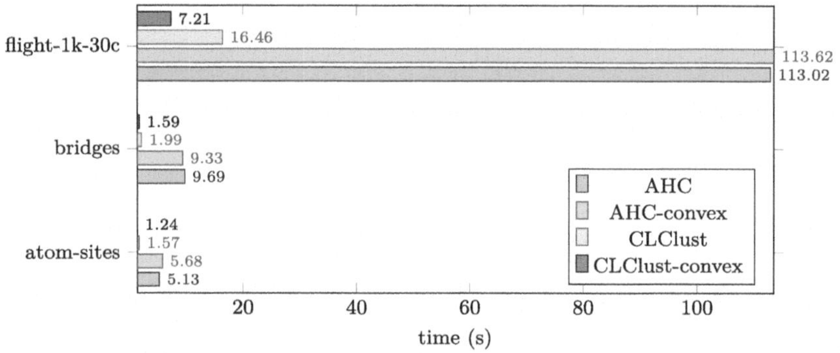

Fig. 4. Clustering running times in different configurations.

The study of the quality of a cluster partition built by CLClust is based on three criteria, namely compression rate, object preservation, and convexity. In the configurations involving CLClust and CLClust-convex, the cutting level is changed from 0 to 1 in steps of size 0.1. For every cut level, the three criteria are monitored. Figure 6 shows the evolution of the three criteria as a function of the cut level while the observations that can be made on these datasets also apply to the other datasets.

For each dataset, we can observe that, initially, compression increases faster than preservation decreases. With the exception of flight-1k-30c, a compression ratio of at least 0.5 can be achieved before preservation begins to decrease. As Fig. 6 shows, when convexity is not enforced, the decrease of preservation is greater than the increase in the compression ratio. This observation can be made for all datasets except fd-reduced-250k-30 and wine datasets, for which preservation remains maximum.

With the exception of the iris dataset, convexity, when not enforced, is also stable in low cut levels, but tends to decrease earlier and faster than preservation. The stability of both preservation and convexity in low cut levels can be explained by the fact that most clusters are made up of two concepts at most (the medoid is always the top concept of such sublattices).

When convexity is required, the preservation of objects is higher and compression rate is only slightly reduced. The object preservation is higher because imposing convexity implies that every cluster has a supremum, increasing the probability that the medoid is the supremum and thus increasing the preservation of objects. For example, considering the atom-site dataset with a cut level of 0.8, the ratio of clusters whose medoid is a supremum increases from 17% to 21% when convexity is enforced.

Among the ten datasets considered in the experiments, eight datasets achieve high compression rates such as atom-site. Only two datasets show low compression rates (< 0.5 with a cut level at 0.8), namely wine and fd-reduced-250k-30. These differences cannot be explained either by the size of datasets or by the number of concepts. More probably the reasons are related to the shapes of the lattices. Indeed, wide but shallow lattices imply many incomparable concepts, meaning that many clusters contain less than three concepts (91% in the case of fd-reduced-250k-30). This also explains why convexity is preserved in such lattices.

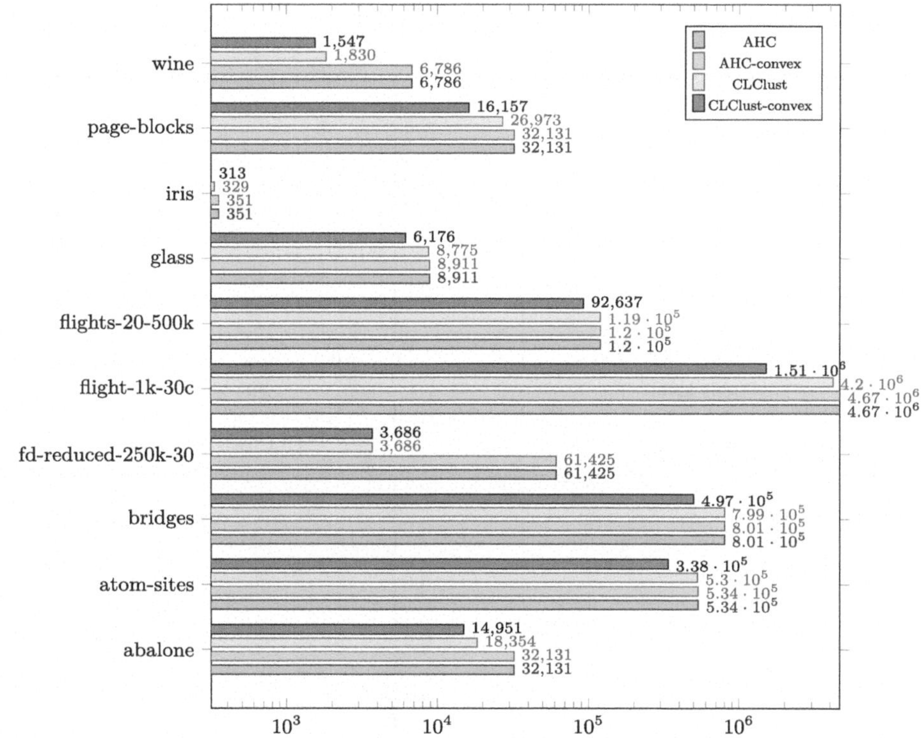

Fig. 5. The numbers of dissimilarities required in the different configurations (log scale).

To sum up, these results show that CLClust is more efficient than a classical version of AHC. In addition, combining CLClust with the convexity constraint provides the best computation times, preserves almost all the objects, with a weak effect on the compression rate.

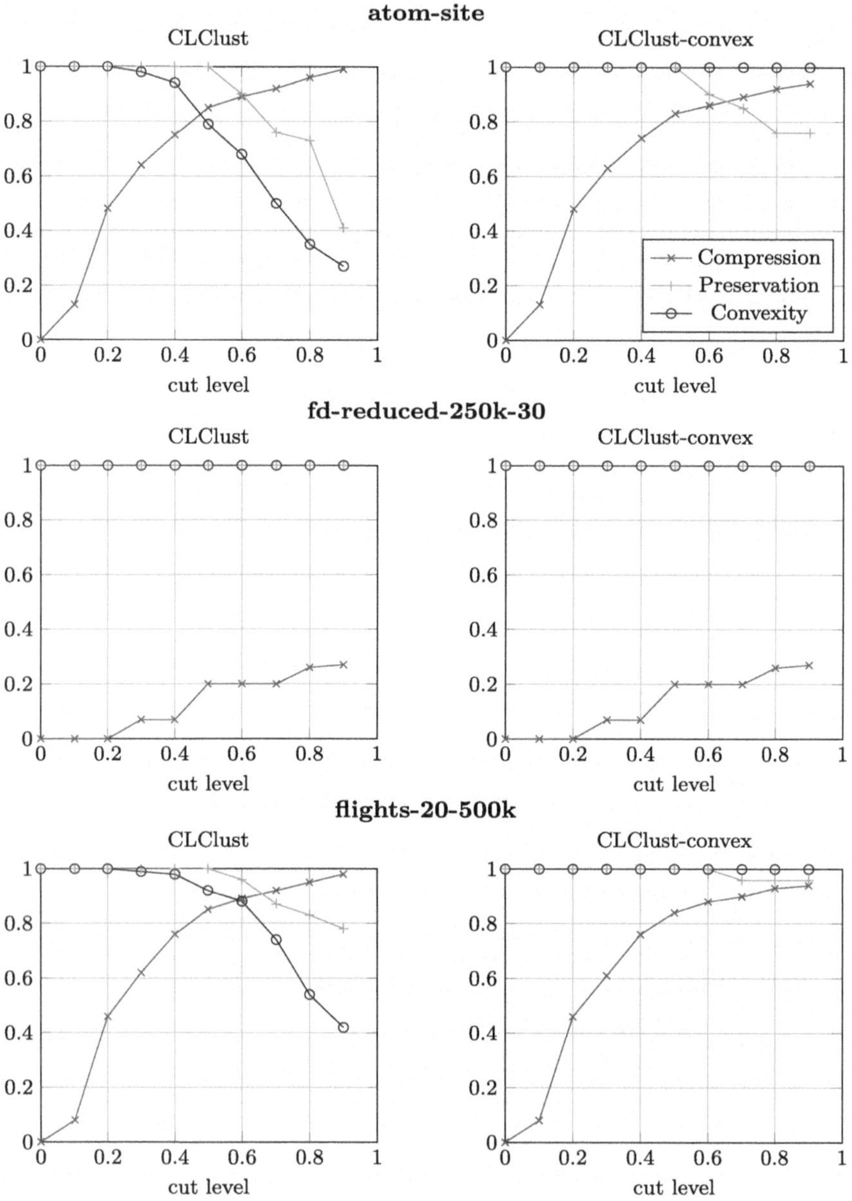

Fig. 6. The variations of compression, object preservation, and convexity w.r.t the cutting level.

6 Conclusions and Perspectives

In this paper, we are interested in reducing a concept lattice in building a representative set of clusters, named RepSet, composed of medoid concepts, for facilitating the visualization and interpretation of possibly large concept lattices. The RepSet is obtained thanks to the CLClust algorithm based on AHC, and depends on three main properties, i.e., a low number of clusters, a hight number of preserved objects, and the local preservation of the original lattice ordering.

As future work, many elements remain to be more precisely studied and several research directions can be explored. Firstly, we would like to extend the experiments and to examine alternative clustering algorithms and dissimilarity measures, and as well to investigate the impacts of the size and of the density of the dataset at hand. Then the preservation of attributes along with objects should also be questioned using alternative dissimilarity measures as proposed in [12]. Finally, we would like to more deeply study the impact of the cut level tuning on the RepSet, and the preservation of the concept lattice ordering in the clusters, possibly using congruence relations.

Acknowledgements. Jaume Baixeries is supported by a recognition 2021SGR-Cat (01266 LQMC) from AGAUR (Generalitat de Catalunya) and the grants AGRUPS-2022 and AGRUPS-2023 from Universitat Politécnica de Catalunya. Alexandre Bazin and Amedeo Napoli are carrying out this research work as part of the French ANR-21-CE23-0023 SmartFCA Research Project.

References

1. Abbas, N., Bazin, A., David, J., Napoli, A.: Discovery of link keys in resource description framework datasets based on pattern structures. Int. J. Approximate Reasoning **161**, 108978 (2023)
2. Abbas, N., Bazin, A., David, J., Napoli, A.: Discovering a representative set of link keys in rdf datasets. In: Alam, M., Rospocher, M., van Erp, M., Hollink, L., Gesese, G.A. (eds.) Proceedings of the 24th International Conference EKAW. Lecture Notes in Computer Science, vol. 15370, pp. 53–68. Springer (2024)
3. Alqadah, F., Bhatnagar, R.: Similarity measures in formal concept analysis. In: International Symposium on Artificial Intelligence and Mathematics (ISAIM) (2010)
4. Alwersh, M., Kovàcs, L.: Survey on attribute and concept reduction methods in formal concept analysis. Indonesian J. Electr. Eng. Comput. Sci. **30**(1), 366–387 (2023)
5. Aragón, R.G., Medina, J., Ramírez-Poussa, E.: Reducing concept lattices by means of a weaker notion of congruence. Fuzzy Sets Syst. **418**, 153–169 (2021)
6. Aswanikumar, C., Srinivas, S.: Concept lattice reduction using fuzzy K-Means clustering. Expert Syst. Appl. **37**(3), 2696–2704 (2010)
7. Bakkelund, D.: Order preserving hierarchical agglomerative clustering. Mach. Learn. **111**(5), 1851–1901 (2022)

8. Buzmakov, A., Kuznetsov, S.O., Napoli, A.: Fast generation of best interval patterns for nonmonotonic constraints. In: Proceedings of the European Conference on Machine Learning and Knowledge Discovery in Databases (ECML-PKDD), pp. 157–172. LNCS 9285, Springer (2015)
9. Cheung, K.S.K., Vogel, D.R.: Lattice-based information retrieval application. In: The Seventh Pacific Asia Conference on Information Systems (PACIS), p. 78. AISeL (2003)
10. Dias, S.M., Vieira, N.J.: A methodology for analysis of concept lattice reduction. Inf. Sci. **396**, 202–217 (2017)
11. Dudyrev, E., Zueva, M., Kuznetsov, S.O., Napoli, A.: Clustering with stable pattern concepts. In: Napoli, A., Rudolph, S. (eds.) Proceedings of the 12th International Workshop FCA4AI (co-located with ECAI 2024). CEUR Workshop Proceedings, vol. 3911, pp. 47–58. CEUR-WS.org (2024)
12. Formica, A.: Ontology-based concept similarity in formal concept analysis. Inf. Sci. **176**(18), 2624–2641 (2006)
13. Ganter, B., Kuznetsov, S.O.: Pattern structures and their projections. In: Delugach, H.S., Stumme, G. (eds.) ICCS-ConceptStruct 2001. LNCS (LNAI), vol. 2120, pp. 129–142. Springer, Heidelberg (2001). https://doi.org/10.1007/3-540-44583-8_10
14. Ganter, B., Wille, R.: Formal Concept Analysis. Springer (1999)
15. Kaufman, L., Rousseeuw, P.J.: Finding groups in data: an introduction to cluster analysis. Wiley (2009)
16. Kovács, L.: Conceptual clustering with application on FCA context. Expert Syst. Appl. **245**, 123013 (2024)
17. Krupka, M.: On complexity reduction of concept lattices: three counterexamples. Inf. Retrieval **15**(2), 151–156 (2012)
18. Kuznetsov, S.O.: Clustering with Axialities. In: Napoli, A., Rudolph, S. (eds.) Proceedings of the 12th International Workshop FCA4AI (co-located with ECAI 2024). CEUR Workshop Proceedings, vol. 3911, pp. 59–66. CEUR-WS.org (2024)
19. van der Merwe, D., Obiedkov, S.A., Kourie, D.G.: AddIntent: A new incremental algorithm for constructing concept lattices. In: Eklund, P.W. (ed.) Proceedings of the Second International Conference on Formal Concept Analysis (ICFCA), pp. 372–385. Lecture Notes in Computer Science 2961, Springer (2004)
20. Monjardet, B.: Metrics on partially ordered setsa survey. Discret. Math. **35**(1), 173–184 (1981)
21. Murtagh, F., Contreras, P.: Algorithms for hierarchical clustering: an overview. Wiley Interdisc. Rev. Data Min. Knowl. Discovery **2**(1), 86–97 (2012)
22. Pérez-Suárez, A., Martínez-Trinidad, J.F., Carrasco-Ochoa, J.A.: A review of conceptual clustering algorithms. Artif. Intell. Rev. **52**(2), 1267–1296 (2019)
23. Siff, M., Reps, T.W.: Identifying modules via concept analysis. IEEE Trans. Software Eng. **25**(6), 749–768 (1999)

24. Viaud, J., Bertet, K., Demko, C., Missaoui, R.: Subdirect decomposition of contexts into subdirectly irreducible factors. In: Ojeda-Aciego, M., Baixeries, J., Sacarea, C. (eds.) Proceedings of the International Workshop on Formal Concept Analysis and Applications (FCA&A, co-located with ICFCA 2015). CEUR Workshop Proceedings, vol. 1434, pp. 49–64. CEUR-WS.org (2015)
25. Viaud, J., Bertet, K., Missaoui, R., Demko, C.: Using congruence relations to extract knowledge from concept lattices. Discret. Appl. Math. **249**, 135–150 (2018)

Atomic Patterns for Efficient Computation with Pattern Structures

Egor Dudyrev[1,4(✉)], Miguel Couceiro[1,2], Mehdi Kaytoue[3], Sergei O. Kuznetsov[4], and Amedeo Napoli[1]

[1] Univ. Lorraine, CNRS, Loria, 54000 Nancy, France
egor.dudyrev@loria.fr
[2] IST, Univ. Lisbon, INESC-ID, 1000-029 Lisbon, Portugal
[3] Univ. Lyon, INSA Lyon, CNRS, LIRIS UMR 5205, 69621 Lyon, France
[4] HSE University, 20 Myasnitskaya St., Moscow 101000, Russian Federation

Abstract. Pattern Structures is a framework in FCA allowing objects to have complex descriptions, only requiring that the set of descriptions forms a complete meet-semi-lattice. However, some particular descriptions or patterns, such as subgraphs and subsequences, do not necessarily ensure that every pair of descriptions has a unique infimum and ask for additional operations, e.g., antichain completion. Moreover, meet-based approaches struggle to generate non-trivial implications for complex data since, in general, they only output closed descriptions. For overcoming such limitations, we introduce in this paper an alternative view of pattern structures based on the join operation and the so-called "atomic patterns". Such atomic patterns correspond to join-irreducible descriptions in the join-semi-lattice of all possible descriptions. They enable an efficient traversal of the description space and the computation of closures, minimal generators, pseudo-intents, implications among others, while showing very good computational performance.

Keywords: Formal Concept Analysis · Pattern Structures · Description Space · Join-Irreducible Element · Atomic Patterns

1 Introduction

Formal Concept Analysis [10] (FCA) is a framework useful in several fields, such as in information and knowledge processing including visualization, knowledge management, machine learning, and data mining [11]. Data are represented by a binary relation from which concepts are extracted and organized into a concept lattice. The latter supports in particular conceptual knowledge discovery in databases: finding frequent patterns, implications or association rules, concepts and structures in the data, to elicit hypotheses and insights from the data.

When it comes to non binary data –say numerical attributes, texts, sequences of item(set)s, hierarchies, graphs– FCA properly defines *conceptual scaling* which allows one to transform the original data into a binary table from which any FCA

P. Cellier et al. (Eds.): CONCEPTS 2025, LNAI 15941, pp. 178–194, 2025.
https://doi.org/10.1007/978-3-032-03364-2_11

algorithm for extracting concepts, implications and building concept lattices can be used. In some applications, working with scaling is hard or even impossible. For example, in the analysis of gene expression data, interordinal scaling produces huge binary data that cannot be analysed with basic tools of FCA [13]. For finding parts of molecules specific to a target, i.e., finding frequent subgraphs, working directly with FCA and ordinal scaling is not feasible due to overwhelming amount of candidate subgraphs [8, 14, 15]. To apply FCA to these types of data, Pattern Structures were introduced [9]. However, they are still facing challenges when it comes to efficiently mine not only closed patterns, but also minimal generators, proper premises, and pseudo-intents.

In this paper, we present a general approach for mining patterns like closed patterns, minimal generators, and pseudo-intents from a pattern structure using "*Atomic Patterns*". These are join-irreducible elements in a pattern structure's description space, which forms a complete semi-lattice. The approach leverages a well-known fact from lattice theory: any description or pattern can be obtained by the join of a subset of atomic patterns. The name "Atomic Patterns" suggests that join-irreducible elements of a description space are not given in advance and need to be computed. The key idea behind atomic patterns is the following: any pattern structure can be broken into pieces, namely atomic patterns, the latter being then enumerated with a particular traversal based on *atomic patterns antichains.* The proposed framework simplifies the mining process and outperforms specialized solutions in various cases.

The rest of the paper is organized as follows. First, we present basic notations and definitions through a running example in Sect. 2. In Sect. 3, we introduce atomic patterns, the way they characterize patterns of interest. Section 4 presents our algorithm based on the traversal of the antichains of atomic patterns. Finally, we present preliminary experimental results showing the potential of atomic patterns for mining different kinds of patterns and we conclude.

2 Basic Definitions and Problem Formulation

In this section we introduce basic definitions about pattern structures and an illustrative example.

Definition 1. *A* ***Pattern Structure*** *[9] is a triple* $(G, (\mathbb{D}, \sqcap), \delta)$ *where* G *is a set of objects,* $(\mathbb{D}, \sqcap)$ *is a complete meet-semi-lattice of object descriptions or patterns, and* $\delta : G \to D$ *is a mapping providing any object* $g \in G$ *with a description* $d \in (\mathbb{D}, \sqcap)$.

As $(\mathbb{D}, \sqcap)$ *or, equivalently,* $(\mathbb{D}, \sqsubseteq)$ *is a semi-lattice, the following Galois connection, denoted by* $\{(.)^{\square}, (.)^{\square}\}$*, between* $(2^G, \subseteq)$ *and* $(D, \sqsubseteq)$*, gives rise to a complete lattice called the pattern concept lattice of* $(G, (D, \sqcap), \delta)$.

The first derivation operator takes a set of objects and returns a maximal description (pattern) shared by all objects. The second derivation operator takes a description and returns the maximal set of objects sharing this description.

Pattern concepts in $(G, (D, \sqcap), \delta)$ *are pairs of the form* (A, d)*,* $A \subseteq G$*,* $d \in (D, \sqcap)$*, such that* $A^{\square} = d$ *and* $A = d^{\square}$*. For a pattern concept* (A, d) *the* *component d is called pattern intent and it is the maximal common description of all objects in A, called pattern extent.*

When partially ordered by $(A_1, d_1) \leq (A_2, d_2) \Leftrightarrow A_1 \subseteq A_2 \quad (\Leftrightarrow d_2 \sqsubseteq d_1)$*, the set of all pattern concepts forms a complete lattice called a pattern concept lattice.*

Let us remark that, since the semi-lattice $(\mathbb{D}, \sqcap)$ is complete, we can define the join operation on patterns such as $d \sqcup_{\mathbb{D}} e = \sqcap\{x \mid d, e \sqsubseteq x\}$, and then the description language is actually the complete lattice $(\mathbb{D}, \sqcap, \sqcup_{\mathbb{D}})$. It should be also noticed that we use $\sqcup_{\mathbb{D}}$ for join operation on $\mathbb{D}$ to differentiate it from the other join operation $\sqcup$ defined on the set of closed patterns and used throughout the original publication on Pattern Structures [9]. In contrast to the join operation $\sqcup$, the new join operation $\sqcup_{\mathbb{D}}$ is defined over a description space , so it is independent of object descriptions or data.

In pattern mining, one is generally interested in computing (frequent) closed patterns. For some purposes, such as rule discovery and rule-based classification [17], one is also interested in patterns called *minimal generators.*

	m_1	m_2	m_3
g_1	5	7	6
g_2	6	8	4
g_3	4	8	5
g_4	4	9	8
g_5	5	8	5

Table 1. Data example

Definition 2 (Closed patterns and minimal generators). *Given a pattern structure* $(G, (\mathbb{D}, \sqcap), \delta)$*, closed patterns are precisely pattern intents. Also, given a closed pattern d, its equivalence class based on common support is made of all patterns e such that* $e^{\Box} = d$*. Minimal elements w.r.t.* $\sqcap$ *are called the minimal generators.*

Remark. Note that in the original paper [9] *all patterns* are supposed to be closed w.r.t. a pattern structure. However, in this paper a *pattern* is an element of description space $(\mathbb{D}, \sqcap)$, so it may be closed or non-closed w.r.t. a particular pattern structure $(G, (\mathbb{D}, \sqcap), \delta)$. In case a pattern is closed in a pattern structure, it is called a *closed pattern* of this pattern structure.

Example 1. Pattern structures can represent various types of data. For instance, on a numerical tabular dataset, an interval pattern structure [13] is a particular pattern structure where descriptions are vectors of values, and where each dimension corresponds to an attribute. Here, the description space can be understood as the finite set of all possible n-rectangles in the Euclidean space having their borders meeting data points. In this case, the meet operation $\sqcap$ is the convex hull of point sets, while the join operation $\sqcup$ is the intersection of the point sets. This may be misleading, but remember that more general patterns are those covering most of the objects. The first derivation operator returns the set of objects that are inside a rectangle while the second derivation operator returns the smallest rectangle containing all data points given in argument. In Table 1, a closed pattern is given by $\{g_1, g_2, g_5\}^{\Box} = \delta(g_1) \sqcap \delta(g_2) \sqcap \delta(g_3) = \langle[5, 6], [7, 8], [4, 6]\rangle$. In this equivalence class, the only minimal generator is given by $\langle[5, 6], [7, 9], [4, 8]\rangle$ that we can also write as $\{m_1 \geq 5\}$. Other examples can be found in [12].

3 Atomic Patterns as Seeds to Mine Patterns

The key idea developed here is that any pattern of the description space, including closed and minimal patterns, can be characterized as the join of a minimal subset of *atomic patterns*, the latter being join-irreducible elements of the finite and complete semi-lattice of descriptions.

Definition 3 (Atomic Pattern). *An* ***atomic pattern*** *is a join-irreducible element in the complete lattice of patterns* $(\mathbb{D}, \sqcap, \sqcup_{\mathbb{D}})$. *The set of atomic patterns is denoted by* $\mathbb{A} \subseteq \mathbb{D}$. *Every pattern from* $\mathbb{D}$ *can be represented as the join of a subset of atomic patterns from* $\mathbb{A}$, *while no atomic pattern from* $\mathbb{A}$ *can be represented as a join of any other patterns from* $\mathbb{D}$:

$$\begin{aligned} &1)\ \forall d \in \mathbb{D}, \quad && \exists \mathcal{A} \subseteq A, \bigsqcup_{\mathbb{D}} \mathcal{A} = d \\ &2)\ \forall a \in \mathbb{A}, \quad && \nexists \mathcal{D} \subseteq \mathbb{D} \setminus \{a\}, \bigsqcup_{\mathbb{D}} \mathcal{D} = a \end{aligned} \tag{1}$$

Example 2. Consider the interval pattern structure from Table 1 restricted to the first attribute only. The description space is given by $\mathbb{D} = \{[4,4], [5,5], [6,6], [4,5], [5,6], [4,6]\}$ which can also be written as constraints $\mathbb{D} = \{\{m_1 \leq 4, m_1 \leq 5, m_1 \leq 6, m_1 \geq 4\}, \ldots, \{m_1 \geq 4, m_1 \leq 6\}\}$ as shown in [13] with equivalent interordinal scaling. Removing redundant attributes, as for example $m_1 \leq 6$ is implied by $m_1 \leq 5$, the set can be simplified as $\mathbb{D} = \{\{m_1 \leq 4\}, \ldots, \{m_1 \geq 4, m_1 \leq 6\}\}$. Note that we can observe here two maximal chains of patterns $\{[4,4], [4,5], [4,6]\}$ and $\{[6,6], [5,6], [4,6]\}$ which actually correspond to the set of binary attributes of the interordinal scale $\{m_1 \leq 4, m_1 \leq 5, m_1 \leq 6\} \cup \{m_1 \geq 4, m_1 \geq 5, m_1 \geq 6\}$. Finally, the set of atomic patterns is given by $\{[4,4], [4,5], [5,6], [6,6]\}$.

We formalize this key idea in the following proposition.

Proposition 1. *Let* $(\mathbb{D}, \sqcap, \sqcup_{\mathbb{D}})$ *be a description language and let* $\mathbb{A} \subseteq \mathbb{D}$ *be the set of atomic patterns of this set. Then, every pattern* $d \in \mathbb{D}$ *can be given as the join of:*

- *a minimal subset of atomic patterns* $\mathcal{A}$ *whose join equals pattern* d:

$$\forall d \in \mathbb{D}, \exists \mathcal{A} \subseteq \mathbb{A} \text{ s.t. } \bigsqcup_{\mathbb{D}} \mathcal{A} = d, \text{ and } \forall \mathcal{A}_* \subset \mathcal{A}, \bigsqcup_{\mathbb{D}} \mathcal{A}_* \neq d \tag{2}$$

In case $(\mathbb{D}, \sqcap, \sqcup_{\mathbb{D}})$ *is a distributive lattice, this minimal subset is unique.*

- *a unique maximal subset of atomic patterns* $\mathcal{B}$ *whose join equals pattern* d:

$$\forall d \in \mathbb{D}, \exists! \mathcal{B} \subseteq \mathbb{A} \text{ s.t. } \bigsqcup_{\mathbb{D}} \mathcal{B} = d, \text{ and } \forall \mathcal{B}_* \supset \mathcal{B}, \bigsqcup_{\mathbb{D}} \mathcal{B}_* \neq d \tag{3}$$

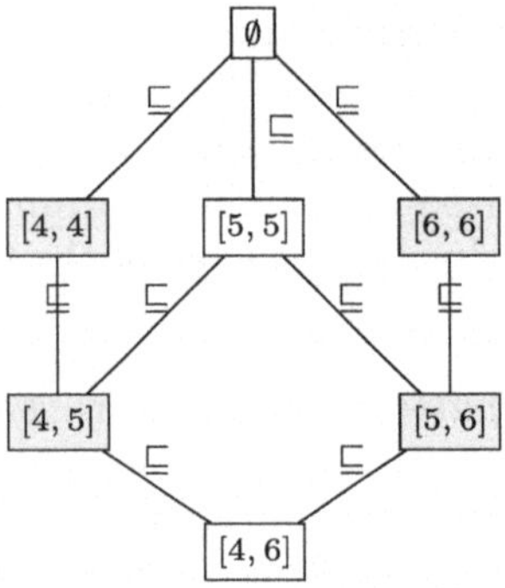

Fig. 1. Description space of the pattern structure of Table 1 for attribute m_1. Elements with grey background are atomic patterns. Emptyset ∅ represents the empty interval which is more precise and more restrictive than any other interval.

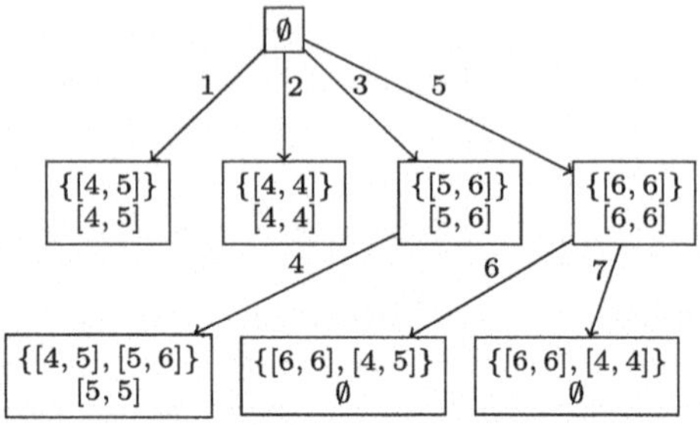

Fig. 2. Traversal of the antichains of atomic patterns used in Algorithm 1. The first line of each node gives the set representation while the second gives the interval representation (join of the elements of the set). Emptyset ∅ represents empty antichain of atomic patterns.

Proof. As recalled in the introduction, any description can be obtained by the join of a subset of atomic patterns. Then, for any element x of $(\mathbb{D}, \sqcap, \sqcup_{\mathbb{D}})$, there is a minimal set of atomic patterns whose join is element x. In a distributive lattice any element can be represented as a join of a unique minimal set of maximal join-irreducible elements smaller than the element. Moreover, the set of all atomic patterns smaller than element x composes the unique maximal set of atomic patterns whose join is element x.

Example 3. In the previous example restricted to attribute m_1, the set of atomic patterns is given by $\{[4,4], [4,5], [4,6], [5,6], [6,6]\}$. The only pattern of the description space that is missing is $[5,5]$, given by the join atomic patterns $[4,5] \sqcup_{\mathbb{D}} [5,6] = [5,5]$ (recalling that in our interval pattern structure definition $\sqcup_{\mathbb{D}}$ corresponds to interval intersection).

It means that we can design an algorithm which only enumerates atomic patterns (including closed and minimal patterns). More precisely, we can restrict the enumeration strategy to antichains of atomic patterns. For that, we denote the antichains $\mathcal{A}$ of atomic patterns of a pattern d in Proposition 1 as $\texttt{atcs}[d]$ (short for "atomic antichains"), and the order ideal of atomic patterns $\mathcal{B}$ as $\texttt{atp}(d)$ (short for "atomic pattern"):

$$\begin{aligned} \texttt{atp}(d) &= \{a \in \mathbb{A} \mid a \sqsubseteq d\}, \\ \texttt{atcs}[d] &= \{\mathcal{A} \subseteq \mathbb{A} \mid \bigsqcup_{\mathbb{D}} \mathcal{A} = d, \mathcal{A} \text{ is an antichain}\} \end{aligned} \tag{4}$$

The set of atomic patterns $\mathbb{A}$ contains two particularly interesting types of atomic patterns: namely support-maximal and support-minimal atomic patterns.

Definition 4 (Support-minimal and support-maximal atomic patterns). *Let $(G, (\mathbb{D}, \sqcap), \delta)$ be a pattern structure and let $\mathbb{A} \subseteq \mathbb{D}$ be a set of atomic patterns. An atomic pattern is called* ***support-maximal*** *(resp.* ***support-minimal****) when any greater (resp. smaller) atomic pattern has smaller (resp. greater) extent:*

$$\begin{aligned} a \in \mathbb{A} \text{ is support-maximal} &\iff \forall b \in \mathbb{A}, (a \sqsubset b) \implies (b^{\square} \subset a^{\square}), \\ a \in \mathbb{A} \text{ is support-minimal} &\iff \forall b \in \mathbb{A}, (b \sqsubset a) \implies (a^{\square} \subset b^{\square}). \end{aligned} \tag{5}$$

Proposition 2. *Let $(G, (\mathbb{D}, \sqcap), \delta)$ be a pattern structure and let $\mathbb{A} \subseteq \mathbb{D}$ be a set of atomic patterns. Every closed (resp. minimal) pattern $d \in \mathbb{D}$ can be given as a join of an antichain of support-maximal (resp. support-minimal) atomic patterns: For $d \in \mathbb{D}$,*

$$\begin{aligned} d \text{ is closed} &\implies \exists \mathcal{A} \in \mathtt{atcs}[d] \text{ s.t. } \forall a \in \mathcal{A}, a \text{ is support-maximal}, \\ d \text{ is minimal} &\implies \exists \mathcal{A} \in \mathtt{atcs}[d] \text{ s.t. } \forall a \in \mathcal{A}, a \text{ is support-minimal}. \end{aligned} \tag{6}$$

Proof. Let us prove two parts of the proposition independently.

Firstly, consider closed pattern $d \in \mathbb{D}$ and the respective antichain $\mathcal{A} \subseteq \mathbb{A}$ constructed as $\mathcal{A} = \{a \in \mathtt{atp}(d) \mid \nexists b \in \mathtt{atp}(d), a \sqsubset b\}$. Since the pattern is closed, its join with any atomic pattern out of the set $\mathtt{atp}(d)$ will make the resulting pattern describe fewer objects: $\forall b \in \mathbb{A} \setminus \mathtt{atp}(d), d^{\square} \cap b^{\square} \subset d^{\square}$. Consider an atomic pattern $a \in \mathcal{A}$. All its greater atomic patterns lie in set $\mathbb{A} \setminus \mathtt{atp}(d)$. If an atomic pattern a is not support-maximal, then there is an atomic pattern $b \in \mathbb{A} \setminus \mathtt{atp}(d)$ with the same support $a^{\square} = b^{\square}$. This would imply that the support of $d^{\square} \cap b^{\square}$ equals $d^{\square}$, which contradicts the assumption that d is closed.

Second, consider minimal pattern $d \in \mathbb{D}$ and the respective antichain $\mathcal{A}$, such that all smaller antichains describe smaller patterns: $\forall b \in \mathcal{A}, \forall a \in \mathbb{A}, (a \sqsubset b) \implies (\bigsqcup_{\mathbb{D}} \mathcal{A} \setminus \{b\} \cup \{a\} \neq d)$. If an atomic pattern $b \in \mathcal{A}$ is not support-minimal, then there exists smaller atomic pattern $a \in \mathbb{A}$ with the same support: $a^{\square} = b^{\square}$. Then, pattern $\bigsqcup_{\mathbb{D}} \mathcal{A} \setminus \{b\} \cup \{a\}$ is smaller than d but matches the same set of objects. This contradicts the initial assumption that pattern d is minimal.

Example 4. Consider the first attribute in Table 1 and let us define the following description space with both open and closed intervals $\mathbb{D} = \{ [4,6], (4,6], [4,6), [5,6], (4,6), [4,5], (5,6], [5,6), (4,5], [4,5), [6,6], [5,5], [4,4], \emptyset\}$. The set of atomic patterns of this description space is $\mathbb{A} = \{ (4,6], [4,6), [5,6], [4,5], (5,6], [4,5), [6,6], [4,4] \}$. Notice that for any atomic pattern with an open bound (e.g. $(4,6]$ describing $(4,6]^{\square} = \{g_1, g_2, g_5\}$) there is always a more precise atomic pattern with two closed bounds and the same extent (e.g. $[5,6]$ describing $[5,6]^{\square} = \{g_1, g_2, g_5\}$). Analogously, fow any interval with two closed bounds (e.g. $[5,6]$ describing $[5,6]^{\square} = \{g_1, g_2, g_5\}$) there is always a more precise interval describing fewer objects (e.g. $[5,6)$ describing $[5,6)^{\square} = \{g_1, g_5\}$). Naturally, in order to mine intents, one should only traverse support-maximal atomic intervals from $\mathbb{A}$ (i.e. the ones having both closed bounds), and one should only traverse support-minimal atomic intervals from $\mathbb{A}$ (i.e. the ones having one open bound) in order to mine minimal generators. Traces of the same idea can be found in interordinal scaling and in publications on (support-)maximal subsequences [7] and support-closed patterns [2].

4 A General Algorithm for Pattern Structures

We have shown that the set of all patterns can be obtained by joins of atomic patterns. Thus, one can enumerate all patterns by efficiently traversing the partially ordered set of atomic patterns. This raises new questions which are discussed below, namely: how to enumerate the set of atomic patterns, how to efficiently explore the set of atomic patterns, and how these enumeration and exploration are related to existing research in FCA.

4.1 How to Enumerate Atomic Patterns?

Based on the definition of atomic patterns, we discuss hereafter different ways of enumerating a set of atomic patterns within a pattern structure.

Explicit Enumeration. The simplest way to enumerate the set of atomic patterns $(\mathbb{A}, \sqsubseteq)$ is to provide it explicitly. Then, the set of all patterns $\mathbb{D}$ will arise from joins of subsets of $\mathbb{A}$. Atomic patterns are often explicitly defined in discretization of numerical data. For example, one can decide to treat attribute "Person's age" with atomic patterns $\mathbb{A} = \{[0, 10], [0, 20], \dots [0, 90], [10, 100], [20, 100], \dots, [90, 100]\}$, where the minimal interval would be $[0, 100]$.

Enumeration of Object Descriptions. Another way of enumerating the set of atomic patterns is by explicitly providing the function `atp` that outputs all atomic patterns smaller than a given pattern d. Then, one can obtain the set of all atomic patterns $\mathbb{A}$ by applying function `atp` to the description of every object from a pattern structure.

$$\text{Given } \delta : G \mapsto \mathbb{D} \text{ and } \mathtt{atp} : \mathbb{D} \to 2^{\mathbb{D}}, \quad \mathbb{A} = \bigcup_{g \in G} \mathtt{atp}(\delta(g)) \tag{7}$$

For example, let us consider the pattern lattice in Fig. 1 and two objects x, y where $\delta(x) = [4, 4]$ and $\delta(y) = [5, 6]$. Then the set of extracted atomic patterns $\mathbb{A}_{xy}$ is $\mathtt{atp}(\delta(x)) \cup \mathtt{atp}(\delta(y)) = \{[4, 4], [4, 5], [5, 6]\}$. Atomic pattern $[6, 6]$ highlighted in Fig. 1 is not extracted in the set $\mathbb{A}_{xy}$ as it describes neither object x nor object y. In this case, the enumeration method guarantees that all resulting atomic patterns $\mathbb{A}$ have non-zero support. This method of enumerating atomic patterns is currently the main method used in the Paspailleur package [6] and in the experimental section of the paper.

Dynamic Enumeration. When the set of atomic patterns is too large, one can generate them in an incremental way, one by one. For example, in the case of Graph Pattern Structures, every object in a pattern structure can be described by a (connected) graph of a hundred vertices. Then every connected subgraph of all provided graphs can be considered as an atomic pattern. Various graph pattern mining algorithms, e.g., gSofia algorithm [3], tackle this problem by navigating the set of subgraphs: at every step of the algorithm, given a current graph, it is checked whether a supergraph of this current graph should be considered or not. In terms of atomic patterns, such algorithm defines a function `next.aps` that takes an atomic pattern (e.g., a graph) and outputs the following atomic patterns or successors, e.g., graphs with one more node.

Given $\top \in \mathbb{D}$ and $\texttt{next.aps} : \mathbb{D} \to 2^{\mathbb{D}}$:

$$\mathbb{A} = \bigcup_{i=1}^{\infty} \mathbb{A}_i, \quad \mathbb{A}_i = \begin{cases} \{b \in \texttt{next.aps}(a) \mid a \in \mathbb{A}_{i-1}\}, & \text{if } i > 1 \\ \texttt{next.aps}(\top), & \text{otherwise} \end{cases} \tag{8}$$

The set of all atomic patterns $\mathbb{A}$ can be upper-bounded by the object descriptions $\delta[G]$, i.e., $\mathbb{A} = \{a \in \bigcup_i \mathbb{A}_i \mid \exists g \in G, a \sqsubseteq \delta(g)\}$.

Enumeration from Attributes in a Formal Context. Finally, the set of attributes M of a formal context (G, M, I) can be considered as an unordered set of atomic patterns: $\mathbb{A} = \{\{m\} \mid m \in M\}$. Then, the join operation over the set of atomic patterns exactly corresponds to the union of atomic patterns, giving rise to the description space $\mathbb{D}$ which is the lattice of all subsets of M. When M is equipped with a partial order $\leq_M$, the pattern lattice $\mathbb{D}$ can be constructed with antichain completion of the partially ordered set $(M, \leq_M)$. Then, atomic patterns would again be singleton sets of attributes $\mathbb{A} = \{\{m\} \mid m \in M\}$.

In particular, the idea of exploring the partially ordered set of attributes for efficient mining of formal concepts was explored in [1]. The problem of converting a partially ordered set of attributes into a pattern structure was studied within the framework of pattern setups [18] and pattern multistructures [2].

The reverse is also true: given a pattern structure $(G, (\mathbb{D}, \sqcap), \delta)$, once its atomic patterns $\mathbb{A}$ are enumerated, the partially ordered set of atomic patterns can be considered as a partially ordered set of attributes in the formal context $(G, \mathbb{A}, I)$ where $I = \{(g, a) \in G \times \mathbb{A} \mid a \sqsubseteq \delta(g)\}$. Thus, the task of enumerating patterns of a pattern structure becomes reduced to the task of enumerating the antichains of partially ordered set of attributes of a formal context.

4.2 Antichain Enumeration Algorithm

Pattern enumeration in a pattern lattice $(\mathbb{D}, \sqsubseteq)$ can be reduced to antichain enumeration in the partially ordered set of atomic patterns $(\mathbb{A}, \sqsubseteq)$ related to $(\mathbb{D}, \sqsubseteq)$. Below we show how to design an efficient antichain traversal.

We impose one restriction on the order of traversing the pattern set: the exploration starts with the smallest pattern i.e., the least precise pattern, and finishes with the most precise pattern. We also want to ensure that we can only generate a pattern once all its smaller patterns were generated. More formally, we want to enumerate patterns in an order that is a linear extension of the partial order over patterns $\sqsubseteq$:

$$\mathbb{D} = \langle d_i \rangle_{i=1}^{|\mathbb{D}|} \text{ such that } \forall d_i, d_j \in \mathbb{D}, (d_i \sqsubseteq d_j) \implies (i \leq j). \tag{9}$$

Suppose that the set of atomic patterns $\mathbb{A}$ is enumerated w.r.t. the partial order on patterns: $\forall a_i, a_j \in \mathbb{A}, (a_i \sqsubseteq a_j) \implies (i \leq j)$. Then we can enumerate the set of patterns $\mathbb{D}$ using *reverse lectic traversal* of the set of antichains of atomic patterns $\mathbb{A}$. This traversal can be considered as a mirrored version of "reverse pre-order traversal" proposed in [19]. Reverse lectic traversal, applied to antichains, starts by initialising a stack that contains the empty antichain, then it takes an element $\mathcal{A}$ from the top of the stack and replaces it with `next_antichains`($\mathcal{A}$):

$$\texttt{next\_antichains}(\mathcal{A}) = \langle \mathcal{A} \cup \{a_i\} \mid \forall a_j \in \mathcal{A}, i < j \text{ and } a_i \not\sqsubseteq a_j \rangle_{i=1}^{|A|}. \tag{10}$$

The first antichain returned by `next_antichains`($\mathcal{A}$) becomes the new top of the stack. A more formal description of the traversal can be found in Algorithm 1.

This traversal is inspired by the reverse prefix traversal of Talky-G algorithm [19] that was used for enumerating minimal generator candidates with one guarantee: a subset of attributes should be visited only if all its proper subsets were already visited. The same idea applies for traversing antichains of atomic patterns: with reverse lectic traversal, we can guarantee that we visit an antichain only if all antichains of less precise patterns were already visited.

Example 5. Consider the example from Fig. 2 that traverses antichains of atomic patterns from Fig. 1. In order to reconstruct this traversal, let us put the atomic patterns in a topological order, so that greater patterns would have greater indices: $\mathbb{A} = \langle [4,5], [4,4], [5,6], [6,6] \rangle$. The traversal starts with empty stack $S = \emptyset$ and empty antichain $\mathcal{A} = \emptyset$. Then it computes `next_antichains`($\mathcal{A}$) that are singleton sets of intervals $\{[4,5]\}, \{[4,4]\}, \{[5,6]\}, \{[6,6]\}$ and puts them into stack S. The next iteration starts with taking antichain $\mathcal{A} = \{[4,5]\}$ from the head of stack S. However, there are no atomic patterns in $\mathbb{A}$ that are placed "to the left of" interval $[4,5]$, so function `next_antichains`($\mathcal{A}$) would return the emptyset. The next iteration considers antichain $\mathcal{A} = \{[4,4]\}$ from the head of stack S. The only atomic pattern placed "to the left of" atomic pattern $[4,4]$ is interval $[4,5]$ comparable to $[4,4]$. So function `next_antichains`($\mathcal{A}$) again returns the emptyset. Then we consider antichain $\mathcal{A} = \{[5,6]\}$. Finally, the topologically ordered set $\mathbb{A}$ contains atomic patterns that have smaller indices than $[5,6]$ and that are incomparable to it. Function `next_antichains`($\mathcal{A}$) returns two new antichains $\{[5,6],[4,5]\}, \{[5,6],[4,4]\}$ that are placed at the head of the stack. The next iteration would consider the newly placed antichain $\mathcal{A} = \{[5,6],[4,5]\}$ and the traversal would continue until the stack becomes empty.

Algorithm 1: Reverse lectic traversal

Input: Atomic patterns $\mathbb{A} = \{a_1, a_2, \ldots, a_n\}$ with a partial order $\sqsubseteq \subseteq \mathbb{A} \times \mathbb{A}$
Data: Ensure that $\forall a_i, a_j \in \mathbb{A}, (a_i \sqsubseteq a_j) \implies i \leq j$
Result: Descriptions $\mathbb{D}$, s.t. $\forall d_i, d_j \in \mathbb{D}, (d_i \sqsubseteq d_j) \implies i \leq j$

```
D_atc ← ∅ ;                                  /* Queue of traversed antichains */
S ← ⟨∅⟩;                                      /* Stack's head is on the left */
while S ≠ ∅ do
    𝒜 ← Q.pop() ;                 /* Antichain of atomic patterns to process */
    /* Use "reverse" to put the first next antichain on top of S         */
    for 𝒜_next ∈ reverse(next_antichains(𝒜)) do
        S.push(𝒜_next);
    end
    D_atc.push(𝒜);
end
D ← ⟨⊔𝒜 | 𝒜 ∈ D_atc⟩;
```

4.3 Mining Intents and Minimal Generators

Previous sections described how one can scale a pattern structure $(G, (\mathbb{D}, \sqsubseteq), \delta)$ into a formal context $(G, \mathbb{A}, I)$, where $\mathbb{A}$ are atomic patterns in $(\mathbb{D}, \sqsubseteq)$ and are partially ordered. Then, the enumeration of all complex patterns of $(\mathbb{D}, \sqsubseteq)$ can be substituted by an efficient enumeration of antichains of the partially ordered attribute set of the scaled context $(G, \mathbb{A}, I)$. We argue that this technique of antichains enumeration can improve not only the algorithms related to Pattern Structures, but (almost) any algorithm in Formal Concept Analysis. To provide an example of such improvement, we discuss below two algorithms that mine intents and minimal generators in a formal context $(G, \mathbb{A}, I)$ where the set of attributes $\mathbb{A}$ is partially ordered by $\sqsubseteq$.

The first algorithm is Close-by-One-with-Implications, CbOI for short, presented in [1]. The authors described a transactional database with a set of binary implications invlving items. Then they proposed CbOI that is based on the classical Close-by-One algorithm but uses implications between items to generate fewer non-canonical descriptions: when considering a closed subset of items B, they generate the next possible descriptions $B \cup \{m\}$ such that item m is directly implied by at least one of the items from B. It is clear that a transactional database can be mapped into a formal context and implications between items can be represented with a partial order on attributes. Then, we can reuse CbOI algorithm for mining intents on the scaled context $(G, \mathbb{A}, I)$ with a partially ordered set of attributes $(\mathbb{A}, \sqsubseteq)$. The interested reader can check the original algorithm in [1] and look over the source code of our implementation of CbOI provided in Paspailleur package [6].

The second algorithm is Talky-G-with-Implications, Talky-GI for short. The original Talky-G algorithm was presented in [19] as an efficient algorithm for mining frequent minimal generators in a formal context. The main optimisation provided in Talky-G is the efficient exploration of the set of minimal generator candidates using reverse pre-order traversal. We further optimise the algorithm by applying a reverse lectic traversal of the set of antichains of a partially ordered attribute set. Again, due to the page limit, we do not formally describe our algorithm Talky-GI in this paper. The interested reader can examine the original algorithm in [19], and also refer to the source code of our implementation of Talky-GI provided in Paspailleur package [6].

5 Experimental Evaluation and Discussion

We evaluate the computational advantages provided by atomic patterns, by examining the efficiency in enumeration of (1) all intents (closed patterns), (2) frequent intents, and (3) frequent minimal generators.

5.1 Experimental Setup

We run all experiments on the famous Titanic dataset[1]. It is interesting for two reasons: 1) it contains 891 objects whose descriptions can be scaled into thousands of binary attributes, that makes the dataset hard for FCA, 2) many-valued attributes (i.e., columns) of the dataset correspond to two different data types: numerical and sequential.

Table 2 presents the information on the many-valued attribute from Titanic dataset. Some many-valued attributes give rise to many atomic patterns. Fortunately, not all atomic patterns should be used for all computations. For example, as it was shown in the theoretical section, we only need support-closed atomic patterns to enumerate closed patterns, and we only need support-minimal atomic patterns to enumerate minimal generators. Moreover, when searching for frequent patterns w.r.t. a predefined minimal support threshold, one can filter out all non-frequent atomic patterns, as they will never generate frequent patterns.

All experiments are conducted with Python 3.11 on a MacBook Pro 2023 with Apple M2 Pro chip and 16 GB RAM. The Jupyter Notebook with experiments is available by the link: https://github.com/EgorDudyrev/expailleur/blob/main/CONCEPTS25%20experiments.ipynb.

5.2 Q1. Efficiency in Enumerating All Intents

The framework of Pattern Structures was originally developed for mining all intents (or closed patterns) on small but complex data. So our first experiment measures how efficient is the approach in mining all intents.

The traditional approach for mining pattern intents is represented by *meet-CbO*: our implementation of Close-by-One algorithm that iterates over subsets of objects and computes their most common patterns using pattern meet operation $\sqcap$. The use of $\sqcap$ allows the algorithm to work directly on pattern structure $(G, (\mathbb{D}, \sqcap), \delta)$ with complex descriptions.

[1] https://www.kaggle.com/c/titanic/data.

Table 2. Many-valued attributes in Titanic dataset, their data types and how many atomic patterns can be extracted from the attribute's values.

attribute	type	# atomic patterns		
		in total	supp. minimal	supp. maximal
Ticket	Sequence	11,601	2,359	1790
Name	Sequence	7,279	2,517	1427
Cabin	Sequence	1,281	318	276
Fare	Interval	362	182	182
Age	Interval	350	176	176
SibSp	Interval	26	14	14
Parch	Interval	26	14	14
Pclass	Interval	10	6	6
Survived	Interval	6	4	4
Sex	Interval	6	4	4
Total	Cartesian	20,947	5,594	3,893

All other algorithms in comparison work on the scaled formal context $(G, \mathbb{A}, I)$ where attributes $\mathbb{A}$ are support-maximal atomic patterns from pattern structure $(G, (\mathbb{D}, \sqcap), \delta)$. Among the compared algorithms are: 1) our implementation of Close-by-One-with-Implications algorithm (*CbOI*) that enumerates intents on scaled context $(G, \mathbb{A}, I)$ by traversing order ideals of the set of atomic patterns $\mathbb{A}$; 2) our implementation of CbOI algorithm that got no information on the partial order on atomic patterns, thus being equivalent to classical *CbO* algorithm; 3) LCM algorithm for mining closed itemsets implemented in Scikit-mine package [4], that serves as a state-of-the-art benchmark.

Table 3 presents the running time of algorithms (in seconds) that mined all intents from the first 5, 10, 15, ..., 100 objects from Titanic dataset. The only controlled variable in the experiment is the "#objects". By varying the number of objects, we vary the number of all atomic patterns that can be extracted from the patterns of these objects, and we also vary the number of intents that can be mined from the data. Recall that only *meet-CbO* algorithm can directly work with pattern structure, while all other algorithms work require three steps to construct pattern intents: 1) extraction of atomic patterns from the pattern structure, 2) mining formal intents on scaled data, and 3) joining atomic patterns from scaled intents to output final pattern intents.

It can be noticed that, for very small data (with # objects = 5), the original *meet-CbO* algorithm works faster than the other algorithms (considering that the other algorithms require the atomic patterns to be extracted beforehand). However, for all other numbers of objects, the proposed *CbOI* algorithm works much faster than all other algorithms, even considering the time it takes to extract the atomic patterns. To our surprise, our implementation of *CbO* algorithm beats *LCM* algorithm, which is often considered as state-of-the-art. We

Table 3. Comparison of time (in seconds) required to enumerate *all* intents of a pattern structure built on top of the first n objects of Titanic dataset. Algorithm meet-CbO is the only algorithm that can be run directly on patterns. The running times of all other algorithms should be summed up with the time taken for extracting and joining atomic patterns. Empty cells correspond to algorithms that took more than ten minutes to run.

#objects	#atomic patterns	#intents	meet-CbO	CbOI	CbO	LCM	atomic extraction	join atomic patterns
5	1,000	28	0.183	0.002	0.003	0.089	1.393	0.015
10	1,283	321	2.613	0.017	0.045	0.135	1.275	0.148
15	1,498	1,438	30.181	0.076	0.273	0.678	1.416	0.628
20	1,656	3,794	150.704	0.225	0.902	2.133	1.548	1.705
25	1,784	8,753	444.397	0.550	2.404	5.714	1.683	3.896
50	2,852	57,273		6.298	28.390	70.762	2.575	25.038
100	4,573	1,054,138		155.541			4.264	473.960

attribute these results to our extensive use of vertical mining approach where we reduce all computations to bit-wise operations on extents of atomic patterns. However, more elaborate comparisons should be made before deriving any strong conclusions.

5.3 Q2. Efficiency in Enumerating Frequent Pattern Concepts

The previous question studied the mining of *all* intents from small datasets. It is known (and can be observed in Table 3) that the number of intents exponentially grows with the number of objects. Thus, the task of mining intents is often reduced to mining only *frequent intents*, that are intents whose support is greater than some provided threshold. In this section we evaluate the time needed for computing the set of frequent intents on Titanic data.

Table 4. Comparison of running times (in seconds) to enumerate intents, frequent w.r.t. the varied minimal support threshold. Empty cells represent the algorithms that took more than ten minutes to compute.

min. support	#sup. max. atomic patterns	#intents	CbOI	CbO	LCM
800	57	2,409	0.20	0.30	0.57
700	100	7,558	0.22	0.54	1.86
600	152	604,632	31.23	108.17	217.10
500	185	3,444,140	159.80		
400	212	8,053,643	370.78		

Table 4 presents the running times of algorithms *CbOI*, *CbO* (i.e. CbOI with no provided information on the partial order on atomic patterns), and *LCM*. We can no longer use *meet-CbO* in the experiments, as it can only mine *all* intents. In our experiments we control the minimal support threshold starting with 800 objects and going down to 400 objects. This changes the number of frequent support maximal atomic patterns and the number of frequent intents in the data, and consequently this changes the time required to enumerate the frequent intents. It can be noticed that it takes less time for *CbOI* algorithm to enumerate eight million frequent intents with min.support = 500, than for *CbO* and *LCM* algorithms to enumerate one million frequent intents with min.support = 600. Moreover, *CbO* and *LCM* algorithms could not enumerate frequent intents for min.support = 500 and min.support = 400 in under ten minutes. Therefore, we leave the corresponding cells in Table 4 empty.

5.4 Q3. Efficiency in Computing Frequent Minimal Generators

Another important task in data-mining is mining frequent minimal generators (also called "keys"). Recall that minimal generators are patterns such that all their smaller patterns have greater support. Together with maximal patterns (intents) they encompass classes of equivalent descriptions in the data.

Table 5. Comparison of running times (in seconds) to enumerate minimal generators, frequent w.r.t. the varied minimal support threshold.

min. support	#sup. min. atomic patterns	#keys Talky-GI	time Talky-GI	#keys Talky-G	time Talky-G
800	57	2,409	0.17	2,425	0.27
700	100	7,612	0.30	7,735	0.56
600	152	608,342	29.09	701,639	59.46
500	185	3,459,158	183.90	4,147,580	346.35
400	212	8,115,532	426.56		

The setup for this experiment is similar to the one from Question 2. We control minimal support threshold, starting from 800 objects and going down to 500 objects, and this changes the number of support-minimal atomic patterns and consequently the number of minimal generators. We compare the *Talky-G* algorithm presented in [19] with its modified version *Talky-GI* (Talky-G-with-Implications) that uses the partial order on atomic patterns for iterating antichains of atomic patterns instead of subsets of atomic patterns. In fact, both algorithms are run by the same function, with the only difference that we inform *Talky-GI* about the partial order on atomic patterns, while *Talky-G* algorithms considers atomic patterns to be unordered.

Table 5 presents the computation time and the number of minimal generators (keys) enumerated by each algorithm. It can be seen that *Talky-GI* algorithm always operates faster than *Talky-G*. Moreover, it also enumerates fewer minimal generators, as it skips some "redundant" generators. For example, *Talky-G* algorithm outputs two minimal generators with the same extent: "Fare $<$ 263, SibSp $<$ 2" and "Fare $<$ 262, SibSp $<$ 2". Clearly, only the former minimal generator is really "minimal" because atomic pattern "Fare $<$ 263" is less precise than atomic pattern "Fare $<$ 262". *Talky-GI* algorithm is informed of the partial order of atomic patterns, thus it does not make this error and outputs only one minimal generator, i.e., "Fare $<$ 263, SibSp $<$ 2". It should be noted that the analogous decrease of "redundant" minimal generators was found in [12] but was only applied to numerical pattern mining and not the general pattern structure formalism.

6 Conclusion

In this paper, we introduced the notion of Atomic Patterns to enhance the efficiency and applicability of Pattern Structures. We illustrated the role of atomic patterns as building blocks in the join-semi-lattice of descriptions and showed that any description or pattern can be derived from the join of a subset of these atomic elements, thereby simplifying the process of pattern generation. Indeed, atomic patterns provide a robust way for enumerating descriptions and more importantly computing closures, minimal generators, and implications with improved computational performance. The experimental study provides initial evidence supporting these advantages.

Future work will focus on consolidating the present work and on exploring how Atomic Patterns can be applied to Pattern Multi-Structures and Pattern Setups. Indeed, several work in the literature [5,7,16] can be addressed with our methodology and further links and comparisons can be established. Additionally, investigating how the set of atomic patterns evolves with respect to pattern structure projections is also worth to be addressed.

Acknowledgments. Egor Dudyrev, Amedeo Napoli, Miguel Couceiro, and Mehdi Kaytoue are carrying out this research work as part of the French ANR- 21-CE23-0023 SmartFCA Research Project. The work by S.O. Kuznetsov in preparing this article was supported by the Basic Research Program of HSE University, Moscow.

References

1. Belfodil, A., Belfodil, A., Kaytoue, M.: Mining formal concepts using implications between items. In: Cristea, D., Le Ber, F., Sertkaya, B. (eds.) ICFCA 2019. LNCS (LNAI), vol. 11511, pp. 173–190. Springer, Cham (2019). https://doi.org/10.1007/978-3-030-21462-3_12
2. Belfodil, A., Kuznetsov, S.O., Kaytoue, M.: On pattern setups and pattern multi-structures. Int. J. Gen Syst **49**(8), 785–818 (2020)
3. Buzmakov, A., Kuznetsov, S.O., Napoli, A.: Efficient mining of subsample-stable graph patterns. In: 17th IEEE International Conference on Data Mining (ICDM), pp. 757–762. IEEE (2017)

4. Cellier, P.: Scikit-mine: a pattern mining library in Python. In: SMiLe 2023 - Spring Workshop on Mining and Learning (2023)
5. Cellier, P., Ferré, S., Ridoux, O., Ducassé, M.: A parameterized algorithm for exploring concept lattices. In: Kuznetsov, S.O., Schmidt, S. (eds.) ICFCA 2007. LNCS (LNAI), vol. 4390, pp. 114–129. Springer, Heidelberg (2007). https://doi.org/10.1007/978-3-540-70901-5_8
6. Dudyrev, E.: Paspailleur (2025). https://doi.org/10.5281/zenodo.15639146. https://smartfca.github.io/paspailleur
7. Ferré, S.: The efficient computation of complete and concise substring scales with suffix trees. In: Kuznetsov, S.O., Schmidt, S. (eds.) ICFCA 2007. LNCS (LNAI), vol. 4390, pp. 98–113. Springer, Heidelberg (2007). https://doi.org/10.1007/978-3-540-70901-5_7
8. Ganter, B., Grigoriev, P.A., Kuznetsov, S.O., Samokhin, M.V.: Concept-based data mining with scaled labeled graphs. In: Wolff, K.E., Pfeiffer, H.D., Delugach, H.S. (eds.) ICCS-ConceptStruct 2004. LNCS (LNAI), vol. 3127, pp. 94–108. Springer, Heidelberg (2004). https://doi.org/10.1007/978-3-540-27769-9_6
9. Ganter, B., Kuznetsov, S.O.: Pattern structures and their projections. In: Delugach, H.S., Stumme, G. (eds.) ICCS-ConceptStruct 2001. LNCS (LNAI), vol. 2120, pp. 129–142. Springer, Heidelberg (2001). https://doi.org/10.1007/3-540-44583-8_10
10. Ganter, B., Wille, R.: Formal Concept Analysis - Mathematical Foundations. Springer, Heidelberg (1999)
11. Kaytoue, M., Codocedo, V., Buzmakov, A., Baixeries, J., Kuznetsov, S.O., Napoli, A.: Pattern structures and concept lattices for data mining and knowledge processing. In: Bifet, A., et al. (eds.) ECML PKDD 2015. LNCS (LNAI), vol. 9286, pp. 227–231. Springer, Cham (2015). https://doi.org/10.1007/978-3-319-23461-8_19
12. Kaytoue, M., Kuznetsov, S.O., Napoli, A.: Revisiting numerical pattern mining with formal concept analysis. In: Proceedings of the 22nd International Joint Conference on Artificial Intelligence (IJCAI), pp. 1342–1347 (2011)
13. Kaytoue, M., Kuznetsov, S.O., Napoli, A., Duplessis, S.: Mining gene expression data with pattern structures in formal concept analysis. Inf. Sci. **181**(10), 1989–2001 (2011)
14. Kuznetsov, S.O.: Galois connections in data analysis: contributions from the soviet era and modern Russian research. In: Ganter, B., Stumme, G., Wille, R. (eds.) Formal Concept Analysis. LNCS (LNAI), vol. 3626, pp. 196–225. Springer, Heidelberg (2005). https://doi.org/10.1007/11528784_11
15. Kuznetsov, S.O.: Computing graph-based lattices from smallest projections. In: Wolff, K.E., Palchunov, D.E., Zagoruiko, N.G., Andelfinger, U. (eds.) KONT/KPP -2007. LNCS (LNAI), vol. 6581, pp. 35–47. Springer, Heidelberg (2011). https://doi.org/10.1007/978-3-642-22140-8_3
16. Kuznetsov, S.O., Samokhin, M.V.: Learning closed sets of labeled graphs for chemical applications. In: Kramer, S., Pfahringer, B. (eds.) ILP 2005. LNCS (LNAI), vol. 3625, pp. 190–208. Springer, Heidelberg (2005). https://doi.org/10.1007/11536314_12
17. Li, J., Li, H., Wong, L., Pei, J., Dong, G.: Minimum description length principle: generators are preferable to closed patterns. In: Proceedings 21st National Conference on Artificial Intelligence and the Eighteenth Innovative Applications of Artificial Intelligence, pp. 409–414. AAAI Press (2006)

18. Lumpe, L., Schmidt, S.E.: Pattern structures and their morphisms. In: Yahia, S.B., Konecny, J. (eds.) Proceedings of 12th International Conference on Concept Lattices and Their Applications (CLA), vol. 1466, pp. 171–179. CEUR Workshop Proceedings (2015)
19. Szathmary, L., Valtchev, P., Napoli, A., Godin, R., Boc, A., Makarenkov, V.: A fast compound algorithm for mining generators, closed itemsets, and computing links between equivalence classes. Ann. Math. Artif. Intell. **70**(1–2), 81–105 (2014)

Layout Decisions for Tabular Euler Diagrams

Uta Priss(✉)

Fakultät Informatik, Ostfalia University, Wolfenbüttel, Germany
u.priss@ostfalia.de
http://www.upriss.org.uk

Abstract. Euler diagrams as a means for visualising sets and their intersections tend to be easy to learn to read but difficult or even impossible to draw. Algorithms for automated drawing exist but do not necessarily produce optimal layouts. This short paper describes a method for creating a well-readable layout for certain types of Euler diagrams. The method consists of translating an Euler diagram into an *Attribute Relationship Graph (ARG)* which is defined in this paper. An ARG is then evaluated by applying a set of rules using standard graph drawing software. This semi-automated method produces better layouts than automated layouts and is much faster than complete manual construction.

1 Introduction

Euler diagrams are a well-known means for visualising sets and their intersections or, in other words, for partially ordered sets. Formal Concept Analysis (FCA) is a technique for generating partially ordered sets (or more precisely 'concept lattices') from data (Ganter and Wille 1999). Traditionally, FCA employs Hasse[1] diagrams for visualisations but using Euler diagrams instead has the advantage of requiring less user training (Priss 2017). A disadvantage of Euler diagrams is that they are much more difficult to automatically generate and that in some cases workarounds (such as 'splitting attributes') are required in order for a diagram to be drawable at all. Software for automated drawing of Euler diagrams exists but tends to not emphasise well-readable layouts[2] because just generating diagrams is already challenging.

We have previously suggested that Euler diagrams in the shape of tables, called *tabular diagrams*, are preferable (Priss 2021). In our experience, it can take hours of trial and error to draw a tabular diagram by hand without tools because depending on its layout, a diagram can be visually appealing or difficult to read. FCA software[3] exists that lets users manipulate Hasse diagrams by clicking on nodes and dragging them around. Similar software for tabular diagrams would be very challenging to implement because there are more restrictions for what is allowed for Euler diagrams. Furthermore, if a diagram is not drawable without a workaround then the diagram could not be displayed at

[1] The diagrams should not be named after Hasse because he did not invent them, but the name is widely established in the literature.

[2] For example, Paetzold et al. (2023) add unnecessary zones; Rodgers (2014) mentions several software tools that mostly produce irregular, concave shapes.

[3] https://upriss.github.io/fca/fcasoftware.html.

P. Cellier et al. (Eds.): CONCEPTS 2025, LNAI 15941, pp. 195–202, 2025.
https://doi.org/10.1007/978-3-032-03364-2_12

all unless some workaround had been preselected which would limit the users' choices on how to proceed. Therefore, Euler diagram drawing algorithms often consider not the diagram itself but a graph (in the sense of mathematical graph theory) that shows adjacency. The method suggested in this paper also employs a mathematical graph but it is a somewhat different construction and thus a novel approach.

The idea is to generate an *Attribute Relationship Graph (ARG)*, which focuses on some core features of the data. Because an ARG is a mathematical graph, it can be imported into existing graph drawing software where its vertices can be moved around until some rules are met. If the rules cannot be met then it is quite likely that a tabular diagram without workarounds is not drawable at all. In the future, software could be implemented that automates the rules. But manipulating an ARG by hand with existing graph drawing software already significantly reduces the amount of time required to create an appealing layout for a tabular diagram as demonstrated by the examples in this paper. Several generalisations of the approach suggested in this paper are possible: applications to other types of diagrams but also extending the use of ARGs by incorporating further types of relationships.

Because this paper continues our previous research of representing concept lattices with Euler diagrams not everything that was defined by Priss and Dürrschnabel (2024) is repeated. But the main notions are explained using examples. Similarly, the definitions of FCA are not repeated in this paper but can be found in the book by Ganter and Wille (1999). Although some FCA terminology is used in this paper, for example, the data is collected in *formal contexts* and the sets of an Euler diagram are called *attributes*, this paper should be mostly comprehensible without any FCA knowledge. The following section defines tabular Euler diagrams. Section 3 describes the method for constructing Euler diagrams as the main contribution of this paper. The paper finishes with a concluding section.

2 Tabular Euler Diagrams

Euler diagrams are a means for visualising sets and their partial orders where attributes (or sets) are represented by closed curves with objects (or elements) enclosed by the curves. Priss (2021) argues that *tabular diagrams* are preferable. In a rectangular Euler diagram (or *rectangular diagram*) each set is represented by a rectangle – sometimes with rounded corners for better discernibility. A tabular diagram is a rectangular diagram where all rectangles are either adjacent sets of rows or of columns of a table. A one-dimensional tabular diagram consisting of a single row or single column is called a *linear diagram*. In order to draw a tabular diagram for a given formal context, the set of attributes needs to be divided into two partitions so that each partition is drawable as a linear diagram (one for the rows and one for the columns). If that is impossible then a tabular diagram is not drawable. Dürrschnabel and Priss (2024) discuss criteria for deciding drawability. More details about and an overview of Euler diagrams in general are provided by Rodgers (2014) and Alsallakh et al. (2016).

The main notions of Euler diagrams can be illustrated using an example of a lattice of types of triangles (cf. Ganter and Wille 1999) and its modelling as a tabular diagram in Fig. 1. Rectangles that are contained in each other indicate a subset relationship.

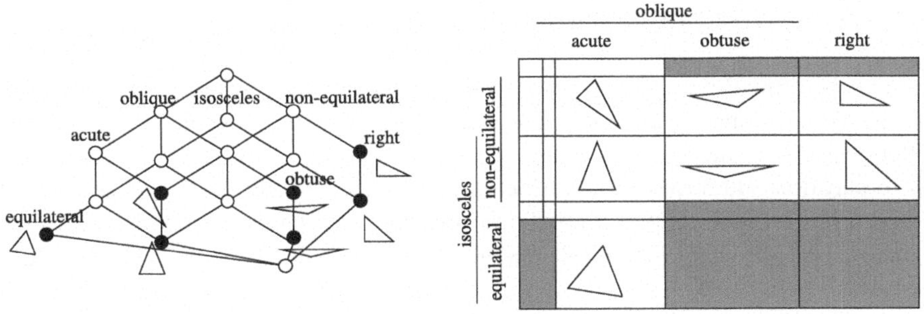

Fig. 1. A lattice for types of triangles and its corresponding tabular diagram

In Fig. 1 the rectangle for 'oblique' includes the rectangles for 'acute' and 'obtuse'. Thus the set of acute objects is a subset of the set of oblique objects and the attribute 'acute' implies the attribute 'oblique'. The cells of the table are called *zones*. Each zone either contains an object (e.g. the triangles in Fig. 1) or is empty (corresponding to a concept without immediate objects) or is shaded (not corresponding to a formal concept). A well-formedness condition for tabular diagrams in this paper is a one-to-one correspondence between non-shaded zones and concepts of an FCA lattice apart from the bottom concept which can be omitted. In Fig. 1, the top concept is the small zone in the top left corner, the bottom concept is omitted. In other applications the top concept can also be the zone outside of the table. Euler diagrams are more general than Venn diagrams which have as many zones as a complete powerset.

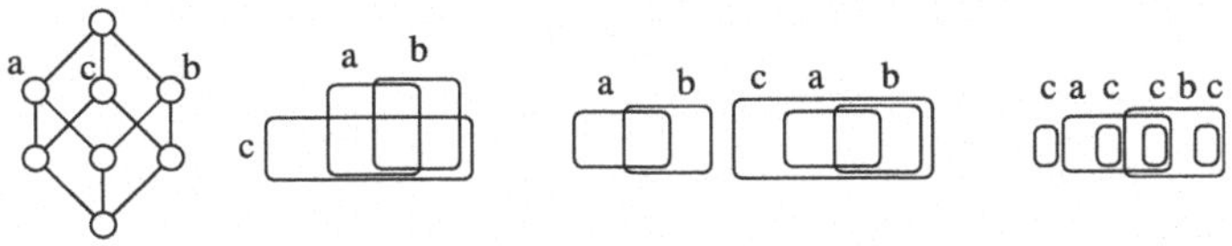

Fig. 2. Hasse diagram and tabular diagrams with different layouts

Unfortunately, not all partial orders are drawable as tabular diagrams. For example, a Boolean lattice with 4 attributes is drawable as a tabular diagram but not with 5 attributes unless some workarounds are applied, such as splitting attributes. Figure 2 displays a Boolean lattice with 3 attributes as a Hasse diagram, as a tabular diagram with 4 columns and two linear diagrams with split attributes. All four diagrams are *zone-equivalent* because they represent the same set of zones. In these tabular diagrams, attribute c is treated visually differently from a and b which should ideally correspond to a semantic difference as well. Thus the meaning of attributes can be relevant for deciding which tabular diagram is most appropriate and certainly more important for the layout of Euler diagrams than it is for Hasse diagrams.

3 Layered Attribute Relationship Graphs

Dürrschnabel and Priss (2024) provide criteria for deciding whether or not a lattice is drawable as a tabular diagram. But even if a lattice is drawable it can still be a challenging task to determine a well-readable layout. Therefore a method for deciding how to partition and arrange the attributes as presented in this section is helpful. The method relies on investigating the relationship between the extensions for all pairs of attributes. The following definitions assume that a and b are attributes with non-empty extensions[4].

a and b are ...	if this is true for their extensions:	this implies ...
comparable	$a' \subseteq b'$ or $b' \subseteq a'$	not contrary, not co-related
contrary	$a' \cap b' = \emptyset$	not comparable, not co-related
co-related	$a' \cap b' \neq \emptyset$ and $a' \not\subseteq b'$ and $b' \not\subseteq a'$	not contrary, not comparable
equal	$a' = b'$	comparable
dichotomic	$\forall o$: either $o \in a'$ or $o \in b'$	contrary

The property 'equal' is a special case of 'comparable', and 'dichotomic' is a special case of 'contrary'. For equal attributes, one can be omitted from the data. An attribute with an empty extension must either be omitted or some 'placeholder' object must be added to its extension. Evaluating properties for all pairs of attributes does not significantly increase the computational complexity because there are only $n(n-1)/2$ pairs for n attributes. Furthermore, FCA software computes extensions and visualisations are usually only of interest for smallish numbers of attributes (e.g. less than 20) anyway.

Lemma 1. *Two attributes a and b (with non-empty extensions) are always either* comparable *or* contrary *or* co-related.

Proof. Further logical combinations of the properties yield nothing different. For example, ($a' \cap b' \neq \emptyset$ and ($a' \subseteq b'$ or $b' \subseteq a'$)) is equivalent to ($a' \subseteq b'$ or $b' \subseteq a'$).

It would also be possible to consider relationships between triples or larger sets of attributes but it is not clear whether the additional effort provides much additional benefit. One can define a set of attributes as *independent* if every possible conjunction occurs which means that the attributes form a Boolean lattice. Instead of 'dichotomic', similar properties 'trichotomic' and so on can be defined. The first three properties are collected in an *Attribute Relationship Graph (ARG)* which has attributes as vertices and an edge for each pair that is comparable or co-related. Furthermore, the edges for comparable attributes are drawn as dashed arrows (pointing to the superset) and the edges for co-related attributes as normal lines. In addition, a list of dichotomic pairs can

[4] Using FCA terminology: an attribute (or 'set label') a defines an extension a' which is a set of its elements (or objects.).

be collected (notated as $a <> b$). Figure 3 shows the attribute relationship graph for the example in Fig. 1. The layers are explained below. Vertices that are not connected by an edge are contrary. The ARG supports layout decisions as explained below and also often determines whether a tabular diagram is drawable at all.

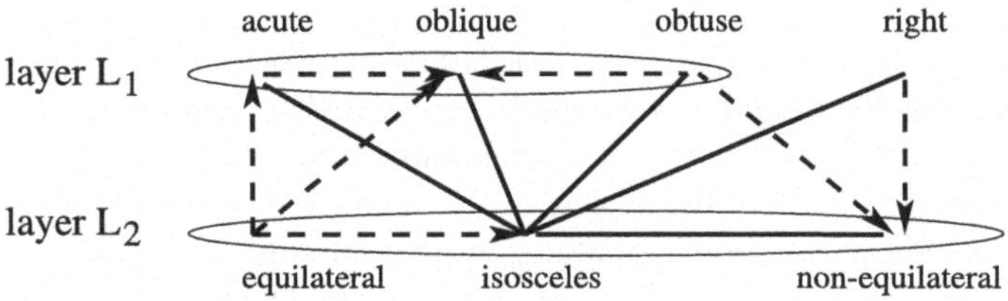

Fig. 3. Attribute Relationship Graph

It is known from FCA that if one divides a set of attributes into two partitions, generates a lattice for each partition and creates the direct product of these two lattices, then the original lattice can be embedded into the product lattice (Theorem 7 of Ganter and Wille (1999)). Traditionally, this principle is used in FCA for creating nested line diagrams. It also applies to tabular diagrams if each of two lattices is drawable as a linear diagram.

Lemma 2. *A tabular diagram of a concept lattice is drawable if and only if the set of attributes of a formal context can be divided into two partitions so that the lattice of each partition is drawable as a linear diagram.*

Proof. Each zone of a table belongs to exactly one row and one column. The index of each zone corresponds to a pair of column and row index. Thus the zones correspond to a direct (or Cartesian) product of rows and columns which is exactly the same situation as in Theorem 7 of Ganter and Wille (1999).

A *layered attribute relationship graph (or LARG)* is an ARG where the vertices are arranged in two horizontal layers[5] (L_1 and L_2) corresponding to the two partitions of the set of attributes as in Fig. 3. The following rules for checking a LARG support layout decisions as explained below. The rules should be processed in the provided order, jumping back from R6 to R1 if a resulting diagram is not drawable until the diagram is drawable or no further possibilites of partitioning the attributes are feasible.

R1 Both layers should contain roughly the same number of vertices.
R2 Within L_1 and L_2 only neighbouring vertices can have a solid edge between them. (If not possible, go back to R1 or STOP)
R3 Within L_1 and L_2 there should be as few solid edges as possible.

[5] An alternative but more traditional graph theoretical modelling might use edge colouring instead of layers: one colour for the edges amongst vertices in L_1, another colour for edges within L_2 and a third colour for the remaining edges.

R4 Dashed edges should be contained within one layer but edge crossings should be minimised.
R5 If it is not possible to have all dashed edges from one vertex in one layer, then it may be better to minimise the number of dashed edges within each layer.
R6 Dichotomic attributes should be in the same layer.
R7 The meaning of the attributes can be considered for sorting them within the layers.

The reason for R2 is that if the extensions of two attributes have a non-empty intersection, a zone for this intersection needs to be placed between the attributes. If three attributes are mutually co-related but not comparable then a linear diagram is only drawable if the extension of one of the attributes is contained in the union of the extensions of the others which means some potential zones are missing. In some rare cases missing zones are not problematic (as discussed by Priss and Dürrschnabel (2024)). But for applications, the probability is extremely high that a tabular diagram is not drawable if R2 cannot be fulfilled. Thus, even though R2 is not strictly necessary from a mathematical view, it can be treated as a necessary condition in applications. Furthermore the readability of a tabular diagram that contradicts R2 is likely to be poor.

The other six rules are not necessary but impact the readability of tabular diagrams and are therefore crucial for determining a layout. Quite often they cannot all be fulfilled simultaneously and need to be balanced against each other. Rules R1 and R3 both make it more likely that linear diagrams are drawable and reduce the numbers of zones of the table in total which implies fewer shaded zones. Rule R4 also reduces shading and improves readability. For example, R4 is contradicted in Fig. 3 by several attributes and as a consequence, it is much easier in Fig. 1 to see that 'acute' and 'obtuse' are comparable with 'oblique' than it is to see that 'right' and 'obtuse' are comparable with 'non-equilateral'. R5, R6 and R7 are the weakest rules and should only be applied if there is anything left to decide. R3 already implies that contrary attributes tend to be in the same layer because there is no edge between them. R6 is therefore a special case of R3.

Figure 4 shows LARGs that were drawn following the rules. In the first example, R2 determines that the 4 attributes in the middle must be distributed across the 2 layers. Initially any of the 4 remaining attributes could be in the same layer. R3 determines that 'running' and 'artificial' should be in different layers. R5 then determines that 'stagnant' and 'natural' should also be in different layers and the locations of 'temporary' and 'maritime'. The attributes 'constant' and 'inland' could be switched which would also switch 'temporary' and 'maritime' but the resulting tabular diagram would have a similar layout that is neither better nor worse. In the second example, R4 is the driving force. The ordering of the first and last two attributes in each layer is determined by R7. Both LARGs correspond to tabular diagrams presented by Priss (2021) which confirms that these previously manually designed diagrams were quite likely optimal with respect to reducing the number of shaded zones and good readability apart from trivial changes such as mirroring the diagrams or moving attributes that do not impact the overall layout structure.

Figure 5 shows an example from Ganter[6] (2013, p. 76) which contains a Boolean lattice with 4 attributes (f inj, g inj, f surj and g surj). The LARG on the right side

[6] This example was chosen because Bernhard Ganter mentioned to me that this was maybe the lattice which he found most difficult to draw with a layout that he liked.

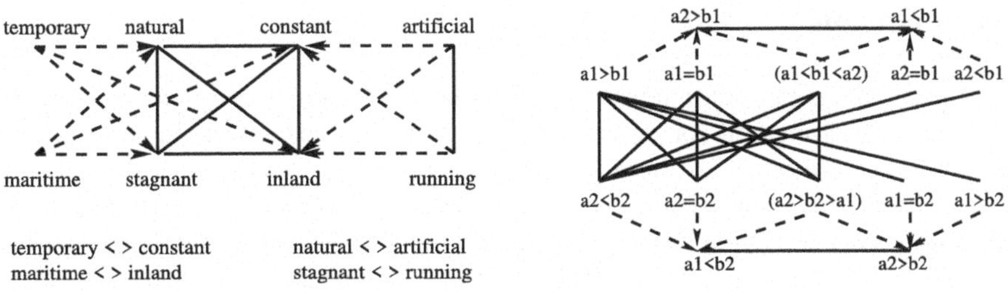

Fig. 4. LARGs that follow the rules

is determined by R2 and R4 and results in the tabular diagram shown in Fig. 6. Thus while there may be many choices for the layout of the Hasse diagram in this example, the layout of the tabular diagram is fairly deterministic. In our opinion, the tabular diagram shows the underlying Boolean lattice with 4 attributes more clearly than the Hasse diagram.

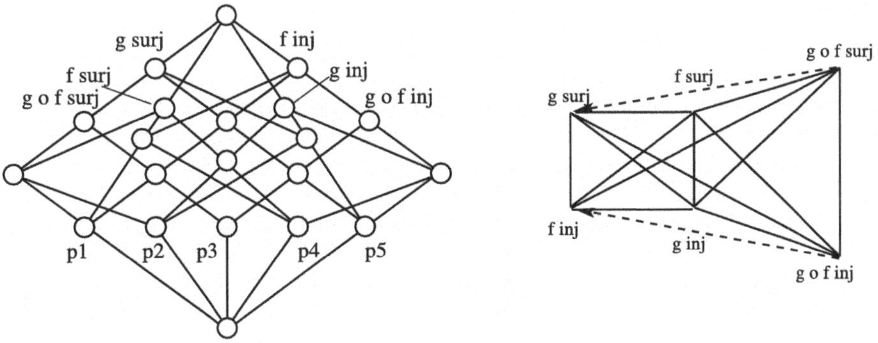

Fig. 5. Hasse diagram and LARG for an example from Ganter (2013, p. 76)

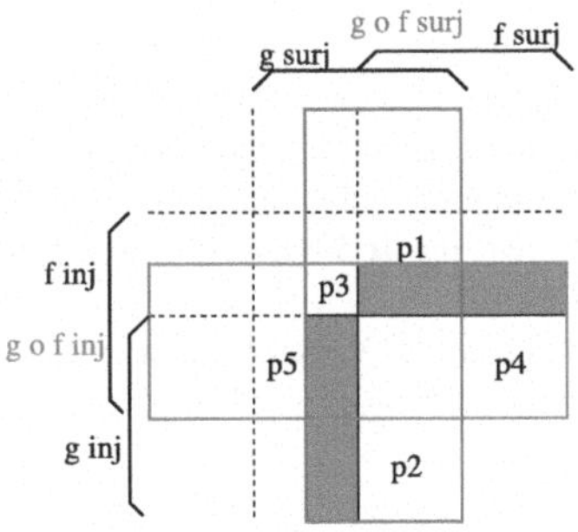

Fig. 6. Tabular diagram derived from the LARG in Fig. 5

4 Conclusion

In summary, this paper continues previous research on tabular diagrams by providing a semi-automated method for deriving layouts that minimise shaded zones and support visual recognition of attribute implications. It is interesting to note that all of the 'famous' lattice[7] examples from Ganter and Wille (1999) and Ganter (2013) that we have looked at so far appear to be drawable as tabular diagrams even though many random concept lattices are not drawable. It is possible that whatever made these examples appealing to Ganter and Wille also makes them more likely to be drawable as tabular diagrams. The reasons are probably symmetry and sufficient attributes that are comparable or contrary to each other.

For future research it would be of interest to explore whether there are further applications for ARGs. An advantage of ARGs is that properties can either be derived from a formal context or, in case of incomplete data, asserted for the data based on background knowledge.

References

Alsallakh, B., Micallef, L., Aigner, W., Hauser, H., Miksch, S., Rodgers, P.: The state-of-the-art of set visualization. Comput. Graph. Forum **35**(1), 234–260 (2016)

Dürrschnabel, D., Priss, U.: Realizability of rectangular euler diagrams. In: Cabrera, I.P., et al. (eds.) Conceptual Knowledge Structures. Proceedings of Concepts 2024, LNAI, vol. 14914, pp. 149–165. Springer, Heidelberg (2024). https://doi.org/10.1007/978-3-031-67868-4_11

Ganter, B., Wille, R.: Formal Concept Analysis. Mathematical Foundations, Springer, Heidelberg (1999)

Ganter, B.: Diskrete Mathematik: Geordnete Mengen. Springer, Heidelberg (2013)

Paetzold, P., Kehlbeck, R., Strobelt, H., Xue, Y., Storandt, S., Deussen, O.: Recteuler: visualizing intersecting sets using rectangles. Comput. Graph. Forum **42** (2023)

Priss, U.: Learning thresholds in formal concept analysis. In: Bertet, K., Borchmann, D., Cellier, P., Ferré, S. (eds.) ICFCA 2017. LNCS (LNAI), vol. 10308, pp. 198–210. Springer, Cham (2017). https://doi.org/10.1007/978-3-319-59271-8_13

Priss, U.: Visualising lattices with tabular diagrams. In: Basu, A., Stapleton, G., Linker, S., Legg, C., Manalo, E., Viana, P. (eds.) Diagrams 2021. LNCS (LNAI), vol. 12909, pp. 378–386. Springer, Cham (2021). https://doi.org/10.1007/978-3-030-86062-2_38

Priss, U., Dürrschnabel, D.: Rectangular euler diagrams and order theory. In: Proceedings of Diagrams 2024. LNAI, vol. 14981, pp. 165–181. Springer, Heidelberg (2024). https://doi.org/10.1007/978-3-031-71291-3_14

Rodgers, P.: A survey of Euler diagrams. J. Visual Lang. Comput. **25**(3), 134–155 (2014)

[7] The lattice for the left LARG of Fig. 4 is on the title page of Ganter and Wille (1999).

Spanning Concept Trees: Enhanced Algorithm and Visualisation

Tim Pattison[1(✉)]

Defence Science and Technology Group, West Ave, Edinburgh 5111, South Australia
tim.pattison@defence.gov.au

Abstract. Describing the recursive execution of a Close-by-One algorithm, the Concept Tree can be derived efficiently from a formal context. However, its use as a proxy for interaction with the concept lattice digraph is problematic, since it can include "bypass" arcs which are not in the digraph. I have previously proposed two algorithms which remediate these bypass arcs to yield a Spanning Concept Tree. This tree resembles a Concept Tree in that the children of a vertex are in reverse lectic order of intents, but differs in that the parent of each vertex in the former is also its first upper cover in this order. In this paper, I present a third remediation algorithm which significantly improves on the computational efficiency of the first two.

The spanning tree of Kuznetsov and Obiedkov can be derived both directly and efficiently from a formal context. Its natural lack of bypass arcs recommends it as an alternative proxy for interaction with the lattice digraph. The properties of this tree are explored, and visualisation techniques are proposed which compensate for the absence from the spanning tree of some lattice digraph arcs.

Each of these trees has both top-down and bottom-up variants, rooted at the lattice top and bottom respectively. Permuting the formal context into a Jointly Reverse Lectic (JRL) order appears to mitigate not only topological incompatibility between top-down and bottom-up trees, but also bypass arcs in the Concept Tree. However, I demonstrate that not all JRL orders of a formal context are equally effective at doing so. The pros and cons of searching for an optimal JRL order, vice remediating the bypass arcs of one which is good enough, are accordingly canvassed.

1 Introduction

A tree spans the concept lattice digraph if it includes all of its vertices and a subset of its arcs. A spanning tree can be derived directly and efficiently from a formal context. Of particular interest is the spanning tree – henceforth "K&O Spanning Tree" – produced by Kuznetsov and Obiedkov [5] as a by-product of their modified Bordat's algorithm for constructing the lattice digraph. In contrast, a Concept Tree [2] can include arcs which are not in the lattice digraph [7], and hence also fewer arcs which are. A Concept Tree is an ordered tree which describes the recursive execution of a Close-by-One algorithm [1,4]; its pre-order traversal reflects the order of those recursive calls which yield canonical

P. Cellier et al. (Eds.): CONCEPTS 2025, LNAI 15941, pp. 203–218, 2025.
https://doi.org/10.1007/978-3-032-03364-2_13

concepts, and its post-order traversal reflects the Reverse Lectic Order (RLO) of the resultant intents [7]. Accordingly, the children of a vertex in the Concept Tree are in RLO of intents. A Spanning Concept Tree is a spanning tree which exhibits the same ordering of its children, and in which the parent of each vertex is also its first upper cover in this RLO.

The Concept Tree has been proposed as a proxy for interaction with the lattice digraph [2]. This approach exploits established user intuition regarding interaction with trees. However, interaction with a Concept Tree containing "bypass" arcs – viz. those absent from the lattice digraph – can disrupt the user's mental model of the digraph. I have previously proposed two algorithms which construct a Spanning Concept Tree from an existing Concept Tree, and thereby remediate these bypass arcs [7]. In this paper I present a third such algorithm which exploits a result by Lindig [6] to efficiently screen for bypass arcs, and thereby significantly improve on the computational efficiency of the first two. Motivated by its natural lack of bypass arcs, I also investigate the K&O Spanning Tree as an alternative proxy for interaction with the lattice digraph. Various properties of this tree are established, and visualisation techniques are proposed which compensate for the absence of some lattice digraph arcs.

The Concept Tree, Spanning Concept Tree and K&O Spanning Tree are "top-down" in the sense that they are rooted at the lattice top and their arcs are oriented downwards. Each also has a "bottom-up" analogue rooted at the bottom with arcs oriented upward. Permuting the formal context into a Jointly Reverse Lectic (JRL) order appears to mitigate not only topological incompatibility [7] between top-down and bottom-up trees, but also bypass arcs in the Concept Tree [7]. I demonstrate that not all JRL orders are equally effective at doing so, and canvas the pros and cons of searching for an optimal JRL order, vice remediating the bypass arcs of one which is good enough.

2 Efficient Remediation of Bypass Arcs

In [7] I proposed two algorithms which exploit the Concept Tree $\mathbb{C}$ to produce a Spanning Concept Tree $\mathbb{S}$. The first constructed $\mathbb{S}$ from scratch using only the topological order of $\mathbb{C}$, while the second morphed $\mathbb{C}$ into $\mathbb{S}$. Creation or remediation of each tree arc incurred a computational cost of $\mathcal{O}(|\mathfrak{B}|)$, where $\mathfrak{B}$ is the set of formal concepts, and each was visited exactly once, yielding overall upper-bound complexity $\mathcal{O}(|\mathfrak{B}|^2)$ subsumption tests, or $\mathcal{O}(|\mathfrak{B}|^2|M|)$ bit comparisons, and lower bound complexity $\Omega(|\mathfrak{B}||\mathfrak{B}-2||M|)$ for a nominal scale. However, the indiscriminate, preemptive remediation of all arcs by the second algorithm missed the opportunity afforded by the availability of $\mathbb{C}$ to avoid costly "remediation" of arcs which do not require it. In this section, I exploit a result by Lindig [6] to efficiently test whether a Concept Tree child is also a lower cover. Only if this test fails do the remaining concepts need to be searched for its preferred upper cover. An algorithm is then proposed which exploits this test to efficiently screen for, and selectively remediate, bypass arcs.

2.1 Preliminaries

Let $X = (1, \ldots, n)$ be an ordered set, whose elements are arbitrarily denoted by the integers $1, \ldots, n$.

Definition 1 (Reverse Lectic Order). *For $A, B \subseteq X$, $i \in X$ and $Y_i :- (1, \ldots, i-1) \subset X$:*

1. *$A <_i B$ if $i \in A \setminus B$ and $A \cap Y_i = B \cap Y_i$*
2. *$A < B$ if $A <_i B$ for some i.*

Definition 2. *A formal context (G, M, I) is in* Jointly Reverse Lectic *(JRL) order if the attribute and object sets M and G are ordered such that for all pairs $a, b \in M$ and $\alpha, \beta \in G$, $a < b \iff a' < b'$ and $\alpha < \beta \iff \alpha' < \beta'$.*

A JRL order can be computed for any formal context in linear time [9]. Substituting M for X in Definition 1 and choosing A, B to be concept intents defines the Reverse Lectic Order (RLO) of intents. Similarly, substituting G for X and choosing A, B to be concept extents defines the RLO of extents. Definition 2 significantly overloads the relation $<$ to denote: the RLO of attribute extents; the induced total order over the corresponding attributes; the RLO of object intents; and the induced total order over the corresponding objects.

2.2 Sub-context Equivalence Class Test

Let (G, M, I) be a formal context with object set G, attribute set M, binary relation $I \subseteq G \times M$, and formal concept set $\mathfrak{B}(G, M, I)$ obtained using the usual derivation operator(s) $'$. Denote by $\leq$ the order relation between concepts corresponding to the inclusion relation $\subseteq$ between their extents, by $\langle \mathfrak{B}, \leq \rangle$ the concept lattice, and by $\top$ and $\bot$ the lattice top and bottom elements, respectively.

Theorem 1 ([6]). *Let $(A, B) \in \mathfrak{B}(G, M, I)$ and $(A, B) < \top$. Then for $g \in G \setminus A$: $(A, B) \prec ((A \cup \{g\})'', B \cap g') \iff (A \cup \{\gamma\})'' = (A \cup \{g\})'' \quad \forall \gamma \in (A \cup \{g\})'' \setminus A$.*

Corollary 1. *Let $(A, B) \in \mathfrak{B}(G, M, I)$ and $(A, B) < \top$. Then for $g \in G \setminus A$: $(A, B) \prec ((A \cup \{g\})'', B \cap g') \iff B \cap \gamma' = B \cap g' \quad \forall \gamma \in (A \cup \{g\})'' \setminus A$.*

Corollary 2. *Let $(C, D) \in \mathfrak{B}(G, M, I)$ and $\bot < (C, D)$. Then for $m \in M \setminus D$: $(C \cap m', (D \cup \{m\})'') \prec (C, D) \iff C \cap \mu' = C \cap m' \quad \forall \mu \in (D \cup \{m\})'' \setminus D$.*

Lemma 1. *For $(A, B), (C, D) \in \mathfrak{B}(G, M, I)$ and $(A, B) < (C, D)$:*

$$\begin{aligned}(A, B) \prec (C, D) &\iff \text{sub-matrix } I \cap (C \setminus A) \times B \text{ has identical rows } \mathbf{d}^T \\ &\iff \text{sub-matrix } I \cap C \times (B \setminus D) \text{ has identical columns } \mathbf{a}\end{aligned}$$

where $\mathbf{d}$ and $\mathbf{a}$ are the indicator vectors for $D \subset B$ and $A \subset C$ respectively, and the superscript ^{T} denotes the vector transpose.

Proof. Identifying C with $(A \cup \{g\})''$ and D with $B \cap g'$ on the right-hand side of Corollary 1 yields $B \cap \gamma' = D$ for each $\gamma \in C \setminus A$. Similarly, identifying A with $C \cap m'$ and B with $(D \cup \{m\})''$ on the right-hand side of Corollary 2 yields $C \cap \mu' = A$ for each $\mu \in B \setminus D$.

Lemma 1 provides an efficient test – henceforth the "sub-context equivalence class test" – whereby a candidate $(A, B) < (C, D)$ can be either confirmed or eliminated as a lower cover of (C, D).

Proposition 1. *It is sufficient to test the rows or columns in Lemma 1 for* mutual *equality, rather than equality with the known vectors* $\mathbf{d}^T$ *and* $\mathbf{a}$ *respectively.*

Proof. For $g \in G \setminus A$ and $C :- (A \cup \{g\})''$, we have $g \in C \setminus A$ in Corollary 1, so that the known vector $\mathbf{d}$ is a row of $I \cap (C \setminus A) \times B$. Similarly for $m \in M \setminus D$ and $B :- (D \cup \{m\})''$, we have $m \in B \setminus D$ in Corollary 2, so that the known vector $\mathbf{a}$ is a column of $I \cap C \times (B \setminus D)$. Mutual equality of the rows and columns, respectively, is therefore sufficient for equality with the known vector.

Proposition 2. *The alternative tests in Lemma 1 require at most* $(|C \setminus A| - 1) \times |B| \ll |G||M|$ *and* $|C| \times (|B \setminus D| - 1) \ll |G||M|$ *bit comparisons respectively.*

Proposition 2 gives the number of bit comparisons required to pass the two alternative tests in Lemma 1; in contrast, failure may be decidable after fewer than the specified number of rows and columns, respectively. The *apriori* less expensive of the two tests should be chosen in each case. The looseness of the upper bound $|G||M|$ on either product in Proposition 2 follows from the pessimistic assumption that the upper bounds $|G|$ and $|M|$ on the two multiplicands may occur *simultaneously*. On the contrary, intent cardinality $|M| \geq |B| \geq |B \setminus D| \geq 1$ is known to increase as extent cardinality $|G| \geq |C| \geq |C \setminus A| \geq 1$ decreases with path length from the lattice top, and vice versa from the lattice bottom. Thus the upper bound on one is attained only with the *lower* bound on the other.

Proposition 3. *The condition in Lemma 1 is automatically satisfied if* $|C \setminus A| = 1$ *or* $|B \setminus D| = 1$.

Proposition 3 states the circumstances under which no computation is required. Prior standardisation of (G, M, I) makes these circumstances more likely.

Proposition 4. *Let* (G, M, I) *be a clarified formal context whose Concept Tree contains an arc between concepts* $(A, B), (C, D) \in \mathfrak{B}$ *which satisfy* $(A, B) \prec (C, D)$. *Then the positive result of the tests in Lemma 1 can be decided without computation if either* (C, D) *is join irreducible or* (A, B) *is meet irreducible.*

Proof. For a clarified context and $(A, B) \prec (C, D)$, $|C \setminus A| = 1$ if (C, D) is join irreducible, while $|B \setminus D| = 1$ if (A, B) is meet irreducible. Proposition 3 ensures that the test in Lemma 1 is positive in both cases.

The lattice – and hence also Concept Tree – of a standardised formal context has up to $|M| + |G|$ distinct irreducible elements. Furthermore, any top-down *spanning* tree must include each digraph arc to an object concept – which is join irreducible – from its sole lower cover unless the object concept is a leaf node, and each digraph arc from an attribute concept – which is meet irreducible – to its sole upper cover. Similarly, any bottom-up spanning tree must include each arc from an attribute concept to its sole upper cover unless the attribute concept is a leaf, and each arc to an object concept from its sole lower cover. To the extent that a given Concept Tree approximates a spanning tree, it too will contain many of the digraph arcs whose adjacent vertices satisfy the irreducibility conditions of Proposition 4. The co-atoms $(A, B) \prec \top$ are a special case of Proposition 4 for the top-down Concept Tree $\mathbb{C}$, whose arcs reverse the lattice order. Similarly, the atoms $(C, D) : \bot \prec (C, D)$ are a special case of Proposition 4 for the bottom-up Concept Tree $\mathbb{B}$, whose arcs respect the lattice order.

Proposition 5. *Testing all parent-child arcs in the Concept Tree using Lemma 1 requires* $\mathcal{O}(|\mathfrak{B}||G||M|)$ *bit comparisons.*

Proof. The Concept Tree contains $|\mathfrak{B}|$ vertices, and hence $|\mathfrak{B}| - 1$ arcs. As per Proposition 2, testing each for the cover relation using Lemma 1 requires $\mathcal{O}(|G||M|)$ bit comparisons per arc.

Proposition 5 indicates how the problem of testing all arcs scales with the sizes of the formal context and its lattice. Since it is based on what we have argued is a significant overestimate of the computation required to test each arc, however, significantly less computation will likely be required for any given problem.

Proposition 6. *Remediating the identified bypass arcs of the Concept Tree has computational complexity* $\mathcal{O}(|\mathfrak{B}||\mathcal{K}||M|)$ *bit comparisons where* $\mathcal{K}$ *is the set of bypass arcs and* $|\mathcal{K}| < |\mathfrak{B}|$.

Proof. The cost of remediating each of the $|\mathcal{K}|$ bypass arcs using either of the algorithms in [7] is $\mathcal{O}(|\mathfrak{B}||M|)$ bit comparisons. There are $|\mathfrak{B}| - 1$ arcs in the Concept Tree, and hence $|\mathcal{K}| \leq |\mathfrak{B}| - 1$.

Since bypass arcs are empirically rare for contexts in JRL order [7], we expect $|\mathcal{K}| \ll |\mathfrak{B}|$.

2.3 Improved Algorithm

Algorithm 1 shows how the efficient sub-context equivalence class test developed in Sect. 2.2 can be applied to detect and remediate only bypass arcs in the top-down Concept Tree $\mathbb{C}$. Its adaptation to instead remediate the bottom-up Concept Tree $\mathbb{B}$ is straightforward. For each arc in $\mathbb{C}$, the less expensive of the two tests of Proposition 1 is applied, and computation is avoided where possible as per Proposition 3. The test for differing rows or columns should be aborted after the first difference is detected. The nesting of conditional statements in lines

Algorithm 1. Screen for and Remediate Bypass Arcs in ℂ

```
Require: The top-down Concept Tree ℂ.
Ensure: The top-down Spanning Concept Tree 𝕊.
 1: function FINDCOVER(parent,target,child)
 2:     repeat
 3:         ▷ get first child if child is null; null if child is last; else next child ◁
 4:         child ← NEXTCHILD(parent,child)
 5:         if child == null then
 6:             return parent
 7:     until child > target
 8:     return FINDCOVER(child,target,null)

 9: 𝕊 ← ∅
10: for arc (C, D) → (A, B) in ℂ do
11:     bypass ← False
12:     if |C \ A| × |B| < |C| × |B \ D| then
13:         if |C \ A| > 1 then
14:             if rows of I ∩ (C \ A) × B differ then
15:                 bypass ← True
16:     else
17:         if |B \ D| > 1 then
18:             if columns of I ∩ C × (B \ D) differ then
19:                 bypass ← True
20:     if not(bypass) then
21:         𝕊 ← 𝕊 ∪ {(C, D) → (A, B)}                  ▷ copy arc from ℂ to 𝕊
22:     else                                  ▷ search ℂ for parent (E, F) of (A, B) in 𝕊
23:         (E, F) ← FINDCOVER((C,D),(A,B),(A,B))
24:         𝕊 ← 𝕊 ∪ {(E, F) → (A, B)}                  ▷ add remediated arc to 𝕊
```

13–15 and lines 17–19 can also be simplified if the implementation supports lazy evaluation of logical conjunctions. Clearly the sets $C \setminus A$ and $B \setminus D$, along with their cardinalities, need only be calculated once for each arc, and the results re-used in the various tests.

In Algorithm 1, $\leftarrow$ denotes assignment, while $\rightarrow$ denotes an arc of the Concept Tree $\mathbb{C}$. For notational convenience, $\mathbb{S}$ is represented as an arc list, to which new arcs are simply appended through set union. NEXTCHILD() returns: the first child of its `parent` argument if its `child` argument is `null`; `null` if `child` is the last child of `parent`; and the next child of `parent` otherwise. The `for` loop at line 10 is a notational convenience: specifically, the arcs of $\mathbb{C}$ should be discovered and tested during a pre-order traversal so as to avoid having to re-acquire the source vertex (C, D) in $\mathbb{C}$ during arc remediation. Code for this re-acquisition is accordingly omitted.

The first upper cover of (A, B) in the RLO of intents [7], and hence its parent in the Spanning Concept Tree $\mathbb{S}$ [7], is the first concept which both succeeds (A, B) in the post-order and is comparable with it. This upper cover is a descendant in $\mathbb{C}$ of (A, B)'s parent (C, D) [7]. To find it, FINDCOVER() tests the right siblings of (A, B) in $\mathbb{C}$ in order until a superconcept $(E, F) > (A, B)$ is identified, and recursively searches the corresponding subtree. The tree descendants of each rejected right sibling – or more generally child of the `parent` argument – are eliminated from the search apriori, because the (reversed) arcs of $\mathbb{C}$ respect the lattice partial order. Recursively searching the subtree of the first qualifying child ensures that the identified cover is the first in the RLO of intents.

Each call to NEXTCHILD() returns a concept whose intent introduces an attribute not previously encountered during the recursive search invoked at line 23. The number of subsumption tests at line 7 is therefore bounded by $\mathcal{O}(|M|)$, yielding a total of $\mathcal{O}(|M|^2)$ bit comparisons – c.f. $\mathcal{O}(|\mathfrak{B}||M|)$ in Proposition 6.

3 K&O Spanning Tree

The FCA algorithm of Bordat [3] was modified by Kuznetsov and Obiedkov [5] to construct a top-down spanning tree as an adjunct to lattice construction, during which the lower covers of each concept are also computed. This ordered tree supports efficient storage and retrieval of a concept, and hence also of its stored lower covers, allowing top-down construction of the lattice digraph. Their algorithm can be trivially adapted to work bottom-up, and thereby generate a bottom-up spanning tree whose vertices store references to its upper covers. These K&O Spanning Trees are potentially attractive alternatives to their (Spanning) Concept Tree counterparts, since they are by-products of lattice digraph construction and do not require remediation. In this section I investigate: visualisation of the K&O Spanning Trees as proxies for interaction with the lattice digraph; a coordinated overview of the lattice digraph whose layout is consistent with either tree; and topologically consistent layout of both trees.

3.1 Tree Properties

Lemma 2 (Kuznetsov and Obiedkov [5]). *In the top-down K&O Spanning Tree, let concept (E, F) be a descendant of (S, T), (X, Y) a left sibling of (S, T), and (V, W) the parent of (S, T) and (X, Y). Then $F \cap Y = W$ and hence $F \not\supseteq Y$.*

Kuznetsov and Obiedkov [5] achieved efficient storage and retrieval of a concept (E, F) in their top-down spanning tree by: starting at the root of the tree; testing the children of the current concept (V, W) in order until the first child (S, T) is discovered whose intent satisfies $T \subset F$; repeating this process for the children of (S, T); and iterating until the selected child has intent F. If no child intent of (V, W) is a subset of F, then concept (E, F) is not yet stored in the tree; it belongs as the next – and currently last – child of (V, W).

A concept (E, F) is added as a tree child of (V, W) provided only that: it does not already exist in the tree; it is a lattice descendant of (V, W); and it is not a lattice descendant of any existing tree child (S, T) of (V, W). To ensure that also $(E, F) \prec (V, W)$, Bordat's algorithm generates the novel lattice descendants of (V, W) in depth-first pre-order, starting with a novel lower cover. In particular, of the lower covers of (V, W) which are not already in the tree, the first in the

RLO of extents is added, followed by *its* first novel lower cover, and so on. The resultant top-down K&O Spanning Tree is an ordered tree, in which the tree children of (V, W) are its novel lower covers in RLO of extents.

In the remainder of this subsection, I use Lemma 2 to prove that post-order traversal of the top-down K&O Spanning Tree is consistent with the lattice partial order, and hence that it achieves a topological sort of the vertices of the lattice digraph. The statement and proof of corresponding properties of the bottom-up tree are left as an exercise for the reader.

Proposition 7. *Let (K, J) be a (possibly improper) descendant of (X, Y) in the top-down K&O Spanning Tree under the circumstances described in Lemma 2. Then $F \not\supseteq J$.*

Proof. Firstly, $J \supseteq Y$ since (K, J) is a possibly improper tree descendant of (X, Y). If we assume that $F \supseteq J$, then $F \supseteq J \supseteq Y \Rightarrow F \supseteq Y$, which contradicts Lemma 2. Hence $F \not\supseteq J$.

Proposition 8. *Let $x, y \in \mathfrak{B}$ have least common ancestor v in the top-down K&O Spanning Tree, and let x lie on an earlier branch from v than y. Then $y \not< x$ in the lattice partial order.*

Proof. This follows from Proposition 7 through the choice of $v = (V, W)$, $y = (E, F)$ and $x = (K, J)$.

A post-order traversal of the top-down K&O Spanning Tree starts at the root and visits the sub-trees rooted at each of the children in their assigned order, followed by their parent. Denote by $\langle \mathfrak{B}, \sqsubset \rangle$ the induced total order over $\mathfrak{B}$.

Lemma 3. *For each $(x, y) \in \mathfrak{B} \times \mathfrak{B}$, $x < y \Rightarrow x \sqsubset y$.*

Proof. $x \sqsubset y \Rightarrow y \not< x$ follows from Proposition 8 and the fact that any tree descendant x of y satisfies $x < y$, so that here too $y \not< x$. Hence $y < x \Rightarrow x \not\sqsubset y \Rightarrow y \sqsubset x$, from which the result follows by exchanging the labels x and y.

The lattice digraph has an arc between each vertex pair (x, y) for which $x \prec y$, where $\prec$ is the cover relation for $\langle \mathfrak{B}, \leq \rangle$. The following result establishes that the total order $\langle \mathfrak{B}, \sqsubset \rangle$ achieves the objective $x \prec y \Rightarrow x \sqsubset y$ of a topological sort of the vertices of the lattice digraph.

Corollary 3. *For all $(x, y) \in \mathfrak{B} \times \mathfrak{B}$, $x \prec y \Rightarrow x \sqsubset y$.*

Proof. $x \prec y \Rightarrow x < y$ and by Lemma 3, $x < y \Rightarrow x \sqsubset y$.

Lemma 4. *The parent of a concept in the top-down K&O Spanning Tree is its upper cover in $\langle \mathfrak{B}, \leq \rangle$ which is first in $\langle \mathfrak{B}, \sqsubset \rangle$.*

Proof. Denote by $\mathcal{U} :- \{z : z \succ x\}$ the set of upper covers of a concept x in $\langle \mathfrak{B}, \leq \rangle$. By Corollary 3, $z \in \mathcal{U} \Rightarrow x \sqsubset z$. Since the elements of $\mathcal{U}$ are not comparable in $\langle \mathfrak{B}, \leq \rangle$, neither are they comparable in the K&O Spanning Tree. In particular, the elements of $\mathcal{U} \setminus y$ are neither ancestors nor descendants of the parent $y \in \mathcal{U}$ of x in the spanning tree. Since the only elements between $x \sqsubset y$ and y in $\langle \mathfrak{B}, \sqsubset \rangle$ are descendants of y, which precludes the elements of $\mathcal{U} \setminus y$, $z \in \mathcal{U} \setminus y \Rightarrow y \sqsubset z$.

Table 1. Example JRL order for the `Lives-in-water` context.

	can_move	lives_in_water	has_limbs	lives_on_land	breast_feeds	needs_chlorophyll	monocotyledon	dicotyledon
frog	✓	✓	✓	✓				
bream	✓	✓	✓					
fish_leech	✓	✓						
dog	✓		✓	✓	✓			
reed		✓		✓		✓	✓	
water_weeds		✓				✓	✓	
corn				✓		✓	✓	
bean				✓		✓		✓

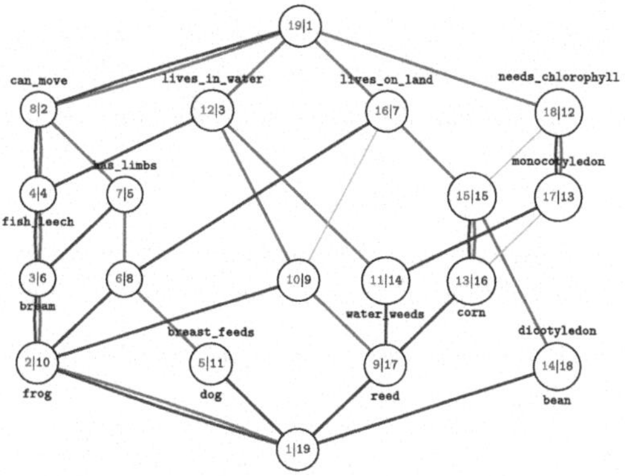

Fig. 1. Top-down (red) and bottom-up (blue) K&O Spanning Trees for the JRL-ordered formal context shown in Table 1. The red and blue numbers inside each vertex indicate its rank in $\langle \mathfrak{B}, \sqsubset \rangle$ for the top-down and bottom-up trees, respectively. (Color figure online)

While the correctness of Lemma 2 and the ensuing results does not depend on the unspecified order in which the lower covers of a concept are processed, the structure of the top-down K&O Spanning Tree – and hence also the order $\sqsubset$ – do. Assuming that they are processed in the order in which they are generated by the `LowerNeighbours()` procedure [5], which by Lemma 5 below is the Reverse Lectic Order of extents, the structure of the tree becomes dependent on the arbitrary initial order of the objects in the input context. Under this assumption, Kuznetsov and Obiedkov conjectured – in effect – that the tree parent is the first upper cover in the RLO of extents. The object concept for `corn` in the top-down (red) spanning tree in Fig. 1 for the context shown in Table 1 constitutes a counter-example to their conjecture. Its tree parent has extent `{reed,corn,bean}`, whereas its first upper cover in the RLO of extents has extent `{reed,water_weeds,corn}`. The RLO of extents differs more generally from $\sqsubset$, since a lower cover – and hence extent subset – comes after its upper covers in the RLO of extents, but, by Corollary 3, before them in $\sqsubset$.

Order $\sqsubset$ Induced by `LowerNeighbours()` Given a parent concept (A, B), `LowerNeighbours()` incrementally constructs subsets $E_i \subset A$, while ensuring that $F_i :- \bigcap_{g \in E_i} g'$ retains at least one novel attribute. Comparing joins, $\vee_{g \in A}(g'', g') = (A, B)$ while $(K_i, F_i) :- \vee_{g \in E_i}(g'', g') \leq (A, B)$ with $K_i :- E_i''$. E_i is constructed by selecting the first object $g \in A$ in the arbitrary order over G whose intent $g' \not\subseteq C_i$ has at least one novel attribute, and accumulating subsequent objects so as to retain (some of) this novelty. Once all objects $g \in A$ have been tested for inclusion in K_i – and added to E_i if the test succeeds – $E_i = E_i'' = K_i$. An attribute is "novel" if it is not included in the intents

$\{F_j : j < i\}$ of any of the sub-concepts generated so far, including $F_0 :- B$. The requirement that $F_i \setminus C_i \neq \emptyset$, where $C_i :- \bigcup_{j<i} F_j$, prevents regeneration of previous candidates (E_j, F_j) for lower covers. Such novelty becomes increasingly harder to attain, since $C_{i+1} \supset C_i$. Candidate (E_i, F_i) is added to the set of lower covers iff $F_i \cap C_i = B$.

Lemma 5. *The lower covers generated by* `LowerNeighbours()` *are in RLO of extents.*

Proof. Let object $\gamma \in G$ be the first element by which E_{i+1} and E_i differ, so that

$$C_i \not\supseteq \bigcap_{\substack{g \in E_i \\ g < \gamma}} g' = \bigcap_{\substack{g \in E_{i+1} \\ g < \gamma}} g' \not\subseteq C_{i+1} \tag{1}$$

Now since $C_{i+1} \supset C_i$, the criteria for exclusion of γ from E_i and E_{i+1} respectively are related by

$$\bigcap_{\substack{g \in E_i \cup \{\gamma\} \\ g \leq \gamma}} g' \subseteq C_i \Rightarrow \bigcap_{\substack{g \in E_{i+1} \cup \{\gamma\} \\ g \leq \gamma}} g' \subseteq C_{i+1} \tag{2}$$

so that $\gamma \notin E_i \Rightarrow \gamma \notin E_{i+1}$ and $\gamma \in E_{i+1} \Rightarrow \gamma \in E_i$. Thus the only permissible (first) difference is $\gamma \in E_i$ and $\gamma \notin E_{i+1}$, from which we conclude that E_{i+1} succeeds E_i in the RLO of extents. Since the sub-concepts are generated in RLO of extents, and of these, each lower cover is added immediately to the set of lower covers, that set must be in RLO of extents.

The subset of lower covers of a concept which are its children in the top-down K&O Spanning Tree are added to the tree in the order in which they are processed. Lemma 5 therefore ensures that $\sqsubset$ differs from the RLO of intents, except possibly where – either by chance or design – the RLO of intents agrees with the RLO of extents with respect to the children of each concept. Exceptionally, however, post-order traversals of the top-down and bottom-up K&O Spanning Trees of Fig. 1 coincide with the RLO of intents and extents, respectively. It follows by Lemma 4, that the parent of each vertex is first in, and by the nature of post-order traversal that its children are sorted into, these respective orders. Hence these particular K&O Spanning Trees satisfy the definitions [7] of top-down and bottom-up Spanning Concept Trees respectively, and have the same degree of topological incompatibility.

3.2 Tree and Digraph Visualisation

If visualisation of the K&O Spanning Tree is to aid comprehension of the modified version of Bordat's algorithm [5], or serve as a proxy for interaction with the lattice digraph in the manner of the Concept Tree of Andrews and Hirsch [2], the topological order of this ordered tree should be preserved in its layout. Of the digraph arcs originating from concept x, only that which connects x to its tree parent y is included in the tree. A visual search to identify candidates for any remaining upper covers of x can be safely constrained to concepts $c \sqsupset x$

Table 2. Formal context from [1] in JRL order.

	0	4	3	2	1
a	✓	✓	✓		
c	✓			✓	
b		✓	✓	✓	✓
d		✓		✓	✓

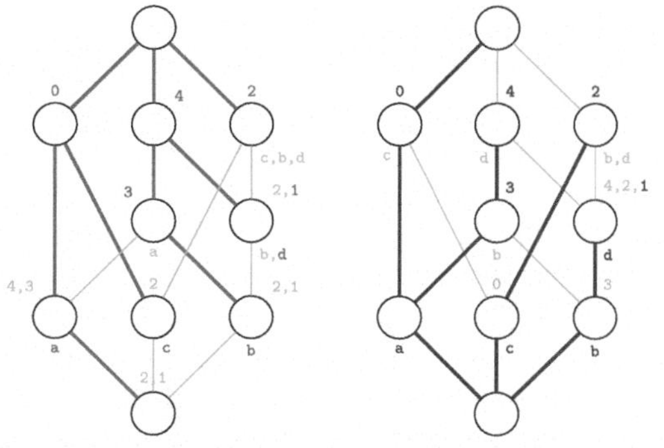

(a) Top-down (b) Bottom-up

Fig. 2. Lattice digraph for context in Table 2, with (a) arcs of the top-down K&O Spanning Tree and reduced labels shown red and (b) arcs of the bottom-up K&O Spanning Tree and reduced labels shown blue. The partially-reduced labels include the elements in grey. (Color figure online)

which are not tree ancestors of y. Preserving the topology of the tree in its layout facilitates the visual application of this constraint. Layering the tree vertices according to their longest directed path to the root through the lattice digraph further constrains the search for upper covers, since any missing arcs must then also be upward. The parts of the corresponding partition of $\mathfrak{B}$ are antichains of $\langle \mathfrak{B}, \leq \rangle$ while the number of parts is the length of its maximal chain.

A coordinated overview of the digraph overlaid with the K&O Spanning Tree would provide valuable context – at least for relatively small digraphs – and a scaffold for displaying lattice details-on-demand requested through tree interaction, such as revealing covers or inheritance of objects and attributes. This scaffold should be consistent with the left-right order of tree children, and the assignment of vertices to layers within the scaffold should be reflected in a layered drawing of the tree. It is also desirable that labelling of the concepts provides clues as to missing digraph arcs and that the direction of any such arcs can be inferred from the tree drawing. Hypotheses formed with the aid of these cues can then be tested through details-on-demand. To compensate for disrupted multiple inheritance in the Concept Tree, Andrews and Hirsch [2] approximated the reduced labelling scheme of the line diagram by labelling a concept with the set difference between its intent and that of its parent, and with the set difference between its extent and the union of those of its tree children. In contrast, the fully-reduced labels exclude the intents of *all* upper covers and the extents of *all* lower covers respectively. Since the reduced labels are unique in the line diagram, repeated labels in the Concept Tree provide clues as to missing arcs. Figure 2 provides a simple example of this labelling scheme applied to both the top-down (Fig. 2a) and bottom-up (Fig. 2b) K&O Spanning Trees. The attribute label `2,1` in Fig. 2a, for example, appears on three concepts, suggesting that these concepts are somehow related by paths through the lattice digraph involving arcs not included in the spanning tree. Superimposition of the top-down and bottom-up trees would need to accommodate – perhaps using modal details-on-demand – the evident discrepancies between their partially-reduced labels.

While the depth of a concept x in the K&O Spanning Tree corresponds to the length of a directed path from $\top$ to x through the lattice digraph, it need not be the *longest* such path, on which decisions about the direction of digraph arcs must be based. Since the source and destination vertices of the digraph arc from $\perp$ to its upper cover labelled `2,1` in Fig. 2a have the same depth in the K&O Spanning Tree, the direction of this arc cannot be inferred from the labelled tree alone. In contrast, the longest path to the infimum has length 4, one more than to the upper cover. This ambiguity is exacerbated in the Concept Tree, where even the *shortest* directed path from $\top$ through the lattice digraph to concept x may exceed its depth in the tree. Off-the-shelf software components for tree visualisation would require modification to accept an assignment of vertices to layers based on the extraneous calculation of longest lattice path vice the endogenous calculation of tree depth.

The longest directed path through the lattice digraph to a given concept from $\perp$ can be calculated as follows in $\mathcal{O}(|\mathfrak{B}|+|R|)$ time, where R is the cover relation. Initialise the path length $l_\uparrow(x)$ of each concept x to 0. For each concept x in the total order $\sqsubset$, and each lattice arc (x, y), assign $l_\uparrow(y) \leftarrow \max(l_\uparrow(y), l_\uparrow(x)+1)$. For this purpose, each concept in the top-down tree should also store references to its *upper* covers. Corollary 3 ensures that $l_\uparrow(x)$ has been finalised before being used to update $l_\uparrow(y)$ for each upper cover y. The vertices of the digraph can then be assigned to the layers $\{l_\uparrow(x) : x \in \mathfrak{B}\}$ – numbered from 0 at $\perp$ – of a layered drawing of the lattice digraph. Repeating this procedure using either the reverse of $\sqsubset$ or the total order induced by post-order traversal of the *bottom-up* K&O Spanning Tree yields a corresponding layering $\{l_\downarrow(x) : x \in \mathfrak{B}\}$ of the concepts numbered from 0 at $\top$. Here, $l_\uparrow(x)$ and $l_\downarrow(x)$ are properly interpreted as lower bounds on the layer assigned to concept x when counted from $\perp$ and $\top$, respectively. Within these bounds, there remains discretion in the assignment of concepts to layers in a layered drawing of the digraph. Even for a drawing having the minimum height $\max_{x\in\mathfrak{B}}(l_\uparrow(x) + l_\downarrow(x))$ necessary to ensure that all digraph arcs are upward, the assignment of any concepts $\{y : y \in \mathfrak{B} \setminus \arg\max_{x\in\mathfrak{B}}(l_\uparrow(x)+l_\downarrow(x))\}$ to layers is not uniquely determined. Thus although the bottom-up and top-down layer assignments $\{l_\uparrow(x) : x \in \mathfrak{B}\}$ and $\{l_\downarrow(x) : x \in \mathfrak{B}\}$ from their respective roots are safe, they need not be mutually consistent.

The reduced labelling scheme for concepts can be calculated in the same pass through the data as is used for labelling. The object label set γ_x of each concept x is initialised to its extent $\mathcal{E}(x)$. Then for each concept x, and each lattice arc (x, y), $\gamma_y \leftarrow \gamma_y \setminus \mathcal{E}(x)$. While the correctness of this procedure relies on all lower covers of concept x being visited, it does not depend on them having been visited before x. Consequently, the attribute label set μ_x can also be calculated in the same pass. It should be initialised to intent $\mathcal{I}(x)$, and then for each arc (x, y),

$\mu_x \leftarrow \mu_x \setminus \mathcal{I}(y)$. The partially-reduced labelling scheme used by Andrews and Hirsch [2] for their Concept Tree can be computed for the K&O Spanning Tree by applying the above procedures to tree arcs only, rather than all digraph arcs.

Orienting the arcs of the top-down and bottom-up K&O Spanning Trees downward and upward, respectively, and treating the order of a concept's children as the left-to-right order of the corresponding rooted sub-trees, yields a planar drawing of each tree. Either drawing, which can be constructed incrementally during a post-order traversal of the tree, could serve as the basis of a drawing of the corresponding lattice digraph, in which the arcs of the spanning tree are guaranteed not to cross. The planarity and width of this heuristic solution would be unaffected by the subsequent vertical translation of vertices into the layers calculated above so as to ensure that the vertical component of each digraph arc is upwards. The more general problem of ordering the vertices of a directed acyclic graph (DAG) within a layered drawing so as to minimise *all* edge crossings is NP-hard. Privileging instead the vertex order and arc crossings of the K&O Spanning Tree is justified by use of the latter as a proxy for interaction with the lattice digraph in the manner of the Concept Tree of Andrews and Hirsch [2]. The K&O Spanning Tree is preferrable for this purpose to the Concept Tree in that user comprehension of the lattice digraph cannot benefit from computational effort spent on avoiding crossings involving bypass arcs.

For K&O Spanning Trees whose branches have disparate lengths, however, this layout may be wider than necessary, since a short branch reserves the horizontal space below it which could safely be occupied by the more distal elements of a longer branch. The latter point is illustrated by the concepts labelled `2,1` and `2` on the branch rooted at the concept labelled `0` in Fig. 2a, which sit below but not to the left of the concept labelled `3` on the later branch rooted at the concept labelled `4`. Since the excessive width will manifest itself at the leaves, the above drawings of the top-down and bottom-up trees will broadly resemble isosceles triangles which are upright and inverted respectively. These are neither mutually compatible nor compatible with a compact drawing of the lattice digraph. Geometric consistency between all three requires the superimposition of both trees on a drawing of the lattice digraph.

3.3 Topological Consistency

If the top-down and bottom-up K&O Spanning Trees are to be navigated simultaneously or alternately for exploration of the concept lattice, any inconsistencies between their topological orders – and hence also left-to-right orders assigned by the above layout – should be minimised [7]. To do otherwise would counteract the user's objective of constructing a consistent mental model of the lattice digraph. I have previously described a technique for mitigating such inconsistencies between the top-down and bottom-up Concept Trees by permuting the context into JRL order [7]. However, the K&O Spanning Tree differs from a Concept Tree in that the topological order $\sqsubset$ of its vertices need not be the RLO of their intents for the top-down tree or extents for the bottom-up tree. Thus mitigating topological incompatibility between those Reverse Lectic Orders by

JRL ordering the context need not result in topological compatibility of the K&O Spanning Trees.

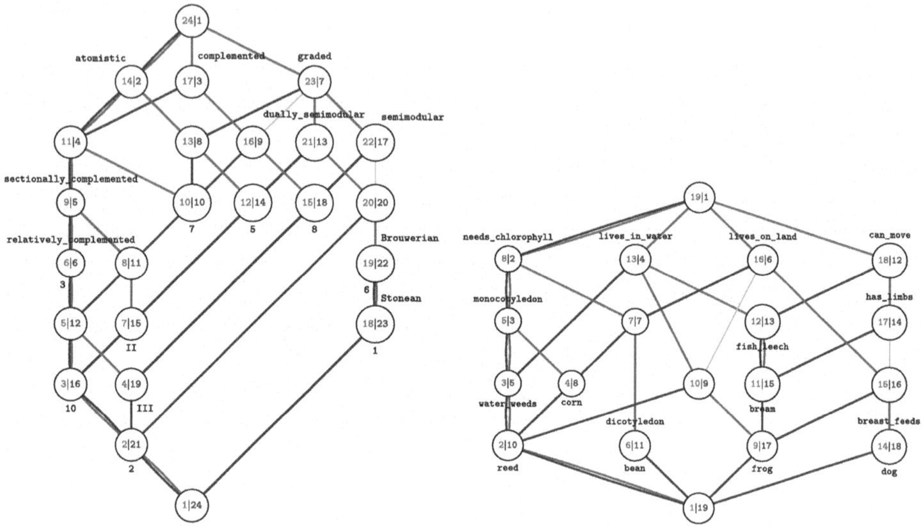

(a) `Lattices` (b) `Lives-in-water`

Fig. 3. Concept lattices and top-down (red arcs) and bottom-up (blue arcs) Concept Trees for the `Lattices` and `Lives-in-water` contexts in JRL order. Red and blue numbers indicate rank in the RLO of intents and extents, respectively. (Color figure online)

For the JRL-ordered context in Table 2, the top-down K&O Spanning Tree shown in Fig. 2a coincides with both the top-down Concept Tree and top-down Spanning Concept Tree, and the bottom-up K&O Spanning Tree shown in Fig. 2b coincides with both the bottom-up Concept Tree and bottom-up Spanning Concept Tree. Accordingly, the topological order $\sqsubset$ coincides with the RLO of intents for the top-down K&O Spanning Tree, and with the RLO of extents for the bottom-up. For this context, the chosen JRL order eliminates topological incompatibility between top-down and bottom-up variants of both the K&O Spanning Tree and the Spanning Concept Tree.

When the top-down (red) and bottom-up (blue) K&O Spanning Trees for the example context in Table 1 are overlaid on the lattice digraph in Fig. 1, their topological incompatibility manifests as a single crossing of blue arcs. Here the intra-layer ordering has been chosen to reflect that of the top-down tree.

4 JRL Order is not Unique

JRL ordering of the formal context prior to computation of the Concept Tree can reduce the number of bypass arcs requiring remediation and mitigate topological incompatibility between the top-down and bottom-up Concept Trees [7].

Conversion of the Concept Tree into the corresponding Spanning Concept Tree removes all bypass arcs, but cannot fix topological incompatibilities which are manifested as crossings between non-bypass arcs. JRL ordering of the example contexts in Tables 1 and 2 appears equally effective at mitigating topological incompatibility between the top-down and bottom-up K&O Spanning Trees as for the corresponding Spanning Concept Trees.

The JRL order for a given formal context need not be unique, since for example any permutation of the peer blocks of a CARVE-decomposable formal context results in an alternate JRL order [8]. This observation raises the possibility that alternate JRL orders may be relatively more or less effective at mitigating – and potentially even eliminating – either bypass arcs or topological incompatibility. This hypothesis is confirmed by comparing Fig. 3a with [7, Figure 1a]. Both show layouts of the lattice digraph and top-down (red arcs) and bottom-up (blue arcs) Concept Trees for JRL-ordered variants of the `Lattices` context [10]. However, both bypass arcs – shown dashed in the latter – and crossings between arcs of the same colour are noticeably absent from the former. Figure 3b shows the same information for the `Lives-in-water` formal context [10]; for the chosen JRL order, both bypass arcs and topological incompatibility are again absent. Since a Concept Tree which lacks bypass arcs is also a Spanning Concept Tree, as is a K&O Spanning Tree whose order $\sqsubset$ coincides with RLO, Fig. 3b can be fairly contrasted with Fig. 1, which contains a crossing of blue arcs. Here again, different JRL orders of the same formal context produce differing degrees of topological incompatibility.

Exhaustive search of the space of all possible JRL orders of a given formal context for one which eliminates both bypass arcs and topological incompatibility is potentially fruitless and likely prohibitive. Instead, we might search only until we find one with suitably few topological incompatibilities, and then remediate any bypass arcs. Systematic investigation into the effect of JRL ordering on topological incompatibility between the top-down and bottom-up K&O Spanning Trees might also obviate Concept Tree remediation.

5 Conclusion

Section 2 presented an improved algorithm for remediation of bypass arcs in the Concept Tree of Andrews and Hirsch [2] based on an efficient test for the cover relation between candidate covers. Future computational studies should test whether the argued improvements in computational complexity are realised for empirical contexts. Section 3 motivated the use of the K&O Spanning Tree, which avoids bypass arcs altogether, as an alternative proxy for interaction with the lattice digraph. Section 3.1 detailed the properties of the K&O Spanning Tree, while Sect. 3.2 discussed visualisation techniques which compensate for the absence from the spanning tree of some lattice digraph arcs. Section 3 also provided two examples in which the top-down and bottom-up K&O Spanning Trees enigmatically coincide with their counterpart Spanning Concept Trees, whose topological incompatibility is known to be mitigated by permutation of the context matrix into JRL order. This anecdotal evidence suggests that K&O Spanning Trees might be preferrable for JRL-ordered contexts, at least, because with no apparent detriment to topological compatibility they avoid the computational cost of mitigating bypass arcs in Concept Trees. Responsive computation is important when an interactive user has chosen a formal context, but cannot commence exploration of the resultant, potentially large tree until it has been constructed and, if necessary, remediated. Section 4 demonstrated that the JRL order is not unique for a given context, and that different JRL orders are not equally effective at mitigating bypass arcs and topological incompatibility between the top-down and bottom-up Concept Trees. Further work should determine whether topological incompatibility can always be eliminated and how suitable JRL orders can be generated without exhaustive search.

Acknowledgement. I am grateful to the insightful reviewer who suggested the procedure now encapsulated in the FINDCOVER() function of Algorithm 1.

References

1. Andrews, S.: A 'best-of-breed' approach for designing a fast algorithm for computing fixpoints of Galois connections. Inf. Sci. **295**, 633–649 (2015). https://doi.org/10.1016/j.ins.2014.10.011
2. Andrews, S., Hirsch, L.: A tool for creating and visualising formal concept trees. In: S. Andrews, S. Polovina (eds.) Proceedings 5th Conceptual Structures Tools & Interoperability Wkshp (CSTIW), pp. 1–9 (2016). http://ceur-ws.org/Vol-1637/
3. Bordat, J.: Calcul pratique du trellis de Galois d'une correspondance. Mathematiques, Informatiques et Sciences Humaines **24**(94), 31–47 (1986)
4. Kuznetsov, S.: A fast algorithm for computing all intersections of objects in a finite semi-lattice. Autom. Document. Math. Linguist. **27**(5), 11–21 (1993)
5. Kuznetsov, S.O., Obiedkov, S.A.: Comparing performance of algorithms for generating concept lattices. J. Exp. Theor. Artif. Intell. **14**(2–3), 189–216 (2002). https://doi.org/10.1080/09528130210164170
6. Lindig, C.: Algorithmen zur Begriffsanalyse und ihre Anwendung bei Softwarebibliotheken. Ph.D. thesis, Technischen Universität Braunschweig (1999). https://www.st.cs.uni-saarland.de/publications/files/lindig-phd-1999.pdf
7. Pattison, T.: Spanning concept trees: algorithms and interaction. In: Cabrera, I.P., Ferré, S., Obiedkov, S. (eds.) Conceptual Knowledge Structures. CONCEPTS 2024. LNCS, vol. 14914. Springer, Heidelberg (2024). https://doi.org/10.1007/978-3-031-67868-4_12
8. Pattison, T., Nataraja, A.: Doubly-lexical order supports standardisation & recursive partitioning of formal context. In: Dürrschnabel, D., López Rodríguez, D. (eds.) ICFCA 2023. Springer, Heidelberg (2023). https://doi.org/10.1007/978-3-031-35949-1_2
9. Spinrad, J.P.: Doubly lexical ordering of dense 0–1 matrices. Inf. Process. Lett. **45**(5), 229–235 (1993). https://doi.org/10.1016/0020-0190(93)90209-R
10. Wille, R.: Concept lattices and conceptual knowledge systems. Comput. Math. Appl. **23**(6–9), 493–515 (1992). https://doi.org/10.1016/0898-1221(92)90120-7

Closure Versus Dualization: A Comparison of Software Tools for Formal Concept Analysis

Imen Ben Sassi and Alexandre Bazin(✉)

LIRMM, Univ. Montpellier, CNRS, Montpellier, France
{imen.ben-sassi,alexandre.bazin}@lirmm.fr

Abstract. Formal concept analysis revolves around the notion of formal concept. Many tools have been developed to compute these concepts, based on the fact that the extents and intents are closed under the closure operators given by the context. However, concepts are also dual to the complement of the incidence relation of the context, a fact that is rarely discussed in the community. In this paper, we compare tools developed in the FCA community against dualization-based tools on runtime in both real and artificial datasets. The experimental observations show that dualization-based tools are competitive and more resistant to increases in context density.

Keywords: Formal concept analysis · Dualization · Comparison · Runtime

1 Introduction

Formal Concept Analysis (FCA) provides a structured framework for extracting meaningful patterns from data by identifying formal concepts, which consist of extent-intent pairs. These concepts, emerging from the closure operators induced by a given context, are useful as interpretable pieces of knowledge. Over the years, various computational tools have been developed to efficiently extract these concepts[1], leveraging the properties of closure operators. While most approaches focus on these properties, an alternative perspective remains largely overlooked. Formal concepts can also be understood through their duality with the complement of the incidence relation of the context. While this viewpoint offers additional insights into the concept computation, it has received relatively little attention in the FCA community.

In this paper, we evaluate the performance of FCA-based tools and dualization-based approaches by comparing their runtime across a range of datasets. Our analysis includes both real-world datasets, which reflect practical applications of FCA, and synthetic datasets, designed to test scalability with

[1] https://upriss.github.io/fca/fcasoftware.html.

P. Cellier et al. (Eds.): CONCEPTS 2025, LNAI 15941, pp. 219–227, 2025.
https://doi.org/10.1007/978-3-032-03364-2_14

density. We focus solely on offline FCA tools that compute all formal concepts. In other words, we do not consider tasks such as computing and visualizing the concept lattice or deriving any base of implications. We also consider the problem of computing n-concepts in polyadic concept analysis, a problem for which the number of available tools is much smaller.

The reported experimental observations show that SHD (for *Sparsity-based Hypergraph Dualization*), the dualization-based tool, is competitive and more resilient to increasing context density, while also supporting the polyadic case.

The rest of the paper is organized as follows. We start by briefly summarizing the preliminaries of FCA in Sect. 2. Next, we overview FCA-based tools and dualization-based approaches in Sect. 3. Section 4 shows the experimental comparison of FCA and dualization tools. Finally, Sect. 5 summarizes our study with a discussion of our results.

2 Formal Concept Analysis

2.1 The Basics

We briefly recall the basics of formal and polyadic concept analysis.

Definition 1 (Formal context). *A* formal context *is a triple* $(\mathcal{O}, \mathcal{A}, \mathcal{I})$, *where* $\mathcal{O}$ *is a set of* objects, $\mathcal{A}$ *is a set of* attributes *and* $\mathcal{I} \subseteq \mathcal{O} \times \mathcal{A}$ *is an incidence relation between objects and attributes. When* $(o, a) \in \mathcal{I}$, *we say that object* a *is described by attribute* a.

From a formal context two *derivation operators* $\cdot'$ are defined:

$$\cdot' : 2^{\mathcal{A}} \rightarrow 2^{\mathcal{O}}$$
$$A' = \{o \in \mathcal{O} \mid \forall a \in A, (o, a) \in \mathcal{I})\}$$
$$\cdot' : 2^{\mathcal{O}} \rightarrow 2^{\mathcal{A}}$$
$$O' = \{a \in \mathcal{A} \mid \forall o \in O, (o, a) \in \mathcal{I})\}$$

The compositions of derivations operators, $\cdot''$ are closure operators.

Definition 2 (Formal concept). *In a formal context, a* formal concept *is a pair* (E, I) *where* E *is a set of objects,* I *is a set of attributes,* $E = I'$ *and* $I = E'$. *We call* E *the* extent *of the concept and* I *its* intent.

Importantly, $E = E''$ and $I = I''$.

The formal concepts of a formal context can be ordered by inclusion of their extents: $(E_1, I_1) \leq (E_2, I_2) \Leftrightarrow E_1 \subseteq E_2$. The set of all formal concepts of a formal context ordered in such a way forms a complete lattice called the concept lattice of the context [3].

Polyadic concept analysis [15] is the generalisation of FCA in which the context contains more than two dimensions. We then speak of n-contexts and n-concepts.

Definition 3 (n-context). *An* n-context *is a tuple* $(D_1, \ldots, D_n, \mathcal{I})$ *where the* D_i *are finite sets called* dimensions *and* $\mathcal{I} \subseteq \prod_{i=1}^{n} D_i$ *is an incidence relation between elements of the dimensions.*

Definition 4 (n-concept). *In an n-context* $(D_1, \ldots, D_2, \mathcal{I})$*, an* n-concept *is a tuple* $(X_1, \ldots, X_n)$ *where the* $X_i \subseteq D_i$ *are maximal such that* $\prod_{i=1}^{n} X_i \subseteq \mathcal{I}$.

There exists an equivalent, arguably cleaner definition of n-concepts using closure operators in [15] but it is too complex for our needs here.

2.2 Concepts as Complements of Minimal Transversals of Holes

Formal concepts and n-concepts also happen to be dual to the complement of the incidence relation of their contexts.

Definition 5 (Hypergraph Transversal). *Let* $\mathcal{E}$ *be a ground set and* $\mathcal{H} \subseteq 2^{\mathcal{E}}$ *be a set of subsets of* $\mathcal{E}$*. The pair* $(\mathcal{E}, \mathcal{H})$ *is then a hypergraph. A* transversal *of* $(\mathcal{E}, \mathcal{H})$ *is a set* $T \subseteq \mathcal{E}$ *such that* $T \cap H \neq \emptyset$ *for all* $H \in \mathcal{H}$.

Let $(\mathcal{O}, \mathcal{A}, \mathcal{I})$ be a formal context and let us construct the hypergraph $(\mathcal{O} \cup \mathcal{A}, \{\{o, a\} \mid o \in \mathcal{O}, a \in \mathcal{A}, (o, a) \notin \mathcal{I}\})$, in which the hyperedges are the "holes" in the context. Then, for each *minimal transversal* T of this hypergraph, the pair $(\{o \in \mathcal{O} \mid o \notin T\}, \{a \in \mathcal{A} \mid a \notin T\})$ is a formal concept. Reciprocally, every formal concept of the context corresponds to a minimal transversal of the hypergraph. Indeed, the minimal transversals are minimal sets of attributes and objects that contain either the object o or the attribute a for each hole (o, a). Therefore, their complements are maximal sets of attributes and objects that do not contain o and a simultaneously. By then partitioning these complements into their sets of objects and attributes, we obtain maximal pairs (E, I) such that $(o, a) \notin E \times I$, for all holes (o, a), i.e. formal concepts. The same holds for n-concepts.

	a	b
1	×	×
2	×	

Fig. 1. A simple formal context.

Using the context depicted in Fig. 1 as an example, the hypergraph would then be $(\{1, 2, a, b\}, \{\{2, b\}\})$. It has a single hyperedge, $\{2, b\}$, and two minimal transversals, $\{2\}$ and $\{b\}$. Their complements are $\{1, a, b\}$ and $\{1, 2, a\}$, which correspond to the two formal concepts of our context, $(\{1\}, \{a, b\})$ and $(\{1, 2\}, \{a\})$.

Dualisation is a very important problem that has been extensively studied and efficient algorithms exist for computing minimal transversals, but this property of concepts is seldom used in the FCA community.

Table 1. Comparison of the FCA tools.

Tool	Language	Input	Concepts		Order		Algorithm
			2D	nD	Optional	Complete	
caspailleur[a]	Python	Binary cxt	×		×		LCM [13]
fcatng[b]	Python	Binary cxt	×			×	Norris' [12]
conexp-clj[c] [5]	Clojure	Binary cxt	×		×		Close-by-One [9]
fcaR[d] [2]	R	Binary cxt	×		×		NextClosure [3]
Concepts[e]	Python	Binary cxt	×			×	Lindig's [10]
fca4j[f] [4]	Java	Binary cxt	×			×	AddExtent [14]
PCbO[g] [8]	Java	Transaction csv	×		×		Close-by-One
DATA-PEELER[h] [1]	C++	csv	×	×	×		Data-Peeler
SHD[i] [11]	C	csv	×	×	×		SHD

[a] https://github.com/EgorDudyrev/caspailleur
[b] https://github.com/tomhanika/fcatng
[c] https://github.com/tomhanika/conexp-clj
[d] https://malaga-fca-group.github.io/fcaR
[e] https://github.com/xflr6/concepts
[f] https://gite.lirmm.fr/gutierre/fca4j-project
[g] https://fcalgs.sourceforge.net/pcbo-amai.html
[h] https://homepages.dcc.ufmg.br/~lcerf/fr/prototypes.html
[i] https://research.nii.ac.jp/~uno/code/shd.html

3 Tools

We selected a number of tools for computing formal concepts, the first 7 developed in the FCA community. Our main criteria for selection were whether the tool is usable in command line (for automatising experiments) and whether we could actually compile and run it. Table 1 presents the tools we compared. Their important characteristics are the number of dimensions they are limited to and whether they allow computing only concepts without the lattice order.

The first 7 tools use closure-based algorithms. DATA-PEELER is a special case as it has not been developed in the FCA community but it works in the polyadic case. The authors were unable to run TRIAS [7]. SHD is a tool for computing the minimal transversals of hypergraphs that offers two algorithms: reverse search and depth-first search. We included both in our experiments as their runtimes are significantly different. The input file for SHD must contain one element of the incidence relation per line, with components separated by commas.

4 Experiments

We ran the tools presented in Table 1 on different datasets, both real (2D) and artificial (2D and 3D), and measured their runtimes. The artificial datasets are used to evaluate the impact of the density on the tools, as real datasets tend to be fairly sparse. Experiments were run from a laptop equipped of an Intel Core i7-1165G7 CPU and 16 GB of RAM. All tools were called from a Python 3.10.12 script. It is worth noting that this disadvantages conexp-clj as its initialisation time of around 3 s is included in the runtime.

4.1 Real Datasets

Datasets Description. We use three real-world datasets (D1, D2, and D3) from the formal context repository[2] [6], as well as two bigger datasets (D4[3] and D5[4]). Their main characteristics are presented in Table 2.

Table 2. Dataset statistics.

Dataset	Description	Objects	Attributes	Density	Concepts
D1 - missmarple	Methods of murder in Miss Marple novels	12	6	0.3056	13
D2 - animals	Animals and their characteristics	35	11	0.3636	35
D3 - seasoning planner	Spices and herbs together and the meals they match	56	37	0.1993	532
D4 - bob-ross	Bob Ross paints and their recurring elements	403	67	0.1193	3,463
D5 - zoo	Animals and their characteristics	101	43	0.3953	4,579

Results. We computed the concepts in the datasets using the tools and measured their runtimes. When applicable, we only computed concepts without the lattice order. The results are depicted in Table 3.

The results show some disparity between FCA tools. We observe that PCBO is the overall best performer. SHD is not far behind, especially with its depth-first version.

4.2 Artificial Datasets

Datasets Description. As SHD stands for *Sparsity-based Hypergraph Dualization*, it stands to reason that it should be more efficient on sparse hypergraph,

[2] https://github.com/fcatools/contexts.
[3] https://github.com/xflr6/concepts/blob/master/examples/bob-ross.cxt.
[4] A binarized version of https://archive.ics.uci.edu/dataset/111/zoo.

Table 3. Empirical comparison of runtimes on 2D contexts.

Tool	Runtime (seconds)				
	D1	D2	D3	D4	D5
caspailleur	0.0031	0.0049	0.044	0.32	0.31
fcatng	0.0001	0.0011	0.216	13.33	52.38
conexp-clj	3.2984	3.6407	3.713	4.49	3.77
fcaR	0.7215	0.8232	0.931	4.32	1.12
Concepts	0.0003	0.0046	0.115	31.50	3.20
fca4j	0.8980	0.0977	0.147	0.32	0.28
PCBO	0.0004	0.0006	0.001	0.003	0.005
data-peeler	0.0015	0.0023	0.004	0.026	0.03
SHD[a]	0.0006	0.0014	0.010	1.89	0.13
SHD[b]	0.0007	0.0010	0.009	0.95	0.06

[a] reverse search approach
[b] depth-first search approach

i.e. dense contexts. To test this hypothesis, we randomly generated formal contexts of sizes 50×20 with densities between 0.1 and 0.9, by coin-flipping. For each density, we generated 50 such contexts and computed their concepts with most of the tools, with the exception of fcatng that was deemed too slow for such task.

Results. The average runtimes are presented in Fig. 2 where the x-axis is the density and the y-axis is the runtime in seconds.

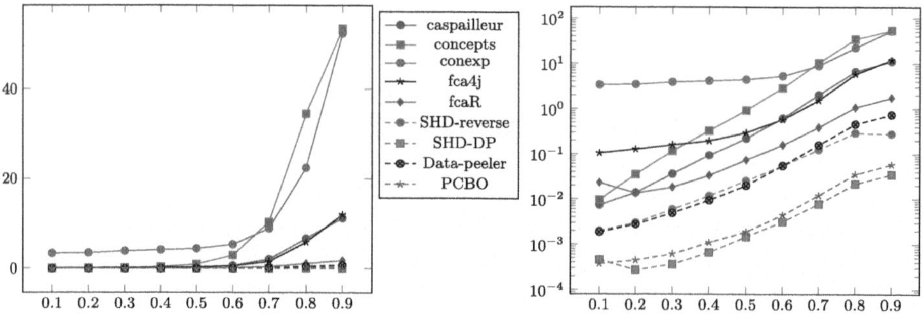

Fig. 2. Comparison of FCA software tools on random datasets. The x-axis is the context density. The y-axis is the runtime in seconds presented with a linear scale (left) and a logarithmic scale (right).

We observe that our hypothesis was indeed correct, the two dualisation-based algorithm are generally more resistant to increases in context density than FCA tools. Our interpretation is that the decrease in the size of their input counteracts the increased number of concepts they have to output. On the FCA side, only PCBO and fcaR exhibit similar behaviours, with PCB being nearly equivalent to SHD's depth-first version.

4.3 Triadic Datasets

Datasets Description. For the triadic case, we randomly generated $20 \times 20 \times 20$ triadic contexts, using the same coin-flipping method, with densities ranging from 0.1 to 0.9. For each density, we generated 20 such contexts and then computed their triadic concepts using DATA-PEELER and SHD.

Results. The average runtimes for each density are presented in Fig. 3. We observe that, contrary to the 2D case, the depth-first version of SHD is less effective. Both SHD and DATA-PEELER appear to resist increases in density until it exceeds 0.8, at which point the reverse search version of SHD begins outperforming other tools.

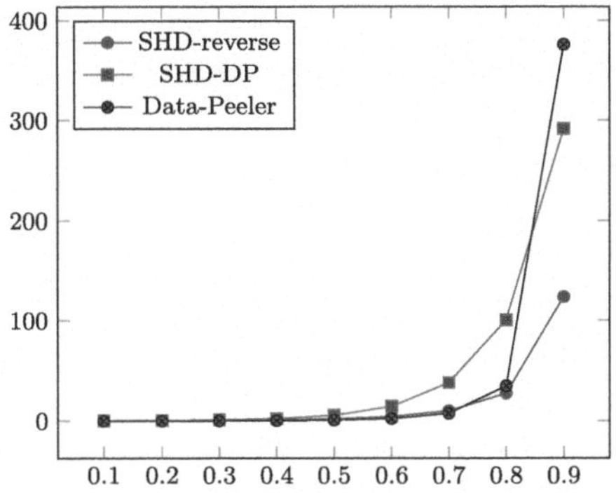

Fig. 3. Comparison of FCA tools for triadic concepts on random datasets. The x-axis is the context density and the y-axis is the runtime in seconds.

We also present the runtimes per numbers of concepts for each tools in Fig. 4. We observe that SHD's runtime increases more slowly than DATA-PEELER's with the number of concepts. We believe that this is due to the decreasing size of SHD's input with increasing density and, thus, increasing numbers of concepts.

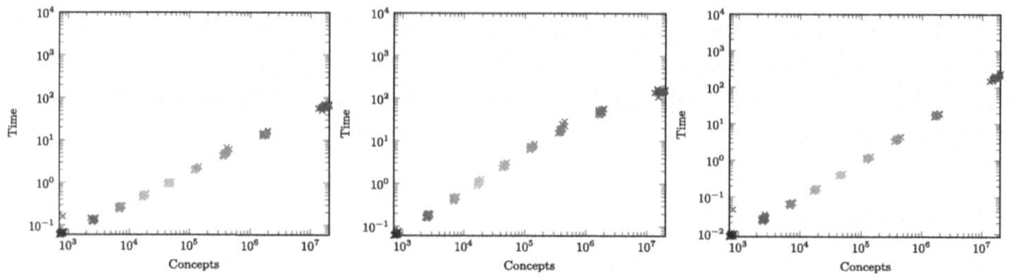

Fig. 4. Runtimes (x-axis) for SHD-reverse (left), SHD-DP (middle) and Data-peeler (right) according to the number of computed concepts (y-axis).

5 Conclusion

Our experiments show that SHD, the dualisation-based tool, is competitive and more resistant to increases in context density, in addition to being usable in the polyadic case. While it is true that real datasets tend to be sparse, this property could be leveraged to make FCA more scalable. Furthermore, this tool is made for hypergraph dualisation in general and not just the specific case of FCA in which the hypergraphs are n-partite and n-regular. It would probably be possible to further optimise the algorithm to be even more efficient at computing formal concepts. We argue that the FCA community should take an interest in integrating dualisation in its algorithms.

References

1. Cerf, L., Besson, J., Robardet, C., Boulicaut, J.-F.: Closed patterns meet n-ary relations. ACM Trans. Knowl. Disc. Data **3**(1), 1–36 (2009)
2. Cordero, P., Enciso, M., López-Rodríguez, D., Mora, Á.: fcaR, formal concept analysis with r. R J. **14**(1), 341–360 (2022)
3. Ganter, B., Wille, R.:Formal Concept Analysis - Mathematical Foundations. Springer, Heidelberg (1999)
4. Gutierrez, A., Huchard, M., Martin, P.: FCA4J: a java library for relational concept analysis and formal concept analysis. In: Proceedings of the Sixteenth International Conference on Concept Lattices and Their Applications (CLA 2022) Tallinn, Estonia, 20–22 June 2022, vol. 3308, pp. 207–212 (2022)
5. Hanika, T., Hirth, J.: Conexp-clj - a research tool for FCA. In: Proceedings of ICFCA 2019 Conference and Workshops, Frankfurt, Germany, 25–28 June 2019, vol. 2378, pp. 70–75 (2019)
6. Hanika, T., Jäschke, R.: A repository for formal contexts. In: Conceptual Knowledge Structures, pp. 182–197. Springer, Cham (2024). https://doi.org/10.1007/978-3-031-67868-4_13
7. Jäschke, R., Hotho, A., Schmitz, C., Ganter, B., Stumme, G.: Trias–an algorithm for mining iceberg tri-lattices. In: Sixth International Conference on Data Mining (ICDM'06), pp. 907–911. IEEE (2006)
8. Krajca, P., Outrata, J., Vychodil, V.: Parallel algorithm for computing fixpoints of galois connections. Ann. Math. Artif. Intell. **59**(2), 257–272 (2010)

9. Kuznetsov, S.O.: A fast algorithm for computing all intersections of objects from an arbitrary semilattice. Nauchno-Tekhnicheskaya Informatsiya Seriya 2-Informatsionnye Protsessy i Sistemy (1), 17–20 (1993)
10. Lindig, C.: Fast concept analysis. In: Working with Conceptual Structures-Contributions to ICCS 2000, pp. 152–161 (2000)
11. Murakami, K., Uno, T.: Efficient algorithms for dualizing large-scale hypergraphs. In: Proceedings of the 15th Meeting on Algorithm Engineering and Experiments, ALENEX 2013, New Orleans, Louisiana, USA, pp. 1–13 (2013)
12. Norris, E.M.: An algorithm for computing the maximal rectangles in a binary relation. Rev. Roumaine Math. Pures Appl. **23**(2), 243–250 (1978)
13. Uno, T., Kiyomi, M., Arimura, H., et al.: LCM ver. 2: efficient mining algorithms for frequent/closed/maximal itemsets. In: FIMI, vol. 126 (2004)
14. van der Merwe, D., Obiedkov, S., Kourie, D.: AddIntent: a new incremental algorithm for constructing concept lattices. In: Eklund, P. (ed.) ICFCA 2004. LNCS (LNAI), vol. 2961, pp. 372–385. Springer, Heidelberg (2004). https://doi.org/10.1007/978-3-540-24651-0_31
15. Voutsadakis, G.: Polyadic concept analysis. Order **19**(3), 295–304 (2002)

Data Analysis

Comparative Analysis of COVID-19 Vaccines Applied in Mexico Through FCA

Edith Vargas-García(✉)

Department of Mathematics, ITAM Río Hondo, Mexico City, Mexico
edith.vargas@itam.mx

Abstract. In this paper, we use Formal Concept Analysis to carry out a comparative analysis between the adverse effects present among the vaccines that were applied massively in Mexico during 2022. FCA allows us to reveal relationships between certain vaccines and certain groups of vaccines through shared core properties: Specifically, we discover connections by the fact that every common (positive or negative) side effect of the group also appears with some specific vaccine under consideration. We also investigate a relationship between the ability to neutralize antibodies and the efficacy of the vaccine. Moreover, we construct a more comprehensive concept lattice considering only vaccines applied in Mexico combined with positive and negative side effects and taking also into account the technological platform on which the vaccines were developed and their dosage.

Keywords: Applications of FCA · Vaccines · COVID-19 · Implications

1 Introduction

Formal Concept Analysis (FCA) is a method for data analysis that combines *the theory of ordered sets* and *lattices* with the notion of *formal concept*. In this work we use FCA to build hierarchical structures, called *concept lattices*, of the COVID-19 vaccines applied massively in Mexico during 2022, taking into account their attributes such as *technological platform, safety, immunogenicity* and *efficacy*, in order to perform a comparative analysis of those COVID-19 vaccines and find biological affinities between them.

For sets G and M and any binary relation $I \subseteq G \times M$ between G and M the triple (G, M, I) is called a *formal context*, and I is its *incidence relation*. The elements of G are called *objects* and those of M are interpreted as *attributes*. The incidence relation induces a Galois correspondence between G and M in the

The author gratefully acknowledges financial support by *the Asociación Mexicana de Cultura A.C.* to *Prof. Mike Behrisch* for his constant support, to *Héctor Vela Toriz* for providing the papers on which this research is based and finally to *Prof. Mariana Espinoza* and *Prof. Carlos Segovia* for their useful comments.

P. Cellier et al. (Eds.): CONCEPTS 2025, LNAI 15941, pp. 231–246, 2025.
https://doi.org/10.1007/978-3-032-03364-2_15

natural way. Corresponding pairs (A, B) of Galois closed sets are called *formal concepts* and they can be ordered by inclusion in the first component. When G and M are finite, a formal context can be represented by a cross table. The elements on the left-hand side (row labels) are the objects, the elements at the top (column labels) are the attributes, and the incidence relation is represented by the crosses. In this paper we build formal contexts (see Tables 2, 4 and 6) where the rows will be labelled with COVID-19 vaccines applied massively in Mexico and the attributes will be *the most common adverse reactions, immunogenicity, efficacy, the technological platform and the dosage of the vaccines*, respectively. We carry out a comparative analysis between the adverse effects among the vaccines that were applied during the COVID-19 pandemic in Mexico. This allows us to reach conclusions about the vaccines for COVID-19, in particular, to identify which vaccine shows more incidence of adverse effects or has more reactogenicity. We also investigate relationships between the strength of the ability to neutralize antibodies and the level of efficacy of the vaccines.

Finally, we formulate attribute implications using different transposed contexts in order to study the feasible attribute combinations. These implications assert a certain relationship between two attribute sets called premise and conclusion, and our goal is to understand the level of biological affinities among the set of COVID-19 vaccines, e.g., finding which vaccines had a greater number of adverse reactions when they were applied to the test subjects. Interpreting the implications, we also determine vaccines and groups of vaccines that exhibit the relationship that every side effect which is a common side effect to the group is also present in other vaccine. These latter findings and interpretations are new compared to the observations in [1].

This work demonstrates an interesting application of FCA for extracting meaningful properties from small data sets that could potentially be of use to take different perspectives in the analysis of medical data.

2 Contexts and Concept Lattices of Vaccines Applied Massively in Mexico

The following information is used as our main source of data. It is derived from the phase 3 trials of the vaccines below. The trials considered participants from different countries, people from different age groups, HIV positives and pregnant individuals. According to reports by the World Health Organization (WHO) [5, 7–10] we have the following information.

- For *AstraZeneca* a large phase 3 trial involving about 30000 participants took place in Argentina, Chile, Colombia, Peru and the USA [5].
- For *Janssen* the study was conducted in Argentina, Brazil, Chile, Colombia, Mexico, Peru, South Africa and the USA and it had 193000 participants [7].
- For *Moderna* the pivotal phase 3 registration trial was conducted in 99 centres across the USA and involved about 30000 participants [8].
- For *Pfizer* the phase 3 trial was conducted in Argentina, Brazil, Germany, South Africa, Turkey, and the USA and involved about 43000 participants [9].

- For *Sinovac-CoronaVac* the phase 3 trial took place in Brazil, Chile, China, Indonesia, Turkey, and involved about 62336 participants [10].

For *Sputnik V* the phase 3 trial was conducted at 25 hospitals and polyclinics in Moscow, Russia, and involved 21977 participants [11]. Finally, for *CanSino-Vaccines* the first study outside of clinical trials was performed in Guadalajara, Mexico, with 346 participating people [6].

In Table 1 we present (in percentage) the most common adverse reactions among participants of the phase 3 trial vaccination.

Table 1. Percentage of subjects in the study exhibiting the most common adverse reactions

	Astra Zeneca	Cansino	Janssen	Moderna	Pfizer BNT162b2	Sinovac	Sputnik V
Serious adverse events (SAE)	0.7–0.8%	<1%	<2%	0.2–9.7%	0–4.6%	0.53%	0.31%
Fever >38° (FE)	7.9%	21%		15.5%	14.2%	11.6%	15.2%
Nausea (N)	21.9%	2.2%		23%	1.1%	<1%	
Chills (Ch)	31.9%	23.6%	2.0%	45.4%	31.9%	11.6%	15.2%
Arthralgia (A)	26.4%	19.7%	1.0%	46.4%	23.6%		
Myalgia (M)	44%	35.8%	1.5%	61.5%	38.3%	24.2%	15.2%
Headache (H)	52.6%	46.7%	2.1%	64.7%	55.1%	24.2%	15.2%
Fatigue (Fa)	53.1%	40.2%	1.9%	70%	62.9%	24.2%	94%
Pain at the injection side (P)	54.2%	1.3%	1.3%	92%	84.1%	42.7%	15.2%

The data in Table 1 is not given in the form of formal contexts. Therefore, we use the method of *conceptual scaling* presented in [2, p. 60], to transform the data from Table 1 into a cross table. The following scales clarify how we chose to interpret the many-valued original data as a binary incidence relation.

SAE %	*Improbable* $\leq 1\%$	*Possible* $> 1\%$
0.31	×	
0.53	×	
0.7 – 0.8	×	
< 1	×	
< 2		×
0 – 4.6		×
0.2 – 9.7		×

Fever Fe%	*Fe few*	*Fe some*	*Fe ?*
7.9	×		
11.6		×	
14.2		×	
15.2		×	
15.5		×	
21		×	
––			×

Nausea N%	*N few*	*N some*	*N ?*
< 1	×		
1.1	×		
2.2	×		
21.9		×	
23		×	
––			×

Chills *Ch%*	*Ch* *few*	*Ch* *some*	*Ch* *many*	*Ch* *very many*
2	×			
11.6		×		
15.2		×		
23.6		×		
31.9			×	
45.4			×	×

Arthralgia *A%*	*A* *few*	*A* *some*	*A* *very many*	*A* *?*
1	×			
19.7		×		
23.6		×		
26.4		×		
46.4			×	
−−				×

Myalgia *M%*	*M* *few*	*M* *some*	*M* *many*	*M* *very many*
1.5	×			
15.2		×		
24.2		×		
35.8			×	
38.3			×	
44			×	
61.5			×	×

Headache *H%*	*H* *few*	*H* *some*	*H* *very many*
2.1	×		
15.2		×	
24.2		×	
46.7			×
52.6			×
55.1			×
64.7			×

Fatigue *Fa%*	*Fa* *few*	*Fa* *very many*	*Fa* *almost all*
1.9	×		
24.2	×		
40.2		×	
53.1		×	
62.9		×	
70		×	
94			×

Pain at the injection side *P%*	*P* *few*	*P* *some*	*P* *many*	*P* *very many*
1.3	×			
15.2		×		
42.7			×	
54.2			×	
84.1			×	×
92			×	×

We continue with the second step in the process of *scaling*, that is, by putting together the individual scales. We chose the method known as *plain scaling*, see [2, p. 60], which combines the scales into a one-valued context without further interconnecting them.

The one-valued context $\mathbb{K} = (V, AR, I)$ of adverse reactions, where the set of objects V consists of the 7 vaccines listed in Table 1 and the set of attributes, denoted by AR, are all the attributes in the individual scales put together, is given in Table 2: a cross in the position (i, j) indicates that the i-th vaccine causes the j-th reaction. The concept lattice arising from the context in Table 2 is given in Fig. 1, and it has 32 concepts.

An example of a concept in the lattice shown in Fig. 1 is the pair (S, R) where

$$(S, R) = (\{\text{Pfizer, CanSino, Sinovac}\}, \{\textit{Fe some, N few}\}).$$

This means that each of the vaccines Pfizer, CanSino, Sinovac caused nausea and fever to certain vaccinated subjects.

Table 2. Context of adverse reactions

	SAE improbable	*SAE possible*	*Fe few*	*Fe some*	*Fe ?*	*N few*	*N some*	*N ?*	*Ch few*	*Ch some*	*Ch many*	*Ch very many*	*A few*	*A some*	*A very many*	*A ?*	*M few*	*M some*	*M many*	*M very many*	*H few*	*H some*	*H very many*	*Fa few*	*Fa very many*	*Fa almost all*	*P few*	*P some*	*P many*	*P very many*
Astra Zeneca	×		×				×				×			×					×				×		×				×	
Cansino	×			×		×				×				×					×				×		×		×			
Janssen		×			×			×	×				×				×				×			×			×			
Moderna		×		×			×				×	×			×				×	×			×		×				×	×
Pfizer		×		×		×					×			×					×				×		×				×	×
Sinovac	×			×		×				×						×		×				×		×					×	
SputnikV	×			×				×		×						×		×				×				×		×		

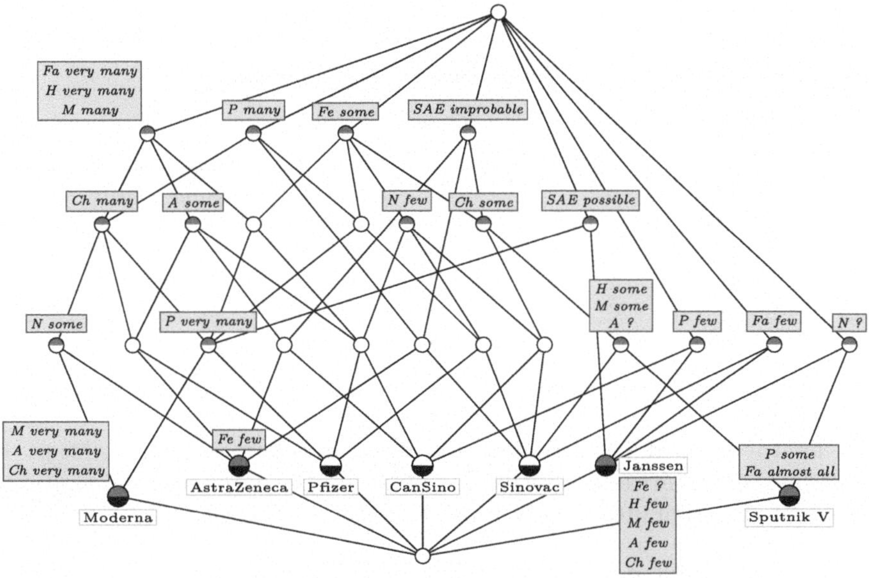

Fig. 1. Lattice of adverse events

In Fig. 1 one can read that every vaccine that causes nausea to some of the vaccinated subjects also causes chills to many vaccinated subjects. One can also read off that every vaccine that causes chills to many vaccinated subjects also causes headache to very many. In the lattice one can observe that myalgia, fatigue, headache (present in many probands) belong to one concept intent shown on the top left of Fig. 1, which we interpret as follows: If a vaccine causes one of myalgia, fatigue or headache to a significant degree, then it will also cause the other two.

We construct a second context $K = (V, EI, I)$ in order to find positive effects and affinities between vaccines. The data to build the context is taken from Table 3 and was again obtained from the phase 3 trials. The same vaccines as before are taken as objects, and the set of attributes, denoted by EI, contains the efficacy, the immunogenicity and the dosage of the COVID-19 vaccines.

Table 3. Percentage of efficacy and immunogenicity

Vaccine, Reference	Efficacy	Immunogenicity
AstraZeneca [5]	after a second dose 63.09%	Neutralizing antibodies (Nabs). 98%
CanSino [6]	after one dose 71%	Neutralizing antibodies (Nabs). 94%
Janssen [7]	after one dose 66.9%	Neutralizing antibodies (Nabs). 93%
Moderna [8]	after a second dose 94.1%	Neutralizing antibodies (Nabs). 95%
Pfizer-BNT162b2 [9]	after a second dose 94.6%	Neutralizing antibodies (Nabs). 98%
Sinovac [10]	after a second dose 67%	Neutralizing antibodies (Nabs). 96%
Sputnik V [11]	after a second dose 91.6%	Neutralizing antibodies (Nabs). 98%

Once again the data in Table 3 is not given in the form of formal contexts, wherefore we need to scale it. Our scales are the following:

Efficacy E%	*E medium* for ≈ 70%	*E high* > 80%	*Only* 1 *Dose*
63.09	×		
66.9	×		×
67	×		
71	×		×
91.6		×	
94.1		×	
94.6		×	

Nabs *Nabs*%	*Nabs medium*	*Nabs high*
93	×	
94	×	
95	×	
96		×
98		×

As for the context from Table 2, we use again plain scaling, cf. [2, p. 60]. The vaccines in the arising one-valued context are the ones applied massively in Mexico and the attributes are given by the individual scales.

Table 4. Context of Efficacy and Immunogenicity.

	E medium	*E high*	*1 Dose*	*Nabs medium*	*Nabs hi*
AstraZeneca	×				×
Cansino	×		×	×	
Janssen	×		×	×	
Moderna		×		×	
Pfizer		×			×
Sinovac	×				×
Sputnik V		×			×

The concept lattice of Table 4 is shown in Fig. 2 and has 10 concepts. One of its concepts is the pair ({CanSino, Jansen, Moderna}, {Nabs medium}), which means that the vaccines CanSino, Jansen, Moderna are comparatively not as effective to produce neutralizing antibodies as the others. In the lattice one can also read that Sinovac and AstraZeneca produce a lot of neutralizing antibodies but pay for it with a lower efficacy.

In the same lattice, one can read that vaccines of one dose are less effective than the others, in particular, they are less effective than the mRNA vaccines. We can moreover see that the vaccines of one dose are also less effective to produce neutralizing antibodies than the other viral vector vaccines.

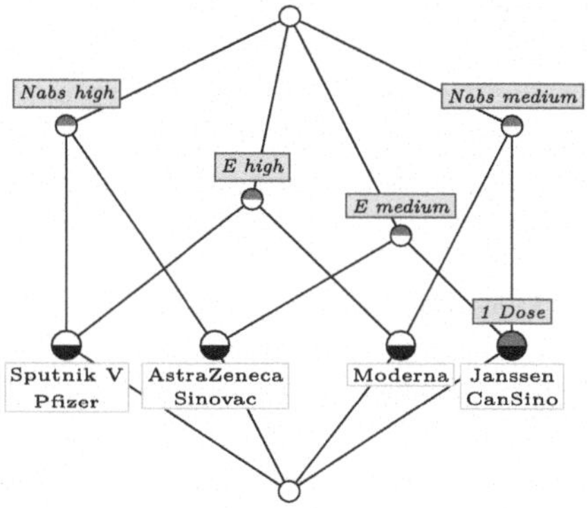

Fig. 2. Lattice of efficacy and immunogenicity

The interaction between the efficacy of the vaccines and the level of neutralizing antibodies, obtained from Fig. 2 can be schematized through the bi-plot of Fig. 3.

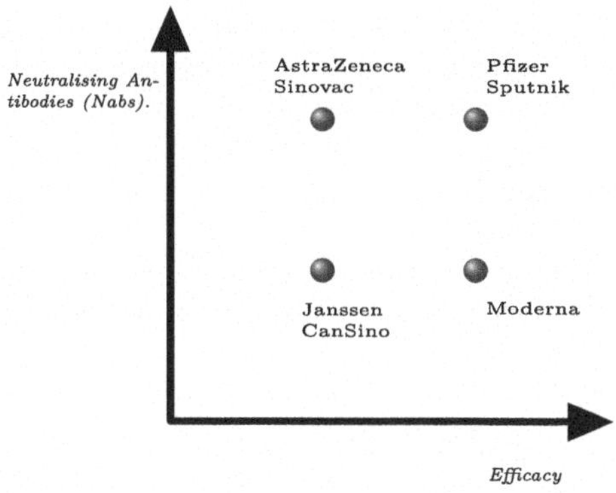

Fig. 3. Bi-plot between efficacy and immunogenicity

3 Implications of the Two Previous Formal Contexts

Below, we concern ourselves with the implications of the previously introduced formal contexts in order to study the feasible attribute combinations and to identify the affinities of (adverse reactions) between vaccines.

We briefly recall the necessary notions. Let M be the set of attributes of the formal context (G, M, I). An *implication between attributes* in M is a pair of subsets of M, denoted by $A \Longrightarrow B$. The set A is the *premise* of the implication $A \Longrightarrow B$, and B is its *conclusion*.

We say that $A \Longrightarrow B$ holds in a context (G, M, I) if every object intent respects $A \Longrightarrow B$, that is, if each object that has all the attributes from A has all the attributes from B as well. We then also say that $A \Longrightarrow B$ is a (valid) implication of (G, M, I) [3].

We start by calculating the implications of the context of Table 4. Using Concept Explorer [4], we derived a total of four formal implications, which we present subsequently together with a reading in ordinary language. The numbers in angle brackets denote the support of each implication.

- `< 2 > 1 Dose` $\Longrightarrow$ `E medium Nabs medium` It means that every vaccine working with only one dose has medium efficacy and produces a medium number of neutralizing antibodies. Moreover, there are 2 vaccines that support this implication.
- `< 2 > E medium Nabs medium` $\Longrightarrow$ `1 Dose` It means that every vaccine that has medium efficacy and produces a medium number of neutralizing antibodies, works with a single dose. Again, there are 2 vaccines that support this implication. Together with the previous implication we infer that according to our scaled data the vaccines manufactured to work with a single dose can actually be characterized as those with medium efficacy and medium number of neutralizing antibodies.
- There are two more implications with no vaccine to support them, which means that they represent contradictory attribute combinations in the premise. Indeed, the combination of a quantity being medium and high at the same time clearly never happens by our choice of scales making "medium" and "high" dichotomic qualifiers.
  `< 0 > Nabs medium Nabs high` $\Longrightarrow$ `E medium E high 1 Dose;`
  `< 0 > E medium E high` $\Longrightarrow$ `1 Dose Nabs medium Nabs high;`

Next, we calculate the implications that can be obtained from the transposed context of Table 4, in which the previous attributes are now objects and vice versa, see Table 5.

The implications of Table 5 allow us to compare and to cluster the vaccines according to the degree of positive effects (with respect to efficacy and immunogenicity) caused by them. An implication of the form `V1` $\Longrightarrow$ `V2` roughly means that vaccine `V2` shares the degree of salience of all positive effects with `V1` and possibly also has additional properties. Since, in essence, we used dichotomic scaling for the two many-valued properties "Efficacy" and "Immunogenicity" of

Table 5. Transposed context of efficacy and immunogenicity

	AstraZeneca	CanSino	Janssen	Moderna	Pfizer	Sinovac	Sputnik V
E medium	×	×	×			×	
E high				×	×		×
1 Dose		×	×				
Nabs medium		×	×	×			
Nabs high	×				×	×	×

Table 3, as a rule of thumb, we expect at most $2^2 = 4$ groups of vaccines to manifest from the implications, but the inclusion of the dosage information in the scale for "Efficacy" could lead to further splits of these groups. We shall see that this does, in fact, not happen. Again we used Concept Explorer [4] to calculate the implications, of which there are eight:

```
< 3 > CanSino  ⟹ Janssen;
< 3 > Janssen  ⟹ CanSino;
< 2 > AstraZeneca  ⟹ Sinovac;
< 2 > Sinovac  ⟹  AstraZeneca;
< 2 > Sputnik V ⟹ Pfizer;
< 2 > Pfizer  ⟹ Sputnik V;
< 0 > AstraZeneca Moderna Sinovac ⟹ CanSino Janssen Pfizer Sputnik V;
< 0 > CanSino Janssen Pfizer Sputnik V ⟹ AstraZeneca Moderna Sinovac;
```

Together the implications

$$\texttt{< 3 > Janssen} \Longrightarrow \texttt{CanSino} \text{ and } \texttt{< 3 >Janssen} \Longrightarrow \texttt{CanSino}$$

mean that Janssen and CanSino are equivalent in their level of efficacy and their capacity to produce neutralizing antibodies (medium performance in both categories), and that they also share the same dosage.

In the same way, by the following four implications, AstraZeneca and Sinovac, and Sputnik V and Pfizer, respectively, are equivalent under our scaling of the data. These three clusters of two vaccines each show that each pair of vaccines exhibits similar performance regarding the two studied qualities efficacy and immunogenicity (Nabs). The seventh vaccine, Moderna, is placed in its own group, but this does not cause any relevant implications to be calculated.

The last two implications have again zero support, which means that they correspond to contradictory situations. For example, note that there are no full rows of crosses in Table 5. Therefore, none of the characteristics efficacy and immunogenicity (and also dosage) is pronounced to the same degree in all three of AstraZeneca, Moderna and Sinovac, for otherwise it were also present in the exact same degree in the remaining four (and hence all) vaccines. The final one of the eight implications can be explained in a similar manner.

We caution against reading the above implications, e.g., `< 2 > Sinovac` $\Longrightarrow$ `AstraZeneca`, in a sharp numerical way. For example, with respect to the given implication, it is not valid to say that in both categories AstraZeneca numerically performs at least as well as Sinovac: this is exactly true for the percentage of neutralizing antibodies since 98% > 96%, but only approximately holds in the sense 63.09% $\sim$ 67% for the efficacy (and fails under a strict numerical interpretation). Thus the clustering of the vaccines into four categories clearly is a product of the similarity levels determined by our scales. Considering that there are only 7 vaccines altogether, choosing the scales finer, that is, closer to the numerical values, would likely have resulted in singleton groups and no interesting implications at all. In this respect we consider our scaling of Table 3 as satisfactory.

We point out that according to the limited view on reality shining through our data, the cluster formed by Pfizer and Sputnik V is the leading group among the seven vaccines, performing both well with respect to efficacy and immunogenicity, and the group of the two vaccines with only one dose is at the rear end with only medium performance in both aspects. This observation agrees well with Fig. 3. On the other hand, this simple classification does, of course, not consider any of the adverse effects caused by the vaccines.

To include not only efficiency but also potential risks into the view, we calculate with Concept Explorer [4] the implications in the basis of the implication theory of the transposed context of Table 2. We hence identify affinities of the vaccines with respect to adverse reactions, obtaining 17 implications. Note that Table 1 contains nine distinct rows of many-valued adverse effects, which after scaling resulted in 30 Boolean attributes in Table 2, i.e., 30 objects in the transposed context. Among the 17 implications there are only three having a support of more than one out of thirty (or out of nine many-valued objects). Even for these three, which we choose to interpret below, the support is quite low (at most four out of thirty). Hence the affinities with respect to adverse effects expressed through these implications are less strong than those resulting from the consideration of efficacy and immunogenicity, which had supports of 40%–60%.

```
< 4 > CanSino Moderna ⟹ Pfizer;
< 3 > CanSino Sputnik V ⟹ Sinovac;
< 2 > Moderna Sinovac ⟹ Pfizer;
< 1 > Janssen Moderna ⟹ Pfizer;
< 1 > Janssen Pfizer ⟹ Moderna;
< 1 > AstraZeneca Sputnik V ⟹ CanSino Sinovac;
< 1 > Moderna Sputnik V ⟹ CanSino Pfizer Sinovac;
< 1 > Pfizer Sputnik V ⟹ CanSino Moderna Sinovac;
< 1 > AstraZeneca Pfizer Sinovac ⟹ Moderna;
< 1 > AstraZeneca CanSino Sinovac ⟹ Sputnik V;
< 1 > CanSino Moderna Pfizer Sinovac ⟹ Sputnik V;
< 0 > Janssen Sinovac Sputnik V ⟹ AstraZeneca CanSino Moderna Pfizer;
```

`< 0 > AstraZeneca Janssen` $\Longrightarrow$ `CanSino Moderna Pfizer Sinovac Sputnik V;`

`< 0 > CanSino Janssen Moderna Pfizer` $\Longrightarrow$ `AstraZeneca Sinovac Sputnik V;`

`< 0 > CanSino Janssen Sinovac` $\Longrightarrow$ `AstraZeneca Moderna Pfizer Sputnik V;`

`< 0 > Janssen Moderna Pfizer Sinovac` $\Longrightarrow$ `AstraZeneca CanSino Sputnik V;`

`< 0 > AstraZeneca CanSino Moderna Pfizer Sinovac Sputnik V` $\Longrightarrow$ `Janssen;`

The implication `< 4 > CanSino Moderna` $\Longrightarrow$ `Pfizer` can be interpreted to say that whichever negative side effect happens with CanSino and Moderna also happens with Pfizer to the same degree. The four effects supporting this implication are fever for some probands, myalgia, headache for many and fatigue for very many test subjects. There is an extra adverse effect present in Pfizer that is not jointly present in CanSino and Moderna (although it appeared with Moderna), which is a non-negligible possibility of serious adverse events. Indeed, the WHO reports confirm participants in the study who presented lymphadenopathy and Bell's palsy [9, p. 6]. There is also a reverse relationship, which however can only be observed directly from the cross table (Table 2), not from the implications: Every side effect that occurred with participants vaccinated with Pfizer, was reported to the same degree with at least the CanSino or Moderna test subjects.

Likewise, the implication `< 3 > CanSino Sputnik V` $\Longrightarrow$ `Sinovac` is interpreted to say that every common side effect that appears with CanSino and Sputnik V, also appears in Sinovac to the same degree. The three effects underlying this are that serious adverse effects were rather improbable with all three vaccines, and that fever and chills occurred to some test subjects. In contrast to the previous implication, in this case we can find two effects that happened for Sinovac to a different extent than for both CanSino and Sputnik V. Namely, many people felt pain at the injection side with Sinovac, but only some with Sputnik V and few with CanSino. Moreover, only few participants vaccinated with Sinovac reported fatigue, while very many did this for CanSino and almost all for Sputnik V.

Finally, the implication `< 2 > Moderna Sinovac` $\Longrightarrow$ `Pfizer` means that every bad effect common to Moderna and Sinovac was also observed for the Pfizer test subjects; the two common effects witnessing this similarity are that fever was reported by some test subjects and pain at the injection side was felt by many.

Next we calculate the logical implications of the context presented in Table 1. Using Concept Explorer [4] we derived 57 implications in the basis of the implication theory. We present only those that have more than two vaccines supporting the implication.

```
< 4 > M many ⟹ H very many Fa very many;
< 4 > H very many ⟹ M many Fa very many;
< 4 > Fa very many ⟹ M many H very many;
< 3 > Ch some ⟹ SAE improbable Fe some;
< 3 > SAE improbable Fe some ⟹ Ch some;
< 3 > N few ⟹ Fe some;
< 3 > A some ⟹ M many H very many Fa very many;
< 3 > Ch many ⟹ M many H very many Fa very many P many;
< 3 > M many H very many Fa very many P many ⟹ Ch many;
```

The first three implications tell that myalgia felt by many, headache felt by very many and fatigue reported by very many are equivalent observations during the phase 3 trials. This is clearly visible in Fig. 1 since the three attribute concepts coincide with the object concept of Moderna.

In the lattice in Fig. 1 we see that the attribute concept of "Ch some" is the meet of the attribute concepts "Fe some" and "SAE improbable". This explains that, in the phase 3 trials, for any vaccine the fact that chills were reported by some subjects was equivalent to the fact that SAE were very infrequent together with fever reported by just some probands. This equivalence is expressed by the fourth and fifth implication.

The implication `< 3 > N few ⟹ Fe some` means that every vaccine that caused nausea to only few subjects also caused fever to some.

With respect to the bottom three implications, we first note from Fig. 1 that within the phase 3 trial data the observation of each of myalgia by many, headache by very many, and fatigue by very many test subjects was equivalent to the two respective others since again the attribute concepts coincide. Moreover, these observations appeared for every vaccine that caused arthralgia to some subjects, as confirmed by the third-to-last implication.

Finally, the bottom two implications express again an equivalence, namely that the attribute concept of "Ch many" is the intersection of those of "P many" with "M many". That is, for the vaccines in the phase 3 trials it was equivalent to cause chills for many probands or to cause pain at the injection side for many subjects together with myalgia for many (or equivalently headache for very many or fatigue for very many).

To end this section, we present a more complete lattice of the COVID-19 vaccines applied in Mexico. To build the lattice we first construct the more comprehensive context given in Table 6 by combining the contexts of Tables 4 and 2, and by also taking into account the technological platform on which the vaccines were developed and the dosage of the vaccines.

Table 6. Context of vaccines

	SAE improbable	*SAE possible*	*Fe few*	*Fe some*	*Fe ?*	*N few*	*N some*	*N ?*	*Ch few*	*Ch some*	*Ch many*	*Ch very many*	*A few*	*A some*	*A very many*	*A ?*	*M few*	*M some*	*M many*	*M very many*	*H few*	*H some*	*H very many*	*Fa few*	*Fa very many*	*Fa almost all*	*P few*	*P some*	*P many*	*P very many*	*E medium*	*E high*	*1 Dose*	*Nabs medium*	*Nabs hi*	*Inact virus*	*mRNA vaccine*	*Vectored vaccine*
AstraZeneca	×		×				×				×			×					×				×		×				×		×				×			×
Cansino	×			×		×				×				×					×				×		×		×				×		×	×				×
Janssen		×			×			×	×				×				×				×			×			×				×		×	×				×
Moderna		×		×			×				×	×			×				×	×			×		×				×	×		×		×			×	
Pfizer		×		×		×					×			×					×				×		×				×	×		×			×		×	
Sinovac	×			×		×				×						×		×				×		×					×		×				×	×		
Sputnik V	×			×				×		×						×		×				×				×		×				×			×			×

The concept lattice of the COVID-19 vaccines obtained from the context of Table 6 is given in Fig. 4 and has 48 concepts.

We investigated which new information can be obtained from analyzing the context of Table 6. We sought to obtain new implications that complement those already obtained from the contexts of Tables 2 and 4. We found 81 implications, many of which are repetitions of the previous ones; only two of them do not have any vaccine to support them. Here we focus on four implications with new attributes in their premises.

```
< 2 > Nabs high Vectored vaccines ⟹ SAE improbable;
< 2 > Nabs medium Vectored vaccines ⟹ P few E medium 1 Dose;
< 2 > Fe some Vectored vaccines ⟹ SAE improbable Ch some;
```

The first implication can be interpreted to say that every vectored vaccine that has a high level of neutralizing antibodies is improbable to cause serious adverse events. The second implication means that every vectored vaccine with a medium level of neutralizing antibodies is of one dose, has medium efficacy, and causes pain at the injection side for only few vaccinated subjects. The third implication states that vectored vaccines causing fever to some probands also cause chills to some and have a low frequency of causing serious adverse effects.

The implication

```
< 2 > mRNA vaccine ⟹
        SAE possible Fe some Ch many M many H very many
                            Fa very many P many P very many E high;
```

can be interpreted as the statement that Pfizer and Moderna, which are mRNA-based vaccines, have high efficacy, but produced chills, myalgia, headache, fatigue, and pain in the injection side for the majority of the vaccinated subjects, and had possible serious adverse events.

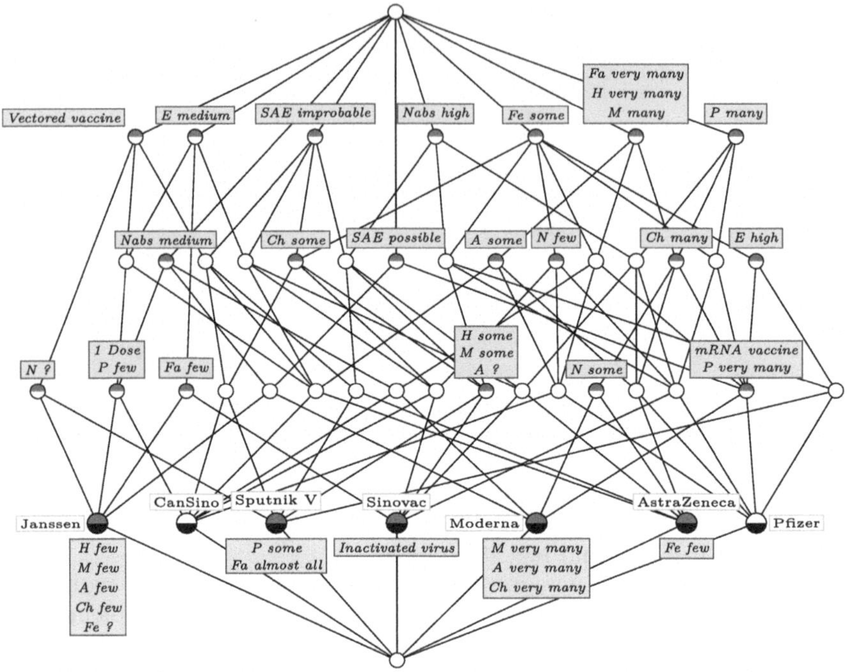

Fig. 4. The concept lattice of COVID-19 vaccines

Finally, from the following implication we obtain that the inactivated virus vaccine, namely Sinovac, has medium efficacy but a high level of neutralizing antibodies, that serious adverse events among the subjects vaccinated with Sinovac were improbable and that it caused fever, nausea, chills, fatigue and headache to some of the vaccinated subjects. This is essentially a listing of the object intent defined by Sinovac.

```
< 1 > Inactivated virus ==>
          SAE improbable Fe some N few Ch some
        A ? M some H some Fa few P many E medium Nabs high;
```

4 Conclusion

We used formal concept analysis (FCA) to analyze certain attributes of the vaccines against COVID-19. From the transposed context of adverse reactions, we built a concept lattice that allowed us to investigate the level of affinity between vaccines with respect to adverse effects. Under this aspect no strong commonalities were visible from the data, which may have been a consequence of our scaling of the many-valued data. Coarser scales could potentially change this situation, but care has to be taken to not over-simplify the data. We also studied the positive side effects by comparing efficacy and immunogenicity within the set of vaccines. Here four clusters of vaccines appeared, three with two members, and one with a single vaccine.

With our work we continued the investigations of [1], and we constructed a comprehensive COVID-19 vaccine concept lattice, focusing on the vaccines applied in Mexico and combining positive and negative side effects with the technological platform on which the vaccines were developed and the dosage of the vaccines. This lattice has 48 concepts and is still very well readable. Some interesting implications based on the technological platform of the vaccines were found to hold in this lattice. Whether these represent connections that are specific to the situation studied in this paper or contain a general relationship that extends to other vaccines with the same technological platform remains to be investigated when more trial data on vaccines with the same technology becomes available.

Alternative pattern extraction methods to the data such as (Boolean matrix factorisation and fuzzy methods) are potential tasks for further investigation.

References

1. Burgos-Salcedo, J.: A comparative analysis of clinical stage 3 COVID-19 vaccines using knowledge representation. medRxiv, Cold Spring Harbor Laboratory Press, 2021–03 (2021)
2. Ganter, B., Wille, R.: Formal Concept Analysis. Mathematical foundations. Springer Nature (2024)
3. Ganter, B., Obiedkov, S., Rudolph, S., Stumme, G.: Conceptual Exploration. Springer, Cham (2016)
4. (Con Exp) The Concept Explorer. https://conexp.sourceforge.net/. Accessed 5 Mar 2025
5. World Health Organization. Background document on the AZD1222 vaccine against COVID-19 developed by Oxford University and AstraZeneca: background document to the WHO interim recommendations for use of the AZD1222 (ChAdOx1-S [recombinant]) vaccine against COVID19 developed by Oxford University and AstraZeneca, 1 March 2021
6. Hernandez-Bello, J., et al.: Neutralizing antibodies against SARS-CoV-2, anti-Ad5 antibodies, and reactogenicity in response to Ad5-nCoV (CanSino Biologics) vaccine in individuals with and without prior SARS-CoV-2. Vaccines **9**(9), 1047 (2021)
7. World Health Organization. Background document on the Janssen Ad26. COV2. S (COVID-19) vaccine: background document to the WHO interim recommendations for use of Ad26. COV2. S (COVID-19) vaccine, 17 March 2021
8. World Health Organization. Background document on the mRNA-1273 vaccine (Moderna) against COVID-19: background document to the WHO interim recommendations for use of the mRNA-1273 vaccine (Moderna), 3 February 2021
9. World Health Organization. Background document on the mRNA vaccine BNT162b2 (Pfizer-BioNTech) against COVID-19: background document to the WHO interim recommendations for use of the Pfizer–BioNTech COVID-19 vaccine, BNT162b2, under emergency use listing, 14 January 2021

10. World Health Organization. Background document on the inactivated vaccine Sinovac-CoronaVac against COVID-19: background document to the WHO interim recommendations for use of the inactivated COVID-19 vaccine, CoronaVac, developed by Sinovac, 24 May 2021
11. Logunov, D.Y., et al.: Safety and efficacy of an rAd26 and rAd5 vector-based heterologous prime-boost COVID-19 vaccine: an interim analysis of a randomised controlled phase 3 trial in Russia. Lancet **397**(10275), 671–681 (2021)

Metatheoretic Structuralism Meets Formal Concept Analysis

Mariana Espinosa Aldama(✉) and Eduardo Robles Belmont

Instituto de Investigaciones en Matemáticas Aplicadas y en Sistemas, UNAM, Mexico City, Mexico
mariana.espinosa@iimas.unam.mx
https://mmss.iimas.unam.mx/

Abstract. Metatheoretic structuralism and Formal Concept Analysis (FCA) offer complementary approaches to analyzing scientific theories. Both frameworks share a hierarchical and set-theoretic foundation, making FCA a powerful tool for visualizing theoretical networks. Through the Space-Time Theories Exploratorium, we show how FCA enhances the mapping of conceptual dependencies and theoretical hierarchies. Our findings demonstrate its potential to refine structuralist methods and advance the formal study of scientific knowledge.

Keywords: FCA applications · metatheoretic structuralism · theory-nets · concept exploration

1 Introduction

There is genuine interest by many philosophers of science in representing the structure of scientific theories; especially since there is a considerable amount of reconstructions that have been done following the criteria established by the structuralist view of metatheoretical analysis [4]. In previous works [10–14] we have proposed to analyze and visualize such reconstructions using the methodologies of Formal Concept Analysis (FCA), a mathematical theory developed by Rudolf Wille, Bernhard Ganter et al., that restructures and reinterprets Birkhoff's lattice theory and Galois connections to define a notion of formal concept and a concept lattice that could serve practical purposes [17,18]. Both approaches are hierarchical and set-theoretic based. Structuralism takes as units of analysis several classes of models as well as theoretical networks (or theory-nets), which can be compared with concept lattices. Our aim now is to bring metatheoretical structuralism to the FCA community as a possible application of such mathematical theory.

In order to make progress in our eagerness to map science, construct and validate contexts, we've been using and developing the software Exploratorium.[1,2]

[1] https://remo.cua.uam.mx/vis/Exploratorium/.
[2] https://github.com/pupitetris/Exploratorium/.

Supported by IIMAS-UNAM.

P. Cellier et al. (Eds.): CONCEPTS 2025, LNAI 15941, pp. 247–263, 2025.
https://doi.org/10.1007/978-3-032-03364-2_16

This platform integrates data from a SQL database, enabling seamless management of multiple networks and controlling data changes and inputs. It enhances user experience by streamlining editing processes, preserving previous configurations to facilitate corrections and iterative refinements. A full screen option displays results as an interactive map for exhibitions, called *macroscope*, that can be navigated with gestures on a touch sensitive screen [5]. These macroscopes facilitate expert supervision and exploration. We invite the reader to explore some of the networks presented here at the Space-time Theories Exploratorium web page.

In this paper we introduce metatheoretical structuralism as a branch of scientific philosophy and its basic units of analysis. We recall how it came to Spanish-speaking countries, how it met with FCA, and the insights that such analysis has brought. Finally we will recapitulate on how visualizations in the *Exploratorium* have facilitated expert explorations of theoretical networks and the accompaniment that they bring in reading the texts.

2 The Origins of the Metatheoretic Structuralist View

The structuralist view in philosophy of science has its origins before the Second World War, when members of the Vienna Circle (the logical positivists), the Berlin Circle (logical empiricists) and the Lwów-Warsaw school seriously discussed the nature of scientific knowledge. The Vienna Circle (1924–1936) was directed by Moritz Schlick, philosopher and physicist, student of Planck, who arrived at the University of Vienna thanks to the efforts of the mathematician Hans Hahn and a direct recommendation from Einstein, who had been impressed by his analysis of special relativity. Schlick was also captivated by the works of Wittgenstein and his rejection of metaphysics, as well as by the positivist ideas of Mach. In 1929 they organized the first congress on philosophy of science, focusing their work on the analysis of language, discarding metaphysics and proposing a demarcation criterion between it and science. Among the members of the Vienna Circle we find H. Feigl, O. Neurath, F. Kaufmann, K. Gödel, A. J. Ayer, C. Morris and R. Carnap. The latter also frequented the meetings of the Berlin Circle, directed by Hans Reichenbach. Also called the *Society of Scientific Philosophy* (1928–1933), this group stood out for its greater inclination towards physics and mathematics and the formalization of theories and their axioms. They were strongly influenced by the works of Einstein, Boltzmann, Tarski, Hilbert and Russell, who frequently attended their meetings. Other members were K. Grelling, W. Dubislav, G. Hempel and R. von Mises. The logical empiricists gave great weight to the discoveries and advances of science, taking scientific observations, experiments and theories as the sole sources of knowledge and not *a priori* judgments or sensory data. The theories were treated with an axiomatic-syntactic approach, through linguistic analysis of protocol statements, which form a basis for contrast that allowed theoretical terms to be related to observational terms through correspondence rules [8]. The Vienna Circle disbanded in 1936 after Schlick's murder and the Nazi persecution. Weissmann and Neurath emigrated to England, while Carnap emigrated to California where he continued the school of *analytical philosophy* in the company of his students W. Quine and D. Davidson, and more inclined to linguistic matters. For their part, Reichenbach and Hempel also emigrated to California and together with H. Putnam, A. Grünbaum, W. Salmon, B. van Fraassen and J. Earmann developed what is today known as *scientific philosophy* [23].

It was not until 1944, when Alfred Tarski published his foundations of semantics [32] and his contextual concept of truth, that semantics could be formalized. Given a series of problems and limitations that the syntactic approach entails, exposed in 1954 by Patrick Suppes [29] and later on by Frederick Suppe [27,28], Suppes proposed to analyze the theoretical structures, not through linguistic or meta-mathematical means but mathematical ones: through set theory, and adding semantic criteria of meaning and contextual truth. The meaning is prior and not subsequent to the criterion of truth, and references to theories must be included as constitutive parts of them [31].

The Argentinian physicist and philosopher Mario Bunge published in 1967 his *Foundations of Physics* [6], an extraordinary book where the most general theories such as Particle Mechanics, Electrodynamics, Relativity, and Quantum Mechanics are formally axiomatized. Bunge's work also introduces the concepts of protophysics and zerological principles to characterize such statements that conform, along with the mathematical theories, semantics, and logic, physics' background. The introduction offers a useful toolbox for the physics foundations researcher, wherein Bunge already exhibits the idea of theoretical structures of partial order and lattices. The reader may find three lattice visualizations that represent some of Bunge's axiomatizations at the *Exploratorium*.

Bunge's axiomatizations are presented through definitions of set predicates, a methodology devised by Suppes [30], which is distinguished from the logical-formal axiomatization of Hilbert and Carnap [19]. The axiomatic-semantic approach of [6] abandons the rules of correspondence, protocol statements, and the distinction of theoretical from observational terms to include a series of interpretation axioms that give meaning to the terms. The axioms are presented as set predicates, and the Tarskian concept of truth is included. The conception of meaning is synthetic and makes use of set theory to make meaningful calculations. Gustavo E. Romero is also an heir of this conception [24].

The model-theoretical semantic view includes most of these proposals, but characterizes theories based on models instead of axiomatic statements. That is, although the axioms may persist, they are not what characterizes scientific theories, but rather their models. In *The Structure of Science*, Ernest Nagel (1961) [20] already tries to enrich the syntactic vision by introducing a third component to the description of the theories that would give a more familiar or visualizable interpretation to the abstract formulas, emphasizing the relevance of the role of models in the characterization of scientific theories.

At the end of the seventies, the model-theoretical semanticist school spread mainly in Europe and America, highlighting Dalla Chiara and Toraldo di Francia in Italy. In the United States, they were headed by Patrick Suppes, Fredrick Suppe, Joseph Sneed, van Fraassen, and Ronald Giere. Michael Friedman can be cast under this tradition. His *Foundations of Space-Time Theories* [16] has provided much of the data used in the Exploratorium, as he explicitly exhibits the models and their elements in two formulations (dependent and independent of coordinates) for the Leibnizian, Newtonian, Newton-Cartan, Galilean, and Lorentzian space-time, as well as for special relativity and general relativity.

At the University of Munich, Wolfgang Stegmüller ran a center for analytical philosophy. He convinced two of his doctorate students to drop their interest in Carnapian philosophy and to study Joseph Sneed's work [25] of which he had recently encountered in his trips to Harvard. In a titanic effort, Wolfgang Balzer and Carlos Ulises Moulines sistematized and made comprehensible Sneed's semantic view in the landmark book "An Architectonic for Science" [4]. Moulines, born in Venezuela, educated in Barcelona and Munich, brought structuralism to Spanish-speaking countries, along with Jose Díez in Spain, Newton Da Costa in Brazil, César Lorenzano and Pablo Lorenzano in Argentina, Juan Manuel Jaramillo and Germán Guerrero Pino in Colombia, Mario Casanueva and Diego Méndez in Mexico... to name a few [2].

Casanueva and Méndez, both philosophers of biology and students of Moulines at Universidad Autónoma Metropolitana (UAM), were the first ones that we have notice of to make use of FCA as such to represent the relations between domains of biological inheritance theories under the structuralist view [21]. Méndez was looking for techniques to order concepts and find distances between different conceptual architectures when he came across Rudolf Wille's work. Mariana Espinosa's doctoral thesis at UAM [11] was supervised by Méndez and Casanueva and deals with the use of FCA to represent theoretical networks of physical theories.

For more than fifty years the structuralists have reconstructed multiple theories, many of which can be found in an extensive anthology edited by Balzer, Moulines and Sneed [3], and in the bibliographic compilation by Abreu, Lorenzano and Moulines [1]. In physics the works of Thomas Bartelborth (general relativity), Thomas Brückner (theory of elementary particles and quantum mechanics), Ulrich Gähde (astronomy), C. Ulises Moulines (thermodynamics), and Martin Rotter (wave mechanics and matrix mechanics) stand out. However, many other sciences are being reconstructed, all the way from measurement theory [9] to nursing models [15].

3 Models, Classes of Models and Typifications

Metatheoretical structuralism may not want to enter the discussion on what a theory is, being such a polysemic term, and rather define a *theoretical element*, its central unit of analysis, along with *models* and *theory-nets*. By analyzing the relations between these units, it seeks to describe the internal structures of knowledge. The classical distinction between theoretical and observational terms is not an issue for structuralists either, since all terms are considered theoretical of some theory. Theoreticity of terms is in relation to a specific theory. The important issue is where in the network of theoretical elements a *theorization* happens, that is, when a new domain, property, or fundamental constant enters the game. A hierarchical presupposition is made, but general inquiry goes in the sense of trying to falsify this presupposition or to find proof of some kind of holism or vicious circles. Inter-theoretical relations, questions about unification, development, and construction of standard classes of models, are all issues of interest to structuralist philosophers that may be enlightened by the visualization of complex theory-nets.

The term "model" is used by structuralists in an opposite sense as it is used by empirical scientists. In this semantic view, a model is the thing (a pendulum, a lady, a geometrical object) depicted by a picture (an equation, a photograph, a graph). They argue this is the case for logicians and mathematicians too. On the other hand, physicists and other empirical scientists usually think of models as the "picture", for example, a certain set of equations and conditions that describe the thing [7,24]. This is important to note because we will frequently consult original sources written by scientists and not necessarily by meta-theoretical philosophers, which talk about their proposed models.

From the structuralist point of view, being there infinite possible models or realizations of a theory, we ought to define classes of model-structures by means of set-theoretic predicates, identifying types of axioms and common elements.[1] They begin by identifying three classes of models: *potential models* (M_p) that set up the conceptual structure by stating its domains and typifications;[2] the class of *actual models* (M) which includes relations between theoretical domains. Partial potential models (M_{pp}) are subsets of M_p that contain non-theoretical domains and relations that may be shared by other theories.

So, x is a model of the class of potential models $x \in M_p$ if its elements have the form

$$x = \langle D_1, , ...D_k, A_1, ...A_l, R_1, ...R_m \rangle$$

where D_k are the *principal base sets* that receive an empirical interpretation, A_i are the *auxiliary base sets* that have a purely mathematical interpretation, and R_m are relations between non-theoretical basic terms.

Likewise, x is a model of the class M if its elements have the form

$$x = \langle D_1, , ...D_k, A_1, ...A_l, R_1, ...R_m, r_1, ...r_n \rangle$$

where r_n are relations between domains of T.

Structuralists define many other classes of models as well as relations between them. There may be classes of *partial models* (M_{pp}), auxiliary models (Aux), or *specialized models* (M_e), as well as a set of so-called *links* and *constraints* (L) between models; together they convey the *formal nucleus* or *theory-core* (K) of a theory. Classes of models are distinguished by the types of axioms or premises

[1] We present here a simplified version of the reasoning behind the construction of models and classes of models. For a complete explanation see [4].

[2] A weaker variant of Bourbaki's concept of "structure species" that does not require formulas to be invariant under transformations is used to conceive the notion of potential model.

the models fulfill. For example, a partial model for Classical Particle Mechanics ($M_{pp}(CPM)$) would describe kinematics, referring to time, positions, and velocities. Proper theoretical terms such as mass and force are found in $M_p(CPM)$, opening the possibility of multiple relations between variables. $M(CPM)$ states the relations between theoretical and non-theoretical variables, such as Newton's second law of dynamics that relates force with mass and acceleration (a non-theoretical term of CPM). Models of a more specialized class (M_e) account for specific conditions and relations, such as the universal law or Hooke's law.

Following the typology of Moulines [22], we can classify the classes of axioms as follows:

- **Primitive or basic concepts:** These are symbols or placeholders that can receive a variety of interpretations depending on the theory in which they are embedded. For example, the symbol E might be used as a primitive sign. In itself, E does not yet denote a specific concept such as energy or Euclidean space—it is simply an uninterpreted token within the formal structure.
- **Axioms of interpretation:** These specify how primitive concepts are to be interpreted in a given domain. For instance, an axiom might state that the primitive token *E3* refers to three-dimensional Euclidean space. This interprets a previously undefined symbol as denoting a specific mathematical structure.
- **Typifications**: These describe how an entity or function is constructed (its internal structure and domain-codomain relations). For example, a mass function $\mathbb{M}(\sigma, s) = m$ takes a physical system $\sigma \in \Sigma$ (a particle, a star, a black hole), and a unit system $s \in S$ (International Unit System, Imperial Unit System), and assigns a value $m \in \mathbb{R}^+$, where Σ denotes the class of all possible physical systems and S the class of scale-cum-unit systems and $\mathbb{R}^+$ the positive real numbers. The general theoretical mass concept would be $\mathbb{M} : \Sigma \times S \to \mathbb{R}^+$. Typifications thus specify the set-theoretical level at which a concept or relation is defined and indicate its ontological status in the reconstruction (see [6] p. 31 for a detailed explanation).
- **Characterizations or conditions**: These are stipulations on the essential mathematical properties of each of the basic terms. For example: having zero curvature, having a positive signature, being univocal on the right, being doubly differentiable, etc. The characterizations have, even if only to a minimal degree, a certain factual content. However, these are not directly empirical statements such as the affirmation of the blackness of crows. And above all, their empirical content is very poor because they always refer to a single concept.
- **Synoptic laws**: These are the most important axioms, since they express the connections that exist between primitive concepts, summarizing all the essential information of the theory. For example force equations.
- **Links, Ligatures or Binding conditions**: These are links between models. For example, the statement that the mass of particles before (model 1) and after (model 2) an inelastic collision in collision mechanics is preserved.
- **Special laws:** These are laws that apply only to some models of the theory, and can be synoptic. For example, Hook's law in Newtonian theory.

- **Distinguished elements**: Such as fundamental constants (the constant of gravitation or the spring's constant), or additive and multiplicative identities (0 and 1 in set theory, algebra and others).

Some of these classes of axioms may come together. Primitive concepts, axioms of interpretation and typification generally define domains such as geometric objects, variables, or fields. "Domain" is then a class of attribute that we are interested in. We have also chosen to distinguish as much as possible classes of synoptic laws: equations of motion, field equations, equations of state, minimum action principles, force laws, etc.

As we compare models, we can easily identify how classes of axioms accompany each other and their hierarchy in the theory-nets. Our approach to construct theory-nets using FCA (those would be theory-lattices) is to take axioms as attributes $a \in A$, and models as objects $M \in B$ where $(M, a) \in i \iff a \in M$.[3] This high granularity allows tracking exactly which axioms a model satisfies. These considerations are important in order to clarify the formal context $\mathbb{K} = \langle M, a, i \rangle$. In our analysis, we may group attributes into meaningful families to facilitate the interpretation of the concept lattice. For example, we may take all the attributes that define a model for General Relativity, after realizing that all the cosmological models that are being studied comply with it, and condense them into a single attribute.

So different classes of models are taken as objects and are called *object-models. Object-concepts* are those concepts that carry the object's label. We shall call those *concept-models.* A central inquiry will be to try to identify concept-models of a certain type in a theory-lattice built from specialized models, or to justify the artificial inclusion of potential, partial, or actual model-objects into a formal context as in the example of Sect. 5.

4 Theoretical Elements, Theory-Nets and Theory-Lattices

The set of all models of a theory comprises its formal nucleus:

$K(T)$ is a *theory-core* of the theory T iff there exists $M_{pp}(T)$, $M_p(T)$, $M(T)$, Me, and $L(T)$ such that:

$$K(T) = \langle M_{pp}(T), M_p(T), M(T), M_e(T), L(T) \rangle$$

where $M_{pp} \subseteq M_p \subseteq M \subseteq M_e$, $L \subseteq M_p$.

Figure 1. shows the predicted relations between classes of models and the classes of attributes that are expected to be found in the network hierarchy.[4] It is important to notice that most relations between elements are based on comparisons that reflect the intentional sense of the classes of models. The term

[3] We are not using the traditional notation of G and M as the sets of objects and attributes in order to avoid confusion with models. Anyhow, the list of possible attributes and models is usually much bigger than the subsets that have been selected to be studied.

[4] L is not depicted.

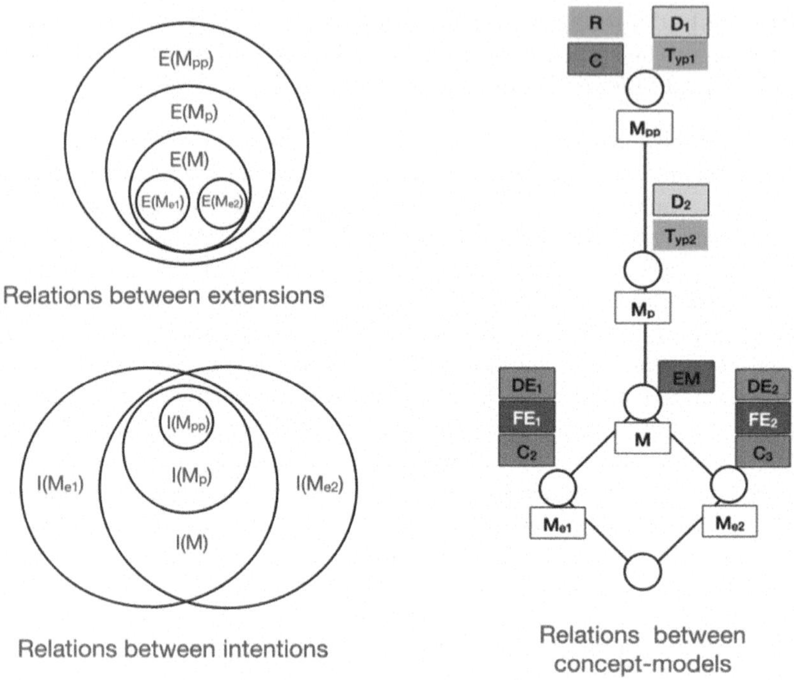

Fig. 1. Upper left side: Relations between extensions of concept-models. Lower left side: Relations between intentions of concept-models. These correspond to the relations between classes of models as defined by metatheoretical structuralism. Right side: Lattice representation of relations between concept-models. Expected locations of classes of attributes. M: Actual Models; M_p: Potential Models, M_{pp}: Partial Potential Models; M_e: Specialized Models; D: Domain; Typ: typification; C: conditions; DE: Distinguished Elements; EM: Equations of Motion; FE: Field Equations. $E(M)$: extension of a concept-model; $I(M)$: intention of a concept-model.

"formal concept", as it is understood in FCA as a pair of extensions and intentions, is not found in classical books of metatheoretical structuralism. One can easily get confused about what level of modeling one is working on, and if the relations between models are in the intentional or extensional sense. A question that FCA easily clarifies.

This theoretical core does not answer the question: What is the theory for? It's like deconstructing a piano, and understanding how each piece fits with every other piece, and yet, not knowing a piano is for playing music. This important aspect of theories is described through informal premises called *intentional applications* I stated with non-theoretical terms of T, but proper to $M_{pp}(T)$, hence $I \subseteq M_{pp}$.

A theoretical element (TE) is a quadruple:

$$TE = \langle K, I, CC, H \rangle$$

where CC is a set that characterizes the *scientific community*, and H is a set of *historical data*. CC and H come into play in diachronic analysis.[5]

Classes of models and complete or partial theoretical elements (I, CC and H may be omitted for simplified versions) can be related in *theoretical networks* (or *theory-nets*) by a specialization relation. A network of theory-nets is called a *holon* (see Fig. 4).

The *specialization relation* is defined as follows:

If $TE = \langle M_{pp}, M_p, M, L, I\rangle$ and $TE' = \langle M'_{pp}, M'_p, M', L', I'\rangle$ are theoretical elements, then TE' is a specialization of TE iff

1. $M'_p = M_p$ and $M'_{pp} = M_{pp}$
2. $M' \subseteq M$, $L' \subseteq L$, and $I' \subseteq I$

The specialization relationship $\sigma \subseteq \widetilde{TE} \times \widetilde{TE}$ is reflexive, transitive, and antisymmetric, thus partially ordering the set of theoretical elements. A theoretical network is then defined as an ordered set $N = \left\langle \widetilde{TE}, \sigma \right\rangle$, where $\widetilde{TE}$ is a set of (complete or partial) theoretical elements (see [4], p. 226–231). Specialized models can form theoretical elements of their own, branching around the intended applications of the model.

5 A Classical Example

The theoretical network of Classical Particle Mechanics (CPM) is a favorite among the structuralist examples. We have taken its formal reconstruction as it is presented in [4], and built a formal context using models as objects. The concept lattice obtained (Fig. 3) is almost identical to the theoretical network the structuralists have drawn by hand (Fig. 2).

The upper part of the lattice shows a chain of nodes corresponding to the partial potential model M_{pp}, the potential model M_p, an auxiliary model, and the actual model M. It is very informative to display such previous models as they will be the connection to other physical theories and theoretical networks.

Assigning individual axioms as attributes will turn a theoretical network into a concept lattice that displays extra nodes for shared axioms. Such has been the case for the node corresponding to the external force f and for the electric charge Q in Fig. 3. Such attributes are shared by more than one theoretical element, producing nodes that are not to be ignored. The extra node for external forces distinguishes a branch apart from those that follow Newton's 3rd law of action and reaction. The node corresponding to the electric charge shows us that distinguished elements might belong to higher-level models like potential models M_p, highlighting nature's fundamental constraints.

Attribute labels may be color-coded indicating classes of attributes. This asset allows us to easily identify where a new domain appears in the lattice, and how classes of attributes are displayed along the network. Domains are

[5] We will center here on the synchronic analysis, taking into account dates and authors as part of the meta descriptions of objects that will later appear in object labels.

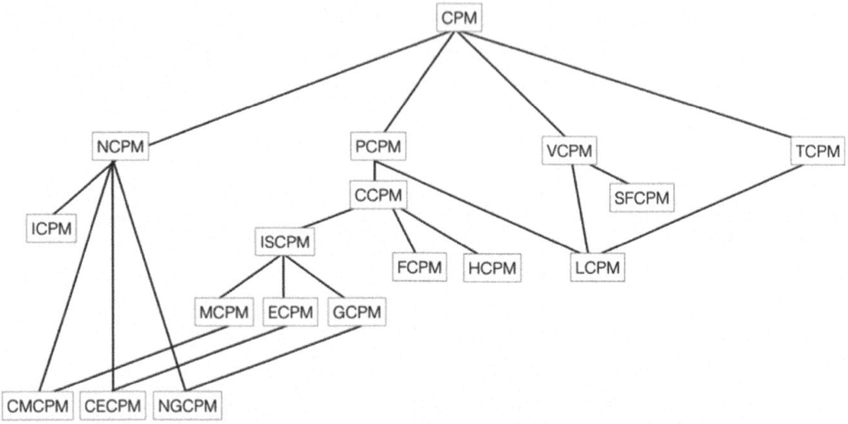

Fig. 2. Theoretical network for Classical Particle Mechanics (CPM). Figure copied from [4]. Nodes are theoretical elements and links are relations of specialization. All of the elements are specialized models of CPM, classified according to the characteristics of the special laws. Force equations types are: dependent on position (CPMP), time-dependent (TCPM), velocity-dependent (VCPM), acceleration-dependent (ACPM), Newtonian (NCPM) (includes 3rd law), conservative (CCPM), of free fall (FCPM), of Hook (HCPM), of Lorentz (LCPM), simple frictional force (SFCPM), inverse-square (ISCPM), magnetostatic (MCPM), electrostatic (ECPM), gravitational (GCPM), isolated (ICPM), position-dependent (PCPM), Newtonian gravitational (NGCPM), Coulombian magnetic (CMCPM) and Coulombian electric (CECPM).

frequently defined in previous and potential models, while force equations are found in specialized models at the bottom of the lattice. The equation of motion (Newton's 2nd law) finds its place at a more fundamental level. Two models are missing in Fig. 3 due to a lack of data. Nevertheless, the similarity and logic of the two representations have encouraged us to continue visualizing and analyzing theoretical networks with FCA.

A comparison between specialized models in a concept lattice should show nodes that correspond to different classes of models. Dis-aggregating sets of axioms may show how some of them are shared by different models. When comparing alternative theories, some aspects of previous and potential models may be shared, connecting the network with other theoretical elements and networks forming a *theoretical holon* as in Fig. 4.

Structuralism has also studied the dynamics of theoretical networks, visualizing different stages of the network as time passes. The known complexity of theoretical networks and their analysis is desperately in need of mathematical and computational tools that will propel our mapping and comprehension of the structure of theories.

Table 1. Formal context for Classical Particle Mechanics, where models are objects and axioms are attributes. Data retrieved from [4].

	Mpp(CPM))	Aux (CPM)	Mp (CPM)	M (CPM)	M (ICPM)	M (HCPM)	M (FCPM)	M (NCPM)	M (PCPM)	M (CCPM)	M (ISCPM)	M (NGCPM)	M (GCPM)	M (ECPM)	M (VCPM)	M (SFCPM)	M (TCPM)	M (LCPM)
TIV-6(b)					x													
TIV-6(a)					x													
LCPM Eq.4																		x
TCPM Eq.2																	x	x
SFCPM Eq.3																x		
VCPM Eq.4															x	x		x
VCPM Eq.3															x	x		x
ECPM Eq.3														x				
GCPM Eq.3												x	x					
ISCPM Eq.3											x	x	x	x				
HCPM Eq.3						x												
CCPM Eq.3						x	x			x	x	x	x	x				
PCPM Eq.3-2						x	x		x	x	x	x	x	x				x
PCPM Eq.3-1						x	x		x	x	x	x	x	x				x
NCPM Eq.5-2					x			x				x						
NCPM Eq.5-1					x			x				x						
2nd Law				x	x	x	x	x	x	x	x	x	x	x	x	x	x	x
g							x											
c																		x
B																		x
E																		x
l																x		
b																x		
ε														x				
Q														x				x
G												x	x					
φ												x						
h											x	x	x	x				
k						x												
F						x	x		x	x	x	x	x	x	x	x	x	x
α		x		x	x	x	x	x	x	x	x	x	x	x	x	x	x	x
r		x		x	x	x	x	x	x	x	x	x	x	x	x	x	x	x
P*					x			x				x						
N*					x			x				x						
m			x	x	x	x	x	x	x	x	x	x	x	x	x	x	x	x
l			x	x	x	x	x	x	x	x	x	x	x	x	x	x	x	x
c1	x	x	x	x	x	x	x	x	x	x	x	x	x	x	x	x	x	x
c2	x	x	x	x	x	x	x	x	x	x	x	x	x	x	x	x	x	x
P	x	x	x	x	x	x	x	x	x	x	x	x	x	x	x	x	x	x
S	x	x	x	x	x	x	x	x	x	x	x	x	x	x	x	x	x	x
T	x	x	x	x	x	x	x	x	x	x	x	x	x	x	x	x	x	x
R	x	x	x	x	x	x	x	x	x	x	x	x	x	x	x	x	x	x
N	x	x	x	x	x	x	x	x	x	x	x	x	x	x	x	x	x	x

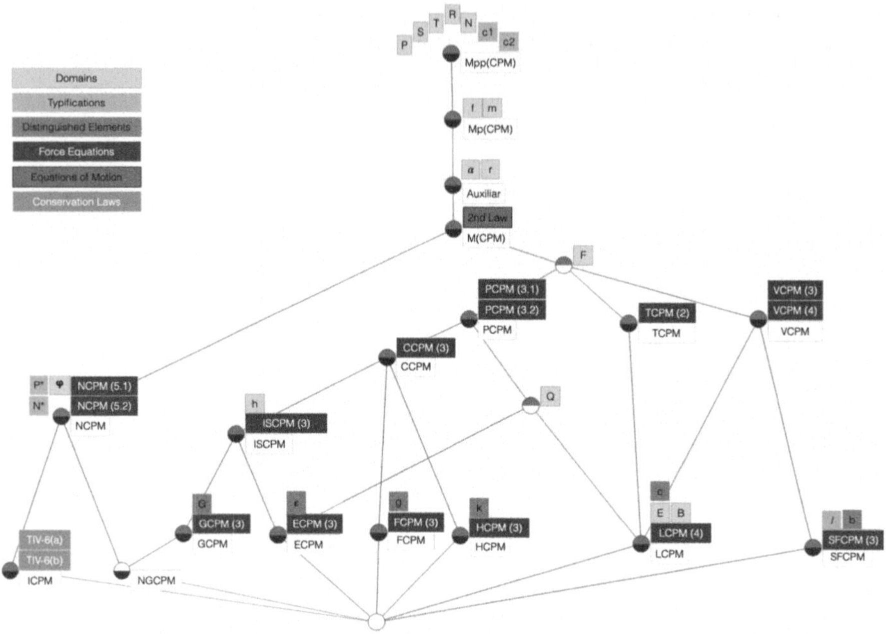

Fig. 3. Theoretical lattice for Classical Particle Mechanics built from the formal context presented in Table 1, using Concept Explorer. Objects are labeled according to the actual models of theoretical elements, as presented in Fig. 2. Attribute labels represent the premises presented by the structuralist reconstruction in [4]. The partial potential model, the potential model and the auxiliary model are also included in the context. CMPCM, CECPM, MCPM are not included here due to missing data in the original text. We can notice that besides the infimum node, there are two extra nodes in the theory-lattice that are not in Fig. 2, corresponding to the external force and the electric charge. We can also identify theorizations, when lower levels present a new domain, colored in light gray, or the distinguished position of the equation of motion (gray), as opposed to the specialized equations (dark gray) in lower levels. Here P: a set of particles or mass-points; S: space points; c_1, c_2 are coordinatizations of time and space respectively and separately; s: distance function; $\mathbb{R}$: real numbers; $\mathbb{N}$: natural numbers referring to dimensions; T: time points; f: sum of forces; m: mass; α: a real-valued time coordinate (after applying the time coordinatization c_1); $r(p, \alpha)$: position of particle p at real-valued time α; F: external force; E: electric field; B: magnetic field; Q: electric charge; c: velocity of light; G: constant of gravitation; g: gravitational acceleration; h: a positive real-valued function encoding the interaction strength between two particles; k: spring constant b: friction parameter; l: the exponent allowing different friction regimes; ϵ: dielectric constant in vacuum; $P* \subseteq P$; $\mathbb{N}^* \subseteq \mathbb{N}$ enumerates indices for counterbalanced forces; φ relation expressing that forces are counterbalanced.

6 Meeting the Exploratorium

At the *Exploratorium*, a simplified theoretical element is considered:

$$T^* = \langle K^* \rangle ,$$

$$K^* = \langle M_{pp}, M_p, M, M_e \rangle$$

where K^* can consist of any of the known classes of models. We have not considered yet ligatures, intentional applications, dates, or names.

Data for the *Exploratorium* is sourced mainly from Michael Friedman's *Foundations of Space-Time Theories* [16], Mario Bunge's *Foundations of Physics* [6], Clifford Will's *Theory and Experiment in Gravitational Physics* [33], and Farahoni and Sotiriou's *f(R) Theories* [26]. Not all of these are structuralist reconstructions per se, but they follow many of their criteria, facilitating the selection of the corresponding attributes.

To date, the Exploratorium web page enables users to delve into ten interactive visualizations, encompassing over 50 theories of space-time and gravitation. It facilitates the location of groups of theories, their foundations, and classes of models. Through hierarchical networks, users learn the logic of interconnected concepts, becoming adept at navigating the conceptual structure of physical theories. It has always been well received as a fresh view to understand the internal structure of physical theories, their foundations and commonalities, and a synthesis of the vast sea of proposed alternative theories of gravitation.

The Exploratorium has been of special interest for science communicators who find in concept networks a creative way of aiding our understanding of theories. It has been presented in several forums to diverse audiences as a tool for conceptual exploration, since clicking on labels will provide pop-up infoboxes with extra information and hyperlinks. This asset encourages experts to navigate in more detail the produced network and validate results. By showcasing dozens of alternative theories of gravitation, it has effectively communicated the diversity of scientific exploration beyond mainstream narratives. This has, in turn, emphasized the importance of providing fair consideration to alternative theories, encouraging a more inclusive, non-dogmatic, and open-minded approach to scientific inquiry.

7 What Follows

We have seen that structuralism and FCA are both set-based theories that aim to semantically classify domains. Both theoretical networks and concept lattices have hierarchical, transitive, reflexive, and antisymmetric relations, which makes us conclude that we can make use of all the analytical power of FCA in the internal study of scientific theories.

For the FCA community, metatheoretical structuralism may show a way to present and interpret data in a more rational way, understanding the classes of attributes that are more likely to appear in certain circumstances. Visualization techniques developed at the example of the Exploratorium with the goal of communicating hierarchical dependencies exhibited by metatheoretic structuralism could also prove to be inspirational, in particular in order to make conceptual data more accessible to non-expert users outside the community.

For the structuralist family, FCA is an open window for major lines of research on theoretical network analysis and exploration. It will surely benefit from the use of new definitions based on ordered pairs of intentions and

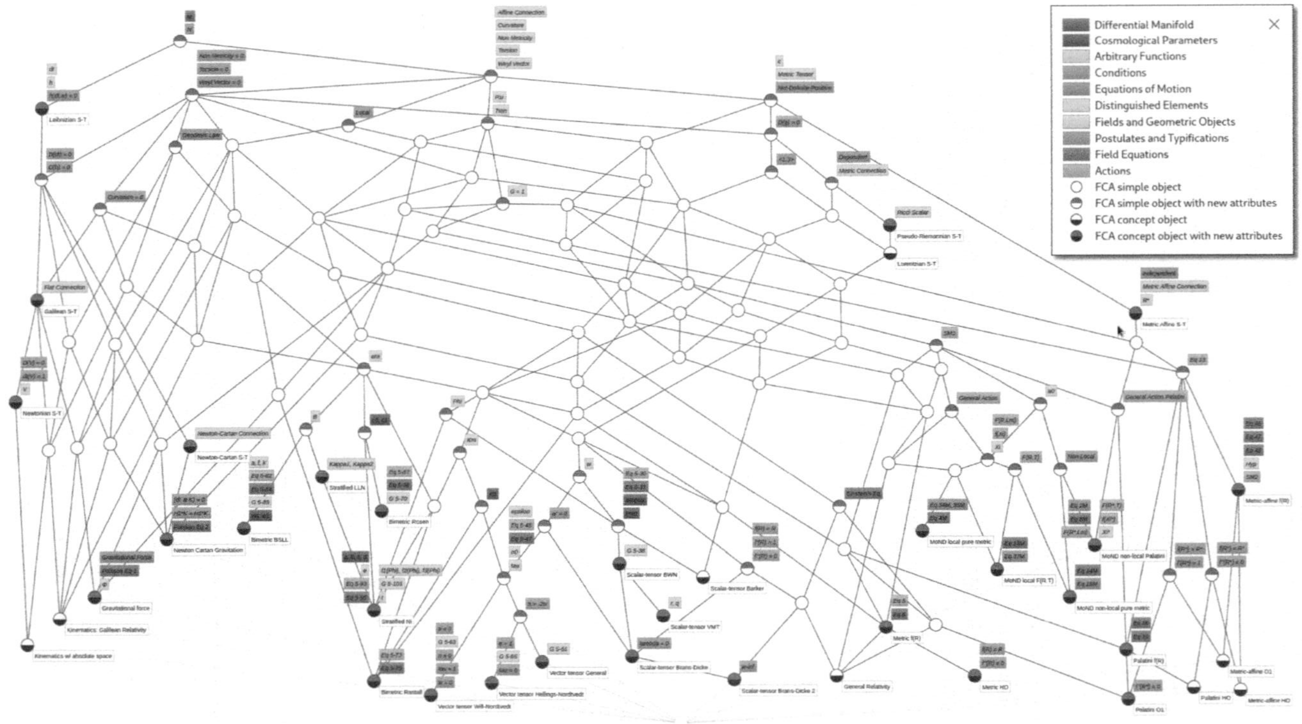

Fig. 4. Holon of gravitational theories made up of 32 actual models and six partial potential models. The upper nodes correspond to topological and geometrical matters where many of the domains are defined. Physical attributes rest in lower nodes where field equations and constrictions are more frequent. Several branches can be identified as metric theories, MoNDian theories and metric affine theories. There is a temporal ordering too, being the earlier proposals resting in the left side of the image, while more recent proposals rest in the right side of the figure. This configuration is due to the parsimony followed by scientific and concept development. This network can be better visualized at https://remo.cua.uam.mx/vis/Exploratorium/theories/en/holon/index.html

extensions and not just extensions. FCA produces visualizations of theoretical networks that comply with all the structuralist requirements and offers tools for network analysis that have not been used just yet in structuralist studies, such as concept distancing, separation indexes, concept probabilities, etc. Current efforts are now directed to diachronic analysis of theoretical elements, looking for some indicators of theoretical progress.

Databases collected and curated for these kinds of science maps may be uploaded to entity stores such as Wolfram Mathematica's entity store, where automated functions may call information and recreate relationship graphs. Artificial intelligence may also be used to look for data, construct and explore contexts, label nodes or solve implications. For the moment, only guided explorations with AI (ChatGPT) have proven useful, since it may not follow strict logical reasoning, may get confused on which set of objects we are considering, give wrong answers to please the user, get confused with notation, etc. Nevertheless, these are problems that more specialized AIs will quickly overcome.

Acknowledgements. This project continues to be developed at the Instituto de Investigaciones en Matemáticas Aplicadas y en Sistemas (IIMAS-UNAM) thanks to SECIHTI support through the program "Estancias Posdoctorales por México Convocatoria 2023(1)" with the application No. 5991306, CVU: 232297 and under the supervision of Dr. Eduardo Robles Belmont.

References

1. Abreu, C., Lorenzano, P., Moulines, C.U.: Bibliography of structuralism III (1995-2012, and additions). Metatheoria–Revista de Filosofía e Historia de la Ciencia **3**(2), 1–36 (2013)
2. Abreu, C., Lorenzano, P.: Conversaciones con C. Ulises Moulines. Metatheoria – Revista de Filosofía e Historia de la Ciencia **11**(1), 1–31 (2020). https://metatheoria.unq.edu.ar/index.php/m/article/view/262
3. Balzer, W., Sneed, J.D., Moulines, C.U.: Structuralist Knowledge Representation: Paradigmatic Examples. Poznań studies in the philosophy of the sciences and the humanities. Rodopi (2000)
4. Balzer, W., Moulines, C., Sneed, J.D.: Una arquitectonica para la ciencia: el programa estructuralista. Universidad Nacional de Quilmes (2012)
5. Borner, K., Record, E., Theriault, T.: Atlas of Macroscopes, Interactive Data Visualizations. MIT Press (2025)
6. Bunge, M.: Foundations of Physics. Springer Tracts in Natural Philosophy. Springer, Cham (1967)
7. Bunge, M.: Semantics I: sense and reference, In: Treatise on Basic Philosophy. Springer, Cham (2012)
8. Creath, R.: Logical empiricism. In: Zalta, E.N., Nodelman, U. (eds.) The Stanford Encyclopedia of Philosophy (Winter 2023). https://plato.stanford.edu/archives/win2023/entries/logical-empiricism/
9. Díez, J.A., Moulines, C.U.: Theories as nets: combinatorial measurement theory. In: Humphreys, P. (ed.) Patrick Suppes, Mathematical Philosopher, pp. 275–297. Kluwer Ac. P., Dordrecht (1994)

10. Espinosa, M., Casanueva, M.: Retículos teóricos y el análisis de conceptos formales, herramientas para el estructuralismo metateórico. Theoria: Int. J. Theory Hist. Found. Sci. (2023). https://doi.org/10.1387/theoria.24078
11. Espinosa, M.: Visualizaciones de retículos conceptuales de teorías del espacio-tiempo y la gravitación mediante el análisis de conceptos formales. Ph.D. thesis, Universidad Autónoma Metropolitana-Cuajimalpa, (2022)
12. Espinosa, M.: Retículos conceptuales de teorías físicas: El Exploratorium. Lilian Al-Chueyr Pereira Martins, Luz Marina Duque Martínez, Lucía Federico, Germán Guerrero Pino, María de las Mercedes O'Lery (eds.) Universidad del Valle, Colombia (2023)
13. Espinosa, M.: The space-time theories exploratorium. In: Scientific Legacy of Professor Zbigniew Oziewicz, pp. 225–245. World Scientific (2023)
14. Espinosa, M.: Mapping gravity with hierarchical networks. In Proceedings: 15th Marcel Grossmann Meeting on Recent Developments in Theoretical and Experimental General Relativity, Astrophysics, and Relativistic Field Theories (2018)
15. Federico, L., Giri, L.: Organizing nursing knowledge from metatheoretical structuralism's point of view. In: Philosophy of Science in the 21st Century: Contributions of Metatheoretical Structuralism. Universidade Federal de Santa Catarina. Núcleo de Epistemologia e Lógica (2023)
16. Friedman, M.: Foundations of Space-Time Theories: Relativistic Physics and Philosophy of Science. Princeton University Press (1983)
17. Ganter, B., Obiedkov, S.: Conceptual Exploration. Springer, Heidelberg (2016)
18. Ganter, B., Wille, R.: Formal Concept Analysis: Mathematical Foundations. Springer, Heidelberg (1999)
19. Giovannini, E.N.: David Hilbert y los fundamentos de la geometría (1891–1905). College Publications (2015)
20. Nagel, E.: The Structure of Science: Problems in the Logic of Scientific Explanation. Harcourt, Brace and Company, New York (1961)
21. Méndez, D., Casanueva, M.: Representación de dominios teóricos mediante retículos: el dominio de la herencia biológica durante el periodo 1865-1902. In: Agora, Papeles de Filosofia **31**(2), 109–141 (2012)
22. Moulines, C.: Tipología axiomática de las teorías empíricas. In: Crítica: Revista Hispanoamericana de Filosofía **17**(51), 41–69 (1985)
23. Reichenbach, H.: La Filosofía Científica. Filosofía Series. Fondo de Cultura Económcia (1990)
24. Romero, G.E.: Scientific Philosophy. Springer, Cham (2018)
25. Sneed, J.D.: The Logical Structure of Mathematical Physics, revised edn. Reidel, Dordrecht (1979)
26. Sotiriou, T.P., Faraoni, V.: f(R) theories of gravity. Rev. Mod. Phys. **82**, 451–497 (2010)
27. Suppe, F.: The search for philosophic understanding of scientific theories. Struct. Sci. Theories **2**, 1–241 (1977)
28. Suppe, F.: The Semantic Conception of Theories and Scientific Realism. University of Illinois Press, Urbana (1989)
29. Suppes, P.: Some remarks on problems and methods in the philosophy of science. Philos. Sci. **21**(3), 242–248 (1954)
30. Suppes, P.: Introduction to Logic. Van Nostrand, New York (1957)
31. Suppes, P.: A comparison of the meaning and uses of models in mathematics and the empirical sciences. Synthese **12**, 287–301 (1960). https://doi.org/10.1007/BF00485107

32. Tarski, A.: The semantic conception of truth: and the foundations of semantics. Philos. Phenomenological Res. **4**(3), 341–376 (1944). https://doi.org/10.2307/2102968
33. Will, C.: Theory and Experiment in Gravitational Physics. Cambridge University Press (1993)

Qualitative and Quantitative Analyses of *C. elegans'* Perception with Concept Lattices as Information Channels

Emma Reyner-Fuentes[1(✉)], Carmen Peláez-Moreno[1], and Francisco J. Valverde-Albacete[2]

[1] Depto. Teoría de Señal y Comunicaciones, Univ. Carlos III de Madrid, Madrid, Spain
emma.reyner@alumnos.uc3m.es, carmen@tsc.uc3m.es

[2] Depto. Teoría de Señal y Comunicaciones y Sistemas Telemáticos y Computación, Univ. Rey Juan Carlos, Madrid, Spain
francisco.valverde@urjc.es

Abstract. In this paper we continue with our exploration of Concept Lattices as Channels of information by analysing the quantitative content of formal contexts. We correlate the qualitative information provided by concept lattices with quantitative information described by an information-theoretical balance equation and visualised by entropy triangles in multi-valued formal contexts. Using the technique of $\mathcal{K}$-Formal Concept Analysis ($\mathcal{K}$-FCA), we extract binary formal contexts by sweeping in a threshold parameter φ, but the choice of this parameter for an optimal visualisation of the information contained in the formal context is difficult and prone to error. With entropy triangles we can visualise informational quantities and therefore choose values for φ so that the concept lattice captures the most information possible. This is shown and validated on real data from an odorant perception task about the nervous system of *Caenorhabditis elegans*.

1 Introduction: Information Transmission by Means of Signs

A number of entities in our cognitive sphere—call them *signs*, $S \subseteq K^G \times K^M$—have a dual nature $S = (\overline{a}, \overline{b})$: one of its natures—let's call it the *significant*, $\overline{a} \in K^G$—determines the other—let's call it the *meaning* $\overline{b} \in K^M$—and *vice-versa*, and this dual nature can be efficiently captured as a relation between them that we call *(mutual) determination* $I \subseteq K^{G \times M}$. The sets G and M may receive multiple names depending on the modelling application: physical indices, features or patterns for G and meaning features or semes for M, with K just being a number-like domain.

For whatever reasons, each of these natures may be differently *selected for* by cognitive processes: e.g. significants are used for *physical transmission and/or sensory reception*, while meaning is used for *understanding*, although we leave such processes without further characterization. Since the sign relation is *conventional*—subject to convention—but must be *realised*—made personal by every different user of signs—the following situation depicted in Fig. 1 is bound to appear:

- User 1 will try to convey meaning $\overline{y}$,
- by lexically *encoding* it as significant $\overline{x}$.

P. Cellier et al. (Eds.): CONCEPTS 2025, LNAI 15941, pp. 264–280, 2025.
https://doi.org/10.1007/978-3-032-03364-2_17

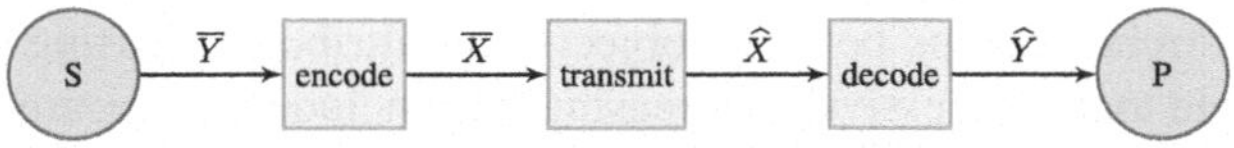

Fig. 1. Basic transmission of information associated with signs.

- Through a communication channel this can be *communicated and transformed* into $\hat{x}$ in the sensory apparatus of user 2,
- and finally decoded as meaning $\hat{y}$ by this user.

With other researchers we believe that mutual determination can be qualitatively modelled with Formal Concept Analysis (FCA) [8,14], and we have recently proposed an accompanying quantitative model [19]. Note that our use of vector notation for each nature is consistent with our later suggesting that they can be modelled using FCA, since this is just linear algebra over a fancy algebra $\mathcal{K}$ with support in K [18], including Boolean algebra [20], idempotent semifields [12] and fuzzy semirings [2,4].

In this paper we would like to explore both qualitatively and quantitatively the transmission relation between different significants $\overline{x}$ and $\hat{x}$, that is, *not* mutually determined, in principle. This is relevant, for instance, for the transformation of representations in DNN (Deep Neural Networks), or, in our examples, for the representation of sensory inputs to brains.

2 Previous Work

2.1 $\mathcal{K}$-Formal Concept Analysis

$\mathcal{K}$-FCA (Formal Concept Analysis over idempotent semifields) extends classical FCA by generalizing binary object–attribute relations into *graded* ones, where associations can take values from a complete idempotent semifield $\overline{\mathcal{K}}$. Instead of asking whether an object has an attribute (as in classical FCA), $\mathcal{K}$-FCA asks *to what degree* the object exhibits the attribute. This allows for richer, quantitative modeling of data. A key parameter, the *threshold of existence* φ, controls the minimum strength of association required for an object–attribute pair to be considered. By adjusting φ, one can explore the data at different levels of granularity.

Formally, the $\mathcal{K}$-FCA framework considers a context $\mathbb{K} = (G, M, R)$ where $R \in \overline{\mathcal{K}}^{G\times M}$ is a relation with values in an idempotent semifield $\overline{\mathcal{K}} = \langle K, \oplus, \otimes, \bot, e, \top\rangle$. For vectors $x \in \overline{\mathcal{K}}^G$ and $y \in \overline{\mathcal{K}}^M$, a dot product is defined as $\langle x \mid R \mid y\rangle = x^\top \otimes R \otimes y$. The associated Galois connection is constructed via the polar operations:

$$(x)^{\uparrow}_{R,\varphi} = \bigvee\{y \in M \mid \langle x \mid R \mid y\rangle_{\overline{\mathcal{K}}} \le \varphi\}, \quad (y)^{\downarrow}_{R,\varphi} = \bigvee\{x \in G \mid \langle x \mid R \mid y\rangle_{\overline{\mathcal{K}}} \le \varphi\}.$$

A pair (a, b) is a *φ-formal concept* if $(a)^{\uparrow}_{R,\varphi} = b$ and $(b)^{\downarrow}_{R,\varphi} = a$. The set of all such pairs forms the *φ-concept lattice*, denoted $\mathfrak{B}^{\varphi}(G, M, R)_{\overline{\mathcal{K}}}$.

By sweeping the threshold φ across its domain, a series of lattices can be generated, revealing how the structure of concepts evolves. This approach enables a multiscale exploration of data complexity. When working within the $\overline{\mathbb{R}}_{\max,+}$ semiring, we can explore *negative* relationships between objects and attributes, starting from the most negative threshold and progressively increasing it to include less negative associations. Analogously, when using the $\overline{\mathbb{R}}_{\min,+}$ semiring, we explore *positive* relationships, starting from the highest threshold and progressively lowering it to include weaker positive associations. In both explorations, analyzing the evolution of the number of concepts as a function of the threshold reveals the underlying structure and complexity of the data.

An example of what a basic $\mathcal{K}$-formal context would look like is presented in Table 1. The sample lattices obtained when sweeping the threshold of existence, ϕ, are presented in Fig. 2. However, a deeper and more thorough explanation on $\mathcal{K}$-FCA can be found in [15].

Table 1. Example of a $\overline{\mathbb{R}}_{\min,+}$ context

$R(g,m)$	m_1	m_2	m_3
g_1	1	0.4	0.2
g_2	0.1	0.9	0.8

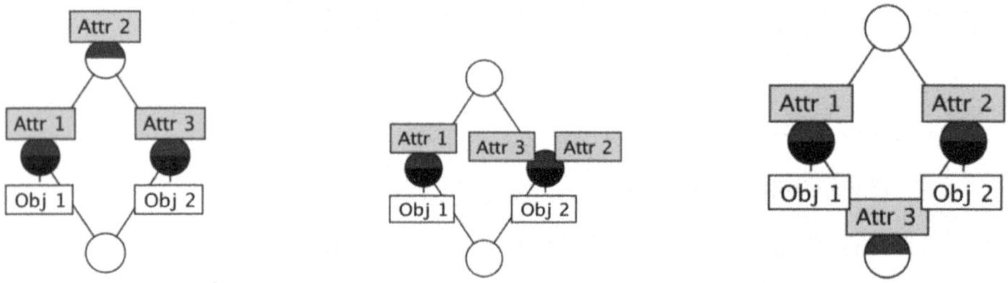

(a) $\phi = 0.3$ (b) $\phi = 0.5$ (c) $\phi = 0.9$

Fig. 2. Evolution of the lattice structure for different ϕs in the $\overline{\mathbb{R}}_{\min,+}$ framework. As the threshold increases, only stronger object–attribute connections are retained.

2.2 Measuring Information by Means of Entropy Triangles

Entropy triangles are *quantitative and visual* tools to measure the information in random variables or vectors. They were originally proposed in [17] to measure the performance in classification tasks, but have since been extended to quantify and visually represent multivariate information sources [16] and channels [13]. Formal *contexts* as sources of information were previously introduced in [19].

The Source Multivariate Entropy Triangle (SMET) is designed to visualise the *distribution of entropy* for a source of information, a random vector $\overline{X} \sim P_{\overline{X}}$ with marginals $X_i \sim P_{X_i}$ providing a geometric representation of how information is stored

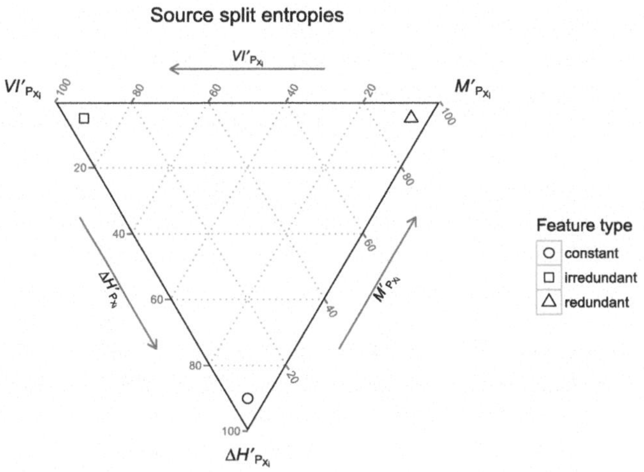

Fig. 3. Schematic ternary representation of SMET analysis.

and shared across the random variables in the vector. This triangle is constructed using three key entropy-based components or *entropic coordinates* that form a 2-simplex [16]:

$$\Delta H'_{P_{X_i}} + M'_{P_{X_i}} + VI'_{P_{X_i}} = 1, \forall i \in I \tag{1}$$

hence the SMET represents these coordinates in a 2-d planar triangle, Fig. 3, where:

- $VI'_{P_{X_i}}$ represents the normalized the *(normalized) privative information* of each random variable in the random vectors.
- $M'_{P_{X_i}}$ measures the *(normalized) bound information*[1] between elements, revealing the extent to which knowledge about one entity reduces uncertainty about others.
- $\Delta H'_{P_{X_i}} =$ measures *(normalized) distance (of P_{X_i}) from uniformity.*

To understand the meaning of these figures, we must first clarify what each region of the SMET triangle means:

- **Proximity to $\Delta H'_{P_{X_i}} = 1, M'_{P_{X_i}} = 0$ (lower vertex of the entropy triangle):** Points located near the lower vertex of the triangle correspond to scenarios where the feature under analysis exhibits deterministic behavior—either consistently active or inactive. In such cases, the feature does not contribute to information transmission, as its state is entirely predictable and lacks entropy.
- **Proximity to $\Delta H'_{P_{X_i}} = 1, M'_{P_{X_i}} \neq 0$ (right region of the entropy triangle):** As data points shift towards the right region of the triangle, bound information increases, signifying strong statistical dependencies between elements in the system. This region is associated with high redundancy, where distinct features (such

[1] Technically this is the normalized addition of the total and dual total correlations [16].

as neurons or odorants) convey overlapping or correlated information. This redundancy may facilitate a more robust encoding but also implies that certain features are not contributing unique information.

- **Proximity to** $VI'_{P_{X_i}} = 1, \Delta H'_{P_{X_i}} \neq 1$ **(left region of the entropy triangle):** Data points near the left region of the triangle indicate a random variable In this scenario, each feature contributes maximally to the overall information content. This configuration supports an efficient encoding scheme where information is maximally preserved and ambiguity is minimized, but less robust to transmission errors.

The Channel Multivariate Entropy Triangle (CMET). While the SMET describes how information is structured within random vectors, the CMET focuses on the *transmission of information* between input $\overline{X}$ and output $\overline{Y}$ random vectors. Again, this triangle is constructed using three key entropy-based components that form a 2-simplex:

$$\Delta H_{P_{\overline{XY}}} + 2 * I_{P_{\overline{XY}}} + VI_{P_{\overline{XY}}} = H_{U_{\overline{X}}} + H_{U_{\overline{Y}}} \tag{2}$$

- $H_{U_{\overline{X}}}$ and $H_{U_{\overline{Y}}}$ would be the entropies of $\overline{x}$ and $\overline{Y}$ if they were uniform.
- $\Delta H_{P_{\overline{XY}}} = \Delta H_{P_{\overline{X}}} + \Delta H_{P_{\overline{Y}}}$ describes how far input and output distributions are from being uniform individually, e.g. $\Delta H_{P_{\overline{X}}} = H_{U_{\overline{X}}} - H_{P_{\overline{X}}}$.
- $VI_{P_{\overline{XY}}} = H_{P_{\overline{X}|\overline{Y}}} + H_{P_{\overline{Y}|\overline{X}}}$, measures the sum of remanent entropy in each $\overline{X}$ and $\overline{Y}$ individually.
- $2 * I_{P_{\overline{XY}}}$ represents the shared information between input and output.

We typically represent the *split triangles*, normalised by $H_{U_{\overline{X}}}, H_{U_{\overline{Y}}}$, respectively:

$$\Delta H'_{P_{\overline{X}}} + I'_{P_{\overline{XY}}} + H'_{P_{\overline{X}|\overline{Y}}} = 1 \qquad \Delta H'_{P_{\overline{Y}}} + I'_{P_{\overline{XY}}} + H'_{P_{\overline{Y}|\overline{X}}} = 1 \tag{3}$$

in which both input and output-related entropies can be displayed apart within the 2-d planar triangle, as shown in Fig. 4:

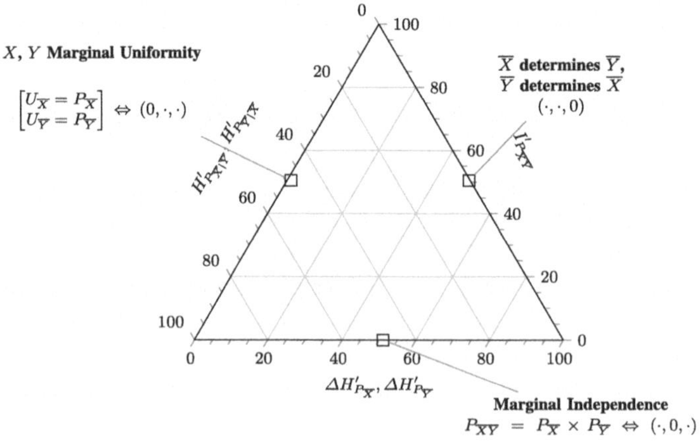

Fig. 4. Schematic ternary representation of CMET analysis.

Analogously to SMET, the geometric layout of points within CMET corresponds to different information transmission regimes within a multivariate system:

- **The apex of the triangle** is associated with configurations in which mutual information between input and output is maximized relative to the total entropy budget, suggesting strong determination between them. In the context of neural encoding of sensory stimuli, such as in olfaction, this region reflects a situation where each output (odorant) is determined by specific combinations of neural activation patterns, facilitating robust discrimination, and *vice-versa.*
- **Left-hand side of the triangle** is where points with long remanent entropy lie. This may either imply failure to capture the variability of the input, or failure to transmit it, possibly due to noisy mappings or non-informative input patterns. The closer to the bottom, the more the system behaves as a random (forgetting) transformation from input to output.
- **Right-hand side of the triangle** describes configurations with no remanent information but a variable degree of uniformity (maximum informativeness) the less so the closer to the bottom.

3 Findings: Concept-Lattices-as-Information-Channels

In this section we put forward the analysis leading to our main finding: *formal contexts and their concept lattices can be seen as information channels*, a perspective we call *Concept-Lattices-as-Information-Channels (CLaIC).*

3.1 Mutual Determination Is Enough to Model Information Transmission

Figure 1, allows us to see the formal similarities, e.g. between transmitting $\overline{x}$ and receiving $\hat{x}$, and between receiving $\hat{x}$ and decoding $\hat{y}$. Apparent differences would be:

- A distinction in the *type* of information being represented: the physical one appealing to the senses, and the semantic one appealing to our understanding capabilities.
- A nuance of "causation" or "induction" that seems to be merely physical in the case of physical representations, but something more "psychological" in the case of meaning [5].
- Also, we may claim that there is no mutual determination between physical representations like the one within the sign relation described in the Introduction.

But, the type of information cannot be an objection to an inclusive formal modelling using dual determination that can cater to many types thereof. In fact, *we can decide to focus only the forward-determination of the model—from objects to attributes—and deem that backwards determination comes for free.*

Note that this also solves the issue of what "nature" determines the causation of the dual one: *whichever we decide to consider the "forward one"*. For instance, in *encoding problems*, it is the meaning which precedes the significant, while in *decoding problems* it is the physical representation that is primary. Both cases, though, can be modelled by the dually-determined model of formal contexts and concept lattices.

Likewise, representation of acoustic channels by means of their confusion matrices [7], for instance—or indeed communication channels by means of conditional probability tables [10], easily transformed into joint distributions—debunks the idea that physical representations are not mutually determined: all accept as representations weighted bipartite graphs—one of the cryptomorhisms of formal contexts [1]—and in our opinion this is actually the mathematical basis for dual determination, or at least a good way to look at it.

3.2 Information Transmission in Concept Lattices

The standard framework for describing communication channels is Information Theory (IT) [10], intimately related to applied Probability Theory. For the purpose of measuring information transmission we have to describe a joint probability model, and we introduce the following *approximate* model:

- Consider an input random vector of binary variables $G = [g_i]_{i \in I}$, and an output random vector of binary variables $M = [m_j]_{j \in J}$. The *decoding events* we are modelling are "receiving an input binary word $\overline{a} \in 2^G$ and decoding an output binary word $\overline{b} \in 2^M$".
- The problem is then to estimate the joint probability model $P_{GM}(\overline{a}, \overline{b})$. For this purpose, suppose that we have measured co-occurrence data for such vectors $\{(\overline{a}^{\psi}, \overline{b}^{\psi})\}_{\psi \in \Psi}$, and that these can be completed to two dually ordered lattices. Then, we can summarise the data in the form of a formal context: $\mathbb{K} = (G, M, I)$.
- Finally, the estimation proceeds by considering the contigency matrix $M(\overline{a}, \overline{b})$ of all possible concepts in $\mathfrak{B}(G, M, I)$. For this procedure notice that:
  - Despite the actual data, we extend the estimation of the probability to *all* the extents and intents of the formal context.
  - We can modify the probabilities by the prior distribution on extents and intents observed.
  - We may use smoothing techniques for *hapax legomena*, if so deemed.
- Once we have $P_{GM}(\overline{a}, \overline{b})$, we can estimate the SMET and CMET for the random vectors G, M and the channel, as per the techniques in Sect. 2.2.

Notice that,

1. In practice, recording tabular data works on the assumption that the M dimensions of observation are fixed and we subject the system to selective input, e.g. inputting one $g_i = 1$ at a time and then measuring its output $\overline{b}(g_i)$. In this manner we accrue data row-by-row. Typically this is then *conditioned data*, i.e. it resembles $P_{M|G}(\overline{b}|\overline{a} = \delta(g_i))$ where $\delta(g_i)$ is Kronecker's delta. But we can multiply this conditioned distribution by a prior on the g_i to obtain the joint probability. This prior distribution is dictated by the experimental presentation of stimuli.
2. Non-binary data can be subjected to binarization via thresholding or some other principled procedure.
3. It is the nature of the application that tells us whether the lattices are both increasing or one increasing and the other decreasing. We may thus choose any of the four possible types of Galois connections or adjunctions to model the co-ordering of the lattices [11].

3.3 Application: Measuring Information in Sensory Tasks

In this section we use CLaIC to describe the information contained in a data table recording the presentation of stimuli at different concentrations and the activities evoked in the neurons of *C.elegans*.

Data Description. The dataset includes neural responses from 11 bilateral chemosensory neuron pairs, identified as ADF, ADL, ASE, ASG, ASH, ASI, ASJ, ASK, AWA, AWB, and AWC [6]. The list of odorants can be consulted in [6]. Responses were recorded during exposure to and removal of odorants at three concentrations: 10^{-4}, 10^{-5}, and 10^{-6}, referred to as *concentrations*[2]. The analysis only considers *pairs* as previous studies show strong correlations between left and right neurons in each pair [3].

Neural activity is recorded as the peak response during odorant exposure. The temporal trace of activity is processed to identify the maximum absolute value, preserving the sign, and averaging it over a 4s neighborhood around the peak. This preprocessing does not differentiate between *ON* responses (activation during odorant presentation) and *OFF* responses (activation upon odorant removal). The trace represents the average of multiple instances recorded under the same conditions.

Contextualization. Let G be the set of odorants ($n = 23$) and M the set of neuronal pairs ($p = 11$). The data is captured as matrices over completed idempotent semifields, $R \in \overline{\mathcal{K}}^{n\times p}$, interpreted as linear mappings between semivector spaces. To model the last step of Fig. 1, we define:

- A column vector in $\mathcal{X} = \overline{\mathcal{K}}^{n\times 1}$ as a *$\mathcal{K}$-set of odorants.*
- A column vector in $\mathcal{X} = \overline{\mathcal{K}}^{p\times 1}$ as a *$\mathcal{K}$-set of neuron activations.*
- A row vector in $\overline{\mathcal{K}}^{1\times p}$ as an *odorant activity profile* (odorant presence).
- A row vector in $\overline{\mathcal{K}}^{1\times n}$ as a *neuronal activation profile* (responses to odorants).

Therefore lattices or systems of extents will be called *lattices of odorants (stimuli)* and lattices or systems of intents will be called *lattices of neurons (or activations).*

In previous work we revealed complementary aspects of the neural code by exploring the data through the lens of $\overline{\mathbb{R}}_{\min,+}$ and $\overline{\mathbb{R}}_{\max,+}$ semirings within the $\mathcal{K}$-FCA framework [9]. $\overline{\mathbb{R}}_{\min,+}$ exploration, illustrated in Fig. 5a, captures excitatory associations between odorants and neurons, enabling us to identify specific patterns of neural activation in response to particular chemical stimuli. In contrast, the $\overline{\mathbb{R}}_{\max,+}$ exploration of Fig. 5b focuses on revealing how certain odorants inhibit neural responses. This dual analysis allowed us to disentangle the dynamics of the sensorium, offering a novel lattice-based view of how olfactory information is functionally structured in *C. elegans*.

[2] Actually, there is data also for 10^{-7}, and 10^{-8} but measures are too weak and after preliminary analysis we decided not to use them for the purposes of this paper.

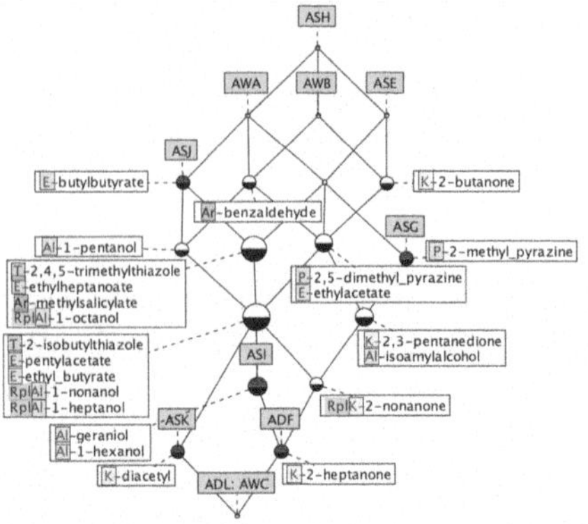

(a) Example lattice for $\overline{\mathbb{R}}_{\min,+}$ analysis at 10^{-4} concentration with $\phi = 0.259$

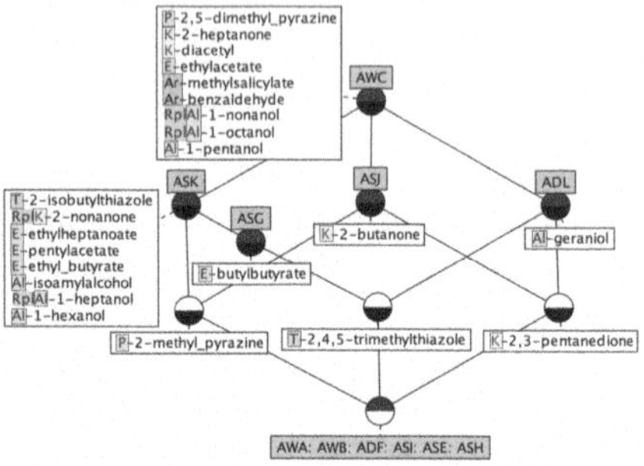

(b) Example lattice for $\overline{\mathbb{R}}_{\max,+}$ analysis at 10^{-4} concentration with $\varphi = 0.0375$

Fig. 5. Example lattices for $\overline{\mathbb{R}}_{\min,+}$ and $\overline{\mathbb{R}}_{\max,+}$ analysis at 10^{-4} concentration from our previous work in [9].

A critical challenge in applying $\mathcal{K}$-FCA is the selection of a free parameter, the *threshold of existence* ϕ. Based on expert intuition and prior experimentation, in our previous work we focused on the three most "relevant" ϕ values: $\phi = 0.257$, $\phi = 0.575$ and $\phi = 0.145$. These thresholds yield concept lattices that reveal meaningful qualitative structures, as introduced above [9].

In this study, we focus mainly on the *quantitative analysis* of the information content of odorant and neuron lattices obtained by $\overline{\mathbb{R}}_{\min,+}$-analysis of the stimuli presented at 10^{-4} concentration. Our goal in this work is to *quantify* the information actually contained in lattices of odorants and neurons by using entropy-based representations. We use the entropy triangles of Sect. 2.2, the SMET and CMET, to explore how information is contained in neuron and odorant lattices, and transmitted by concept lattices.

The Information Balances in Systems of Extents and Intents corresponding to lattices of neurons and odorants are depicted side by side for the different concentrations of odorants in Fig. 6. Each shading point within the entropy triangles represents a formal context and lattice constructed for a specific value of the threshold parameter ϕ, hence the accumulation of points shows regions in SMET space where most concept lattices for odorants (left) and neurons (right) lie.

The lowest apex corresponds to situations in which all attributes are either consistently present (for lower ϕ, reflecting a more permissive threshold for existence) or entirely absent (for higher ϕ, corresponding to a more stringent threshold). In both cases, the resulting lattices convey minimal information, as their structure becomes overly homogeneous.

Across concentrations we see a grouping of odorant lattice entropies towards lower concentrations perhaps indicative of the lack of variability of responses due to lowered *causes*. This tendency is inverted in neuron lattices, which are the *results* of stimulation, whereby we see a wider distribution of responses in the lowest concentration at 10^{-6}.

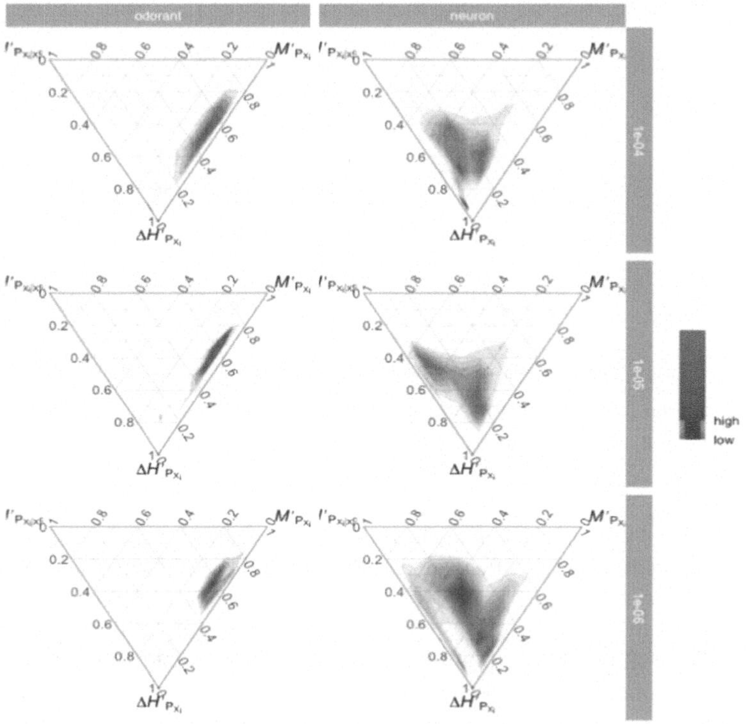

Fig. 6. Odorant (left) and neuron (right) SMETs showing the exploration of all ϕ at different concentrations.

But the most striking difference between lattices of odorants and neurons—across all concentrations—is that the former are collected close to the right margin of the triangle suggesting very redundant information between different odorants. This is good in controlled experiments, since we want to repeatedly obtain similar results for *similar stimuli* and these stimuli seem to be so. However, for lattice of results (neural activations) we obtain much more uncorrelated outputs in the neurons. This is of interest, in principle, since it may be showing a tendency towards decorrelation among neural responses showing either specialization of individual neurons upon chemically-related groups of odorants for univocal coding, or widespread decorrelation in distributed coding (see below).

Henceforth we focus in concentration 10^{-4} which produces the specific evolution with ϕ shown in Fig. 7. This allows us to visualize the evolution of information content across the entire $\overline{\mathbb{R}}_{\min,+}$ exploration. We observe that both the lowest and highest values of ϕ are located near the lower vertex of the triangle. As ϕ increases from its lowest values, the corresponding points ascend within the triangle, indicating a rise in entropy and, consequently, in the informational richness of the lattices. It is important to note that these points represent the average entropy across the 11 neurons (right) and 23 odorants (left) included in the $\overline{\mathbb{R}}_{\min,+}$ analysis.

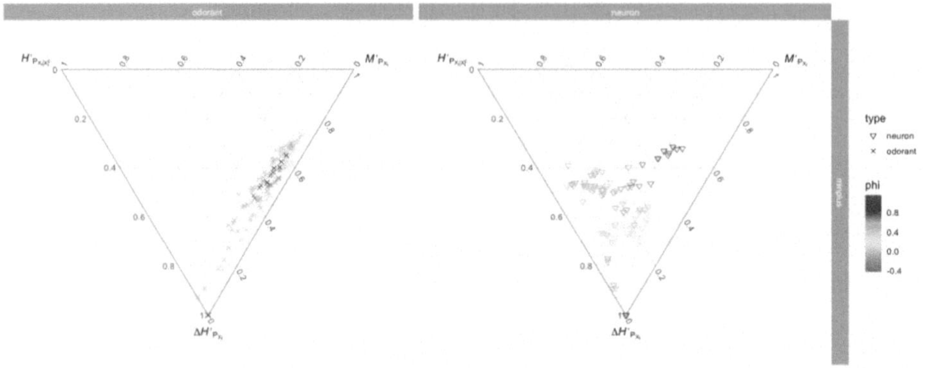

Fig. 7. Detail of the evolution of the *average* SMETs for odorants and neurons for Min-plus analysis at an odorant concentration of 10^{-4}.

Consider the lattice of neuron activations to the right of Fig. 7. Certain neurons, such as AWC, exhibit deterministic behavior (e.g., always inactive), which in turn pulls the overall average downward. Notably, a dense cluster of points emerges in the central region of the triangle, corresponding to ϕ values approximately in the range $[0.15, 0.6]$. The position of these points—central within the triangle—implies a compromise between redundancy and specificity: the neurons are neither highly redundant nor entirely uncorrelated. Instead, they encode complementary information that supports the discrimination of odorants in combination. This configuration is consistent with known biological mechanisms whereby odor identity is encoded through distributed patterns of neuronal activity. Importantly, the central cluster contains all three ϕ values previously identified as qualitatively relevant through expert knowledge ($\phi = 0.145$, 0.257, and 0.575). Their alignment with the region of maximum informational content provides strong validation for their selection and confirms that the corresponding lattices successfully capture meaningful and non-redundant structure in the underlying data.

Regarding the lattices of odorants at this concentration, to the left of Fig. 7,

- The progression of ϕ values unfolds almost entirely along the right-hand side of the entropy triangle. This positioning indicates a high degree of redundancy among odorant representations across the $\overline{\mathbb{R}}_{\min,+}$ exploration. In other words, the odorants tend to activate overlapping or similar patterns across the neural population, resulting in bound information dominating the overall entropy decomposition. Such redundancy is consistent with the biological nature of olfactory coding: while individual neurons contribute to the discrimination of odorants, the representation of each odorant arises from distributed patterns of activity, rather than unique, neuron-specific responses.
- As ϕ increases from lower values, we observe a rise in the overall information content, reaching a peak near $\phi \approx 0.26$. This point corresponds precisely to one of the ϕ values previously selected as qualitatively relevant through expert knowledge. The fact that this value coincides with the configuration of maximal entropy con-

firms its informativeness from a quantitative perspective as well, further validating the rationale behind its initial selection.

- Beyond this optimal point, information content begins to decline as ϕ continues to increase. Nevertheless, the range of ϕ values approximately between 0.15 and 0.6 remains located in the upper third of the triangle, denoting high entropy levels. This suggests that the lattices derived from this interval still preserve substantial informational structure and balance in the representation, thereby supporting the idea that these ϕ values collectively yield the most informative and biologically relevant lattice configurations.

The Information Transmitted by Concept Lattices. The ternary plots displayed in Fig. 8 represent the evolution of the entropies transmitted from the lattice of odorants to the lattice of neuron activations across each of the different thresholds of ϕ. Each point corresponds to a lattice (left: odorants; right: neurons) derived from a specific ϕ value and is colored accordingly. We have presented the split CMET to emphasize the apparent incongruence in transmitted information: the lopsidedness in the distributions of points comes from the fact that the right coordinate $I'_{P_{XY}}$ in the split version, is divided in the case of odorants by $H_{U_{\overline{G}}} = |G| = 23$ and by $H_{U_{\overline{M}}} = |M| = 11$ in the case of neuron activations. Their averages in this case, are less meaningful than when both are of the same cardinality, and that is why we do not report it.

Also, there is a distinct cluster located near the center of the triangle corresponding to extreme values of ϕ, where all elements are either active or inactive. These configurations result in either fully connected or entirely disconnected lattices, and thus fail to convey meaningful information within the system.

These distributions reveal several key insights:

- Strikingly, all points are distributed along the right-hand side of the triangle for both series of lattices. Following the reading guide on the CMET, from the left triangle we extract that odorant extents determine neuron activations intents, and *vice-versa* from the right triangle. This is not surprising, since we have *surmised* in our application that there was *mutual determination* between both types of random vectors, and this is how the data to estimate the transmission of information was obtained. The split variation of information at $VI'_{P_{\overline{XY}}} = 0$ show that residual information is null, concordant with mutual determination.
- The lack of points near the $I'_{P_{\overline{XY}}}$ vertex (top) suggests that transmitted information is relatively low, and therefore, neurons and odorants are redundantly coupled, that is, we are (probably) considering many more neurons than would be required to account for the odorants in the experiment. However, mutual determination is also saying that there are *more* odorants than required to discriminate between neurons.
- The dominance of $\Delta H'_{P_{\overline{X}}}$ and $\Delta H'_{P_{\overline{Y}}}$ implies that most information in the input-output channel comes from differentiable entropy patterns among outputs, rather than mutual information. In other words, each odorant is represented in a sufficiently distinct way across neurons, according with the reading stemming from the transmitted information information.

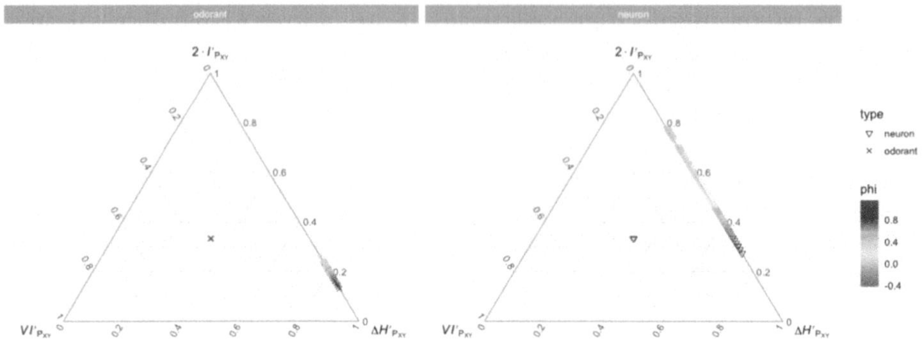

Fig. 8. CMET of concept lattices for the minplus exploration of the 10^{-4} concentration (split for better viewing)

Additionally, the progression of ϕ values along the entropy-dominated axis reveals that while varying ϕ changes the structure of the lattices, it does not significantly shift the informational regime in which the system operates. Interestingly, the point corresponding to $\phi \approx 0.26$—previously identified as highly informative through expert knowledge—lies within the densest cluster of high-information configurations. This further validates the interpretability and significance of that particular threshold.

Application-Related Findings. These findings align with what is known about the olfactory coding strategies in *Caenorhabditis elegans*. Odorants are typically not represented through single-neuron specificity, but rather through distributed and combinatorial patterns of activation. The results presented in the CMET suggest that:

- Odorant representations in the worm are highly *discriminative and redundant*—each neuron contributes a specific signal without overlapping with others. This is the case with mutual determination of sets of different size which are, however, just a partial take on the whole problem (the worm reacts to more odorants and there might possibly be other neurons with olfactory function).
- The neural code emphasizes differentiation among odorants rather than compression or redundancy. This reflects a design where the nervous system aims for coverage and separability in the olfactory space rather than efficiency or redundancy.
- The robustness of high-information transmission across a wide range of ϕ values indicates that the system is resilient to variations in sensitivity thresholds, allowing the worm to maintain informative representations across different conditions.

Altogether, the CMET analysis shows that the formal concept lattices capture meaningful and biologically relevant information structures, and that the values of ϕ previously highlighted by domain experts correspond to configurations where information transmission is maximal. This supports the use of FCA-based frameworks for studying distributed representations in biological systems.

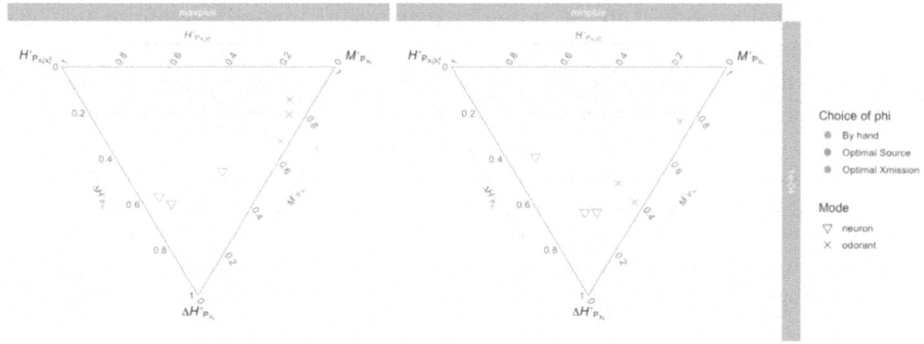

(a) Source entropies

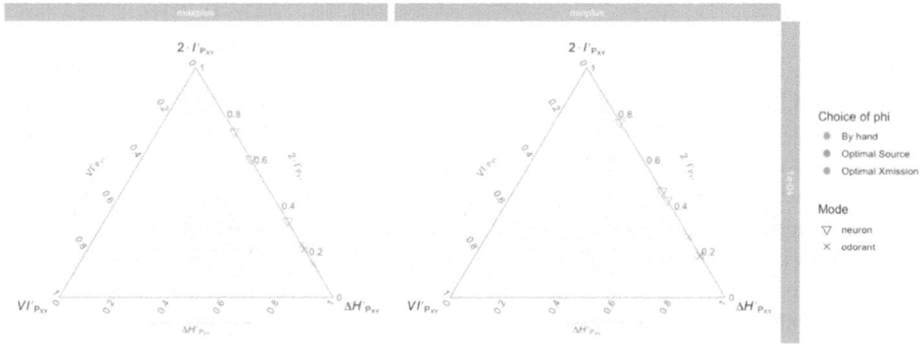

(b) Channel entropies

Fig. 9. Source and channel entropy triangles for the explored choices of ϕ. In all cases, odorant concentration was 10^{-4}. Different choice strategies for ϕ serve different purposes after the SMET, CMET and user intuitions, in all likelihood.

Application Technique: Choosing the ϕ. We next explored the affordances of choosing a ϕ in the following instances:

1. The ϕ_u producing the most "readable" concept lattice—the method in [9].
2. The ϕ_x producing the *most average information transfer* from inputs to outputs.
3. The ϕ_s producing *the most average information-filled* odorant and neuron lattices.

Of course, 1 is the most time-consuming, but has the appeal that it is the most effective at transmitting information to other users. Strategies 2 and 3 have the advantage of being almost automatic.

Figure 9a displays the information content of the sources for these choices of ϕ while Fig. 9b displays the information transferred by the same choices:

- We can see that the maxplus and minplus user choices have different characteristics: while the maxplus choice captures more information for odorants, albeit rather redundant, the information captured for neurons is more or less the same. However, both captured in the case of min-plus analysis are rather low, and also redundant.

- The information of the lattices chosen by maximising transmitted information also have different character in the maxplus and minplus case. The SMET shows that choosing the ϕ_s to maximise source information is effective, but less so in the case of choosing ϕ_x to masimise transmitted information, as was to be expected.
- Likewise, in the CMET we can clearly see that choosing the ϕ_x for maximal transmission is effective and advantageous. Less so choosing for maximal information in individual lattices, and the least so for user-justified choices.

We conclude from this example, that indeed max-plus and min-plus analyses look at different types of quantitative information from lattices. That both the SMET and the CMET are needed for a complete outlook in the quantitative-informational landscape of each application, and that intuitions developed in choosing ϕ_u for some applications do not necessarily transport for other applications.

Discussion. The results from the SMET and CMET analyses offer a principled and quantitative characterization of the informational structure underlying the neural representations of olfactory stimuli in *C. elegans*. Through the systematic variation of the threshold parameter ϕ, we explored a continuum of formal concept lattices, revealing how information is encoded and transmitted across neuronal and stimulus dimensions.

From a biological standpoint, these findings support the notion that olfactory coding in *C. elegans* is not built upon hardwired, one-to-one mappings, but rather emerges from structured, distributed patterns of neural co-activation. The redundancy observed in the odorants' SMET—where multiple odorants yield similar neural patterns—may reflect a form of efficient compression in a limited nervous system, enabling generalization and robustness. Meanwhile, the central zone in the neurons' SMET captures the delicate balance between specificity and redundancy, critical for achieving discriminability without overfitting. Altogether, these information-theoretic landscapes not only quantify the representational richness of concept lattices derived from neural data, but also point to biologically plausible regimes that reflect the efficient encoding principles governing the nematode's sensory system.

Together, the results of SMET and CMET analyses illustrate the nuanced interplay between redundancy, specificity, and information transfer in the conceptual organization of odor perception. By embedding the exploration of formal lattices into an information-theoretic framework, we demonstrate how specific parameterizations—particularly within a restricted range of ϕ—yield maximally informative and biologically coherent structures. These findings contribute to a deeper understanding of olfactory processing in *C. elegans*, and highlight the potential of concept lattices as compact and interpretable representations of complex distributed codes.

4 Conclusion and Further Work

We proposed a new way of measuring the quantitative information balances involved in the mutual determination of objects an attributes in concept lattices by using source and channel entropy triangles—the SMET and CMET—and we applied them to measuring both the immanent information in each of the modes of tabular data, as well as the transport of information from mode to mode, with data obtained from a neuroscience task. By leveraging these entropy-based representations, we provide a principled framework for validating the selection of ϕ in K-FCA, and noticed that this clashes with learnt practice of selecting the ϕ so that the concept lattice is more interpretable.

Future work will extend this analysis to other concentrations and $\overline{\mathbb{R}}_{\max,+}$ entropy transformations, further refining our understanding of information transfer in *C. elegans'* sensory system.

Acknowledgments. This research was funded by the Spanish Ministerio de Ciencia e Innovación grant PID2021-125780NB-I00 funded by MICIU/AEI/10.13039/501100011033 and, by "ERDF A way of making Europe".

Disclosure of Interests. The authors have no competing interests to declare that are relevant to the content of this article.

References

1. Behrendt, G.: Maximal antichains in partially ordered sets. Ars Combinatoria **25**(C), 149–157 (1988). http://scholar.google.com/scholar?q=related:11542WglhckJ:scholar.google.com/&hl=en&num=20&as_sdt=0,5
2. Belohlavek, R.: Fuzzy Galois connections. Technical report. 13, Universit of Ostrava (1998). http://ac030.osu.cz/irafm/ps/rep13.ps.gz
3. Bokman, E., Pritz, C.O., Ruach, R., Itskovits, E., Sharvit, H., Zaslaver, A.: Intricate response dynamics enhances stimulus discrimination in the resource-limited *C. elegans* chemosensory system (2024). https://doi.org/10.1101/2024.01.14.575365
4. Burusco, A., Fuentes-González, R.: The study of the L-fuzzy concept lattice. Mathware Soft Comput. **3**, 209–218 (1994). http://www.raco.cat/index.php/Mathware/article/viewArticle/84628/109625
5. Erk, K.: What is word meaning, really?: (and how can distributional models help us describe it?). In: GEMS 2010: Proceedings of the 2010 Workshop on Geometrical Models of Natural Language Semantics, pp. 17–25. Association for Computational Linguistics (2010). http://portal.acm.org/citation.cfm?id=1870516.1870519&coll=DL&dl=ACM&CFID=184286426&CFTOKEN=84196972
6. Lin, A., et al.: Functional imaging and quantification of multineuronal olfactory responses in C. elegans. Sci. Adv. **9**(eade1249), 1–16 (2023)
7. Peláez-Moreno, C., García-Moral, A.I., Valverde-Albacete, F.J.: Analyzing phonetic confusions using formal concept analysis. J. Acoust. Soc. Am. **128**(3), 1377–1390 (2010). https://doi.org/10.1121/1.3458854
8. Priss, U., Old, L.J.: Modelling lexical databases with formal concept analysis. J. Univ. Comput. Sci. **10**(8), 967–984 (2004). http://www.jucs.org/jucs_10_8/modelling_lexical_databases_with
9. Reyner-Fuentes, E., Peláez-Moreno, C., Valverde-Albacete, F.J.: Discovering the structure of odorants in caenorhabditis elegans using formal concept analysis. In: Cabrera, I.P., Ferré, S., Obiedkov, S. (eds.) Conceptual Knowledge Structures, vol. 14914, pp. 254–269. Springer, Cham (2024). https://doi.org/10.1007/978-3-031-67868-4_17
10. Shannon, C.E.: A mathematical theory of Communication. Bell Syst. Tech. J. **XXVII**(3), 379–423 (1948). http://www3.alcatel-lucent.com/bstj/vol27-1948/articles/bstj27-3-379.pdf

11. Valverde-Albacete, F.J., Peláez-Moreno, C.: Extending conceptualisation modes for generalised Formal Concept Analysis. Inf. Sci. **181**, 1888'1909 (2011). https://doi.org/10.1016/j.ins.2010.04.014
12. Valverde-Albacete, F.J., Peláez-Moreno, C.: Towards a generalisation of formal concept analysis for data mining purposes. In: Missaoui, R., Schmidt, J. (eds.) ICFCA 2006. LNCS (LNAI), vol. 3874, pp. 161–176. Springer, Heidelberg (2006). https://doi.org/10.1007/11671404_11
13. Valverde-Albacete, F., Peláez-Moreno, C.: Assessing information transmission in data transformations with the channel multivariate entropy triangle. Entropy **20**(7), 498 (2018). https://doi.org/10.3390/e20070498
14. Valverde-Albacete, F.J.: Explaining the structure of framenet with concept lattices. In: Ganter, B., Godin, R. (eds.) ICFCA 2005. LNCS (LNAI), vol. 3403, pp. 79–94. Springer, Heidelberg (2005). https://doi.org/10.1007/978-3-540-32262-7_6
15. Valverde-Albacete, F.J., González-Calabozo, J.M., Peñas, A., Peláez-Moreno, C.: Supporting scientific knowledge discovery with extended, generalized Formal Concept Analysis. Expert Syst. Appl. **44**, 198–216 (2016). https://doi.org/10.1016/j.eswa.2015.09.022
16. Valverde-Albacete, F.J., Peláez-Moreno, C.: The evaluation of data sources using multivariate entropy tools. Expert Syst. Appl. **78**, 145–157 (2017). https://doi.org/10.1016/j.eswa.2017.02.010
17. Valverde-Albacete, F.J., Peláez-Moreno, C.: Two information-theoretic tools to assess the performance of multi-class classifiers. Pattern Recogn. Lett. **31**(12), 1665–1671 (2010)
18. Valverde-Albacete, F.J., Peláez-Moreno, C.: The linear algebra in formal concept analysis over idempotent semifields. In: Baixeries, J., Sacarea, C., Ojeda-Aciego, M. (eds.) ICFCA 2015. LNCS (LNAI), vol. 9113, pp. 97–113. Springer, Cham (2015). https://doi.org/10.1007/978-3-319-19545-2_6
19. Valverde-Albacete, F.J., Peláez-Moreno, C.: A formalization of multilabel classification in terms of lattice theory and information theory: concerning datasets. Math. MDPI **12**(2), 1–31 (2024). https://doi.org/10.3390/math12020346
20. Wille, R.: Restructuring lattice theory: an approach based on hierarchies of concepts. In: Ferré, S., Rudolph, S. (eds.) ICFCA 2009. LNCS (LNAI), vol. 5548, pp. 314–339. Springer, Heidelberg (2009). https://doi.org/10.1007/978-3-642-01815-2_23

Image Processing in Boolean Matrix Factorization

Martin Trnecka[1] and Marketa Trneckova[1,2](✉)

[1] Department of Computer Science, Palacký University Olomouc, Olomouc, Czech Republic
marketa.trneckova@gmail.com

[2] Department of Mathematical Analysis and Applications of Mathematics, Palacký University Olomouc, Olomouc, Czech Republic

Abstract. Boolean matrix factorization (BMF) is a data mining method that decomposes a binary matrix into the Boolean product of two smaller matrices, revealing hidden patterns in that matrix. Traditional BMF algorithms overlook visual aspects, limiting their ability to identify natural factors. This paper explores the use of image processing methods to enhance BMF. We propose treating Boolean matrices as black-and-white images and applying methods such as analysis connected component, SLIC segmentation, Quad tree, spatial filtering, and morphological operations. Experiments on real and synthetic datasets demonstrate that these methods highlight relevant structures in data and improves factor computation.

Keywords: Boolean matrix factorization · Image processing · Pattern detection

1 Motivation

Boolean matrix factorization (BMF), also referred to as a Boolean matrix decomposition, is a data mining method for decomposing a binary matrix representing object-attribute relationships into the Boolean product of two smaller matrices. This decomposition helps uncover hidden patterns within the data. The BMF methods try to find factors that have up to permutation of rows and columns the shape of a dense rectangle–a rectangle full of 1 s except for a reasonable amount of 0 s. This visual perspective, a crucial aspect of BMF, is surprisingly underutilized in contemporary BMF methods.

However, existing BMF algorithms (see an overview in [19]) are relatively advanced, some natural patterns may be undiscoverable for them. To address this issue, we created a small real-world dataset which falls into a community analysis area. We collect gaming data from the National Hockey League (NHL) season 2022/2023. Namely, we count the number of games between each of the 32 NHL teams, which are divided into Western and Eastern conferences. Each conference contains two divisions: Pacific and Central in the Western and Atlantic

P. Cellier et al. (Eds.): CONCEPTS 2025, LNAI 15941, pp. 281–294, 2025.
https://doi.org/10.1007/978-3-032-03364-2_18

and Metropolitan in the Eastern. Teams play 26 within-division games, 24 non-divisional within-conference games, and 32 inter-conference games. Note that within a division, each of the eight teams plays four games with five opponents and three games with two opponents.[1] If the number of games between two particular teams was equal to four, we put 1 to a particular row and column of data. The resulting data are shown in Fig. 1.

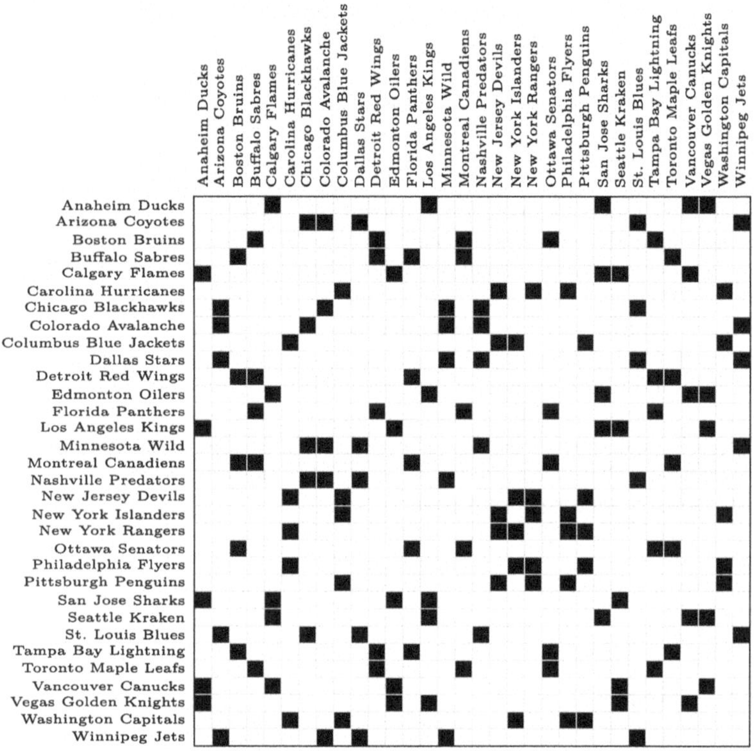

Fig. 1. The NHL data. Black squares represent 1 s; white squares represent 0 s in the data.

Obviously, one may expect divisions to be natural factors in such data, i.e., factors should correspond with existing communities shown as a graph in Fig. 2.

Generally, BMF algorithms, different from humans, fail to find such factors as they are not able to "see" them. Of course, humans cannot observe the factors directly from the matrix too (see Fig. 3a). Nevertheless, the factors are significantly more straightforward to see if we group objects that share attributes and attributes that are common for some objects (Fig. 3b). Even though they do not have the shape of nice rectangles (Fig. 3c), humans can figure them out. Note

[1] For more details see https://en.wikipedia.org/wiki/Season_structure_of_the_NHL.

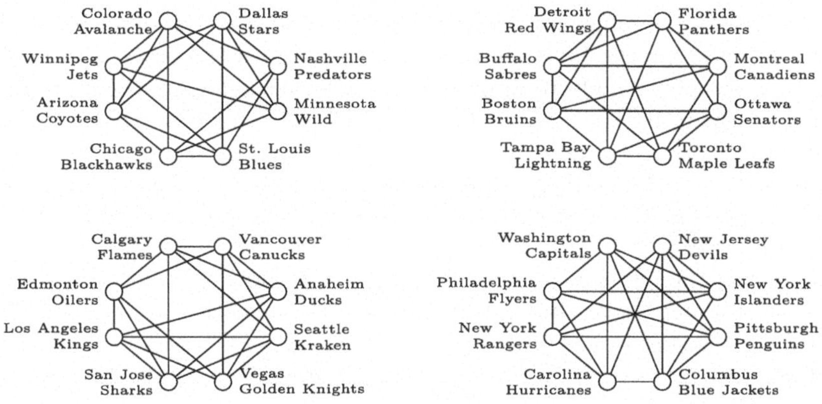

Fig. 2. Four clearly separated communities (divisions) in NHL data.

that BMF algorithms work in the same vein. They simultaneously group objects and attributes and tolerate some disruption in the shape of nice rectangles, i.e., they consider dense rectangles. More precisely, BMF algorithms introduce some errors (they consider ones as zeros and vice versa) when performing such tasks. However, existing BMF algorithms are not able to find natural factors in NHL data.

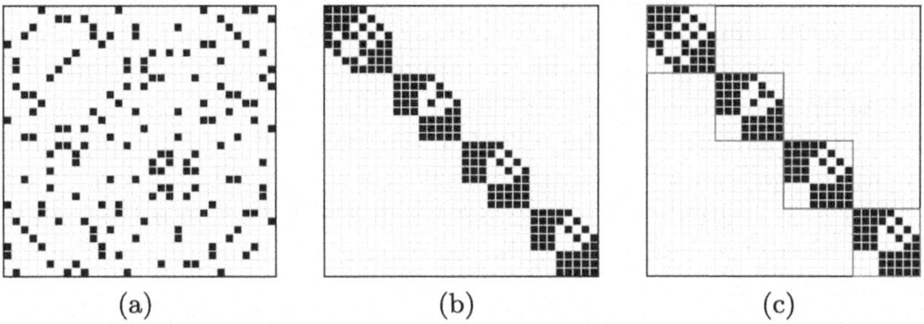

Fig. 3. (a) The original NHL data. (b) Data after permutation of rows and columns. (c) Natural factors in the data.

There is a difference between a human view of data and a BMF algorithm's view. Humans do not work directly with errors. Note that in the case of the NHL data, there is no error in the data. Instead of this, humans rather suppress less relevant information. For example, if some 1 s are missing, we imagine that they are present; similarly, if some 1 s are extra, we imagine that they are not present in the data. In other words, humans try to find rectangles in data. Another difference is that, during factor computation, algorithms process rows or columns one at a time without considering the "big picture", whereas humans perceive the data as a whole.

In the paper, we empathize with the visual aspect of the data. Specifically, we propose handling the Boolean data as a black-and-white image and applying image processing methods to suppress less relevant information. This reveals hidden patterns in the data, so the factors may be directly observable. Moreover, computing factors from data where the less relevant information was removed is much easier, as the BMF method has to do less work. The main aim of the paper is to present this concept along with promising preliminary results from ongoing research.

The rest of the paper is organized as follows. In Sect. 2, we outline a scheme for the use of image processing in BMF. In Sect. 3, we discuss preliminary results obtained via selected image processing methods. In Sect. 4, we discuss an extension of our scheme to data over a finite scale. Section 5 concludes the paper and outlines potential research directions.

2 How to Apply Image Processing in BMF?

Image processing [9] is a common designation for various methods of analyzing, modifying, and enhancing digital images, such as noise removal, segmentation, or pattern recognition.

However, any Boolean matrix with m rows and n columns can be seen as a black-and-white digital image with $m \times n$ pixels, and thus, the image processing can be simply applied to them; we first have to make natural patterns in data visible. This is crucial, as image processing relies on the existence of a structure in the image. For example, if we take data depicted in Fig. 3a, there is no visible structure, and thus, we are not able to separate the important information (the visible structure) from the less relevant.

The existing patterns can be revealed via rows and columns permutations. Namely, we can permute the matrix to reveal a so-called banded structure [11] (also known as a staircase pattern). The banded structure in a Boolean matrix is a pattern where the 1 s are concentrated around the main diagonal and create a "band" (see Fig. 3b).

We cannot expect a perfect banded structure in real-world data. However, reasonable data naturally arises in a pattern close to the perfect banded structure since such data have many similar objects and attributes, leading to clusters of related items. As a consequence the meaningful factors (or at least their parts) will naturally appear on the band.

There exist many methods for computation of banded structure (see an overview in [8]). We choose three representative methods of the most important groups, namely the Spectral ordering [2], the Barycenter [17], and the Alternating [11]. We applied them to various data and compared the resulting banded structure. An example of such comparison on Paleo data[2] is shown on Fig. 4. Although there are small differences between these methods, all of them perform well and can find a meaningful banded structure.

[2] Available at https://nowdatabase.org/.

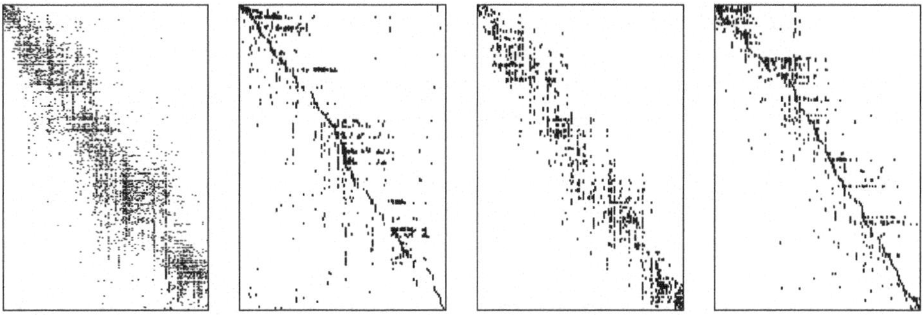

(a) (b) (c) (d)

Fig. 4. Banded structure in Paleo data. (a) Original data. (b) Banded structure obtained via Alternatig method. (c) Banded structure obtained via Barycenter method. (d) Banded structure obtained via Spectral ordering method.

When the existing patterns are visible in the data, we may directly applied the image processing.

3 Preliminary Results

Generally in our settings the role of the image processing is to enhance the banded structure and thus reveals the factors in the data. Namely, we want to suppress less relevant information, i.e., remove small groups of 1 s that are usually not a part of the band and fill 0 s (flip them to 1 s) that violating a shape of nice rectangles. In what follows, we discuss use of selected image processing methods in BMF as well as results from experiments showing the advantages of this.

Although we used various data, the experimental evaluation of each method follows a common scheme. First, we reorder data to obtain the banded structure. We used all three methods from the previous section, but only selected results are present since there are only small differences between them. Then, we applied the image processing method. We also computed factors via the standard BMF methods, namely via GreConD [7] and Asso [18] algorithms, as they are both representatives of two major approaches to BMF and use them for comparison.

In the next subsections, we use image processing terminology, namely, image instead of Boolean matrix and pixel instead of matrix entry.

3.1 Connected Components

Analysis of connected components [9] is a method that identifies groups (or components, hence the method's name) of similar adjacent pixels in digital image. The method scans through the image and groups pixels based on a connectivity criterion (e.g., 4-neighborhood or 8-neighborhood).

We use this method with 4-neighborhood connectivity, meaning that only the pixels with value one directly next to each other in the vertical or horizontal directions are connected. After detecting connected components, we filter out small components, i.e., components containing a small amount of pixels. Namely, we filter out components that have less than six pixels. The remaining significant components are then enclosed in a bounding box to extract rectangular structures from the data. The bounding box is a standard tool in image processing that identifies a rectangular part of the image, and thus, it can be interpreted as a factor.

The resulting bounding boxes for the NHL data are shown in Fig. 3c. We can see that the method identifies the natural factors in the data. Both GreConD and Asso are not able to find these factors. Note that the analysis of connected components provides non-overlapping factors.

3.2 Simple Linear Iterative Clustering

Simple linear iterative clustering (SLIC) [1] is a widely used method for segmenting an image into compact and perceptually meaningful clusters, known as superpixels. SLIC is based on the k-means clustering algorithm optimized for efficiency and spatial consistency.

We applied the method to Zoo dataset [15] (see Fig. 5a). The obtained clusters are shown in Fig. 5c (each cluster has a different color). Each pixel within a cluster is then replaced with the median value of all pixels in that cluster, resulting in data shown in Fig. 5d.

One can easily observe that the banded structure has significantly improved compared to the original one (Fig. 5b). Moreover, there is a notable reduction in the number of obtained factors. For instance, when using the GreConD algorithm, we obtain 23 factors instead of the original 29. We may also interpret the bounding boxes of clusters (see Fig. 5e) directly as factors. In such a case, there are only 14 factors. We observe a similar behavior in the case of Asso algorithm.

3.3 Quad Tree

Another widely used method in image segmentation is a Quad tree method [9], where the image is recursively divided into quadrants until a stop criterion is reached. Traditionally, the image is split in half, both vertically and horizontally, regardless of the underlying content. The stop criterion is a size or a homogeneity of quadrants. This fixed, symmetric division can be a disadvantage because it does not always align with the natural boundaries in the image.

To overcome this limitation, we used a modified version of the Quad tree, where the splitting point that made the split parts as different as possible is selected. The difference is measured in a way similar to the between-class variance used in Otsu's method [20].

Figure 6b shows blocks containing at least 95% of ones (the stop criterion) obtained via the modified Quad tree method. The Zoo dataset contains 101

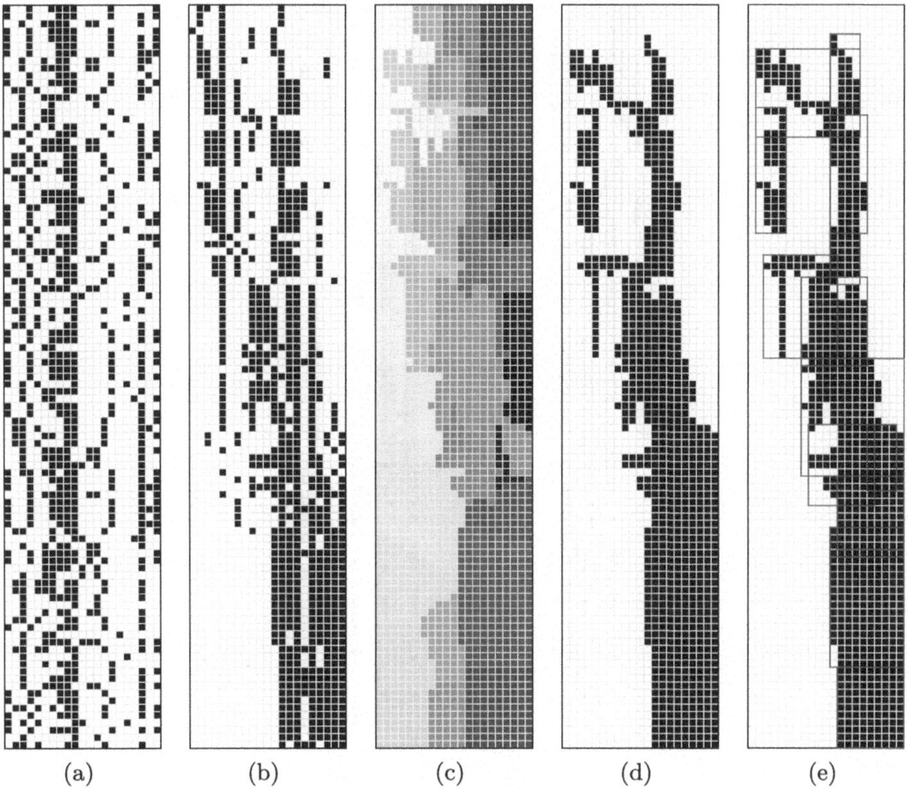

Fig. 5. (a) The original Zoo data. (b) Data after permutation of rows and columns via Barycenter method. (c) Clusters obtained via SLIC method (each cluster has a different color). (d) Clusters after binarization. (e) Bounded boxes for non-zero clusters.

objects representing different species. It includes 17 binary attributes describing various characteristics, such as whether an animal has fur, is born from an egg, or lives in water. Additionally, a numerical attribute that categorizes animals into seven groups is provided. We used this attribute for an evaluation of the quality of factors. We discovered that several blocks consist exclusively of one animal type. In our analysis, we were able to identify almost all mammals, as well as birds and fish.

Interestingly, one block contains all the birds and nearly all the insects, essentially grouping together all animals capable of flight. This result indicates that the extracted factors are semantically meaningful.

3.4 Spatial Filtering

Spatial filtering is a fundamental image processing method that modifies pixel values based on their spatial relationship with neighboring pixels. It operates

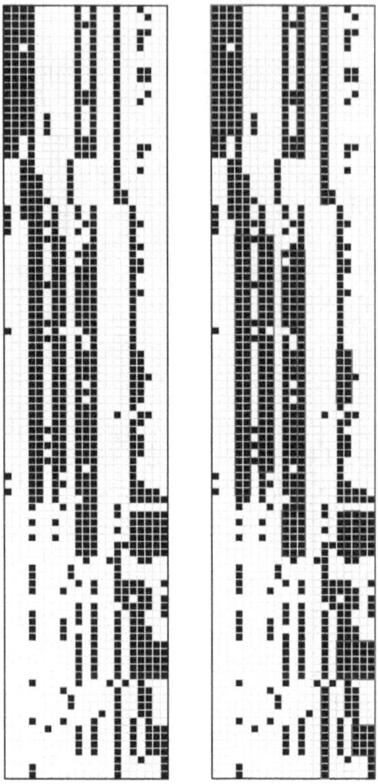

(a) (b)

Fig. 6. (a) The Zoo data reordered via Spectral ordering method. (b) Non-zero blocks obtained via the modified Quad tree method.

directly on the image by applying a filter (or mask) over a local region of pixels. The filter moves across the image, computing new pixel values based on a predefined mathematical operation.

There are two main types of spatial filtering: linear and non-linear. Linear filtering involves weighted averaging of neighboring pixels, and it is commonly used for blurring, sharpening, and edge detection. Non-linear filtering uses operations that are not based on simple weighted sums, e.g., median, which is effective for noise reduction, especially for impulse noise (salt-and-pepper noise). Unlike mean filtering, which can blur edges, median filtering effectively smooths the image while maintaining sharp transitions [9].

We used median filtering, which is more suitable for our purpose. The filter works by replacing each pixel value with the median of the pixel values in its local neighborhood. Note that we are not limited to the median operation. In general, any desired percentile can be used. To prevent the corners of rectangles from becoming rounded, we applied the filter twice: first with a column vector-shaped filter and then with a row vector-shaped filter defining the local neighborhood–

both of length five. The same results can be alternatively achieved via classical mean filtering followed by thresholding.

Generally, the purpose of spatial filtering is to remove noise from the image. This task is very similar to the error handling in BMF. We adapt the experimental scenario from [10]. Gupta et al. in [10] generate several 1000×50 binary datasets involving various cases of overlapping patterns. These are widely used to assess the ability of error (or noise) handling in BMF [5].

We used data 4, data 6, and data 7 from [10] as these capture nontrivial relations between patterns involved. We follow the usual scenario. To each dataset, we introduced errors, i.e., we changed n percent of entries (1 s to 0 s and vice versa). We limit the values of n to a maximum of 15%, which is relatively high according to [5]. We investigated the influence of various kind of errors, namely we considered additive error (0 s are changed to 1 s), subtractive error (1 s are changed to 0 s) and general error (1 s are changed to zeros and vice versa).

Then we applied the median filter and evaluated the ability to remove the introduced error and discover the original patterns. Figure 7 shows the number of different entries divided by the number of changed entries, i.e., divided by the error. This tells us how large a portion of the error remains in the data after filtration. One may see that despite a large error, only a very small amount of errors remains undetected.

While additive and general noise are removed relatively well, we see worse results with subtractive noise. This is partly due to the fact that the patterns in the data are relatively narrow (they have only a few attributes).

3.5 Morphology

Image morphology [9] is a widely used method for processing geometrical structures in images. In our experiments, we used closing and opening operations. The primary purpose of the closing operation is to fill small gaps without affecting the overall shape and size of structures in the image. The primary purpose of the opening operation is to remove small parts from the image while preserving the shape and size of larger structures in the image. In both cases, the result is driven by the structuring element's size and shape.

We start with applying the closing operation twice. First, using a structuring element in the shape of a column vector (3×1) and then using a structuring element in the shape of a row vector (1×3). Generally, the column vector sets the pixel to 1 if the pixels in the preceding or following row (or both) have a value equal to 1 in that column. Similarly, the row vector sets the pixel to 1 if the pixels in the preceding or following column (or both) have a value equal to 1 in that row.

After this phase, we apply the opening operation once. In our experiments, we used a structuring element of size 3×2.

We used in BMF well-known real-world benchmark data: DNA with dimension 4590×392 [16]; Mushroom with dimension 8124×119 [14]; and already mentioned Paleo with dimension 501×139. On each dataset, we first computed

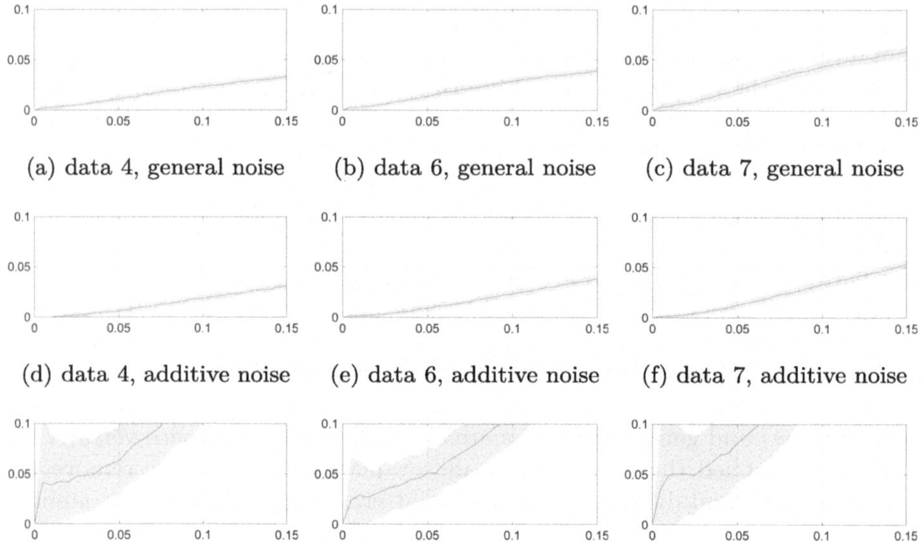

(a) data 4, general noise (b) data 6, general noise (c) data 7, general noise

(d) data 4, additive noise (e) data 6, additive noise (f) data 7, additive noise

(g) data 4, subtractive noise (h) data 6, subtractive noise (i) data 7, subtractive noise

Fig. 7. The ability of spatial filtering to remove introduced errors. The x-axis represents the error size from 0 to 15%. The y-axis shows how many percent of the error remains in the data. The average values over 1000 iterations as well as the standard deviation (shaded areas) are show.

the banded structure via the method mentioned in Sect. 2, and then, on each banded structure, we applied the above-mentioned morphology.

First, we study how large portion of data was changed. Table 1 columns marked by "morphology" show differences between data and data after morphology. Columns "Spec.", "Bary." and "Alter." correspond with methods for computing banded structure. 0 means that the data after morphology and original data are the same, and 1 means that they are complementary. We may see that the morphology causes only small changes in the data.

Table 1. Summarization of results of experiments with morphology.

data	morphology			GreConD				Asso			
	Spec.	Bary.	Alter.	orig.	Spec.	Bary.	Alter.	orig.	Spec.	Bary.	Alter.
dna	0.013	0.009	0.004	173	36	92	117	–	33	78	86
mushroom	0.103	0.116	0.109	48	25	36	24	37	22	26	19
paleo	0.041	0.045	0.039	112	48	63	56	–	45	62	52

Then, we study how image processing affects factorization. Namely, we compared the number of factors required to explain 90% of the data. Columns

"GRECOND" and "ASSO" in Table 1 show the numbers of factors required for the explanation of 90% of data. The value "" means that ASSO is not able to explain such a portion of data. We may see that the reduction of the number of factors (column "orig." in Table 1) is significant.

3.6 Discussion

Generally, BMF can benefit from image processing in two ways. First, image processing can be used for factor extraction. We showed that the analysis of connected components, SLIC, and Quad tree methods could be used for this task. We demonstrated that these methods can help discover meaningful factors that remain undetected via classical BMF algorithms.

Second, image processing can remove less relevant information and thus simplify factor computation and interpretation. We showed that spatial filtering and morphology are suitable for this. Both only slightly change the data while significantly decreasing the number of factors within the data.

Note that analysis of connected components, SLIC, and Quad tree can also be used to remove less relevant information, by filtering out small components (or clusters or split parts).

Overall, the presented results show that image processing is beneficial in BMF.

4 Beyond the Boolean Case

Boolean matrix factorization is a special case of matrix factorization of data containing values from a finite ordinal scale [3]. The most common case is that we have data where the values contain degrees to which objects possess particular attributes. In such case, data can be seen as a grayscale image. Various algorithms for extracting factors from such data exist; an overview can be found, e.g., in [6]. We used modifications of GRECOND and ASSO for factorization of data over a finite scale called GRECOND$_L$ [3] and ASSO$_L$ [4]. The following section briefly discusses how to apply image processing in such a case.

In fact, all methods presented in the previous section are applicable not only to black-and-white images but also to grayscale images. Let us assume the NHL dataset introduced in Sect. 1, with the difference that we do not binarize it. Instead, we take the data and divide each value by the maximum value, which is four. The resulting value represents the degree of membership that a team has often played matches against another team (see Fig. 8a).

Even though the methods for computing the banded structure are defined and used on binary data, they can be directly used on data over a finite ordinal scale. More precisely, the Barycenter method uses the so-called Barycentr metric, the Alternating method uses the maximal subarray problem, and the Spectral ordering uses the Fiedler's eigenvalue. All of these concepts can be used on non-binary data.

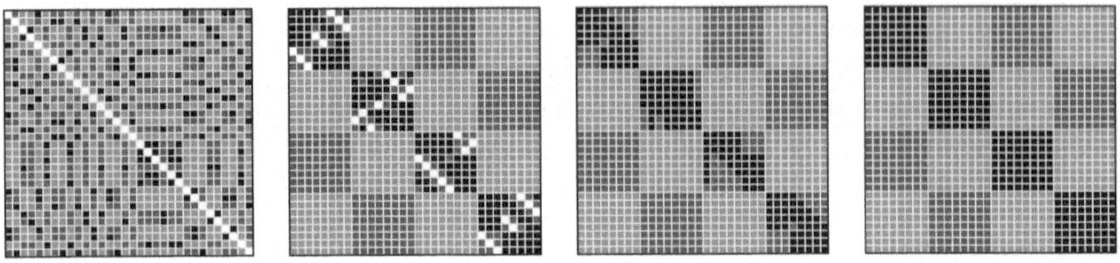

(a) (b) (c) (d)

Fig. 8. (a) The original NHL data. There are five values in the data; each is represented by a different color. A darker color means a bigger value. (b) Data after permutation of rows and columns. (c) Data after applying mathematical morphology. (d) Data after applying mathematical morphology and hit-or-miss operation

One may easily observe natural factors after reordering the data (Fig. 8b). Factorization algorithms do not reveal these factors like in the binary case.

Applying grayscale morphology on such data in the same way as in the case of binary data in Sect. 3.5, we obtain the result shown in Fig. 8c. Additionally, by adding a hit-or-miss operation [9] for corner detection, we are able to achieve the result shown in Fig. 8d.

In what follows, we use in the clustering community the well-known Iris dataset [13] presented in [12]. The original dataset contains 150 samples (we selected 30 of them) from three species of iris (Virginica, Versicolor, and Setosa). Each sample is described by features that characterize its appearance, such as *sepal_length*, *sepal_width*, *petal_length*, and *petal_width*. Additionally, we introduced derived attributes including *sepal_area* (*sepal_length* · *sepal_width*), *petal_area* (*petal_length* · *petal_width*), and ratio attributes like *ratio_pl_sl* and *ratio_pw_sw*. These attributes are numerical, and we scaled them to values 0, 0.5, and 1. The resulting dataset is shown in Fig. 9a. After reordering, we obtained the data depicted in Fig. 9b. In Fig. 9c, we can see the clusters obtained by applying the SLIC algorithm (each cluster has a different color). Replacing every pixel in each cluster with the median of the values within that cluster results in the output shown in Fig. 9d. When we apply $\textsc{GreConD}_L$ on such data, the overall number of factors remains unchanged, but the factors explain a larger portion of the data. For example, on original data, the first two factors explain 83%; meanwhile, when the algorithm is applied to the modified data, the first two factors explain 88%. Moreover, to explain 99% of the data, only six factors are needed, whereas on the original data, seven factors are needed.

In Fig. 9e, the blocks obtained by applying the modified Quad tree method are shown. The stop criterion was that at least 95% of values within the split part are the same. Among the blocks are three blocks, each corresponding with a particular species of iris. Note $\textsc{GreConD}_L$ and $\textsc{Asso}_L$ are not able to find factors that correspond with species Versicolor and Setosa. The factor corresponding with the species Virginica is found.

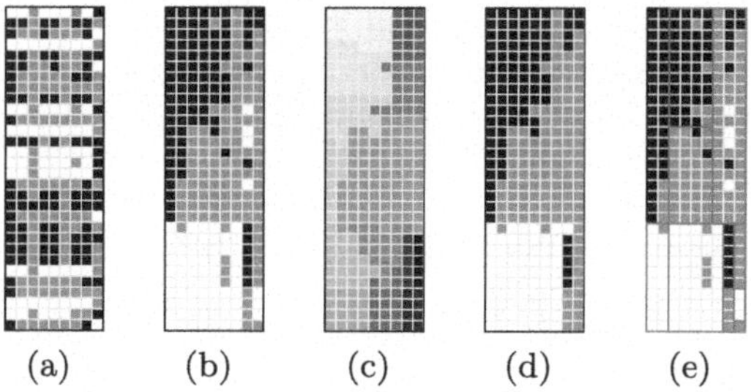

Fig. 9. (a) The original Iris data. (b) Data after reordering via Barycenter method. (c) Clusters obtained using SLIC algorithm (each cluster has a different color). (d) Data after SLIC preprocessing. (e) Block obtained using Quad tree. (Color figure online)

5 Conclusion

In this paper, we proposed a novel idea, emphasizing the visual aspect of data, for handling Boolean data as black-and-white images. We proposed a scheme using a banded structure and image processing to improve Boolean matrix factorization (BMF). We demonstrated that methods such as analysis of connected components, SLIC segmentation, Quad tree, spatial filtering, and morphological operations could significantly enhance the banded structure. These methods either facilitate the extraction of meaningful factors that remain hidden to classical BMF algorithms or simplify the data by suppressing less relevant information, thereby reducing the number of factors. Moreover, we extended our approach to data over finite ordinal scales, showing that grayscale adaptations of the proposed methods yield similar benefits. The experiments confirm that image processing can be beneficial in BMF.

The promising results suggest that this perspective opens new research directions in BMF. The presented results are relatively broad, and further research should provide a more in-depth analysis of the proposed methods. For example, in the case of morphology, we used the most basic setting of the structuring element. However, the results are already very promising, a more detailed study focusing on the impact of the structuring element's size should be conducted. Additionally, many other image processing methods could be beneficial in this context. One of the main candidates is convolutional neural networks (CNNs).

References

1. Achanta, R., et al.: SLIC superpixels compared to state-of-the-art superpixel methods. IEEE Trans. Pattern Anal. Mach. Intell. **34**(11), 2274–2282 (2012)
2. Atkins, J.E., Boman, E.: A spectral algorithm for seriation and the consecutive ones problem. SIAM J. Comput. **28**(1), 297–310 (1998). https://doi.org/10.1137/S0097539795285771
3. Belohlavek, R.: Optimal decompositions of matrices with entries from residuated lattices. J. Logic Comput. **22**, 1405–1425 (2012)

4. Belohlavek, R., Krmelova, M.: Beyond Boolean matrix decompositions: toward factor analysis and dimensionality reduction of ordinal data. In: 2013 IEEE 13th International Conference on Data Mining (ICDM), pp. 961–966. IEEE (2013). https://doi.org/10.1109/ICDM.2013.81
5. Belohlavek, R., Trnecka, M.: Handling noise in Boolean matrix factorization. Int. J. Approximate Reasoning **96**, 78–94 (2018). https://doi.org/10.1016/j.ijar.2018.03.006
6. Belohlavek, R., Trneckova, M.: Factorization of matrices with grades with overcovering. IEEE Trans. Fuzzy Syst. **32**(4), 1641–1652 (2023). https://doi.org/10.1109/TFUZZ.2023.3330760
7. Belohlavek, R., Vychodil, V.: Discovery of optimal factors in binary data via a novel method of matrix decomposition. J. Comput. Syst. Sci. **76**(1), 3–20 (2010). https://doi.org/10.1016/j.jcss.2009.05.002
8. Behrisch, M., et al.: Matrix reordering methods for table and network visualization. Comput. Graph. Forum **35**(3), 693–716 (2016). https://doi.org/10.1111/cgf.12935
9. Gonzalez, R., Woods, R.: Digital Image Processing, 4th edn. Pearson, New York (2018)
10. Gupta, R., et al.: Quantitative evaluation of approximate frequent pattern mining algorithms. In: Proceedings of the 14th ACM SIGKDD International Conference on Knowledge Discovery and Data Mining (KDD 2008), pp. 301–309. ACM, New York (2008)
11. Garriga, G.C., Junttila, E., Mannila, H.: Banded structure in binary matrices. Knowl. Inf. Syst. **28**, 197–226 (2011). https://doi.org/10.1007/s10115-010-0319-7
12. Fisher, R.A.: The use of multiple measurements in taxonomic problems. Ann. Eugen. **7**(2), 179–188 (1936)
13. Fisher, R.A.: The UCI Machine Learning Repository. https://archive.ics.uci.edu
14. Kelly, M., Longjohn, R., Nottingham, K.: The UCI Machine Learning Repository. https://archive.ics.uci.edu
15. Lichman, M.: UCI Machine Learning Repository. University of California, School of Information and Computer Science, Irvine (2013). http://archive.ics.uci.edu/ml
16. Myllykangas, S., et al.: DNA copy number amplification profiling of human neoplasms. Oncogene **25**(55), 7324–7332 (2006)
17. Mäkinen, E., Siirtola, H.: The barycenter heuristic and the reorderable matrix. Informatica **29**, 357–363 (2005)
18. Miettinen, P., et al.: The discrete basis problem. IEEE Trans. Knowl. Data Eng. **20**(10), 1348–1362 (2008). https://doi.org/10.1109/TKDE.2008.53
19. Miettinen, P., Neumann, S.: Recent developments in Boolean matrix factorization. In: Proceedings of the 29th International Joint Conference on Artificial Intelligence (IJCAI 2020), pp. 4922–4928 (2020). https://doi.org/10.24963/ijcai.2020/685
20. Otsu, N.: A threshold selection method from gray-level histograms. IEEE Trans. Syst. Man Cybern. **9**(1), 62–66 (1979)

On Distance Functions Between Closure Systems and Their Application in Industrial Maps

Ľubomír Antoni[1(✉)], Peter Eliaš[2], Ján Guniš[1], Dominika Kotlárová[1], Stanislav Krajči[1], Ondrej Krídlo[1], Viktor Pristaš[1], Ľubomír Šnajder[1], and Vít Voženílek[3,4]

[1] Faculty of Science, Institute of Computer Science, Pavol Jozef Šafárik University in Košice, Jesenná 5, 04001 Košice, Slovak Republic
lubomir.antoni@upjs.sk

[2] Mathematical Institute, Slovak Academy of Sciences, Grešákova 6, 04001 Košice, Slovak Republic

[3] Faculty of Sciences, Department of Geoinformatics, Palacky University in Olomouc, 17. listopadu 50, 779 00 Olomouc, Czech Republic

[4] Faculty of Earth Sciences and Spatial Management, Department of Geoinformatics and Cartography, University of Maria Curie-Sklodowska, Al. Kraśnicka 2D, 20-031 Lublin, Poland

Abstract. By measuring the distance between closure systems, we can assess how closely two datasets or knowledge structures are related. In this paper, we propose distance functions for comparing closure systems, which can also be applied to concept lattices built on the same set of objects with varying attribute sets. Our proposed methods were implemented in the Go programming language. In our practical application, we examined industry maps from 63 school world atlases, originating from 23 countries and 40 publishers, from 1938 to 2018. We compare the distances between concept lattices constructed from three sets of map attributes: industrial sectors (13 attributes), power plants, pipelines, and material transport (12 attributes), and minerals (45 attributes). Our results demonstrate that the proposed distance functions could effectively capture structural differences between thematic layers of industrial maps, reflecting their varying conceptual complexity.

Keywords: Closure Systems · Concept Lattices · Cartography · Distance · Meet-irreducible elements

1 Introduction

Formal Concept Analysis is a mathematical framework that is used to extract meaningful hierarchies from relational data [1–3]. By measuring similarities or dissimilarities between concept lattices on the same set of objects, we can assess

P. Cellier et al. (Eds.): CONCEPTS 2025, LNAI 15941, pp. 295–306, 2025.
https://doi.org/10.1007/978-3-032-03364-2_19

how closely related two datasets or knowledge structures are. Domenach and Portides [4,5] introduced a novel measure to compare concept lattices on the same set of objects and attributes and investigated randomly generated Boolean matrices. Their dissimilarity measure between concept lattices considers the so-called overhanged pairs of objects (the overhanging relation). Moreover, they introduced a similarity measure between lattices based on correspondences between objects and between attributes [6]. Bazin and Kahn [7] explored Minkowski-like distance measures between concept lattices, implication bases, and formal contexts on the same sets of objects and attributes, as well. They define the distance measure between concept lattices as a distance measure between the concept forming operators.

The aim of our paper is to propose distance functions between closure systems to compare concept lattices on the same set of objects but with different sets of attributes. The proposed distance functions are natural in the Formal Concept Analysis setting because they compare closure systems, the fundamental structures from which concept lattices are derived, thereby preserving the conceptual nature of formal contexts even when attribute sets differ. We aim to investigate the theoretical properties of the proposed distance functions between closure systems. As a practical application, we aim to use the proposed functions in compiling the content of industry maps in school world atlases from different world producers. In Sect. 2, we remind the basic notions of Formal Concept Analysis. In Sect. 3, we define the distance functions between closure systems and explore their theoretical properties. In Sect. 4, we introduce the application of our proposed methods in real-world industrial map data.

2 Formal Concept Analysis and Its Basic Notions

Formal Concept Analysis is grounded in several core notions, including the formal context, the concept-forming operator, formal concepts, and the structure known as the concept lattice [3].

Definition 1. *Consider sets B, A and a binary relation $I \subseteq B \times A$. Thus, a triple $\langle B, A, I\rangle$ is called a formal context. The elements of the sets B, A are called objects and attributes, respectively. A relation I is called an incidence relation.*

We can imagine a formal context as a binary object-attribute table, representing the relationships between objects and their corresponding attributes. Moreover, we recall the operators that act in a formal context to establish the conceptual structure:

Definition 2. *Consider a formal context $\langle B, A, I\rangle$ and $X \in \mathcal{P}(B)$, $Y \in \mathcal{P}(A)$ of power sets of objects and attributes, respectively. Two mappings $\uparrow\colon \mathcal{P}(B) \to \mathcal{P}(A)$ and $\downarrow\colon \mathcal{P}(A) \to \mathcal{P}(B)$ given by*

$$\uparrow(X) = X^{\uparrow} = \{y \in A : (\forall x \in X)\langle x, y\rangle \in I\}$$

and

$$\downarrow(Y) = Y^{\downarrow} = \{x \in B : (\forall y \in Y)\langle x, y\rangle \in I\}$$

are called concept-forming operators of a formal context $\langle B, A, I\rangle$.

The concept-forming operators enable the construction of so-called formal concepts [3]:

Definition 3. *Consider a formal context* $\langle B, A, I\rangle$ *and concept-forming operators* $\uparrow$, $\downarrow$. *Consider the subsets of objects and attributes* $X \in \mathcal{P}(B)$, $Y \in \mathcal{P}(A)$. *A pair* $\langle X, Y\rangle$ *such that it holds* $X^{\uparrow} = Y$, $Y^{\downarrow} = X$ *is called a formal concept of* $\langle B, A, I\rangle$. *Moreover, in a formal concept* $\langle X, Y\rangle$, *the set of objects* X *is referred to as the extent (denoted as* $\text{ext}\langle X, Y\rangle$*), while the set of attributes* Y *is called the intent (denoted as* $\text{int}\langle X, Y\rangle$*).*

Moreover, we denote the set of all formal concepts in the formal context $\langle B, A, I\rangle$ as:

$$\mathfrak{B}(B, A, I) = \{\langle X, Y\rangle \in \mathrm{P}(B) \times \mathrm{P}(A) : X^{\uparrow} = Y, Y^{\downarrow} = X\}.$$

Definition 4. *Consider two formal concepts* $\langle X_1, Y_1\rangle, \langle X_2, Y_2\rangle \in \mathfrak{B}(B, A, I)$ *of* $\langle B, A, I\rangle$. *Consider a partial order* $\preceq$ *such that* $\langle X_1, Y_1\rangle \preceq \langle X_2, Y_2\rangle$ *iff* $X_1 \subseteq X_2$. *A partially ordered set* $\langle \mathfrak{B}(B, A, I), \preceq\rangle$ *is called a concept lattice of* $\langle B, A, I\rangle$. *We denote the concept lattice of* $\langle B, A, I\rangle$ *by* $\underline{\mathfrak{B}}(B, A, I)$. *We denote by* $\text{Ext}(\underline{\mathfrak{B}})$ *and* $\text{Int}(\underline{\mathfrak{B}})$ *the set of all the extents and intents, of* $\underline{\mathfrak{B}}(B, A, I)$, *respectively.*

Within the framework of Formal Concept Analysis, the Basic Theorem [3] establishes that every concept lattice is a complete lattice.

3 Distance Functions Between Closure Systems

In this section, we propose distance functions between closure systems and explore their properties.

If $\mathcal{A}$ is a system of subsets of the set S, we denote by $[\mathcal{A}]_S$ the closure system on S generated by $\mathcal{A}$ (i.e., the intersection of all closure systems on S that contain $\mathcal{A}$).

Definition 5. *If* $\mathcal{A}, \mathcal{B}$ *are closure systems on* S, *we denote by* $h(\mathcal{A}, \mathcal{B})$ *the size of the smallest system of subsets* $\mathcal{S} \subseteq \mathcal{P}(S)$ *such that* $[\mathcal{A} \cup \mathcal{S}]_S \supseteq \mathcal{B}$. *Moreover, we define the function* $d(\mathcal{A}, \mathcal{B}) = h(\mathcal{A}, \mathcal{B}) + h(\mathcal{B}, \mathcal{A})$.

If $\mathcal{A}$ is a closure system on S, denote by $M(\mathcal{A})$ the system of all $\cap$-irreducible elements of $\mathcal{A}$, i.e.,

$$M(\mathcal{A}) = \left\{A \in \mathcal{A} \colon A \subset \bigcap\{B \in \mathcal{A} \colon A \subset B\}\right\}.$$

Here, $\subset$ denotes the proper inclusion, and the intersection of an empty family of subsets of S is equal to S.

The following lemma shows that the family $M(\mathcal{A})$ can be considered as an optimal representation of the closure system $\mathcal{A}$ [8].

Lemma 1. *Let $\mathcal{A}$ be a closure system on a finite set S, and let $\mathcal{B} \subseteq \mathcal{A}$. The following conditions are equivalent.*

1. $\mathcal{A} = [\mathcal{B}]_S$,
2. $M(\mathcal{A}) \subseteq \mathcal{B}$.

Proof. (1) $\Rightarrow$ (2). Assume the opposite, that is, $\mathcal{A} = [\mathcal{B}]_S$ and $M(\mathcal{A}) \setminus \mathcal{B} \neq \emptyset$. Let A be an element of $M(\mathcal{A}) \setminus \mathcal{B}$. We have $A \in [\mathcal{B}]_S$, hence there exists a family $\mathcal{B}' \subseteq \mathcal{B}$ such that $A = \bigcap \mathcal{B}'$. For every $B \in \mathcal{B}'$ we have $B \in \mathcal{A}$ and $A \subset B$. It follows that $\bigcap\{B \in \mathcal{A} \colon A \subset B\} \subseteq \bigcap \mathcal{B}' = \mathcal{A}$. But then $A \notin M(\mathcal{A})$, a contradiction.

(2) $\Rightarrow$ (1). Assume the opposite, that is, $M(\mathcal{A}) \subseteq \mathcal{B}$ and $[\mathcal{B}]_S \neq \mathcal{A}$. Since $\mathcal{A}$ is a closure system, we have $[\mathcal{B}]_S \subseteq \mathcal{A}$, hence $\mathcal{A} \setminus [\mathcal{B}]_S$ is nonempty. Let A be a maximal element of $\mathcal{A} \setminus [\mathcal{B}]_S$. Denote $\mathcal{A}' = \{B \in \mathcal{A} \colon A \subset B\}$. By the maximality of A we have $\mathcal{A}' \subseteq [\mathcal{B}]_S$, hence $\bigcap \mathcal{A}' \in [\mathcal{B}]_S$. It follows that $A \subset \bigcap \mathcal{A}'$, hence $A \in M(\mathcal{A})$. But then $A \in [\mathcal{B}]_S$, a contradiction.

Theorem 1. *The function d from Definition 5 defines a metric on the space of all closure systems on a set S.*

Proof. We verify the metric axioms:

By definition, $h(\mathcal{A}, \mathcal{B})$ is the cardinality of the smallest system required to extend $\mathcal{A}$ to include $\mathcal{B}$, which is always non-negative. Thus, we have

$$d(\mathcal{A}, \mathcal{B}) = h(\mathcal{A}, \mathcal{B}) + h(\mathcal{B}, \mathcal{A}) \geq 0 \qquad \text{(non-negativity)}.$$

If $\mathcal{A} = \mathcal{B}$, then $\mathcal{A}$ already contains $\mathcal{B}$, implying $h(\mathcal{A}, \mathcal{B}) = 0$ and analogously $h(\mathcal{B}, \mathcal{A}) = 0$. Thus,

$$d(\mathcal{A}, \mathcal{B}) = 0.$$

Conversely, if $d(\mathcal{A}, \mathcal{B}) = 0$, then both $h(\mathcal{A}, \mathcal{B}) = 0$ and $h(\mathcal{B}, \mathcal{A}) = 0$, meaning $\mathcal{A}$ and $\mathcal{B}$ mutually contain each other, which implies $\mathcal{A} = \mathcal{B}$ (identity of indiscernibles).

Since addition is commutative, from definition

$$d(\mathcal{A}, \mathcal{B}) = h(\mathcal{A}, \mathcal{B}) + h(\mathcal{B}, \mathcal{A}).$$

we obtain that

$$d(\mathcal{A}, \mathcal{B}) = d(\mathcal{B}, \mathcal{A}) \quad \text{(symmetry)}.$$

Consider any closure systems $\mathcal{A}, \mathcal{B}, \mathcal{C}$. Consider $\mathcal{S}_1 \subseteq \mathcal{P}(S)$ such that $[\mathcal{A} \cup \mathcal{S}_1]_S \supseteq \mathcal{B}$ and $|\mathcal{S}_1| = h(\mathcal{A}, \mathcal{B})$. Analogously, let $\mathcal{S}_2 \subseteq \mathcal{P}(S)$ be such that $[\mathcal{B} \cup \mathcal{S}_2]_S \supseteq \mathcal{C}$ and $|\mathcal{S}_2| = h(\mathcal{B}, \mathcal{C})$. Now, $\mathcal{S}_3 = \mathcal{S}_1 \cup \mathcal{S}_2$ is such that $[\mathcal{A} \cup \mathcal{S}_3]_S \supseteq \mathcal{C}$. It means that $h(\mathcal{A}, \mathcal{C}) \leq |\mathcal{S}_3| \leq |\mathcal{S}_1| + |\mathcal{S}_2|$.

Thus, we obtain that

$$h(\mathcal{A},\mathcal{C}) \leq h(\mathcal{A},\mathcal{B}) + h(\mathcal{B},\mathcal{C}).$$

Similarly, we can show that

$$h(\mathcal{C},\mathcal{A}) \leq h(\mathcal{C},\mathcal{B}) + h(\mathcal{B},\mathcal{A}).$$

From both inequalities, we obtain:

$$h(\mathcal{A},\mathcal{C}) + h(\mathcal{C},\mathcal{A}) \leq (h(\mathcal{A},\mathcal{B}) + h(\mathcal{B},\mathcal{C})) + (h(\mathcal{C},\mathcal{B}) + h(\mathcal{B},\mathcal{A})).$$

which is equivalent to

$$d(\mathcal{A},\mathcal{C}) \leq d(\mathcal{A},\mathcal{B}) + d(\mathcal{B},\mathcal{C}) \qquad \text{(triangle inequality)}.$$

We obtain that $d(\mathcal{A},\mathcal{B})$ satisfies all four metric properties.

Example 1. labelexe1 Let $S = \{0,1\}$, $\mathcal{A} = \{\{1\},\{0,1\}\}$, $\mathcal{B} = \{\emptyset,\{0\},\{0,1\}\}$. Then $h(\mathcal{A},\mathcal{B}) = 1$, since $\mathcal{A} \not\supseteq \mathcal{B}$ but $[\mathcal{A} \cup \{\{0\}\}]_S \supseteq \mathcal{B}$. Similarly $h(\mathcal{B},\mathcal{A}) = 1$, hence $d(\mathcal{A},\mathcal{B}) = 2$.

We will now compare the above distance function d with two similarly defined distance functions.

Definition 6. *Let $\mathcal{A},\mathcal{B}$ be closure systems on S. Let us define $h_1(\mathcal{A},\mathcal{B}) = |M(\mathcal{B}) \setminus M(\mathcal{A})|$, $h_2(\mathcal{A},\mathcal{B}) = |M(\mathcal{B}) \setminus \mathcal{A}|$, and let $d_1(\mathcal{A},\mathcal{B}) = h_1(\mathcal{A},\mathcal{B}) + h_1(\mathcal{B},\mathcal{A})$, $d_2(\mathcal{A},\mathcal{B}) = h_2(\mathcal{A},\mathcal{B}) + h_2(\mathcal{B},\mathcal{A})$.*

The following example shows that the distance functions d, d_1, d_2 are different.

Example 2. Let $S = \{0,1,2\}$, $\mathcal{A} = \{\emptyset,\{0\},\{1\},\{2\},S\}$, $\mathcal{B} = \{\emptyset,\{0,1\},S\}$. Then $h(\mathcal{A},\mathcal{B}) = 1$ since $\mathcal{A} \not\supseteq \mathcal{B}$ but $[\mathcal{A} \cup \{0,1\}]_S \supseteq \mathcal{B}$. We have also $h(\mathcal{B},\mathcal{A}) = 2$, since $[\mathcal{B} \cup \{\{0,2\},\{1,2\}\}]_S \supseteq \mathcal{A}$, but there is no set $A \subseteq S$ such that $[\mathcal{B} \cup \{A\}]_S \supseteq \mathcal{A}$. Hence $d(\mathcal{A},\mathcal{B}) = 3$. Further, we have $M(\mathcal{A}) = \{\{0\},\{1\},\{2\}\}$, $M(\mathcal{B}) = \{\emptyset,\{0,1\}\}$, hence $h_1(\mathcal{A},\mathcal{B}) = 2$, $h_1(\mathcal{B},\mathcal{A}) = 3$, $h_2(\mathcal{A},\mathcal{B}) = 1$, $h_2(\mathcal{B},\mathcal{A}) = 3$, thus $d_1(\mathcal{A},\mathcal{B}) = 5$ and $d_2(\mathcal{A},\mathcal{B}) = 4$.

Example 2 shows that the distance functions d, d_1, and d_2 can give different results, and this also points to why these differences might matter in practice when comparing concept lattices. For instance, we saw that $d_1(\mathcal{A},\mathcal{B}) = 5$, while $d(\mathcal{A},\mathcal{B}) = 3$. This suggests that d_1 tends to count more differences, since it is based on the symmetric difference of irreducible generators, even if fewer additions are enough to generate the full closure system. So there's a trade-off: d gives a more precise measure of the minimal transformation needed, but it's harder to compute, while d_1 is simpler to calculate but could make two systems seem more different than they actually are. In applications like comparing lattices from school atlas data, such differences can affect how we interpret similarity between contexts—whether we see them as fundamentally different or not.

Choosing which distance to use depends on whether we prioritize precision or computational simplicity.

It is well known that the distance function d_1 satisfies the triangle inequality, hence it is a metric:

$$d_1(\mathcal{A}, \mathcal{C}) = |M(\mathcal{A}) \triangle M(\mathcal{C})| \leq |M(\mathcal{A}) \triangle M(\mathcal{B})| + |M(\mathcal{B}) \triangle M(\mathcal{C})| =$$

$$= d_1(\mathcal{A}, \mathcal{B}) + d_1(\mathcal{B}, \mathcal{C})$$

for all closure systems $\mathcal{A}, \mathcal{B}, \mathcal{C}$ on some set S. We have proved in Theorem 1 that d_1 is also a metric. The following example shows that the distance d_2 is not a metric.

Example 3. labelexe3 Let $S = \{0, 1\}$, $\mathcal{A} = \{\{0\}, S\}$, $\mathcal{B} = \mathcal{P}(S)$, and $\mathcal{C} = \{\emptyset, \{1\}, S\}$. Then $M(\mathcal{A}) = \{\{0\}\}$, $M(\mathcal{B}) = \{\{0\}, \{1\}\}$, $M(\mathcal{C}) = \{\emptyset, \{1\}\}$, and we obtain $d_2(\mathcal{A}, \mathcal{B}) = 1$, $d_2(\mathcal{B}, \mathcal{C}) = 1$, but $d_2(\mathcal{A}, \mathcal{C}) = 3$.

The following theorem shows that functions d_1, d_2 can be considered as estimations of d.

Theorem 2. *Let S be a set and let $\mathcal{A}, \mathcal{B}$ be closure systems on S. Then $d(\mathcal{A}, \mathcal{B}) \leq d_2(\mathcal{A}, \mathcal{B}) \leq d_1(\mathcal{A}, \mathcal{B})$.*

Proof. It suffices to show that $h(\mathcal{A}, \mathcal{B}) \leq h_2(\mathcal{A}, \mathcal{B}) \leq h_1(\mathcal{A}, \mathcal{B})$. We have $M(\mathcal{A}) \subseteq \mathcal{A}$, hence $d_2(\mathcal{A}, \mathcal{B}) = |M(\mathcal{B}) \setminus \mathcal{A}| \leq |M(\mathcal{B}) \setminus M(\mathcal{A})| = d_1(\mathcal{A}, \mathcal{B})$, and the second inequality follows. To prove the first one, let us take $\mathcal{S} = M(\mathcal{B}) \setminus \mathcal{A}$. Then $\mathcal{A} \cup \mathcal{S} \supseteq M(\mathcal{B})$ and hence we have $[\mathcal{A} \cup \mathcal{S}]_S \supseteq \mathcal{B}$. It follows that $d_2(\mathcal{A}, \mathcal{B}) \leq |\mathcal{S}| = d_2(\mathcal{A}, \mathcal{B})$.

Sufficient literature is available in which it is shown that the closure systems on a fixed set S can be understood as concept extents of the formal context $(\mathcal{P}(S), \mathrm{Imp}(S), \models)$, where $\mathcal{P}(S)$ is the power set, $\mathrm{Imp}(S)$ the set of all implications $A \to b$, and $\models$ the "respects" relation (see, e.g., Caspard and Monjardet [9]). Moreover, note that the metric introduced in Definition 5 could be formulated much more generally, namely as the distance between closures of an arbitrary closure system (Definition 5 would then represent the special case of the closure system of all closure systems on S).

While Theorem 2 establishes that $d \leq d_2 \leq d_1$, it is helpful to interpret these distances in terms of their operational behavior. The distance d captures the minimal number of subsets that need to be added to one closure system to obtain the other and is thus *sensitive to the global structure* of the systems. In contrast, d_1 and d_2 are defined using the sets of $\cap$-irreducible elements, which play a central role in the implication theory of Formal Concept Analysis. Specifically, d_1 measures the symmetric difference between the generating sets of two closure systems and is *more coarse* but computationally simpler. The function d_2 penalizes generators from one system not present in the other and is *more sensitive to directional inclusion*, making it suitable when one system is treated as a baseline or reference.

4 Application in Industrial Maps

Industrial maps from 63 school atlases of the world, selected from the private collection of one of the authors, were used to illustrate the proposed distance functions d_1 and d_2 (Definition 6). The atlases, published between 1938 and 2018, represent 40 publishers from 23 countries (see Tables 1 and 2). The maps ranged in scale from 1:25 million to 1:90 million. The maps were selected based on four main criteria: (i) geographic diversity (to ensure global representation); (ii) publisher variety (to reflect different editorial standards); (iii) temporal coverage—from 1938 to recent editions; and (iv) thematic clarity, assessed by the map's visual organization, presence of labeled industrial symbols, and the completeness of the legend. Maps that lacked clearly distinguishable industrial content or used ambiguous graphical symbols were excluded.

Table 1. Number of atlases from the author's private collection by country of publication (we used ISO 3166-1 alpha-3 country codes for consistency)

Number of atlases	Country of publication
10	CZE, GBR
6	AUT, DEU, USA
3	BEL, ZAF
2	POL, SVN, SVK
1	CAN, HRV, ESP, FIN, HUN, LVA, LTU, NLD, PRT, RUS, SGP, CHE, SWE
63	Total

It is important to acknowledge that thematic maps in school atlases are shaped not only by cartographic conventions but also by educational, cultural, and other influences. For instance, certain atlases emphasize heavy industry (e.g., metallurgy, coal mining), reflecting historical industrial pride, while others highlight high-tech sectors or environmental concerns. Similarly, the presence or absence of certain resources or sectors may reflect national priorities, curricular emphases, or geopolitical framing. These underlying factors likely influence the structure of the resulting concept lattices and should be considered when interpreting observed differences.

Since a map functions as a communication tool, its core significance lies in the message it conveys. The content of the map (see Fig. 1) refers to the set of elements it includes, i.e., *what is represented* on the map.

We denote the set of 63 industrial maps from school atlases of the world as the set of objects B. The attributes used to encode map content were created through a systematic review of recurring industrial elements across all maps. For example, the 45 attributes for mineral resources were derived by identifying all distinct mineral types (e.g., coal, iron ore, bauxite, etc.) explicitly shown

Table 2. Number of atlases by publication period

Number of atlases	Publication period
2	1938–1945
9	1946–1989
11	1990–2000
30	2001–2010
11	2011–2018
63	Total

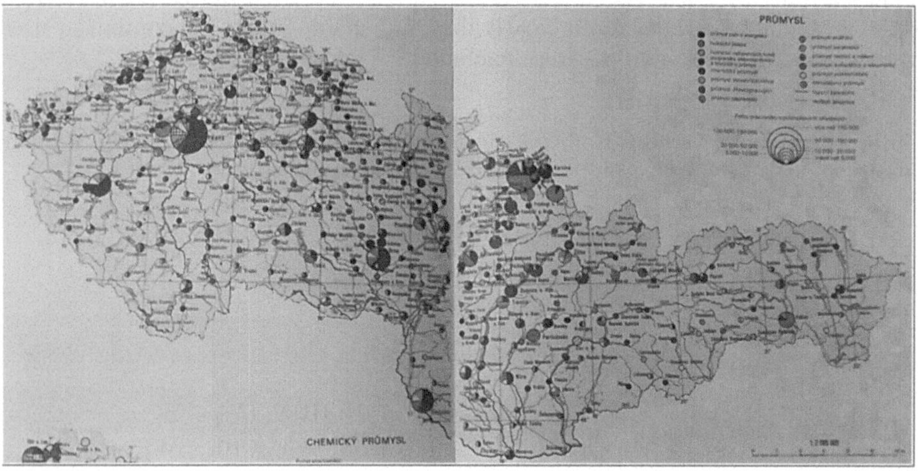

Fig. 1. Example of a complex thematic map, map of the industry of Czechoslovakia, published in the school atlas, used here as a representative example of mid-20th-century cartographic depiction of industrial distribution.

on at least one map. Minerals were grouped individually if they were treated separately in legends or symbolized independently. The same principle applied to power infrastructure and industrial sectors. Thus, we categorized the content of the industrial maps into three groups of attributes: the set of 13 attributes for industrial sectors (denoted A_1), the set of 12 attributes of power plants, product pipelines, raw material transport (denoted A_2), and the set of 45 attributes of mineral resources (denoted A_3).

We use a binary indication for each map to record whether each specific element was included in the map's content. In Fig. 2, we present the part of source data with five industrial maps and their 33 attributes. We can see that the School Atlas of the World from 1998 includes iron metallurgy, non-ferrous metallurgy, engineering, chemical, building materials, wood processing, and the food industry from the group of industrial sectors.

Industrial sectors

	iron metallurgy	non-ferrous metallurgy	engineering	chemical	building materials	wood processing	food industry	unspecified	textile	leather industry	electrical industry	glass industry	rubber industry
1998 School Atlas of the World/CART	1	1	1	1	1	1	1	1	0	0	0	0	0
1989 School Atlas of the World/CART	1	1	1	1	1	1	1	1	1	1	0	0	0
1978 School Atlas of the World/CART	1	1	1	1	0	0	1	1	1	0	0	0	0
2012 School Atlas of the World/CART	0	0	0	0	0	0	0	0	0	0	0	0	0
2004 School Atlas of the World/SHO	0	0	0	0	0	0	0	0	0	0	0	0	0

Power plants and transport

	thermal power plant	hydroelectric power plant	nuclear power plant	geothermal power plant	tidal power plant	oil pipeline	gas pipeline	port	airport	road routes	railway routes	river navigability
1998 School Atlas of the World/CART	1	1	0	0	0	1	1	1	0	0	0	0
1989 School Atlas of the World/CART	1	1	0	0	0	1	1	1	0	0	0	0
1978 School Atlas of the World/CART	1	1	0	0	0	1	1	1	1	0	0	0
2012 School Atlas of the World/CART	0	0	0	0	0	1	1	1	1	1	1	1
2004 School Atlas of the World/SHO	0	1	1	0	0	0	0	0	0	0	0	0

Mineral resources

	hard coal	lignite coal	petroleum	natural gas	iron ore	manganese	chrom	antimon
1998 School Atlas of the World/CART	1	0	1	1	1	1	1	1
1989 School Atlas of the World/CART	1	0	1	1	1	1	1	1
1978 School Atlas of the World/CART	1	0	1	1	1	1	1	1
2012 School Atlas of the World/CART	1	0	1	1	1	1	1	0
2004 School Atlas of the World/SHO	1	0	1	1	1	1	1	1

Fig. 2. Part of coded data from industrial maps of school atlases

We use the full shape of our coded data to obtain three incidence relations $I_1 \subseteq B \times A_1$, $I_2 \subseteq B \times A_2$, and $I_3 \subseteq B \times A_3$. These incidence relations on the same set of objects B were used to construct three concept lattices of formal contexts $\langle B, A_1, I_1 \rangle$, $\langle B, A_2, I_2 \rangle$, $\langle B, A_3, I_3 \rangle$, respectively.

In Table 3, we present the characteristics of concept lattices of three mentioned formal contexts. In particular, $|\underline{\mathfrak{B}}|$ is the number of formal concepts of the concept lattice $\underline{\mathfrak{B}}$ in the selected group of attributes. $|M(\underline{\mathfrak{B}})|$ is the number of meet-irreducible elements of the concept lattice $\underline{\mathfrak{B}}$ in the selected set of attributes.

Table 3. Characteristics of concept lattices of three formal contexts

Formal context	$\lvert\underline{\mathfrak{B}}\rvert$	$\lvert M(\underline{\mathfrak{B}})\rvert$
$\langle B, A_1, I_1 \rangle$	88	14
$\langle B, A_2, I_2 \rangle$	42	12
$\langle B, A_3, I_3 \rangle$	2,244	35

In Table 4, we compare the concept lattices between three attribute groups derived from the content of the industrial maps using distance functions d_1 and d_2 from Definition 6.

Our proposed methods were implemented in the Go programming language, which offers efficient concurrency support and lightweight goroutines. These features are particularly advantageous when processing large concept lattices or multiple formal contexts in parallel, allowing scalable and high-performance computation.

Table 4. Distances between concept lattices of three formal contexts

Formal contexts	d_1	d_2
$\langle B, A_1, I_1\rangle$ vs. $\langle B, A_2, I_2\rangle$	24	24
$\langle B, A_1, I_1\rangle$ vs. $\langle B, A_3, I_3\rangle$	47	47
$\langle B, A_2, I_2\rangle$ vs. $\langle B, A_3, I_3\rangle$	45	44

4.1 Interpretation of Results

The analysis of 63 industrial maps, systematically categorized into three thematic attribute groups, i.e., industrial sectors (A_1), energy infrastructure and transport (A_2), and mineral resources (A_3), reveals substantial variation in the structural complexity of the corresponding concept lattices. As shown in Table 3, the concept lattice derived from mineral resource attributes, i.e., $\langle B, A_3, I_3\rangle$, exhibits a significantly larger number of extents (2,244 each), indicating a high level of attribute differentiation and conceptual richness. In contrast, the lattices constructed from industrial sectors (A_1) and energy-related infrastructure (A_2) are considerably simpler, with 88 and 42 concepts, respectively. Since the sets A_1 and A_2 contain 13 and 12 attributes, respectively, we obtain that energy-related infrastructure attributes provide more homogeneous or overlapping representations within those thematic domains.

The numbers of meet-irreducible elements, representing the minimal building blocks of the concept lattices, show relatively small differences across the three contexts. For instance, the industrial sectors lattice has 14 meet-irreducible elements, while the energy infrastructure lattice has 12. The mineral resources lattice, despite its much larger overall size, has 35 meet-irreducible elements. These values suggest that while the lattices vary significantly in their overall complexity, their underlying logical architecture, captured by the distribution of meet-irreducibles, remains comparatively stable across thematic domains.

The computed distance measures d_1 and d_2 between pairs of concept lattices, summarized in Table 4, quantitatively affirm these qualitative observations. The smallest distance is between industrial sectors and energy infrastructure ($d_1 = d_2 = 24$), suggesting a higher degree of thematic overlap and structural similarity in the way these topics are depicted across atlases. In contrast, the largest distances occur between energy infrastructure and mineral resources ($d_1 = 45$, $d_2 = 44$), as well as between industrial sectors and mineral resources ($d_1 = d_2 = 47$), pointing to a considerable semantic divergence. For example, the distance of 47 between A_1 and A_3 confirms that mineral-related content is much less aligned with industrial sector depictions. This may reflect the fact that mineral resources are often presented as separate geological layers, with distinct cartographic styles and symbology, whereas industry and energy infrastructure are more frequently integrated or co-located on the same maps.

These findings demonstrate that the proposed distance functions effectively capture the semantic and structural dissimilarities between thematic layers of school atlases. The high conceptual complexity of the mineral resource layer, with 2,244 extents, could be interpreted in two ways. On one hand, it may reflect genuinely rich geological detail and a wide variety of mineral types explicitly represented. On the other hand, it may also stem from inconsistencies in symbology, labeling, or data granularity across different atlas publishers and periods. Unlike industrial and energy infrastructure themes, which often rely on standardized symbols and shared conventions, the portrayal of mineral resources may vary more significantly, especially across different national cartographic traditions. This variance could impact both map readability and the clarity of educational messaging, particularly for students trying to understand global patterns. Distinguishing between detailed representation and visual inconsistency is therefore an important direction for future work, potentially involving visual symbol analysis or deeper legend parsing.

5 Conclusions

In this paper, we presented distance functions between closure systems, which can be applied to compare concept lattices defined over the same set of objects but different sets of attributes. We demonstrated the practical relevance of these functions through an application to the compilation of industrial maps in school world atlases from various global publishers.

Our approach provides a novel bridge between abstract lattice-theoretic structures and concrete cartographic data, enabling systematic comparison of thematic content across educational resources. The distance functions we proposed offer a formal tool for detecting similarities and differences in how knowledge is encoded and visualized in atlases.

In our future work, we aim to investigate whether school atlases from different countries and publishers present a uniform depiction of particular phenomena, in this case, industrial distribution. If such convergence is confirmed, one could argue for the existence of an implicit, standardized cartographic convention.

It is worth noting that the distance function introduced in Definition 5 operates at the level of closure systems, and we applied it to formal contexts sharing the same object set. A more elegant formulation could define such a distance directly on formal contexts, using the notion of scale measures.

Beyond industrial maps, this method holds potential for comparative analyses of various thematic cartographic layers, such as historical vs. modern thematic maps, educational representations across curricula, or environmental data from different sources. Such applications highlight the generality of our framework in supporting knowledge comparison across domains.

Acknowledgments. This work was supported by the Slovak Research and Development Agency under contract No. APVV-21-0468 (L'. Antoni). This article was supported by the Scientific Grant Agency of the Ministry of Education, Science, Research and Sport of the Slovak Republic under contract VEGA 1/0539/25 (O. Krídlo, S. Krajči). This article was partially supported by the project KEGA 010-UPJŠ-4/2024 (J. Guniš, L'. Šnajder, D. Kotlárová). P. Eliaš was supported by the Slovak Research and Development Agency under the contract no. APVV-20-0069, and by the Scientific Grant Agency (VEGA) under grant no. VEGA 2/0104/24.

Disclosure of Interests. The authors have no competing interests to declare that are relevant to the content of this article.

References

1. Wille, R.: Restructuring lattice theory: an approach based on hierarchies of concepts. In: Rival, I. (ed.) Ordered Sets, pp. 445–470. Reidel, Dordrecht-Boston (1982)
2. Wille, R.: Formal concept analysis as applied lattice theory. In: Yahia, S.B., Nguifo, E.M., Belohlavek, R. (eds.) CLA 2006. LNCS (LNAI), vol. 4923, pp. 42–67. Springer, Heidelberg (2008). https://doi.org/10.1007/978-3-540-78921-5_3
3. Ganter, B., Wille, R.: Formal Concept Analysis: Mathematical Foundation. Springer, Cham (1999)
4. Domenach, F., Portides, G.: Similarity measures on concept lattices. In: Wilhelm, A., Kestler, H. (eds.) Analysis of Large and Complex Data. STUDIES CLASS, Springer, Cham (2016). https://doi.org/10.1007/978-3-319-25226-1_14
5. Domenach, F., Portides, G.: Similarity measures on concept lattices. In: Wilhelm, A.F.X., Kestler, H.A. (eds.) Analysis of Large and Complex Data. SCDAKO, pp. 159–169. Springer, Cham (2016). https://doi.org/10.1007/978-3-319-25226-1_14
6. Domenach, F., Rajabi, Z.: Correspondence-based lattice similarity measure. Arch. Data Sci. Ser. A **2**(1), 109–123 (2017). https://publikationen.bibliothek.kit.edu/1000065969
7. Bazin, A., Kahn, G.: Distances Between Formal Concept Analysis Structures (2024). https://hal.archives-ouvertes.fr/hal-04475242
8. Davey, B.A., Priestley, H.A.: Introduction to Lattices and Order, 2nd edn. Cambridge University Press, Cambridge (2002)
9. Caspard, N., Monjardet, B.: The lattices of closure systems, closure operators, and implicational systems on a finite set: a survey. Discret. Appl. Math. **127**(2), 241–269 (2003). https://doi.org/10.1016/S0166-218X(02)00209-3

Theory

When Horn is All You Need

Sergei Obiedkov[1,2](✉) and Sebastian Rudolph[1,2]

[1] TU Dresden, Dresden, Germany
[2] Center for Scalable Data Analytics and Artificial Intelligence (ScaDS.AI), Dresden/Leipzig, Germany
{sergei.obiedkov,sebastian.rudolph}@tu-dresden.de

Abstract. In classical formal concept analysis, *attribute logic* refers to the study of implications that hold between the attributes of a formal context. In some scenarios, attributes may be logically interdependent *a priori* by definition, particularly when they are defined by logical formulae. This paper examines various settings in which attributes are logically defined and explores the resulting effects on attribute logic and on the structure of the concept lattice. We also investigate under which conditions the implicational theory of a context with logically defined attributes is as informative as the underlying context itself for deciding the validity of logical formulae.

Keywords: FCA · attribute logic · compound attributes

1 Introduction

One way to understand formal contexts in formal concept analysis (FCA) [3] is to assume that the objects correspond to different conceivable scenarios or situations, while the attributes represent statements that may or may not hold in these scenarios. Such a perspective gives rise to a logical, model-theoretic view on FCA, where the context's objects are associated with logical interpretations and the attributes are logical formulae that may or may not hold in each of the considered interpretations.

Clearly, attributes logically defined in this way must follow certain constraints regarding their (co-)occurrence in object intents. For instance, the attribute $p \vee q$ must always be present when the attribute q is. Likewise, the attributes p and $\neg p$ can never co-exist in an object intent.

In such a setting, there are different ways to describe the "logical content" of a formal context in the sense of a formula that summarizes the "logical commonalities" of all present objects. Two typical ways to obtain such descriptions are (1) directly from the context via an object-wise disjunction or (2) from (a representation of) the context's implicational theory. The latter is always implied by the former, but might be logically weaker, given that it can only express Horn-like relationships between the attributes.

In this paper, we formally introduce the aforementioned approach of "logical contexts", where objects represent interpretations and attributes represent

P. Cellier et al. (Eds.): CONCEPTS 2025, LNAI 15941, pp. 309–324, 2025.
https://doi.org/10.1007/978-3-032-03364-2_20

logical statements. We then investigate the relationship between the two different types of logical "summaries", first focusing on two specific cases from propositional logic (referred to as literal contexts and disjunctive contexts), and then presenting a general criterion for determining when the two summaries are logically equivalent.

2 Preliminaries

2.1 Lattices

Recall that a *lattice* is a partially ordered set $(L, \leq)$ in which every pair of elements $a, b \in L$ has a meet and a join. The *meet* or *infimum*, denoted $a \sqcap b$, is the unique largest element among elements $x \in L$ such that $x \leq a$ and $x \leq b$. Similarly, the *join* or *supremum*, denoted $a \sqcup b$, is the unique smallest element among elements $y \in L$ such that $a \leq y$ and $b \leq y$.[3]

The meet and join operations can be extended to arbitrary subsets of L in a straightforward way. For example, $\bigsqcup A$ for $A \subseteq L$ is the unique smallest element in the set $\{y \in L \mid \forall a \in A\colon a \leq y\}$. Such an element does not always exist. Lattices where joins and meets exist for all subsets are called *complete.* All finite lattices are complete. Every complete lattice has the least element, denoted 0, and the greatest element, denoted 1.

An element $x \in L$ is said to be *join-irreducible* if $x = \bigsqcup A$ implies $x \in A$. *Meet-irreducible* elements are defined similarly.

An *atom* in L is a minimal nonzero element, i.e., an element $a \neq 0$ such that, if $b \leq a$, then either $b = 0$ or $b = a$. A lattice is *atomistic* if every join-irreducible element is an atom.

A lattice L is *distributive* if the distributive laws hold for all $a, b, c \in L$:

$$a \sqcap (b \sqcup c) = (a \sqcap b) \sqcup (a \sqcap c), \qquad a \sqcup (b \sqcap c) = (a \sqcup b) \sqcap (a \sqcup c).$$

2.2 Contexts, Concepts, Implications

In FCA, data is organized in a *(formal) context*, which defines a relation between a set of objects and a set of attributes [3]. This is represented as a triple $\mathbb{K} = (G, M, I)$, where G is the set of objects, M is the set of attributes, and $I \subseteq G \times M$ is a binary relation indicating whether an object has a certain attribute.

For a set of objects $A \subseteq G$, the *derivation operator* $(\cdot)'$ applied to A produces the set of attributes that are common to all objects in A:

$$A' = \{m \in M \mid \forall g \in A\colon (g, m) \in I\}.$$

Similarly, for a set of attributes $B \subseteq M$, the derivation operator $(\cdot)'$ applied to B yields the set of objects that possess all attributes in B:

$$B' = \{g \in G \mid \forall m \in B\colon (g, m) \in I\}.$$

[3] While $\vee$ and $\wedge$ are commonly used to denote join and meet in the literature, we reserve these symbols for logical conjunction and disjunction.

A *(formal) concept* of a formal context is a pair (A, B), where A (the *extent*) is a set of objects and B (the *intent*) is a set of attributes, satisfying $A' = B$ and $B' = A$. That is, A consists of all objects sharing the attributes in B, and B consists of all attributes common to the objects in A. For $g \in G$, the set $\{g\}'$, often written g', is the *object intent* of g. Similarly, for $m \in M$, the set $m' = \{m\}'$ is the *attribute extent* of m.

A concept (A, B) is said to be at least as *general* as a concept (C, D) if $C \subseteq A$ or, equivalently, if $B \subseteq D$. This is denoted by $(C, D) \leq (A, B)$. The set of all concepts of a context $\mathbb{K}$, ordered in this way, forms a complete lattice called the *concept lattice* of $\mathbb{K}$.

For $A, B \subseteq M$, the *implication* $A \to B$ is said to *hold* in the context $\mathbb{K}$ if $A' \subseteq B'$. A set $X \subseteq M$ *respects* $A \to B$ if $A \nsubseteq X$ or $B \subseteq X$. It respects an implication set Σ (denoted $X \Vdash \Sigma$) if it respects every implication in Σ. It is easy to see that all implications in Σ hold in $\mathbb{K}$ if and only if every object intent of $\mathbb{K}$ respects Σ.

An implication $A \to B$ *follows from* or *is entailed by* an implication set Σ if every attribute set $C \subseteq M$ that respects Σ also respects $A \to B$. Given a context $\mathbb{K}$ and an implication set Σ, we call Σ

- *sound* w.r.t. $\mathbb{K}$ if all implications in Σ hold in $\mathbb{K}$;
- *complete* w.r.t. $\mathbb{K}$ if all implications that hold in $\mathbb{K}$ follow from Σ;
- *non-redundant* if no implication in Σ follows from the others;
- an *implication basis* of $\mathbb{K}$ if it is sound, complete, and non-redundant.

Among the multiple bases of a context, the *canonical* or *Duquenne–Guigues* basis, as defined in [4], has the fewest implications.

2.3 Logics and Model-Theoretic Semantics

From a very generic perspective, a *logic* is defined as a pair $(\mathcal{L}, \dot{\models})$ where $\mathcal{L}$ is a set containing the *formulas* of the logic and $\dot{\models} \subseteq 2^{\mathcal{L}} \times \mathcal{L}$ is the *entailment relation* where $\Phi \dot{\models} \varphi$ means that φ is a logical consequence of Φ.[4] An entailment relation gives rise to a so-called *consequence operator* $\mathrm{Cn} : 2^{\mathcal{L}} \to 2^{\mathcal{L}}$, defined via $\mathrm{Cn}(\Phi) = \{\varphi \mid \Phi \dot{\models} \varphi\}$.

An important subclass of logics, comprising the classical logics including propositional, first-order, and higher-order logics, are the *Tarskian logics* which are characterized by the fact that the entailment relation can be defined in a model-theoretic way by means of a *satisfaction system* $(\mathcal{I}, \mathcal{L}, \models)$ where $\mathcal{I}$ is some set called *interpretations* and $\models \subseteq \mathcal{I} \times \mathcal{L}$ is the *satisfaction relation*. For $\varphi \in \mathcal{L}$ and $\mathfrak{I} \in \mathcal{I}$, we read $\mathfrak{I} \models \varphi$ as "$\mathfrak{I}$ satisfies φ" and we also call $\mathfrak{I}$ a *model* of φ. If such a satisfaction system is provided, it gives rise to an entailment relation by letting $\Phi \dot{\models} \psi$ whenever every model of all $\varphi \in \Phi$ is also a model of ψ. For any entailment relation defined in this way, the corresponding consequence operator is a closure operator (often referred to as the *deductive closure*).

[4] In the literature, $\dot{\models}$ is often denoted $\models$, coinciding with the notation for satisfaction. For better clarity, we prefer to distinguish the two symbols. Also, we may write $\phi \dot{\models} \psi$ for $\{\phi\} \dot{\models} \psi$.

3 Attribute Logic of Contexts with Logically Defined Attributes

Given a logic with model-theoretic semantics represented by a satisfaction system $\mathbb{S} = (\mathcal{I}, \mathcal{L}, \models)$, an $\mathbb{S}$-*context* is a context (G, M, I), where

- each object $g \in G$ is associated with some interpretation $\mathfrak{I}_g \in \mathcal{I}$;
- attributes are $\mathcal{L}$-formulas, i.e., $M \subseteq \mathcal{L}$; and
- gIm if and only if $\mathfrak{I}_g \models m$.

In such a setting, the objects of the context represent situations, scenarios or possible worlds, while the attributes are statements that may or may not hold in these situations, scenarios, or possible worlds.

Example 1. Chapter 2 of [6] presents a collection of puzzles set in the world of Lewis Carroll's *Alice in Wonderland.* In these puzzles, the King of Hearts asks the Queen of Hearts to prepare some tarts, only to discover that various ingredients are missing. Among them is jam, which is found in the house of the March Hare, the Mad Hatter, and the Dormouse. The three are brought to trial. Assuming that at least one of them is guilty and—why not?—that the Dormouse always steals alone, this scenario can be described using the $\mathbb{S}$-context shown in Fig. 1.

Who Stole the Jam?	*hare*	*hatter*	*dormouse*	*hare* ∨ *hatter*	¬*dormouse*
March Hare	×			×	×
Mad Hatter		×		×	×
March Hare and Mad Hatter	×	×		×	×
Dormouse			×		

$$\neg dormouse \to hare \vee hatter$$
$$hare \vee hatter \to \neg dormouse$$
$$hare \to \neg dormouse$$
$$hatter \to \neg dormouse$$
$$dormouse, \neg dormouse \to hare, hatter$$

Fig. 1. A propositional-logic context and its implication basis. Here and below, we omit curly brackets around sets when their omission does not cause confusion.

We work here with $\mathbb{S}$ being propositional logic, where our language includes three propositional variables: *hare*, *hatter*, and *dormouse*. Each variable represents the claim that the corresponding suspect has stolen the jam. We have the freedom to choose which sentences involving these three variables to include in the $\mathbb{S}$-context. In this case, we include the atomic sentences, a single disjunction of two of them, and the negation of the third. Each is associated with an attribute of the $\mathbb{S}$-context. Under our assumptions, only four out of the eight possible interpretations remain admissible, corresponding to the four objects of the context.

In this framework, it is clear that attributes can be a priori logically interdependent. In particular, not every combination $A \subseteq M$ of attributes can occur as an object intent (for instance, in the above example, a scenario where *hare* $\vee$ *hatter* holds but neither *hare* nor *hatter* does, would be nonsensical). Consequently, an attribute set $A \subseteq M$ is called $\mathbb{S}$-M-*coherent* (or just *coherent*, if $\mathbb{S}$ and M are clear) if there exists some $\mathfrak{I} \in \mathcal{I}$ such that $\mathfrak{I} \models m$ for all $m \in A$ and $\mathfrak{I} \not\models m$ for all $m \in M \setminus A$. If the considered logic $\mathbb{S}$ supports conjunction and negation (at least on the sentence level), the $\mathbb{S}$-M-coherence of A corresponds to the satisfiability of the sentence

$$\Big(\bigwedge_{m \in A} m\Big) \wedge \Big(\bigwedge_{m \in M \setminus A} \neg m\Big)$$

in the logic $\mathbb{S}$. Clearly, by definition, the object intents of an $\mathbb{S}$-context (G, M, I) are always $\mathbb{S}$-M-coherent.

From now on, we will assume that the logic $\mathbb{S}$ is Boolean-closed and that it supports the connectives $\neg$, $\wedge$, $\vee$, $\rightarrow$ with their usual semantics. We note that the symbol $\rightarrow$ is then slightly overloaded, since it is also used as a syntactic element in FCA implications. However, the two notions are closely related, and we believe there is no danger of confusion.

A useful notion in logical contexts is the following: an $\mathcal{L}$-formula φ is *valid* in $\mathbb{K} = (G, M, I)$ if every $g \in G$ satisfies $\mathfrak{f}_{\mathbb{K}}(g) \models \varphi$, where

$$\mathfrak{f}_{\mathbb{K}}(g) = \Big(\bigwedge_{m \in g'} m\Big) \wedge \Big(\bigwedge_{m \in M \setminus g'} \neg m\Big).$$

Note that a formula does not need to be contained in M to be valid in $\mathbb{K}$. Defining

$$\Phi(\mathbb{K}) = \bigvee_{g \in G} \mathfrak{f}_{\mathbb{K}}(g),$$

we can express validity in a context by means of logical entailment:

Proposition 1. *Given* $\mathbb{S} = (\mathcal{I}, \mathcal{L}, \models)$*, a formula* $\varphi \in \mathcal{L}$ *is valid in an* $\mathbb{S}$*-context* $\mathbb{K} = (G, M, I)$ *if and only if* $\Phi(\mathbb{K}) \models \varphi$.

Proof. Suppose that φ is valid in $\mathbb{K}$, i.e., $\mathfrak{f}_{\mathbb{K}}(g) \models \varphi$ for all $g \in G$. Every interpretation that satisfies $\Phi(\mathbb{K})$ also satisfies $\mathfrak{f}_{\mathbb{K}}(g)$ for some $g \in G$ and, therefore, must satisfy φ. It follows that $\Phi(\mathbb{K}) \models \varphi$.

Conversely, suppose that φ is not valid in $\mathbb{K}$. Then there exists some $g \in G$ such that $\mathfrak{f}_{\mathbb{K}}(g) \not\models \varphi$. This means that there must be an interpretation $\mathfrak{I}$ that satisfies $\mathfrak{f}_{\mathbb{K}}(g)$—and thus $\Phi(\mathbb{K})$—but not φ. Consequently, $\Phi(\mathbb{K}) \not\models \varphi$. □

It will also be useful to represent an implication set Σ as a formula, analogous to the $\Phi(\mathbb{K})$ representation of an $\mathbb{S}$-context $\mathbb{K}$. A natural choice is

$$\Psi(\Sigma) = \bigwedge_{A \rightarrow B \in \Sigma} \mathfrak{g}(A \rightarrow B), \quad \text{where} \quad \mathfrak{g}(A \rightarrow B) = \Big(\bigwedge_{m \in A} m\Big) \rightarrow \Big(\bigwedge_{m \in B} m\Big).$$

Note that $\mathfrak{g}(A \rightarrow B)$ and $\Psi(\Sigma)$ can be rewritten as a conjunction of *Horn clauses*, i.e., disjunctions of literals with at most one occurring without negation.

Proposition 2. *Given $\mathbb{S} = (\mathcal{I}, \mathcal{L}, \models)$ and an implication set Σ over an attribute set $M \subseteq \mathcal{L}$, we have $\mathfrak{I} \models \Psi(\Sigma)$ for $\mathfrak{I} \in \mathcal{I}$ if and only if $\{m \in M \mid \mathfrak{I} \models m\} \Vdash \Sigma$.*

Proof. The set $\{m \in M \mid \mathfrak{I} \models m\}$ respects $A \to B$ if and only if $\mathfrak{I} \not\models m$ for some $m \in A$ or $\mathfrak{I} \models m$ for all $m \in B$, which occurs if and only if $\mathfrak{I} \models \mathfrak{g}(A \to B)$. The result follows. □

Proposition 3. *Let $\mathbb{K} = (G, M, I)$ be an $\mathbb{S}$-context and Σ be an implication set over M. Then $\Psi(\Sigma)$ is valid in $\mathbb{K}$ if and only if all implications in Σ hold in $\mathbb{K}$.*

Proof. An object intent g' respects an implication $A \to B \in \Sigma$ if and only if $m \notin g'$ for some $m \in A$ or $m \in g'$ for all $m \in B$. This is equivalent to $\mathfrak{f}_{\mathbb{K}}(g) \models \mathfrak{g}(A \to B)$. It follows that $g' \Vdash \Sigma$ if and only if $\mathfrak{f}_{\mathbb{K}}(g) \models \Psi(\Sigma)$. Thus, all implications in Σ hold in $\mathbb{K}$ if and only if $\Psi(\Sigma)$ is valid in $\mathbb{K}$. □

Corollary 1. *Let $\mathbb{K} = (G, M, I)$ be an $\mathbb{S}$-context and Σ be an implication set over M. Then $\Phi(\mathbb{K}) \dot{\models} \Psi(\Sigma)$ if and only if all implications in Σ hold in $\mathbb{K}$.*

The fact that attributes in an $\mathbb{S}$-context can be logically interdependent through the underlying logic suggests introducing revised versions of entailment, completeness, redundancy, and basis. Given a logic $\mathbb{S}$, we say that an implication $A \to B$, where $A, B \subseteq M$, *$\mathbb{S}$-follows from* or *is $\mathbb{S}$-entailed by* (or, if $\mathbb{S}$ is clear, *logically follows from, is logically entailed by*) an implication set Σ if $\Psi(\Sigma) \dot{\models} \mathfrak{g}(A \to B)$. Given a context $\mathbb{K}$, we say that an implication set Σ is *$\mathbb{S}$-complete* (or *logically complete*), if every implication that holds in $\mathbb{K}$ $\mathbb{S}$-follows from Σ. Σ is *$\mathbb{S}$-non-redundant* (or *logically non-redundant*), if no implication in Σ $\mathbb{S}$-follows from the others. Finally, we call Σ an *$\mathbb{S}$-implication basis* (or *logical implication basis*) of $\mathbb{K}$ if it is sound, $\mathbb{S}$-complete, and $\mathbb{S}$-non-redundant.

Example 2. Consider the $\mathbb{S}$-context from Example 1. The assumptions used to build it—that at least one character is guilty and that the Dormouse always steals alone—can be expressed as follows:

$$\mathit{hare} \lor \mathit{hatter} \lor \mathit{dormouse} \qquad \mathit{dormouse} \land (\mathit{hare} \lor \mathit{hatter}) \to \bot,$$

or, using the attributes of our $\mathbb{S}$-context, as an $\mathbb{S}$-implication basis:

$$\neg \mathit{dormouse} \to \mathit{hare} \lor \mathit{hatter} \qquad \mathit{hare} \lor \mathit{hatter} \to \neg \mathit{dormouse}.$$

However, as shown in Fig. 1, the canonical basis of this context consists of five implications. Like any basis, it is non-redundant in the sense defined in Section 2.2. Still, it is not *logically* non-redundant, as the last three implications logically follow from the first two. This redundancy can be reduced or eliminated by computing a basis *relative to background knowledge* that captures the logic underlying the attributes [2], which is beyond the scope of this paper.

In FCA literature, propositional-logic formulae are sometimes referred to as *compound attributes* [2,3]. The difference from our set-up is that compound attributes are not assumed to be part of the attribute set M of a formal context:

they are Boolean combinations of attributes from M, which are treated as independent propositional variables. In this setting, an object intent fully determines an interpretation by assigning values to each variable in M. The *extent of a compound attribute* φ in $\mathbb{K} = (G, M, I)$ is defined as the subset A of G such that the interpretations corresponding to objects in A satisfy ϕ. A compound attribute is *all-extensional* in $\mathbb{K}$ if its extent is G. Two compound attributes are said to be *extensionally equivalent over* $\mathbb{K}$ if they have the same extents in $\mathbb{K}$ and *globally equivalent* if they have the same extents in any context with attribute set M. Globally equivalent compound attributes are precisely those that are extensionally equivalent in the *test context* $(\mathfrak{P}(M), M, \ni)$. They correspond to equivalent propositional formulae.

A set of compound attributes can be added to $\mathbb{K}$. If this is done so that their extents are preserved, the resulting context is called a *Boolean enrichment* of $\mathbb{K}$, which is, in our terms, an $\mathbb{S}$-context. Compound attributes that are all-extensional in $\mathbb{K}$ are precisely the formulae we call valid in $\mathbb{K}$ (or, equivalently, in any of its Boolean enrichments). Note, however, that our $\mathbb{S}$-contexts are slightly more general because they are not required to include all atoms as attributes.

While, in our framework, the selection of M from $\mathcal{L}$ is arbitrary, most usage scenarios will require it to follow certain principles. In the case of propositional logic, for instance, one reasonable assumption is that M contains all propositional atoms. In that case, the attribute extent of every non-atomic attribute can be determined from the extents of the atomic attributes.

Another common assumption is that M is closed under certain Boolean operations. In such cases, one may also investigate the effects on the attribute logic, the structure of the resulting concept lattices, and the properties of implication bases. In particular, we examine the settings where $\Phi(\mathbb{K}) \equiv \Psi(\Sigma)$, with Σ being an implication basis of $\mathbb{K}$. We begin by studying the specific cases where M is closed under negation or disjunction.

4 The Case of Negated Attributes

Let us consider the case where M is closed under negation. As a basic example, M might consist of *literals*, that is, of atomic propositions and their negations: $M = P \cup \{\neg p \mid p \in P\}$ for some set P of propositional atoms. In the following, we will call such propositional logic contexts *literal contexts*.

We note that, in this case, no object can have all attributes of M simultaneously (as M contains atoms and their negations); therefore, M as a whole describes falsity, denoted $\bot$, which we will sometimes use instead of M for clarity. We also note in Proposition 4 that the implications that hold in a literal context fully determine which attribute sets appear as object intents of that context – which does not hold for arbitrary contexts.

Proposition 4. *Let $\mathbb{K} = (G, M, I)$ be a literal context for some set P of propositional atoms. Then an attribute set S is an object intent of $\mathbb{K}$ if and only if it is of the form $A \cup \{\neg p \mid p \in P \setminus A\}$ for some $A \subseteq P$ and all implications that hold in $\mathbb{K}$ are respected by S.*

Proof. **(Only if)**: Consider an arbitrary object $g \in G$ and its corresponding interpretation $\mathfrak{I}_g$. Clearly, for every $p \in P$, exactly one of $\mathfrak{I}_g \models p$ or $\mathfrak{I}_g \models \neg p$ holds, whence g' must have the form $A \cup \{\neg p \mid p \in P \setminus A\}$ $(*)$. The fact that g' respects all implications of $\mathbb{K}$ is trivial.
(If): Consider a set of the form $S = A \cup \{\neg p \mid p \in P \setminus A\}$ that respects all implications of $\mathbb{K}$. It must be an intent and consequently be obtained as the intersection of object intents. If S itself is an object intent, the claim has been proven. In case it were not, there would have to be an object intent that is a strict superset of S, which is impossible in the view of $(*)$. □

We observe that, for a literal context $\mathbb{K} = (G, M, I)$, the formula $\Phi(\mathbb{K})$ is in full disjunctive normal form (DNF), except for repeated literals:

$$\Phi(\mathbb{K}) \equiv \bigvee_{g \in G} \bigwedge g',$$

whereas, for a set Σ of implications over M, the formula $\Psi(\Sigma)$ can be easily rewritten in conjunctive normal form (CNF):

$$\Psi(\Sigma) \equiv \bigwedge_{A \to B \in \Sigma} \bigwedge_{m \in B} \left((\bigvee_{\ell \in A} \neg \ell) \vee m \right).$$

Here and in the following, we silently assume that double negation is eliminated, that is, applying $\neg$ to $\neg m$ results in m.

Proposition 5. *Let $\mathbb{K} = (G, M, I)$ be a literal context for some set P of propositional atoms, and let Σ be an implication basis of $\mathbb{K}$. Then $\Phi(\mathbb{K}) \equiv \Psi(\Sigma)$.*

Proof. By Corollary 1, it suffices to show that $\Psi(\Sigma) \models \Phi(\mathbb{K})$. Let $\mathfrak{I}$ be an interpretation such that $\mathfrak{I} \models \Psi(\Sigma)$, and define $T_{\mathfrak{I}} = \{\ell \in M \mid \mathfrak{I} \models \ell\}$. By Proposition 2, we have $T_{\mathfrak{I}} \Vdash \Sigma$.

By Proposition 4, there exists $g \in G$ such that $g' = T_{\mathfrak{I}}$. Consequently, $\Phi(\mathbb{K})$ includes the conjunction $\bigwedge T_{\mathfrak{I}}$. Thus, $\mathfrak{I} \models \Phi(\mathbb{K})$, proving the claim. □

Combining Propositions 1 and 5, we obtain

Corollary 2. *Let $\mathbb{K}$ be a literal context for some set P of propositional atoms. Let φ be an arbitrary propositional formula over P. Then φ is valid in $\mathbb{K}$ if and only if it is logically entailed by $\Psi(\Sigma)$, where Σ is an implication basis of $\mathbb{K}$.*

Thus, if Σ is an implication basis of such context $\mathbb{K}$, then $\Phi(\mathbb{K})$ and $\Psi(\Sigma)$ provide two equivalent representations of $\mathbb{K}$'s logic: any such context's implication basis will be sufficient to decide for any Boolean combination of attributes if it is valid in the context.

In line with our earlier considerations, we should note that, while any implication basis Σ of a literal context $\mathbb{K}$ is sound (every of its implications holds in every $\mathfrak{I}_g$) and logically complete (any implication that holds in every $\mathfrak{I}_g$ logically follows from Σ), it is not necessarily logically non-redundant. For example, for two propositional atoms p and q, the implications $p \to q$ and $\neg q \to \neg p$ are logically equivalent. However, an implication basis in the traditional FCA sense would contain (representatives of) both, whenever it contains one. Likewise, implication bases would include implications expressing tautologies, such as $p \wedge \neg p \to \bot$. As discussed above, this is because the classical definition of an implication basis in FCA assumes no logical interdependencies between attributes, and thus no prior relationships between attributes like p and $\neg p$.

One obvious way to turn a sound and logically complete implication set into a logical implication basis is to iteratively remove logically redundant implications. Note that the result of such a procedure is not necessarily unique and may depend on the order of removals.

Example 3. A literal context corresponding to the scenario of Example 1, along with its implication basis, is shown in Fig. 2. It can be readily verified that this implication set is indeed sound and logically complete with respect to the given context. However, it is not logically non-redundant, as, for instance, the first three implications are merely different ways of expressing the disjunction $\mathit{hare} \vee \mathit{hatter} \vee \mathit{dormouse}$. To obtain a logical implication basis, one may select any of the first three implications and either the fourth or the next two.

Who Stole the Jam?	*hare*	*hatter*	*dormouse*	*¬hare*	*¬hatter*	*¬dormouse*
March Hare	×				×	×
Mad Hatter		×		×		×
March Hare and Mad Hatter	×	×				×
Dormouse			×	×	×	

$$\neg \mathit{hare}, \neg \mathit{hatter} \to \mathit{dormouse}$$
$$\neg \mathit{hare}, \neg \mathit{dormouse} \to \mathit{hatter}$$
$$\neg \mathit{hatter}, \neg \mathit{dormouse} \to \mathit{hare}$$
$$\mathit{dormouse} \to \neg \mathit{hare}, \neg \mathit{hatter}$$
$$\mathit{hare} \to \neg \mathit{dormouse}$$
$$\mathit{hatter} \to \neg \mathit{dormouse}$$
$$\mathit{hare}, \neg \mathit{hare} \to \bot$$
$$\mathit{hatter}, \neg \mathit{hatter} \to \bot$$

Fig. 2. A literal context and its implication basis

Implications with a $\bot$ on the right-hand side are often called *integrity constraints*. When considering the attribute logic in a literal context, we can focus entirely on integrity constraints, as every implication is logically equivalent to a set of them. Specifically, an implication $A \to B$ holds in a context if and only if all implications in the set $\{A \to \{b\} \mid b \in B\}$ hold, or equivalently, if all implications in the set $\{A \cup \{\neg b\} \to \bot \mid b \in B\}$ hold.

In fact, any CNF of the form $\bigwedge_{A \in \mathcal{A}} \bigvee A$, with $\mathcal{A}$ a family of subsets of M, gives rise to a sound and logically complete set $\{\{\neg m \mid m \in A\} \to \bot \mid A \in \mathcal{A}\}$ of integrity constraints, provided the CNF is logically equivalent to $\Phi(\mathbb{K})$. Thus, the search for logical implication bases consisting of integrity constraints is closely related to the problem of minimizing formulae in conjunctive normal form.

Another interesting question is how the addition of negated attributes to a context affects the structure of the corresponding concept lattice. In fact, this very question has already been investigated from a slightly different perspective, providing us with a ready-made answer in the finite case [5].

Definition 1. *Given a finite lattice, the* opposite element *of a lattice element* ℓ*, denoted* ℓ^{op}*, is defined by* $\ell^{\text{op}} = \bigsqcup\{x \mid x \sqcap \ell = 0\}$*. A lattice is said to be* $\sqcap$-complemented *if all its* $\sqcap$*-irreducible elements* ℓ *satisfy that* ℓ^{op} *is a complement of* ℓ*, i.e.,* $\ell^{\text{op}} \sqcap \ell = 0$ *and* $\ell^{\text{op}} \sqcup \ell = 1$.

Note that ℓ^{op} coincides with the pseudocomplement of ℓ [1] if the latter exists.

Theorem 1. *A finite lattice is isomorphic to the concept lattice of a literal context if and only if it is atomistic and* $\sqcap$*-complemented.*

A curious reader can refer to Fig. 3 to verify that the concept lattice of the literal context from our running example satisfies the theorem.

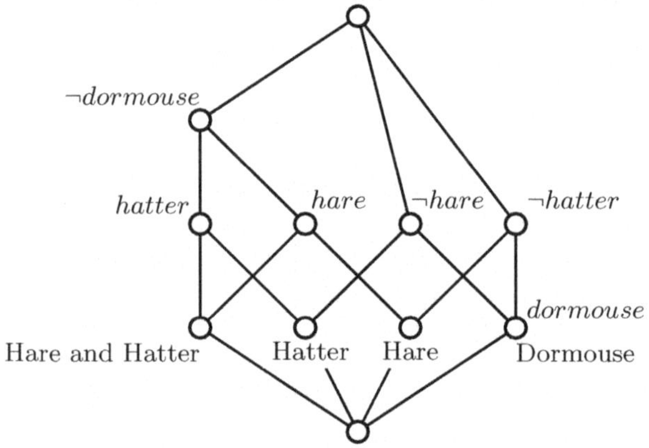

Fig. 3. A concept lattice diagram of the literal context in Fig. 2

5 The Case of Disjunctions

Another interesting case arises when M consists of all possible disjunctions of atomic propositions, i.e., $M = \{\bigvee Q \mid Q \subseteq P\}$ for some set P of propositional atoms. We call propositional logic contexts with such attribute sets *disjunctive contexts* over P. Note that $\bigvee \varnothing \equiv \bot$ and $\bigvee\{p\} \equiv p$ for every $p \in P$, so we will sometimes use $\bot$ and p to denote the attributes $\bigvee \varnothing$ and $\bigvee\{p\}$, respectively.

Proposition 6. *Let* $\mathbb{K} = (G, M, I)$ *be a disjunctive context over some set* P *of propositional atoms. Then a set* $S \subseteq M$ *is an object intent of* $\mathbb{K}$ *if and only if it is of the form* $S = \{\bigvee B \mid A \cap B \neq \varnothing\}$ *for some* $A \subseteq P$ *and respects all implications that hold in* $\mathbb{K}$.

Proof. **(Only if)**: Consider an object $g \in G$. Since $\mathfrak{I}_g \models \bigvee B$ if and only if $\mathfrak{I}_g \models p$ for some $p \in B$, it follows that $g' = \{\bigvee B \mid A \cap B \neq \varnothing\}$, where $A = \{p \mid \mathfrak{I}_g \models p\}$. As g' is an object intent, it respects all implications of $\mathbb{K}$.

(If): Suppose that $S = \{\bigvee B \mid A \cap B \neq \varnothing\}$ for some $A \subseteq P$ and S respects all implications of $\mathbb{K}$. Then S must be an intent. If S is an object intent, the claim follows. Otherwise, let $\mathcal{T}$ be a collection of object intents such that $S = \bigcap \mathcal{T}$. Since $S \subsetneq T$ for all $T \in \mathcal{T}$, there exists $\bigvee B_T \in T \setminus S$ with $A \cap B_T = \varnothing$ for each $T \in \mathcal{T}$. As $B_T \neq \varnothing$, we pick $p_T \in B_T$ and let $Q = \{p_T \mid T \in \mathcal{T}\}$. Then $S \cap Q = \varnothing$, but, since $\bigvee Q \in T$ for all $T \in \mathcal{T}$, we have $\bigvee Q \in S$.

This contradicts the assumption that $S = \{\bigvee B \mid A \cap B \neq \varnothing\}$, as it requires $A \cap Q \neq \varnothing$ and $p_T \in A$ for some $T \in \mathcal{T}$. Hence, S must be an object intent. □

We can easily compile the interpretations associated with objects of $\mathbb{K}$ into a full DNF equivalent to $\Phi(\mathbb{K})$ by leaving out all but atomic attributes:

$$\Phi(\mathbb{K}) \equiv \bigvee_{g \in G} \left(\left(\bigwedge_{m \in g' \cap P} m \right) \wedge \left(\bigwedge_{m \in P \setminus g'} \neg m \right) \right).$$

Proposition 7. *Let $\mathbb{K} = (G, M, I)$ be a disjunctive context over some set P, and let Σ be an implication basis of $\mathbb{K}$. Then $\Phi(\mathbb{K}) \equiv \Psi(\Sigma)$.*

Proof. The proof follows a similar reasoning as in Proposition 5. Again, it is sufficient to show that $\Psi(\Sigma) \models \Phi(\mathbb{K})$. For an interpretation $\mathfrak{I}$, define

$$T_{\mathfrak{I}} = \{m \in M \mid \mathfrak{I} \models m\} = \{\bigvee B \in M \mid P_{\mathfrak{I}} \cap B \neq \varnothing\},$$

where $P_{\mathfrak{I}} = \{p \in P \mid \mathfrak{I} \models p\}$. If $\mathfrak{I} \models \Psi(\Sigma)$, then $T_{\mathfrak{I}}$ respects Σ by Proposition 2. By Proposition 6, this implies that $g' = T_{\mathfrak{I}}$ for some $g \in G$, in which case $\mathfrak{I} = \mathfrak{I}_g$ and $P_{\mathfrak{I}} = g' \cap P$. By examining the clause for g in the above representation of $\Phi(\mathbb{K})$, we conclude that $\mathfrak{I} \models \Phi(\mathbb{K})$, proving that $\Psi(\Sigma) \models \Phi(\mathbb{K})$. □

The equivalence established in Proposition 7, combined with Proposition 1, warrants the following corollary:

Corollary 3. *Let $\mathbb{K} = (G, M, I)$ be a disjunctive context over P. Let φ be an arbitrary propositional formula over P. Then φ is valid in $\mathbb{K}$ if and only if it is logically entailed by $\Psi(\Sigma)$, where Σ is an implication basis of $\mathbb{K}$.*

Thus, for contexts where attributes are defined through disjunction, the logic of the context is captured entirely by its implication basis—just as for contexts where attributes are defined through negation. And just as in that case, an implication basis can be logically redundant—an example of such redundancy appears in Fig. 4.

Figure 5 shows a concept lattice diagram for the disjunctive context in Fig. 4. We can see that the lattice is distributive. Is this always true for disjunctive contexts? Proposition 8 provides some insight.

Who Stole the Jam?	$\bot$	*hare*	*hatter*	*dormouse*	*hare* $\vee$ *hatter*	*hare* $\vee$ *dormouse*	*hatter* $\vee$ *dormouse*	*hare* $\vee$ *hatter* $\vee$ *dormouse*
March Hare		×			×	×		×
Mad Hatter			×		×		×	×
March Hare and Mad Hatter		×	×		×	×	×	×
Dormouse				×		×	×	×

$$\begin{aligned} \varnothing &\to \textit{hare} \vee \textit{hatter} \vee \textit{dormouse} \\ \textit{hare} &\leftrightarrow \textit{hare} \vee \textit{hatter}, \\ & \ \textit{hare} \vee \textit{dormouse} \\ \textit{hatter} &\leftrightarrow \textit{hare} \vee \textit{hatter}, \\ & \ \textit{hatter} \vee \textit{dormouse} \\ \textit{dormouse} &\to \textit{hare} \vee \textit{dormouse}, \\ & \ \textit{hatter} \vee \textit{dormouse} \\ \bot &\leftrightarrow M \end{aligned}$$

Fig. 4. A disjunctive context and its implication basis. The notation $A \leftrightarrow B$ represents the set of two implications: $\{A \to B, B \to A\}$.

Proposition 8. *Let $\mathbb{K} = (G, M, I)$ be a disjunctive context over P. Given an arbitrary set*

$$\{(X_t, Y_t) \mid t \in T\}$$

of formal concepts of $\mathbb{K}$, where T is some index set, the supremum in the concept lattice is given by

$$\bigsqcup_{t \in T} (X_t, Y_t) = (\bigcup_{t \in T} X_t, \bigcap_{t \in T} Y_t).$$

Proof. Suppose, for contradiction, that this does not hold for some index set T. Define

$$(X, Y) = \bigsqcup_{t \in T} (X_t, Y_t).$$

By the basic theorem on concept lattices [3], we have

$$\bigcup_{t \in T} X_t \subseteq X \qquad \text{and} \qquad \bigcap_{t \in T} Y_t = Y.$$

Under our assumption, $\bigcup_{t \in T} X_t \subsetneq X$, i.e., the inclusion is proper. Then, there exists some $g \in G$ such that $Y \subseteq g'$ but $g \in X_t$ for no $t \in T$. The latter implies that $Y_t \subseteq g'$ for no $t \in T$.

For $t \in T$, let $Q_t \subseteq P$ be such that $\bigvee Q_t \in Y_t \setminus g'$ and denote $Q = \bigcup_{t \in T} Q_t$. For $h \in X_t$, we have $\mathfrak{I}_h \models \bigvee Q_t$ and therefore $\mathfrak{I}_h \models \bigvee Q$. Thus, $\bigvee Q \in Y_t$ for all $t \in T$, $\bigvee Q \in Y$, and $\bigvee Q \in g'$. It follows that $\mathfrak{I}_g \models p$ for some $p \in Q$. However, this p must belong to Q_t for some $t \in T$, and then $\mathfrak{I}_g \models \bigvee Q_t$. Therefore, $\bigvee Q_t \in g'$, leading to a contradiction. □

Thus, the concept extents of a disjunctive context are closed under union. By the basic theorem on concept lattices, they are also closed under intersection. This suggests the following characterization:

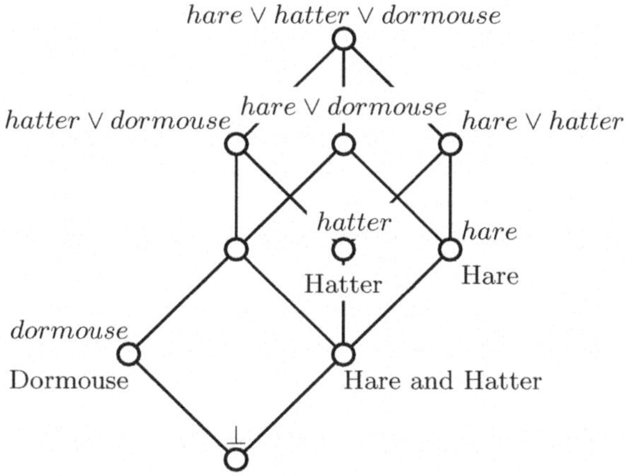

Fig. 5. A concept lattice diagram of the disjunctive context in Fig. 4

Theorem 2. *The concept lattice of a disjunctive context is distributive. Every distributive lattice is isomorphic to the concept lattice of a disjunctive context.*

Proof. The first part is straightforward. For the second part, recall that every distributive lattice is isomorphic to a lattice of sets closed under intersection and union. Let $\mathcal{F}$ be such a family of subsets of the ground set G. We build a disjunctive context $\mathbb{K} = (G, M, I)$ over $P = \{p_S \mid S \in \mathcal{F}\}$ by defining $\mathfrak{I}_g$ for $g \in G$ so that $\mathfrak{I}_g \models p_S$ if and only if $g \in S$.

The concept extents of $\mathbb{K}$ are precisely the sets in $\mathcal{F}$. To see this, observe that

$$\{p_S\}' = S$$

and, more generally,

$$(\bigvee_{S \in \mathcal{H} \subseteq \mathcal{F}} p_S)' = \bigcup \mathcal{H}.$$

Since $\mathcal{F}$ is closed under union, it follows that all attribute extents of $\mathbb{K}$ belong to $\mathcal{F}$. All other concept extents are intersections of attribute extents, and, since $\mathcal{F}$ is closed under intersection, they also belong to $\mathcal{F}$. As the order on concepts coincides with the subset order on their extents, the concept lattice of $\mathbb{K}$ is isomorphic to $\mathcal{F}$. □

6 The General Case

The two previous cases share the property that, for a context whose attribute set is logically defined in a certain way, the set of its implications (e.g., represented by its implication basis) provides sufficient knowledge to verify whether an arbitrary Boolean formula φ is valid in that context. On a more abstract level, this raises the question of which sets of logically defined attributes exhibit this property.

Definition 2. *A set M of propositionally defined attributes is called* implication-exact *if, for every propositional context $\mathbb{K}$ with attribute set M, the validity of any propositional formula φ in $\mathbb{K}$ can be determined from the implications of $\mathbb{K}$.*

While this definition precisely captures the property we would like to diagnose for a given attribute set, it is rather impractical: (1) showing that some set M is implication-exact appears to require considering all propositional contexts and all formulae; and (2) it remains unclear what exactly the method of "determining" validity from the context's implications would be.

To address these issues, we propose an alternative criterion that is much easier to verify, and we show that it coincides with implication-exactness.

Definition 3. *A set M of propositionally defined attributes is called* exclusion-precise *if, for every coherent subset $C \subseteq M$, there exists an implication $A \to B$ over M respected by all coherent subsets of M except C.*

Theorem 3. *A set M of propositionally defined attributes is implication-exact if and only if it is exclusion-precise.*

Proof. For the following, let $\mathcal{C}$ denote the set of all coherent subsets of M and note that, by definition of coherence, for every coherent subset $D \in \mathcal{C}$, there is (at least) one interpretation $\mathfrak{I}_D$ satisfying $\mathfrak{I}_D \models m$ for all $m \in D$ and $\mathfrak{I}_D \not\models m$ for all $m \in M \setminus D$.

(Only if): We prove this direction by contraposition. Assume that M is not exclusion-precise. This means that there exists a $C \in \mathcal{C}$ that respects every implication over M respected by all $D \in \mathcal{C} \setminus \{C\}$. Now consider two propositional contexts:

- $\mathbb{K}_1 = (G_1, M, I_1)$ for which $\{\mathfrak{I}_g \mid g \in G_1\} = \{\mathfrak{I}_D \mid D \in \mathcal{C}\}$ and
- $\mathbb{K}_2 = (G_2, M, I_2)$ for which $\{\mathfrak{I}_g \mid g \in G_2\} = \{\mathfrak{I}_D \mid D \in \mathcal{C} \setminus \{C\}\}$.

Obviously, every implication that holds in $\mathbb{K}_1$ also holds in $\mathbb{K}_2$. On the other hand, due to our assumption, there cannot be any implication that holds in $\mathbb{K}_2$ but not in $\mathbb{K}_1$. Consequently, exactly the same implications must hold in $\mathbb{K}_1$ and $\mathbb{K}_2$. Now consider the propositional formula

$$\varphi_{\overline{C}} = \bigvee\{\neg m \mid m \in C\} \vee \bigvee\{m \mid m \in M \setminus C\}.$$

We observe that $\varphi_{\overline{C}}$ is valid in $\mathbb{K}_2$ but not in $\mathbb{K}_1$. Since the two contexts have the same implicational theories, M cannot be implication-exact.

(If): Assume that M is exclusion-precise. Given some $C \in \mathcal{C}$, let $Exc(C)$ denote an implication respected by all coherent sets but C (which is guaranteed to exist by definition). Now, given an arbitrary propositional context $\mathbb{K} = (G, M, I)$, we define $\Sigma_{\mathbb{K}} = \{Exc(C) \mid C \in \mathcal{C} \setminus \{g' \mid g \in G\}\}$. We observe that all implications of $\Sigma_{\mathbb{K}}$ hold in $\mathbb{K}$, and we also obtain, for any $D \in \mathcal{C}$, that D respects $\Sigma_{\mathbb{K}}$ precisely if $D = g'$ for some $g \in G$. We now find that M is implication-exact, since any propositional formula φ is valid in $\mathbb{K}$ if and only if it logically follows from $\Sigma_{\mathbb{K}}$.

For the "if" part, note that all implications in $\Sigma_{\mathbb{K}}$ hold in $\mathbb{K}$, which, by Corollary 1, means that $\Psi(\Sigma_{\mathbb{K}})$ is a logical consequence of $\Phi(\mathbb{K})$. Hence, any φ that is a logical consequence of $\Psi(\Sigma_{\mathbb{K}})$ is also a logical consequence of $\Phi(\mathbb{K})$ and must thus be valid in $\mathbb{K}$ due to Proposition 1.

For the "only if" part, suppose, toward a contradiction, that φ is valid in $\mathbb{K}$ (and hence a logical consequence of every $\mathfrak{f}_{\mathbb{K}}(g)$) but does not logically follow from $\Psi(\Sigma_{\mathbb{K}})$. This means there must exist an interpretation $\mathfrak{I}$ such that $\mathfrak{I} \models \Psi(\Sigma_{\mathbb{K}})$ but $\mathfrak{I} \not\models \varphi$. Now consider the set $D = \{m \in M \mid \mathfrak{I} \models m\}$, which must be coherent by construction. Moreover, D must respect $\Sigma_{\mathbb{K}}$, and, therefore, by our above argument, we have $D = g'$ for some $g \in G$. It follows that $\mathfrak{I} \models \mathfrak{f}_{\mathbb{K}}(g)$ must hold. Since we also know by assumption that φ is a logical consequence of $\mathfrak{f}_{\mathbb{K}}(g)$, we can conclude $\mathfrak{I} \models \varphi$, which is a contradiction. □

Example 4. For a set P of atomic propositions, choose $Q \subset P$ and define

$$M = \{\bigvee A \mid A \subseteq Q, A \neq \varnothing\} \cup \{p, \neg p \mid p \in P \setminus Q\}.$$

That is, we split the atoms into two sets, one of which we close under disjunction and the other of which we close under negation. Note that we do not need to include $\bigvee \varnothing$, because falsity can be represented by M (as discussed in Section 4).

We show that any such attribute set is exclusion-precise and, hence, implication-exact. Since $P \subseteq M$, coherent sets are in one-to-one correspondence with interpretations. For an arbitrary coherent set corresponding to some interpretation $\mathfrak{I}$, let $P_{\text{true}} = \{p \in P \mid \mathfrak{I} \models p\}$. Then, consider the implication $A \to B$, where

$$A = P_{\text{true}} \cup \{\neg p \mid p \in P \setminus (P_{\text{true}} \cup Q)\}$$

and

$$B = \begin{cases} M & \text{if } Q \subseteq P_{\text{true}}; \\ \{\bigvee(Q \setminus P_{\text{true}})\} & \text{otherwise.} \end{cases}$$

It can be readily checked that $\mathfrak{I}$ is the only interpretation that does not satisfy $\mathfrak{g}(A \to B)$, and, consequently, the coherent set associated with $\mathfrak{I}$ is the only one not that does not respect $A \to B$.

We remark that the choice of attributes in Fig. 1 fits the above description, which guarantees that any context based on this attribute selection would have a fully informative implication set.

As a "byproduct" of this consideration, we can make the somewhat counterintuitive observation that the attribute set of a literal context remains implication-exact even if one of the negated atoms is removed from M. To see this, consider the case where Q contains only a single element. As a minimal example, let $P = \{p, q\}$ and $M = \{p, \neg p, q\}$. We show that M is implication-exact by demonstrating that any interpretation (and thus any coherent set) can be "ruled out" by an implication that holds in all other interpretations:

interpretation	p	q	ruled out by
$\mathfrak{I}_1$	false	false	$\{\neg p\} \to \{q\}$
$\mathfrak{I}_2$	false	true	$\{q\} \to \{p\}$
$\mathfrak{I}_3$	true	false	$\{p\} \to \{q\}$
$\mathfrak{I}_4$	true	true	$\{p, q\} \to \{p, \neg p, q\}$

Example 5. In all examples of implication-exact attribute sets M considered so far, we had $P \subseteq M$, and consequently, each coherent set corresponded to a single interpretation. However, neither of these conditions is necessary for M to be implication-exact.

Consider $P = \{p, q\}$ and $M = \{p \vee q, \neg p \vee \neg q, \bot\}$. There are three coherent sets: $C_0 = \{\neg p \vee \neg q\}$, $C_1 = \{p \vee q, \neg p \vee \neg q\}$, and $C_2 = \{p \vee q\}$. Here, each C_i corresponds to the set of interpretations that satisfy exactly i atoms of P. For C_1, there are two such interpretations – those assigning different truth values to p and q. The implication $C_1 \to \bot$ rules out exactly these two interpretations while being respected by C_0 and C_2. For $i \neq 1$, the implication $C_i \to C_{2-i}$ is respected by every coherent set except C_i. Therefore, M is exclusion-precise and hence implication-exact. By a similar argument, the same conclusion holds for $M = \{\bigvee_{p \in P} p, \bigvee_{p \in P} \neg p, \bot\}$, for any set P of propositional atoms.

7 Conclusion

In this paper, we studied the effect of logically defined attributes on a context's attribute logic. We identified examples and a general criterion for when the selection of attributes guarantees that the context's implicational knowledge is maximally informative.

Future work on this subject may include the question if concept lattices that arise from contexts with implication-exact attribute sets satisfy special properties (or even if there is a characterization similar to the ones for literal and disjunctive contexts). Moreover, one might ask how or under which circumstances a logical implication basis can be efficiently obtained directly from the context or from a (logic-oblivious) implication basis.

Acknowledgments. This work is partly supported by DFG in project 389792660 (TRR 248, Center for Perspicuous Systems), by BMBF in ScaDS.AI, and by BMBF and DAAD in project 57616814 (SECAI).

References

1. Blyth, T.S.: Pseudocomplementation; stone and heyting algebras. In: Lattices and Ordered Algebraic Structures, pp. 103–118. Springer London, London (2005)
2. Ganter, B., Obiedkov, S.: Conceptual Exploration. Springer (2016)
3. Ganter, B., Wille, R.: Formal Concept Analysis – Mathematical Foundations. Springer Cham, 2 edn. (2024)
4. Guigues, J.L., Duquenne, V.: Famille minimale d'implications informatives résultant d'un tableau de données binaires. Mathématiques et Sciences Humaines **24**(95), 5–18 (1986)
5. Rodríguez-Jiménez, J.M., Cordero, P., Enciso, M., Rudolph, S.: Concept lattices with negative information: A characterization theorem. Inf. Sci. **369**, 51–62 (2016)
6. Smullyan, R.: Alice in Puzzle-Land: A Carrollian Tale for Children Under Eighty. Dover Recreational Math, Dover Publications (2011)

Rational Inference in Formal Concept Analysis

Lucas Carr[1], Nicholas Leisegang[1], Thomas Meyer[1], and Sergei Obiedkov[2,3](✉)

[1] University of Cape Town and CAIR, Cape Town, South Africa
{lucas,tmeyer}@airu.org.za, lsgnic001@myuct.ac.za
[2] TU Dresden, Dresden, Germany
sergei.obiedkov@tu-dresden.de
[3] Center for Scalable Data Analytics and Artificial Intelligence (ScaDS.AI) Dresden/Leipzig, Dresden, Germany

Abstract. Defeasible conditionals are a form of non-monotonic inference which enable the expression of statements like "if ϕ then normally ψ". The KLM framework defines a semantics for the propositional case of defeasible conditionals by construction of a preference ordering over possible worlds. The pattern of reasoning induced by these semantics is characterised by consequence relations satisfying certain desirable properties of non-monotonic reasoning. In FCA, implications are used to describe dependencies between attributes. However, these implications are unsuitable to reason with erroneous data or data prone to exceptions. Until recently, the topic of non-monotonic inference in FCA has remained largely uninvestigated. In this paper, we provide a construction of the KLM framework for defeasible reasoning in FCA and show that this construction remains faithful to the principle of non-monotonic inference described in the original framework. We present an additional argument that, while remaining consistent with the original ideas around non-monotonic reasoning, the defeasible reasoning we propose in FCA offers a more contextual view on inference, providing the ability for more relevant conclusions to be drawn when compared to the classical case.

Keywords: Formal Concept Analysis · Non-monotonic Reasoning · Attribute Implications · Preference Relations

1 Introduction

Formal Concept Analysis (FCA) [10,12] applies lattice theory to the long-standing philosophical view of concepts as a duality between extension—referring to the instances of a concept—and intension—the meaning ascribed to that concept. This dualism is elegantly modelled using Galois connections between sets of objects and attributes. The strength of this modelling has made FCA a popular tool for knowledge representation and reasoning, information retrieval, rule mining, and ontology engineering. The connective $\rightarrow$ expresses a relationship between two sets of attributes such that the *attribute implication* $A \rightarrow B$ means "all objects possessing attributes A also possess attributes B".

P. Cellier et al. (Eds.): CONCEPTS 2025, LNAI 15941, pp. 325–341, 2025.
https://doi.org/10.1007/978-3-032-03364-2_21

Attribute implications are considered satisfied only when consistent with all available information. As a result, a single counterexample can prevent a relationship between attributes from being recognised. However, data is often error-prone, and some counterexamples may be tolerated; alternatively, in certain domains, it may be useful to express relationships that only partially hold. The canonical example in non-monotonic reasoning involving penguins and flying birds illustrates this latter point: imagine a context with many objects that may have the attributes 'bird' and 'flying'; only one of these objects is a penguin, which is a 'bird' but not 'flying'. In such a case, expressing a partial correspondence between the attributes 'bird' and 'flying' remains valuable, despite the exception posed by the penguin.

Defeasible conditionals represent a particular kind of non-monotonic inference relation: for example, `bird` $\mid\!\sim$ `flying` expresses the information that "typical birds fly, while non-typical birds may not". In the original framework proposed by Kraus, Lehmann, and Magidor (commonly referred to as the KLM framework), these conditionals are given a semantics via a preference-relation $\prec$ over possible worlds. The above conditional holds if `flying` is satisfied in every $\prec$-minimal world that also satisfies `bird` [15, 18]. This semantics induces consequence relations satisfying properties that are argued to consitute a reasonable account of non-monotonic inference. In particular, *preferential* and *rational* consequence relations are distinguished and discussed.

In this paper, we introduce the $\mid\!\sim$ operator into formal concept analysis, adapting it from its original setting in propositional logic. We show that the consequence relation induced in the FCA setting is faithful to its classical counterpart and that an equivalent non-monotonic entailment relation can be defined. On the other hand, we argue that the FCA setting provides an intuitive restriction on possible worlds through the formal context. This restriction allows for non-monotonic reasoning, in accordance with rational consequence, offering a more contextual world-view than in the classical case.

Paper Outline: In Sect. 2, we provide the basic notions in FCA relevant to this work, along with a more detailed discussion of non-monotonic reasoning and the KLM framework for propositional logic. In Sect. 3, we adapt the FCA setting to accommodate preferential and rational consequence relations; proofs of the theorems and lemmas presented there can be found in the full technical report. Next, we introduce a defeasible conditional to the logic and show that, for each system (preferential and rational), our definitions are sound and complete. Section 4 discusses a more applied approach to defeasible reasoning in FCA and defines rational closure—a non-monotonic entailment relation—for FCA. Section 5 provides a detailed example and discusses how rational closure in FCA differs from the classical case. Section 6 reviews related work, while Sect. 7 concludes and outlines directions for future research.

2 Preliminaries

In what follows, we refer to the languages of propositional logic and FCA's *attribute logic*. In the setting of propositional logic, lower-case Latin letters are used to denote propositional variables, while Greek letters denote formulae in the language $\mathcal{L}$, which is defined in the usual way by $\alpha :: \top \mid \bot \mid a \mid \neg\alpha \mid \alpha \wedge \alpha \mid \alpha \vee \alpha \mid \alpha \rightarrow \alpha \mid \alpha \leftrightarrow \alpha$.

The set of all *valuations* (i.e., assignments of truth values to variables) is denoted by $\mathcal{U}$; when a valuation $v \in \mathcal{U}$ satisfies a propositional formula α, we write $v \Vdash \alpha$.

In FCA, subsets of objects and attributes are denoted by capital letters. Lowercase letters denote individual elements of these sets. We return to Greek letters for the language of compound attributes introduced in Sect. 3.1.

2.1 Formal Concept Analysis

Formal Concept Analysis is a framework for reasoning about conceptual structures in data [10, 12]. We introduce only the basic notions relevant to this work. The typical starting point in FCA, *a formal context*, is a triple $\mathbb{K} = (G, M, I)$ comprised of a set of objects G, a set of attributes M, and a binary relation $I \subseteq G \times M$. An object–attribute pair in the relation, $(g, m) \in I$, is interpreted as saying that *"object g has attribute m"*. Formal contexts are usually visualized by cross-tables, as shown in Example 1.

Example 1. The context in Fig. 1 represents a portion of the 1984 United States Congressional Voting Records, sourced from the UCI Machine Learning Repository [3]. The objects are individual congressmen, and the attributes correspond to various issues on which they voted, as well as to the two political parties represented in Congress. A cross indicates that the corresponding congressman voted in favor of a particular issue or belongs to the corresponding party.

Congress	dem	rep	hci	wpc	abr	pff	esa	rgs	ast	anc	mxm	imm	scc	edu	rts	crm	dfe	aas
Con-1		×		×		×	×	×				×		×	×	×		×
Con-4	×			×	×			×					×		×			×
Con-9		×		×		×	×	×						×	×	×		×
Con-17	×		×		×			×		×		×	×	×				×
Con-18	×		×		×				×	×	×				×		×	×

Fig. 1. A formal context with attributes dem: *democrat*, rep: *republican*, hci: *handicapped-infants*, wpc:*water-project-cost-sharing*, abr: *adoption-of-the-budget-resolution*, pff: *physician-fee-freeze*, esa: *el-salvador-aid*, rgs: *religious-groups-in-schools*, ast: *anti-satellite-test-ban*, anc: *aid-to-nicaraguan-contras*, mxm: *mx-missile*, imm: *immigration*, scc: *synfuels-corporation-cutback*, edu: *education*, rts: *superfund-right-to-sue*, crm: *crime*, dfe: *duty-free-exports*, aas: *export-administration-act-south-africa*

Two *derivation operators* provide a way of describing the set of attributes (*resp.* objects) shared by certain subsets of objects (*resp.* attributes). They are given by $(\cdot)^{\uparrow} : 2^G \to 2^M$ and $(\cdot)^{\downarrow} : 2^M \to 2^G$ so that, for $A \subseteq G$ and $B \subseteq M$,

$$A^{\uparrow} = \{m \in M \mid \forall g \in A,\ (g, m) \in I\},$$
$$B^{\downarrow} = \{g \in G \mid \forall m \in B,\ (g, m) \in I\}.$$

An *attribute implication* over M is a pair of attribute sets, denoted $A \to B$, where A is the *premise* and B is the *conclusion*. It is *satisfied* by a set of attributes C (notation: $C \models A \to B$) if $A \not\subseteq C$ or $B \subseteq C$ and *supported* by C if $A \cup B \subseteq C$.

$A \rightarrow B$ *is satisfied* or *holds* in $\mathbb{K}$ if $\{g\}^{\uparrow} \models A \rightarrow B$ for all $g \in G$. This is equivalently expressed by $A^{\downarrow} \subseteq B^{\downarrow}$ or $B \subseteq A^{\downarrow\uparrow}$. An implication is *supported* by $\mathbb{K}$ if it is supported by $\{g\}^{\uparrow}$ for some $g \in G$.

An implication i over M is a *logical consequence* of a set of implications $\mathcal{T}$ if, for every subset $X \subseteq M$, we have $X \models i$ whenever $X \models \mathcal{T}$ (meaning $X \models j$ for all $j \in \mathcal{T}$); we then write $\mathcal{T} \models i$. The Armstrong axioms are a syntactic counterpart to semantic entailment of attribute implications [4].

2.2 Association Rules

Association rules are essentially attribute implications that may admit counterexamples [16]. Given a context $\mathbb{K} = (G, M, I)$ and an attribute set $X \subseteq M$, the *(relative) support* of X in $\mathbb{K}$ is the frequency of objects possessing attributes X, i.e., $supp(X) = |X^{\downarrow}|/|G|$. The *(relative) support* of an association rule $X \rightarrow Y$ is defined as $supp(X)$, while its *confidence* is given by $supp(X \cup Y)/supp(X)$. In association rule mining, the goal is typically to identify all rules with support and confidence above specified thresholds.

Association rules not only admit exceptions; they may also exhibit non-monotonic behaviour. Consider the context in Example 1. If the confidence threshold is set at 0.6, the rule $\{\texttt{edu}\} \rightarrow \{\texttt{imm}\}$, with a confidence of 0.67, satisfies the threshold, whereas the rule $\{\texttt{edu}, \texttt{rep}\} \rightarrow \{\texttt{imm}\}$, with a confidence of 0.5, does not. That is, adding an attribute to the premise of a rule can invalidate its conclusion.

Nevertheless, association rules are not well-suited to our purposes of defeasible reasoning, where we wish to interpret a rule $X \rightarrow Y$ as stating that "typical instances of X are also instances of Y". Association rules may behave undesirably under this interpretation. For instance, consider the rules $\{\texttt{edu}\} \rightarrow \{\texttt{imm}\}$ and $\{\texttt{edu}\} \rightarrow \{\texttt{wpc}\}$, which both satisfy the theshold of 0.6 in Example 1. From a typicality perspective, we would expect the rule $\{\texttt{edu}\} \rightarrow \{\texttt{imm}, \texttt{wpc}\}$ to hold as well. However, with a confidence of only 0.33, it fails to meet the threshold.

The underlying issue is that association rules are agnostic to which specific objects contribute towards the acceptance of a rule. In Sect. 2.3, we will see that this pattern of reasoning is precisely captured by the *And* postulate, guaranteed by preferential and rational consequence relations.

2.3 Defeasible Reasoning

Non-monotonic reasoning is concerned with developing formal reasoning processes whereby a conclusion drawn under a premise can be withdrawn under the addition of another premise. More precisely, defeasible reasoning aims to express notions that, while normal things behave in a certain way, there may be atypical things that do not.

Kraus et al. [15] introduce a collection of consequence relations for non-monotonic reasoning in propositional logic, which satisfy certain properties—considered to represent a good account of non-monotonic reasoning—called the *rationality postulates*. We use $\mid\!\sim_X$ to denote a defeasible consequence relation, where the subscript indicates which postulates the relation satisfies. A *preferential consequence relation*, denoted $\mid\!\sim_P$, is one that satisfies the postulates in Table 1.

Table 1. KML postulates for preferential consequence relations

(REF) Reflexivity	$\phi \mid\sim \phi$
(LLE) Left Logical Equivalence	$\phi \equiv \psi$ and $\psi \mid\sim \gamma$ implies $\phi \mid\sim \gamma$
(RW) Right Weakening	$\psi \to \gamma$ and $\phi \mid\sim \psi$ implies $\phi \mid\sim \gamma$
(AND) And	$\phi \mid\sim \psi$ and $\phi \mid\sim \gamma$ implies $\phi \mid\sim \psi \wedge \gamma$
(OR) Or	$\phi \mid\sim \gamma$ and $\psi \mid\sim \gamma$ implies $\phi \vee \psi \mid\sim \gamma$
(CUT) Cut	$\phi \wedge \psi \mid\sim \gamma$ and $\phi \mid\sim \psi$ implies $\phi \mid\sim \gamma$
(CM) Cautious Monotonicity	$\phi \mid\sim \psi$ and $\phi \mid\sim \gamma$ implies $\phi \wedge \psi \mid\sim \gamma$

Preferential consequence relations are given a semantics by construction of preferential interpretations. In the following, we restrict discussion to the finite case.

Definition 1 (Preferential Interpretation). *A* preferential interpretation $\mathcal{P}$ *is a triple* $(S, l, \prec)$ *with a set of states* S*, a function* $l\colon S \to \mathcal{U}$ *mapping states to valuations, and a strict partial order* $\prec$ *on* S. $\mathcal{P}$ satisfies $\phi \mid\sim \psi$ *if the* $\prec$*-minimal states among the elements of* S *satisfying* ϕ*, denoted* $[\![\phi]\!]$*, also satisfy* ψ.

The stronger system of *rational consequence relations* ($\mid\sim_R$) is introduced in [18]. It satisfies all the above postulates with the addition of

(RM) Rational Monotonicity $\phi \mid\sim \psi$ and $\phi \not\mid\sim \neg\gamma$ implies $\phi \wedge \gamma \mid\sim \psi$

It is obvious that rational consequence relations are a type of preferential relations. The additional property (RM) is read as "If, under normal circumstances, the presence of ϕ implies ψ but not the negation of γ, then I should be able to take γ as true without causing the retraction of ψ". Rational consequence relations are given a semantics by means of *ranked interpretations* [7,18].

Definition 2 (Ranked Interpretation). *A preferential interpretation* $(S, l, \prec)$ *is called* ranked *if there exists a* ranking function $\mathsf{R}\colon S \to \mathbb{N} \cup \{\infty\}$ *such that* $s \prec t$ *is equivalent to* $\mathsf{R}(s) < \mathsf{R}(t)$*, where* $<$ *is the usual order on* $\mathbb{N} \cup \{\infty\}$.

The distinction between preferential and rational consequence is discussed in more depth in Sect. 3.2. The ordering derived from a ranking function can be considered as stratifying the states into "rankings"— equivalence classes over which there is a linear order.

Satisfaction of a defeasible conditional under a ranked interpretation, like under any preferential interpretation, depends only on the $\prec$-minimal valuations. The soundness and completeness results from [15,18] establish that preferential and rational consequence relations correspond to preferential and ranked interpretations, respectively:

Theorem 1 (Soundness). *If* $\mathcal{P}$ *is a preferential (resp.* $\mathcal{R}$ *is a ranked) interpretation, the induced consequence relation* $\mid\sim_{\mathcal{P}}$ *(resp.* $\mid\sim_{\mathcal{R}}$*) is preferential (resp. rational).*

Theorem 2 (Completeness). *A consequence relation is preferential (resp. rational) if and only if it is induced by a preferential (resp. ranked) interpretation.*

Entailment of defeasible conditionals from a set Δ of defeasible conditionals has yet to be discussed. The classical approach would be to consider all ranked interpretations satisfying Δ and suggest that a conditional $\alpha \mid\!\sim \beta$ to be entailed by Δ if it were satisfied by each of these interpretations. Such an entailment relation is Tarskian, and it would introduce monotonicity on the meta-level in the sense that any $\Gamma \supseteq \Delta$ would retain all consequences of Δ.

A different approach, due to Lehmann and Magidor [18], suggests that only a subset of ranked interpretations satisfying Δ should be used for entailment, based on the *presumption of typicality*—that, we should, as far as possible, regard things as typical. This induces a preference relation $\preceq_{\mathcal{R}}$ over ranked interpretations: if $\mathcal{R}_1$ and $\mathcal{R}_2$ are ranked interpretations over the same set of states S, with ranking functions R_1 and R_2, then $\mathcal{R}_1 \preceq_{\mathcal{R}} \mathcal{R}_2$ if and only if $\mathsf{R}_1(u) \leq \mathsf{R}_2(u)$ for all $s \in S$.

It was shown by Giordano et al. [14] that, when restricted to the finite case, such an ordering over ranked interpretations satisfying a given set Δ of defeasible conditionals will always have a minimum element, denoted $\mathcal{R}^{\Delta}_{RC}$. *Rational closure* [14,18] is the entailment relation induced by considering only what is satisfied in $\mathcal{R}^{\Delta}_{RC}$.[1]

3 Defeasible Reasoning in FCA

In the previous section, we outlined the KLM approach to defeasible reasoning in propositional logic. This section introduces a relatively simple translation of these ideas into FCA. We adopt a scaffolded approach: first, we present the structures needed to support preferential reasoning; then, we show why preferential consequence is undesirable and how a small adjustment to the preference relation yields rational inference instead. Proofs for the results in this section are found in the accompanying technical report on arXiv.[2]

Before this begins, some necessary changes to the typical FCA setting require discussion. The reader might have doubts regarding what a rational consequence relation might mean in FCA, given that certain postulates—namely, (OR) and (RM)—require a logic which has negation and disjunction, the expressivity for which is beyond the attribute logic underlying FCA.

3.1 Contextual Attribute Logic

In the usual setting, implications are defined over sets of attributes $\{m_1, \ldots, m_n\}$ with a conjunctive view. Essentially, implications can be considered analogous to conjunctions of definite Horn clauses which share the same negated literals [10]. A result of this is that the expressivity for disjunction or negation on either side of the implication is not present. Moreover, FCA typically restricts the meaning of the incidence relation to

[1] Independently, Pearl [20] proposed *System Z*, which coincides with rational closure.

[2] arxiv.org/pdf/2504.16938.

positive information. Several attempts to extend the expressivity of FCA's attribute logic are well documented [10,11,21,23], but a single approach is yet to be widely accepted.

We adopt the idea of *compound attributes*, due to Ganter [11] over a finite context. Compound attributes allow for the construction of more complex formulae defined by the extension of (normal) attributes and other compound attributes. The language, denoted $\mathcal{L}(M)$, is defined recursively by $\phi :: \{m\} \mid \neg\phi \mid \phi_1 \wedge \phi_2 \mid \phi_1 \vee \phi_2 \mid \phi_1 \rightarrow \phi_2$.

Definition 3 (Compound Attributes). *Given a context* $\mathbb{K} = (G, M, I)$, *its attribute-to-object operator is extended to compound attributes as follows:*

$$(\neg\phi)^{\downarrow} = G \backslash \phi^{\downarrow}; \quad (\phi \vee \psi)^{\downarrow} = \phi^{\downarrow} \cup \psi^{\downarrow}; \quad (\phi \wedge \psi)^{\downarrow} = \phi^{\downarrow} \cap \psi^{\downarrow}; \quad (\phi \rightarrow \psi)^{\downarrow} = (\neg\phi \vee \psi)^{\downarrow}.$$

Here, $\phi, \psi \in \mathcal{L}(M)$. *We say that an object* $g \in G$ satisfies *a compound attribute* ϕ *(notation:* $g \Vdash \phi$*) if* $g \in \phi^{\downarrow}$.

Definition 4 (Implications over Compound Attributes). *An implication* $\phi \rightarrow \psi$ *over* $\mathcal{L}(M)$ holds *in* $\mathbb{K} = (G, M, I)$ *if* $g \Vdash \phi \rightarrow \psi$ *for all* $g \in G$ *or, equivalently, if* $\phi^{\downarrow} \subseteq \psi^{\downarrow}$. *We write* $g \Vdash \Sigma$ *if* $g \Vdash \phi \rightarrow \psi$ *for every implication* $\phi \rightarrow \psi$ *in an implication set* Σ.

It is easy to see that an attribute implication $A \rightarrow B$, where $A, B \subseteq M$, holds in $\mathbb{K}$ if and only if so does the implication over compound attributes $\bigwedge A \rightarrow \bigwedge B$.

Example 2. For the context in Example 1, the compound attribute $\phi := \texttt{mxm} \vee \neg\texttt{imm}$ may be constructed to capture those who were either in favour of maintaining the US' stock of intercontinental ballistic missiles or in opposition to the *Immigration Reform and Control Act*, which (in part) sought to penalise employers who knowingly employed illegal immigrants [1,2]. The extent of this compound attribute consists of `Con-4`, `Con-9`, and `Con-18`.

3.2 Defeasible Conditionals over Compound Attributes

We now introduce the '$\mid\!\sim$' as a connective over compound attributes. Then, $\phi \mid\!\sim \psi$ is to be interpreted as "The typical objects that satisfy the (compound) attribute ϕ also satisfy ψ". Implicit in this reading is that a suitable structure for defining a semantics must have an explicit notion of when an object is 'typical' and when it is not; i.e., a preference relation. It is then obvious that a formal context alone is insufficient.

We introduce a *preferential context* as an extension to the formal context, which provides such a relation on objects. Definition 5 provides a useful notation for referring the minimal (preferred) objects from a set.

Definition 5 (Minimisation). *Let* A *be a set equipped with a strict partial order* $\prec$. *The* minimisation *is a selection function* $\underline{(\cdot)} : 2^A \mapsto 2^A$ *that maps each subset* $B \subseteq A$ *to the set of all* $\prec$*-minimal elements of* B, *i.e.,*

$$\underline{B} = \{g \in B \mid \nexists h \in B \text{ such that } h \prec g\}$$

We can then introduce a preferential context, as well as a notion for when a defeasible conditional is satisfied.

Definition 6 (Preferential Context). *A preferential context $\mathbb{P} = (G, M, I, \prec)$ is a quadruple where (G, M, I) is a formal context and $\prec$ is a strict partial order over the set of objects G representing a preference relation.*

A defeasible conditional $\psi \mid\sim \phi$ over the set $\mathcal{L}(M)$ of compound attributes is satisfied *by a preferential context $\mathbb{P}$ if and only if for each object $g \in \underline{(\psi^{\downarrow})}$ it is also the case that $g \Vdash \phi$; which can be expressed equivalently as $\underline{(\psi^{\downarrow})} \subseteq \phi^{\downarrow}$, or $\phi^{\downarrow} \subseteq \underline{(\psi^{\downarrow})}^{\uparrow}$*

At the object level, it makes little sense to speak of the validity of defeasible conditionals as distinct from the validity of implications. Therefore, we will use the notation $g \Vdash \psi \mid\sim \phi$ to mean $g \Vdash \psi \rightarrow \phi$ and, as with implications, extend this notation to sets of defeasible conditionals. We will also say that a preferential context *supports* a defeasible conditional $\psi \mid\sim \phi$ whenever the underlying formal context supports the implication $\psi \rightarrow \phi$.

Example 3. We present a subcontext of the context from Example 1 featuring three congressmen along with their party affiliations and voting records on the following bills: (i) the Immigration Reform and Control Act, (ii) the Education Amendments Act, and (iii) the Comprehensive Crime Control Act.

Congress	dem	rep	imm	edu	crm
Con-1		×	×	×	×
Con-9		×		×	×
Con-17	×		×	×	

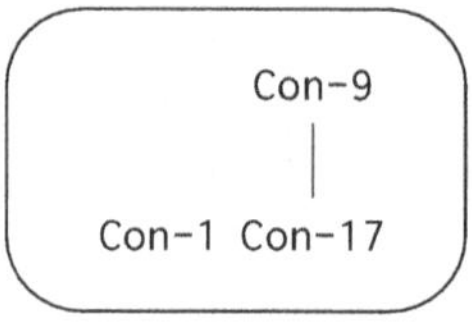

It is clear that the classical implication `edu` $\rightarrow$ `imm` is not satisfied in this context, due to the counter-example of `Con-9`. If we instead consider the defeasible counterpart, `edu` $\mid\sim$ `imm`, alongside the preferential context induced by the order on objects described by Example 3, the conditional is satisfied by the context.

We let $\mid\sim_{\mathbb{P}}$ refer to the consequence relation induced by the semantics from Definition 6 for defeasible conditionals. It should be quite clear that $(\phi, \psi) \in \mid\sim_{\mathbb{P}}$ (or, $\phi \mid\sim_{\mathbb{P}} \psi$) if and only if $\mathbb{P}$ satisfies $\phi \mid\sim \psi$.

It remains to be shown that these defeasible conditions are a faithful translation of the original KLM framework. For our soundness result we now show that every relation $\mid\sim_{\mathbb{P}}$ induced by a preferential context $\mathbb{P}$ is a preferential consequence relation. The following lemma is a reasonably obvious result of the semantics we have given to defeasible conditionals, and is helpful for the soundness result.

Lemma 1. *If $\mathbb{P}$ is a preferential context, then it satisfies the defeasible conditional $\phi \mid\sim \psi$ if and only if $\underline{(\phi^{\downarrow})} = \underline{(\phi^{\downarrow} \cap \psi^{\downarrow})}$.*

Theorem 3 (Soundness of Preferential Contexts). *For any preferential context $\mathbb{P}$, the induced relation $\mid\sim_{\mathbb{P}}$ defines a preferential consequence relation, i.e., $\mid\sim_{\mathbb{P}}$ is closed under (REF), (LLE), (RW), (AND), (OR), (CUT), and (CM).*

We now show that for any preferential consequence relation $\mid\!\sim_{\mathcal{P}}$, there exists a preferential context $\mathbb{P}$ such that the induced consequence relation $\mid\!\sim_{\mathbb{P}}$ coincides exactly with $\mid\!\sim_{\mathcal{P}}$. This yields our completeness result. Our approach relies on the completeness result for preferential interpretations from [15], as recalled in Theorem 2.

As a preliminary step, we show that for any preferential interpretation $\mathcal{P}$ over the set $\mathcal{M}$ of propositional atoms, one can construct a preferential context $\mathbb{P}$ over the attribute set M such that the consequence relation $\mid\!\sim_{\mathbb{P}}$ induced by $\mathbb{P}$ corresponds to $\mid\!\sim_{\mathcal{P}}$ via a translation between propositional formulae and compound attributes. In this sense, $\mid\!\sim_{\mathbb{P}}$ reflects the pattern of reasoning described by $\mid\!\sim_{\mathcal{P}}$.

The translation is described by construction of a *derived context*. To avoid ambiguity, we adopt the following notational convention: Greek letters $\phi, \psi, \ldots$ denote compound attributes in the language $\mathcal{L}(M)$, whereas $\phi_{\mathcal{M}}, \psi_{\mathcal{M}}, \ldots$ denote propositional formulae over the set $\mathcal{M}$ of propositional atoms.

Definition 7 (Derived Context). *For a preferential interpretation $\mathcal{P} = (S, l, \prec)$ over propositional atoms $\mathcal{M}$, the* derived preferential context *is given by $\mathbb{P}^{\mathcal{P}} = (G, M, I, \prec_*)$ where $G = \{g_s \mid s \in S\}$, $M = \mathcal{M}$, $(g_s, m) \in I$ if and only if $l(s) \Vdash m_{\mathcal{M}}$, and $g_s \prec_* g_t$ if and only if $s \prec t$.*

The following lemmas establish the link, in terms of consequence relations, between preferential interpretations and derived preferential contexts.

Lemma 2. *For any propositional formula $\phi_{\mathcal{M}}$, $l(s) \Vdash \phi_{\mathcal{M}}$ if and only if $g_s \Vdash \phi$.*

Lemma 3. *A defeasible implication $\phi_{\mathcal{M}} \mid\!\sim \psi_{\mathcal{M}}$ over $\mathcal{M}$ is satisfied by a preferential interpretation $\mathcal{P}$ if and only if the compound attribute counterpart $\phi \mid\!\sim \psi$ is satisfied in the derived preferential context $\mathbb{P}^{\mathcal{P}}$.*

While the consequence relation induced by a derived preferential context is not strictly equivalent to that of the corresponding propositional interpretation; Lemma 2 and Lemma 3 establish a systematic correspondence between the two. These results show that the inferential structure of a propositional consequence relation can be faithfully reflected in the compound attribute language of a preferential context.

Theorem 4 (Completeness of Preferential Contexts). *A consequence relation is preferential if and only if it can be induced by some preferential context $\mathbb{P}$.*

We use this correspondence to show that completeness for preferential contexts directly follows from the completeness result of preferential interpretations in [15] (recalled in Theorem 2). Theorem 3 and Theorem 4 provide a representation result for preferential consequence relations in FCA. However, preferential consequence relations allow for some unintuitive consequences.

As an illustration, consider the following scenario: at a university, a typical student graduates. Suppose that at least one of these typical students—call her Alice—is also clever. Alice should then be considered a typical clever student (in fact, this follows from Lemma 1).

Suppose another student, Bob, is not a typical student because, despite being clever, he never works and will not graduate. It seems strange to accept that Bob might be a typical clever student: by virtue of Alice being a typical student and Bob being an atypical one, it seems reasonable to suggest that Alice is more typical than Bob, and thus Bob should not be a typical clever student (since Alice is one too).

This line of reasoning is not sound with respect to preferential contexts, as described earlier. In fact, Example 3 demonstrates precisely how preferential reasoning may fail to guarantee rational monotonicity: it has already been established that $\mathtt{edu} \mid\!\sim \mathtt{imm}$ is satisfied by the preferential context induced by the order in Example 3. That $\mathtt{edu} \not\mid\!\sim \neg\mathtt{rep}$ holds is shown by Representative-1 who is minimal in the set of education amendments voters while also being a Republican. From rational monotonicity it should follow that $\mathtt{edu} \wedge \mathtt{rep} \mid\!\sim \mathtt{imm}$; but this is clearly not satisfied by the context as Representative-9 is minimal with respect to Republican-education amendment voters but did not vote for immigration reform.

A solution to this issue is to require that the preference relation on objects be a *strict weak order* rather than simply a partial order [22].

Definition 8. *A strict partial order $\prec$ on a set G is a* strict weak order *if and only if it also satisfies the property that the incomparability of two elements is transitive. Then, if g_0 and g_1 are incomparable, and g_0 is incomparable with g_2, then also g_1 is incomparable with g_2 for all $g_0, g_1, g_2 \in G$.*

Under a strict weak order, incomparability forms equivalence classes on elements. In the context of preference relations, we consider an equivalence class to contain objects that have the same degree of typicality. Objects from another equivalence class are then less or more typical. It is helpful to view strict weak orders as inducing a ranked structure where each 'rank' corresponds to some degree of typicality [13, 18]. If we consider some $g_0, g_1 \in \underline{(\phi^{\downarrow})}$ (and so g_0 and g_1 are incomparable) where also $g_0 \in \underline{(\phi \wedge \psi)^{\downarrow}}$, there cannot be another $g_2 \in \underline{(\phi \wedge \psi)^{\downarrow}}$ such that $g_1 \prec g_2$ by the transitivity of incomparability.

Definition 9 (Ranked Context). *A* ranked context $\mathbb{R} = (G, M, I, \prec)$ *is a preferential context where $\prec$ is a strict weak order.*

Strict weak orders can be represented by a ranking function $\mathsf{R}\colon G \to \mathbb{N}$, where $\mathbb{N}$ is equipped with its usual order. For all $g_0, g_1 \in G$ we then have $g_0 \prec g_1$ iff $\mathsf{R}(g_0) < \mathsf{R}(g_1)$. We additionally require that $\mathsf{R}(g) = 0$ for some $g \in G$, and whenever $\mathsf{R}(g) = j > 0$, there exists a $g_0 \in G$ with $\mathsf{R}(g_0) = j - 1$. In future, we may denote a ranked context by $\mathbb{R} = (G, M, I, \mathsf{R})$ and, when the context is clear, write $\mathbb{R}(g)$ for $\mathsf{R}(g)$.

We denote the consequence relation induced by a ranked context $\mathbb{R}$ as $\mid\!\sim_{\mathbb{R}}$. From the definition it is clear that ranked contexts are a subset of preferential contexts, and so every $\mid\!\sim_{\mathbb{R}}$ is at least preferential consequence relation. Then, all that is required to show that $\mid\!\sim_{\mathbb{R}}$ is a rational consequence relation is to show that it satisfies (RM).

Theorem 5 (Soundness of Ranked Contexts). *If $\mid\!\sim_{\mathbb{R}}$ is the consequence relation induced by a ranked context $\mathbb{R}$, then $\mid\!\sim_{\mathbb{R}}$ is closed under (RM).*

The completeness result for ranked contexts with respect to rational consequence relations follows a similar trajectory to the result for preferential contexts: a derived ranked context, $\mathbb{R}^{\mathcal{R}}$, can be constructed from a ranked interpretation, $\mathcal{R}$, such that for any consequence relation, $\mid\!\sim_{\mathcal{R}}$, induced by a ranked interpretation there is another consequence relation $\mid\!\sim_{\mathbb{R}}$ induced by its derived context that corresponds to an analogous pattern of reasoning.

Lemma 4. *If $\mathcal{R}$ is a ranked interpretation and $\mathbb{R}^{\mathcal{R}}$ is the derived ranked context, then $\mathcal{R} \Vdash \phi_{\mathcal{M}} \mid\!\sim \psi_{\mathcal{M}}$ if and only if $\mathbb{R}^{\mathcal{R}} \Vdash \phi \mid\!\sim \psi$.*

Theorem 6 (Completeness of Ranked Contexts). *A consequence relation is* rational *if and only if the consequence relation induced by a ranked context.*

4 Non-monotonic Entailment in Ranked Contexts

In the previous section, we examined how a formal context can be extended to provide semantics for defeasible conditionals and demonstrated that this extension represents a faithful translation of propositional rational consequence relations. We now turn to the matter of defeasible entailment within FCA: that is, given a set Δ of defeasible conditionals, what else should be inferred? Recall from the discussion in Sect. 2.3 that Tarskian notions of consequence remain monotonic. Consequently, a notion of entailment based on the set of all ranked contexts satisfying Δ fails to capture the non-monotonicity of defeasible inference.

4.1 Finding Order

As an intermediary step, we propose `ObjectRank` as an approach to constructing a preference relation over objects, which is a derivation of BaseRank [7,9]. Thus far, we have remained agnostic regarding how any preference relation over objects might be constructed. However, manually constructing a suitable order is not necessarily a trivial task: it is not always obvious when one object should be considered more typical than another. Instead, our proposed approach considers background information that represents a perspective on how the domain is expected to behave.

The background information is encoded as a set Δ of defeasible conditionals. For instance, `crm` $\mid\!\sim$ `imm` represents the expectation that typical representatives who vote in favour of the 'Comprehensive Crime Control Act' also vote in favour of the 'Immigration Reform and Control Act'. The rank of an object is then determined by how consistent it is with Δ.

It may happen that the given formal context admits no ranking that satisfies Δ. If this is the case, the algorithm must report so.

Definition 10 (Δ-Compatibility). *For a set Δ of defeasible conditionals, a formal context (G, M, I) is* Δ-compatible *if there is a ranked context (G, M, I, R) where all conditionals from Δ hold.*

`ObjectRank` starts by temporarily assigning the rank $|G|$ to all objects. Objects with rank $|G|$ should be considered as unranked. The rank 0 is then assigned to all objects that satisfy all conditionals in Δ. Conditionals supported by 0-ranked objects are then removed from Δ, and the process is repeated, now considering a reduced set of

Algorithm 1: `ObjectRank`

Input: A context $\mathbb{K} = (G, M, I)$ and a set Δ of defeasible conditionals over $\mathcal{L}(M)$
Result: A ranking $\mathsf{R}\colon G \to \mathbb{N}$ such that Δ holds in (G, M, I, R) if $\mathbb{K}$ is Δ-compatible; $\bot$, otherwise

1 $i := 0$
2 initialize $\mathsf{R}(g) := |G|$ for all $g \in G$
3 $\Gamma := \Delta$
4 **while** $\exists g \in G\colon \mathsf{R}(g) = |G|$ **do**
5   **forall** $g \in G$ *with* $\mathsf{R}(g) = |G|$ **do**
6   **if** $g \Vdash \Gamma$ **then**
7   update $\mathsf{R}(g) := i$
8   **if** $\forall g \in G\colon \mathsf{R}(g) \neq i$ **then**
9   **return** $\bot$
10     $\Gamma := \{(\phi \mathrel{|\!\sim} \psi) \in \Gamma \mid g \nVdash \phi \text{ for all } g \in G \text{ with } \mathsf{R}(g) = i\}$
11     $i := i + 1$
12 **return** R

unranked objects and reduced Δ. As there are at most $|G|$ iterations of the **while** loop and each iteration requires time $O(|G||\Delta|)$, the algorithm runs in time polynomial in the size of the input context $\mathbb{K}$ and Δ.

Example 4. Consider the `ObjectRank` algorithm with the context from Example 1 and the set $\Delta := \{\texttt{imm} \mathrel{|\!\sim} \texttt{crm}, \texttt{wpc} \mathrel{|\!\sim} \texttt{scc}\}$ as inputs. On the first iteration, the objects which satisfy Δ are `Con-18` and `Con-4` and are thus assigned rank 0. Additionally, `Con-4` supports the conditional $\texttt{wpc} \mathrel{|\!\sim} \texttt{scc}$, which is then removed from Δ. On the next iteration, only objects `Con-1` and `Con-9` satisfy the reduced set of conditionals and are thus assigned rank 1. Further, `Con-1` supports the conditional $\texttt{imm} \mathrel{|\!\sim} \texttt{crm}$ and so it is removed from Δ. The set Δ is now empty, and so all remaining objects satisfy it, and are assigned rank 3 (namely, `Con-17`). The ranked context derived from this process is shown by Example 5.

Proposition 1. *Let* $\mathbb{R} = (G, M, I, \mathsf{R})$ *be a ranked context. For* $i \in \mathbb{N}$, *define* $\mathbb{R}_k$ *to be the context obtained by restricting* $\mathbb{R}$ *to objects* $g \in G$ *with* $\mathsf{R} \leq k$. *That is,*

$$\mathbb{R}_k = (G_k, M, I \cap (G_k \times M), \mathsf{R}),$$

where $G_k = \{g \in G \mid \mathsf{R}(g) \leq k\}$. *The following invariant holds for* `ObjectRank`*: At the start and at the end of each iteration of the* ***while*** *loop, the context* $\mathbb{R}_i$

1. *satisfies all defeasible conditionals in* Δ;
2. *supports all defeasible conditionals in* $\Delta \setminus \Gamma$;
3. *supports none of the defeasible conditionals in* Γ.

Proof. The statement holds trivially before the first iteration, when $i = 0$, $G_0 = \emptyset$, and $\Delta \setminus \Gamma = \emptyset$. Suppose that it holds at the start of some iteration (before line 5), when $i = k$ for some $0 \leq k < |G|$. Note that, at this point, $\mathsf{R}(g) < k$ for all $g \in G_k$. We show that the statement holds after the iteration (after line 11), when $i = k + 1$.

The body of the loop changes the ranking $\mathsf{R}(g)$ of some objects $g \in G$ from $|G|$ to k. Consider a conditional $\phi \mid\!\sim \psi \in \Delta$. If $\phi \mid\!\sim \psi \notin \Gamma$ at the start of the iteration, it is supported by $\mathbb{R}_k$ by assumption, which means there exists an object $h \in G_k$ with $\mathsf{R}(h) < k$ such that $h \Vdash \phi$. Hence, no object g with $\mathsf{R}(g) = k$ belongs to $\underline{(\phi^{\downarrow})}$. Since $\mathbb{R}_k$ satisfies $\phi \mid\!\sim \psi$ by assumption, the conditional remains satisfied in $\mathbb{R}_{k+1}$.

If $\phi \mid\!\sim \psi \in \Gamma$ at the start of the iteration, then it is satisfied by every object g with $\mathsf{R}(g) = k$ due to the test in line 6. Therefore, it again remains satisfied in $\mathbb{R}_{k+1}$, which proves condition 1 of the invariant.

A conditional is removed from Γ in line 10 at this iteration if and only if it is supported by at least some object g with $\mathsf{R}(g) = k$. The conditionals removed from Γ at earlier iterations are supported by $\mathbb{R}_k$—and hence by $\mathbb{R}_{k+1}$—by assumption, while the conditionals remaining in Γ are not supported by $\mathbb{R}_k$. Thus, conditions 2 and 3 of the invariant are also satisfied. □

Corollary 1. *If the* `ObjectRank` *algorithm returns a ranking* R *on input* Δ *and* $\mathbb{K} = (G, M, I)$*, then the ranked context* (G, M, I, R) *satisfies* Δ.

Proposition 2. *Consider an execution of the* `ObjectRank` *algorithm on* Δ *and a* Δ*-compatible context* $\mathbb{K} = (G, M, I)$. *Let* R *be the ranking just before the termination of the algorithm and* $\mathbb{R} = (G, M, I, \mathsf{R})$. *Also, let* $\mathbb{R}^* = (G, M, I, \mathsf{R}^*)$ *be such that* $\mathbb{R}^* \Vdash \Delta$. *Then,* $\mathsf{R}(g) \leq \mathsf{R}^*(g)$ *for all* $g \in G$.

Proof. We prove this by induction on $\mathsf{R}^*(g)$. For the base case, if $\mathsf{R}^*(g) = 0$, then $g \Vdash \Delta$, and `ObjectRank` assigns g rank 0.

Now we assume that the statement holds for all $\mathsf{R}^*(g) < k < |G|$ and show that it must then hold for $\mathsf{R}^*(g) = k$.

Suppose, towards contradiction, that $\mathsf{R}(g) > \mathsf{R}^*(g) = k$ for some $g \in G$, and consider the iteration of `ObjectRank` when $i = \min(k, t)$, where t is the value of i just before the termination of the algorithm. We have $\mathsf{R}(g) = |G|$ both at the start and at the end of this iteration. This means that g does not satisfy some conditional $\phi \mid\!\sim \psi$ that belongs to Γ at the start of the iteration. From Proposition 1, it follows that $\phi \mid\!\sim \psi$ is not supported by $\mathbb{R}_{k-1}$. Since $\mathsf{R}(g) \leq \mathsf{R}^*(g)$ whenever $\mathsf{R}^*(g) < k$, it is not supported by $\mathbb{R}^*_{k-1}$ either. That is, there is no $h \in G$ with $h \Vdash \phi$, $h \Vdash \psi$, and $\mathsf{R}^*(h) < k$. Therefore, $g \in \underline{(\phi^{\downarrow})}$ in $\mathbb{R}^*$ and $\mathbb{R}^* \nVdash \phi \mid\!\sim \psi$, a contradiction. □

Corollary 2. *If a context* $\mathbb{K} = (G, M, I)$ *is* Δ*-compatible and* $(G, M, I, \mathsf{R}^*) \Vdash \Delta$*, then, on input* Δ *and* $\mathbb{K}$*, the* `ObjectRank` *algorithm returns a ranking* R *such that* $\mathsf{R}(g) \leq \mathsf{R}^*(g)$ *for all* $g \in G$.

Thus, we have

Theorem 7. *Assume that* $\mathbb{K} = (G, M, I)$ *and* Δ *are the input to the* `ObjectRank` *algorithm. If* $\mathbb{K}$ *is* Δ*-compatible,* `ObjectRank` *returns a ranking* $\mathsf{R}\colon G \to \mathbb{N}$ *such that* Δ *holds in* (G, M, I, R). *Otherwise,* `ObjectRank` *returns* $\bot$.

4.2 Rational Closure

We can now describe the rational closure of a Δ-compatible formal context. The first point is to show that, by the same argument as in the propositional case, a preference over ranked contexts can be constructed.

Definition 11 (Preference Relation on Contexts). *Let $\mathbb{R}^\Delta$ denote the set of ranked contexts over the same (G, M, I) that satisfy Δ. For two contexts $\mathbb{R}_1, \mathbb{R}_2 \in \mathbb{R}^\Delta$, we write $\mathbb{R}_1 \preceq_\mathbb{R} \mathbb{R}_2$ if and only if $\mathbb{R}_1(g) \leq \mathbb{R}_2(g)$ for all $g \in G$.*

Ranked contexts that consider objects as typical as possible are preferred, such that we continue to reason classically unless required. In the propositional setting, we described rational closure as being the entailment relation determined by considering the minimum element with respect to the preference relation on ranked interpretations. With this in mind, we present the following proposition, the proof of which is a direct result of Proposition 2.

Proposition 3. *If $\mathbb{R}^\Delta$ is the set of all ranked contexts derived from a formal context (G, M, I) satisfying Δ, and $\mathbb{R}^\Delta_{\mathsf{OR}} \in \mathbb{R}^\Delta$ is the ranked context derived from the* `ObjectRank` *algorithm, then $\mathbb{R}^\Delta_{\mathsf{OR}}$ is the unique $\preceq_\mathbb{R}$-minimum ranked context.*

There is a subtle observation that has thus far been omitted from the discussion. The aim of this section was to show that a faithful construction of rational closure in FCA is possible. We note that where, in the propositional case, a ranked interpretation contains a complete set of valuations populating the ranks, we only consider the objects of a formal context. It is not a guarantee that the set of object intents are representative of the entire attribute space. With this in mind, we define *contextual rational closure* as

Definition 12 (Contextual Rational Closure). *Given a ranked context $\mathbb{R}^\Delta_{\mathsf{OR}}$, obtained through* `ObjectRank` *applied to Δ and a formal context (G, M, I), we state that $\phi \mid\sim \psi$ is in the* contextual rational closure *of $\mathbb{R}^\Delta_{\mathsf{OR}}$ if and only if $\mathbb{R}^\Delta_{\mathsf{OR}}$ satisfies $\phi \mid\sim \psi$. We denote this by $\mathbb{R}^\Delta_{\mathsf{OR}} \mid\approx_{CRC} \phi \mid\sim \psi$.*

That the definition of contextual rational closure describes a rational consequence relation follows immediately from the fact that it is the consequence relation described by some ranked context; and so, on both the object and meta level, ranked contexts satisfy the rationality postulates.

5 Discussion

Example 5. The context describes the same U.S. Congress representatives alongside their party affiliations and voting records in 1984. This is, however, a ranked context which has been derived from the `ObjectRank` algorithm with respect to the set Δ given in Example 5. This encodes the assumption that, in the 1984 Congress, typical representatives who supported immigration reform legislation also endorsed a tough-on-crime position, and that those who favoured the Water Project Cost-Sharing Act further supported the Synfuels Corporation Cutback.

R	Congress	dem	rep	hci	wpc	abr	pff	esa	rgs	ast	anc	mxm	imm	scc	edu	rts	crm	dfe	aas
0	Con-18	×		×		×				×	×	×				×		×	×
0	Con-4	×			×	×			×					×		×			×
1	Con-1		×		×		×	×	×				×		×	×	×		×
1	Con-9		×		×		×	×	×						×	×	×		×
2	Con-17	×		×		×			×		×		×	×	×				×

(a) Ranked Context derived from `ObjectRank` with Δ

$$\Delta = \begin{Bmatrix} \texttt{imm} \mid\!\sim \texttt{crm}, \\ \texttt{wpc} \mid\!\sim \texttt{scc} \end{Bmatrix}$$

(b) A set of conditionals describing a normative view on congressional voting

$$\mathbb{R}^{\Delta}_{\mathsf{OR}} \mid\!\approx_{\mathsf{CRC}} \texttt{dem} \mid\!\sim \texttt{rts},$$

$$\mathbb{R}^{\Delta}_{\mathsf{OR}} \mid\!\approx_{\mathsf{CRC}} \texttt{imm} \mid\!\sim \texttt{rep},$$

$$\mathbb{R}^{\Delta}_{\mathsf{OR}} \not\mid\!\approx_{\mathsf{CRC}} \texttt{crm} \mid\!\sim \texttt{imm}$$

(c) Additional conditionals that are entailed under contextual rational closure

Fig. 2. Illustration of contextual rational closure

That the entailment relation defined by contextual rational closure is indeed non-monotonic, observe that in Example5—which defines the contextual rational closure of (G, M, I) and Δ—$\mathbb{R}^{\Delta}_{\mathsf{OR}} \mid\!\approx \texttt{dem} \wedge \texttt{hci} \mid\!\sim \texttt{dfe}$ holds, as `Con-18` is the minimal `dem-hci`-object and also satisfies `dfe`. If we add the conditional $\texttt{anc} \mid\!\sim \texttt{scc}$ to Δ and recompute the ranking, the new ordering would be the same for all objects except `Con-18`, who would now occupy a new third rank. The consequence being that `Con-17` becomes the minimal `dem-hci` object, and does not satisfy `dfe`; and so, $\mathbb{R}^{\Delta}_{\mathsf{OR}} \not\mid\!\approx \texttt{dem} \wedge \texttt{hci} \mid\!\sim \texttt{dfe}$.

We make one final remark on the distinction between the entailment system of propositional rational closure, where a complete set of valuations is considered, and the FCA-centric contextual rational closure. If the set of objects in Example 5 were extended so as to become representative of the entire attribute space, then every defeasible conditional in Δ would be non-trivially satisfied on the 0th rank: at least the object that satisfies all attributes would satisfy every conditional and corresponding premise in Δ. This reflects what would unfold in the propositional case, as Δ is distinct from the canonical flying birds example, as there are no implications which "clash" with one another.

This is not a problem per se, but rather illustrates how by restricting the models under consideration—a second-order effect of considering Δ with respect to a formal context—allows one to get non-monotonic behaviour without negation, or clashes between rules.

6 Related Works

As mentioned in the introduction, the inclusion of defeasibility into FCA represents a relatively new line of research. This paper describes a further development of the ideas initially presented by Carr et al. [5]. Independently of this work, Ding et al. [8] and

Liang et al. [19] developed an approach to KLM-style defeasible reasoning in FCA. While their work falls within a similar domain, it focuses on developing a defeasible relation between concepts (i.e., allowing exceptions in the sub/super-concept relation), whereas our work discusses defeasible attribute implications. Moreover, their approach is limited to *cumulative consequence relations*, which do not support negation or disjunction, whereas we explore preferential and rational consequence relations.

7 Conclusion

In this paper, we presented an approach to defeasible reasoning in FCA that faithfully reconstructs the KLM framework, originally developed for propositional logic. This enables the identification of *defeasible* dependencies between sets of attributes in FCA, modelled as implication-like defeasible conditionals. These dependencies are characterised by rational consequence relations and follow a describable pattern of reasoning.

We extended this result to the more abstract notion of non-monotonic entailment by providing an interpretation of rational closure in the FCA setting. Our approach diverges from the original definition in that a formal context restricts consideration to the objects present in a given context, rather than to all possible objects, the latter scenario being a more direct translation of rational closure. This leads to an entailment relation based on contextually relevant information, excluding possible but absent information from consideration.

Future research directions include developing a perspective on *typical concepts*, which incorporate the preference relation on objects in their construction, and examining the corresponding concept lattices. An early notion of this was introduced in a previous paper [5], but there remains significant scope for further investigation. Also, since rational closure represents only one form of defeasible entailment, exploring alternative notions, such as *lexicographic* closure [17] and *relevant* closure [6], may also prove interesting.

Acknowledgments. This work is based on the research supported wholly/in part by the National Research Foundation of South Africa (REFERENCE NO: SAI240823262612).

References

1. Department of defense authorization act, 1984 (1983). https://www.congress.gov/bill/98th-congress/senate-bill/675. Senate Bill
2. Immigration reform and control act of 1986 (1986). https://www.congress.gov/bill/99th-congress/senate-bill/1200. Senate Bill
3. Congressional Voting Records. UCI Machine Learning Repository (1987). https://doi.org/10.24432/C5C01P
4. Armstrong, W.: Dependency structure of data base relationships. In: Proceedings of IFIP Congress, pp. 580–583 (1974)
5. Carr, L., Leisegang, N., Meyer, T., Rudolph, S.: Non-monotonic extensions to formal concept analysis via object preferences. In: Gerber, A., Maritz, J., Pillay, A.W. (eds.) SACAIR 2024. CCIS, vol. 2326, pp. 476–492. Springer (2024). https://doi.org/10.1007/978-3-031-78255-8_28

6. Casini, G., Meyer, T., Moodley, K., Nortjé, R.: Relevant closure: a new form of defeasible reasoning for description logics. In: Fermé, E., Leite, J. (eds.) JELIA 2014. LNCS (LNAI), vol. 8761, pp. 92–106. Springer, Cham (2014). https://doi.org/10.1007/978-3-319-11558-0_7
7. Casini, G., Meyer, T., Varzinczak, I.: Taking defeasible entailment beyond rational closure. In: Calimeri, F., Leone, N., Manna, M. (eds.) JELIA 2019. LNCS (LNAI), vol. 11468, pp. 182–197. Springer, Cham (2019). https://doi.org/10.1007/978-3-030-19570-0_12
8. Ding, Y., Manoorkar, K., Wayan Switrayni, N., Wang, R.: Defeasible reasoning on concepts. arXiv e-prints arXiv:2409.04887 (2024). https://doi.org/10.48550/arXiv.2409.04887
9. Freund, M.: Preferential reasoning in the perspective of Poole default logic. Artif. Intell. **98**(1–2), 209–235 (1998)
10. Ganter, B., Obiedkov, S.: Conceptual Exploration. Springer, Heidelberg (2016)
11. Ganter, B., Wille, R.: Contextual attribute logic. In: Tepfenhart, W.M., Cyre, W. (eds.) ICCS-ConceptStruct 1999. LNCS (LNAI), vol. 1640, pp. 377–388. Springer, Heidelberg (1999). https://doi.org/10.1007/3-540-48659-3_23
12. Ganter, B., Wille, R.: Formal Concept Analysis – Mathematical Foundations, 2 edn. Springer Cham (2024). https://doi.org/10.1007/978-3-031-63422-2
13. Ginsberg, M.L.: Counterfactuals. Artif. Intell. **30**(1), 35–79 (1986)
14. Giordano, L., Gliozzi, V., Olivetti, N., Pozzato, G.: Semantic characterization of rational closure: from propositional logic to description logics. Artif. Intell. **226**, 1–33 (2015)
15. Kraus, S., Lehmann, D., Magidor, M.: Nonmonotonic reasoning, preferential models and cumulative logics. Artif. Intell. **44**(1–2), 167–207 (1990)
16. Lakhal, L., Stumme, G.: Efficient mining of association rules based on formal concept analysis. In: Ganter, B., Stumme, G., Wille, R. (eds.) Formal Concept Analysis. LNCS (LNAI), vol. 3626, pp. 180–195. Springer, Heidelberg (2005). https://doi.org/10.1007/11528784_10
17. Lehmann, D.: Another perspective on default reasoning (2002). https://arxiv.org/abs/cs/0203002
18. Lehmann, D., Magidor, M.: What does a conditional knowledge base entail? Artif. Intell. **55**(1), 1–60 (1992)
19. Liang, F., Manoorkar, K., Palmigiano, A., Tzimoulis, A.: KLM-style defeasible reasoning on concepts. In: Napoli, A., Rudolph, S. (eds.) FCA4AI 2024 What can FCA do for Artificial Intelligence 2024, pp. 9–14. CEUR-WS (2024)
20. Pearl, J.: System Z: a natural ordering of defaults with tractable applications to nonmonotonic reasoning. In: Proceedings of the 3rd Conference on Theoretical Aspects of Reasoning About Knowledge, TARK 1990, pp. 121–135. Morgan Kaufmann Publishers Inc., San Francisco (1990)
21. Pérez-Gámez, F., Cordero, P., Enciso, M., Mora, A.: A new kind of implication to reason with unknown information. In: Braud, A., Buzmakov, A., Hanika, T., Le Ber, F. (eds.) ICFCA 2021. LNCS (LNAI), vol. 12733, pp. 74–90. Springer, Cham (2021). https://doi.org/10.1007/978-3-030-77867-5_5
22. Roberts, F.S., Tesman, B.: Applied Combinatorics. CRC Press, Boca Raton (2024)
23. Rodriguez-Jimeneza, J., Corderoa, P., Encisoa, M., Moraa, A.: Negative attributes and implications in formal concept analysis. Procedia Comput. Sci. **31**, 758–765 (2014)

Incomplete Formal Contexts and Their Intrinsic Dimension

Tobias Hille[1,2(✉)] and Tom Hanika[3]

[1] Knowledge and Data Engineering Group, University of Kassel, Kassel, Germany
hille@cs.uni-kassel.de
[2] Interdisciplinary Research Center for Information System Design, University of Kassel, Kassel, Germany
[3] Intelligent Information Systems, University of Hildesheim, Hildesheim, Germany
tom.hanika@uni-hildesheim.de

Abstract. While the notion of geometric intrinsic dimension has been studied for complete formal contexts, its behavior in the presence of incomplete data was not investigated until now. In this paper, we investigate the geometric intrinsic dimension of incomplete formal contexts, where the object-attribute relationship is partially unknown or undefined. Specifically, we introduce a theoretical upper bound on the intrinsic dimension of the completion of such contexts, derived from so-called stable certain concepts. These are defined by well-known patterns of incompleteness from the literature. We validate our theoretical results through computational experiments and discuss their implications. We also show that certain concepts can be a universal tool for analyzing incomplete formal concepts (The Source code is available under https://www.codeberg.org/thille/ic-gid).

Keywords: FCA · Incomplete Formal Context · Geometric Data Set · Intrinsic Dimension

1 Introduction

Incomplete knowledge is a pervasive challenge in many domains, from data analysis to formal concept exploration. The absence of complete information often leads to uncertainty and imprecision. This complicates the task of modeling and understanding complex systems. In Formal Concept Analysis (FCA), incomplete formal contexts arise when relationships between objects and attributes are explicitly modeled as being unknown. In order to gain meaningful insights, these gaps in the data must be addressed.

This paper investigates the Intrinsic Dimension (ID) of incomplete formal contexts. As introduced, the ID is as a measure that captures the complexity and structure of a data set even in the presence of missing information. The objective of this study is to quantify the extent to which data incompleteness affects intrinsic dimensionality. Specifically, we explore how one can estimate an upper

P. Cellier et al. (Eds.): CONCEPTS 2025, LNAI 15941, pp. 342–358, 2025.
https://doi.org/10.1007/978-3-032-03364-2_22

bound for the ID of (complete) formal context $\mathbb{K}$ based on an incomplete context $\mathbb{K}_i$ with $\mathbb{K}_i \leq \mathbb{K}$. To this end, we compare the ID of complete formal contexts with an upper bound derived from corresponding incomplete contexts. We prepare these using various methods to create the incompleteness. Through theoretical analysis and experimental investigations, this paper provides insights into the challenges posed by incomplete formal contexts and offers tools for understanding their intrinsic properties. By addressing these issues, we contribute to the broader effort to manage uncertainty in FCA and related fields. This work provides first steps into the direction of the development of a machine learning algorithm that is capable of detecting low-dimensional completions of incomplete formal contexts without having to test each one individually. Our contributions are:

- Introduction of the notion of *stable certain* concepts and presentation of their utility for the analysis of incomplete formal contexts.
- Theoretical demonstration how an upper bound on the ID of possible completions of an incomplete formal context (Sect. 4) can be derived.
- Experimental investigations into the quality of this upper bound when applied to incomplete contexts derived from real world data sets using different methods for constructing the incompleteness (Sect. 5).

2 Preliminaries

Our work is rooted within the field of FCA introduced by Ganter and Wille [13]. For sets G (objects) and M (attributes) and an incidence relation $I \subset G \times M$ the formal context $\mathbb{K} :- (G, M, I)$ gives rise to the object and attribute derivation operators $\cdot' : \mathcal{P}(G) \to \mathcal{P}(M), A \mapsto A' :- \{m \in M \mid \forall g \in A : (g, m) \in I\}$ and $\cdot' : \mathcal{P}(M) \to \mathcal{P}(G), B \mapsto B' :- \{g \in G \mid \forall m \in B : (g, m) \in I\}$. The set of formal concepts is then defined by $\mathfrak{B}(\mathbb{K}) :- \{(A, B) \in \mathcal{P}(G) \times \mathcal{P}(M) \mid A' = B, B' = A\}$. In a formal concept (A, B) the sets A and B are called *extent* and *intent*, respectively. Using the order relation $(A, B) \leq (C, D) :\Leftrightarrow A \subseteq C$ the encompassing concept lattice $(\mathfrak{B}(\mathbb{K}), \leq)$ is found.

The element $(g, m) \in I$ encodes that the object g has the attribute m. Yet the meaning of the absence of (g, m) is often not quite clear. Burmeister and Holzer [5] introduced a natural extension to these definitions having concrete interpretations. They introduced the case that it could not be decided at the time of creating the incidence relationship whether the object g has the attribute m or not. They called the contexts introduced above *one valued* or *complete* formal contexts and defined *incomplete* formal contexts as follows. Given the set $W :- \{\times, o, ?\}$, an incomplete formal context $\mathbb{K}_i :- (G, M, W, J)$ uses a map $J : G \times M \to W$ (instead of an incidence relation) to encode whether an object g has an attribute m ($\times$), does not have it (o), or whether it is unknown if it has the attribute (?). It is quite natural to build operators suited for this setting of incompleteness similar to the object and attribute derivations ($'$) mentioned above. For a set $A \subseteq G$ the *certain* and *possible* intents generated by A are defined as $A^\Box :- \{m \in M \mid \forall g \in A : J(g, m) = \times\}$ and $A^\Diamond :- \{m \in M \mid \forall g \in$

$A : J(g,m) \neq o\}$ respectively. The notions of *certain* and *possible* extent generated by a subset B of M are defined in a dual way by exchanging the roles of objects and attributes above. It is known that the pairs of maps $(^\square,^\square)$ and $(^\diamond,^\diamond)$ both form a Galois connection [17]. We introduce the notion of certain and possible concepts based on the corresponding certain and possible intents or extents. Of special interest is the *information order* (also called Kripke-Semantics) on W, namely $\leq_W := \{(o,o),(?,o),(?,?),(?,\times),(\times,\times)\}$ [11,12]. This notion facilitates the establishment of a *completion order* between incomplete contexts as follows: Consider two incomplete contexts $j \in \{1,2\} : \mathbb{K}_i^j = (G,M,W,J_j)$. We define $\mathbb{K}_i^1 \leq \mathbb{K}_i^2 :\Leftrightarrow \forall(g,m) \in \ G \times M : J_1(g,m) \leq_W J_2(g,m)$ and say that $\mathbb{K}_i^2$ is an extension of $\mathbb{K}_i^1$. The maximal elements with regards to this order are called the *completions* of an incomplete context $\mathbb{K}_i$ and we denote their set by $\mathcal{C}(\mathbb{K}_i) := \{\mathbb{K}_i^c = (G,M,W,J_c) \mid \nexists(g,m) \in G \times M : J_c(g,m) = ?, \mathbb{K}_i \leq \mathbb{K}_i^c\}$. Inversely, we call the set $\mathcal{C}_i(\mathbb{K}) := \{\mathbb{K}_i \mid \mathbb{K}_i \leq \mathbb{K}\}$ the *incompletions* of a complete formal context. Sometimes it is helpful to consider the natural identification of a specific completion with a corresponding complete context, e.g. $\mathbb{K}_i^c \sim \mathbb{K} :\Leftrightarrow \forall(g,m) \in G \times M : (J(g,m) = \times \Leftrightarrow (g,m) \in I) \wedge (J(g,m) = o \Leftrightarrow (g,m) \notin I)$. Note that in those cases it holds that $A' = A^\square = A^\diamond$ and $B' = B^\square = B^\diamond$ for $A \subseteq G, B \subseteq M$.

In the field of data science, the process of completing missing data is known as *imputation*, while constructing an incomplete data set from a complete one is known as *amputation*. A first formalization using the above notions is produced by choice maps $\mathcal{A} : \mathbb{K} \mapsto \mathcal{A}(\mathbb{K}) \in \mathcal{C}_i(\mathbb{K})$ and $\mathcal{I} : \mathbb{K}_i \mapsto \mathcal{I}(\mathbb{K}_i) \in \mathcal{C}(\mathbb{K}_i)$. Although parameterized or non-deterministic processes may require notation extensions, these are not necessary for the presented work. We focus on scenarios where neither imputation nor amputation alter the number of objects or attributes.

As we are interested in investigating the intrinsic dimension related to incomplete formal contexts, we now briefly recapitulate the mathematical foundations as introduced by Hanika et al. [16]. Consider a finite (non-trivial) set X (called *data points*), a finite set $F \subseteq \mathbb{R}^X$ (called *feature functions*) and a map $d_F(x,y) := \sup_{f \in F} |f(x) - f(y)|$. As F and X are finite, $\sup_{x,y \in X} d_F(x,y)$ exists, ensuring that (X, d_F) is a complete and separable pseudo metric space. Together with a measure μ on X we call the triple $\mathscr{D} = (X, F, \mu)$ a *(finite) geometric data set.* This notion allows for thoroughly defining a family of dimension functions.

As formal concepts are integral to FCA we use them to define the intrinsic dimension of a finite formal context $\mathbb{K} = (G,M,I)$. For subsets (not just intents or extents) $A \subseteq G$ and $B \subseteq M$ we define the normalized counting measures $\nu_G(A) = |A|/|G|$ and $\nu_M(B) = |B|/|M|$ on G and M respectively. Let us consider $X = M$ as space of data points. On M we then define the feature functions in the set $F(\mathbb{K}) := \{\nu_G(A) \cdot \mathbb{1}_B \mid (A,B) \in \mathfrak{B}(\mathbb{K})\}$. From these ingredients we define the geometric data set representation $\mathscr{D}(\mathbb{K}) := (M, F(\mathbb{K}), \nu_M)$. In other words, we will measure a set of data points using the concepts it contains. An advantage over other intrinsic dimension methods is that this can be done without the need to introduce an artificial metric to the relational data.

Hanika et al. [16] introduce for this representation an explicit formula to compute the intrinsic dimension. For each feature function $\nu_G(A) \cdot \mathbb{1}_B$ a *partial diameter* is derived by

$$\operatorname{PartDiam}((\nu_G(A) \cdot \mathbb{1}_B)_\star(\nu_M), 1-\alpha) :- \begin{cases} \nu_G(A) & \text{if } \alpha < \nu_M(B) < 1-\alpha \\ 0 & \text{otherwise} \end{cases}$$

where $(\nu_G(A) \cdot \mathbb{1}_B)_\star(\nu_M)$ is the push-forward measure of ν_M. This is then used to derive a representation of the *observable diameter* of a finite context $\mathbb{K}$:

$$\operatorname{ObsDiam}(\mathscr{D}(\mathbb{K}); -\alpha) = \sup\{\nu_G(A) \mid (A,B) \in \mathfrak{B}(\mathbb{K}), \alpha < \nu_M(B) < 1-\alpha\}$$

The resulting value can be interpreted as the fraction of the data that the features (i.e., the formal concepts) can observe. However, only those features are considered that have an intent size of more than α and less than $1-\alpha$. It may be noted that in the case of finite contexts, $\operatorname{ObsDiam}(\mathscr{D}(\mathbb{K}); -\alpha)$ attains only finitely many possible values, for there is only a finite number of concepts in $\mathfrak{B}(\mathbb{K})$. Using these notions the *intrinsic dimension* of a (complete) formal context $\mathbb{K}$ is defined as $\partial(\mathscr{D}(\mathbb{K})) :- (\Delta(\mathscr{D}(\mathbb{K})))^{-2}$ where

$$\Delta(\mathscr{D}(\mathbb{K})) :- \int_0^{\frac{1}{2}} \operatorname{ObsDiam}(\mathscr{D}(\mathbb{K}); -\alpha)\, d\alpha.$$

We want to close this section by addressing the representation of data in complete formal contexts. In this study, both our theoretical framework and experimental approach consider the data "as is". The primary focus of our work is situated within the domain of formal concept analysis. Consequently, our attention is oriented towards the concept lattice structure as opposed to the pure lattice structure. Therefore, we will not consider reduced and/or clarified formal contexts, as these transformations inadvertently alter row and attribute counts, consequently affecting measures and the intrinsic dimension. By maintaining the original data structure, we preserve features that accurately measure the underlying ID to ensure representation of the data set's inherent characteristics.

3 Related Work

In addition to the works referenced in the previous Sect. 2 we provide the reader with pointers to other works that investigated related and adjacent research questions to the ones tackled in this work.

The development of incomplete formal contexts has followed a multifaceted trajectory since its origins in *attribute exploration* and *knowledge acquisition* [5,17]. Several works have expanded this area, creating connections with *possibility theory* and exploring the details of *certain* and *possible attribute implications* [2]. In parallel, investigations into the characteristics of randomly distributed complete formal contexts have produced valuable insights [4,10]. Recently, these disparate research threads have intersected, with random context modeling used in evaluating collaborative exploration techniques for completing incomplete formal contexts [11]. Additionally, in the realm of concept enumeration and estimation, studies have established expected number of concepts [19] or lower bounds for the average number of concepts in random contexts [24].

The field of intrinsic dimensionality is of high interest in the broad machine learning community, which lead to an abundance of works discussing different notions of intrinsic dimension of data sets. Starting from rather simple approaches, such as that of Chavez et al. [8], which use comparatively basic statistics, and progressing to slightly more involved ones, such as the approach followed by Carter [7], who proposed considering a local variant of the intrinsic dimension, we see a range of methodologies. Sutton et al. [25], on the other hand, propose a relative intrinsic dimension between data distributions. These works have in common that they require the data set in question to have (meaningful) metric functions. Formal contexts, naturally, do not exhibit such metrics. Although such metrics can be artificially introduced, e.g., using Hamming distances, their meaningfulness is debatable.

More sophisticated works link the intrinsic dimension to the mathematical phenomenon of measure concentration [22,23]. From this Hanika et al. [16] derived an axiomatization which resulted into a practically computable dimension function as mentioned above. Previous experimental investigations of the intrinsic dimension of geometric data sets constructed from formal contexts were done in [15], where formal concepts were used to explore data sets.

A substantial body of research has explored various imputation methods for handling missing data in the field of data science and machine learning [6]. While simple techniques such as mean, median, or hot-deck are commonly used, we conjecture that they often rely on assumptions about data density that may not hold true in practice. Furthermore, these methods frequently fail to meet the required levels of measurement typically demanded in formal contexts. Thus, when applying them to incomplete formal contexts, these implicit assumptions would lead to replacing ? with o in most cases. This issue becomes particularly significant when dealing with larger, sparse data sets, where the limitations of these basic imputation methods become more pronounced and potentially problematic.

4 Intrinsic Dimension for Incomplete Formal Contexts

In the context of incomplete formal contexts, a pertinent question concerns the existence of an intrinsic dimension. From a philosophical standpoint, it may be argued that the dimension of an incomplete context is more akin to an interval or maybe even a distribution than a fixed value, produced by the ID's of all possible completions. Nevertheless, assigning an intrinsic dimension value to an incomplete formal context can prove both interesting and useful. For instance, this could be employed to evaluate potential completions. The objective of this study is to establish an upper limit for the intrinsic dimension of all possible completions, representing the worst-case scenario. The central concept is to confine our analysis to the so-called *stable certain* concepts, which are those that cannot disappear under any completion. This definition is founded on the notion of *certain* intents, as introduced earlier.

Definition 1. *Let* $\mathfrak{B}^{\square}(\mathbb{K}_i) :- \{(A, B) \in \mathcal{P}(G) \times \mathcal{P}(M) \mid A^{\square} = B, B^{\square} = A\}$. *We call elements of this set* certain *concepts.*

Remark 1. The set is well-defined and possesses a lattice order that is identical with the one generated by the completion, wherein all ? are replaced by o.

Definition 2. *A certain concept* $(A, B) \in \mathfrak{B}^{\square}(\mathbb{K}_i)$ *is called* stable *if*

$$\nexists m \in M \setminus B : \forall g \in A : J(g, m) \neq o$$

which is equivalent to

$$\forall m \in M \setminus B : \exists g \in A : J(g, m) = o.$$

We denote with $\mathfrak{B}_s^{\square}(\mathbb{K}_i)$ *the set of all certain concepts that are stable.*

Remark 2. The set constructed in this way is a partially ordered set but no longer a lattice. It is straightforward to see that the intersection of two stable certain concepts does not necessarily yield a concept that is certain and stable.

Using these stable certain concepts we can follow the derivations from Hanika et al. outlined in Sect. 2. Starting with a corresponding set of feature functions $F(\mathbb{K}_i) :- \{\nu_G(A) \cdot \mathbb{1}_B \mid (A, B) \in \mathfrak{B}_s^{\square}(\mathbb{K}_i)\}$ we can create a notion of a *geometric data set for the incomplete formal context* $\mathbb{K}_i$ by $\mathscr{D}(\mathbb{K}_i) :- (M, F(\mathbb{K}_i), \nu_M)$. Continuing, we obtain the observable diameter of the incomplete formal contexts:

$$\text{ObsDiam}(\mathscr{D}(\mathbb{K}_i), -\alpha) = \sup\{\nu_G(A) \mid (A, B) \in \mathfrak{B}_s^{\square}(\mathbb{K}_i), \alpha < \nu_M(B) < 1 - \alpha\}$$

Correspondingly, the geometric ID of $\mathbb{K}_i$ is then given by $\partial(\mathscr{D}(\mathbb{K}_i)) :- (\Delta(\mathscr{D}(\mathbb{K}_i)))^{-2}$ where $\Delta(\mathscr{D}(\mathbb{K}_i)) :- \int_0^{\frac{1}{2}} \text{ObsDiam}(\mathscr{D}(\mathbb{K}_i), -\alpha)\mathrm{d}\alpha$.

In essence, the ID in the conventional sense is exclusive to the complete formal context. However, given an incomplete context, the IDs of completions can vary widely. As stated earlier, the objective is to establish an upper bound on the potential values. Indeed, the ID of the incomplete formal context can delineate a boundary that remains insurmountable regardless of the method employed to complete the context.

Proposition 1. *Let* $\mathbb{K}_i :- (G, M, W, J)$ *be an incomplete formal context and* $\mathcal{C}(\mathbb{K}_i)$ *the set of all its possible completions. It holds that*

$$\forall \mathbb{K} \in \mathcal{C}(\mathbb{K}_i) : \partial(\mathscr{D}(\mathbb{K})) \leq \partial(\mathscr{D}(\mathbb{K}_i)).$$

Proof. Let us fix α and consider a stable certain concept (A, B) with an intent in the interval $(\alpha, 1 - \alpha)$. Because (A, B) is stable, there is no $m \in M \setminus B$ such that for all elements of the current extent A there is a ? or $\times$ available. This in turn means that in every completion the initial stable certain concept can only be changed into a concept of the form (A^c, B) with $A \subseteq A^c$. Thus the ObsDiam can only grow larger for the given α which in turn means $\Delta(\mathscr{D}(\mathbb{K})) \geq \Delta(\mathscr{D}(\mathbb{K}_i))$. This reversed inequality shows the claim. □

The above proof highlights the reasoning of the name choice, as a stable concept is tightly connected to a "normal" concept in every completion. With the same reasoning as in Remark 1 we can state the following about a completion that realizes the value at the boundary.

Corollary 1. *Let* $\mathbb{K}_i = (G, M, W, J)$ *be an incomplete formal context and the completion* $\mathbb{K} \in \mathcal{C}(\mathbb{K}_i)$ *be defined by replacing every ? in* $\mathbb{K}_i$ *by o. Then* $\partial(\mathscr{D}(\mathbb{K})) = \partial(\mathscr{D}(\mathbb{K}_i))$.

5 Experimental Investigations

We start the experimental investigations with a focus on the used measurement instruments, the stable certain concepts. Subsequently, the perspective will be shifted to examine the same underlying data through the lens of intrinsic dimension in both complete and incomplete formal contexts. The structure of the experiments will remain consistent throughout.

5.1 Methods

The following experimental procedure is designed to generate a multitude of incomplete formal concepts with varying number of missing entries for several formal context based on real world data. The initial step will be to encode a given data set as a formal context, followed by the generation of a Boolean *incompleteness* mask of identical extrinsic dimensions. In locations where this mask yields a value of one, the corresponding entry in the formal context is replaced with a question mark (?), thereby creating an incomplete context. For researchers interested in reproducibility, we note that this method, together with the set of hyperparameters explained below and through the source code linked above, will produce intermediate artifacts totaling around 30 GB in size.

Data Preprocessing. A collection of data sets was sourced from the *UCI Machine Learning Repository* [18] using an (unofficial) Python library[1], which facilitated the download and filtering process. The initial selection underwent a refinement process, excluding data sets with errors and those of excessive size that were incompatible with current processing methods. Further data preparation involved removing rows containing any NaN values and applying nominal scaling across all attribute types, regardless of their original nature. The final selection criterion limited the inclusion to contexts where the product of the number of objects and attributes ($|G||M|$) did not exceed 20 000. This comprehensive procedure ultimately yielded a curated set of 27 data sets.

[1] https://github.com/uci-ml-repo/ucimlrepo/.

Generating Incomplete Contexts. The process of generating incomplete contexts involves several methods for introducing missing entries, denoted by ?. The *uniform* method randomly samples a number of missing entries between 0 and the total number of elements of the incidence matrix ($|G||M|$), then distributes these uniformly across the matrix. The *binomial* approach uses a Bernoulli random process with a given probability p to decide whether an entry should be replaced by a ?. The *dirichlet* method samples a categorical distribution from a Dirichlet distribution with uniform concentration of scale b, then for each object, it samples the number of missing entries and distributes them randomly across attributes. This method is based on the algorithm for sampling from a null-model for formal contexts [10][2]. Experiments were conducted using different values of probability p, equally spaced between 0.01 and 0.1, and scale b, logarithmically spaced from 0.001 to 10.0, to explore the impact of these parameters on the properties of the generated incomplete contexts. Each sampling procedure defined by the combination of initial context, method and parameter was replicated 20 times to ensure the robustness and reliability of the findings.

Calculating Concepts and Intrinsic Dimension. The above procedure resulted both in complete contexts and a multitude of incomplete contexts. In the case of complete contexts, the *PCbO* algorithm [20,21][3] was used to calculate the intents. As *PCbO* can not handle incomplete contexts, a small additional step of preprocessing is required. By building a complete context from a given incomplete context by replacing all ? with o, it is possible to calculate intents with *PCbO* too *as if* one would calculate the certain intents of the incomplete context. The set of certain intents (and extents) is then filtered down to the set of stable certain concepts in a straightforward procedure. Since it is not required, we do not calculate the concept lattice nor the full sets of (stable) certain concepts and instead only store the sizes of the ex- and intents. To calculate the intrinsic dimension, a straightforward computational approach using the ex- and intent sizes was employed, as described in [15][4]. The main idea is to iteratively compute the "steps" at which the observable diameter changes. Since we are working in a finite setting, we are guaranteed to perform an exact computation, except for possible floating-point issues. To simplify the internal bookkeeping and prevent errors through floating point precision, the supremum of the empty set is zero and the ID for $\Delta(\mathcal{D}(\mathbb{K})) = 0$ is set to infinity.

Identifying Computational Artifacts. We will refer with *incompleteness method* to one of the methods used for introducing the missing entries, and *parameter* to indicate the chosen parametrization of the method. In the following, when speaking of a *configuration*, we mean the tuple (data set, incompleteness method, parameter, seed) to specify a specific element of the possible

---

[2] https://github.com/maximilian-felde/formal-context-generator.
[3] https://fcalgs.sourceforge.net/pcbo-amai.html.
[4] https://codeberg.org/thille/bd-gid.

combinations of experimental artifacts, where *seed* represents the initial state of the underlying pseudo random number generator used for sampling from the distributions. Furthermore, a configuration can be used to identify a pair $(\mathbb{K}, \mathbb{K}_i)$ consisting of a complete (from the initial data set) and generated incomplete formal context. For this pair, we additionally group together secondary artifacts such as the number of concepts $|\mathfrak{B}(\mathbb{K})|$, number of certain concepts $|\mathfrak{B}^{\square}(\mathbb{K}_i)|$ and the number of stable certain concepts $|\mathfrak{B}^{\square}_s(\mathbb{K}_i)|$, and later the (original) ID $\partial(\mathscr{D}(\mathbb{K}))$ and newly introduced bounding ID $\partial(\mathscr{D}(\mathbb{K}_i))$. Additionally, we can derive further artifacts as follows. The relative frequency of $\times$ in the incidence of a complete formal context is usually called *density*. Similarly, we will give the value based on a similar notion for incomplete formal contexts the same name and calculate it through $|\{(g,m) \mid J(g,m) = \times\}|/|G||M|$. Furthermore, the relative frequency of ? in the incomplete setting, namely $|\{(g,m) \mid J(g,m) = ?\}|/|G||M|$, might be of interest and will be called the *incompleteness density* in the following.

5.2 Investigating Stable Certain Concepts

For a first investigation we count the certain and stable certain concepts in the created incomplete contexts. We observe that in almost all configurations the number of certain concepts is non-zero (no figure), whereas this is not the case for stable certain concepts, as shown in Fig. 1. By grouping configurations according to incompleteness method and parameter, it becomes quite apparent that the *dirichlet* method leads to a very high percentage of empty set of stable certain concepts. This effect increases in strength the lower the parameter b (uniform scale) is set. For the *uniform* method it can be observed that on

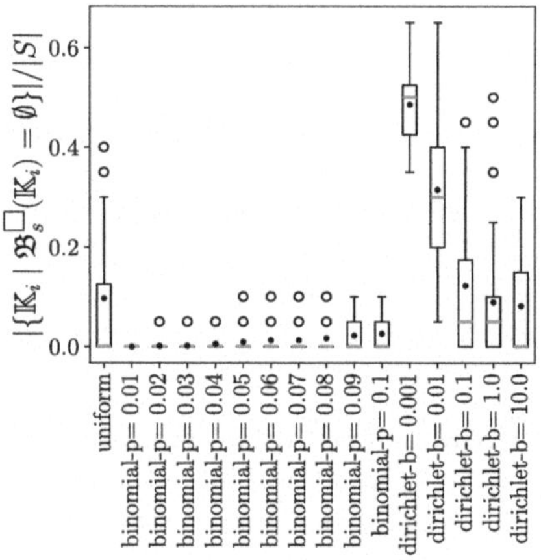

Fig. 1. For each configuration, we check if $\mathfrak{B}^{\square}_s(\mathbb{K}_i) = \emptyset$, averaged over different seeds S of otherwise identical configurations. The different configurations are grouped by incompleteness method and parameter.

average (over data sets) no stable certain concepts exists in 10% of configurations. In contrast, the *binomial* incompleteness method produces only for a few of the selected data sets or/and the highest investigated parameter values of p any configurations, which do not include stable certain concepts at all. To contextualize this more, we plot for each configuration the number of certain concepts against the number of stable certain concepts (see Fig. 2). A clear clustering by data set (each tip on the $x = y$ line) and staggered layers according to the parameter p emerge for the *binomial* incompleteness method. Configurations with *dirichlet* incompleteness show a slightly different behavior. They fill out most of the possible area, without very strong clusters emerging. Notably, it is hard to distinguish the different parameter values b by different global patterns, whereas they all have in common that only a few are placed in the rightmost section. The *uniform* configurations behave quite similarly.[5] At the bottom several large cluster (for sets of size one, two and larger) can clearly be seen. They contain configurations of several incompleteness methods, which is expected from the appearance of empty sets as calculated and shown in Fig. 1 earlier.

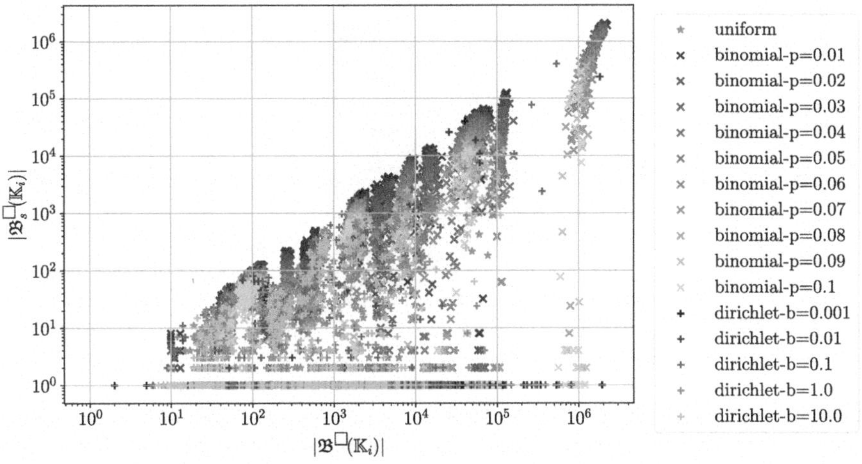

Fig. 2. For each configuration, the tuple consisting of the number of certain concepts and the number of stable certain concepts is visualized. For example, a point on the line $y = 1$ means that only one stable certain concept was found in the incomplete context.

Another interesting observation can be made by plotting the ratio between the density of the incomplete context and the incompleteness density.[6] Thus the x-value of a configuration is calculated as

[5] Separate plots showing only the point clouds for a single incompleteness method each are omitted due to space limitations.

[6] Both indicators were briefly introduced in the last paragraph of Sect. 5.1.

$|\{(g,m) \mid J(g,m) = \times\}|/|\{(g,m) \mid J(g,m) = ?\}|$. We plot these x-values against the number of certain stable concepts $|\mathfrak{B}_s^{\square}(\mathbb{K}_i)|$ of the configuration artifacts in Fig. 3. The clusters described earlier for the *binomial* incompleteness method emerge very clearly again. But more striking is the almost perfect separation by incompleteness method of the configurations with *binomial* on the right side and *dirichlet* together with *uniform* on the left side of the line $x = 1$. This overall separation remains intact when plotting these x-values against the fraction of stable certain concepts among the certain concepts of the incomplete context of the configuration (see Fig. 4). Unsurprisingly, all the different (data set based) clusters of the *binomial* configurations get mapped together. Similarly the *dirichlet* configurations (and hidden underneath the *uniform* ones too) emerge as much denser point cloud. One hypothesis to explain parts of the overall picture emerging from Fig. 3 and 4 might be that the less dense an incomplete context, the lower the chance of finding certain concepts that are not stable.

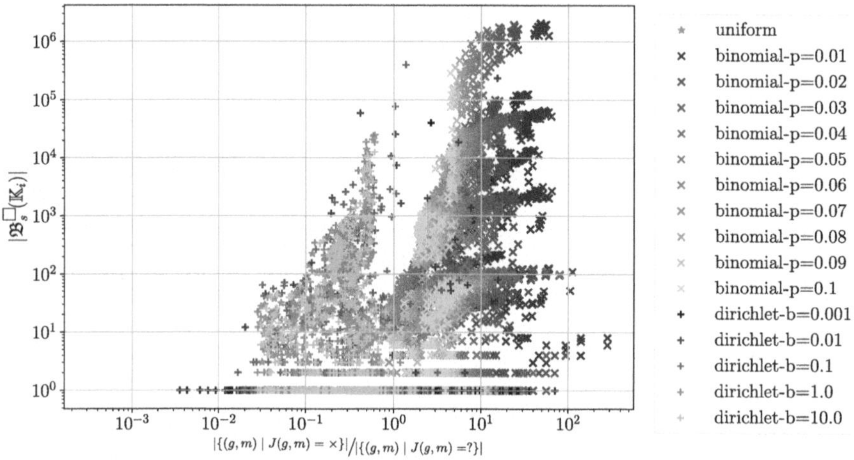

Fig. 3. For each configuration, we plotted the point obtained by calculating the ratio between density and incompleteness density of the incomplete context and the number of stable certain concepts. For example, incomplete formal contexts with the same number of $\times$ and ? land on the line $x = 1$.

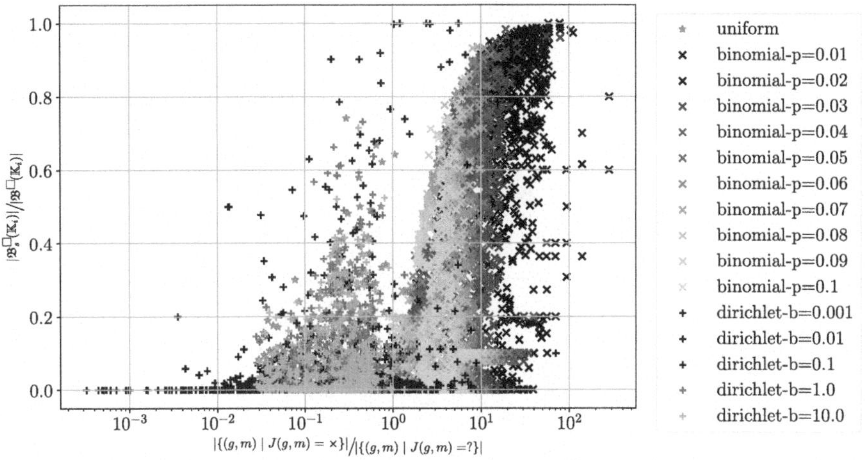

Fig. 4. For each configuration, we plotted the point obtained by calculating the ratio between density and incompleteness density of the incomplete context and the fraction of stable certain concepts among the certain concepts. Thus, a point on $y = 1$ means that every certain concept is stable for this incomplete context.

5.3 Bounding the Intrinsic Dimension from Above

We now turn our investigation to the ID, both in the case of complete and incomplete contexts. Naturally, the presented analysis will have parallels to the one in the previous section, as the notions of stable certain concepts and ID are very much linked together. Thus, comparable to the initial investigation done for the empty sets of stable certain concepts, we count the configurations where the obtained ID (of the incomplete context) goes to infinity. Figure 5 shows the collected statistics, where configurations are grouped according to incompleteness method and parameter. Differences arise from the fact that although an empty set of stable certain concepts leads to an infinite ID, the ID can also be infinite if there are only stable certain concepts of a special form, namely those where the intent is either empty or the full attribute set. With that in mind, the general trends as in Fig. 1 can be observed again.

It becomes quite apparent that the *dirichlet* method leads to a very high percentage of cases with infinite ID and that this effect increases in strength the lower the parameter b is set. For the value $b = 0.001$ on average almost all configurations have very few cases with finite ID. Again, the *uniform* method is similar to the last *dirichlet* parameter setting of $b = 10.0$, where the average of configurations with infinite ID is around 40%. A strong change occurred for the set of *binomial* incompleteness methods. Although the mean and median show a clear trend increase from lower to higher values of p, other elements of the boxes strongly indicate that the variance between data sets is far larger than before.

Using the interesting x-axis introduced in the previous section, we can now take a look at how "well" empirically the upper bound works. For this, we calcu-

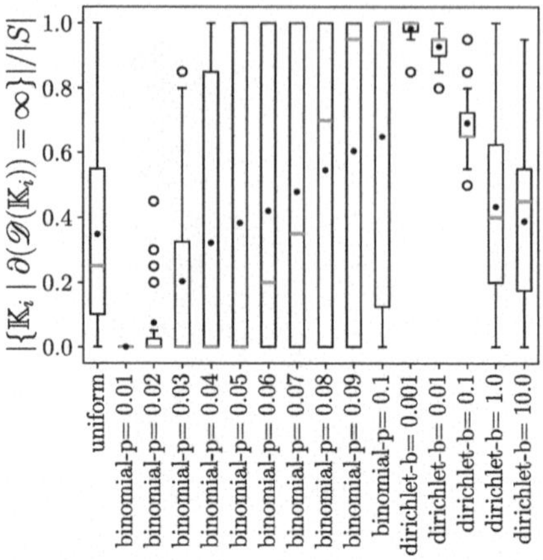

Fig. 5. For each configuration, we check if the obtained $\partial(\mathscr{D}(\mathbb{K}_i))$ is infinite, averaged over different seeds S of otherwise identical configurations. The different configurations are grouped by incompleteness method and parameter.

late the ratio of the ID for the complete context $\partial(\mathscr{D}(\mathbb{K}))$ and the ID (bound) for the incomplete context $\partial(\mathscr{D}(\mathbb{K}_i))$.[7] In Fig. 6, these values are then plotted against the aforementioned ratio between density and incompleteness density (both for the incomplete context). Notably, the homogeneous spread of the *dirichlet* and *uniform* point clouds is significantly reduced, with points mapped to a zero ID ratio value, when comparing to Fig. 4. Importantly, there are no configurations with a density ratio less than one where the ID ratio equals one. As observed in Fig. 4 and again here in Fig. 6, only a small number of *dirichlet* crosses can be seen on the side where the density ratio exceeds one. Among those, only a very small number obtain an ID ratio of one.

The *binomial* point cloud exhibits a disrupted structure, with a small but highly dense cluster near the ID ratio of zero, an unsurprising observation when taking the previous Figure 5 into account. Most remaining points of these configurations form a large cluster in the upper half, where the density of the cluster increases progressively toward the upper limit of the ID ratio of one.

As a final step, we provide an alternative global perspective on the configurations by using a different ratio. Specifically, we divide the number of stable certain concepts by the number of concepts induced by the initial complete context. Figure 7 shows these values plotted against the ID ratio introduced above, offering a complementary view of the relationships within the data. Under this lens, the distinction between the different incompleteness methods is blurred, but it does provide an insight into the empirical quality of the upper bound of the ID. A general trend of more stable certain concepts leading to a tighter bound on the ID can be observed, albeit mainly for the *binomial* incompleteness method. We can also see that for these incompleteness configurations even

[7] To simplify computation, we set $x/\infty = 0$.

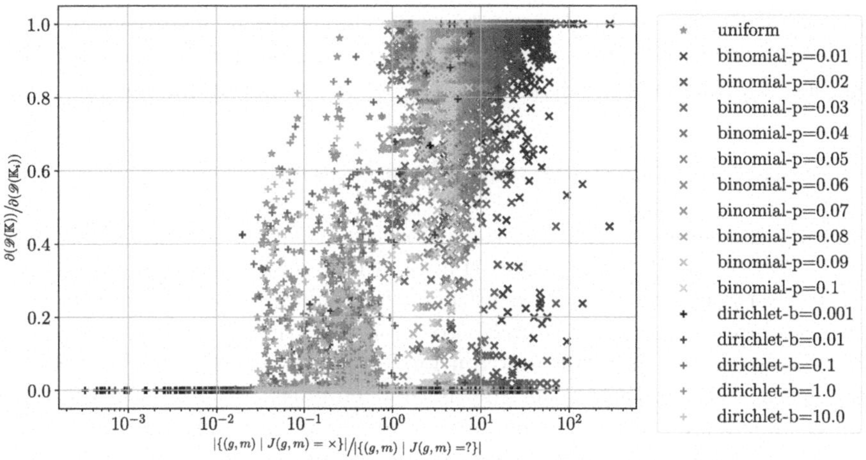

Fig. 6. For each configuration, we plotted the point obtained by calculating the ratio between density and incompleteness density of the incomplete context, and ratio of initial ID of the complete context and the upper bound of the ID of the incomplete context. For example, a point on the line $y = 1$ means that the ID bound is exact wrt. the initial complete context.

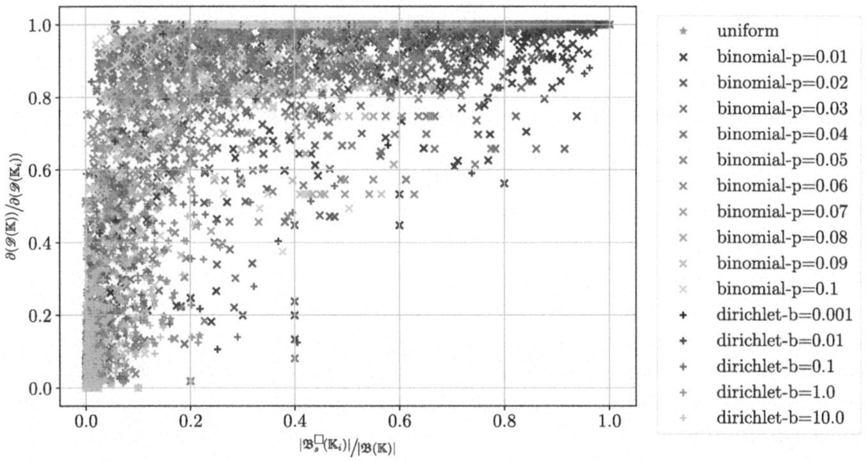

Fig. 7. For each configuration, we used the ratio between density and incompleteness density together with the ratio of stable certain concepts when compared to the original number of concepts in the complete context. For example, a point on the line $y = 1$ means that the ID bound is exact w.r.t. the initial complete context.

for low number of stable certain concepts the ID might be approximated quite closely. In contrast, the *dirichlet* configurations (and also the *uniform* configurations, as before) cluster almost exclusively in the lower left corner, which means that using the few stable certain concepts available leads to an inability to obtain a tight upper bound. A fundamental insight that emerges from this analysis is that stable certain concepts serve as a reliable foundation for comprehending incomplete formal contexts characterised by *binomial* incompleteness.

6 Further Discussions and Conclusion

This study has shown a first approach for investigating the ID of incomplete contexts. We found that the proportion of stable certain concepts is positively correlated with the accuracy of the estimate for the ID. Moreover, it appears that stable certain concepts are a valuable tool for analyzing incomplete contexts.

It is noteworthy that the distribution and number of stable certain concepts are strongly contingent on the method employed to generate the incompleteness. For all methods a substantial fraction of all configurations leads to very small sets of stable certain concepts and thus to very high (or even infinite) upper bounds on the ID. This happens to a lesser extent in the case of *binomial* incompleteness where the stable certain concepts usually appear in enough quantities to give a reasonable upper bound.

It appears that the missing entries introduced by the *dirichlet* and the *uniform* methods result in the destruction of nearly all (original) concepts, in many cases. By modifying these methods in such a manner that the number of missing entries is more strictly limited, it might be possible to introduce more stable concepts. However, since it has not yet been researched how real-world incomplete formal contexts relate to complete formal contexts, the implications of this observation are difficult to assess at this stage. Furthermore, it is important to note that the described preprocessing techniques, particularly the scaling of nominal attributes, may significantly influence the observed effects. Altogether, exploring alternative approaches to the introduction of missing entries (real and synthetic) have to be investigated.

For future work we may note the following observations. The introduced upper bound is sometimes quite close to the highest possible ID among the completions. Its dependency on the set of stable certain concepts is very restrictive, especially in cases where a large fraction of entries is missing. This hints at a possible way for refining the presented upper bound. It might be possible to define a broader class of certain concepts. One might consider those that are close to being stable. For example, one could count the number of different ways in which a *certain* concept is not stable.

Finally, it can be empirically observed that real-world data sets tend to have a low intrinsic dimension. This phenomenon is known by different names in different fields. For example, in the field of deep learning it is known as the manifold hypothesis [9], and in the field of statistical inference it is known as the blessing of dimensionality [1,3,14]. A more thorough examination of the empirical distribution of the ID of possible completions could provide further insight into the interplay between incomplete and complete contexts. Hence, the results of this and the present research can guide the design of an algorithm that will complete an incomplete context such that the result is of low intrinsic dimension.

References

1. The blessing of dimensionality: separation theorems in the thermodynamic limit. IFAC-PapersOnLine **49**(24), 64–69 (2016). 2th IFAC Workshop on Thermodynamic Foundations for a Mathematical Systems Theory TFMST 2016
2. Ait-Yakoub, Z., Djouadi, Y., Dubois, D., Prade, H.: From a possibility theory view of formal concept analysis to the possibilistic handling of incomplete and uncertain contexts. In: 5th International Workshop "What can FCA do for Artificial Intelligence?" (FCA4AI 2016), La Hague, Netherlands, pp. 79–88 (2016). hal-01445243
3. Anderson, J., Belkin, M., Goyal, N., Rademacher, L., Voss, J.R.: The more, the merrier: the blessing of dimensionality for learning large gaussian mixtures. In: Annual Conference Computational Learning Theory (2013)
4. Borchmann, D., Hanika, T.: Some experimental results on randomly generating formal contexts. In: International Conference on Concept Lattices and their Applications (2016)
5. Burmeister, P., Holzer, R.: On the treatment of incomplete knowledge in formal concept analysis. In: Ganter, B., Mineau, G.W. (eds.) ICCS-ConceptStruct 2000. LNCS (LNAI), vol. 1867, pp. 385–398. Springer, Heidelberg (2000). https://doi.org/10.1007/10722280_27
6. Cabrera-Sánchez, J.F., Cruz-Corona, C., Yáñez Escolano, A., Silva-Ramírez, E.L.: A benchmark for missing data imputation techniques: development perspectives and performance comparative. In: Dorronsoro, B., Zagar, M., Talbi, E.G. (eds.) OLA 2024. CCIS, vol. 2311, pp. 140–153. Springer, Cham (2025). https://doi.org/10.1007/978-3-031-77941-1_11
7. Carter, K.M., Raich, R., Hero, A.O., III.: On local intrinsic dimension estimation and its applications. IEEE Trans. Signal Process. **58**(2), 650–663 (2010)
8. Chávez, E., Navarro, G., Baeza-Yates, R., Marroquín, J.L.: Searching in metric spaces. ACM Comput. Surv. **33**(3), 273–321 (2001)
9. Fefferman, C., Mitter, S., Narayanan, H.: Testing the manifold hypothesis (2013). https://arxiv.org/abs/1310.0425
10. Felde, M., Hanika, T.: Formal context generation Using Dirichlet distributions. In: Endres, D., Alam, M., Şotropa, D. (eds.) ICCS 2019. LNCS (LNAI), vol. 11530, pp. 57–71. Springer, Cham (2019). https://doi.org/10.1007/978-3-030-23182-8_5
11. Felde, M., Stumme, G.: Interactive collaborative exploration using incomplete contexts. Data Knowl. Eng. **143**, 102104 (2023)
12. Fitting, M.: Kleene's logic, generalized. J. Log. Comput. **1**(6), 797–810 (1991)
13. Ganter, B., Wille, R.: Formal Concept Analysis, 2 edn. Springer, Cham (2024)
14. Gorban, A.N., Tyukin, I.Y.: Blessing of dimensionality: mathematical foundations of the statistical physics of data. Philos. Trans. Roy. Soc. A: Math. Phys. Eng. Sci. **376** (2018)
15. Hanika, T., Hille, T.: What is the intrinsic dimension of your binary data? – and how to compute it quickly. In: Cabrera, I.P., Ferré, S., Obiedkov, S. (eds) CONCEPTS 2024. LNCS, vol. 14914, pp. 97–112. Springer, Cham (2024). https://doi.org/10.1007/978-3-031-67868-4_7
16. Hanika, T., Schneider, F.M., Stumme, G.: Intrinsic dimension of geometric data sets. Tohoku Math. J. **74**(1), 23–52 (2022)
17. Holzer, R.: Knowledge acquisition under incomplete knowledge using methods from formal concept analysis: part I. Fundam. Inform. **63**(1), 17–39 (2004)
18. Kelly, M., Longjohn, R., Nottingham, K.: The UCI machine learning repository. https://archive.ics.uci.edu. Accessed 24 Mar 2025

19. Kovács, L.: Efficient approximation for counting of formal concepts generated from formal context. Miskolc Math. Notes **19**(2), 983–996 (2018)
20. Krajca, P., Outrata, J., Vychodil, V.: Parallel recursive algorithm for FCA. In: Belohlavek, R., Kuznetsov, S.O. (eds.) Proceedings of the CLA 2008. CEUR WS, vol. 433, pp. 71–82. CEUR-WS.org (2008)
21. Krajca, P., Outrata, J., Vychodil, V.: Parallel algorithm for computing fixpoints of Galois connections. AMAI **59**, 257–272 (2010)
22. Pestov, V.: Intrinsic dimension of a dataset: what properties does one expect? In: IJCNN, pp. 2959–2964 (2007)
23. Pestov, V.: An axiomatic approach to intrinsic dimension of a dataset. Neural Netw. **21**(2–3), 204–213 (2008)
24. Sakurai, T.: On formal concepts of random formal contexts. Inf. Sci. **578**, 615–620 (2021)
25. Sutton, O.J., Zhou, Q., Gorban, A.N., Tyukin, I.Y.: Relative intrinsic dimensionality is intrinsic to learning. CoRR (2023)

The E-Base of Finite Semidistributive Lattices

Kira Adaricheva[1] and Simon Vilmin[2](✉)

[1] Department of Mathematics, Hofstra University, Hempstead, NY 11549, USA
kira.adaricheva@hofstra.edu
[2] Aix-Marseille Université, CNRS, LIS, Marseille, France
simon.vilmin@lis-lab.fr

Abstract. Implicational bases (IBs) are a well-known representation of closure spaces and their closure lattices. This representation is not unique, though, and a closure space usually admits multiple IBs. Among these, the canonical base, the canonical direct base as well as the D-base aroused significant attention due to their structural and algorithmic properties. Recently, a new base has emerged from the study of free lattices: the E-base. It is a refinement of the D-base that, unlike the aforementioned IBs, does not always accurately represent its associated closure space. This leads to an intriguing question: for which classes of (closure) lattices do closure spaces have a valid E-base? Lower bounded lattices are known to form such a class. In this paper, we prove that for semidistributive lattices, the E-base is both valid and minimum.

Keywords: Implicational bases · Closure spaces · E-base · Semidistributive lattices

1 Introduction

Implicational bases (IBs) are a well-known representation of finite closure spaces and their closure lattices. Indeed, implications go by many names in a broad range of fields, e.g. attribute implications in Formal Concept Analysis [16], functional dependencies in database theory [22,23], Horn clauses in propositional logic [12], or join-covers in lattice theory [15,18]. Since a closure space admits several IBs in general, a rich development of implications, summarized in two surveys [8,31], emerged from this variety of perspectives. Moreover, recent contributions [6,7,10] show that IBs are still an active topic of research. Among possible IBs, two have attracted interest due to their structural and algorithmical properties. First, the canonical (or Duquenne-Guigues) base [14,19,30], has a minimum number of implications and is reflected in any other (minimum) IB by means of pseudo-closed sets. Second, the canonical direct base, surveyed in [9], is the smallest (unit) IB enjoying directness, being the property of computing closures with only one pass over the implications.

Translating the language of join-covers in (free) lattices [15] into implications, Adaricheva et al. [5] recently introduced two new specimens in the zoo of IBs:

P. Cellier et al. (Eds.): CONCEPTS 2025, LNAI 15941, pp. 359–374, 2025.
https://doi.org/10.1007/978-3-032-03364-2_23

the D-base and the E-base. These bases find their origin in lattice theory where special relations between join-irreducible elements were developed to tackle notoriously hard problems. The history begins at the cross-section of P. Whitman's conjecture[1] related to lattices of partitions [29] and B. Jónsson's conjecture about the structure of finite sublattices of free lattices [20]. On their way to solve the first problem, Pudlàk and Tůma used a special binary relation on join-irreducible elements, called the C-relation [27]. Only a few years later, they solved Whitman's problem in a celebrated paper [28]. While working on Jónsson's conjecture, Day [13] used the C-relation, which became the D-relation when the solution to the problem—brought by Nation in his famous paper [25]—was incorporated to the monograph on free lattices of Freese, Nation and Ježek [15]. There, the authors highlighted the connection between the D-relation and the so-called minimal join-covers that will later become the D-base. In investigating lattices without D-cycles (cycles in the D-relation, see Sect. 5 for a more formal definition), they also unveiled an important subset of minimal join-covers along with a subset of the D-relation, which they called the E-relation. This subset of join-covers will become what is now known as the E-base.

The D-base is a subset of the canonical direct base that still enjoys directness as long as implications are suitably ordered. It already proved its efficiency in a handful of data analysis applications [1,3,4,26] and its algorithmic aspects have been addressed in a recent paper [6]. The E-base on the other hand is a refinement of the D-base obtained by retaining implications satisfying a minimality criterion within the closure lattice. Borrowing tools from free lattices [15], especially the D-relation, Adaricheva et al. [5] show that in closure spaces without D-cycles, the E-base is a valid IB. Furthermore, the main property of the D-base, its feature of directness, is still retained in the E-base of such spaces. Even more importantly, the number of implications in the (aggregated) E-base is the same as in the canonical base, making it minimum. Yet, unlike the D-base and other mentioned IBs, the E-base does not always encode faithfully its closure space. This prompts the next stimulating question, which constitutes the main motivation of our paper:

Question 1. *For what classes of (closure) lattices do closure spaces have valid E-base?*

For such classes, the E-base could be a base of choice given that it is shorter than the D-base and may still possess the advantages the D-base has over other existing bases. Surprisingly, a seemingly unrelated result of Wild [30, Theorem 11] yields as a direct corollary that the E-base is also valid in closure lattices of binary matroids. With lattices without D-cycles, these are to our knowledge the only (major) classes of lattices whose associated closure spaces have valid E-base.

In this contribution, we investigate closure spaces with semidistributive closure lattices, that is, closure lattices satisfying both meet and join-

[1] He asked his question in the same paper where he solved the fundamental problem of G. Birkhoff [11] about representing lattices by equivalence relations.

semidistributive laws SD_m and SD_j (resp.). These laws are intimately connected with classes of lattices involved into Whitman's and Jónsson's conjectures. Our main result is the next theorem.

Theorem 1. *The (aggregated) E-base of a standard closure space with a semidistributive closure lattice is valid and minimum.*

Remark that the E-base might not be valid in a closure lattice enjoying only one law, SD_j or SD_m (see Examples 2 and 5). Since SD lattices do have D-cycles, we cannot leverage from the approach used in [5,15] to prove Theorem 1. Instead, we show how the E-base relates to the pseudo-closed sets of the canonical base [19] using the properties of semidistributivity.

Organization of the Paper. In Sect. 2 we give necessary definitions and properties regarding closure spaces, lattices and implications. In Sect. 3, we introduce the E-base. We provide examples to illustrate how it can fail being a valid IB of its associated closure. Moreover, we put the light on its relationships with other IBs, especially the canonical base. Section 4 is devoted to the proof of Theorem 1. We conclude the paper in Sect. 5 with a question for future works.

Remark 1. Due to space limitations, most proofs are omitted. They can be found in the `arXiv` version of the paper: arXiv:2502.04146.

2 Preliminaries

All the objects we consider in this paper are finite. We assume basic familiarity with lattices and closure systems and redirect the reader to [18] for an introduction to the topic. If S is a set, $\mathbf{2}^S$ denotes its powerset. Whenever a singleton set $\{X\}$ or $\{x\}$ is used, we may withdraw brackets and use X and x to simplify notations. Sometimes, mostly in examples, we write a set as the concatenation of its elements, e.g. abc instead of $\{a, b, c\}$.

Closure Spaces. A *closure operator* over S is a map $\phi \colon \mathbf{2}^S \to \mathbf{2}^S$ that satisfies the following properties for all $X, Y \subseteq S$: (1) $X \subseteq \phi(X)$, (2) $\phi(\phi(X)) = \phi(X)$ and (3) $\phi(X) \subseteq \phi(Y)$ if $X \subseteq Y$. The pair (S, ϕ) is a *closure space*. Let $\mathcal{C}$ denote the fixpoints of ϕ, i.e. $\mathcal{C} = \{C : C \subseteq S, \phi(C) = C\}$. The members of $\mathcal{C}$ are called *closed sets*. The pair $(S, \mathcal{C})$ is a *closure system*, that is $S \in \mathcal{C}$ and $C_1 \cap C_2 \in \mathcal{C}$ whenever $C_1, C_2 \in \mathcal{C}$. Note that $\phi(X) = \min_{\subseteq}\{C : C \in \mathcal{C},\ X \subseteq C\} = \bigcap\{C : C \in \mathcal{C}, X \subseteq C\}$ for all $X \subseteq S$. The closure space (S, ϕ) is *standard* if $\phi(x) \setminus \{x\}$ is closed for every $x \in S$.

Remark 2. Unless otherwise stated, we assume that all closure spaces are standard.

Let $C \in \mathcal{C}$. A *spanning set* of C is any subset X of S such that $\phi(X) = C$. We say that X *spans* C. For $x \in S$, a *(non-trivial) generator* of x is a subset Y of S such that $x \notin Y$ but $x \in \phi(Y)$. We say that Y *generates* x. The family of inclusion-wise minimal generators of x is denoted $\text{gen}(x)$.

Let (S, ϕ) be a closure space. The *binary part* of (S, ϕ) is the closure space (S, ϕ^b) defined for all $X \subseteq S$ by:

$$\phi^b(X) = \bigcup_{x \in X} \phi(x)$$

Observe that any closed set of $\mathcal{C}$ is also closed for ϕ^b, or equivalently, $\phi^b(X) \subseteq \phi(X)$ for all $X \subseteq S$. Given $X, Y \subseteq S$, X is a *ϕ^b-refinement* of Y if $\phi^b(X) \subseteq \phi^b(Y)$. If $\phi^b(X) \subset \phi^b(Y)$, X is a *proper* ϕ^b-refinement of Y. Let $C \in \mathcal{C}$. A ϕ^b-minimal spanning set of C is a spanning set A of C such that for any proper ϕ^b-refinement B of A, B does not span C. Since $B \subseteq A$ entails $\phi^b(B) \subseteq \phi^b(A)$, a ϕ^b-minimal spanning set of C is also a minimal spanning set of C. Let $x \in S$. A *(non-trivial) ϕ^b-generator* A of x is a set A such that $x \in \phi(A)$ but $x \notin \phi^b(A)$. In particular, a ϕ^b-generator A of x is a *D-generator* of x if it is ϕ^b-minimal for this property, that is, $x \notin \phi(B)$ for any proper ϕ^b-refinement B of A. The collection of D-generators of x is denoted $\text{gen}_D(x)$. Observe that a ϕ^b-generator of x which is at the same time a ϕ^b-minimal spanning set of its closed set needs not be a D-generator of x. A set $Q \subseteq S$ is *quasi-closed* w.r.t. ϕ if for $X \subseteq Q$, $\phi(X) \subset \phi(Q)$ entails $\phi(X) \subseteq Q$. Remark that if $\phi(Q) \neq \phi(x)$ for any $x \in S$, then Q is ϕ^b-closed. Indeed, for $x \in Q$, $\phi^b(x) = \phi(x) \subset \phi(Q)$ holds by assumption, so that $\phi^b(x) \subseteq Q$ follows. If $P \subseteq S$ is not closed and an inclusion-wise minimal quasi-closed set among the spanning sets of $\phi(P)$, it is *pseudo-closed*. The closed set $\phi(P)$ is *essential*.

Closure Lattices. Let (S, ϕ) be a closure space. The poset $(\mathcal{C}, \subseteq)$ is a *(closure) lattice* where $C_1 \wedge C_2 = C_1 \cap C_2$ and $C_1 \vee C_2 = \phi(C_1 \cup C_2)$. It is well-known that each lattice is isomorphic to a closure lattice. In $(\mathcal{C}, \subseteq)$, a *predecessor* of $C \in \mathcal{C}$ is a closed set C_* such that $C_* \subset C$ and for every closed set C', $C_* \subset C' \subseteq C$ means $C' = C$. The *successors* of C are defined dually. We write $C_* \prec C$ to denote that C_* is a predecessor of C and $C^* \succ C$ to denote that C^* is a successor of C. For $\mathcal{C}' \subseteq \mathcal{C}$, the *ideal* $\downarrow\mathcal{C}'$ of $\mathcal{C}'$ in $(\mathcal{C}, \subseteq)$ is given by $\downarrow\mathcal{C}' = \{C : C \in \mathcal{C}, C \subseteq C' \text{ for some } C' \in \mathcal{C}'\}$. The *filter* $\uparrow\mathcal{C}'$ of $\mathcal{C}'$ is defined dually.

We define irreducible closed sets. A closed set J is *join-irreducible*, *ji* for short, if $J \neq \emptyset$ and for every $C_1, C_2 \in \mathcal{C}$, $J = C_1 \vee C_2$ implies $J = C_1$ or $J = C_2$. Equivalently, J is ji iff it has a unique predecessor J_*. Since $(\mathcal{C}, \subseteq)$ is assumed standard, J is ji if and only if $J = \phi(x)$ for some $x \in S$. As $\phi(x) \neq \phi(y)$ for $x \neq y$, ϕ is a bijection between S and the ji's of $(\mathcal{C}, \subseteq)$. Thus, for simplicity, we will identify x with its closure $\phi(x)$ and say that x is ji in $\mathcal{C}$ with predecessor x_*. A closed set M is *meet-irreducible*, *mi* for short, if $M \neq S$ and $M = C_1 \cap C_2$ implies $M = C_1$ or $M = C_2$ for any $C_1, C_2 \in \mathcal{C}$. Similarly to ji's, M is mi if and only if it has a unique successor M^*. An *atom* of $(\mathcal{C}, \subseteq)$ is a successor of $\emptyset$ ($\emptyset \in \mathcal{C}$ since (S, ϕ) is standard). Dually, a *coatom* is a predecessor of S in $(\mathcal{C}, \subseteq)$. Atoms are ji singletons, while coatoms are mi.

We move to arrow relations [16]. Let $J, M \in \mathcal{C}$. We write $J \uparrow M$ if M is an inclusion-wise maximal closed set not containing J as a subset, that is $J \nsubseteq M$ but $J \subseteq M'$ for every $M' \in \mathcal{C}$ such that $M \subset M'$. Note that $J \uparrow M$ implies that M is mi. Dually we write $J \downarrow M$ if $J \not\subseteq M$ but $J' \subseteq M$ for every $J' \subset J$ in $\mathcal{C}$. Similarly, $J \downarrow M$ entails that J is join-irreducible. We write $J \updownarrow M$ if $J \uparrow M$ and $J \downarrow M$. If J is ji, we may write $x \uparrow M$, $x \downarrow M$ and $x \updownarrow M$ where x is the unique element of S such that $J = \phi(x)$. We turn our attention to prime and coprime elements [24][2]. A closed set C is *prime* in $(\mathcal{C}, \subseteq)$ if for every $C_1, C_2 \in \mathcal{C}$, $C \subseteq C_1 \vee C_2$ implies $C \subseteq C_1$ or $C \subseteq C_2$. Prime elements must be ji, hence we say $x \in S$ is prime if $\phi(x)$ is. Equivalently, x is prime if and only if there exists a unique mi M such that $x \uparrow M$, in particular $x \updownarrow M$ must hold. Moreover, x is prime if and only if it admits only singleton minimal generators, i.e. gen(x) contains only singleton sets. Dually, a closed set M is *coprime* if for all $C_1, C_2 \in \mathcal{C}$, $C_1 \cap C_2 \subseteq M$ implies $C_1 \subseteq M$ or $C_2 \subseteq M$. A coprime M must be mi and there is a unique J such that $M \downarrow J$, in particular it holds $J \updownarrow M$. If J is prime, the unique M such that $J \updownarrow M$ is coprime. Thus, $\updownarrow$ is a bijection between prime and coprime closed sets.

A lattice $(\mathcal{C}, \subseteq)$ is *join-semidistributive* (SD$_j$) if for all $C_1, C_2, C_3 \in \mathcal{C}$, $C_1 \vee C_2 = C_1 \vee C_3$ entails $C_1 \vee C_2 = C_1 \vee (C_2 \wedge C_3)$. *Meet-semidistributivity* (SD$_m$) is defined dually by flipping $\wedge$ and $\vee$ operations. The lattice $(\mathcal{C}, \subseteq)$ is *semidistributive* (SD) if it is both meet and join-semidistributive. We now recall useful properties regarding semidistributivity.

Theorem 1 (Theorem 2.1, Corollary 2.2 in [20], Corollary 1 in [17]). *The lattice of a (finite) closure space (S, ϕ) is* SD$_j$ *if and only if each closed set C has a unique ϕ^b-minimal spanning set.*

In the rest of the paper, we call this unique ϕ^b-minimal spanning set the *canonical spanning set* of C.

Proposition 1 (Proposition 49 in [2]). *In a closure space with* SD$_j$ *lattice, each essential closed set is spanned by a unique pseudo-closed set.*

This pseudo-closed subsumes the canonical representation of its closure.

Theorem 2 (Corollary 2.55, Theorem 2.56 in [15]). *Let (S, ϕ) be a closure space with lattice $(\mathcal{C}, \subseteq)$.*

(1) $(\mathcal{C}, \subseteq)$ is SD$_j$ *if and only if for every meet-irreducible M there exists a unique $x \in S$ such that $x \updownarrow M$.*
(2) $(\mathcal{C}, \subseteq)$ is SD$_m$ *if and only if for every $x \in S$, there exists a unique meet-irreducible M such that $x \updownarrow M$.*
(3) $(\mathcal{C}, \subseteq)$ is SD *if and only if $\updownarrow$ is bijection between S and meet-irreducible closed sets.*

Theorem 3 (Theorem 1 in [17]). *Let (S, ϕ) be a (finite) closure space with* SD$_j$ *lattice $(\mathcal{C}, \subseteq)$. Let $M_1, \dots M_k$ be the coatoms of $(\mathcal{C}, \subseteq)$. Then, for all $1 \leq i \leq k$, M_i is coprime and $A = \{a_1, \dots, a_k\}$, where a_i is the unique (prime) a_i such that $a_i \updownarrow M_i$, is the canonical spanning set of S.*

Observe that the last statement is proved in the more general case of complete strongly atomic lattices with the continuity condition.

[2] The definition of primes and coprimes is switched w.r.t. [24]. In our context it is more natural to consider elements of S as primes rather than coprimes, since we will mostly use this aspect of primality.

Implicational Bases (IBs). We refer to [8,31] for a more detailed introduction to the topic. An *implication* over S is a statement $A \to X$, with $A, X \subseteq S$. In $A \to X$, A is the *premise* and X the *conclusion*. An implication $A \to x$, $x \in S$, is a *(right) unit implication*. If both A and X are singletons, the implication is *binary*. An *implicational base* (IB) is a pair (S, Σ) where Σ is a set of implications over S. An IB is unit (resp. binary) if all its implications are unit (resp. binary). The *aggregation* or *aggregated form* of a unit IB (S, Σ) is obtained by replacing all implications with the same premise by a single implication with unified conclusions.

An IB induces a closure space (S, ϕ) where a subset C of S is closed if and only if $A \subseteq C$ implies $X \subseteq C$ for all $A \to X \in \Sigma$. Dually, each closure space (S, ϕ)—each lattice $(\mathcal{C}, \subseteq)$—can be represented by several *equivalent* IBs. An implication $A \to X$ holds in (S, ϕ) if and only if $X \subseteq \phi(A)$. In particular, the binary part of (S, ϕ) can be represented by the binary IB (S, Σ^b) gathering all valid (non-trivial) binary implications, that is $\Sigma^b = \{a \to x : x \in \phi(a), x \neq a\}$. An IB (S, Σ) is *valid* for (S, ϕ) if the closure space associated to (S, Σ) is indeed (S, ϕ). Among the possible IBs of (S, ϕ), and besides the E-base, we will mention three:

- the *canonical* or *Duquenne-Guigues base* (S, Σ_{DG}) [19]. It is defined from pseudo-closed sets as follows:

$$\Sigma_{DG} = \{P \to \phi(P) \setminus P : P \text{ is pseudo-closed}\}.$$

  This IB is *minimum*, it has the least number of implications among all other IBs. The following theorem is well-known and will be useful in the next sections.

Theorem 4 (e.g. Theorem 5 in [30]). *Let (S, ϕ) be a closure space and let (S, Σ) be an IB for (S, ϕ). Then, for any pseudo-closed set P of (S, ϕ), Σ contains an implication $A \to B$ such that $A \subseteq P$ and $\phi(A) = \phi(P)$.*

- the *canonical direct base* (S, Σ_{cd}) [9]. It relies on minimal generators of each element of S. More precisely,

$$\Sigma_{cd} = \{A \to x : x \in S, A \in \text{gen}(x)\}.$$

- the *D-base* (S, Σ_D) [5]. It is defined from D-generators and binary implications representing the binary part of (S, ϕ):

$$\Sigma_D = \Sigma^b \cup \{A \to x : x \in S, A \in \text{gen}_D(x)\}.$$

  Remark that $\Sigma_D \subseteq \Sigma_{cd}$.

3 The *E*-Base and Some of Its Properties

In this section, we first introduce the E-base in the line of seminal works on these objects [5,15]. Then, we exhibit further properties of the E-base and connect it with other IBs, especially the canonical base.

We start with the definitions of E-generators and E-base of a given closure space (S, ϕ). These definitions translate those of [5,15] within our terms.

Definition 1 (E-generator). *Let (S, ϕ) be a closure space and let $x \in S$. A subset A of S is a* E-generator *of x if A is a D-generator of x and $\phi(A)$ is inclusion-wise minimal in $\{\phi(B) : B \in \text{gen}_D(x)\}$. We denote by $\text{gen}_E(x)$ the family of E-generators of x. We have*

$$\text{gen}_E(x) = \{A : A \in \text{gen}_D(x) \textit{ and } \phi(A) \in \min_{\subseteq}\{\phi(B) : B \in \text{gen}_D(x)\}\}.$$

In general $\text{gen}_E(x)$ may be empty, much as $\text{gen}_D(x)$. In fact, this will happen precisely if x is prime in $(\mathcal{C}, \subseteq)$. Moreover, as pointed out in [31], E-generators share common points with critical generators of convex geometries [21]. Convex geometries form a well-known class of closure spaces. For a convex geometry, a critical generator of some x is a minimal generator A of x whose closure is minimal among the closures of other minimal generators of x. Thus, E-generators and critical circuits both ask for minimality in the closure lattice. Yet, the two objects differ in that E-generators rely on ϕ^b while critical generators do not.

Definition 2 (E-base). *The* E-base *of a closure space (S, ϕ) is the IB (S, Σ_E) where*

$$\Sigma_E = \Sigma^b \cup \{A \to x : x \in S, A \in \text{gen}_E(x)\}.$$

By definition, the E-base is a subset of the D-base. Henceforth, it is also a subset of the canonical direct base. Intuitively, the E-base is obtained from the D-base by ruling out implications spanning closed sets "too high" in the closure lattice with respect to a fixed element x. More formally, one obtains the E-base from the D-base by repeatedly applying the following operation: if $A_1 \to x, A_2 \to x$ lie in the non-binary part of Σ_D and $\phi(A_1) \subset \phi(A_2)$, then remove $A_2 \to x$.

Example 1 (see Fig. 5.5, p. 111 in [15]). Let $S = \{a, b, c, d, e, f, g\}$ and consider the closure space (S, ϕ) associated to the lattice of Fig. 1. This lattice is semidistributive. We build the E-base by identifying, for each x, $\text{gen}(x)$, $\text{gen}_D(x)$ and finally $\text{gen}_E(x)$.

- $\text{gen}(a) = \{c, e, f, g\}$. Since $\text{gen}_D(x)$ takes into account only non-singleton minimal generators, we have $\text{gen}_D(a) = \emptyset$ and hence $\text{gen}_E(a) = \emptyset$ as well (a is prime).
- $\text{gen}(b) = \{d\}$. As for b, we have $\text{gen}_E(b) = \emptyset$ (b is prime too).
- $\text{gen}(c) = \{ad, e, f, g\}$. Since ad is the unique non-singleton minimal generator of c, it must be at the same time a D-generator and a E-generator for it is ϕ^b-minimal and minimal with respect to ϕ. Thus, $\text{gen}_E(c) = \{ad\}$.
- $\text{gen}(d) = \{be, bg\}$. We have $\phi^b(bg) = abcfg$ and $\phi^b(be) = abce$. Thus both are ϕ^b-minimal and $\text{gen}_D(d) = \{be, bg\}$. Now to identify $\text{gen}_E(d)$ we need to compare the closures of the D-generators of d. We have $\phi(bg) = abcdfg \subset S = \phi(be)$. Ruling out be, we get $\text{gen}_E(d) = \{bg\}$.
- $\text{gen}(e) = \emptyset$ so that $\text{gen}_E(e) = \emptyset$.

- gen$(f) = \{bc, be, cd, ad, de, g\}$. Among them, we have $\phi^b(bc) = abc \subset abce = \phi^b(be)$ and $\phi^b(ad) = abd \subset abcd = \phi^b(cd) \subset abcde = \phi^b(de)$. Keeping only the ϕ^b-minimal generators leads to $\text{gen}_D(f) = \{ad, bc\}$. We have $\phi(bc) = abcf \subset abcdf = \phi(ad)$ which leads to withdraw ad. Hence $\text{gen}_E(f) = \{bc\}$.
- gen$(g) = \{be, de, ef\}$. We have $\phi^b(be) = abce \subset abcde = \phi^b(de)$. On the other hand $\phi^b(ef) = acef$. We obtain $\text{gen}_D(g) = \{be, ef\}$. Now $\phi(ef) = acefg \subset abcdefg = \phi(be)$. Henceforth, $\text{gen}_E(g) = \{ef\}$.

Putting all the parts together, we can build the E-base (S, Σ_E) of (S, ϕ). For readability we aggregate the binary implications:

$$\Sigma_E = \left\{ \begin{matrix} g \to acf, & f \to ac, & e \to ac, \\ d \to b, & c \to a & \end{matrix} \right\} \cup \left\{ \begin{matrix} ad \to c, & bg \to d \\ bc \to f, & ef \to g \end{matrix} \right\}.$$

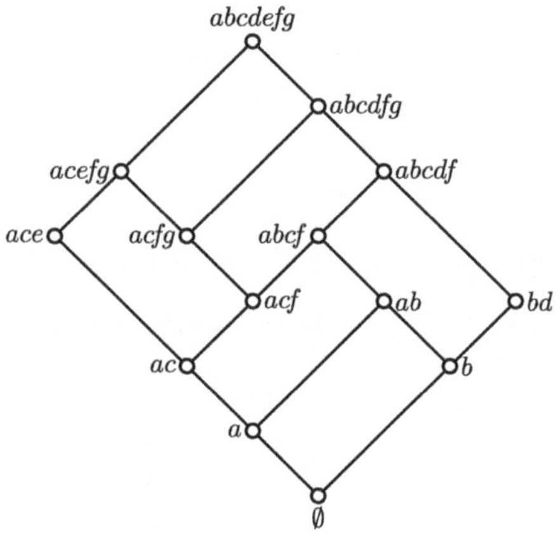

Fig. 1. The closure lattice of Example 1. It is semidistributive.

Unlike the D-base though, and as mentioned in the introduction, the E-base of a closure space does not always constitute a valid IB. We give below three increasingly demanding examples that illustrate how the E-base can fail to describe a closure space by comparing it to the canonical base.

Example 2 (Example 27 in [5]*).* Let $S = \{a, b, c, d\}$ and consider the closure space (S, ϕ) whose closure lattice is given in Fig. 2. It is SD_j but not SD_m. We have $\Sigma_{DG} = \{ad \to bc, ac \to b, bd \to c\}$. This coincides with the (aggregated) D-base. The E-base is (S, Σ_E) with $\Sigma_E = \{ac \to b, bd \to c\}$. The implication $ad \to bc$ does not belong to the (aggregated) E-base of (S, ϕ). Indeed, for $ad \to c$, we have $bd \to c$ with $\phi(bd) = bcd \subset abcd = \phi(ad)$. Similarly for $ad \to b$, we have $ac \to b$ in Σ with $\phi(ac) = abc \subset abcd = \phi(abcd)$. It follows that no implication of the E-base describes the essential closed set $abcd$. Since essential sets must be described by any IB, the E-base is not valid.

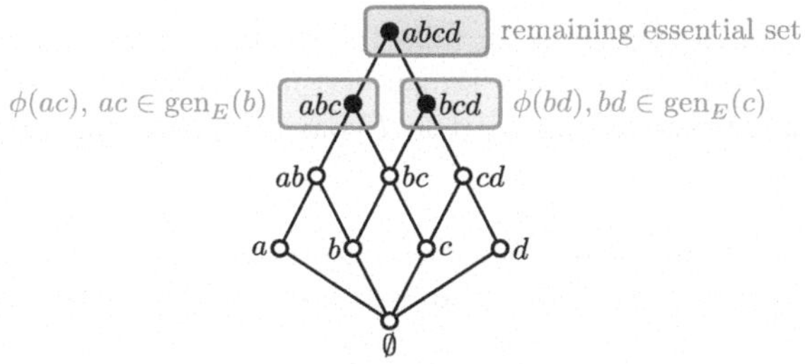

Fig. 2. The SD_j closure lattice of Example 2. Black dots are the essential sets: *abc*, *bcd* and *abcd*. Among them, two are described by the *E*-base. They are highlighted in green. The essential set *abcd*, highlighted in red, is not the closure of any *E*-generators. (Color figure online)

The previous example suggests that the *E*-base of a closure space may not be valid because it fails to describe an essential set. Yet, the next example shows that describing all essential sets is not sufficient for the *E*-base to be valid.

Example 3. Let $S = \{a, b, c, d, e\}$ and consider the closure space (S, ϕ) corresponding to the closure lattice of Fig. 3. Its canonical base (S, Σ_{DG}) has:

$$\Sigma_{DG} = \{d \to c, e \to c\} \cup \{ac \to b, bc \to a, cde \to ab, abce \to d\}.$$

On the other hand, the *E*-base (S, Σ_E) is defined with:

$$\Sigma_E = \{d \to c, e \to c\} \cup \{ac \to b, bc \to a, ae \to d, be \to d\}.$$

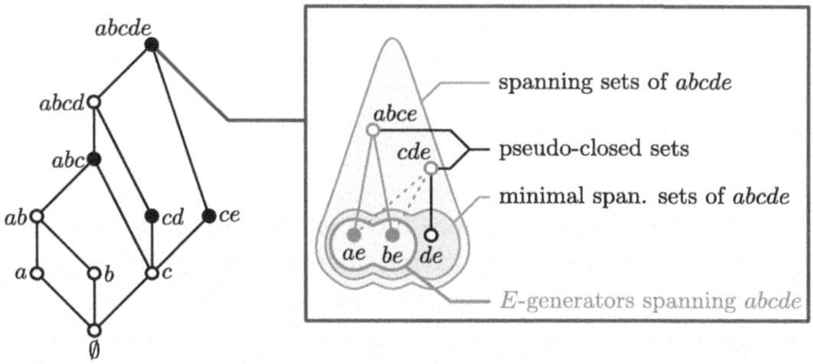

Fig. 3. The closure lattice of Example 3. The black dots are the essential sets: *abc*, *cd*, *ce* and *abcde*. All are described by the *E*-base. Yet, one of the pseudo-closed set spanning *abcde* does not contain any *E*-generator. This is shown in the box on the right picturing the spanning sets of *abcde*. The pseudo-closed set *abce* subsumes *E*-generators *ae* and *be*, while *cde* subsumes none.

The essential sets are *cd*, *ce*, *abc*, and *abcde*. They are all described by the *E*-base. The pseudo-closed set *cde* does not contain any *E*-generator as shown in the box of Fig. 3. Henceforth, (S, Σ_E) is not valid. In fact, *cde* is even closed w.r.t. (S, Σ_E).

In the last example, the E-base fails to describe the closure space because one of the pseudo-closed sets is not subsumed by any E-generator spanning the same essential set. However, even if the E-base satisfies this condition, it does not need to be valid.

Example 4. Consider the closure space (S, ϕ) associated to the lattice of Fig. 4. We have $S = \{a, b, c, d, e, f\}$. The canonical base (S, Σ_{DG}) has:

$$\Sigma_{DG} = \{d \to c, f \to ec, e \to c\} \cup \{ac \to bd, bc \to ad, cde \to abf\}.$$

The (aggregated) E-base (S, Σ_E) has:

$$\Sigma_E = \{d \to c, f \to ec, e \to c\} \cup \{ac \to bd, bc \to ad, ae \to f, be \to f, de \to f\}.$$

In this case, the pseudo-closed set cde indeed includes the E-generator cd subsuming the same essential set $abcdef$. However, the closure of de in Σ_E does not reach a and b. This is because $\phi(ac) = abcd \subset abcdef$ and similarly $\phi(bc) = abcd \subset abcdef$. Thus de cannot be a E-generator of a and b and the E-base is not valid despite faithfully capturing pseudo-closed sets.

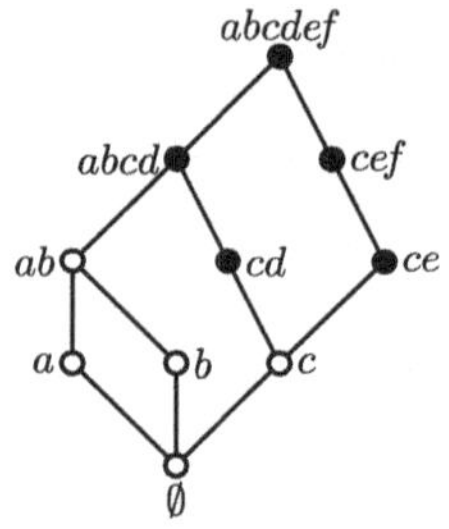

Fig. 4. The closure lattice of Example 4. Black dots represent essential sets.

Understanding which closure spaces have valid E-base is an intriguing problem, and constitutes the main motivation for our contribution. Before investigating this question, we give a characterization of E-generators in Lemma 1. It comes from the observation that if $A \in \text{gen}_E(x)$, any closed set $C \subset \phi(A)$ generating x can only contain singleton minimal generators of x. This makes x prime in the lattice $(\downarrow C, \subseteq)$.

Lemma 1. *Let (S, ϕ) be a closure space with lattice $(\mathcal{C}, \subseteq)$ and let $x \in S$. A subset A of S is a E-generator of x if and only if the following conditions hold:*

(1) A is a ϕ^b-minimal spanning set of $\phi(A)$
(2) A is a non-trivial ϕ^b-generator of x
(3) for every $C \in \mathcal{C}$ such that $C \subset \phi(A)$, $x \in C$ implies that x is prime in $(\downarrow C, \subseteq)$.

Remark 3. Recall from the preliminaries that conditions (1) and (2) in Lemma 3 are not equivalent to be a D-generator. While a D-generator A of x satisfies these conditions it also needs to be ϕ^b-minimal in the sense that no proper ϕ^b-refinement of A generates x too.

Condition (3) in the last lemma is equivalent to the condition (3') below:

(3') for every $C \in \mathcal{C}$ such that $C \prec \phi(A)$, $x \in C$ implies that x is prime in $(\downarrow C, \subseteq)$.

In words, Lemma 1 describes, by means of ϕ^b-minimal spanning sets, the inclusion-wise minimal closed sets above which x stops being prime, i.e. when it starts admitting non-singleton minimal generators. This is formally stated in the subsequent corollary.

Corollary 1. *Let (S, ϕ) be a closure space with lattice $(\mathcal{C}, \subseteq)$ and let $x \in S$. The family $\{C : C \in \mathcal{C}$ and x is not prime in $(\downarrow C, \subseteq)\}$ is a filter of $(\mathcal{C}, \subseteq)$ whose inclusion-minimal members are exactly the closed sets of the E-generators of x:*

$$\{\phi(A) : A \in \text{gen}_E(x)\} = \min_{\subseteq}\{C : C \in \mathcal{C} \text{ and } x \text{ is not prime in } (\downarrow C, \subseteq)\}.$$

□

Lemma 1 also stresses on the fact that any ϕ^b-minimal spanning set A of the closure of some E-generator of x is also a E-generator of x, as long as $x \notin \phi^b(A)$.

Corollary 2. *Let $(S, \mathcal{C})$ be a closure space and let $x \in S$. If $C \in \{\phi(B) : B \in \text{gen}_E(x)\}$, then any ϕ^b-minimal spanning set A of C satisfying $x \notin \phi^b(A)$ is a E-generator of x.*

The situation is pictured in Fig. 5. Following Lemma 1 and Corollary 1, for a closed set C and $x \in C$, we say that x is *almost prime* in $(\downarrow C, \subseteq)$ if x is not prime in $(\downarrow C, \subseteq)$ but prime in $(\downarrow C_*, \subseteq)$ for every $C_* \prec C$ such that $x \in C_*$. We thus obtain a new definition of the E-base of a closure space.

Definition 3 (E-base). *Let (S, ϕ) be a closure space with lattice $(\mathcal{C}, \subseteq)$. The E-base of (S, ϕ) is the IB (S, Σ_E) where*

$$\begin{aligned}\Sigma_E = &\Sigma^b \cup \{A \to x : x \in S, A \text{ is a } \phi^b - \text{minimal spanning set of } \phi(A)\\ &\text{s.t. } x \notin \phi^b(A) \text{ and } x \text{ is almost prime in } (\downarrow \phi(A), \subseteq)\}.\end{aligned}$$

To conclude the section, we show that E-generators and their closure relate to any IB representing the closure space. To do so, we highlight the relationships between E-generators and quasi-closed sets. The next lemma can be seen as the analogue for E-generators in any closure space of the Expansion 16 of Wild [31] dedicated to critical generators in convex geometries.

Lemma 2. *Let (S, ϕ) be a closure space with lattice $(\mathcal{C}, \subseteq)$. Let $C \in \mathcal{C}$, $x \in C$, and $Q = C \setminus \{y : x \in \phi^b(y)\}$. Then Q is a quasi-closed set spanning C if and only if $C = \phi(A)$ for some $A \in \text{gen}_E(x)$.*

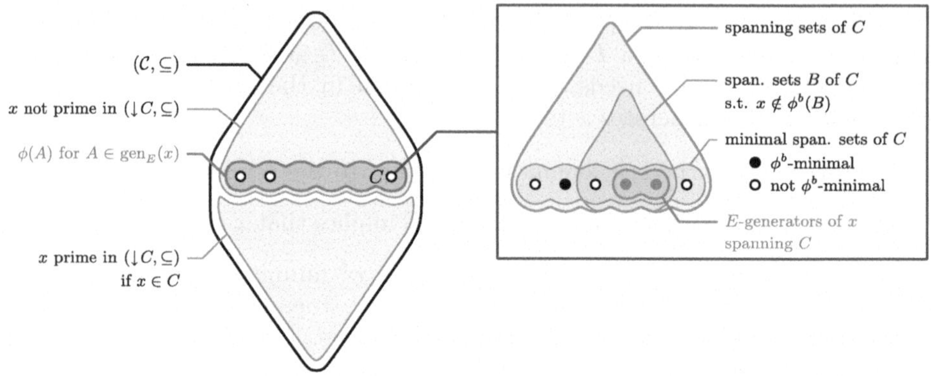

Fig. 5. The E-generators of x in a closure space (S, ϕ). On the left, the lattice $(\mathcal{C}, \subseteq)$ associated with (S, ϕ) is partitioned according to Corollary 1, i.e. according to the filter of closed sets above which x is not prime. The minimal members of this filter are the closure of the E-generators of x. The box on the right illustrates Corollary 2: within the spanning sets of $C = \phi(A)$ for some $A \in \text{gen}_E(x)$, the E-generators of x are the ϕ^b-minimal spanning sets B of C s.t. $x \notin \phi^b(B)$.

As a consequence, the closure of any E-generator must be essential. On the other hand, not all essential need be generated by some E-generator, as shown by Example 2. We can now give a theorem that relates E-generators, hence the E-base, to the canonical base.

Theorem 5. *Let (S, ϕ) be a closure space with canonical base (S, Σ_{DG}) and let $x \in S$. For all $C \in \{\phi(B) : B \in \text{gen}_E(x)\}$ there exists an implication $P \to C \setminus P$ in Σ_{DG} and a E-generator A of x such that $A \subseteq P$ and $\phi(A) = \phi(P) = C$.*

Using Theorem 4 and Theorem 5, we obtain the following straightforward corollary connecting the E-base with other IBs.

Corollary 3. *Let (S, ϕ) be a closure space and let (S, Σ) be an IB for (S, ϕ). For all $x \in S$ and all $C \in \{\phi(B) : B \in \text{gen}_E(x)\}$, there exists an implication $A \to Y$ in Σ such that $x \notin A$ and $\phi(A) = C$.* □

4 Closure Spaces with Semidistributive Lattices

In this section, we give a proof of Theorem 1, our main result. We first give a key lemma.

Lemma 3. *Let (S, ϕ) be a closure space with* SD *lattice $(\mathcal{C}, \subseteq)$. Let E be a non-ji essential set of (S, ϕ) with associated pseudo-closed set P and canonical spanning set A. For each $C \prec E$ in $(\mathcal{C}, \subseteq)$ and each x in the canonical spanning set of C, $x \notin P$ implies that $A \to x$ belongs to the E-base of (S, ϕ).*

We proceed to the proof of Theorem 1 that we first restate.

Theorem 1. *The (aggregated) E-base of a standard closure space with a semidistributive closure lattice is valid and minimum.*

Proof. Let $(S, \mathcal{C})$ be a standard closure space with SD lattice $(\mathcal{C}, \subseteq)$. Let (S, Σ_E) be its E-base. We need to show that for every $X \subseteq S$, $\phi(X) = \Sigma_E(X)$ where $\Sigma_E(\cdot)$ is the closure operator induced by (S, Σ_E). By definition of the E-base, $\Sigma_E(X) \subseteq \phi(X)$ for every $X \subseteq S$.

We prove the Theorem using induction on closed sets ordered by inclusion. As the space is standard, it readily holds for $\emptyset$ and all atoms of $(\mathcal{C}, \subseteq)$. Let $C \in \mathcal{C}$ and assume that for every $X \subseteq C$ such that $\phi(X) \subset C$, we have $\phi(X) = \Sigma_E(X)$. We argue that for every $Y \subseteq C$ such that $\phi(Y) = C$, we have $\Sigma_E(Y) = C$. If $Y = C$ then $\Sigma_E(Y) = C$ readily holds since $\Sigma_E(Y) \subseteq \phi(Y)$. Thus, we can assume that $Y \subset C$. We distinguish three cases:

(1) C is not essential (hence not join-irreducible). Since C is not essential, Y is not quasi-closed. Therefore, there exists $X \subseteq Y$ such that $\phi(X) \subset \phi(Y)$ and $\phi(X) \nsubseteq Y$. However, by inductive hypothesis, $\phi(X) = \Sigma_E(X)$ and hence $\Sigma_E(X) \nsubseteq Y$ so that $Y \subset \Sigma_E(Y)$. Since this holds for every proper subset Y of C spanning C and as $\Sigma_E(Y) \subseteq \phi(Y)$ for all such Y's, we deduce that $\Sigma_E(Y) = \phi(Y) = C$ as required.

(2) C is join-irreducible. Since the system is standard, we thus have that $C = \phi(x)$ for a unique $x \in S$. Moreover, Y contains x since $\{x\}$ is the unique minimal spanning set of C. By definition Σ_E contains an implication $x \to y$ for each y such that $y \in \phi(x)$. we deduce $\phi(Y) = \Sigma_E(Y) = C$.

(3) C is essential but not join-irreducible. As all non-trivial binary implications of (S, ϕ) belongs to Σ_E, we have that $\Sigma_E(Y)$ contains A, the canonical spanning set of C. To show that $\Sigma_E(Y) = C$, we prove that for each of the predecessors $C_i, \ldots, C_k$ of C, the canonical spanning set A_i of C_i is included in $\Sigma_E(Y)$. On this purpose, we first argue that $\Sigma_E(Y)$ is quasi-closed with respect to ϕ. Let $X \subseteq \Sigma_E(Y)$ such that $\phi(X) \subset \phi(\Sigma_E(Y)) = \phi(Y) = C$. By inductive hypothesis, $\Sigma_E(X) = \phi(X)$ so that $\phi(X) = \Sigma_E(X) \subseteq \Sigma_E(\Sigma_E(Y)) = \Sigma_E(Y)$. Therefore, $\Sigma_E(Y)$ is quasi-closed and in particular $P \subseteq \Sigma_E(Y)$ with P the unique pseudo-closed set spanning C obtained from Proposition 1. Now, let C_i be a predecessor of C and consider its canonical spanning set A_i. Let $x \in A_i$. If $x \in P$, then $x \in \Sigma_E(Y)$ by previous argument. If $x \notin P$, then by Lemma 3 we have $A \to x \in \Sigma_E$. Because $A \subseteq P \subseteq \Sigma_E(Y)$, we deduce that $x \in \Sigma_E(Y)$. Therefore $A_i \subseteq \Sigma_E(Y)$ for each $1 \leq i \leq k$.
Now, $\phi(A_i) = C_i \subset C$ for each $1 \leq i \leq k$. By inductive hypothesis, $\Sigma_E(X) = \phi(X)$ for each $X \subseteq C$ such that $\phi(X) \subset C$. Henceforth, $C_i = \Sigma_E(A_i) \subseteq \Sigma_E(Y)$. As C is not join-irreducible and (S, ϕ) is standard, we have $C = \bigcup_{i=1}^{k} C_i \subseteq \Sigma_E(Y) \subseteq \phi(Y) = C$. We deduce that $\Sigma_E(Y) = C$ for every subset Y of C such that $\phi(Y) = C$.

In all three cases, we have that $\Sigma_E(Y) = \phi(Y)$ for every $Y \subseteq C$ such that $\phi(Y) = C$. We deduce using induction that the E-base is valid.

It remains to show that in its aggregated form (S, Σ_E) is minimum. On this purpose, we identify a bijection between Σ_E and Σ_{DG}. Observe first that they have the same binary part by definition. Hence, we need only analyze their non-binary parts. By Lemma 2, the closure of a E-generator is essential. By Lemma 3, the canonical spanning set of each non-ji essential set is a E-generator. Since $(\mathcal{C}, \subseteq)$ is SD, we deduce by Theorem 1 that there is a bijection between E-generators and non-ji essential sets. Again by semidistributivity of $(\mathcal{C}, \subseteq)$, there is a bijection between essential sets and pseudo closed sets by virtue of Proposition 1. We get a bijection between E-generators and non-singleton pseudo-closed sets. Hence, once aggregated, (S, Σ_E) is minimum by Theorem 4. □

We remark that both SD_j and SD_m properties are important. Indeed, in general, neither SD_m lattices nor SD_j lattices have valid E-base. The lattice of Example 2 is SD_j but not SD_m and the E-base of the corresponding closure space is not valid. Below, we give an example of a closure space whose lattice is SD_m and its E-base not valid.

Example 5. Let (S, ϕ) be the closure space of the SD_m lattice of Fig. 6. We have:

- $\Sigma_{DG} = \{e \to ac, f \to ad, ab \to cdef, acde \to f, acdf \to e\}$
- $\Sigma_E = \{e \to ac, f \to ad, ab \to cd, de \to f, cf \to e\}$ (aggregated form).

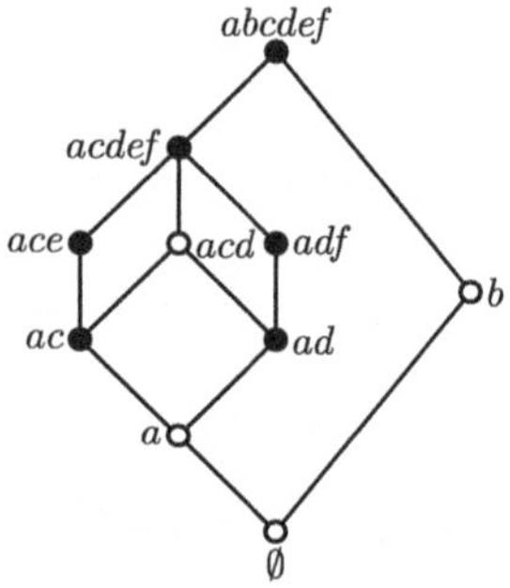

Fig. 6. The closure lattice of Example 5. Black dots are essential sets. The lattice is SD_m yet the E-base is not valid.

The E-base (S, Σ_E) is not valid since ab does not generate ef. This example illustrates the importance of SD_j in Lemma 3. Indeed, $acdef$ is a predecessor of the essential set $abcdef$ which has no canonical representation. Its minimal spanning sets are de, cf and ef but none of them comprises only prime elements of $(\downarrow acdef, \subseteq)$, which are a, c and d. Thus, the E-generator and pseudo-closed set ab does not reach any spanning set of $acdef$ in Σ_E.

5 Conclusion

In this paper, we proved that every closure space with SD lattice has a valid E-base. When such space does not have D-cycles the result was established in [5]. Therefore, the new cases for which E-base is valid are closure spaces that are SD and possess D-cycles.

To conclude, we formulate an open question related to the E-base of any closure space with SD lattice and D-cycles. A D-cycle in (S, ϕ) is a sequence $x_0, x_1, \ldots, x_n = x_0$ of elements from S such that, for each $1 \leq k \leq n$ there exists $A_k \in \text{gen}_D(x_k)$ with $x_{k-1} \in A_k$. In Example 1, we have D-cycle: $x_0 = c, x_1 = f, x_2 = g, x_3 = d, x_4 = x_0 = c$. The non-binary implications in the E-base have exactly these elements and their D-generators A_k. Other examples confirm this observation, which brings us to the following question.

Question 2. *Does the E-base of a closure space with* SD *lattice and D-cycles always include implications $A_k \to x_k$, where some $x_{k-1} \in A_k$ and x_{k-1}, x_k are consecutive members of some D-cycle?*

References

1. Adaricheva, K., Bernhardt, J., Liu, W., Schmidt, B.: Importance of overnight parameters to predict Sea Breeze on Long Island. arXiv preprint arXiv:2309.01803 (2023)
2. Adaricheva, K., Nation, J.B.: On implicational bases of closure systems with unique critical sets. Discret. Appl. Math. **162**, 51–69 (2014)
3. Adaricheva, K., Nation, J.B.: Discovery of the D-basis in binary tables based on hypergraph dualization. Theoret. Comput. Sci. **658**, 307–315 (2017)
4. Adaricheva, K., et al.: Measuring the implications of the D-basis in analysis of data in biomedical studies. In: Baixeries, J., Sacarea, C., Ojeda-Aciego, M. (eds.) ICFCA 2015. LNCS (LNAI), vol. 9113, pp. 39–57. Springer, Cham (2015). https://doi.org/10.1007/978-3-319-19545-2_3
5. Adaricheva, K., Nation, J.B., Rand, R.: Ordered direct implicational basis of a finite closure system. Discret. Appl. Math. **161**(6), 707–723 (2013)
6. Adaricheva, K., Nourine, L., Vilmin, S.: Computing the D-base and D-relation in finite closure systems. arXiv preprint arXiv:2404.07037 (2024). https://doi.org/10.1016/j.tcs.2025.115459
7. Bérczi, K., Boros, E., Makino, K.: Hypergraph Horn functions. SIAM J. Discret. Math. **38**(2), 1417–1437 (2024)
8. Bertet, K., Demko, C., Viaud, J.F., Guérin, C.: Lattices, closures systems and implication bases: a survey of structural aspects and algorithms. Theoret. Comput. Sci. **743**, 93–109 (2018)
9. Bertet, K., Monjardet, B.: The multiple facets of the canonical direct unit implicational basis. Theoret. Comput. Sci. **411**(22–24), 2155–2166 (2010)
10. Bichoupan, T.: Independence of essential sets in finite implication bases. arXiv preprint arXiv:2304.06837 (2023)
11. Birkhoff, G.: On the structure of abstract algebras. In: Mathematical Proceedings of the Cambridge Philosophical Society, pp. 433–454. Cambridge University Press (1935)

12. Crama, Y., Hammer, P.: Boolean Functions: Theory, Algorithms, and Applications. Cambridge University Press (2011)
13. Day, A.: Characterizations of finite lattices that are bounded-homomorphic images or sublattices of free lattices. Can. J. Math. **31**(1), 69–78 (1979)
14. Day, A.: The lattice theory of functional dependencies and normal decompositions. Internat. J. Algebra Comput. **2**(4), 409–432 (1992)
15. Freese, R., Ježek, J., Nation, J.B.: Free Lattices. Mathematical Surveys and Monographs Series, vol. 42. American Mathematical Society (1995)
16. Ganter, B., Wille, R.: Formal Concept Analysis: Mathematical Foundations. Springer, Heidelberg (2012)
17. Gorbunov, V.A.: Canonical decompositions in complete lattices. Algebra Log. **17**(5), 323–332 (1978)
18. Grätzer, G.: Lattice Theory: Foundation. Springer, Heidelberg (2011)
19. Guigues, J.L., Duquenne, V.: Familles minimales d'implications informatives résultant d'un tableau de données binaires. Math. Sci. Hum. **95**, 5–18 (1986)
20. Jónsson, B., Kiefer, J.E.: Finite sublattices of a free lattice. Can. J. Math. **14**, 487–497 (1962)
21. Korte, B., Lovász, L., Schrader, R.: Greedoids. Algorithms and Combinatorics Series, vol. 4. Springer, Heidelberg (2012)
22. Maier, D.: Minimum covers in relational database model. J. ACM **27**(4), 664–674 (1980)
23. Mannila, H., Räihä, K.J.: The Design of Relational Databases. Addison-Wesley (1992)
24. Markowsky, G.: Primes, irreducibles and extremal lattices. Order **9**(3), 265–290 (1992)
25. Nation, J.B.: Finite sublattices of a free lattice. Trans. Am. Math. Soc. 311–337 (1982)
26. Nation, J.B., Cabot-Miller, J., Segal, O., Lucito, R., Adaricheva, K.: Combining algorithms to find signatures that predict risk in early-stage stomach cancer. J. Comput. Biol. **28**(10), 985–1006 (2021)
27. Pudlák, P., Tůma, J.: Yeast graphs and fermentation of algebraic lattices. Colloq. Math. Soc. János Bolyai **14**, 301–341 (1974)
28. Pudlák, P., Tůma, J.: Every finite lattice can be embedded in a finite partition lattice. Algebra Univ. **10**, 74–95 (1980)
29. Whitman, P.: Lattices, equivalence relations, and subgroups. Bull. Am. Math. Soc. **52**, 507–522 (1946)
30. Wild, M.: A theory of finite closure spaces based on implications. Adv. Math. **108**(1), 118–139 (1994)
31. Wild, M.: The joy of implications, aka pure Horn formulas: mainly a survey. Theoret. Comput. Sci. **658**, 264–292 (2017)

A Data Model for Relational Concept Algebras

Jens Kötters(✉) and Stefan E. Schmidt

Technische Universität Dresden, Dresden, Germany

Abstract. A database-theoretic variant of Formal Concept Analysis (FCA) defines the concept lattice of a relational structure. The concept lattice naturally extends to a relational concept algebra; this further deepens the connection between FCA and database theory. It seems possible to axiomatically characterize concept lattices of relational structures using the additional concept operations; partial results have been presented in recent work. This requires to be precise about the underlying data model, as even small details can affect the axiomatization. In this article, we give an up-to-date presentation of our primary relational data model.

Keywords: Relational Concept Algebras · Relational Data Models · Database Theory · Algebraic Logic

1 Motivation

Informally, by a concept algebra, we mean a concept lattice equipped with additional algebraic operations. In Formal Concept Analysis (FCA), when referring to a concept algebra, one usually means the concept algebra of a formal context $\mathbb{K} = (G, M, I)$, as defined by Rudolf Wille [24] (see also [9, Sect. 8.3]). It is an example of such a concept algebra in the wider sense. The *concept algebra* of $\mathbb{K}$ is the algebra $\underline{\mathfrak{A}}(\mathbb{K}) := (\mathfrak{B}(\mathbb{K}), \wedge, \vee, ^{\triangle}, ^{\triangledown}, 0, 1)$, which extends the concept lattice by two unary operations, the *weak negation* $(A, B)^{\triangle} := ((G \setminus A)'', (G \setminus A)')$ and the *weak opposition* $(A, B)^{\triangledown} := ((M \setminus B)', (M \setminus B)'')$, and exposes the bottom concept 0 and the top concept 1. The operations of $\underline{\mathfrak{A}}(\mathbb{K})$ correspond to the operations of propositional logic, i.e. conjunction, disjunction, negation, false and true, except that there are two kinds of negation, as motivated by the definitions.

The Basic Theorem on Concept Lattices [9, Thm. 3] states that every concept lattice $\underline{\mathfrak{B}}(\mathbb{K})$ is a complete lattice, and conversely, every complete lattice is isomorphic to the concept lattice of some formal context $\mathbb{K}$. Likewise, we would expect a Basic Theorem on Concept Algebras to characterize the concept algebras $\underline{\mathfrak{A}}(\mathbb{K})$ up to isomorphism, but finding such a theorem is still an open problem (cf. [9, p. 324]). The conjecture that concept algebras are, up to isomorphism, the complete *weakly dicomplemented lattices* [19], has been refuted by Kwuida and Machida [20].

Over the years, different kinds of concept lattices have been introduced. An inspirational paper by Wille [23] marks the beginning of a new era in FCA, where

P. Cellier et al. (Eds.): CONCEPTS 2025, LNAI 15941, pp. 375–391, 2025.
https://doi.org/10.1007/978-3-032-03364-2_24

different approaches arise, that define concepts over relational data. Relational Concept Analysis [11,12] (RCA) and the combination of FCA with Description Logics [5,4] are two prominent examples of such approaches. A database-theoretic FCA variant by Kötters [16,13] allows to obtain the concept lattice $\underline{\mathfrak{B}}(\mathfrak{G})$ of a relational structure $\mathfrak{G}$. The connection between FCA and database theory is further deepened by the discovery, that $\underline{\mathfrak{B}}(\mathfrak{G})$ naturally admits an external operation, somewhat resembling scalar multiplication on vector spaces, which establishes a variant of SPJR algebra [1, Sect. 4.4], the conjunctive-query fragment of Codd's relational algebra, at the level of concepts. The availability of this additional operation, which we call *right multiplication*, made it seem possible to obtain a "Basic Theorem on Concept Lattices of Relational Structures", which is our main objective. The quotation marks indicate that the name would not be entirely correct, as additional operations are involved, but at this stage, we still want to be flexible about which operations are used.

Informally, by a *relational concept algebra*, we mean a concept lattice of a relational structure, equipped with additional algebraic operations. So far, we have defined two specific kinds of relational concept algebras. The *orbital concept lattice* of $\mathfrak{G}$ extends the concept lattice $\underline{\mathfrak{B}}(\mathfrak{G})$ by the abovementioned external operation, and makes available the bottom concept, top concept, equality concepts, and the domain function (roughly a kind of arity function for concepts), at the abstract level. With these operations, a partial axiomatization result can be stated in [21]. The *conjunctive concept algebra* $\underline{\mathfrak{C}}(\mathfrak{G})$, introduced in [18], replaces the powerful right multiplication with much simpler, elementary operations. This leads to simpler axioms, which compare surprisingly well to the cylindric algebra axioms, well-known in algebraic logic. We call the algebras that satisfy these axioms *projectional semilattices*, and conjecture in [18] that the algebras $\underline{\mathfrak{C}}(\mathfrak{G})$ are, up to isomorphism, the complete projectional semilattices. We would then have arrived at the desired Basic Theorem, but the conjecture is still open.

The purpose of this paper is to provide an improved and up-to-date presentation of the key results and insights obtained so far. A running example, taken from the first paper on concept lattices of relational structures [13], is used for illustrations. Section 2 presents three different relational data models, which have been considered in earlier papers [13,17,14], using distinct formalisms in [14], but all can be formalized as relational structures. There are different representations and variants of conjunctive queries, see [1]. Our formalizations of conjunctive queries in Sect. 3 (logical queries) and Sect. 5 (tableau queries) motivate the orders for the Galois connection, from which the concept lattice is obtained in Sect. 6. The relational concept algebras in Sect. 7 have been introduced in [21] and [18], respectively, and Sect. 8 revisits conceptual scaling, as considered in [15].

2 Relational Data

A *relational signature* is a set M of relation names, where each name $R \in M$ has an *arity* $|R| \in \mathbb{N}^*$. Throughout the paper, we use the relational signature $M_{\text{fam}} := \{\mathsf{male}/1, \mathsf{female}/1, \mathsf{mother}/2, \mathsf{father}/2, \mathsf{parent}/2\}$ in our examples. The notation is somewhat informal, but makes clear that male and female are unary relation names, whereas mother, father and parent are binary relation names.

An *M-structure* $\mathfrak{A}$ has a universe A (denoted by the corresponding Roman letter), and it associates to each n-ary name $R \in M$ an n-ary relation $R^{\mathfrak{A}} \subseteq A^n$. Throughout the paper, we use the M_{fam}-structure $\mathfrak{G}_{\text{fam}}$ for our examples; its universe $G_{\text{fam}} := \{\mathsf{Anne}, \mathsf{Bob}, \mathsf{Chris}, \mathsf{Dora}, \mathsf{Emily}\}$ consists of family members, and it provides the relations $\mathsf{male}^{\mathfrak{G}_{\text{fam}}} := \{\mathsf{Bob}, \mathsf{Chris}\}$, $\mathsf{female}^{\mathfrak{G}_{\text{fam}}} := \{\mathsf{Anne}, \mathsf{Dora}, \mathsf{Emily}\}$, $\mathsf{mother}^{\mathfrak{G}_{\text{fam}}} := \{(\mathsf{Anne}, \mathsf{Bob}), (\mathsf{Anne}, \mathsf{Chris})\}$, $\mathsf{father}^{\mathfrak{G}_{\text{fam}}} := \{(\mathsf{Bob}, \mathsf{Dora}), (\mathsf{Bob}, \mathsf{Emily})\}$ and $\mathsf{parent}^{\mathfrak{G}_{\text{fam}}} := \mathsf{mother}^{\mathfrak{G}_{\text{fam}}} \cup \mathsf{father}^{\mathfrak{G}_{\text{fam}}}$. The pair $(\mathsf{Anne}, \mathsf{Bob}) \in \mathsf{mother}^{\mathfrak{G}_{\text{fam}}}$ expresses that Anne is the mother of Bob, and likewise for the other pairs. A *relational structure* is an M-structure (for some M).

There are different ways to think about a relational structure $\mathfrak{A}$. A database-theorist might think of a relation $R^{\mathfrak{A}}$ as a table, and draw it that way. In this way, a relational structure formalizes a relational database, as essentially a collection of tables. Figure 1 illustrates $\mathfrak{G}_{\text{fam}}$ from this viewpoint. Note however, that the universe must be specified explicitly, if it contains elements not occurring in the tables, and is not given otherwise (as e.g. by a global domain **dom**, cf. [1, p.30]).

A graph-theorist might think of $\mathfrak{A}$ as a graph; the universe A consists of the nodes, and each n-ary relation $R^{\mathfrak{A}}$ is a collection of R-edges, each connecting n nodes (in an ordered way). This viewpoint is illustrated in Fig. 2. We use the obvious abbreviations A, ..., E for the family members, ♂ and ♀ for male and female, and m, f, p for the binary relation names. The five unary edges are simply drawn as node labels. Parallel edges, like the p-edge and the m-edge from A to B, are drawn as a single edge, with their edge labels combined. Further drawing conventions must be introduced to visualize higher-arity edges, but we shall keep it simple here. The tables view is relation-centric, whereas the graph view is object-centric, and may be closer to the human way of thinking.

Finally, a practitioner of FCA might think of $\mathfrak{A}$ as a power context family, i.e. a sequence $(\mathbb{K}_1, \mathbb{K}_2, \mathbb{K}_3, \dots)$ of formal concepts. Figure 3 visualizes $\mathfrak{G}_{\text{fam}}$ as a power context family. The attributes of $\mathbb{K}_n$ are the n-ary relation names of M_{fam}, and its objects are n-tuples from G^n_{fam}, with the obvious incidence relation. Note that the columns of $\mathbb{K}_1$ and $\mathbb{K}_2$ in Fig. 3 correspond to the tables in Fig. 1; whereas the rows of $\mathbb{K}_1$ and $\mathbb{K}_2$ correspond to the labeled nodes and labeled edges, respectively, of the graph in Fig. 2. So the power context family is like a hinge, which connects the other two viewpoints. Our theory supports all these views, but depending on the task, one viewpoint might be better than the other.

3 Logical Queries

A *primitive-positive formula* is a first-order formula which may contain conjunction ($\wedge$) and existential quantification ($\exists$), but no other connectives or quantifiers. We assume a countably infinite set **var** of variables. An *atomic formula* is a *relational atom* $R(x_1, \dots, x_n)$ or an *equality atom* $x{=}y$. The set of primitive-positive formulas over the relational signature M is denoted by $\mathrm{PP}(M)$. The free variables in a formula $\varphi \in \mathrm{PP}(M)$ are collected in the set $\mathrm{free}(\varphi)$.

male
Bob
Chris

female
Anne
Dora
Emily

mother	
Anne	Bob
Anne	Chris

father	
Bob	Dora
Bob	Emily

parent	
Anne	Bob
Anne	Chris
Bob	Dora
Bob	Emily

Fig. 1. Visualizing $\mathfrak{G}_{\text{fam}}$ as Tables

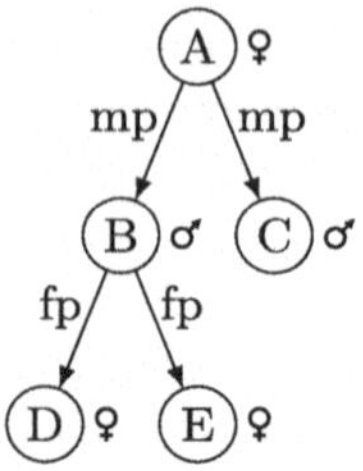

Fig. 2. Visualizing $\mathfrak{G}_{\text{fam}}$ as a Graph

$\mathbb{K}_1$	male	female
Anne		×
Bob	×	
Chris	×	
Dora		×
Emily		×

$\mathbb{K}_2$	parent	mother	father
(Anne,Bob)	×	×	
(Anne,Chris)	×	×	
(Bob,Dora)	×		×
(Bob,Emily)	×		×

Fig. 3. Visualizing $\mathfrak{G}_{\text{fam}}$ as a Power Context Family

Under the standard logical semantics, as described by Ebbinghaus et al. [8], an *M-interpretation* is a pair $(\mathfrak{G}, \alpha)$, consisting of a non-empty M-structure $\mathfrak{G}$ (i.e. the universe G is non-empty), and a *variable assignment* $\alpha : \mathbf{var} \to G$. We assume it is known what it means for φ to *hold* in $\mathfrak{G}$ under α, written $(\mathfrak{G}, \alpha) \models \varphi$. Likewise, we write $\varphi \models \psi$ if φ *implies* ψ, and $\varphi \dashv\models \psi$ if φ and ψ are *equivalent.*

We call $\varphi \in \mathrm{PP}(M)$ a *conjunctive query*, if we intend to interpret it under a different semantics, which we call *tuple semantics.* The difference is that under tuple semantics, the variable assignments are tuples, i.e. they are finite. More specifically, a *named tuple* over a set U is a function $t : X \to U$ defined on a finite set $X \subseteq \mathbf{var}$ of variables. We define $\mathrm{def}(t) := X$, and say that $x \in \mathbf{var}$ is *undefined* under t if $x \notin \mathrm{def}(t)$. The set of named tuples over U is denoted by $\mathrm{NTup}(U)$. An *M-interpretation* under tuple semantics is a pair $(\mathfrak{G}, t)$ consisting of a non-empty M-structure $\mathfrak{G}$ and a *variable assignment* $t \in \mathrm{NTup}(G)$. We now define what it means for φ to *hold* in $\mathfrak{G}$ under t, written $(\mathfrak{G}, t) \models_{\text{tup}} \varphi$. If $\mathrm{free}(\varphi) \subseteq \mathrm{def}(t)$, it is defined in the obvious way, cf. [1, p. 24]. And if $\mathrm{free}(\varphi) \not\subseteq \mathrm{def}(t)$, i.e. some free variable in φ is undefined under t, we stipulate $(\mathfrak{G}, t) \not\models_{\text{tup}} \varphi$. So even $x{=}x$ does not hold, if x is undefined under t. We also want to allow two *special conjunctive queries*, the *tautology* true and the *contradiction* false, with the obvious meaning. We set $\mathrm{CQ}(M) := \mathrm{PP}(M) \cup \{\mathsf{true}, \mathsf{false}\}$ and, for technical reasons, $\mathrm{free}(\mathsf{true}) := \emptyset$ and $\mathrm{free}(\mathsf{false}) := \mathbf{var}$.

For a query $\varphi \in \mathrm{CQ}(M)$ and an M-structure $\mathfrak{G}$, we call

$$\mathrm{res}_{\mathfrak{G}}(\varphi) := \{t \in \mathrm{NTup}(G) \mid (\mathfrak{G}, t) \models_{\text{tup}} \varphi \text{ and } \mathrm{def}(t) = \mathrm{free}(\varphi)\}, \quad (1)$$

$$\mathrm{res}^*_{\mathfrak{G}}(\varphi) := \{t \in \mathrm{NTup}(G) \mid (\mathfrak{G}, t) \models_{\text{tup}} \varphi\}, \quad (2)$$

the *result table* and the *result set*, respectively, of φ in $\mathfrak{G}$. Note that $\mathrm{res}_{\mathfrak{G}}(\mathsf{true}) = \{\langle\rangle\}$, where $\langle\rangle : \emptyset \to G$ denotes the *empty tuple*. On the other hand, $\mathrm{res}^*_{\mathfrak{G}}(\mathsf{true}) = \mathrm{NTup}(G)$, and $\mathrm{res}_{\mathfrak{G}}(\mathsf{false}) = \mathrm{res}^*_{\mathfrak{G}}(\mathsf{false}) = \emptyset$. While $\mathrm{res}_{\mathfrak{G}}(\varphi)$ is our primary notion, $\mathrm{res}^*_{\mathfrak{G}}(\varphi)$ will be of theoretical value. We define *implication* and *equivalence*, respectively, of conjunctive queries by

$$\varphi \models_{\mathrm{tup}} \psi \;:\Leftrightarrow\; \mathrm{res}^*_{\mathfrak{G}}(\varphi) \subseteq \mathrm{res}^*_{\mathfrak{G}}(\psi) \text{ f.a. } M\text{-structures } \mathfrak{G}, \tag{3}$$

$$\varphi \mathrel{=\!\!|\!\models}_{\mathrm{tup}} \psi \;:\Leftrightarrow\; \mathrm{res}^*_{\mathfrak{G}}(\varphi) = \mathrm{res}^*_{\mathfrak{G}}(\psi) \text{ f.a. } M\text{-structures } \mathfrak{G}. \tag{4}$$

The following proposition relates implication and equivalence in the tuple semantics to their counterparts in standard logic (as mentioned above).

Proposition 1 ([16, **Prop. 3**]). *Let* $\varphi, \psi \in \mathrm{PP}(M)$. *Then*

$$\varphi \models_{\mathrm{tup}} \psi \;\Leftrightarrow\; \varphi \models \psi \textit{ and } \mathrm{free}(\varphi) \supseteq \mathrm{free}(\psi), \tag{5}$$

$$\varphi \mathrel{=\!\!|\!\models}_{\mathrm{tup}} \psi \;\Leftrightarrow\; \varphi \mathrel{=\!\!|\!\models} \psi \textit{ and } \mathrm{free}(\varphi) = \mathrm{free}(\psi). \tag{6}$$

In the next section, we have a closer look at tables.

4 Tables

A *table* over a set $G \neq \emptyset$ is a tuple set $T \subseteq \mathrm{NTup}(G)$, such that $\mathrm{def}(s) = \mathrm{def}(t)$ for all $s, t \in T$. This is in accordance with the definition of result tables in (1). The table's *rows* are the elements $t \in T$, and the table's *schema*, defined by

$$\mathrm{schema}(T) := \begin{cases} \mathrm{def}(t) & \text{if } t \in T \\ \mathbf{var} & \text{if } T = \emptyset \end{cases}, \tag{7}$$

is the set of its *column names*. Accordingly, $t(x) \in G$ is the *entry* in row t and column x. The tables over G are collected in the set $\mathrm{Tab}(G)$. For each finite $X \subseteq \mathbf{var}$, the set $\mathrm{Tab}(G)[X] := \mathfrak{P}(G^X)$ is called the X*-slice* of $\mathrm{Tab}(G)$. The X-slice contains all tables with schema X, plus the empty table. For $x, y \in \mathbf{var}$, the *equality table* $E_{xy} \in \mathrm{Tab}(G)[\{x, y\}]$ is the table

$$E_{xy} := \{t \in G^{\{x,y\}} \mid t(x) = t(y)\}. \tag{8}$$

In particular, E_{xx} has a single column x, which contains all objects of G.

A well-known operation on tables is the natural join, cf. [1, p. 58]. The *natural join* of $T_1 \in \mathrm{Tab}(G)[X_1]$ and $T_2 \in \mathrm{Tab}(G)[X_2]$ is the table

$$T_1 \bowtie T_2 := \{t \in G^{X_1 \cup X_2} \mid t|_{X_1} \in T_1 \text{ and } t|_{X_2} \in T_2\}. \tag{9}$$

The natural join is associative and commutative (cf. [1, p. 58]), and trivially idempotent, so by definition $(\mathrm{Tab}(G), \bowtie)$ is a meet-semilattice. As usual, the definition $T_1 \leq T_2 :\Leftrightarrow T_1 = T_1 \bowtie T_2$ retrieves the implicit table order. From the definition of the natural join in (9), we obtain the characterization

$$T_1 \leq T_2 \Leftrightarrow \left\{ \begin{array}{c} \text{schema}(T_1) \supseteq \text{schema}(T_2) \\ \text{and } \{t|_{\text{schema}(T_2)} \mid t \in T_1\} \subseteq T_2 \end{array} \right. . \tag{10}$$

From (10), in turn, we obtain that any family $(T_i)_{i\in I}$ of tables has a supremum

$$\bigotimes_{i\in I} T_i := \bigcup_{i\in I} \{t|_{\bigcap_{i\in I} \text{schema}(T_i)} \mid t \in T_i\}. \tag{11}$$

This shows that $(\text{Tab}(G), \leq)$ is a complete lattice. Now we shall make sense of the table order. The *regular closure* of a table $T \in \text{Tab}(G)$ is the set

$$\text{rc}(T) := \{t \in \text{NTup}(G) \mid s \subseteq t \text{ for some} s \in T\} \tag{12}$$

of all named tuples that extend one of the table rows. On the basis of the following results, a table can be identified with its regular closure $\text{rc}(T)$.

Proposition 2 ([16, Prop. 4]). *The function* $\text{rc} : \text{Tab}(G) \to \text{NTup}(G)$ *is an order embedding, i.e.* $T_1 \leq T_2 \Leftrightarrow \text{rc}(T_1) \subseteq \text{rc}(T_2)$ *for all* $T_1, T_2 \in \text{Tab}(G)$.

As Proposition 2 shows, the table order can be identified with set inclusion. Moreover,

$$\text{rc}(\text{res}_{\mathfrak{G}}(\varphi)) = \text{res}^*_{\mathfrak{G}}(\varphi) , \tag{13}$$

i.e. the result table can be identified with the result set. Finally, the regular closure preserves arbitrary infima, i.e. $\text{rc}(\bowtie_{i\in I} T_i) = \bigcap_{i\in I} \text{rc}(T_i)$, so the natural join can be identified with set intersection, cf. [16, Sect. 3.5]. Using the above results, we can now restate (3) and (4) in terms of the table order:

$$\varphi \models_{\text{tup}} \psi :\Leftrightarrow \text{res}_{\mathfrak{G}}(\varphi) \leq \text{res}_{\mathfrak{G}}(\psi) \text{ f.a. } M\text{-structures } \mathfrak{G}, \tag{14}$$

$$\varphi \mathrel{=\!\!|\!\models}_{\text{tup}} \psi :\Leftrightarrow \text{res}_{\mathfrak{G}}(\varphi) = \text{res}_{\mathfrak{G}}(\psi) \text{ f.a. } M\text{-structures } \mathfrak{G}. \tag{15}$$

Equation (15) states that, as would be expected, conjunctive queries are equivalent if they produce the same result table in all M-structures $\mathfrak{G}$. The corresponding statement for standard semantics does not hold, since $x{=}x$ and $y{=}y$ are then tautologies, and thus equivalent, i.e. $x{=}x \mathrel{=\!\!|\!\models} y{=}y$, but we have $\text{res}_{\mathfrak{G}}(x{=}x) = E_{xx} \neq E_{yy} = \text{res}_{\mathfrak{G}}(y{=}y)$. Insofar, tuple semantics provides a logical underpinning for the natural notion of query equivalence (cf. [1, p. 37]).

5 Graph Queries/Tableau Queries

As illustrated in Sect. 2, a relational structure (e.g. a relational database) can be seen as a graph. It is then natural to also formalize a query as a (usually much smaller) graph, describing a pattern to be matched in the data. Indeed, the logical queries from Sect. 3 can be represented as graphs, and the modeling relation $\models_{\text{tup}}$ corresponds to graph homomorphism. The observation that primitive-positive formulas and implication can be represented by graphs and their homomorphisms, respectively, is widely attributed to Chandra and Merlin [6]. In this section, we reproduce these results in our formalism.

It is well-known [8, Ch. VIII, Thm. 4.4] that every first-order formula φ is equivalent to a formula ψ in *prenex normal form* (i.e. with all quantifiers at the front) where $\text{free}(\varphi) = \text{free}(\psi)$. In particular, every primitive-positive formula $\varphi \in \text{PP}(M)$ can be transformed into an equivalent formula

$$\exists z_1 \ldots \exists z_n (A_1 \wedge \cdots \wedge A_m) , \tag{16}$$

where $A_1, \ldots, A_n$ are atoms. In fact, many authors explicitly require the prenex normal form in their definitions of conjunctive queries.

A *windowed M-structure* is a pair $(\mathfrak{A}, \lambda)$ that consists of an M-structure $\mathfrak{A}$ and a *window* $\lambda \in \text{NTup}(A)$. Every formula $\varphi \in \text{PP}(M)$ can be represented by a finite windowed M-structure $\Gamma(\varphi) = (\mathfrak{A}_\varphi, \lambda_\varphi)$, which conveys its meaning. We present examples in Fig. 4, and refer to [16, Sect. 3.1] for a general procedure.

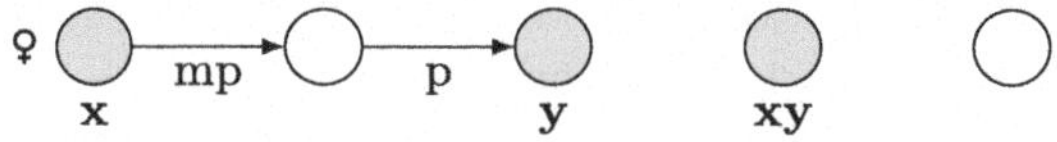

Fig. 4. Graph representations of primitive-positive formulas. Left: $\exists z(\mathsf{female}(x) \wedge \mathsf{parent}(x, z) \wedge \mathsf{mother}(x, z) \wedge \mathsf{parent}(z, y))$, Middle: $x{=}y$, Right: $\exists x\ x{=}x$.

A *homomorphism* $f : (\mathfrak{A}, \lambda) \to (\mathfrak{B}, \mu)$ of windowed M-structures is a homomorphism $f : \mathfrak{A} \to \mathfrak{B}$ which additionally satisfies $f \circ \lambda \subseteq \mu$ (i.e. $\text{def}(\lambda) \subseteq \text{def}(\mu)$ and $f(\lambda(x)) = \mu(x)$ for all $x \in \text{def}(\lambda)$). So f preserves all edges and all distinguished elements. We write $(\mathfrak{A}, \lambda) \lesssim (\mathfrak{B}, \mu)$ if such a homomorphism f exists. This defines a preorder, called the *homomorphism preorder*, and $(\mathfrak{A}, \lambda)$ and $(\mathfrak{B}, \mu)$ are *hom-equivalent*, written $(\mathfrak{A}, \lambda) \simeq (\mathfrak{B}, \mu)$, if $(\mathfrak{A}, \lambda) \lesssim (\mathfrak{B}, \mu)$ and $(\mathfrak{B}, \mu) \lesssim (\mathfrak{A}, \lambda)$. We shall also define $\Gamma(\mathsf{true})$ and $\Gamma(\mathsf{false})$, in such a way that $\Gamma(\mathsf{true})$ is the least, and $\Gamma(\mathsf{false})$ is the greatest element in the homomorphism preorder. More specifically, $\Gamma(\mathsf{true}) = (\mathfrak{A}_{\mathsf{true}}, \langle\rangle)$ is the empty M-structure, i.e. $A_{\mathsf{true}} = \emptyset$, equipped with an empty window. Whereas $\Gamma(\mathsf{false}) = (\mathfrak{A}_{\mathsf{false}}, \lambda_{\mathsf{false}})$ is given by $A_{\mathsf{false}} = \{e\}$, e arbitrary, $R^{\mathfrak{A}_{\mathsf{false}}} = \{(e, \ldots, e)\}$ for all $R \in M$, and $\text{def}(\lambda) = \mathbf{var}$. The windowed M-structure $\Gamma(\mathsf{false})$ is special, in that we allow it to have an infinite window. The following proposition states the equivalence between a logical query φ and its graph representation $\Gamma(\varphi)$. Note here that not only graph queries, but also M-interpretations, are windowed M-structures.

Proposition 3 ([16, Prop. 2]). *Let $\varphi \in \text{CQ}(M)$ and $(\Gamma(\varphi), t)$ be an M-interpretation. Then $(\mathfrak{G}, t) \models_{\text{tup}} \varphi$ if and only if $\Gamma(\varphi) \lesssim (\mathfrak{G}, t)$.*

Note that $\Gamma(\varphi) = (\mathfrak{A}_\varphi, \lambda_\varphi)$ also formalizes a *tableau query*, cf. [1, p. 43f.]. As the name indicates, $\mathfrak{A}_\varphi$ is then usually visualized as in Fig. 1, and λ_φ referred to as the *summary* [1]. The tables in a tableau query usually contain both constants and variables, but in our approach, they contain only variables. This may seem like a severe limitation, but constants can be modeled by unary relations, and can be systematically introduced via conceptual scaling, cf. Sect. 8. The following theorem is the *homomorphism theorem* [1, p. 115] of database theory, translated to our formalism. It states that the (dualized) homomorphism preorder represents implication under tuple semantics.

Theorem 1 ([16, Thm. 2]). *Let $\varphi, \psi \in \mathrm{CQ}(M)$. Then $\varphi \models_{\mathrm{tup}} \psi$ if and only if $\Gamma(\psi) \lesssim \Gamma(\varphi)$.*

As Theorem 1 shows, windowed M-structures naturally generalize the logic of primitive-positive formulas (under tuple semantics) to an infinitary logic. In particular, we may understand an arbitrary windowed M-structure as a graph query or tableau query, and use all three notions interchangeably.

With Proposition 3, the result operations on logical queries, cf. (1) and (2), translate to equivalent operations on tableau queries,

$$\mathrm{res}_{\mathfrak{G}}(\mathfrak{A}, \lambda) := \{t \in \mathrm{NTup}(G) \mid (\mathfrak{A}, \lambda) \lesssim (\mathfrak{G}, t) \text{ and } \mathrm{def}(t) = \mathrm{def}(\lambda)\}\,, \tag{17}$$

$$\mathrm{res}_{\mathfrak{G}}(\mathfrak{A}, \lambda) := \{t \in \mathrm{NTup}(G) \mid (\mathfrak{A}, \lambda) \lesssim (\mathfrak{G}, t)\}\,. \tag{18}$$

The *product* $\prod_{i\in I}(\mathfrak{A}_i, \lambda_i)$ and the *sum* $\sum_{i\in I}(\mathfrak{A}_i, \lambda_i)$ of a family $((\mathfrak{A}_i, \lambda_i))_{i\in I}$ of windowed M-structures, defined and illustrated in [16, Sect. 4], realize an infimum and a supremum, respectively, in the homomorphism preorder (being unique up to hom-equivalence). The binary product is defined as $(\mathfrak{A}, \lambda) \times (\mathfrak{B}, \mu) := (\mathfrak{A} \times \mathfrak{B}, \lambda \times \mu)$, where $\mathfrak{A} \times \mathfrak{B}$ is the direct product of M-structures, see e.g. [8, p. 30], and $(\lambda \times \mu)(x) := (\lambda(x), \mu(x))$ for all $x \in \mathrm{def}(\lambda \times \mu) = \mathrm{def}(\lambda) \cap \mathrm{def}(\mu)$. Figure 5 illustrates a product of two windowed M_{fam}-structures.

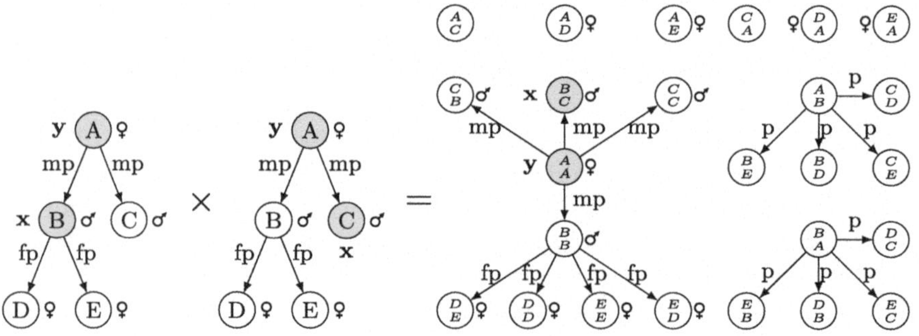

Fig. 5. Example: Product of windowed M_{fam}-structures (adapted from [13])

The binary sum $(\mathfrak{A}, \lambda) + (\mathfrak{B}, \mu)$ corresponds to the conjunction of formulas. It can be visualized by drawing $(\mathfrak{A}, \lambda)$ and $(\mathfrak{B}, \mu)$ side-by-side (disjoint union), and then merging the nodes $\lambda(x)$ and $\mu(x)$, for all $x \in \mathrm{def}(\lambda) \cap \mathrm{def}(\mu)$. Note however, that the window of the sum is defined on $\mathrm{def}(\lambda) \cup \mathrm{def}(\mu)$. The product $\prod_{i\in I}(\mathfrak{A}_i, \lambda_i)$ and sum $\sum_{i\in I}(\mathfrak{A}_i, \lambda_i)$ are defined analogously, cf. [16, Sect. 4].

Let $\mathrm{TQ}(M)$ denote the class of all tableau queries. As shown in [16, Prop. 7], there exists a class function $\mathrm{rep} : \mathrm{TQ}(M) \to \mathrm{TQ}(M)$, such that the proper class $\overline{\mathrm{TQ}}(M) := \{\mathrm{rep}(Q) \mid Q \in \mathrm{TQ}(M)\}$ is a system of representatives w.r.t. hom-equivalence, and the ordered class $(\overline{\mathrm{TQ}}(M), \leq)$ is a complete lattice. We write $[(\mathfrak{A}, \lambda)] := \mathrm{rep}(\mathfrak{A}, \lambda)$ and pretend it is an equivalence class. If $[(\mathfrak{A}, \lambda)] = [(\mathfrak{B}, \mu)]$, then $\mathrm{def}(\lambda) = \mathrm{def}(\mu)$, so $\mathrm{free}([(\mathfrak{A}, \lambda)]) := \mathrm{def}(\lambda)$ is well-defined. For each finite $X \subseteq \mathbf{var}$, the *X-slice* $\overline{\mathrm{TQ}}(M)[X] := \{Q \in \overline{\mathrm{TQ}}(M) \mid \mathrm{free}(Q) = X\} \cup \{\Gamma(\mathsf{false})\}$ contains all queries with the set X of free variables, plus the contradiction.

6 Concept Lattices of Relational Structures

We have defined tables and queries, and their respective orders. These orders might seem rather arbitrary, at first, but their meaning has been revealed in Proposition 2 and Theorem 1, respectively. The result operation $\mathrm{res}_{\mathfrak{G}}$ of (17) naturally extends to query classes, and it has a dual adjoint $\mathrm{info}_{\mathfrak{G}}$, so the pair

$$\mathrm{res}_{\mathfrak{G}}(\mathfrak{A}, \lambda) := \{t \in \mathrm{NTup}(G) \mid [(\mathfrak{A}, \lambda)] \leq [(\mathfrak{G}, t)] \text{ and } \mathrm{def}(t) = \mathrm{def}(\lambda)\} ,$$
$$\mathrm{info}_{\mathfrak{G}}(T) := [\prod_{t\in T}(\mathfrak{G}, t)] ,$$

forms a Galois connection $(\mathrm{info}_{\mathfrak{G}}, \mathrm{res}_{\mathfrak{G}})$ between the given orders, and we obtain a concept lattice in the usual way. For convenience, we denote both operations by $(\cdot)^{\diamond}$. We denote the concept lattice by $\underline{\mathfrak{B}}(\mathfrak{G}) = (\mathfrak{B}(\mathfrak{G}), \leq)$. The *domain* of a concept $(T, Q) \in \mathfrak{B}(\mathfrak{G})$ is the variable set $\mathrm{dom}(T, Q) := \mathrm{schema}(T) = \mathrm{free}(Q)$. The bottom concept is $\bot := (\emptyset, [\Gamma(\mathsf{false})])$, and the top concept is $\top := (\{\langle\rangle\}, [\Gamma(\mathsf{true})]^{\diamond\diamond})$. For each finite $X \subseteq \mathbf{var}$, we define the *X-slice* $\underline{\mathfrak{B}}(\mathfrak{G})[X] := \{C \in \mathfrak{B}(\mathfrak{G}) \mid \mathrm{dom}(C) = X\} \cup \{\bot\}$. Figure 6 shows the whole slice $\underline{\mathfrak{B}}(\mathfrak{G}_{\mathrm{fam}})[\{x\}]$ and three concepts from $\underline{\mathfrak{B}}(\mathfrak{G}_{\mathrm{fam}})[\{x, y\}]$. The intents use a simplified representation, showing only the *support* [16, Sect. 5.6] of each query (i.e. the relevant connected component(s)), and using query minimization [1, p. 118ff.]. The infima and suprema of concepts in $\underline{\mathfrak{B}}(\mathfrak{G})$ are characterized as follows (cf. [16, 13]):

$$\bigwedge_{i\in I}(T_i, Q_i) = (\bowtie_{i\in I} T_i, [\sum_{i\in I} Q_i]^{\diamond\diamond}) , \tag{19}$$

$$\bigvee_{i\in I}(T_i, Q_i) = ((\Join_{i\in I} T_i)^{\diamond\diamond}, [\prod_{i\in I} Q_i]) . \tag{20}$$

Equation (19) for the concept infimum is illustrated in Fig. 7.

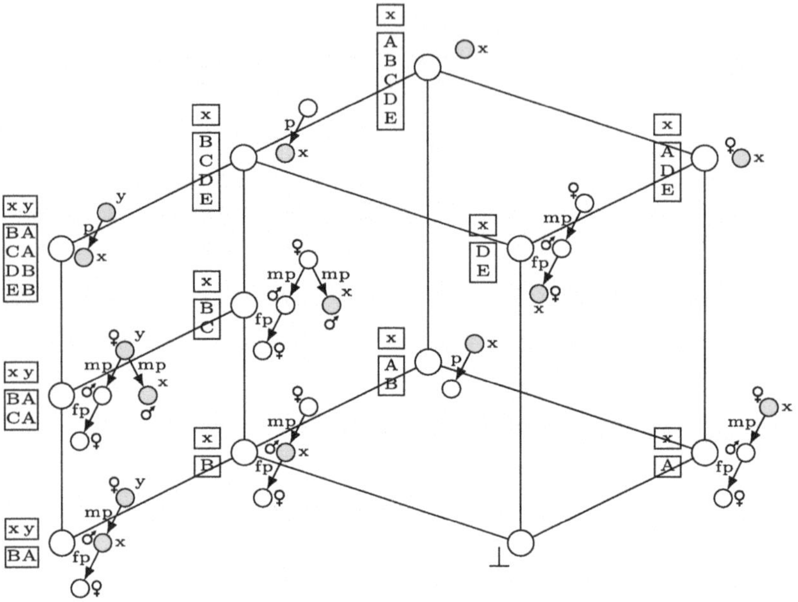

Fig. 6. The slice $\underline{\mathfrak{B}}(\mathfrak{G}_{\mathrm{fam}})[\{x\}]$, and three concepts from the slice $\underline{\mathfrak{B}}(\mathfrak{G}_{\mathrm{fam}})[\{x, y\}]$ (illustration taken from [13])

7 Relational Concept Algebras

7.1 Orbital Concept Lattices

The fragment of Codd's relational algebra that corresponds to conjunctive queries is the SPJR algebra [1]. The name refers to the table operations it provides: (S)election, (P)rojection, Natural (J)oin, and (R)enaming. Actually, it comprises two different kinds of selection, which we denote by $\sigma_{x=y}$ and $\sigma_{x=c}$. The operation $\sigma_{x=y}$ retains only those rows of a table, which have the same value in the columns x and y. It is a partial operation, defined by $\sigma_{x=y}(T) := \{t \in T \mid t(x) = t(y)\}$ on all tables having columns x and y. The operation $\sigma_{x=c}$, for a given constant c, retains only those rows which have the value c in column x. However, from a generic logical viewpoint, which does not adopt the database-theoretic specializations [1, p. 25ff.], we have no constants at our avail, because M is a purely relational signature. So effectively, we are limited to selections $\sigma_{x=y}$. We refer to this weaker variant of SPJR algebra as the *constant-free SPJR algebra.*

In the constant-free SPJR algebra, we can obtain *column duplication* δ_{xy} as a derived operation. It is a partial operation, given by $\delta_{xy}(T) = \{t \cup \{(y, t(x))\} \mid \mathrm{t} \in T\}$ for all tables T which have a column x, but not a column y. The variant of SPJR algebra, which replaces selection with column duplication, shall be called the *DPJR algebra.* But as it turns out, in the DPJR algebra, we can obtain selection $\sigma_{x=y}$ as a derived operation; so the DPJR algebra is equivalent to the constant-free SPJR algebra.

A remarkable aspect of the DPJR algebra is that it naturally arises in a different way. We define the *right multiplication* $T \cdot \lambda := \{t \circ \lambda \mid t \in T\}$, where $X, Y \subseteq \mathbf{var}$ are finite, $T \in \mathrm{Tab}(G)[Y]$ and $\lambda : X \to Y$. Then by definition $T \cdot \lambda \in \mathrm{Tab}(G)[X]$. Projection, renaming and duplication are realized by special cases of $\lambda : X \to Y$. Examples are shown in Fig. 7. We call $\pi : X \to Y$ an *inclusion* if $X \subseteq Y$ and $\pi(x) = x$ for all $x \in X$. If $T \in \mathrm{Tab}(G)[Y]$ and $\pi : X \to Y$ is an inclusion, then $T \cdot \pi \in \mathrm{Tab}(G)[X]$ is the *projection* of T to X. Moreover, if $T \in \mathrm{Tab}(G)[Y]$ and $\xi : X \to Y$ is a *bijection*, then $T \cdot \xi \in \mathrm{Tab}(G)[X]$ has the $\xi(x)$-column of T renamed to x, for all $x \in X$. So the bijections realize *renaming* operations. Finally, we call $\delta : X \to Y$ a *folding* if $X \supseteq Y$ and $\pi(y) = y$ for all $y \in Y$. If $T \in \mathrm{Tab}(G)[Y]$ and $\delta : X \to Y$ is a folding, then $T \cdot \delta \in \mathrm{Tab}(G)[X]$ extends T with a new column x, which duplicates column $\delta(x)$, for each $x \in X \setminus Y$. So the foldings realize *column duplications*. Now let us multiply $T \in \mathrm{Tab}(G)[Y]$ with an arbitrary $\lambda : X \to Y$. By Lemma 1 below, λ can be decomposed into a projection π, a renaming ξ and a column duplication δ, i.e. $\lambda = \pi \circ \xi \circ \delta$. Moreover, we have $T \cdot (\pi \circ \xi \circ \delta) = ((T \cdot \pi) \cdot \xi) \cdot \delta$. So right multiplication exactly formalizes the operations of projection, renaming and column duplication. It remains to state the lemma:

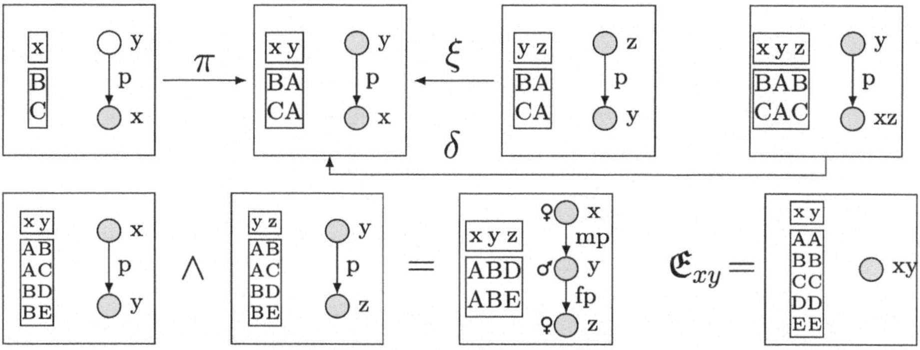

Fig. 7. DPJR Concept Operations with Equality. Projection: $\pi(x) = x$, Renaming: $\xi(y) = x, \xi(z) = y$, Duplication: $\delta(x) = x, \delta(y) = y, \delta(z) = x$

Lemma 1 (Decomposition Lemma [21]**).** *For every $\lambda : X \to Y$, there exists a folding $\delta : X \to Z_1$, a bijection $\xi : Z_1 \to Z_2$ and an inclusion $\pi : Z_2 \to Y$ such that $\lambda = \pi \circ \xi \circ \delta$.*

A matching right multiplication can be defined on the tableau queries. Let $[(\mathfrak{A}, \nu)] \in \overline{\mathrm{TQ}}(M)[Y]$ and $\lambda : X \to Y$. If $[(\mathfrak{A}, \nu)] = [(\mathfrak{B}, \mu)]$, then $[(\mathfrak{A}, \nu \circ \lambda)] = [(\mathfrak{B}, \mu \circ \lambda)]$, so $[(\mathfrak{A}, \nu)] \cdot \lambda := [(\mathfrak{A}, \nu \circ \lambda)]$ is well-defined. The operations π, ξ and δ can be understood if we liken the tableau query $[(\mathfrak{A}, \lambda)]$ to a formula; then π is existential quantification, ξ is one-to-one substitution of free variables, and δ

injects an equality atom $x{=}\delta(x)$ for every $x \in \mathrm{def}(\delta)$, cf. [21]. As for tables, we obtain $[(\mathfrak{A},\nu)]\cdot\lambda = [(\mathfrak{A},\nu)]\cdot(\pi\circ\xi\circ\delta) = ((([(\mathfrak{A},\nu)]\cdot\pi)\cdot\xi)\cdot\delta)$ for an arbitrary $\lambda : X \to Y$, which reduces right multiplication to the three kinds of operations. The right multiplications satisfy

$$\mathrm{res}_{\mathfrak{G}}(Q\cdot\mu) = \mathrm{res}_{\mathfrak{G}}(Q)\cdot\mu\,, \tag{21}$$

$$\mathrm{info}_{\mathfrak{G}}(T\cdot\mu) = \mathrm{info}_{\mathfrak{G}}(T)\cdot\mu\,. \tag{22}$$

As a consequence, if $(T,Q) \in \mathfrak{B}(\mathfrak{G})[Y]$ and $\lambda : X \to Y$, then $(T,Q)\cdot\mu := (T\cdot\mu, Q\cdot\mu) \in \mathfrak{B}(\mathfrak{G})[X]$. Since the natural join represents the concept infimum (cf. (19)), we have thus established the DPJR operations on concepts. The *orbital concept lattice* of $\mathfrak{G}$ is the algebra $(\mathfrak{B}(\mathfrak{G}),\vee,\wedge,\bot,\top,\cdot,\mathfrak{E}_{xy},\mathrm{dom})_{x,y\in\mathbf{var}}$, where $\mathfrak{E}_{xy} := (E_{xy}, E_{xy}^{\diamond\diamond})$ is an *equality concept* for all $x,y \in \mathbf{var}$, cf. Fig. 7.

7.2 Conjunctive Concept Algebras

The right multiplication in Sect. 7.1 seems natural for tableau queries; but for primitive positive formulas, the natural operations are (syntactic) conjunction and existential quantification. In a conjunctive concept algebra [18], these are considered as operations on concepts. While conjunction is simply represented by the concept infimum, existential quantification of $x \in \mathbf{var}$ is a special case of projection (cf. Sect. 7.1), defined for $(T,Q) \in \mathfrak{B}(\mathfrak{G})[X]$ by $C_x(T,Q) := (T,Q)\cdot\pi$, where $\pi : X\setminus\{x\} \to X$. For example, $(T,Q)\cdot\pi = C_y(T,Q)$ in Fig. 7.

The algebra $\underline{\mathfrak{C}}(\mathfrak{G}) := (\mathfrak{B}(\mathfrak{G}),\wedge,\bot,\top,C_x,\mathfrak{E}_{xy},\mathrm{dom})_{x,y\in\mathbf{var}}$ is the *full conjunctive concept algebra* over $\mathfrak{G}$. An algebra $(V,\wedge,0,1,c_x,d_{xy},\mathrm{dom})_{x,y\in\mathbf{var}}$ of the same type is a *projectional semilattice*, if it satisfies the axioms

(PS0) $(V,\wedge,0,1)$ bounded semilattice
(PS1) $c_x(0)=0$
(PS2) $u \le c_x(u)$
(PS3) $c_x(u\wedge c_x(v)) = c_x(u)\wedge c_x(v)$
(PS4) $c_x(c_y(u)) = c_y(c_x(u))$
(PS5) $u \neq 0 \Rightarrow (u \neq c_x(u) \Leftrightarrow u \le d_{xx})$
(PS6) $x \neq y,z \Rightarrow d_{yz} = c_x(d_{yx}\wedge d_{xz})$
(PS7) $x \neq y \Rightarrow d_{xy}\wedge c_x(d_{xy}\wedge u) \le u$
(PS8) $u \neq 0 \Rightarrow \mathrm{dom}(u)$ finite
(PS9) $\mathrm{dom}(u) = \{x \in \omega \mid u \le d_{xx}\}$
(PS10) $\mathrm{dom}(u) = \emptyset \Rightarrow u = 1$
(PS11) $d_{xx} \neq 0$
(PS12) $d_{xy} = d_{yx}$

for all $u,v \in V$ and $x,y,z \in \mathbf{var}$. We have shown in [18, Prop. 11], that the $\bigwedge$-subalgebras of $\underline{\mathfrak{C}}(\mathfrak{G})$ are, up to isomorphism, precisely the complete lattices which satisfy the projectional semilattice axioms. The conjecture is that this also characterizes the algebras $\underline{\mathfrak{C}}(\mathfrak{G})$ up to isomorphism.

8 Conceptual Scaling

As mentioned in Sect. 2, relational structures are used to formalize relational databases. However, as the reader familiar with relational databases would be aware, our example structure $\mathfrak{G}_{\mathrm{fam}}$, illustrated in Fig. 1, is hardly the kind of database we would encounter in practice. The same information would rather be

name	sex	mother	father
Anne	female		
Bob	male	Anne	
Chris	male	Anne	
Dora	female		Bob
Emily	female		Bob

Fig. 8. A relational database consisting of a single table Person

sex	male	female
male	×	
female		×

Fig. 9. A conceptual scale for the enum datatype of sex

stored in a single table Person, like the one in Fig. 8. The name column serves as a primary key, and both the mother and father columns are foreign keys into the same table. There is also a sex column, with an enum datatype, which allows the values male or female. This database can be formalized by a relational structure $\mathfrak{R}_{\text{fam}}$ over the signature $\{\mathsf{Person}/4\}$; its single relation $\mathsf{Person}^{\mathfrak{R}_{\text{fam}}}$ is the 4-ary relation shown in Fig. 8. Obviously, the metadata (i.e. column names and types, primary and foreign key constraints) is not included in this formalization.

While $\mathfrak{G}_{\text{fam}}$ and $\mathfrak{R}_{\text{fam}}$ contain the same information (if we know how to read them), they differ in how the objects of our interest, i.e. the five family members, are represented. In $\mathfrak{G}_{\text{fam}}$ they occur as the table entries, and consequently, the tables represent relations between objects. With the primitive-positive formulas over M_{fam}, we talk about the objects in the universe G_{fam} (i.e. the variables range over G_{fam}, cf. *domain calculus* [1, pp. 39, 74]). In $\mathfrak{R}_{\text{fam}}$, on the other hand, the objects are represented as table rows, i.e. as named tuples, whereas the table fields contain values, such as the object's name, which is a string in the name field, or null values in the empty fields. With SQL queries, we talk about the objects that are represented as tuples (i.e. the variables range over tuples, cf. *tuple calculus* [1, pp. 39, 74]). But if we evaluate primitive-positive formulas in $\mathfrak{R}_{\text{fam}}$, we miss to talk about the objects, talking about the values in R_{fam} instead. In fact, the single relation Person may not seem like a relation intuitively, because it connects values, rather than objects. So from a conceptual perspective, as elaborated in this article, we would certainly prefer $\mathfrak{G}_{\text{fam}}$ as a model.

Using the method of conceptual scaling [9], we can transform a relational structure into another relational structure, switching from the perspective of the tuple calculus to the perspective of the domain calculus. For illustration, we show how $\mathfrak{R}_{\text{fam}}$ is transformed into $\mathfrak{G}_{\text{fam}}$. For this purpose, it is convenient to regard $\mathfrak{G}_{\text{fam}}$ as a power context family (cf. Fig. 3). First, every database table, minus the foreign key columns, can be considered as a many-valued context [9]. This leaves us with the columns name and sex in Fig. 8. For each of the columns, a conceptual scale [9] may be chosen, depending on the column's datatype (the actual SQL type, or some semantic subtype). For the sex column, we choose the conceptual scale in Fig. 9. As usual, the objects of the scale are the possible column values, whereas its attributes are unary relation names that are included in the signature M_{fam}. In this particular example, the values and the relation names coincide. In a practical setting, as described in [15], the power context family $\mathfrak{G}_{\text{fam}}$ is virtual, i.e. it is not actually generated. Instead, each formula over M_{fam} is translated to an equivalent SQL query, which is evaluated in $\mathfrak{R}_{\text{fam}}$. This requires to associate with each relation name an SQL fragment, which gets included in the query's WHERE-clause. The SQL fragments for male and female are `t.sex='male'` and `t.sex='female'`, respectively, where t gets replaced by a table alias for the Person table. For example, the atom male(x) translates to the SQL statement `SELECT x.name FROM Person AS x WHERE x.sex='male';`. The SELECT-clause uses the primary key as the default way of printing an object. The statement also defines the unary relation $\mathsf{male}^{\mathfrak{G}_{\text{fam}}}$, and likewise for $\mathsf{female}^{\mathfrak{G}_{\text{fam}}}$. This establishes the context $\mathbb{K}_1$ in Fig. 3.

The foreign keys mother and father translate to binary relation names, defined by the SQL fragments `s.name=t.mother` and `s.name=t.father`, respectively, where s and t get replaced by table aliases for the Person table. The remaining attribute parent of $\mathbb{K}_2$ is derived from mother and father. It is associated with the SQL fragment `s.name=t.mother OR s.name=t.father`. However, the addition of derived attributes is not described in [15].

We have thus obtained $\mathfrak{G}_{\text{fam}}$ as shown in Fig. 3. Note that we have not scaled the name column in Fig. 8. Choosing a scale as in Fig. 9, the object names are exposed as unary relation names, which can play the role of constants. For example, the atom female(Anne) can then be used as a macro for $\exists z(\mathsf{Anne}(z) \wedge \mathsf{female}(z))$. In order to achieve data-independence, an infinite scale can be used, which introduces all possible strings as constants. We could even use a prefix scale, to enable prefix search on the name column. In summary, while our core mathematical model does not directly allow the use of constants, keeping the theory elegant, conceptual scaling provides for the missing flexibility.

9 Related Work

After FCA was established, Wille started a program of *restructuring mathematical logic*, where the basic notions of traditional philosophical logic, namely *concepts*, *judgments* and *conclusions*, should be formalized based on FCA. The role of FCA, of course, would be to provide the formalization of concepts, whereas John Sowa's theory of Conceptual Graphs [22] was meant to contribute a formalization of judgments and conclusions (cf. [23, Sect. 1]). More specifically, Wille points to the *S-graphs* of Chein and Mugnier [7] for a mathematization of conceptual graphs. As Chein and Mugnier state, S-graphs translate to primitive-positive formulas [7, Sect. 9.1], and conclusions can be expressed by graph homomorphisms [7, Thm. 1]. However, S-graphs are understood as closed formulas (i.e. sentences), and the notion of their homomorphisms is lost in the ensuing theory of *concept graphs*, summarized in [25].

The main difference between S-graphs and conjunctive queries is thus, that conjunctive queries generally represent open formulas. This puts us on a different path, as open formulas naturally support a notion of extension. The homomorphism theorem of database theory [1, Sect. 6.2] provides a characterization of conclusions, analog to [7, Thm. 1] for S-graphs. Moreover, the minimal representation of a conjunctive query [1, Sect. 6.2] corresponds to an *irredundant S-graph* [7]. Insofar, at least from a purely theoretical perspective, our approach realizes Wille's original ideas in the setting of database theory. For further references to FCA-related work, the reader is referred to [16, Sect. 8].

Andréka and Németi [3] also define a notion of *concept algebra* of a relational structure. They denote the relational structure by $\mathfrak{M}$. Their concept algebra consists of the first-order definable relations over $\mathfrak{M}$; its operations are induced by the logical connectives (more precisely, it is a *cylindric set algebra* [10]). This notion of concept algebra is further developed in [2], and in particular, concept algebras are considered for any kind of logic, not just first-order logic. In particular, as we consider a logic of conjunctive queries, our concept algebra $\underline{\mathfrak{C}}(\mathfrak{G})$ is also a concept algebra in that sense. It seems worthwile to investigate more generally, how this algebraic-logical notion of concept algebras combines with FCA's notion of concept lattice.

10 Conclusion

We have presented an overview of previous work based on concept lattices of relational structures. While definitions have evolved over time, the focus on axioms for relational concept algebras requires to be precise, as variations of the definitions, even if they seem practically irrelevant, may have an effect on the axiomatization. Special emphasis lies also on the database-theoretic formalizations, as they are interconnected with the definition of concepts and relational concept algebras. With this paper, we hope to provide a single point of access for the interested reader, as well as a point of reference for future work. Such work may investigate the influence of modeling options on the axiomatizations.

References

1. Abiteboul, S., Hull, R., Vianu, V.: Foundations of Databases. Addison-Wesley (1995)
2. Andréka, H., Gyenis, Z., Németi, I., Sain, I.: Universal Algebraic Logic. Dedicated to the Unity of Science, Birkhäuser (2022)
3. Andréka, H., Németi, I.: How many varieties of cylindric algebras are there. Trans. Am. Math. Soc. **369**(12), 8903–8937 (2017). https://doi.org/10.1090/tran/7083
4. Baader, F.: Least common subsumers and most specific concepts in a description logic with existential restrictions and terminological cycles. In: Gottlob, G., Walsh, T. (eds.) Proceedings of IJCAI 2003, pp. 319–324. Morgan Kaufmann (2003)
5. Baader, F., Molitor, R.: Building and structuring description logic knowledge bases using least common subsumers and concept analysis. In: Ganter, B., Mineau, G.W. (eds.) ICCS-ConceptStruct 2000. LNCS (LNAI), vol. 1867, pp. 292–305. Springer, Heidelberg (2000). https://doi.org/10.1007/10722280_20
6. Chandra, A.K., Merlin, P.M.: Optimal implementation of conjunctive queries in relational databases. In: Proceedings of the Ninth Annual ACM Symposium on Theory of Computing, STOC 1977, pp. 77–90. ACM, New York (1977)

7. Chein, M., Mugnier, M.L.: Conceptual graphs: fundamental notions. Revue d'Intell. Artif. **6**(4), 365–406 (1992)
8. Ebbinghaus, H.D., Flum, J., Thomas, W.: Mathematical Logic, 2nd edn. Springer, New York (1994)
9. Ganter, B., Wille, R.: Formal Concept Analysis: Mathematical Foundations, 2nd edn. Springer, Cham (2024)
10. Henkin, L., Monk, J.D., Tarski, A.: Cylindric Algebras, Part 1. North-Holland (1971)
11. Huchard, M., Hacene, M.R., Roume, C., Valtchev, P.: Relational concept discovery in structured datasets. Ann. Math. Artif. Intell. **49**(1–4), 39–76 (2007)
12. Huchard, M., Roume, C., Valtchev, P.: When concepts point at other concepts: the case of UML diagram reconstruction. In: Proceedings of the 2nd Workshop on Advances in Formal Concept Analysis for Knowledge Discovery in Databases (FCAKDD 2002), pp. 32–43 (2002)
13. Kötters, J.: Concept lattices of a relational structure. In: Pfeiffer, H.D., Ignatov, D.I., Poelmans, J., Gadiraju, N. (eds.) ICCS-ConceptStruct 2013. LNCS (LNAI), vol. 7735, pp. 301–310. Springer, Heidelberg (2013). https://doi.org/10.1007/978-3-642-35786-2_23
14. Kötters, J.: Intension graphs as patterns over power context families. In: Huchard, M., Kuznetsov, S. (eds.) Proceedings of CLA 2016. CEUR Workshop Proceedings, vol. 1624. CEUR-WS.org (2016)
15. Kötters, J., Eklund, P.W.: The theory and practice of coupling formal concept analysis to relational databases. In: Kuznetsov, S.O., Napoli, A., Rudolph, S. (eds.) Proceedings of FCA4AI 2018. CEUR Workshop Proceedings, vol. 2149, pp. 69–80. CEUR-WS.org (2018)
16. Kötters, J., Eklund, P.W.: Conjunctive query pattern structures: a relational database model for formal concept analysis. Discret. Appl. Math. **273**, 144–171 (2020)
17. Kötters, J., Schmidt, H.W.: A database browser based on pattern concepts. In: Carpineto, C., Kuznetsov, S.O., Napoli, A. (eds.) Proceedings of the Workshop Formal Concept Analysis Meets Information Retrieval (FCAIR 2013). CEUR Workshop Proceedings, vol. 977, pp. 47–56. CEUR-WS.org (2013). http://ceur-ws.org/Vol-977
18. Kötters, J., Schmidt, S.E.: Conjunctive concept algebras – named perspective. In: Napoli, A., Rudolph, S. (eds.) Proceedings of FCA4AI (12th Edition). CEUR Workshop Proceedings, vol. 3911, pp. 15–26. CEUR-WS.org (2024)
19. Kwuida, L.: Dicomplemented lattices. a contextual generalization of Boolean algebras. Ph.D. thesis, TU Dresden, Germany (2004)
20. Kwuida, L., Machida, H.: On the isomorphism problem of concept algebras. Ann. Math. Artif. Intell. **59**, 223–239 (2010)
21. Kötters, J., Schmidt, S.E.: Orbital concept lattices. In: Braun, T., Cristea, D., Jäschke, R. (eds.) ICCS 2022. LNCS, vol. 13403, pp. 66–81. Springer, Cham (2022). https://doi.org/10.1007/978-3-031-16663-1_6
22. Sowa, J.F.: Conceptual Structures: Information Processing in Mind and Machine. Addison-Wesley, Reading (1984)
23. Wille, R.: Conceptual graphs and formal concept analysis. In: Lukose, D., Delugach, H., Keeler, M., Searle, L., Sowa, J. (eds.) ICCS-ConceptStruct 1997. LNCS, vol. 1257, pp. 290–303. Springer, Heidelberg (1997). https://doi.org/10.1007/BFb0027878

24. Wille, R.: Boolean concept logic. In: Ganter, B., Mineau, G.W. (eds.) ICCS 2000. LNAI, vol. 1867, pp. 317–331. Springer (2000). https://doi.org/10.1007/10722280_22
25. Wille, R.: Formal concept analysis and contextual logic. In: Hitzler, P., Schärfe, H. (eds.) Conceptual Structures in Practice, pp. 137–173. Chapman & Hall/CRC (2009)

Rises for Measuring Local Distributivity in Lattices

Mohammad Abdulla[1,2], Tobias Hille[1,2], Dominik Dürrschnabel[1,2,3(✉)], and Gerd Stumme[1,2]

[1] Knowledge and Data Engineering Group, University of Kassel, Kassel, Germany
{abdulla,hille,duerrschnabel,stumme}@cs.uni-kassel.de
[2] Interdisciplinary Research Center for Information Systems Design, University of Kassel, Kassel, Germany
[3] Baden Wuerttemberg Cooperative State University Mosbach, Mosbach, Germany

Abstract. Distributivity is a well-established and extensively studied notion in lattice theory. In the context of data analysis, particularly within Formal Concept Analysis (FCA), lattices are often observed to exhibit a high degree of distributivity. However, no standardized measure exists to quantify this property. In this paper, we introduce the notion of rises in (concept) lattices as a means to assess distributivity. Rises capture how the number of attributes or objects in covering concepts change within the concept lattice. We show that a lattice is distributive if and only if no non-unit rises occur. Furthermore, we relate rises to the classical notion of meet- and join distributivity. We observe that concept lattices from real-world data are to a high degree join-distributive, but much less meet-distributive. We additionally study how join-distributivity manifests on the level of ordered sets.

Keywords: Posets · Formal Concept Analysis · Distributive Lattices · Local Distributivity/Join-Distributivity · Join-Rise · Meet-Rise

1 Introduction

In lattice theory, a particular interesting property of a lattice $(L \leq)$ is that of being distributive, i. e., when, for all $x, y, z \in L$, $x \wedge (y \vee z) = (x \wedge y) \vee (x \wedge z)$ and $x \vee (y \wedge z) = (x \vee y) \wedge (x \vee z)$ hold. Distributive lattices are equipped with strong properties that make them particularly useful in data analysis and knowledge representation: They can for instance be embedded into products of total orders, which can be used for a divide-and-conquer approach for data analysis by decompositions or for well readable visualisations; moreover for their implicational theory, only implications with one-element premises—which are thus easy to understand—have to be considered.

Previous studies suggest that lattices arising in data-driven contexts, such as those in Formal Concept Analysis (FCA), exhibit a high degree of distributivity. Wille [25] provides evidence that many concept lattices from real-world data sources are 'mostly distributive'. Despite this observation, there is no widely

P. Cellier et al. (Eds.): CONCEPTS 2025, LNAI 15941, pp. 392–407, 2025.
https://doi.org/10.1007/978-3-032-03364-2_25

accepted measure to quantify the degree of distributivity in such lattices—not to speak of any method for 'repairing' the non-distributive part of the lattice.

For data analysis tasks such as decompositions and visualisations, it might also suffice to consider some weaker form of distributivity, such as semidistributivity, local distributivity, modularity, semimodularity, etc. It should be obvious that 'the right way' of measuring and repairing non-distributivity (and any other algebraic property) will strongly depend on the goal of the data analysis. Therefore a large tool kit with different measures and methods is required.

In [2], we started this approach by proposing the Birkhoff completion, which embeds any (non-distributive) lattice into the smallest possible distributive one by preserving all joins. In this paper, we follow another observation: (structural properties of) neighboring elements in distributive (concept) lattices vary only slightly. When we move in a finite distributive lattice from an element to an upper neighbor, the set of join-irreducible elements below increases exactly by one [and the set of meet-irreducible elements above decreases exactly by one]. (In FCA that means that the cardinalities of the extents and intents of two neighboring concepts of a reduced context differ exactly by one.) Hence whenever a rise (which we will formally define in Sect. 3) is larger than one, then the distributivity law is violated—which could be repaired in a subsequent step.

It turned out that we rediscovered with the property 'all join rises are equal to one' an old concept which has already frequently been rediscovered before [19]—the so-called *local distributivity* or *join-distributivity*. Join-distributivity has initially been introduced by Dilworth in 1940 (see [6]) and has since then been discovered and studied independently from many different perspectives. In particular, join-distributive lattices are equivalent to anti-matroids, convex geometries [7,8,16] and learning spaces [9,24]. The equivalences summarized in Theorem 7 in Sect. 3 are both reason and result of this confluence of perspectives.

In this paper, we will study specific aspects of join- and meet-rises and join-/meetdistributivity that may be beneficial for an analysis of (concept) lattices that are 'almost join-distributive'. Because of the duality principle of lattice theory,[1] it is sufficient to describe our results only for either join-distributivity or meet-distributivity. Because real-world concept lattices are closer to being join-distributive than meet-distributive (see Sect. 5 for details) and because learning spaces are also joindistributive, we will focus on the former ones. We will use the term 'local distributivity' when talking about the overall picture, and the equivalent term 'joindistributivity' for details.

As our research is driven by a data analysis perspective, *all sets and structures in this paper will be finite*, unless explicitly mentioned otherwise.

While the work in this paper is mostly of theoretical nature, we will discuss potential applications in the outlook (Sect. 6). In Sect. 2, we will introduce the necessary background on ordered sets, lattices, and Formal Concept Analysis. In Sect. 3, we will define rises and establish their connection to local distributivity. In Sect. 4, we will extend the study of join-distributivity to posets. Finally,

[1] Every valid statement also holds in its dual version, i. e. when we systematically flip $\leq \leftrightarrow \geq$, 'meet' ($\wedge$) $\leftrightarrow$ 'join' ($\vee$), $\top \leftrightarrow \bot$, etc.

Sect. 5 will analyze real-world datasets to quantify local distributivity in practice. Related work is discussed throughout the paper.

2 Preliminaries

Here we briefly recall the basic notations. For more background on lattice theory and Formal Concept Analysis, we refer to [3,5,11,21]. We follow the notation of [11] whenever possible.

2.1 Ordered Sets and Lattices

An *order* (sometimes also called *partial order*) on a set P is a binary relation $\leq$ on P that is: reflexive (For all $a \in P$, $a \leq a$), antisymmetric (If $a \leq b$ and $b \leq a$, then $a = b$), transitive (If $a \leq b$ and $b \leq c$, then $a \leq c$). $\boldsymbol{P} := (P, \leq)$ is then called an *ordered set.* We call $(x, y) \in P \times P$ a *comparable pair* of P if $x < y$. We call a comparable pair a *covering pair* and write $x \prec y$ if, for all $\mathrm{p} \in P$, $x \leq p < y$ implies $x = p$. A *chain* in $(P, \leq)$ is a set $C \subseteq P$ where, for all $x, y \in C$, $x \leq y$ or $y \leq x$. A chain is called *maximal* if it is not a proper subset of any other chain. The *height* h of a finite ordered set P is the length of its longest chain. The *height of an element* x is given by $\max\{|C| \mid \forall y \in C : y < x$, C is a chain$\}$. For two elements $x, y \in P$, $[x, y] := \{z \mid x \leq z \leq y\}$ is the *interval* between x and y.

If, for $x, y \in P$, the set $\{z \mid z \leq x$ and $z \leq y\}$ has a largest element, then it is the *meet* of x and y, denoted by $x \wedge y$. Dually, if there is a least element in $\{z \in P \mid z \geq x, z \geq y\}$, then it is the *join* of x and y, denoted by $x \vee y$. An ordered set $\boldsymbol{L} : -(L, \leq)$ is called a *lattice* if for any two elements their meet and join exist. It is a *complete lattice* if all subsets $X \subseteq L$ have meet (denoted by $\bigwedge X$) and join (denoted by $\bigvee X$). $\bot := \bigwedge \emptyset$ is the *bottom element* and $\top := \bigvee \emptyset$ is the *top element.* $\bot$ and $\top$ are often denoted by 0 and 1. We refrain from this notation, as it may lead to confusion with our concept of rises.

$x \in \boldsymbol{P}$ is join-irreducible if it is not the join of a set of elements not containing x. It is meet-irreducible if it is not the meet of a set of elements not containing it. The set of all join-irreducible elements of $\boldsymbol{P}$ is denoted by $\mathcal{J}(\boldsymbol{P})$, and the set of all its meet-irreducibles is denoted by $\mathcal{M}(\boldsymbol{P})$. We define $\mathcal{M}^x := \{m \in \mathcal{M}(\boldsymbol{P}) \mid x \leq m\}$. For $x \in P$ let $m(x) = |\mathcal{M}^x|$. Dually, let $\mathcal{J}_x = \{j \in \mathcal{J}(\boldsymbol{P}) \mid j \leq x\}$ and for $x \in P$ let $j(x) = |\mathcal{J}_x|$. $X \subseteq L$ is an *irredundant* $\bigvee$-representation of $a \in L$ if $a = \bigvee X$ and $a \neq \bigvee(X \backslash \{x\})$ for every $x \in X$. A *rank function* in a lattice $(L, \leq)$ is a mapping $r \colon L \to \mathbb{N}$ such that $r(\bot) = 0$ and, for any two elements $x, y \in L$, $x \prec y \Rightarrow r(x) + 1 = r(y)$ holds. A lattice with rank function is *graded.* $K \subseteq L$ is a *sublattice* of lattice $(L, \leq)$ if K is closed under meets and joins. Distributivity, as defined in the introduction, can be characterized by forbidden sublattices, as famously discovered by Birkhoff:

Theorem 1 (Birkhoff [3]). *A lattice* $\boldsymbol{L}$ *is distributive if and only if it has neither* M_3 *nor* N_5 *as a sublattice.*

A lattice is called *modular* if for all $x, y, z \in L$ with $z \leq x$ it follows that $x \wedge (y \vee z) = (x \wedge y) \vee z$. It is well-known that distributive lattices are modular. Modularity can be weakened to *semi-modularity* as follows. A finite lattice $\boldsymbol{L}$ is *semimodular* if, for all $x, y \in L$, $x \wedge y \prec y$ implies $x \prec x \vee y$, and it is *dually semimodular* if $y \prec x \vee y$ implies $x \wedge y \prec x$. The lattice S_7 (see Fig. 1 (c)) is the smallest semimodular lattice which is not modular.

Theorem 2 ([21]). *A finite lattice $\boldsymbol{L}$ is modular if and only if it is both semi-modular and dually semimodular.*

A complete lattice $\boldsymbol{L}$ is called *join-distributive* if it is semimodular and every modular sublattice is distributive (see Definition 6). Lattices satisfying the dual condition are called *meet-distributive*. For these two properties, there are multiple other possible definitions, as listed below in Theorem 7.

2.2 Formal Contexts and Concept Lattices

In this section, we introduce the fundamental definitions and concepts from Formal Concept Analysis (FCA) used throughout this work. A *(formal) context* is a triple $\mathbb{K} = (G, M, I)$, where G and M are sets whose elements are called *objects* and *attributes*, resp., and $I \subseteq G \times M$ is called *incidence relation*. For $A \subseteq G$, we define $A' := \{m \in M \mid \forall g \in A\ (g, m) \in I\}$. Dually, for $B \subseteq M$, we define $B' := \{g \in G \mid \forall m \in B\ (g, m) \in I\}$. A *(formal) concept* of $\mathbb{K}$ is a pair (A, B) such that $A \subseteq G$, $B \subseteq M$, $A' = B$, and $B' = A$. A is the *extent* and B the *intent* of the concept. The set of all concepts of $\mathbb{K}$, ordered by $(A_1, B_1) \leq (A_2, B_2) :\Longleftrightarrow A_1 \subseteq A_2$, forms a complete lattice, the *concept lattice* of $\mathbb{K}$, denoted by $\mathfrak{B}(\mathbb{K})$. A context is *clarified* if, for $g, h \in G$, $g' = h'$ implies $g = h$, and if for $m, n \in M$, $m' = n'$ implies $m = n$. For $g \in G$, (g'', g') is an *object concept* and, for $m \in M$, (m', m'') is an *attribute concept.* A context is *object-reduced* if every object concept is join-irreducible, it is *attribute-reduced* if every attribute concept is meet-irreducible, and it is *reduced* if it is both. For $g \in G$ and $m \in M$ with $(g, m) \notin I$, we write $g \swarrow m$ if, for $h \in G$, $g' \subsetneq h'$ implies $(h, m) \in I$, and $g \nearrow m$ if, for $n \in M$, $m' \subsetneq n'$ implies $(g, n) \in I$. $g \swarrow\!\!\!\nearrow m$ stands for both $g \swarrow m$ and $g \nearrow m$. The *Dedekind-MacNeille completion* of an ordered set $\boldsymbol{P}$, denoted by $DM(\boldsymbol{P})$, is the smallest complete lattice into which $\boldsymbol{P}$ can be order embedded:

Theorem 3 (FCA version of Dedekind s Completion Theorem [11]**).** *For an ordered set $\boldsymbol{P}$, define $\iota(x) := (\{a \in P \mid a \leq x\}, \{a \in P \mid a \geq x\})$ for $x \in P$. This defines an embedding ι of $\boldsymbol{P}$ in $\mathfrak{B}(P, P, \leq)$. Moreover, $\iota(\bigvee X) = \bigvee \iota(X)$ or $\iota(\bigwedge X) = \bigwedge \iota(X)$ if the join or meet of X, respectively, exists in $\boldsymbol{P}$. Furthermore, if κ is any order embedding of $\boldsymbol{P}$ into a complete lattice $\boldsymbol{L}$, then there exists an embedding λ of $\mathfrak{B}(P, P, \leq)$ into $\boldsymbol{L}$ such that $\kappa = \lambda \circ \iota$.*

3 Rises and Local Distributivity

Recall, that the mappings j and m count the number of join-irreducibles and meet-irreducibles below and above an element in a poset, respectively.

Definition 4. *Let* $\mathbf{L} := (L, \leq)$ *be a finite lattice. The* join-rise *of a comparable pair* (x, y) *of* $\mathbf{L}$ *is denoted by* $\Delta_j(x, y) := j(y) - j(x)$ *and the* meet-rise *by* $\Delta_m(x, y) := m(x) - m(y)$. *We call a rise between covering elements* unit *if its value is one, otherwise we call it* non-unit.

We will measure these rises mostly for covering pairs $x \prec y$.

If we already have a clarified and reduced context $\mathbb{K}$, the maps j and m on $\mathfrak{B}(K)$ measure the size of the extent and the intent respectively, i.e., $j(A, B) = |\mathcal{J}_{(A,B)}| = |A|$ and $m(A, B) = |\mathcal{M}_{(A,B)}| = |B|$. This observation gives rise to the following lemma.

Lemma 5. *For two formal concepts* $(A, B) \leq (C, D)$ *of a reduced and clarified context* $\Delta_j((A, B), (C, D)) = |C| - |A|$ *and* $\Delta_m((A, B), (C, D)) = |B| - |D|$ *hold.*

Rises capture how concept extents or intents change when we move up or down in the lattice. For some initial examples, we refer the reader to Fig. 1, which shows six example contexts and the corresponding concept lattices. The concepts are labels with the cardinalities of their extent (below) and of their intent (above). Non-unit rises between covering concepts are highlighted. We see that in the distributive lattice C_2 all rises are unit, whereas the other three lattices—which are all non-distributive—all have at least one non-unit rise. Furthermore, S_7 has some non-unit join-rises, while all its meet-rises are unit. (We will see later in Theorem 10 that the existence of S_7 of sublattice is also a necessary condition for this situation.)

When studying the behavior of non-unit rises, we quickly recognized that the absence of non-unit rises is just another way of looking at a well-known (and, as said before, frequently re-discovered) concept:

Definition 6. *A finite lattice* $\mathbf{L}$ *is* locally distributive *or* join-distributive *(and sometimes also called* upper locally distributive (ULD) *in the literature) if* $\mathbf{L}$ *is semimodular and every modular sublattice is distributive. Lattices satisfying the dual condition are called* meet-distributive.

The following theorem provides different views on this—somewhat complexly defined—concept. It summarizes many well-known results that are stated (sometimes in the dual version), e. g., in [6–8,11,16,19,20,23]. For sake of simplicity and uniformity, we consider finite lattices only.[2] As always in lattice theory, the dual theorem also holds.

Theorem 7. *Let* $\mathbf{L}$ *be a finite lattice. Then the following are equivalent:*

1. $\mathbf{L}$ *is join-distributive.*
2. $\mathbf{L}$ *has a neighborhood-preserving* $\bigvee$*-embedding into a powerset lattice.*
3. *Every element has a unique irredundant* $\bigwedge$*-representation.*
4. *For all* $x, y \in L$ *with* $x \prec y$ *there exists a unique meet-irreducible* z *such that* $x \leq z$ *and* $y \not\leq z$.

[2] For some of the equivalences in the following theorem, the finiteness condition can be relaxed, e. g., to the finite chain condition or to doubly founded lattices.

	m_1	m_2	m_3
g_1	×		
g_2		×	
g_3			×

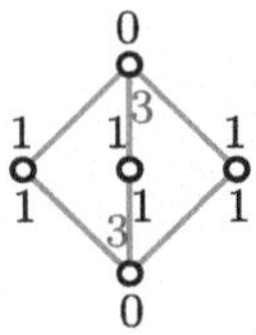

(a) M_3

	m_1	m_2	m_3
g_1	×	×	
g_2	×		
g_3			×

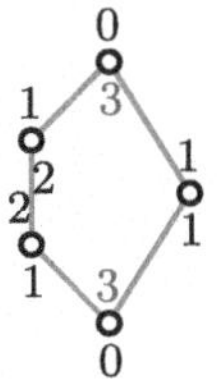

(b) N_5

	m_1	m_2	m_3
g_1	×		
g_2	×	×	
g_3		×	×
g_4			×

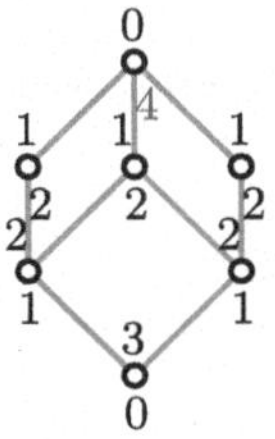

(c) S_7

	m_1	m_2	m_3	m_4
g_1	×	×		
g_2		×	×	
g_3			×	×

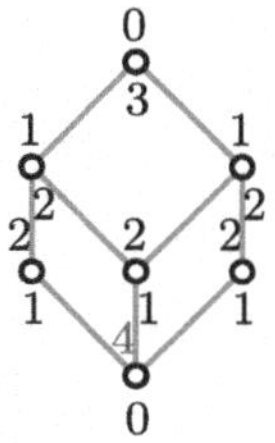

(d) S_7^d

	m_1	m_2	m_3	m_4	m_5
g_1		×		×	
g_2	×	×	×		
g_3		×			×
g_4	×				
g_5			×		

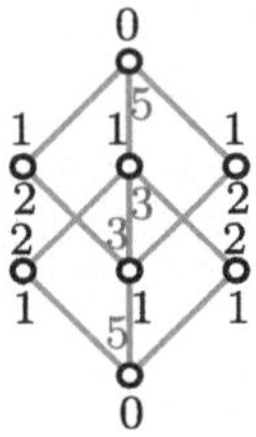

(e) M_3M_3

	m_1	m_2	m_3	m_4
g_1		×	×	×
g_2	×		×	×
g_3	×	×	×	
g_4	×	×		

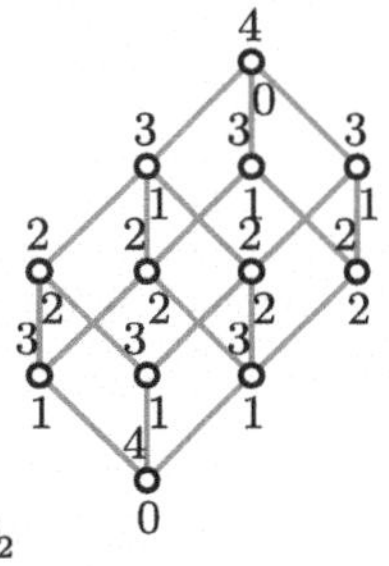

(f) C_2

Fig. 1. Six small reduced and clarified contexts and their concept lattices. The lower label (object) of a concept node is the number of join irreducible elements in the down-set, and correspondingly the upper label (attribute) is the number of meet irreducible elements in the up-set. Non-unit rises (see Lemma 5) between covering concepts are indicated by a colored label.

5. *$\mathbf{L}$ is graded with the rank function $r(x) = |\{m \in \mathcal{M}(\mathbf{L}) \mid m \not\geq x\}|$.*
6. *For every element $x \in L$, the interval $[x, x^\top]$ with $x^\top := \bigvee\{y \in L \mid x \prec y\}$ is Boolean.*

If $\mathbf{L} = \mathfrak{B}(G, M, I)$, then the following conditions are equivalent to those above:

7. *For every concept intent B and for all $m, n \in M \backslash B$ with $m' \neq n'$ we have the* anti-exchange axiom*: $m \in (B \cup \{n\})''$ implies $n \notin (B \cup \{m\})''$.*
8. *Every intent B is the closure of its extremal points, where $m \in M$ is an* extremal point *of B if $m \in B$ but $m \notin (B \backslash \{n \in M \mid m' = n'\})''$.*
9. *If m and n are irreducible attributes then $g \swarrow m$ and $g \swarrow n$ imply $m' = n'$.*

We can now connect our join-rises to this theorem.

Theorem 8. *Let $\mathbf{L}$ be a finite lattice. Then the following condition is equivalent to those stated in Theorem 7:*

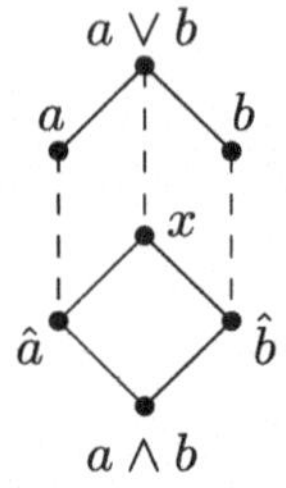

Fig. 2. Visualization of the proof of Theorem 10. Solid lines indicate a covering relation, while dashed lines indicate comparability.

10. *For all $x, y \in L$ with $x \prec y$ it holds $\Delta_m(x, y) = 1$.*

If $\mathbf{L} = \underline{\mathfrak{B}}(G, M, I)$ and (G, M, I) is clarified and reduced, then the following condition is equivalent to those above:

11. *For all concepts $(A, B), (C, D) \in \mathfrak{B}(G, M, I)$ with $(A, B) \prec (C, D)$ it holds $|B| - |D| = 1$*

Proof. (4) ⇔ (10): For all $x, y \in \boldsymbol{L}$ with $x \prec y$, the existence of z in Item 4 of Theorem 7 is equivalent to $\Delta_m(x, y) = 1$.

(10) ⇔ (11) follows from Lemma 5. □

As it is well-known that a finite lattice is distributive if and only if it is both join-distributive and meetdistributive, we obtain the following necessary and sufficient criterion for distributivity.

Corollary 9. *A finite lattice is distributive if and only if for all covering pairs the meet-rises and join-rises are unit.*

It is also well-known (see Theorem 1) that a lattice is distributive if and only if it does not contain M_3 or N_5 (as given in Figs. 1a and 1b) as sublattice. If it contains M_3, then it is neither join- nor meet-distributive and hence must have both non-unit join-rises and non-unit meet-rises (see Fig. 1d for an example). If it contains N_5, then it has a non-unit join-rise or a non-unit meet-rise. It is not necessary that it has both of them, as shown for instance for the lattice S_7^d in Fig. 1d. We now turn to the natural question of the properties that arise from unit rises in a single direction. The following theorem offers a characterization in terms of a sublattice condition.

Theorem 10. *Let $\boldsymbol{L}$ be a finite, join-distributive lattice. Then $\boldsymbol{L}$ is meet-distributive if and only if it does not contain S_7 as a sublattice.*

Proof. "⇒": If $\boldsymbol{L}$ is meet-distributive then it cannot have a non-meet-distributive sublattice. In particular it cannot have S_7 as sublattice, because S_7 is not meet-distributive.

"⇐": Let $\boldsymbol{L}$ be a finite join-distributive lattice that is not meet-distributive. We will construct a sublattice of $\boldsymbol{L}$ that is isomorphic to S_7. First, we show that

$\boldsymbol{L}$ is not dually semimodular: Assume that it were dually semimodular. As dual semimodularity together with join-distributivity implies distributivity, and thus also meet-distributivity, $\boldsymbol{L}$ would also be meet-distributive. $\lightning$.

As $\boldsymbol{L}$ is not dually semimodular, it does in particular not fulfill the weak condition of dual semimodularity since L is finite [21], which would prohibit the existence of two incomparable elements $a, b \in L$ with $a \prec a \vee b$, $b \prec a \vee b$ and $a \wedge b \not\prec a$. Let a and b be two such elements. As $\boldsymbol{L}$ is join-distributive it is, by Item 5 of Theorem 7, graded. Hence also the interval $[a \wedge b, a \vee b]$ is graded. Because of $a \wedge b \not\prec a$ there exists $\hat{a}$ with $a \wedge b \prec \hat{a} < a$, and because of the gradedness of the interval there also exists $\hat{b}$ with $a \wedge b \prec \hat{b} < b$. Let $x := \hat{a} \vee \hat{b}$. In the remainder of the proof we will show that the seven elements $a \vee b, a, b, x, \hat{a}, \hat{b}$ and $a \wedge b$ constitute a sublattice of $\boldsymbol{L}$ which is isomorphic to S_7 (see Fig. 2):

- Note that $\hat{b} \not\leq a$ and $\hat{a} \not\leq b$, otherwise $\hat{a} = a \wedge b$ or $\hat{b} = a \wedge b$. Thus, $a \wedge b \leq \hat{a} \wedge \hat{b} < \hat{a}$, and hence $a \wedge b = \hat{a} \wedge \hat{b}$.
- As $\boldsymbol{L}$ is join-distributive it is also semimodular. Hence $a \wedge b \prec \hat{a}$ and $a \wedge b \prec \hat{b}$ imply $\hat{a} \prec x$ and $\hat{b} \prec x$, resp.
- We have $x \not\leq a$ as otherwise we would have $\hat{b} \leq x \leq a$. The same type of argument yields $x \not\leq b$.
- Furthermore, $x = \hat{a} \vee \hat{b} \leq a \vee b$. Also, $x \neq a \vee b$ as otherwise there would be a maximal chain with three elements from $a \vee b$ to $a \wedge b$, contradicting the gradedness of the interval $[a \wedge b, a \vee b]$.
- As $x \leq a \vee b$, we know that $a \vee x \leq a \vee b$. Furthermore, $a \vee x = a \vee b$, as otherwise $a < a \vee x < a \vee b$ which would contradict $a \prec a \vee b$. By the same argument $b \vee x = a \vee b$.
- Additionally, $a \wedge x = \hat{a}$, as otherwise $x > a \wedge x > \hat{a}$, a contradiction to $x \succ \hat{a}$. Analogously, $b \wedge x = \hat{b}$. □

4 Join-Distributivity in Posets

Earlier in this work, we examined join-distributivity in lattices by measuring the number of non-unit rises. In this section, we transfer this approach to ordered sets. In data analysis contexts, ordered sets can be considered as condensed representation of the full lattice (via the Dedekind-MacNeille completion). To this end, we first need the notion of join-distributivity in ordered sets.

Definition 11. *An ordered set* $(P, \leq)$ *is called* join-distributive, *if* $DM(P, \leq)$ *is join-distributive. Dually, it is called* meet-distributive *if* $DM(P, \leq)$ *is meet-distributive. Finally, it is called* distributive *if it is meet- and join-distributive.*

This definition follows the style of definition of J. Larmerov and J. Rachunek [18] via the Dedekind-MacNeille completion, and our definition of a distributive ordered set coincides with theirs. Other properties of lattices such as being modular, complemented, Boolean, pseudo-complemented, Brouwerian and Stone have been adapted to ordered sets [4,12,18], but up to our knowledge join-distributivity is not among them.

Recall, that join- and meet-irreducible elements in ordered sets, are defined the same way as in lattices and that $\mathcal{J}(\boldsymbol{P})$ and $\mathcal{M}(\boldsymbol{P})$ refers to the set of join-irreducible and meet-irreducible elements respectively. Note that if an ordered set has a smallest element $\perp$, then it is join-reducible as the supremum of the empty set. On the other hand, in an ordered set with multiple minimal elements, each of them is irreducible. With keeping this in mind, *join-rises* and *meet-rises in ordered sets* are defined the same way as in lattices.

Figure 3 shows two ordered sets and their Dedekind-MacNeille completions. The numbers refer to the number of meet-irreducible elements which are larger or equal to each element. It is apparent that in the examples the numbers are preserved, when the Dedekind-MacNeille completion is computed, which implies that the rises between elements are preserved. The following proposition shows that this is indeed the case. The first part of the proposition is only given because it is used to prove the second part. It seems to be folklore in lattice theory, but we couldn't find it stated explicitly in the literature.

Proposition 12. *Let $\boldsymbol{P}$ be a finite ordered set.*

1. $\mathcal{M}(DM(\boldsymbol{P})) = \{\iota(x) \mid x \in \mathcal{M}(\boldsymbol{P})\}$
2. *For $x \in P$ the equality $m_{\boldsymbol{P}}(x) = m_{DM(\boldsymbol{P})}(\iota(x))$ holds.*

Proof. 1. '$\subseteq$': All elements in $DM(\boldsymbol{P})\backslash\{\iota(x) \mid x \in P\}$ are reducible by the construction of the DM completion, as they are created as joins and meets of the original elements. Hence $\mathcal{M}(DM(\boldsymbol{P})) \subseteq \{\iota(x) \mid x \in \mathcal{M}(\boldsymbol{P})\}$.

1. '$\supseteq$': Assume the opposite, i.e., there exists an $x \in \mathcal{M}(P)$ with $\iota(x) \notin \mathcal{M}(DM(\boldsymbol{P}))$. Then there also exists $\hat{K} \subseteq \mathcal{M}(DM(\boldsymbol{P}))$ with $\iota(x) = \bigwedge \hat{K}$. By '$\subseteq$', for each $\hat{k} \in \hat{K}$ there is a $k \in \mathcal{M}(\boldsymbol{P})$ with $\iota(k) = \hat{k}$, and, as ι is an embedding and therefore injective, k is even unique in P. Let $K \subseteq \mathcal{M}(\boldsymbol{P})$ such that $\iota(K) = \hat{K}$. As ι is order-preserving, $x \leq k$ for all $k \in K$. Thus, there is some element y that is a maximal lower bound of K. As ι is order preserving and $\iota(K) = \hat{K}$, it follows that $\iota(y) \leq \bigwedge \hat{K} = \iota(x)$ and therefore $y \leq x$. As $\iota(x) = \bigwedge \hat{K} \leq \iota(k)$ for any $k \in K$, x is a common, lower bound of K. This makes x the unique greatest lower bound of K, i.e., $x = \bigwedge K$, which contradicts the original assumption.

Ad 2: With Item 1 and the fact that ι is an order embedding, we obtain $m_{\boldsymbol{P}}(x) = |\{y \in \mathcal{M}(\boldsymbol{P}) \mid y \geq_{\boldsymbol{P}} x\}| = |\{y \in \mathcal{M}(DM(\boldsymbol{P})) \mid y \geq_{DM(\boldsymbol{P})} \iota(x)\}| = m_{DM(\boldsymbol{P})}(\iota(x))$. □

In the sequel we want to analyze, how unit rises in the ordered set are preserved under the Dedekind-MacNeille completion.

Proposition 13. *Let $\boldsymbol{P} = (P, \leq)$ be a finite ordered set. If $x \prec y$ in $\boldsymbol{P}$ and $\Delta_m(x, y) = 1$ then $\iota(x) \prec \iota(y)$ in $DM(\boldsymbol{P})$.*

Proof. Let $x \prec y$ in $(P, \leq)$ with a unit meet-rise. With Proposition 12(2) follows $\Delta_m(\iota(x), \iota(y)) = \Delta_m(x, y) = 1$. Hence, there cannot exist some $z \in DM(\boldsymbol{P})$ with $\iota(x) < z < \iota(y)$.

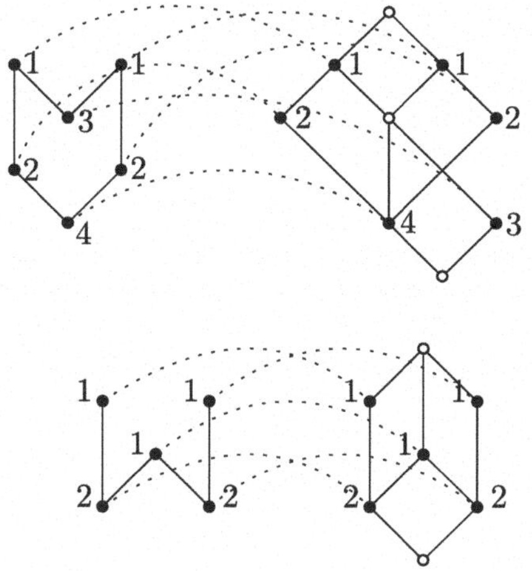

	m_1	m_2	m_3	m_4	m_5
g_1	×	⤢	×	↙	
g_2	⤢	×	↙	×	
g_3	×	×	⤢	⤢	×
g_4	×	×	×	×	⤢

	m_1	m_2	m_3
g_1	×	⤢	↗
g_2	↗	⤢	×
g_3	×	×	⤢
g_4	⤢	×	×

Fig. 3. Two examples for the Dedekind-MacNeille completion, showing that the step numbers stay the same (element wise). Numbers indicate $m(x)$, the white nodes are the ones that are added in the Dedekind-MacNeille completion.

To determine if a finite ordered set is join-distributive, one could compute the lattice completion of the ordered set and then check, if there are no non-unit meet-rises. However, this is potentially expensive, as the number of elements of the Dedekind-MacNeille completion might be exponentially larger than the number of elements in the original ordered set. We thus propose another way, which can be determined in polynomial time with respect to the number of elements of the ordered set, using the following isomorphism that follows directly from the standard context of a lattice as described in [11, Proposition 14].

Lemma 14. *Let $(P, \leq)$ be a finite ordered set. Then $\mathfrak{B}(J, M, \leq|_{J \cup M})$ with $J := \mathcal{J}(\boldsymbol{P})$ and $M := \mathcal{M}(\boldsymbol{P})$ is isomorphic to $DM(P, \leq)$.*

We can thus compute the context $(J, M, \leq|_{J \cup M})$ and then use the equivalence of (1) and (9) in Theorem 7 to determine join-distributivity. As this context is clarified by definition, we only have to check if every row that has a doublearrow has no additional downarrow or doublearrow. Computing the arrow relations can, by their definition, be done in polynomial time (e. g., by checking their definition for each cell), as the necessary inclusion checks between attribute and object vectors are at most quadratic in number, respectively. We thus receive a polynomial-time check for join-distributivity of arbitrary finite ordered sets. As example, the right side of Fig. 3 shows the formal contexts $(J, M, \leq|_{J \cup M})$ and their arrow relations. For the upper ordered set, g_1, g_2 and g_3 have at least one doublearrow and an additional downarrow or doublearrow, thus, the ordered set is not join-distributive. On the other hand there is no attribute with a doublearrow and an additional uparrow or doublearrow which makes the ordered set meet-distributive. The opposite is true for the lower ordered set, which is not meet- but join-distributive.

5 Local Distributivity in Real-World Data

Join- and meet-rises provide us with a straightforward way of measuring non-distributivity in real-world (concept) lattices:[3]

Definition 15. *Let* $\boldsymbol{L}$ *be a finite lattice. Then* $nur_\wedge(\boldsymbol{L}) := |\{(x,y) \in \boldsymbol{L}^2 \mid x \prec y, \Delta_m(x,y) > 1\}|$ *is the* absolute number of non-unit meet-rises. *When normalising this value by dividing it by* $|\prec|$ *(the number of covering pairs), one obtains the* relative number of non-unit meet-rises. *We will abuse the notation by using* $nur_\wedge(\boldsymbol{L})$ *also for the latter, whenever this is clear from the context.* $nur_\vee(\boldsymbol{L})$*, the* (absolute and relative) number of non-unit join-rises *is defined dually.*

The following Lemma follows directly from Theorem 8. It summarizes the relationship between the $nur_\wedge(\boldsymbol{L})$ and the $nur_\vee(\boldsymbol{L})$ and the different forms of distributivity.

Lemma 16. *A finite lattice* $\boldsymbol{L}$ *is*

- *join-distributive iff* $nur_\wedge(\boldsymbol{L}) = 0\,\%$,
- *meet-distributive iff* $nur_\vee(\boldsymbol{L}) = 0\,\%$*, and*
- *distributive iff* $nur_\wedge(\boldsymbol{L}) = nur_\vee(\boldsymbol{L}) = 0\,\%$.

The lattice is thus '100% distributive' if the relative frequency of the meet- and join-rises that are non-unit is 0%. The more these values deviate from 0%, the 'less distributive' is the lattice.

In [25], R. Wille observed that many real-world concept lattices are (mostly) distributive at the top because "everyday thinking predominantly uses logical inferences with one-element premises", and then abruptly break down at the bottom because of conflicting attributes. While this led Wille to introduce truncated distributive lattices, it inspired us to the following assumption:

Assumption A1. Concept lattices of real-world contexts will show a higher degree of join-distributivity than of meet-distributivity.

If this assumption holds we would expect that $nur_\wedge(\boldsymbol{L}) \leq nur_\vee(\boldsymbol{L})$ in most cases. To this end, we have analysed the non-unit rises of all concept lattices of the FCA context repository[4] [13] (top part of Table 1) and of some further datasets (bottom part of the table). The datasets were not preprocessed and all analysis was conducted using custom Python code. In the table, $\boldsymbol{L}$ is the concept lattice $\mathfrak{B}(\mathbb{K})$ of the context at hand, and $|\prec|$ gives the number of covering pairs in $\boldsymbol{L}$.

First of all, we observe that the only distributive concept lattice in this collection is the one about New Zealand (which is isomorphic to $\{0,1,2,3\} \times$

[3] There are many other, equally interesting ways for measuring non-distributivity, which we do not discuss here. Examples include $|\{(x,y,z) \in \boldsymbol{L}^3 \mid x \vee (y \wedge z) \neq (x \vee y) \wedge (x \vee z)\}|$ (and variations thereof which only count the non-trivial tuples) and $|\{a \in \boldsymbol{L} \mid \exists x, y \in \boldsymbol{L} \colon a \wedge x = a \wedge y, a \vee y = a \vee y, x \neq y\}|$.

[4] https://github.com/fcatools/contexts/tree/main/contexts (visited March 25, 2025).

Table 1. *nur*-values for some real-world datasets

$\mathbb{K}$	$\lvert \boldsymbol{L} \rvert$	$\lvert \prec \rvert$	$nur_\vee(\boldsymbol{L})$		$nur_\wedge(\boldsymbol{L})$	
			abs.	rel.	abs.	rel.
officesupplies	5	5	1	0.20	1	0.20
newzealand	8	10	0	0.00	0	0.00
planets	12	18	5	0.28	5	0.28
bodiesofwater	12	18	6	0.33	1	0.06
famous_animals	13	21	6	0.29	5	0.24
missmarple	13	21	12	0.57	5	0.24
livingbeings	19	32	11	0.34	8	0.25
driveconcepts	24	50	2	0.04	12	0.24
gewässer	28	62	30	0.48	8	0.13
animals	35	66	33	0.50	20	0.30
tealady	65	148	48	0.32	31	0.21
music	163	507	311	0.61	56	0.11
seasoningplanner	532	1593	784	0.49	563	0.35
zoo [10]	4 579	19 076	12 228	0.64	3 451	0.18
wikipedia [17]	14 171	70 732	53 342	0.75	6 161	0.09
students [22]	17 603	80 902	67 439	0.83	5 713	0.07
wiki44k [14,15]	21 923	109 698	91 924	0.84	4 526	0.04
mushroom [1]	238 710	1 370 991	1 318 000	0.96	102 519	0.07

$\{0,1\}$), as it is the only one with $nur_\vee(\boldsymbol{L}) = nur_\wedge(\boldsymbol{L}) = 0$. Then we observe that for all datasets (except the drive concepts), we have indeed $nur_\wedge(\boldsymbol{L}) \leq nur_\vee(\boldsymbol{L})$, supporting our assumption. We assume that the concept lattice on drive concepts behaves differently because it has an atypcial small number of objects (5) for a comparatively large number (25) of attributes.

The larger the lattice, the more pronounced is the effect postulated in A1, as can be seen in Fig. 4. With increasing size of the covering relation, the relative number of non-unit meet-rises is (with very few exceptions) decreasing, while the relative number of non-unit join-rises is with almost no exceptions increasing. The extreme case is the mushroom dataset, whose concept lattice is '96% non-meet-distributive' but only '7% non-join-distributive'.

Coming back to Wille's observation that distributivity breaks down at the bottom of a concept lattice because of inconsistent attribute combinations, we assume that the bottom element of the lattice is particularly prone to generate non-unit meet-rises. Therefore, we analyse the count of non-unit meet-rises on the lowest covering pairs (i. e., those between the bottom element of the lattice and the atoms) in the first row of Table 2. This shows that the concept lattices of real-world datasets exhibit almost exclusively non-unit meet-rises at the very bottom. This comes with no surprise, as a unit-rise would only occur if the object

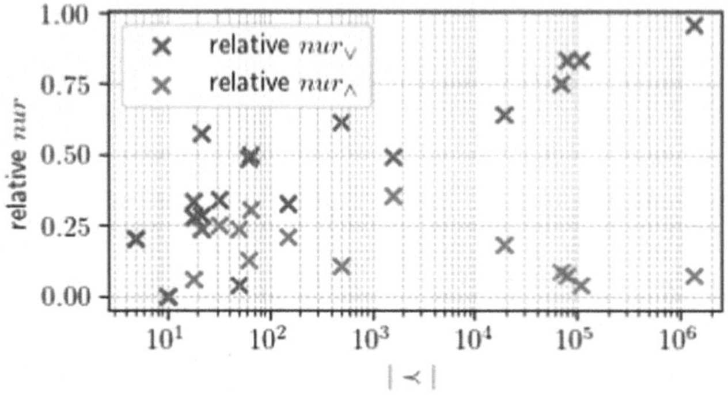

Fig. 4. The plot shows for every lattice its relative $nur_\vee$ (red) and $nur_\wedge$ (blue) values in relation to the size of its covering relation (Color figure online)

Table 2. Relative non-unit rises on the atoms and co-atoms of the concept lattice

	officesupplies	newzealand	planets	bodiesofwater	famous_animals	missmarple	livingbeings	driveconcepts	gewässer	animals	tealady	music	seasoningplanner	zoo	wikipedia	students	wiki44k	mushroom
$nur_\wedge(\boldsymbol{L})$/atoms	$\frac{1}{2}$	$\frac{0}{2}$	$\frac{5}{5}$	$\frac{1}{2}$	$\frac{5}{5}$	$\frac{5}{5}$	$\frac{4}{4}$	$\frac{4}{5}$	$\frac{8}{8}$	$\frac{8}{8}$	$\frac{7}{7}$	$\frac{5}{6}$	$\frac{38}{38}$	$\frac{59}{59}$	$\frac{103}{103}$	$\frac{479}{479}$	$\frac{587}{587}$	$\frac{8124}{8124}$
$nur_\vee(\boldsymbol{L})$/coatoms	$\frac{1}{2}$	$\frac{0}{2}$	$\frac{1}{2}$	$\frac{2}{3}$	$\frac{1}{2}$	$\frac{4}{4}$	$\frac{4}{4}$	$\frac{1}{4}$	$\frac{6}{6}$	$\frac{5}{5}$	$\frac{7}{7}$	$\frac{7}{7}$	$\frac{29}{29}$	$\frac{17}{17}$	$\frac{68}{68}$	$\frac{27}{27}$	$\frac{65}{65}$	$\frac{23}{23}$

that is generating the atom concept at hand has (up to purification) exactly all but one attribute of the formal context which is rarely the case.

The same observation holds for the join-rises between the top-element and the co-atoms of the lattice, as shown in the second row of Table 2. For the ten largest of our datasets (from *gewässer* to *mushroom*), all join-rises between co-atoms and top element are non-unit. This also comes with no real surprise, as a unit join-rise would mean that the attribute that is generating the co-atom under study would match with all objects beside exactly one. However, this effect does not contribute as much to the total count of non-unit join-rises compared to the effect of the atoms to the total count of non-unit meet-rises, as real-world concept lattices tend to be leaner at the top: the wiki44k dataset, for instance, has 587 atoms but only 65 co-atoms, and the mushroom dataset has 8 124 atoms but only 23 co-atoms.

Further insight into the distribution of the non-unit meet-rises is provided by Fig. 5. There we have plotted for all lattices with height 10 or more the distribution of $nur_\wedge$ over the height of the covering pairs in the lattice. (The plots for the smaller lattices look very similar.) The left-most point of each curve corresponds to the 100% entries in Table 2. We observe that the values are then almost everywhere decreasing, which means that the non-join-distributivity in these lattices accumulates towards the bottom of the concept lattice. An extreme case is the mushroom dataset, which is 'join-distributive almost everywhere' with the exception of the atoms of the lattice.

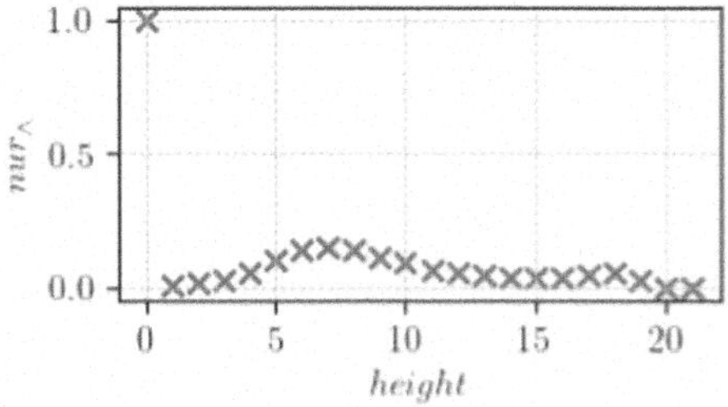

(a) mushroom

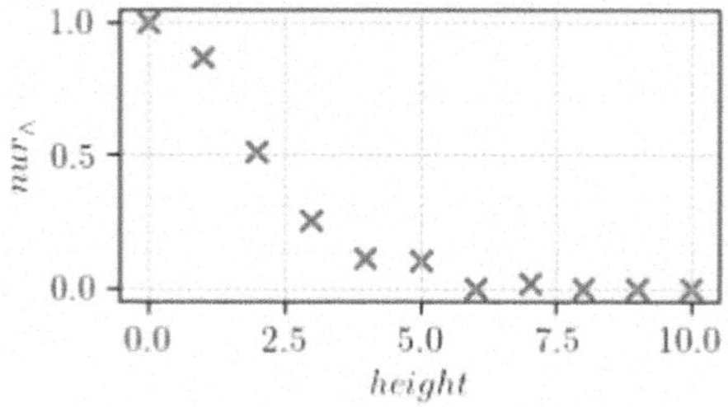

(b) seasoningplanner

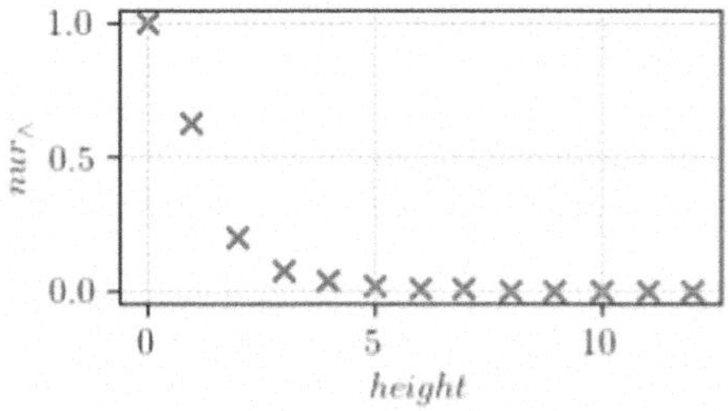

(c) students

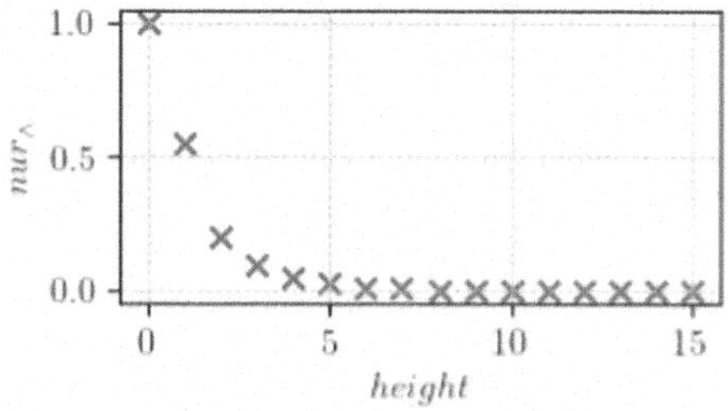

(d) wiki44k

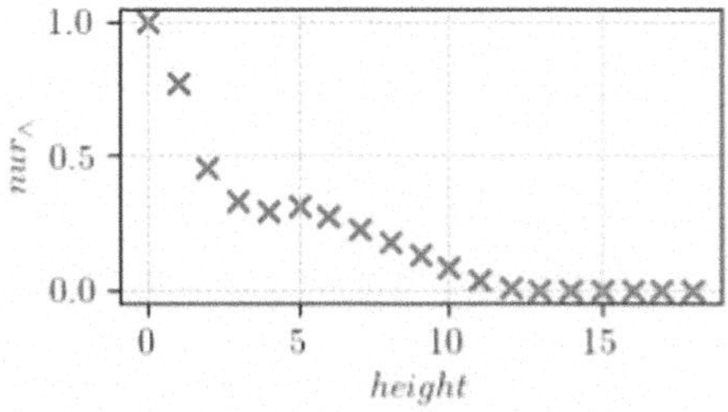

(e) wikipedia

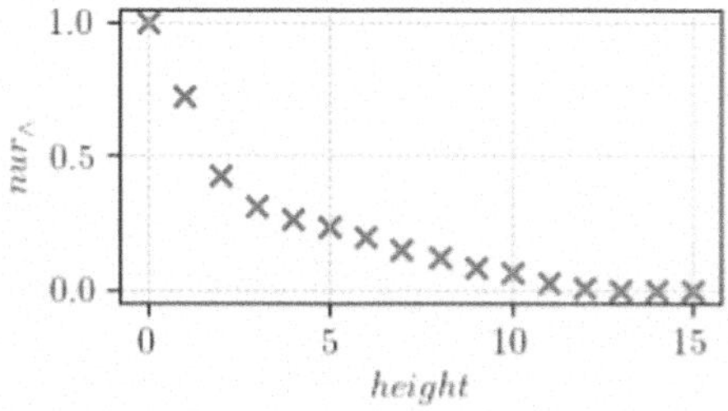

(f) zoo

Fig. 5. Distribution of $nur_\wedge$ over the height for all lattices with height ≥ 10.

6 Conclusion and Future Work

In this paper, we have introduced non-unit rises as indicator and measures for the degree of the presence of local distributivity in (concept) lattices and ordered sets. This opens various lines of research that may at the end lead to algebraic methods for analysing large real-world concept lattices: How can the failure of local distributivity be repaired? How can the result be used for novel drawing algorithms for concept lattices? How can it be exploited for complexity reduction by means of congruence and tolerance relations? Last but not least it is an interesting open question how (join)distributive ordered sets can be defined directly, without the detour via the Dedekind-MacNeille completion.

Acknowledgments. We thank the anonymous reviewers for their valuable comments.

References

1. Mushroom. UCI Machine Learning Repository (1981). https://doi.org/10.24432/C5959T
2. Abdulla, M., Hirth, J., Stumme, G.: The Birkhoff completion of finite lattices. In: Conceptual Knowledge Structures, pp. 20–35. Springer, Cham (2024)
3. Birkhoff, G.: Lattice theory. In: Colloquium Publications, vol. 25. American Mathematical Society, Providence, RI, 3. edn. (1967)
4. Chajda, R.: Forbidden configurations for distributive and modular ordered sets. Order **5**, 407–423 (1989). https://doi.org/10.1007/BF00353659
5. Davey, B.A., Priestley, H.A.: Introduction to Lattices and Order. Cambridge University Press, Cambridge (2002)
6. Dilworth, R.P.: Lattices with Unique Irreducible Decompositions, pp. 93–99. Birkhäuser Boston (1990). https://doi.org/10.1007/978-1-4899-3558-8_10
7. Edelman, P.: Meet-distributive lattices and the anti-exchange closure. Algebra Universalis **10**, 290–299 (1980). https://doi.org/10.1007/BF02482912
8. Edelman, P., Jamison, R.: The theory of convex geometries **19**, 247–270 (1985). https://doi.org/10.1007/BF00149365
9. Falmagne, J.C., Doignon, J.P.: Learning Spaces. Springer, Heidelberg (2010)
10. Forsyth, R.: Zoo. UCI Machine Learning Repository (1990). https://doi.org/10.24432/C5R59V
11. Ganter, B., Wille, R.: Formal Concept Analysis, 2nd edn. Springer, Cham (2024). https://doi.org/10.1007/978-3-031-63422-2
12. Halaš, R.: Pseudocomplemented ordered sets. Archivum Mathematicum **029**(3-4), 153–160 (1993)
13. Hanika, T., Jäschke, R.: A repository for formal contexts. In: Conceptual Knowledge Structures, pp. 182–197. Springer, Cham (2024)
14. Hanika, T., Marx, M., Stumme, G.: Discovering implicational knowledge in Wikidata. In: Cristea, D., Le Ber, F., Sertkaya, B. (eds.) ICFCA 2019. LNCS (LNAI), vol. 11511, pp. 315–323. Springer, Cham (2019). https://doi.org/10.1007/978-3-030-21462-3_21
15. Ho, V.T., Stepanova, D., Gad-Elrab, M.H., Kharlamov, E., Weikum, G.: Rule learning from knowledge graphs guided by embedding models. In: Vrandečić, D., et al. (eds.) ISWC 2018. LNCS, vol. 11136, pp. 72–90. Springer, Cham (2018). https://doi.org/10.1007/978-3-030-00671-6_5
16. Korte, B., Schrader, R., Lovász, L.: Abstract Convexity – Antimatroids. In: Greedoids. Algorithms and Combinatorics, vol. 4, pp. 19–43. Springer, Heidelberg (1991). https://doi.org/10.1007/978-3-642-58191-5_3

17. Kunegis, J.: Konect: the koblenz network collection. In: Proceedings of the 22nd International Conference on World Wide Web, pp. 1343–1350 (2013)
18. Larmerová, J., Rachůnek, J.: Translations of distributive and modular ordered sets. Acta Universitatis Palackianae Olomucensis. Facultas Rerum Naturalium. Mathematica **27**(1), 13–23 (1988). http://eudml.org/doc/23469
19. Monjardet, B.: A use for frequently rediscovering a concept. Order **1**, 415–417 (1985). https://doi.org/10.1007/BF00582748
20. Mühle, H.: Meet-distributive lattices have the intersection property. Mathematica Bohemica **148**(1), 95–104 (2023). https://doi.org/10.21136/MB.2022.0072-21
21. Roman, S.: Lattices and Ordered Sets. Springer, New York (2008). https://doi.org/10.1007/978-0-387-78901-9
22. Seshapanpu, J.: Students performance in exams (2018). https://www.kaggle.com/spscientist/students-performance-in-exams
23. Stern, M.: From Boolean Algebras to Semimodular Lattices, p. 1–72. Encyclopedia of Mathematics and its Applications, Cambridge University Press (1999)
24. Wild, M.: Compressed representation of learning spaces. J. Math. Psychol. **79**, 64–76 (2017). https://doi.org/10.1016/j.jmp.2017.02.002
25. Wille, R.: Truncated distributive lattices: conceptual structures of simple-implicational theories. Order **20**(3), 229–238 (2003). https://doi.org/10.1023/B:ORDE.0000026494.22248.85

A Stone Duality for Pure and Trivial Double Boolean Algebras

Gael Tenkeu Kembang[1], Michel Krebs[2], Leonard Kwuida[2](✉), Etienne Romuald Temgoua Alomo[3], and Yannick Lea Tenkeu Jeufack[1]

[1] Department of Mathematics, University of Yaounde 1, Yaounde, Cameroon
[2] School of Business, Bern University of Applied Sciences, Bern, Switzerland
{michel.krebs,leonard.kwuida}@bfh.ch
[3] Department of Mathematics, University of Yaounde 1, Ecole Normale Supérieure, Yaounde, Cameroon

Abstract. This work provides a topological representation for the class of pure and trivial double Boolean algebras and uses it to show that the category of pure and trivial double Boolean algebras and the category of pure and trivial double Boolean spaces are categorically anti-equivalent.

Keywords: Double Boolean algebra · Topological space · Boolean space · duality

1 Introduction

In 2000, Rudolf Wille [12] introduced logical Boolean concepts as a mathematical theory based on formal concept analysis. The concept lattice is enriched by two new operations; a negation and an opposition, which then lead to a new class of algebras, called double Boolean algebras, which models the algebra of protoconcepts. The class of Boolean algebras is a sub-class of the class of double Boolean algebras. Each protoconcept is a concept generator so that each concept is a representative of a class of protoconcepts for a given context. The study of double Boolean algebras will lead to a better understanding of protoconcept algebras and hence formal concepts that have application in computer sciences and data analysis. Several investigations of double Boolean algebras have since been carried out, as documented in [4,5,7,9,11]. A double Boolean algebra is an algebra $\underline{D} := (D; \sqcap, \sqcup, \neg, \lrcorner, \bot, \top)$ of type $(2, 2, 1, 1, 0, 0)$ verifying twenty three identities (Definition 1). A double Boolean algebra is said trivial if $\bot \sqcup \bot = \top \sqcap \top$. The class of trivial double Boolean algebras is a sub-variety of the variety of double Boolean algebras. This sub-variety plays an important role in construction of double Boolean algebras; more precisely, several double Boolean algebras are obtained as the product of trivial double Boolean algebras with Boolean algebras. It would therefore be interesting to fully understand the variety of trivial double Boolean algebras. This work contributes to this framework by establishing a topological representation for the class of pure and trivial double Boolean

P. Cellier et al. (Eds.): CONCEPTS 2025, LNAI 15941, pp. 408–422, 2025.
https://doi.org/10.1007/978-3-032-03364-2_26

algebras. We then use this topological representation to show that the category of pure and trivial double Boolean algebras and the category of pure and trivial double Boolean spaces (concatenation of two disjoint Boolean spaces) are categorically anti-equivalent.

Our work is organized as follows. Section 2 recalls some basic notions from Boolean algebras and double Boolean algebras, necessary for understanding our contribution. In Sect. 3, we establish a Stone duality for the class of pure and trivial double Boolean algebras. Finally, some perspectives for further research are discussed in the last Section.

2 Preliminaries

We recall some basic notions from topology that can be found in [2]. A **topology** τ on a set X is a family of subsets of X containing $\emptyset$ and X, closed under arbitrary unions and finite intersections. A **topological space** is a pair (X, τ), where X is a set and τ a topology on X. Let (X, τ) be a topological space. The elements of τ are called **open sets** of (X, τ) and the elements of X are called **points** of (X, τ). The complement of an open set of (X, τ) is called **closed set**. We will denote a topological space (X, τ) simply by X. A **base** or **basis** of a topology τ on a set X is any family $\mathcal{B}$ of open sets such that every open set of X is a union of elements of $\mathcal{B}$. Let x be a point of a topological space X. A **neighborhood** of x is any subset $\mathcal{U}$ of X that contains an open set that contains x. A **Hausdorff space or separated space** is a topological space in which different points have disjoint neighborhoods. An open cover of a topological space X is a family $\{U_i\}_{i\in I}$ of open sets such that $X = \underset{i\in I}{U_i}$. Let $\{U_i\}_{i\in I}$ be an open cover of a topological space X. A sub-cover of $\{U_i\}_{i\in I}$ is a subset of $\{U_i\}_{i\in I}$ that still covers X. A topological space X is said to be **compact** if every open cover of X contains a finite sub-cover. A map $f\colon (X, \tau) \to (Y, \sigma)$ between two topological spaces is **continuous** if for all $O \in \sigma$, $f^{-1}(O) \in \tau$. A **homeomorphism** between two topological spaces is a continuous bijection with continuous inverse. A topological space is a **Boolean space** if it is Hausdorff, compact, and has a basis of clopen (i.e. both closed and open) subsets.

Let $\underline{B} := (B; \wedge, \vee, {}', 0, 1)$ be a Boolean algebra. A subset F of B is called **filter** if $1 \in F$ and for all $x, y \in B$: $x, y \in F \implies x \wedge y \in F$, and $(x \in F, x \leq y) \implies y \in F$. The notion of **ideal** is defined dually. The set of all filters of $\underline{B}$ is denoted by $\mathcal{F}(\underline{B})$. A filter F is called **prime filter** if $0 \notin F$ and for all $x, y \in B$, $x \vee y \in F \Rightarrow x \in F$ or $y \in F$. The set of all prime filters of $\underline{B}$ is denoted by $\mathcal{F}_{pr}(\underline{B})$. Define $\underline{B}^*$ to be the topological space whose underlying set is the collection $\mathcal{F}_{pr}(\underline{B})$ of prime filters of $\underline{B}$ and whose topology has a basis consisting of all sets of the form $V(a) := \{F \in B^* : a \in F\}$ for $a \in B$. If X is a topological space, let X^* be the sub-Boolean algebra of $\underline{P}(X)$ whose universe the collection of clopen subsets of X.

The following proposition is the topological representation for Boolean algebras which was proved by *M. Stone* in [8]. In this paper, we use the notation and the version given in [1].

Proposition 1. *1. Let $\underline{B}$ be a Boolean algebra. Then $\underline{B}^*$ is a Boolean space, and $\underline{B}$ is isomorphic to $\underline{B}^{**}$ under the mapping $\mathcal{V}_B \colon B \to B^{**}, x \mapsto V(x)$.*
2. Let X be a Boolean space. Then X^* is a Boolean algebra, and X is homeomorphic to X^{**} under the mapping $\Theta_X \colon X \to X^{**}, x \mapsto \{K \in X^* : x \in K\}$.

Lemma 1. [1]

1. *If $\varphi \colon A \to B$ is a Boolean algebra homomorphism, then the map $\varphi^* \colon B^* \to A^*$, $U \mapsto \varphi^{-1}(U)$ is continuous and satisfies $(\varphi^*)^{-1}(V(a)) = V(\varphi(a))$ for all $a \in A$.*
2. *If $f \colon X \to Y$ is a continuous map between Boolean spaces, then the map $f^* \colon Y^* \to X^*$, $K \mapsto f^{-1}(K)$ is a Boolean algebra homomorphism and satisfies $(f^*)^{-1}(\Theta_X(x)) = \Theta_Y(f(x))$ for all $x \in X$.*

Now we recall some notions from category theory see [6] useful in presenting our results. A **category** $\mathcal{C}$ consists of the following three entities:

- A class $ob(\mathcal{C})$, whose elements are called objects;
- A class $hom(\mathcal{C})$, whose elements are called morphisms. Each morphism f has a source object X and a target object Y. The expression $f \colon X \to Y$ would be verbally stated as "f is a morphism from X to Y". The expression $hom_{\mathcal{C}}(X, Y)$ denotes the *hom*-class of all morphisms from X to Y.
- A binary operation $\circ$, called composition of morphisms, such that for any three objects X, Y and Z, we have

$$\circ \colon hom_{\mathcal{C}}(Y, Z) \times hom_{\mathcal{C}}(X, Y) \to hom_{\mathcal{C}}(X, Z)$$

  governed by two axioms:
  - Associativity: If $f \colon X \to Y$, $g \colon Y \to Z$ and $h \colon Z \to T$, then

$$h \circ (g \circ f) = (h \circ g) \circ f;$$

  - Identity: For every object X, there exists a morphism $id_X : X \to X$, called the identity morphism for X, such that for every morphism $f \colon X \to Y$, we have

$$id_Y \circ f = f \circ id_X.$$

The opposite category $\mathcal{C}^{op}$ of a given category $\mathcal{C}$ is formed by reversing the morphisms, i.e., interchanging the source and the target of each morphism.

Let $\mathcal{C}$ and $\mathcal{D}$ be two categories. A **covariant functor** F from $\mathcal{C}$ to $\mathcal{D}$ is a mapping that associates each object X in $\mathcal{C}$ to an object $F(X)$ in $\mathcal{D}$ and each morphism $f \colon X \to Y$ in $\mathcal{C}$ to a morphism $F(f) \colon F(X) \to F(Y)$ in $\mathcal{D}$ such that:

(i) $F(id_X) = id_{F(X)}$ for every object X in $\mathcal{C}$,

(ii) $F(g \circ f) = F(g) \circ F(f)$ for all morphisms $X \xrightarrow{f} Y \xrightarrow{g} Z$ in $\mathcal{C}$.

A **contravariant functor** from $\mathcal{C}$ to $\mathcal{D}$ is a functor from $\mathcal{C}$ to $\mathcal{D}^{op}$.

If F and G are covariant functors between the categories $\mathcal{C}$ and $\mathcal{D}$, then a **natural transformation** η from F to G is a family of morphisms in $\mathcal{D}$ that satisfies two requirements:

(a) The natural transformation must associate, to every object X in $\mathcal{C}$, a morphism $\eta_X : F(X) \to G(X)$ between objects of $\mathcal{D}$. The morphism η_X is called the component of η at X.
(b) Components must be such that for every morphism $f \colon X \to Y$ in $\mathcal{C}$ we have $\eta_Y \circ F(f) = G(f) \circ \eta_X$.

This last equation can be conveniently expressed by the following commutative diagram:

$$\begin{array}{ccc} F(X) & \xrightarrow{\eta_X} & G(X) \\ {\scriptstyle F(f)}\downarrow & & \downarrow{\scriptstyle G(f)} \\ F(Y) & \xrightarrow[\eta_Y]{} & G(Y) \end{array}$$

If for every object X in $\mathcal{C}$, the morphism η_X is an isomorphism in $\mathcal{D}$, then η is said to be a **natural isomorphism**. Two categories $\mathcal{C}$ and $\mathcal{D}$ are **equivalent** if there exists $F \colon \mathcal{C} \to \mathcal{D}$ and $G \colon \mathcal{D} \to \mathcal{C}$ two covariant functors, and two natural isomorphisms $\varepsilon \colon F \circ G \to id_{\mathcal{D}}$ and $\eta \colon id_{\mathcal{C}} \to G \circ F$.

We end this section by recalling some basic notions on double Boolean algebras. For further information, the reader can see [5,11,13].

Definition 1 [13]. *An algebra* $\underline{D} := (D; \sqcap, \sqcup, \neg, \lrcorner, \bot, \top)$ *of type* $(2, 2, 1, 1, 0, 0)$ *is called* ***double Boolean algebra (dBa)*** *if the following axioms are satisfied:*

$(1a)\ (x \sqcap x) \sqcap y = x \sqcap y$	$(1b)\ (x \sqcup x) \sqcup y = x \sqcup y$
$(2a)\ x \sqcap y = y \sqcap x$	$(2b)\ x \sqcup y = y \sqcup x$
$(3a)\ x \sqcap (y \sqcap z) = (x \sqcap y) \sqcap z$	$(3b)\ x \sqcup (y \sqcup z) = (x \sqcup y) \sqcup z$
$(4a)\ x \sqcap (x \sqcup y) = x \sqcap x$	$(4b)\ x \sqcup (x \sqcap y) = x \sqcup x$
$(5a)\ x \sqcap (x \vee y) = x \sqcap x$	$(5b)\ x \sqcup (x \wedge y) = x \sqcup x$
$(6a)\ x \sqcap (y \vee z) = (x \sqcap y) \vee (x \sqcap z)$	$(6b)\ x \sqcup (y \wedge z) = (x \sqcup y) \wedge (x \sqcup z)$
$(7a)\ \neg\neg(x \sqcap y) = x \sqcap y$	$(7b)\ \lrcorner\lrcorner(x \sqcup y) = x \sqcup y$
$(8a)\ \neg(x \sqcap x) = \neg x$	$(8b)\ \lrcorner(x \sqcup x) = \lrcorner x$
$(9a)\ x \sqcap \neg x = \bot$	$(9b)\ x \sqcup \lrcorner x = \top$
$(10a)\ \neg\bot = \top \sqcap \top$	$(10b)\ \lrcorner\top = \bot \sqcup \bot$
$(11a)\ \neg\top = \bot$	$(11b)\ \lrcorner\bot = \top$

$$(12)\ (x \sqcap x) \sqcup (x \sqcap x) = (x \sqcup x) \sqcap (x \sqcup x)$$

where $x \vee y = \neg(\neg x \sqcap \neg y)$ *and* $x \wedge y = \lrcorner(\lrcorner x \sqcup \lrcorner y)$

On a double Boolean algebra $\underline{D}$, a quasi-order relation $\sqsubseteq$ is defined as follows: $x \sqsubseteq y :\Longleftrightarrow x \sqcap y = x \sqcap x$ and $x \sqcup y = y \sqcup y$. A double Boolean algebra $\underline{D}$ is called : **pure** if for all $x \in D$, $x \sqcap x = x$ or $x \sqcup x = x$, **trivial** if $\top \sqcap \top = \bot \sqcup \bot$ and **regular** if "$\sqsubseteq$" is an order [5,13]. For a double Boolean algebra $\underline{D}$, we set $D_{\sqcap} := \{x \in D \mid x \sqcap x = x\}$, $D_{\sqcup} := \{x \in D \mid x \sqcup x = x\}$, $D_p := D_{\sqcap} \cup D_{\sqcup}$. The algebra $\underline{D}_{\sqcap} := (D_{\sqcap}; \sqcap, \vee, \neg, \bot, \neg\bot)$ (resp. $\underline{D}_{\sqcup} := (D_{\sqcup}; \wedge, \sqcup, \lrcorner, \lrcorner\top, \top)$) is a Boolean algebra whose order relation is the restriction of $\sqsubseteq$ to $\underline{D}_{\sqcap}$ (resp. $\underline{D}_{\sqcup}$). [13]

Example 1. 1. **Algebra of protoconcepts**: Let $\mathbb{K} := (G, M, I)$ be a triple of sets with $I \subseteq G \times M$. For $A \subseteq G$ and $B \subseteq M$, define

$$A' := \{m \in M \mid (a, m) \in I, \forall a \in A\} \text{ and } B' := \{g \in G \mid (g, b) \in I, \forall b \in B\}.$$

A **protoconcept** of $\mathbb{K}$ is a pair (A, B) such that $A'' = B'$. Logical operations are defined on the set $\mathfrak{P}(\mathbb{K})$ of protoconcepts of $\mathbb{K}$ as follows:

$$\begin{array}{rcl} \textbf{meet}: (A,B) \sqcap (C,D) & := & (A \cap C, (A \cap C)') \\ \textbf{join}: (A,B) \sqcup (C,D) & := & ((B \cap D)', B \cap D) \\ \textbf{negation}: \quad \neg(A,B) & := & (G \setminus A, (G \setminus A)') \\ \textbf{opposition}: \quad \lrcorner(A,B) & := & ((M \setminus B)', M \setminus B) \\ \textbf{nothing}: \quad \bot & := & (\emptyset, M) \\ \textbf{all}: \quad \top & := & (G, \emptyset) \end{array}$$

Then $\underline{\mathfrak{P}}(\mathbb{K}) := (\mathfrak{P}(\mathbb{K}); \sqcap, \sqcup, \neg, \lrcorner, \bot, \top)$ is a regular double Boolean algebra. $\underline{\mathfrak{P}}(\mathbb{K})_{\sqcap}$ (resp. $\underline{\mathfrak{P}}(\mathbb{K})_{\sqcup}$) is isomorphic (resp. dual isomorphic) to the powerset algebra of G (resp. M).

2. The algebra $\underline{D}_3 := (\{\bot, a, \top\}; \sqcap, \sqcup, \neg, \lrcorner, \bot, \top)$ defined by the Hasse diagram and the Cayley tables in Fig. 1 is a **pure and trivial dBa**. Moreover $D_{3_{\sqcap}} = \{\bot, a\}$ and $D_{3_{\sqcup}} = \{a, \top\}$.

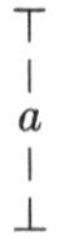

$\sqcap$	$\bot$	a	$\top$
$\bot$	$\bot$	$\bot$	$\bot$
a	$\bot$	a	a
$\top$	$\bot$	a	a

$\sqcup$	$\bot$	a	$\top$
$\bot$	a	a	$\top$
a	a	a	$\top$
$\top$	$\top$	$\top$	$\top$

x	$\bot$	a	$\top$
$\neg x$	a	$\bot$	$\bot$
$\lrcorner x$	$\top$	$\top$	a

Fig. 1. $\underline{D}_3$ and its Cayley tables

3. The algebra $\underline{D}_7 := (\{\bot, a, b, c, d, e, \top\}; \sqcap, \sqcup, \neg, \lrcorner, \bot, \top)$ defined by the Hasse diagram and the Cayley tables in Fig. 2 is a **pure and trivial dBa**. Moreover $D_{7_{\sqcap}} = \{\bot, a, b, e\}$ and $D_{7_{\sqcup}} = \{e, c, d, \top\}$.
4. The algebra $\underline{D}_4 := (\{\bot, a, b, \top\}; \sqcap, \sqcup, \neg, \lrcorner, \bot, \top)$ defined by the Hasse diagram and the Cayley tables in Fig. 3 is a **non-pure and trivial dBa**. Moreover $D_{4_{\sqcap}} = \{\bot,$ a$\}$ and $D_{4_{\sqcup}} = \{a, \top\}$.

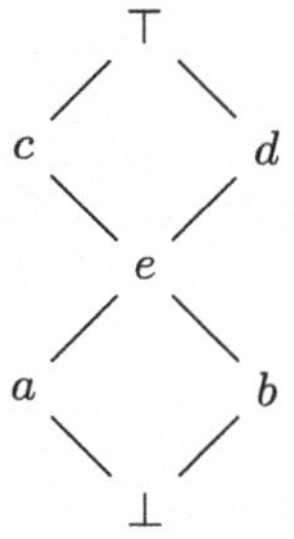

$\sqcap$	$\bot$	a	b	e	c	d	$\top$
$\bot$	$\bot$	$\bot$	$\bot$	$\bot$	$\bot$	$\bot$	$\bot$
a	$\bot$	a	$\bot$	a	a	a	a
b	$\bot$	$\bot$	b	b	b	b	b
e	$\bot$	a	b	e	e	e	e
c	$\bot$	a	b	e	e	e	e
d	$\bot$	a	b	e	e	e	e
$\top$	$\bot$	a	b	e	e	e	e

$\sqcup$	$\bot$	a	b	e	c	d	$\top$
$\bot$	e	e	e	e	c	d	$\top$
a	e	e	e	e	c	d	$\top$
b	e	e	e	e	c	d	$\top$
e	e	e	e	e	c	d	$\top$
c	c	c	c	c	c	$\top$	$\top$
d	d	d	d	d	$\top$	d	$\top$
$\top$	$\top$	$\top$	$\top$	$\top$	$\top$	$\top$	$\top$

x	$\bot$	a	b	e	c	d	$\top$
$\neg x$	e	b	a	$\bot$	$\bot$	$\bot$	$\bot$
$\lrcorner x$	$\top$	$\top$	$\top$	$\top$	d	c	e

Fig. 2. $\underline{D}_7$ and its Cayley tables

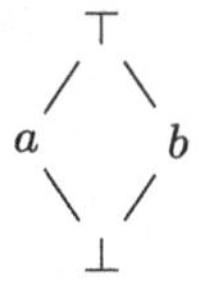

$\sqcap$	$\bot$	a	b	$\top$
$\bot$	$\bot$	$\bot$	$\bot$	$\bot$
a	$\bot$	a	$\bot$	a
b	$\bot$	$\bot$	$\bot$	$\bot$
$\top$	$\bot$	a	$\bot$	a

$\sqcup$	$\bot$	a	b	$\top$
$\bot$	a	a	$\top$	$\top$
a	a	a	$\top$	$\top$
b	$\top$	$\top$	$\top$	$\top$
$\top$	$\top$	$\top$	$\top$	$\top$

x	$\bot$	a	b	$\top$
$\neg x$	a	$\bot$	a	$\bot$
$\lrcorner x$	$\top$	$\top$	a	a

Fig. 3. $\underline{D}_4$ and its Cayley tables

The **ordinal sum** of two disjoint posets $(P; \leq_P)$ and $(Q; \leq_Q)$ is the poset $(P \cup Q; \leq)$ with $\leq := \leq_P \cup \leq_Q \cup P \times Q$. We denote it by $P \oplus Q$. If $(P; \leq_P)$ has a greatest element, say 1_P, and $(Q; \leq_Q)$ has a least element, say 0_Q, then the **glued sum** is obtained by identifying 1_P and 0_Q [3]. We will denote the glued sum of $(P; \leq_p, 1_P)$ and $(Q; \leq_Q, 0_Q)$ by $P \dot{\oplus} Q$. The following proposition shows how to construct pure and trivial dBas from the glued sum of two Boolean algebras.

Proposition 2 [4, *Theorem 3.5*]. *A double Boolean algebra is a pure and trivial dBa if and only if it is a glued sum of two Boolean algebras.*

The following proposition shows that homomorphisms (resp. monomorphisms, isomorphisms) between two pure and trivial dBas $\underline{D}$ and $\underline{E}$ are determined by homomorphisms (resp. monomorphisms, isomorphisms) between Boolean algebras $\underline{D}_\sqcap$ and $\underline{E}_\sqcap$, $\underline{D}_\sqcup$ and $\underline{E}_\sqcup$.

Proposition 3 [10, *Corollary 4.7*]. *A double Boolean algebra morphism (resp. monomorphism, isomorphism) from a pure and trivial double Boolean algebra* $\underline{D}$ *to a pure and trivial double Boolean algebra* $\underline{E}$ *is a map* $f\colon D \to E$ *of the form*

$$f(x) = \begin{cases} f_1(x) \text{ if } x \in D_\sqcap \\ f_2(x) \text{ if } x \in D_\sqcup \end{cases}$$

where $f_1\colon D_\sqcap \to E_\sqcap$ *and* $f_2\colon D_\sqcup \to E_\sqcup$ *are Boolean algebra morphisms (resp. monomorphisms, isomorphisms).*

We can now present our results.

3 Topological Representation of Pure and Trivial Double Boolean Algebras

For any Boolean algebra $\underline{B} := (B; \wedge, \vee, ', 0, 1)$, we denote by $\overline{B}$ its dual, that is $\overline{B} := (B; \vee, \wedge, ', 1, 0)$.

Let $\underline{D}$ be a pure and trivial dBa. For $a \in D$, set

$V(a) := \{F \in \mathcal{F}_{pr}(\overline{D_\sqcap}) : a \in F\}$ if $a \in D_\sqcap$ and $V(a) := \{F \in \mathcal{F}_{pr}(\underline{D_\sqcup}) : a \in F\}$ if $a \in D_\sqcup$. We have $V(\perp) = \mathcal{F}_{pr}(\overline{D_\sqcap})$, $V(\top) = \mathcal{F}_{pr}(\underline{D_\sqcup})$ and $V(\top \sqcap \top) = V(\perp \sqcup \perp) = \emptyset$. Note that if $a \in D_\sqcap \cap D_\sqcup$, then $a = \perp \sqcup \perp = \top \sqcap \top$, since D is pure and trivial.

Definition 2 [1]**.** *Given two disjoint topological spaces X_1 and X_2, we define the union of X_1 and X_2 to be the topological space whose underlying set is $X_1 \cup X_2$ and whose open sets are precisely the subsets of the form $O_1 \cup O_2$ where O_i is open in X_i, $1 \leq i \leq 2$.*

Let X_1 and X_2 be two disjoint sets. We define on $X_1 \cup X_2$ an order relation $\leq_{12}$ as follows:

If $x, y \in X_1$ or $x, y \in X_2$, then $x \leq_{12} y :\Longleftrightarrow x = y$; if $x \in X_1$ and $y \in X_2$, then $x \leq_{12} y$. In this case, we write $X_1 \leq_{12} X_2$. This order allows us to indicate in which order the sets X_1 and X_2 are glued or concatenated.

Given two disjoint topological spaces X_1 and X_2, we denote by $X_1 \bowtie X_2$ the ordered union of X_1 and X_2 in which $X_1 \leq_{12} X_2$. We also call $X_1 \bowtie X_2$ the join or concatenation of X_1 and X_2.

Definition 3. *A topological space X is called* ***pure and trivial double Boolean space*** *if $X = X_1 \bowtie X_2$, where X_1 and X_2 are disjoint Boolean spaces.*

The following lemma is a direct consequence of Definition 3.

Lemma 2. *Let $X = X_1 \bowtie X_2$ and $Y = Y_1 \bowtie Y_2$ be two pure and trivial double Boolean spaces. The maps $f_1 \colon X_1 \to Y_1$ and $f_2 \colon X_2 \to Y_2$ are continuous (resp. homeomorphisms) if and only if the map*

$$f \colon X \to Y, x \mapsto f(x) := \begin{cases} f_1(x) \text{ if } x \in X_1 \\ f_2(x) \text{ if } x \in X_2 \end{cases}$$

is continuous (resp. a homeomorphism).

Definition 4. *1. Let $\underline{D}$ be a pure and trivial dBa. Define $\underline{D}^* := \overline{D}_\sqcap^* \bowtie \underline{D}_\sqcup^*$.*

2. Let $X = X_1 \bowtie X_2$ be a pure and trivial double Boolean space. Let X_1^* (resp. X_2^*) denote the sub-algebra of the Boolean algebra $\overline{P}(X_1)$ (resp. $\underline{P}(X_2)$) whose universe is the collection of clopen subsets of X_1 (resp. X_2). Define $X^* = X_1^* \dot{\oplus} X_2^*$.

Theorem 1 ***(Topological representation for pure and trivial dBas).***

1. *Let $\underline{D}$ be a pure and trivial dBa. Then $\underline{D}^*$ is a pure and trivial double Boolean space. $\underline{D}$ is isomorphic to $\underline{D}^{**}$ under the mapping $\mathcal{V}_D\colon D \to D^{**}, x \mapsto V(x)$.*
2. *Let $X = X_1 \bowtie X_2$ be a pure and trivial double Boolean space. Then X^* is a pure and trivial double Boolean algebra. X is homeomorphic to X^{**} under the mapping $\Theta_X\colon X \to X^{**}, x \mapsto \{K \in X^* : x \in K\}$.*

Proof. 1. By definition, $\underline{D}^* = \overline{D}_\sqcap^* \bowtie \underline{D}_\sqcup^*$; moreover $\overline{D}_\sqcap^*$ and $\underline{D}_\sqcup^*$ are disjoint Boolean spaces (by Proposition 1), hence $\underline{D}^*$ is a pure and trivial double Boolean space. Let us show that $\underline{D}^{**}$ is a pure and trivial double Boolean algebra. By Proposition 1, $\overline{D}_\sqcap^{**}$ and $\underline{D}_\sqcup^{**}$ are Boolean algebras such that $1_{\overline{D}_\sqcap^{**}} = 0_{\underline{D}_\sqcup^{**}}$. Thus $\underline{D}^{**} = \overline{D}_\sqcap^{**} \dot{\oplus} \underline{D}_\sqcup^{**}$ is a pure and trivial double Boolean algebra (by Proposition 2). Now we show that $\mathcal{V}_D$ is a pure and trivial dBa isomorphism. The maps $\mathcal{V}_{D_\sqcap}\colon D_\sqcap \to D_\sqcap^{**}, x \mapsto V(x)$ and $\mathcal{V}_{D_\sqcup}\colon D_\sqcup \to D_\sqcup^{**}, x \longmapsto V(x)$ are Boolean algebra isomorphisms (by Proposition 1) and

$$\mathcal{V}_D\colon D \to D^{**}, x \mapsto \mathcal{V}_D(x) = \begin{cases} \mathcal{V}_{D_\sqcap}(x) \text{ if } x \in D_\sqcap \\ \mathcal{V}_{D_\sqcup}(x) \text{ if } x \in D_\sqcup \end{cases}$$

$\mathcal{V}_D$ is by Proposition 3, a pure and trivial dBa isomorphism.

2. By definition, $X^* = X_1^* \dot{\oplus} X_2^*$ and X_1^* and X_2^* are Boolean algebras (by Proposition 1) such that $1_{X_1^*} = 0_{X_2^*}$. Hence X^* is a glued sum of X_1^* and X_2^*, thus by Proposition 2, X^* is a pure and trivial double Boolean algebra. Let us show that X^{**} is a pure and trivial double Boolean space. By Proposition 1, X_1^{**} and X_2^{**} are Boolean spaces and $X_1^{**} \cap X_2^{**} = \emptyset$. Thus $X^{**} = X_1^{**} \bowtie X_2^{**}$ is a pure and trivial double Boolean space. Now we show that Θ_X is a homeomorphism. The maps $\Theta_{X_1}\colon X_1 \to X_1^{**}, x \mapsto \{K \in X_1^* : x \in K\}$ and $\Theta_{X_2}\colon X_2 \to X_2^{**}, x \mapsto \{K \in X_2^* : x \in K\}$ are homeomorphisms (by Proposition 1) and

$$\Theta_X\colon X \to X^{**} : x \mapsto \Theta_X(x) = \begin{cases} \Theta_{X_1}(x) \text{ if } x \in X_1 \\ \Theta_{X_2}(x) \text{ if } x \in X_2 \end{cases}$$

Θ_X is by Lemma 2, a homeomorphism. ■

Now we illustrate this topological representation by concrete examples.

Example 2. 1. We start with the trivial dBa $\underline{D}_3$ of Example 1. Since $\underline{D}_3$ is trivial, $a = \top \sqcap \top = \bot \sqcup \bot$.

$$\underline{D}_3^* = \overline{D}_{3_\sqcap}^* \bowtie \underline{D}_{3_\sqcup}^*.$$

♦ $\overline{D}_{3_\sqcap}^*$ is the topological space whose underlying set is the collection $\mathcal{F}_{pr}(\overline{D}_{3_\sqcap})$ of all prime filters of $\overline{D}_{3_\sqcap}$ and whose topology τ_1 has a basis consisting of all sets of the form $V(x) = \{F \in \mathcal{F}_{pr}(\overline{D}_{3_\sqcap}) : x \in F\}$.
$\mathcal{F}_{pr}(\overline{D}_{3_\sqcap}) = \{\{\bot\}\}$, $V(\bot) = \mathcal{F}_{pr}(\overline{D}_{3_\sqcap})$, $V(\top \sqcap \top) = \emptyset$ and $\tau_1 = \{\emptyset, \mathcal{F}_{pr}(\overline{D}_{3_\sqcap})\}$.

♦ $\underline{D}^*_{3_\sqcup}$ is the topological space whose underlying set is the collection $\mathcal{F}_{pr}(\underline{D}_{3_\sqcup})$ of all prime filters of $\underline{D}_{3_\sqcup}$ and whose topology τ_2 has a basis consisting of all sets of the form $V(x) = \{F \in \mathcal{F}_{pr}(\underline{D}_{3_\sqcup}) : x \in F\}$.
$\mathcal{F}_{pr}(\underline{D}_{3_\sqcup}) = \{\{\top\}\}$, $V(\top) = \mathcal{F}_{pr}(\underline{D}_{3_\sqcup})$, $V(\top \sqcap \top) = \emptyset$ and $\tau_2 = \{\emptyset, \mathcal{F}_{pr}(\underline{D}_{3_\sqcup})\}$.
Finally, the underlying set of $\underline{D}^*_3$ is $\mathcal{F}_{pr}(\overline{D}_{3_\sqcap}) \cup \mathcal{F}_{pr}(\underline{D}_{3_\sqcup}) = \{\{\bot\}, \{\top\}\}$ and the topology τ of $\underline{D}^*_3$ is $\tau = \{\emptyset, \mathcal{F}_{pr}(\overline{D}_{3_\sqcap}), \mathcal{F}_{pr}(\underline{D}_{3_\sqcup}), \mathcal{F}_{pr}(\overline{D}_{3_\sqcap}) \cup \mathcal{F}_{pr}(\underline{D}_{3_\sqcup})\}$.
Now we evaluate $\underline{D}^{**}_3$.

$$\underline{D}^{**}_3 = \overline{D}^{**}_{3_\sqcap} \dot{\oplus} \underline{D}^{**}_{3_\sqcup}.$$

♦ $\overline{D}^{**}_{3_\sqcap}$ is the sub-algebra of the Boolean algebra $\overline{P}(\mathcal{F}_{pr}(\overline{D}_{3_\sqcap})$ whose universe is the collection of clopen subsets of $\overline{D}^*_{3_\sqcap}$. Hence,

$$\overline{D}^{**}_{3_\sqcap} = (\{\emptyset, \mathcal{F}_{pr}(\overline{D}_{3_\sqcap})\}; \cup, \cap, ^c, \mathcal{F}_{pr}(\overline{D}_{3_\sqcap}), \emptyset).$$

♦ $\underline{D}^{**}_{3_\sqcup}$ is the sub-algebra of the Boolean algebra $\underline{P}(\mathcal{F}_{pr}(\underline{D}_{3_\sqcup})$ whose universe is the collection of clopen subsets of $\underline{D}^*_{3_\sqcup}$. Hence,

$$\underline{D}^{**}_{3_\sqcup} = (\{\emptyset, \mathcal{F}_{pr}(\underline{D}_{3_\sqcup})\}; \cap, \cup, ^c, \emptyset, \mathcal{F}_{pr}(\underline{D}_{3_\sqcup})).$$

Finally, $\underline{D}^{**}_3$ is a pure and trivial dBa as a glued sum of the Boolean algebras $\overline{D}^{**}_{3_\sqcap}$ and $\underline{D}^{**}_{3_\sqcup}$. Its Hasse diagram is given in Fig. 4

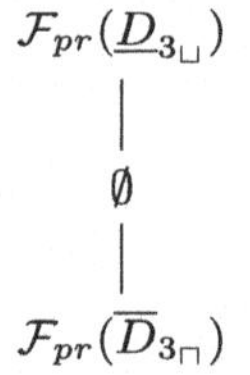

Fig. 4. $\underline{D}^{**}_3$

2. We continue with the trivial dBa $\underline{D}_7$ of Example 1.

$$\underline{D}^*_7 = \overline{D}^*_{7_\sqcap} \bowtie \underline{D}^*_{7_\sqcup}.$$

♦ $\overline{D}^*_{7_\sqcap}$ is the topological space whose underlying set is the collection $\mathcal{F}_{pr}(\overline{D}_{7_\sqcap})$ of all prime filters of $\overline{D}_{7_\sqcap}$ and whose topology τ_1 has a basis consisting of all sets of the form $V(x) = \{F \in \mathcal{F}_{pr}(\overline{D}_{7_\sqcap}) : x \in F\}$.
$\mathcal{F}_{pr}(\overline{D}_{7_\sqcap}) = \{\{\bot, a\}, \{\bot, b\}\}$, $V(\bot) = \mathcal{F}_{pr}(\overline{D}_{7_\sqcap})$, $V(a) = \{\{\bot, a\}\}$, $V(b) = \{\{\bot, b\}\}$, $V(e) = \emptyset$ and $\tau_1 = \{\emptyset, \{\{\bot, a\}\}, \{\{\bot, b\}\}, \mathcal{F}_{pr}(\overline{D}_{7_\sqcap})\}$.
♦ $\underline{D}^*_{7_\sqcup}$ is the topological space whose underlying set is the collection $\mathcal{F}_{pr}(\underline{D}_{7_\sqcup})$ of all prime filters of $\underline{D}_{7_\sqcup}$ and whose topology τ_2 has a basis consisting of all sets of the form $V(x) = \{F \in \mathcal{F}_{pr}(\underline{D}_{7_\sqcup}) : x \in F\}$.

$\mathcal{F}_{pr}(\underline{D}_{7_\sqcup}) = \{\{c,\top\},\{d,\top\}\}$, $V(\top) = \mathcal{F}_{pr}(\underline{D}_{7_\sqcup})$, $V(c) = \{\{c,\top\}\}$, $V(d) = \{\{d,\top\}\}$ $V(e) = \emptyset$ and $\tau_2 = \{\emptyset, \{\{c,\top\}\}, \{\{d,\top\}\}, \mathcal{F}_{pr}(\underline{D}_{7_\sqcup})\}$.
Finally, the underlying set of $\underline{D}_7^*$ is $\mathcal{F}_{pr}(\overline{D}_{7_\sqcap}) \cup \mathcal{F}_{pr}(\underline{D}_{7_\sqcup})$ and the topology τ of $\underline{D}_7^*$ is $\tau = \{O_1 \cup O_2 : O_1 \in \tau_1,\ O_2 \in \tau_2\}$
Now we evaluate $\underline{D}_7^{**}$.

$$\underline{D}_7^{**} = \overline{D}_{7_\sqcap}^{**} \dot{\oplus} \underline{D}_{7_\sqcup}^{**}.$$

♦ $\overline{D}_{7_\sqcap}^{**}$ is the sub-algebra of the Boolean algebra $\overline{P}(\mathcal{F}_{pr}(\overline{D}_{7_\sqcap})$ whose universe is the collection of clopen subsets of $\overline{D}_{7_\sqcap}^*$. Hence,

$$\overline{D}_{7_\sqcap}^{**} = \big(\{\emptyset, \{\{\bot,a\}\}, \{\{\bot,b\}\}, \mathcal{F}_{pr}(\overline{D}_{7_\sqcap})\}; \cup, \cap, ^c, \mathcal{F}_{pr}(\overline{D}_{7_\sqcap}), \emptyset\big).$$

♦ $\underline{D}_{7_\sqcup}^{**}$ is the sub-algebra of the Boolean algebra $\underline{P}(\mathcal{F}_{pr}(\underline{D}_{7_\sqcup})$ whose universe is the collection of clopen subsets of $\underline{D}_{7_\sqcup}^*$. Hence,

$$\underline{D}_{7_\sqcup}^{**} = \big(\{\emptyset, \{\{c,\top\}\}, \{\{d,\top\}\}, \mathcal{F}_{pr}(\underline{D}_{7_\sqcup})\}; \cap, \cup, ^c, \emptyset, \mathcal{F}_{pr}(\underline{D}_{7_\sqcup})\big)$$

Finally, $\underline{D}_7^{**}$ is a pure and trivial dBa as a glued sum of the Boolean algebras $\overline{D}_{7_\sqcap}^{**}$ and $\underline{D}_{7_\sqcup}^{**}$. Its Hasse diagram is given in Fig. 5

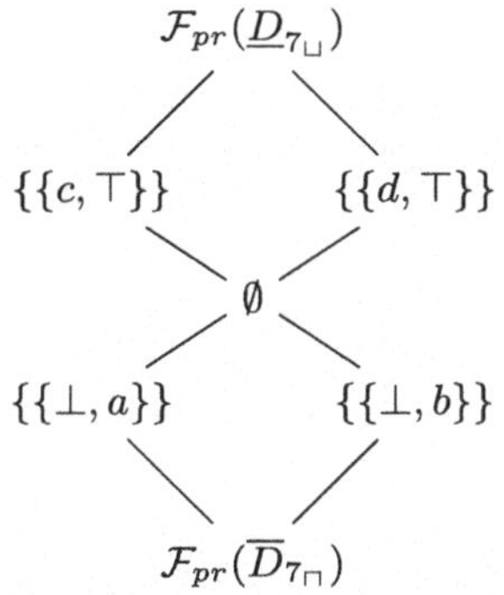

Fig. 5. $\underline{D}_7^{**}$

3. Set $X_1 = \{0,1\}$ and $X_2 = \{2\}$. We consider the topological spaces $(X_1, P(X_1))$ and $(X_2, P(X_2)$, then $(X_1, P(X_1))$ and $(X_2, P(X_2)$ are disjoint Boolean spaces, and hence $X = X_1 \bowtie X_2$ is a pure and trivial double Boolean space.
X_1^* is the sub-algebra of the Boolean algebra $\overline{P}(X_1)$ whose universe is the collection of all clopen subsets of X_1. Hence,

$$X_1^* = \overline{P}(X_1) = \big(\{\emptyset, \{0\}, \{1\}, X_1\}; \cup, \cap, ^c, X_1, \emptyset\big).$$

X_2^* is the sub-algebra of the Boolean algebra $\underline{P}(X_2)$ whose universe is the collection of all clopen subsets of X_2. Hence,

$$X_2^* = \underline{P}(X_2) = \big(\{\emptyset, X_2\}; \cap, \cup, ^c, \emptyset, X_2\big).$$

$$X^* = X_1^* \dot{\oplus} X_2^* = \overline{P}(X_1) \dot{\oplus} \underline{P}(X_2).$$

X^* is a pure and trivial double Boolean algebra as a glued sum of the Boolean algebras X_1^* and X_2^*. Its Hasse diagram is given by Fig. 6.

Now we evaluate X^{**}.

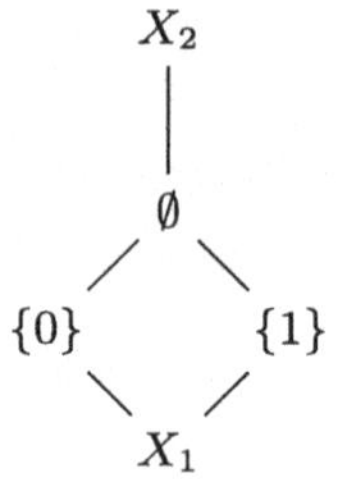

Fig. 6. X^*

$$X^{**} = \overline{X_1^*}^* \bowtie X_2^{**} = \underline{P}(X_1)^* \bowtie \underline{P}(X_2)^*.$$

♦ $\underline{P}(X_1)^*$ is the topological space whose underlying set is the collection $\mathcal{F}_{pr}(\underline{P}(X_1))$ of all prime filters of $\underline{P}(X_1)$ and whose topology τ_1 has a basis consisting of all sets of the form $V(x) = \{F \in \mathcal{F}_{pr}(\underline{P}(X_1)) : x \in F\}$.
$\mathcal{F}_{pr}(\underline{P}(X_1)) = \{\{\{0\}, X_1\}, \{\{1\}, X_1\}\}$, $V(\emptyset) = \emptyset$, $V(\{0\}) = \{\{\{0\}, X_1\}\}$, $V(\{1\}) = \{\{\{1\}, X_1\}\}$, $V(X_1) = \mathcal{F}_{pr}(\underline{P}(X_1))$ and
$\tau_1 = \{V(\emptyset), V(\{0\}), V(\{1\}), V(X_1)\}$

♦ $\underline{P}(X_2)^*$ is the topological space whose underlying set is the collection $\mathcal{F}_{pr}(\underline{P}(X_2))$ of all prime filters of $\underline{P}(X_2)$ and whose topology τ_2 has a basis consisting of all sets of the form $V(x) = \{F \in \mathcal{F}_{pr}(\underline{P}(X_2)) : x \in F\}$.
$\mathcal{F}_{pr}(\underline{P}(X_2)) = \{\{X_2\}\}$, $V(\emptyset) = \emptyset$, $V(X_2) = \mathcal{F}_{pr}(\underline{P}(X_2))$ and $\tau_2 = \{\emptyset, V(X_2)\}$.
Finally the underlying set of X^{**} is $\mathcal{F}_{pr}(\underline{P}(X_1)) \cup \mathcal{F}_{pr}(\underline{P}(X_2)$ and the topology τ of X^{**} is $\tau = \{O_1 \cup O_2 : O_1 \in \tau_1, O_2 \in \tau_2\}$.

In the following, we use the duality for Boolean algebras and Boolean spaces to establish the duality for pure and trivial double Boolean algebras and pure and trivial double Boolean spaces.

We start by stating this lemma which will be useful in what follows.

Lemma 3. *1. If $\varphi \colon \underline{D} \to \underline{E}$ is a pure and trivial dBa homomorphism, then the map $\varphi^* \colon E^* \to D^*$, $U \mapsto \varphi^{-1}(U)$ is continuous and satisfies $(\varphi^*)^{-1}(V(a)) = V(\varphi(a))$ for all $a \in D$.*

2. Let $X = X_1 \bowtie X_2$ and $Y = Y_1 \bowtie Y_2$ be two pure and trivial double Boolean spaces. If $f\colon X \to Y$ is a continuous map, then the map $f^*\colon Y^* \to X^*$, $K \mapsto f^{-1}(K)$ is a pure and trivial dBa homomorphism and satisfies $(f^*)^{-1}(\Theta_X(x)) = \Theta_Y(f(x))$ for all $x \in X$.

Proof. 1. Since φ is a homomorphism of trivial dBas, there exist $\varphi_1\colon D_\sqcap \to E_\sqcap$ and $\varphi_2\colon D_\sqcup \to E_\sqcup$ homomorphisms of Boolean algebras such that

$$\varphi(x) = \begin{cases} \varphi_1(x) \text{ if } x \in D_\sqcap \\ \varphi_2(x) \text{ if } x \in D_\sqcup \end{cases}$$

(by Proposition 3). The maps $\varphi_1^*\colon \overline{E}_\sqcap^* \to \overline{D}_\sqcap^*$, $U \mapsto \varphi_1^{-1}(U)$ and $\varphi_2^*\colon \underline{E}_\sqcup^* \to \underline{D}_\sqcup^*$, $U \mapsto \varphi_2^{-1}(U)$ are continuous and satisfy
$(\varphi_1^*)^{-1}(V(a)) = V(\varphi_1(a))$ for all $a \in D_\sqcap$ and $(\varphi_2^*)^{-1}(V(a)) = V(\varphi_2(a))$ for all $a \in D_\sqcup$ (by Lemma 1). Moreover

$$\varphi^*\colon \underline{E}^* \to \underline{D}^*, U \mapsto \varphi^*(U) = \begin{cases} \varphi_1^*(U) \text{ if } U \in E_\sqcap^* \\ \varphi_2^*(U) \text{ if } U \in E_\sqcup^* \end{cases}.$$

Hence by Lemma 2, $\varphi^*\colon \underline{E}^* \to \underline{D}^*$, $U \mapsto \varphi^{-1}(U)$ is continuous and satisfies $(\varphi^*)^{-1}(V(a)) = V(\varphi(a))$ for all $a \in D$.

2. Since f is a continuous map between pure and trivial double Boolean spaces, there exist $f_1\colon X_1 \to Y_1$ and $f_2\colon X_2 \to Y_2$ continuous maps such that

$$f(x) = \begin{cases} f_1(x) \text{ if } x \in X_1 \\ f_2(x) \text{ if } x \in X_2 \end{cases}$$

(by Lemma 2). The maps $f_1^*\colon Y_1^* \to X_1^*$, $K \mapsto f_1^{-1}(K)$ and $f_2^*\colon Y_2^* \to X_2^*$, $K \mapsto f_2^{-1}(K)$ are Boolean algebra homomorphisms (by Lemma 1). Moreover

$$f^*\colon Y^* \to X^*, U \mapsto f^*(U) = \begin{cases} f_1^*(U) \text{ if } U \in Y_1^* \\ f_2^*(U) \text{ if } U \in Y_2^* \end{cases}.$$

Hence by Proposition 3, $f^*\colon Y^* \to X^*$, $K \mapsto f^{-1}(K)$ is a pure and trivial dBa homomorphism and satisfy $(f^*)^{-1}(\Theta_X(x)) = \Theta_Y(f(x))$ for all $x \in X$. ■

Example 3. We consider the correspondence φ from $\underline{D}_3$ to $\underline{D}_7$ defined by the diagram in Fig. 7.

For any $x \in D_3$, $\varphi(x) = \begin{cases} \varphi_1(x) \text{ if } x \in D_{3_\sqcap} \\ \varphi_2(x) \text{ if } x \in D_{3_\sqcup} \end{cases}$ where $\varphi_1\colon D_{3_\sqcap} \to D_{7_\sqcap}$ and $\varphi_2\colon D_{3_\sqcup} \to D_{7_\sqcup}$ are such that $\varphi_1(\bot) = \bot$, $\varphi_1(\top \sqcap \top) = e$, $\varphi_2(\top \sqcap \top) = e$ and $\varphi_2(\top) = \top$. Since φ_1 and φ_2 are Boolean algebra homomorphisms, we conclude by Proposition 3 that φ is a double Boolean algebra homomorphism.

$$\varphi^*\colon \underline{D}_7^* \to \underline{D}_3^*, U \mapsto \varphi^*(U) = \begin{cases} \varphi_1^*(U) = \varphi_1^{-1}(U) \text{ if } U \in D_{7_\sqcap}^* \\ \varphi_2^*(U) = \varphi_2^{-1}(U) \text{ if } U \in D_{7_\sqcup}^* \end{cases}.$$

$$\varphi^*(\{\bot, a\}) = \varphi_1^*(\{\bot, a\}) = \varphi_1^{-1}(\{\bot, a\}) = \{\bot\},$$
$$\varphi^*(\{\bot, b\}) = \varphi_1^*(\{\bot, b\}) = \varphi_1^{-1}(\{\bot, b\}) = \{\bot\},$$
$$\varphi^*(\{c, \top\}) = \varphi_2^*(\{c, \top\}) = \varphi_2^{-1}(\{c, \top\}) = \{\top\},$$
$$\varphi^*(\{d, \top\}) = \varphi_2^*(\{d, \top\}) = \varphi_2^{-1}(\{d, \top\}) = \{\top\}.$$

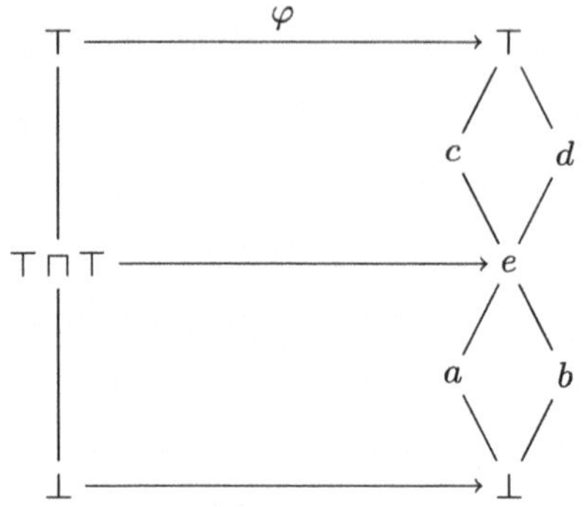

Fig. 7. Homomorphism from $\underline{D}_3$ to $\underline{D}_7$.

Let $\mathcal{PTDBA}$ be the category of pure and trivial double Boolean algebras, which has pure and trivial double Boolean algebras as objects and double Boolean algebra homomorphisms as morphisms. Let $\mathcal{PTDBS}$ be the category of pure and trivial double Boolean spaces, which has pure and trivial double Boolean spaces as objects and continuous maps as morphisms.

Definition 5. *We define a correspondence* $\Phi\colon \mathcal{PTDBA} \to \mathcal{PTDBS}$ *which acts on objects as in the first statement of Definition 4 and on morphisms as in the first statement of Lemma 3, and a correspondence* $\Psi\colon \mathcal{PTDBS} \to \mathcal{PTDBA}$ *which acts on objects as in the second statement of Definition 4 and on morphisms as in the second statement of Lemma 3.*

Lemma 4. *The correspondences* Φ *and* Ψ *of Definition 5 are contravariant functors.*

Proof. We will show that $\Phi\colon \mathcal{PTDBA} \to \mathcal{PTDBS}$ is a contravariant functor. In the same way, one can show that $\Psi\colon \mathcal{PTDBS} \to \mathcal{PTDBA}$ is also a contravariant functor. First of all, $\Phi\colon \mathcal{PTDBA} \to \mathcal{PTDBS}$ is well defined by Theorem 1 and Lemma 3. Let $D \xrightarrow{f} E \xrightarrow{g} F$ be two morphisms in $\mathcal{PTDBA}$. Let us show that $(g \circ f)^* = f^* \circ g^*$. For any $U \in F^*$, $(g \circ f)^*(U) = (g \circ f)^{-1}(U) = (f^{-1} \circ g^{-1})(U) = f^{-1}(g^{-1}(U)) = f^*(g^{-1}(U)) = f^*(g^*(U)) = (f^* \circ g^*)(U)$. Thus, $(g \circ f)^* = f^* \circ g^*$. Moreover, for any pure and trivial dBa D and any $U \in D^*$, $id_D^*(U) = id_D^{-1}(U) = U = id_{D^*}(U)$. We conclude that $\Phi\colon \mathcal{PTDBA} \to \mathcal{PTDBS}$ is a contravariant functor. ∎

We are ready to prove the duality for pure and trivial double Boolean algebras and pure and trivial double Boolean spaces.

Theorem 2. *The category* $\mathcal{PTDBA}$ *of pure and trivial double Boolean algebras and the category* $\mathcal{PTDBS}$ *of pure and trivial double Boolean spaces are anti-equivalent. Explicitly,*

1. *The anti-equivalence is given by the functor* $\Phi\colon \mathcal{PTDBA} \to \mathcal{PTDBS}$ *and its quasi-inverse* $\Psi\colon \mathcal{PTDBS} \to \mathcal{PTDBA}$.

2. *The assignments given by* $D \mapsto \mathcal{V}_D$ *on pure and trivial double Boolean algebras and given by* $X \mapsto \Theta_X$ *on pure and trivial double Boolean spaces define natural transformations* $\mathcal{V}\colon id_{\mathcal{PTDBA}} \to \Phi \circ \Psi$ *and* $\Theta\colon id_{\mathcal{PTDBS}} \to \Psi \circ \Phi$.
3. *The natural transformations* $\mathcal{V}$ *and* Θ *are functor isomorphisms.*

Proof. The first statement is a consequence of the second and third statements.

2. In order to show that $\mathcal{V}$ and Θ are natural transformations we need to verify that for every homomorphism $\varphi\colon D \to E$ of pure and trivial double Boolean algebras and each continuous function $f\colon X \to Y$ of pure and trivial double Boolean spaces the following diagrams commute.

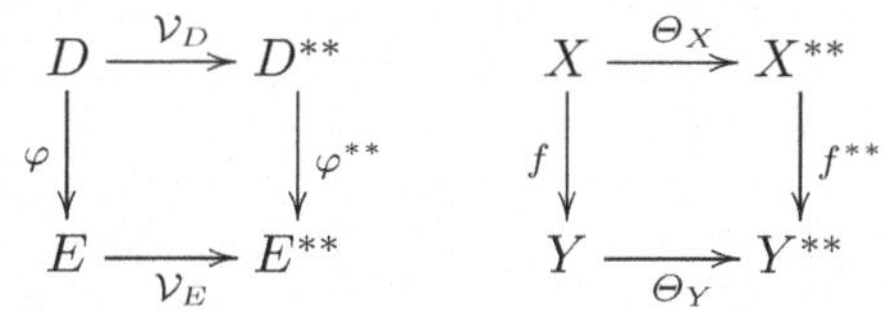

That is $\varphi^{**} \circ \mathcal{V}_D = \mathcal{V}_E \circ \varphi$ and $f^{**} \circ \Theta_X = \Theta_Y \circ f$. For the diagram on the left, take $a \in D$, then $\mathcal{V}_D$ maps a to $V(a)$ and φ^{**} maps $V(a)$ to $(\varphi^*)^{-1}(V(a))$; but this set is equal to $V(\varphi(a))$ by Lemma 3. Since $(\mathcal{V}_E \circ \varphi)(a) = V(\varphi(a))$, the diagram on the left commute. For the diagram on the right, take $x \in X$, then f^{**} maps $\Theta_X(x)$ to $(f^*)^{-1}(\Theta_X(x))$; but again by Lemma 3, this set equal to $\Theta_Y(f(x))$. Hence the diagram of the right commute. We conclude that $\mathcal{V}$ and Θ are natural transformation.
3. The natural transformation $\mathcal{V}$ is an isomorphism by the first statement of Theorem 1 and the natural transformation Θ is an isomorphism by the second statement of Theorem 1. ∎

4 Conclusion

In this work, we have provided a topological representation for pure and trivial double Boolean algebras and use it to show that the category of pure and trivial double Boolean algebras and the category of pure and trivial double Boolean spaces are anti-equivalent. Future work will address the extension of this duality to the category of pure double Boolean algebras.

Acknowledgments. We thank the anonymous referees for their constructive remarks and suggestions which help to improve this work. This work was supported by Swiss National Science Foundation(SNF), Grant Nr.: IZSEZO-219516/1

Disclosure of Interests. The authors have no competing interests to declare that are relevant to the content of this article.

References

1. Burris, S., Sankappanavar, H.P.: A Course in Universal Algebra. Springer, New York (1981)
2. Gamelin, T.W., Greene, R.E.: Introduction to Topology, 2nd edn. Dover Publications, Inc. (1999)
3. Gratzer, G.: Lattice Theory: Foundation. Springer, Berlin (2011). https://doi.org/10.1007/978-3-0348-0018-1
4. Kembang, G.T., Kwuida, L., Temgoua, E.R.A, Tenkeu, Y.L.J: Simple and subdirectly irreducible double Boolean algebras. arXiv:2312.13686 (2023). https://doi.org/10.48550/arXiv.2312.13686
5. Kwuida, L.: Prime ideal theorem for double Boolean algebras. Discussiones Math. Gener. Algebra Appl. 263–275 (2007). https://doi.org/10.7151/dmgaa.1130
6. Mac Lane, S.: Categories for the Working Mathematician. Graduate Texts in Mathematics, vol. 5. Springer, New York (1978). https://doi.org/10.1007/978-1-4757-4721-8
7. Howlader, P., Banerjee, M.: Topological representation of double Boolean algebras. Algebra Univ. **84**(2), 1–32 (2023). https://doi.org/10.1007/s00012-023-00811-x
8. Stone, M.H.: Application of the theory of Boolean rings to general topology. Trans. Am. Math. Soc. **84**, 375–481 (1937). https://doi.org/10.2307/1989788
9. Tenkeu, Y.L.J., Tenkeu, G.K., Temgoua, E.R.A., Kwuida, L.: Filters, ideals and power of double Boolean algebras. Discussiones Math. - Gener. Algebra Appl. **44**(2), 451–478 (2024). https://doi.org/10.7151/dmgaa.1466
10. Tenkeu, G.K., Tenkeu, J.Y.L, Temgoua, E.R.A, Kwuida, L: On double Boolean algebras: subalgebras, homomorphisms and some constructions (2024). https://doi.org/10.13140/RG.2.2.35809.11360
11. Vormbrock, B., Wille, R.: Semiconcept and protoconcept algebras: the basic theorems. In: Ganter, B., Stumme, G., Wille, R. (eds.) Formal Concept Analysis. LNCS (LNAI), vol. 3626, pp. 34–48. Springer, Heidelberg (2005). https://doi.org/10.1007/11528784_2
12. Wille, R.,: Restructuring lattice theory: an approach based on hierarchies of concepts. In: Rival, I. (ed.) Ordered Sets. NATO Advanced Study Institutes Series, vol. 83. Springer, Dordrecht (1982). https://doi.org/10.1007/978-94-009-7798-3_15
13. Wille, R.: Boolean concept logic. In: Ganter, B., Mineau, G.W. (eds.) ICCS-ConceptStruct 2000. LNCS (LNAI), vol. 1867, pp. 317–331. Springer, Heidelberg (2000). https://doi.org/10.1007/10722280_22

Concept Multilattices with Truth-Stressing Hedges

Gael Nguepy Dongmo[1(✉)], Blaise Blériot Koguep Njionou[1], and Leonard Kwuida[2]

[1] Department of Mathematics and Computer Science, University of Dschang, Dschang, Cameroon
koguep@univ-dschang.org
[2] School of Business, Bern University of Applied Sciences, Bern, Switzerland
leonard.kwuida@bfh.ch

Abstract. In the context of Formal Concept Analysis (FCA) based on multilattices (M-FCA), the number of derived concepts is often unmanageably large, posing challenges for practical applications. This paper addresses this issue by introducing **truth-stressing linguistic hedges** into M-FCA as a parameterization mechanism for concept-forming operators. We start by defining a generalized pair of antitone operators using hedges such as "very" or "extremely" to refine fuzzy concepts. We establish several properties of these operators and demonstrate that the resulting concept multilattice is isomorphic to a complete multilattice defined via a derived Galois connection. Importantly, we prove that applying stronger hedges results in fewer formal concepts, thereby offering a systematic approach to concept lattice reduction in fuzzy environments.

Keywords: Formal Concept Analysis · Fuzzy Logic · Multilattices · Linguistic Hedge · Concept Reduction

1 Introduction

Formal Concept Analysis (FCA) provides a structured framework for extracting and analyzing conceptual relationships from data. As the theory has evolved, particularly into the fuzzy domain, multilattices have emerged as a robust structure for handling degrees of truth in FCA. Introduced by Medina et al., [11,13] the M-FCA framework replaces classical lattices with multilattices to better model partial and uncertain information. In the same direction, Nguepy et al. [8,14,15] constructed a pair of antitone concept-forming operators and two pairs of isotone concept-forming operators in M-FCA. Another significant work on M-FCA was done by Koguep et al. [16], they have used residuated multilattices to evaluate objects and attributes in FCA setting, and shown that the structure of the set of corresponding formal concepts is a residuated multilattice.

Linguistic hedges, such as "very," "roughly," or "extremely," are crucial in human reasoning. Zadeh [17,18], a pioneer in fuzzy logic, highlighted their importance and proposed a mathematical model for them in the early 1970s. Since

P. Cellier et al. (Eds.): CONCEPTS 2025, LNAI 15941, pp. 423–436, 2025.
https://doi.org/10.1007/978-3-032-03364-2_27

then, hedges have been extensively studied for their role in approximate reasoning and their linguistic and logical implications. Hedges modify the meaning of natural language expressions. For instance, "very" or "extremely" intensify meaning, as seen in the difference between "a country with a high rate of unemployment" and "a country with an extremely high rate of unemployment." The latter expression applies to a smaller set of countries, thus intensifying hedges narrow the scope of the concept they modify. Conversely, hedges such as "roughly" or "more or less" broaden and emphasize the scope, therefore introducing uncertainty.

A major challenge in fuzzy FCA, including M-FCA, is the proliferation of formal concepts, which can hinder interpretability and computational efficiency. As we have seen in the previous paragraph, Linguistic hedges terms like "very," "extremely," or "roughly" have long been recognized as powerful tools in fuzzy logic for modulating truth values. These hedges, especially truth-stressing ones, narrow the scope of membership functions and are therefore promising candidates for concept reduction [1,4,10]. While hedges have been employed in FCA over residuated lattices (L-FCA), their potential in M-FCA has not yet been explored. This paper fills that gap by introducing hedge-based antitone concept-forming operators in M-FCA. We prove that the resulting structure retains completeness and forms a concept multilattice isomorphic to one built from a hedge-based Galois connection. Moreover, we show that stronger hedges systematically reduce the number of fuzzy concepts, offering both theoretical insights and practical benefits for fuzzy data analysis.

The paper is organized as follow. Section 2 recalls some basic notions of multilattice theory, fuzzy logic and Formal Concept Analysis via multilattice. Section 3 presents our new operators parametrized with truth-stressing hedges, the concept multilattice with hedges and some properties. Section 4 provides an illustrative Example with a Truth-Stressing Hedge and Sect. 5 concludes the paper.

2 Preliminaries

This section recalls several basic notions on multilattices, adjoint pairs and truth-stressing hedges. Let $(P, \leq)$ be a poset and X be any non-empty subset of P. We denote by $U(X)$ (resp. $L(X)$) the set of upper (resp. lower) bounds of X. The supremum (resp. infimum) of X is denoted by $\vee X$ or sup$X$ (resp. $\wedge X$ or inf$X$).

2.1 Multilattices Theory

We present some definitions that help introduce multilattices. Figure 1 shows an example of a complete lattice. In fact, c, e and $\top$ are in $U(\{a, b\})$, and the least element is $\{c\}$. Then $\vee\{a, b\} = c$. Looking at Fig. 2, we observe that c, d, e and $\top$ are in $U(\{a, b\})$, but $\vee\{a, b\}$ does not exist since c and d are not comparable. This shows that the diagram is not a lattice. However, the minimal elements of $U(\{a, b\})$ are c and d, we therefore need to introduce new concepts to handle such situations.

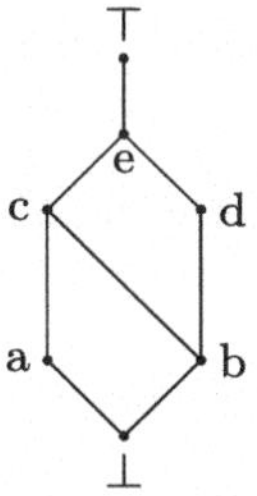

Fig. 1. An example of a complete lattice.

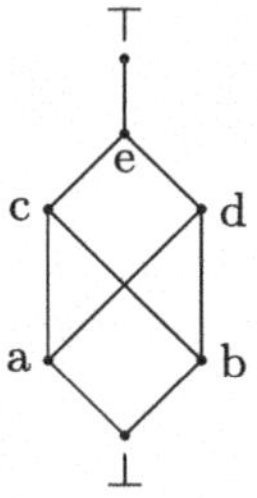

Fig. 2. An example of a complete multilattice.

Definition 1. *[5] Let $(P, \ \leq)$ be a poset and X be any non-empty subset of P. A* ***multisupremum*** *(resp.* ***multiinfimum****) of X is a minimal (resp. maximal) element of $U(X)$ (resp. $L(X)$).*

The set of multisuprema (resp. multiinfima) of X is denoted by $\sqcup X$ (resp. $\sqcap X$). For $x, \ y \in P$ we simply write $U(x), \ L(x), \ x \sqcup y, \ x \sqcap y$ for $U(\{x\}), \ L(\{x\})$, $\sqcup\{x,y\}, \sqcap\{x,y\}$, respectively. Moreover, $\sqcup\{x_i \mid i \in I\}$ will be denoted $\bigsqcup\limits_{i\in I} x_i$ (and $\bigsqcap\limits_{i\in I} x_i$ is given similarly).

Example 1. When we return to Fig. 2 as we said, c, d, e and $\top$ are in $U\{a,b\}$, but c and d are not comparable. Hence, $\{a,b\}$ has minimal upper bounds c and d, that is $a \sqcup b = \{c,d\}$. Analogously, $c \sqcap d = \{a,b\}$.

Now, we can give the definition of a multilattice.

Definition 2. *[6] A* ***multilattice*** *is a poset $(M, \leq)$ in which, for any pair of elements $\{a,b\}$ of M, the following conditions hold:*

- *if $x \in M$ is an element of $U(\{a,b\})$, there exits $m \in a \sqcup b$ such that $m \leq x$,*
- *if $x \in M$ is an element of $L(\{a,b\})$, there exits $m \in a \sqcap b$ such that $x \leq m$.*

If, the pair $\{a,b\}$ is changed by an arbitrary subset $X \subseteq M$, one obtains a ***complete multilattice****.*

Now, we present adjoint pair, which is a generalization of a triangular norm and its residuated implication.

Definition 3. *[7] Let $(P, \leq)$ be a poset, and $(\&, \rightarrow)$ be a couple of binary operations on P such that*

1. *the operation $\&$ is order-preserving in both arguments, i.e., if $a_1 \leq a_2$, then $(a_1 \,\&\, b) \leq (a_2 \,\&\, b)$ and $(c \,\&\, a_1) \leq (c \,\&\, a_2), \forall a_1, a_2, b, c \in P$;*
2. *the operation $\rightarrow$ is order-preserving in first and reversing in second argument, i.e., if $a_1 \leq a_2$, then $(b \rightarrow a_1) \leq (b \rightarrow a_2)$ and $(a_2 \rightarrow c) \leq (a_1 \rightarrow c), \forall a_1, a_2, b, c \in P$;*
3. *and we have:*

$$a \leq (c \rightarrow b) \text{ if and only if } (a \,\&\, c) \leq b$$

for all $a, b, c \in P$.

Then we say that $(\&, \rightarrow)$ forms an ***adjoint pair*** *in $(P, \leq)$.*

In the rest of our article, for any poset P, P_1, P_2, P_3, any operators $\&\colon P \times P \rightarrow P$ and $\otimes : P_1 \times P_2 \rightarrow P_3$ we set:

$$m \,\&\, X := \{m \,\&\, x \mid x \in X\}, \quad \text{where } \emptyset \neq X \subseteq P \text{ and } m \in P;$$
$$X \otimes m := \{x \otimes m \mid x \in X\}, \quad \text{where } \emptyset \neq X \subseteq P_1 \text{ and } m \in P_2;$$
$$Y \leq m :\Longleftrightarrow y \leq m \text{ for all } y \in Y, \quad \text{where } \emptyset \neq Y \text{ and } Y \cup \{m\} \subseteq P_j, 1 \leq j \leq 3.$$

We now define the notion of left-continuity.

Definition 4. *[13] Let $(M_1, \leq_1)$, $(M_2, \leq_2)$ be two multilattices. Let $(P, \leq)$ be a poset, and $\otimes :\ M_1 \times M_2 \rightarrow P$ be a map. We say that $\otimes$ is:*

(i) left-continuous in the first argument if $K_1 \otimes m_2 \leq p \Longrightarrow \sqcup K_1 \otimes m_2 \leq p$ for all $K_1 \subseteq M_1$, $m_2 \in M_2$, and $p \in P$,
(ii) left-continuous in the second argument if $m_1 \otimes K_2 \leq p \Longrightarrow m_1 \otimes \sqcup K_2 \leq p$ for all $K_2 \subseteq M_2$, $m_1 \in M_1$ and $p \in P$,
(iii) left-continuous if it is left-continuous in both arguments.

Definition 5. *[13] Let $^{\Uparrow} : P \rightarrow Q$ and $^{\Downarrow} : Q \rightarrow P$ be two maps between the posets $(P, \leq)$ and $(Q, \leq)$. The pair $(^{\Uparrow}, ^{\Downarrow})$ is called a Galois connection if:*

1. *$p_1 \leq p_2$ implies $p_2^{\Uparrow} \leq p_1^{\Uparrow}$ for every $p_1, p_2 \in P$;*
2. *$q_1 \leq q_2$ implies $q_2^{\Downarrow} \leq q_1^{\Downarrow}$ for every $q_1, q_2 \in Q$;*
3. *$p \leq p^{\Uparrow\Downarrow}$ and $q \leq q^{\Downarrow\Uparrow}$ for all $p \in P$ and $q \in Q$.*

To achieve our goal, we need to introduce intensifying linguistic hedge such as "very", "extremely"... etc. As we can see in the documents [1,9], a truth-stressing hedge is a mapping $^* : M \to M$ satisfying the following conditions:

$$\top^* = \top \tag{1}$$

$$a^* \leq a \tag{2}$$

$$a \leq b \Rightarrow a^* \leq b^* \tag{3}$$

$$a^{**} = a^* \tag{4}$$

where a, b are elements of a complete multilattice M with $\top$ as top element, equipped with an adjoint pair $(\&, \to)$.

On the previous hypothesis, one can give an example of two important truth-stressing hedges:

(i): Identity, i.e. $a^* = a$ and (ii): Globalization, i.e. $a^* = \begin{cases} \top, & \text{if } a = \top \\ \bot, & \text{else} \end{cases}$

Throughout this document we will use the notation $A^* = \{a^* : a \in A\}$, for all $A \subseteq M$.

Lemma 1. *A truth-stressing hedge* * *satisfies:*

$$\Big(\underset{j \in J}{\sqcup} a_j^*\Big)^* = \underset{j \in J}{\sqcup} a_j^*$$

for all $\{a_j \mid j \in J\} \subseteq M$.

Proof. Let $x \in \Big(\underset{j \in J}{\sqcup} a_j^*\Big)^*$, then there is $\alpha \in \underset{j \in J}{\sqcup} a_j^*$ such that, $x = \alpha^*$. Therefore $\alpha \geq a_j^*$, then $\alpha^* \geq a_j^{**} = a_j^*$. That is, there exists $\beta \in \underset{j \in J}{\sqcup} a_j^*$ such that $x \geq \beta$. But $x = \alpha^* \leq \alpha$, which leads to $\alpha \geq x \geq \beta$, hence $\alpha = \beta$. Therefore $x = \beta^* \leq \beta$, we finally obtain $x = \beta$. Thus $x \in \underset{j \in J}{\sqcup} a_j^*$.

Conversely, for $x \in \underset{j \in J}{\sqcup} a_j^*$, we have $x \geq a_j^*$ for all $j \in J$. Therefore $x^* \geq a_j^{**} = a_j^*$, which means there exists $\alpha \in \underset{j \in J}{\sqcup} a_j^*$ such that, $x^* \geq \alpha$, that is $x^* = x^{**} \geq \alpha^*$, then $x \geq \alpha^*$. Since, $\alpha \in \underset{j \in J}{\sqcup} a_j^*$, we have $\alpha \geq a_j^*$, then $\alpha^* \geq a_j^*$ which means there is $\beta \in \underset{j \in J}{\sqcup} a_j^*$ such that, $\alpha^* \geq \beta$. We therefore obtain, $x \geq \alpha^* \geq \beta$. Since $x, \beta \in \underset{j \in J}{\sqcup} a_j^*$, we get $x = \beta$ hence $\alpha^* \geq x$. Finally, $x = \alpha^*$, which means that, $x \in \Big(\underset{j \in J}{\sqcup} a_j^*\Big)^*$. □

2.2 Antitone Concept-Forming Operators

In this subsection, we present a fuzzy concept multilattice which is the extension of fuzzy concept lattice introduced by Bělohlávek [2].

Let M be a complete multilattice and $(\&,\to)$ an adjoint pair defined on it such that & is left continuous. Let X and Y be two non-empty sets called objects set and attributes set respectively, and let $I \in M^{X\times Y}$ be an $M-$fuzzy relation between X and Y. A triple (X, Y, I) is called an **M-fuzzy formal context**.

Theorem 1. *[11,13] Let $f \in M^X$ and $g \in M^Y$. Then the following infima exist*

$$\inf\{f(x) \to I(x,y) \mid x \in X\} \text{ and } \inf\{g(y) \to I(x,y) \mid y \in Y\}.$$

Furthermore, the derivation operators $^\lozenge : M^X \to M^Y$ and $^\blacklozenge : M^Y \to M^X$ defined as follow: for $f \in M^X$ and $g \in M^Y$,

$$f^\lozenge(y) := \bigwedge_{x\in X}\Big(f(x) \to I(x,y)\Big) \text{ with } y \in Y$$
$$\text{and}$$
$$g^\blacklozenge(x) := \bigwedge_{y\in Y}\Big(g(y) \to I(x,y)\Big) \text{ with } x \in X,$$

form a Galois connection between M^X and M^Y.

We therefore obtain the following proposition.

Proposition 1. *[11,13] For any $f, f_1, f_2, f_j \in M^X$, $g, g_1, g_2, g_j \in M^Y$, $j \in J$, where J is an index set, we have the following:*

(i) $f_1 \leq f_2 \implies f_2^\lozenge \leq f_1^\lozenge, \quad g_1 \leq g_2 \implies g_2^\blacklozenge \leq g_1^\blacklozenge$;
(ii) $f \leq f^{\lozenge\blacklozenge}, \quad g \leq g^{\blacklozenge\lozenge}$;
(iii) $f^\lozenge = f^{\lozenge\blacklozenge\lozenge}, \quad g^\blacklozenge = g^{\blacklozenge\lozenge\blacklozenge}$;
(iv) $\sqcap_{j\in J}\left(f_j^\lozenge\right) \subseteq \{f^\lozenge, \quad f \in \sqcup_{j\in J} f_j\}$[1], $\quad \sqcap_{j\in J}\left(g_j^\blacklozenge\right) \subseteq \{g^\blacklozenge, \quad g \in \sqcup_{j\in J} g_j\}$.

Theorem 2. *[13] The order set $(\mathcal{C}^{\lozenge\blacklozenge}, \leq)$ is a complete multilattice where, for every set of concepts $\{(f_j, g_j)\}_{j\in J}$:*

$$\sqcap_{j\in J}\{(f_j, g_j)\} = \{(f, f^\lozenge): \quad f \in \sqcap_{j\in J} f_j\}$$
$$\text{and}$$
$$\sqcup_{j\in J}\{(f_j, g_j)\} = \{(g^\blacklozenge, g): \quad g \in \sqcap_{j\in J} g_j\}.$$

3 Concept Multilattices with Truth-Stressing Hedge

In this section, we assume that * is truth-stressing hedge on M, we denote the fix-points of * by;

$$Fix(*) = \{a \in M \mid a^* = a\}.$$

For any universe U, we consider the operators $\lfloor - \rfloor : M^U \to 2^{U\times M}$ and $\lceil - \rceil : 2^{U\times M} \to M^U$ define by: for all $f, g \in M^U$,

$$\lfloor f \rfloor := \{(x,a) \in U \times M \mid a \leq f(x)\}$$

[1] We write $\sqcup_{j\in J} f_j$ to express the multisupremum of the set $\{f_j,\ j \in J\}$.

which represents an area under the membership function $f : U \to M$. For any $B \subseteq U \times M$ and $x \in U$ we define the mapping $\lceil B \rceil \in M^U$ by

$$\lceil B \rceil(x) := b \quad \text{with} \quad b \in \sqcup\{a \in M \mid (x,a) \in B\}$$

where we choose the element b such that the operator $\lceil - \rceil$ increases.

Remark 1. A such b always exists, in fact: for two subsets B_1, B_2 of $U \times M$, if $B_1 \subseteq B_2$, then $\{a \in M \mid (x,a) \in B_1\} \subseteq \{a \in M \mid (x,a) \in B_2\}$. For any $b_2 \in \sqcup\{a \in M \mid (x,a) \in B_2\}$, we have $\{a \in M \mid (x,a) \in B_1\} \leq b_2$, hence there exists $b_1 \in \sqcup\{a \in M \mid (x,a) \in B_1\}$ such that $b_1 \leq b_2$. We take $\lceil B_1 \rceil(x) = b_1$ and $\lceil B_2 \rceil(x) = b_2$.

Now we define

$$B^* = \{(x, a^*) \mid (x,a) \in B\}.$$

For an M-fuzzy formal context (X, Y, I) and the two truth-stressing hedges $*_X$ and $*_Y$ on M, we have the following notations:

$$M^{*_X} := \{a^{*_X} \mid a \in M\} \text{ and } M^{*_Y} := \{a^{*_Y} \mid a \in M\}.$$

For any fuzzy set $f \in M^X$ and $g \in M^Y$, we set:

$$f^*(x) = \big(f(x)\big)^* \text{ and } g^*(y) = \big(g(y)\big)^* \text{ with } x \in X \text{ and } y \in Y.$$

The following definition gives a generalization of Medina et al. [13] antitone concept-forming operator by using truth-stressing hedges.

Remark 2. According to Theorem 1, as $f^* \in M^X$ and $g^* \in M^Y$, then the following infima exist:

$$\inf\{f^*(x) \to I(x,y) \mid x \in X\} \text{ and } \inf\{g^*(y) \to I(x,y) \mid y \in Y\}.$$

Now, we define parametrized antitone concept-operators with the truth-stressing hedge.

Definition 6. *The antitone concept-forming operators parametrized with the truth-stressing hedge* * *are operators* $^\blacktriangle : M^X \to M^Y$ *and* $^\blacktriangledown : M^Y \to M^X$ *defined by: for* $f \in M^X$ *and* $g \in M^Y$,

$$f^\blacktriangle(y) := \bigwedge_{x \in X}\{f^*(x) \to I(x,y)\}, \text{ for } y \in Y$$

and

$$g^\blacktriangledown(x) := \bigwedge_{y \in Y}\{g^*(y) \to I(x,y)\}, \text{ for } x \in X.$$

Remark 3. When the hedge is identity, the pair $(^\blacktriangle, ^\blacktriangledown)$ is exactly the Medina et al. concept-forming operator $(^\diamond, ^\blacklozenge)$.

The fix-point of $(^{\blacktriangle}, ^{\blacktriangledown})$ is called **fuzzy concept** with hedge and the set of all fuzzy concepts is

$$\mathcal{C}^{\blacktriangle\blacktriangledown}(X^*, Y^*, I) := \{(f, g) \in M^X \times M^Y \mid f^{\blacktriangle} = g \text{ and } g^{\blacktriangledown} = f\}.$$

Thus for a fuzzy concept (f, g), f is the collection of all objects that have all the attributes of "very g" and g is the collection of all attributes that are shared by all the objects of "very f".

Now we are going to show some properties of the generalized concept-forming operators with hedge.

Proposition 2. *The pair $(^{\blacktriangle}, ^{\blacktriangledown})$ of concept-forming operators with hedge has the following properties: For $f, f_1, f_2, f_j \in M^X$, $g, g_1, g_2, g_j \in M^Y$, $j \in J$, where J is an index set;*

1. $f^{\blacktriangle} = f^{*\Diamond}$, $\quad g^{\blacktriangledown} = g^{*\blacktriangledown}$;
2. $f^{\blacktriangle} = f^{*\blacktriangle}$, $\quad g^{\blacktriangledown} = g^{*\blacktriangledown}$;
3. $f^{\Diamond} \leq f^{\blacktriangle}$, $\quad g^{\blacklozenge} \leq g^{\blacktriangledown}$;
4. $f^* \leq f^{\blacktriangle\blacktriangledown}$, $\quad g^* \leq g^{\blacktriangledown\blacktriangle}$;
5. $f_1 \leq f_2 \implies f_2^{\blacktriangle} \leq f_1^{\blacktriangle}$, $\quad g_1 \leq g_2 \implies g_2^{\blacktriangledown} \leq g_1^{\blacktriangledown}$;
6. $f^{\blacktriangle\blacktriangledown\blacktriangle\blacktriangledown} = f^{\blacktriangle\blacktriangledown}$, $\quad g^{\blacktriangledown\blacktriangle\blacktriangledown\blacktriangle} = g^{\blacktriangledown\blacktriangle}$;
7. $\underset{j \in J}{\sqcap}\left(f_j^{\blacktriangle}\right) \subseteq \{f^{\blacktriangle},\ \ f \in \underset{j \in J}{\sqcup} f_j^*\}$, $\quad \underset{j \in J}{\sqcap}\left(g_j^{\blacktriangledown}\right) \subseteq \{g^{\blacktriangledown},\ \ g \in \underset{j \in J}{\sqcup} g_j^*\}$.

Proof. 1. Directly, by Definition 6 we obtain the result.

2. We use the fact that, $f^* = f^{**}$.
3. Since $f^* \leq f$ and $g^* \leq g$ and operator $\rightarrow$ is order-reversing for the second argument, we obviously obtain the result.
4. By Proposition 1 item (ii), we have $f^* \leq f^{*\Diamond\blacklozenge}$, and from item 1., $f^{*\Diamond\blacklozenge} = f^{\blacktriangle\blacklozenge}$. Then we obtain $f^* \leq f^{\blacktriangle\blacklozenge}$. By item 3., $f^{\blacktriangle\blacklozenge} \leq f^{\blacktriangle\blacktriangledown}$. Hence $f^* \leq f^{\blacktriangle\blacklozenge}$.
   By the same manner one can obtain $g^* \leq g^{\blacktriangledown\blacktriangle}$.
5. As $f_1 \leq f_2$ and $g_1 \leq g_2$, we have $f_1^* \leq f_2^*$ and $g_1^* \leq g_2^*$, then by the fact that $\rightarrow$ is order-reversing for the second argument, one can obviously obtain the result.
6. From 4., we have $f^* \leq f^{\blacktriangle\blacktriangledown}$, then $f^{*\blacktriangle\blacktriangledown} \leq f^{\blacktriangle\blacktriangledown\blacktriangle\blacktriangledown}$. Hence by 2., we obtain $f^{\blacktriangle\blacktriangledown} = f^{*\blacktriangle\blacktriangledown} \leq f^{\blacktriangle\blacktriangledown\blacktriangle\blacktriangledown}$.
   On the other hand, by 2., we have $f^{\blacktriangle *} \leq f^{\blacktriangle\blacktriangledown\blacktriangle}$, and since $^{\blacktriangledown}$ is antitone, we get $f^{\blacktriangle *\blacktriangledown} \geq f^{\blacktriangle\blacktriangledown\blacktriangle\blacktriangledown}$ and $f^{\blacktriangle *\blacktriangledown} = f^{\blacktriangle\blacktriangledown}$, hence $f^{\blacktriangle\blacktriangledown} \geq f^{\blacktriangle\blacktriangledown\blacktriangle\blacktriangledown}$.
   By the same way, we show that $g^{\blacktriangledown\blacktriangle} = g^{\blacktriangledown\blacktriangle\blacktriangledown\blacktriangle}$.
7. We have $\underset{j \in J}{\sqcap}(f_j^{\blacktriangle}) = \underset{j \in J}{\sqcap}(f_j^{*\Diamond})$ and by Proposition 1 item (iv), we have $\underset{j \in J}{\sqcap}(f_j^{*\Diamond}) = \{f^{\Diamond},\ \ f \in \underset{j \in J}{\sqcup} f_j^*\}$. Now we are going to show that for any $f \in \underset{j \in J}{\sqcup} f_j^*$, we have $f = f^*$.
   Let $f \in \underset{j \in J}{\sqcup} f_j^*$, then $f \geq f_j^*$, so $f^* \geq f_j^{**} = f_j^*$, therefore there is $f_1 \in \underset{j \in J}{\sqcup} f_j^*$, such that $f^* \geq f_1$, then $f \geq f^* \geq f_1$. Therefore $f = f_1$, thus $f^* \geq f$ and by the definition of hedge we obtain $f = f^*$. Since $f = f^*$, we have $f^{\Diamond} = f^{*\Diamond} = f^{\blacktriangle}$.

□

Remark 4. We observe that, the concept-forming operators with hedge $({}^{\blacktriangle},{}^{\blacktriangledown})$ is not always a Galois connection.

In the set $\mathcal{C}^{\blacktriangle\blacktriangledown}(X^*, Y^*, I)$, we define the ordered relation $\leq$ by: $(f_1, g_1) \leq (f_2, g_2)$ if and only if $f_1 \leq f_2$ (if and only if $g_2 \leq g_1$) for the concepts (f_1, g_1) and (f_2, g_2). The following results are about the investigation of the structure of $(\mathcal{C}^{\blacktriangle\blacktriangledown}(X^*, Y^*, I), \leq)$.

Lemma 2. *For all $F \subseteq X \times M^{*_X}$, we have $F \subseteq \lfloor\lceil F\rceil^{*_X}\rfloor^{*_X}$ and if $G = \lfloor g\rfloor$ for some $g \in M^Y$, then $\lceil G^{*_Y}\rceil = \lceil G\rceil^{*_Y}$.*

Proof. Let $(x, a) \in F$. Then there is $b \in M$ such that $a = b^*$. Elsewhere, $(x, a) \in F$ means $a \leq \lceil F\rceil(x)$, that is $a^* \leq \lceil F\rceil^*(x)$, therefore $(x, a^*) \in \lfloor\lceil F\rceil^*\rfloor(x)$, which means $(x, a)^* \in \lfloor\lceil F\rceil^*\rfloor(x)$, then $(x, a)^* \in \lfloor\lceil F\rceil^*\rfloor^*(x)$. Since $(x, a)^* = (x, b)^{**} = (x, b)^* = (x, a)$, we obtain $(x, a) \in \lfloor\lceil F\rceil^*\rfloor(x)$.

For the next, For $x \in X$, let us start by showing that $\lceil\lfloor g\rfloor^*\rceil(x) = g^*(x)$.

We have $\lceil\lfloor g\rfloor^*\rceil(x) \in \sqcup\{a \in M \mid (x, a) \in \lfloor g\rfloor^*\}$. Since, $(x, a) \in \lfloor g\rfloor^*$ then $g(x)$ is an upper bound of the set $\{a \in M \mid (x, a) \in \lfloor g\rfloor^*\}$ and $g^*(x)$ belongs to that set, then $\sqcup\{a \in M \mid (x, a) \in \lfloor g\rfloor^*\} = \{g^*(x)\}$. On the other hand, we can show by the same way that, $\lceil\lfloor g\rfloor\rceil^*(x) = \{g(x)\}^*$. $\square$

Now, we can consider the following pair of operators and prove that it is a Galois connection.

Consider operators ${}^{\Uparrow} : 2^{X\times M^{*_X}} \to 2^{Y\times M^{*_Y}}$ and ${}^{\Downarrow} : 2^{Y\times M^{*_Y}} \to 2^{X\times M^{*_X}}$ as follow:

$$F^{\Uparrow} := \lfloor\lceil F\rceil^{\blacktriangle}\rfloor^{*_Y} \quad \textit{and} \quad G^{\Downarrow} := \lfloor\lceil G\rceil^{\blacktriangledown}\rfloor^{*_X},$$

for all $F \subseteq X \times M^{*_X}$ and $G \subseteq Y \times M^{*_Y}$.

Lemma 3. *The pair $({}^{\Uparrow},{}^{\Downarrow})$ forms a Galois connection between $X \times M^{*_X}$ and $Y \times M^{*_Y}$.*

Proof.
1. Let $F_1, F_2 \subseteq X \times M^{*_X}$ such that $F_1 \subseteq F_2$, then $\{a \in M \mid (x, a) \in F_1\} \subseteq \{a \in M \mid (x, a) \in F_2\}$, therefore $\{a \in M \mid (x, a) \in F_1\} \leq b_2$ with $\lceil F_2\rceil(x) = b_2$. Then by the definition of multilattice there exists $b_1 \in \sqcup\{a \in M \mid (x, a) \in F_1\}$, such that $b_1 \leq b_2$. We take $b_1 = \lceil F_1\rceil(x)$. Then $\lceil F_1\rceil \leq \lceil F_2\rceil$, we therefore obtain $\lceil F_2\rceil^{\blacktriangle} \leq \lceil F_1\rceil^{\blacktriangle}$. As $\lfloor\ \ \rfloor$ is isotone, we get $\lfloor\lceil F_2\rceil^{\blacktriangle}\rceil\rfloor \leq \lfloor\lceil F_1\rceil^{\blacktriangle}\rceil\rfloor$, hence $\lfloor\lceil F_2\rceil^{\blacktriangle}\rceil\rfloor^{*_Y} \leq \lfloor\lceil F_1\rceil^{\blacktriangle}\rceil\rfloor^{*_Y}$. By the same way one can show that, for $G_1, G_2 \subseteq Y \times M^{*_Y}$, if $G_1 \subseteq G_2$ then $\lfloor\lceil G_2\rceil^{\blacktriangledown}\rceil\rfloor^{*_X} \leq \lfloor\lceil G_1\rceil^{\blacktriangledown}\rceil\rfloor^{*_X}$.
2. For extensivity, we proceed the same as in [3] Lemma 2. $\square$

We can therefore have the following theorem.

Theorem 3. *The concept multilattice with hedge $\mathcal{C}^{\blacktriangle\blacktriangledown}(X^{*_X}, Y^{*_Y}, I)$ is isomorphic to the concept multilattice $\mathcal{C}^{\Uparrow\Downarrow}(X \times M^{*_X}, Y \times M^{*_Y}, I')$ induced by the Galois connection $({}^{\Uparrow},{}^{\Downarrow})$. The corresponding isomorphism and its inverse are $h : \mathcal{C}^{\blacktriangle\blacktriangledown}(X^*, Y^*, I) \to \mathcal{C}^{\Uparrow\Downarrow}(X \times M^{*_X}, Y \times M^{*_Y}, I')$ and $h^{-1} : \mathcal{C}^{\Uparrow\Downarrow}(X \times M^{*_X}, Y \times M^{*_Y}, I') \to \mathcal{C}^{\blacktriangle\blacktriangledown}(X^*, Y^*, I)$ as follow:*

$$h((F, G)) = \left(\lfloor F\rfloor^{*_X}, \lfloor G\rfloor^{*_Y}\right) \quad \textit{and} \quad h^{-1}((F', G')) = \left(\lceil F'\rceil^{\blacktriangle\blacktriangledown}, \lceil G'\rceil^{\blacktriangledown\blacktriangle}\right).$$

Proof. This proof can be obtained by the same method as the proof of Theorem 3.17 in [4]. □

Theorem 4. *The multilattice $(\mathcal{C}^{\blacktriangle\blacktriangledown}(X^{*_X}, Y^{*_Y}, I), \leq\ )$ is complete, the multiinfima and multisuprema are given as follows; for every set of concepts $\{(f_j, g_j)\}_{j\in J}$:*

$$\text{there exist } f \in \underset{j\in J}{\sqcap} f_j \text{ and } g \in \text{maximals } \{g_j^{*_Y} \mid j \in J\} \text{ such that}$$
$$\underset{j\in J}{\sqcap}\{(f_j, g_j)\} = (f^{\blacktriangle\blacktriangledown}, g^{\blacktriangledown\blacktriangle})$$
$$\text{and there exist } f \in \text{maximals } \{f_j^{*_X} \mid j \in J\} \text{ and } g \in \underset{j\in J}{\sqcap} g_j \text{ such that}$$
$$\underset{j\in J}{\sqcup}\{(f_j, g_j)\} = (f^{\blacktriangle\blacktriangledown}, g^{\blacktriangledown\blacktriangle}).$$

Proof. Since h defined in the previous theorem is an isomorphism, we have
$$h\Big(\underset{j\in J}{\sqcap}(f_j, g_j)\Big) = \bigcap_{j\in J}\Big(\lfloor f_j\rfloor^{*_X}, \lfloor g_j\rfloor^{*_Y}\Big) = \Big(\Big(\bigcap_{j\in J}\lfloor f_j\rfloor^{*_X}\Big), \Big(\bigcup_{j\in J}\lfloor g_j\rfloor^{*_Y}\Big)^{\Downarrow\Uparrow}\Big),$$
since $\Big(\lfloor f_j\rfloor^{*_X}, \lfloor g_j\rfloor^{*_Y}\Big)$ is a concept. Then we have

$$h^{-1}\Big(\Big(\bigcap_{j\in J}\lfloor f_j\rfloor^{*_X}\Big), \Big(\bigcup_{j\in J}\lfloor g_j\rfloor^{*_Y}\Big)^{\Downarrow\Uparrow}\Big) = \Big(h^{-1}\Big(\Big(\bigcap_{j\in J}\lfloor f_j\rfloor^{*_X}\Big)\Big), h^{-1}\Big(\Big(\bigcup_{j\in J}\lfloor g_j\rfloor^{*_Y}\Big)^{\Downarrow\Uparrow}\Big)\Big).$$

By applying the definition of h^{-1}, we obtain,

$$\Big(h^{-1}\Big(\Big(\bigcap_{j\in J}\lfloor f_j\rfloor^{*_X}\Big)\Big), h^{-1}\Big(\Big(\bigcup_{j\in J}\lfloor g_j\rfloor^{*_Y}\Big)^{\Downarrow\Uparrow}\Big)\Big) = \Big(\Big\lceil\Big(\bigcap_{j\in J}\lfloor f_j\rfloor^{*_X}\Big)\Big\rceil^{\blacktriangle\blacktriangledown}, \Big\lceil\Big(\bigcup_{j\in J}\lfloor g_j\rfloor^{*_Y}\Big)^{\Downarrow\Uparrow}\Big\rceil^{\blacktriangledown\blacktriangle}\Big).$$

On the one hand, let us show that there exists $f \in \underset{j\in J}{\sqcap} f_j$ such that,

$$\Big\lceil\bigcap_{j\in J}\lfloor f_j\rfloor^{*_X}\Big\rceil^{\blacktriangle\blacktriangledown} = f^{\blacktriangle\blacktriangledown}.$$

Let $(x, a) \in \bigcap_{j\in J}\lfloor f_j\rfloor^{*_X}$, then $(x, a) \in \lfloor f_j\rfloor^{*_X}$ for all $j \in J$. We then have $a_1 \leq f_j(x)$ with $a = a_1^{*_X}$ for some $a_1 \in M$, therefore $a = a_1^{*_X} \leq f_j^{*_X}(x) \leq f_j(x)$. Then there exists $y \in \underset{j\in J}{\sqcap} f_j(x)$, such that $a \leq y$. By setting $y = f(x)$ for each $(x, a) \in \lfloor f_j\rfloor^{*_X}$, we have $f \in \underset{j\in J}{\sqcap} f_j$. Hence $a \leq f(x)$, then $(x, a) \in \lfloor f\rfloor$ which gives $(x, a) \in \lfloor f\rfloor^{*_X}$. Conversely if $(x, a) \in \lfloor f\rfloor^{*}$, we will have $(x, a) \in \bigcap_{j\in J}\lfloor f_j\rfloor^{*_X}$. Thus $\bigcap_{j\in J}\lfloor f_j\rfloor^{*} = \lfloor f\rfloor^{*_X}$. We finally have

$$\Big\lceil\Big(\bigcap_{j\in J}\lfloor f_j\rfloor^{*_X}\Big)\Big\rceil^{\blacktriangle\blacktriangledown} = \Big\lceil\lfloor f\rfloor^{*_X}\Big\rceil^{\blacktriangle\blacktriangledown} = f^{\blacktriangle\blacktriangledown}.$$

On the other hand, let us show that there exists $g \in$ maximals $\{g_j^{*_Y} \mid j \in J\}$ such that, $\left\lceil \left(\bigcup_{j\in J} \lfloor g_j \rfloor^{*_Y}\right)^{\Downarrow\Uparrow} \right\rceil^{\blacktriangledown\blacktriangle} = g^{\blacktriangledown\blacktriangle}$.

$$
\begin{aligned}
\left\lceil \left(\bigcup_{j\in J} \lfloor g_j \rfloor^{*_Y}\right)^{\Downarrow\Uparrow} \right\rceil^{\blacktriangledown\blacktriangle} &= \left\lceil \left\lfloor \left\lceil \left\lfloor \left\lceil \bigcup_{j\in J} \lfloor g_j \rfloor^{*_Y} \right\rceil^{\blacktriangledown} \right\rfloor^{*_Y} \right\rceil^{\blacktriangle} \right\rfloor^{*_Y} \right\rceil^{\blacktriangledown\blacktriangle} \\
&= \left\lceil \left\lfloor \left\lceil \left\lfloor \left\lceil \bigcup_{j\in J} \lfloor g_j \rfloor \right\rceil^{*_Y\blacktriangledown} \right\rfloor \right\rceil^{*_Y\blacktriangle} \right\rfloor \right\rceil^{*_Y\blacktriangledown\blacktriangle} \quad \text{By Lemma 2} \\
&= \left\lceil \left\lfloor \left\lceil \left\lfloor \left\lceil \bigcup_{j\in J} \lfloor g_j \rfloor^{*_Y} \right\rceil^{\blacktriangledown} \right\rfloor \right\rceil^{\blacktriangle} \right\rfloor \right\rceil^{\blacktriangledown\blacktriangle} \quad \text{By Proposition 2 item 2.} \\
&= \left\lceil \bigcup_{j\in J} \lfloor g_j \rfloor^{*_Y} \right\rceil^{\blacktriangledown\blacktriangle\blacktriangledown\blacktriangle} \quad \text{since } \lceil\lfloor\ \ \rfloor\rceil \text{ is identity} \\
&= \left\lceil \bigcup_{j\in J} \lfloor g_j \rfloor^{*_Y} \right\rceil^{\blacktriangledown\blacktriangle}.
\end{aligned}
$$

Let $y \in Y$, we have $\left\lceil \bigcup_{j\in J} \lfloor g_j \rfloor^{*_Y} \right\rceil(y) = b$ with $b \in \sqcup\{a \in M \mid (y,a) \in \bigcup_{j\in J} \lfloor g_j \rfloor^{*_Y}\}$, but $\sqcup\{a \in M \mid (y,a) \in \bigcup_{j\in J} \lfloor g_j \rfloor^{*_Y}\} = \sqcup\{a \in M \mid \exists j \in J : (y,a) \in \lfloor g_j \rfloor^{*_Y}\} = \sqcup\{a \in M \mid \exists j \in J : a \leq g_j^{*_Y}(y)\} = \text{maximals}\{g_j^{*_Y}(y) \mid j \in J\}$, since maximal elements of $\{g_j^{*_Y}(y) \mid j \in J\}$ are both elements and upper bounds of the set $\{a \in M \mid \exists j \in J : a \leq g_j^{*_Y}(y)\}$. Then for each $y \in Y$, by setting $b = g(y)$, we have $g \in$ maximals $\{g_j^{*_Y} \mid j \in J\}$, and $\left\lceil \bigcup_{j\in J} \lfloor g_j \rfloor^{*_Y} \right\rceil(y) = g(y)$.

Dually, one can obtain the multisuprema. □

Remark 5. The previous theorem is in accord with the results obtained from the work carried out by Medina et al. <<*On the DedekindMacNeille completion and formal concept analysis based on multilattices*>> [12]. Indeed, they showed that the concept multilattice is always a lattice. That is why here the concept multilattice with truth-stressing hedge gives us a lattice.

The next shows that if $*_X = id$, the concepts from $\mathcal{C}^{\blacktriangle\blacktriangledown}(X, Y^{*_Y}, I)$ are particular concepts from the whole $\mathcal{C}^{\Diamond\blacklozenge}(X, Y, I)$.

Theorem 5. *Let $*_X$ be the identity hedge and $fix(*_{1Y}) \subseteq fix(*_{2Y})$, we have*

$$\mathcal{C}^{\blacktriangle_1\blacktriangledown_1}(X, Y^{*_{1Y}}, I) \subseteq \mathcal{C}^{\blacktriangle_2\blacktriangledown_2}(X, Y^{*_{2Y}}, I)$$

specially we have,

$$\mathcal{C}^{\blacktriangle_1\blacktriangledown_1}(X, Y^{*_{1Y}}, I) \subseteq \mathcal{C}^{\Diamond\blacklozenge}(X, Y, I)$$

which means

$$|\mathcal{C}^{\blacktriangle_1\blacktriangledown_1}(X, Y^{*_{1Y}}, I)| \leq |\mathcal{C}^{\Diamond\blacklozenge}(X, Y, I)|.$$

Proof. Let $(f, g) \in \mathcal{C}^{\blacktriangle_1\blacktriangledown_1}(X, Y^{*_{1Y}}, I)$, it is obvious that $f^{\blacktriangle_2} = g$. It remains to show that, $g^{\blacktriangledown_2} = g$. We have $g^{*_{1Y}*_{1Y}} = g^{*_{1Y}}$ which means $g^{*_{1Y}} \in Fix(*_{1Y}) \subseteq Fix(*_{2Y})$, then $g^{*_{1Y}*_{2Y}} = g^{*_{1Y}}$. Also, since $g^{*_{1Y}*_{2Y}} \leq g^{*_{2Y}}$, we obtain $g^{*_{1Y}} \leq g^{*_{2Y}}$.

On another hand, $f = g^{\blacktriangledown_1} = g^{*_{1Y}\blacktriangledown_2} \geq g^{\blacktriangledown_2} = f^{\blacktriangle_2\blacktriangledown_2} = f$ since f is an extent. Hence, $f = g^{\blacktriangledown_2}$. Thus $(f, g) \in \mathcal{C}^{\blacktriangle_2\blacktriangledown_2}(X, Y^{*_{2Y}}, I)$.

According to the Remark 3 we get the next. □

4 Illustrative Example with a Truth-Stressing Hedge

Let us consider a small M-fuzzy formal context (X, Y, I) with:

- Object set: $X = \{x_1\}$,
- Attribute set: $Y = \{y_1, y_2\}$,
- Multilattice of truth values is:

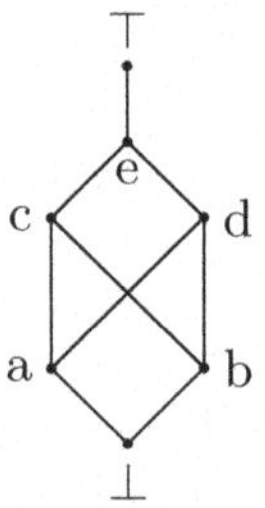

The adjoint pair on M are defined as follows: For $x, y \in M$,

$$x \,\&\, y = \begin{cases} \top & \text{if } x = \top \text{ and } y = \top \\ \bot & \text{if } x \in \{\bot, b\} \text{ or } y \in \{\bot, b\} \\ a & \text{otherwise} \end{cases}$$

and

$$x \to y = \begin{cases} \top & \text{if } x \leq y \\ b & \text{if } x \notin \{\bot, b\} \text{ and } y \in \{\bot, b\} \\ e & \text{if } x = \top \text{ and } y \in \{a, c, d, e\} \\ \top & \text{otherwise} \end{cases}$$

The fuzzy incidence relation $I : X \times Y \to M$ is given by:

I	y_1	y_2
x_1	d	$\top$

Then set of concepts with the classical operators is

$$\mathcal{C}^{\Diamond\blacklozenge}(X, Y, I) = \{(\{e/x\}, \{\top/y_1, \top/y_2\}), (\{\top/x\}, \{e/y_1, \top/y_2\})\}$$

We consider the **globalization hedge** defined on M by:

$$a^* = \begin{cases} \top & \text{if } a = \top, \\ \bot & \text{otherwise.} \end{cases}$$

Then the set of concepts with parametrized operators is:

$$\mathcal{C}^{\blacktriangle\blacktriangledown}(X, Y^*, I) = \{(\{e/x\}, \{\top/y_1, \top/y_2\})\}$$

Effect of the Hedge

When we use the classical concept forming operators all the truth value of a fuzzy set on M^X would be preserved, resulting in more membership degrees and thus more fuzzy concepts. The globalization hedge collapses all non-maximal truth values to $\bot$, thereby **reducing the number of fixpoints** and concepts.

This example illustrates how truth-stressing hedges act as a parameter to control the granularity of concept extraction in M-FCA.

5 Conclusion

This work extends the theory of Formal Concept Analysis via multilattices by incorporating truth-stressing linguistic hedges into the definition of concept-forming operators. The proposed framework demonstrates that such hedges not only preserve the algebraic integrity of M-FCA but also enable effective control over the number of extracted concepts. We showed that the resulting concept multilattice forms a complete multilattice and is isomorphic to one induced by a new Galois connection that integrates hedge-based mappings.

Furthermore, our analysis confirms that stronger hedges lead to fewer concepts, providing a valuable tool for reducing conceptual complexity in fuzzy datasets. These results suggest new directions for both theoretical investigation (e.g., hedge-parameterized isotone operators) and applied research (e.g., experimental validation of hedge effectiveness in real datasets). This work opens promising pathways for semantic granularity control in fuzzy FCA and supports more scalable and interpretable concept analysis.

References

1. Bartl, E., Konecny, J.: Using linguistic hedges in L-rough concept analysis. In: Yahia, S.B., Konecny, J. (eds.) The Twelfth International Conference CLA, vol. 1466, pp. 229–240 (2015)
2. Belohlávek, R.: Fuzzy galois connections. Math. Log. Q. **45**, 497–504 (1999)
3. Belohlavek, R., Vychodil, V.: Reducing the size of fuzzy concept lattices by hedges. In: The 14th IEEE International Conference on Fuzzy Systems, FUZZ 2005, pp. 663–668. IEEE (2005)

4. Belohlavek, R., Vychodil, V.: Formal concept analysis and linguistic hedges. Int. J. Gen. Syst. **41**(5), 503–532 (2012)
5. Benado, M.: Les ensembles partiellement ordonnés et le théorème de raffinement de schreier. ii. théorie des multistructures. Czech. Math. J. **5**(3), 308–344 (1955)
6. Cabrera, I.P., Cordero, P., Gutiérrez, G., Martínez, J., Ojeda-Aciego, M.: On residuation in multilattices: filters, congruences, and homomorphisms. Fuzzy Sets Syst. **234**, 1–21 (2014)
7. Cornejo, M.E., Medina, J., Ramírez, E.: A comparative study of adjoint triples. Fuzzy Sets Syst. **211**, 1–14 (2013)
8. Dongmo, G.N., Njionou, B.K., Kwuida, L., Onabid, M.: Multilattice as the set of truth values for fuzzy rough sets. J. Appl. Non-Classical Logics 1–20 (2024)
9. Hájek, P.: On very true. Fuzzy Sets Syst. **124**(3), 329–333 (2001)
10. Konecny, J.: Isotone fuzzy galois connections with hedges. Inf. Sci. **181**(10), 1804–1817 (2011)
11. Medina, J., Ruiz-Calviño, J.: Fuzzy formal concept analysis via multilattices: first prospects and results. In: Szathmary, L., Priss, U. (eds.) The Ninth International Conference CLA, vol. 972, pp. 69–80 (2012)
12. Medina-Moreno, J., Ojeda-Aciego, M., Pócs, J., Ramírez-Poussa, E.: On the dedekind-macneille completion and formal concept analysis based on multilattices. Fuzzy Sets Syst. **303**, 1–20 (2016)
13. Medina-Moreno, J., Ojeda-Aciego, M., Ruiz-Calviño, J.: Concept-forming operators on multilattices. In: Cellier, P., Distel, F., Ganter, B. (eds.) ICFCA 2013. LNCS (LNAI), vol. 7880, pp. 203–215. Springer, Heidelberg (2013). https://doi.org/10.1007/978-3-642-38317-5_13
14. Nguepy, D.G., Njionou, B.B.K., Kwuida, L., Onabid, M.: Rough fuzzy concept analysis via multilattice. In: Campagner, A., Lenz, O.U., Xia, S., Slezak, D., Was, J., Yao, J. (eds.) IJCRS 2023. LNCS, vol. 14481, pp. 495–508. Springer, Cham (2023). https://doi.org/10.1007/978-3-031-50959-9_34
15. Nguepy Dongmo, G., Koguep Njionou, B., Kwuida, L., Onabid, M.: Roughness in formal concept analysis via multilattices. Fuzzy Sets Syst. **500**, 109179 (2025)
16. Njionou, B.B.K., Kwuida, L., Lele, C.: Formal concepts and residuation on multilattices. Fundamental Informaticae **18**(4), 1–21 (2023)
17. Zadeh, L.A.: A fuzzy-set-theoretic interpretation of linguistic hedges. J. Cybern. **2**(3), 4–34 (1972)
18. Zadeh, L.A.: The concept of a linguistic variable and its application to approximate reasoning-I. Inf. Sci. **8**(3), 199–249 (1975)

Author Index

P. Cellier et al. (Eds.): CONCEPTS 2025, LNAI 15941, pp. 437–438, 2025.
https://doi.org/10.1007/978-3-032-03364-2

The manufacturer's authorised representative in the EU is Springer Nature Customer Service Centre GmbH, Europaplatz 3, 69115 Heidelberg, Germany. If you have any concerns regarding our products, please contact ProductSafety@springernature.com

Printed and bound by CPI Group (UK) Ltd, Croydon, CR0 4YY
30/09/2026
02225585-0010